Correlative
Neuroanatomy
& Functional Neurology

18th edition

Correlative Neuroanatomy & Functional Neurology

JOSEPH G. CHUSID, MD

Professor of Neurology
New York Medical College
(New York City)

Director of Department of Neurology
St. Vincent's Hospital and Medical Center
(New York City)

LANGE Medical Publications LMP Los Altos, California 94022

Italian Edition: *Piccin Editore, Via Altinate, 107, 35100 Padua, Italy*
Japanese Edition: *Kinpodo Publishing Co., Ltd., 34 Nishiteranomae-cho, Shishigatani,*
Sakyo-ku, Kyoto, Japan
Spanish Edition: *El Manual Moderno, S.A., Av. Sonora 206, 06100 Mexico, D.F.*
Portuguese Edition: *Editora Guanabara Koogan, S.A., Travessa do Ouvidor, 11-ZC-00,*
20,040 Rio de Janeiro - RJ, Brazil
Polish Edition: *Panstwowy Zaklad Wydawnictw Lekarskich, P.O. Box 379, 00-950 Warsaw, Poland*
German Edition: *Springer-Verlag, Postfach 10 52 80, D-6900 Heidelberg 1, West Germany*
Serbo-Croatian Edition: *Savremena Administracija, Crnotravska 7-9, 11000 Belgrade, Yugoslavia*

International Standard Book Number: *0-87041-012-1*
Library of Congress Catalogue Card Number: *82-82712*

Correlative Neuroanatomy & Functional Neurology, 18th ed. $15.00
Copyright © 1938, 1939, 1942, 1947, 1950, 1952, 1954, 1956, 1958, 1960,
1962, 1964, 1967, 1970, 1973, 1976, 1979, 1982

A Concise Medical Library for Practitioner and Student

To my wife, Kathryn

Table of Contents

III. PRINCIPLES OF NEURODIAGNOSIS

IV. CENTRAL NERVOUS SYSTEM DISORDERS

Preface

This volume is intended for the beginner in clinical neurology. It is meant to serve as an aid or supplement to standard neurologic texts and literature rather than as a substitute for them. It has become increasingly popular with students, house staff members, and practitioners in this country and abroad over the past 4 decades.

The author's principal objective has been to present briefly and clearly some of the important structural and functional features of the nervous system as they relate to problems encountered in clinical neurology. Concise format, charts, diagrams, and illustrations have been prepared with this purpose in mind, and efforts have been made to include recent important advances in neurology. More than 475 illustrations and over 60 tables have been assembled for this edition.

With the appearance of the Eighteenth Edition, I am pleased to report that Spanish, Italian, Japanese, Portuguese, Polish, German, and Serbo-Croatian editions have been published and have been well received. French and Indonesian editions are now in preparation.

I would like to express my appreciation and gratitude to my friends and colleagues at St. Vincent's Hospital and Medical Center of New York for their continued support. Dr. Michael Garofalo and Dr. Hyman Donnenfeld deserve special mention, and Dr. Gail P. Ballweg provided several fine photographs. Dr. Michael J. Chusid of the Medical College of Wisconsin revised the chapter on infectious diseases of the central nervous system.

I wish to extend my sincere thanks to the publishers, editors, and authors who graciously permitted the reproduction of illustrations and charts in this book. The helpful suggestions and criticisms of students, readers, and physicians from many parts of the world are gratefully acknowledged and are most welcome.

Joseph G. Chusid

New York City
August, 1982

Section I: Central Nervous System

The Brain | 1

The brain is the greatly modified and enlarged anterior portion of the CNS. It is surrounded by 3 protective membranes (meninges) and is enclosed within the cranial cavity of the skull. Division into cerebral cortex, basal ganglia, thalamus and hypothalamus, midbrain, brain stem, and cerebellum provides a useful basis for the study of brain localization.

THE CEREBRAL HEMISPHERES

The 2 cerebral hemispheres, which make up the largest portion of the brain, are separated by the deep **longitudinal cerebral fissure.** The **falx cerebri,** a crescent-shaped extension of dura mater, projects into the longitudinal cerebral fissure. The **corpus callosum** is the great white central commissure that crosses the longitudinal cerebral fissure. The body of the corpus callosum is arched; its anterior curved portion, the genu, continues anteroventrally as the rostrum. The thick posterior portion terminates in the curved splenium, which overlaps the midbrain.

The surfaces of the cerebral hemispheres are dorsolateral, medial, and basal. They contain many grooves, or furrows, known as fissures and sulci. The portions of brain lying between these grooves are called convolutions, or gyri. Some gyri are relatively constant in location and contour, whereas others show considerable variation. The **lateral cerebral fissure** (fissure of Sylvius) separates the temporal from the frontal lobe. Starting at the base of the brain as a deep cleft lateral to the anterior perforated substance, it divides into 3 branches: the anterior horizontal ramus, which ascends into the inferior frontal gyrus; the anterior ascending ramus, which also ascends into the inferior frontal gyrus but farther posteriorly; and the posterior ramus, which continues backward and upward to terminate in the parietal lobe.

The **central sulcus** (fissure of Rolando) arises about the middle of the hemisphere, beginning near the longitudinal cerebral fissure and extending downward and forward to about 2.5 cm above the lateral cerebral fissure. The **parieto-occipital fissure** passes along the medial surface of the posterior portion of the cerebral hemisphere, runs downward and forward as a deep cleft with much buried cortex, and joins the calcarine

fissure. The **calcarine fissure** begins on the medial surface, near the occipital pole, and extends forward to an area slightly below the splenium of the corpus callosum. The rostral portion is deeper and more constant in location and structure. The **cingulate sulcus** begins below the anterior end of the corpus callosum on the medial surface of the hemisphere, continues parallel to the corpus callosum, and finally curves up to the superior medial border a short distance behind the upper end of the central sulcus. The **circular sulcus** (circuminsular fissure) surrounds the **insula,** or island, of Reil and separates it from the adjacent frontal, parietal, and temporal lobes.

Main Divisions of the Cerebrum

The cerebral hemisphere may be divided into the frontal, parietal, occipital, and temporal lobes, the insula, and the rhinencephalon.

A. Frontal Lobe: The frontal lobe extends from the frontal pole to the central sulcus behind and the lateral fissure at the side. The **precentral sulcus** passes anterior and parallel to the central sulcus. It is subdivided into the superior and inferior precentral sulci. The **superior and inferior frontal sulci** extend forward and downward from the precentral sulcus, dividing the lateral surface of the frontal lobe into 3 parallel gyri: the **superior, middle, and inferior frontal gyri.** The inferior frontal gyrus is divided into 3 parts by the anterior horizontal and ascending rami of the lateral cerebral fissure: the orbital part lies rostral to the anterior horizontal ramus; the triangular part is the wedge-shaped portion between the anterior horizontal and anterior ascending rami; the opercular part is between the ascending ramus and the precentral sulcus.

The **orbital sulci and gyri** are irregular in contour and location. The **olfactory sulcus** lies beneath the olfactory tract on the orbital surface; lying medial to it is the gyrus rectus, or **straight gyrus.** The **cingulate gyrus** is the crescentic or arched convolution on the medial surface between the cingulate sulcus and the corpus callosum. The **paracentral lobule** is the quadrilateral gyrus around the end of the central sulcus on the medial surface of the hemisphere.

B. Parietal Lobe: The parietal lobe extends from the central sulcus to the parieto-occipital fissure and laterally to the level of the lateral cerebral fissure. The **postcentral sulcus** extends behind and parallel to the lateral (rolandic) fissure and consists of a superior and

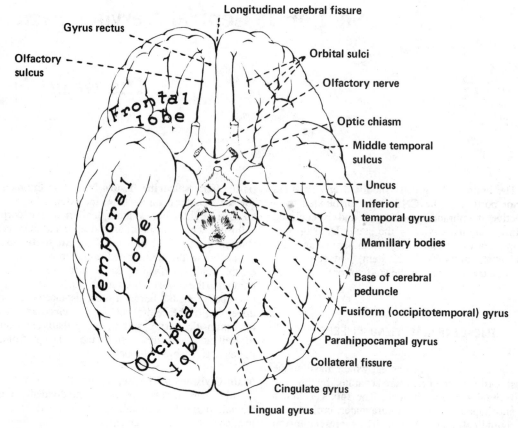

Longitudinal cerebral fissure

Gyrus rectus

Olfactory sulcus

Orbital sulci

Olfactory nerve

Optic chiasm

Middle temporal sulcus

Uncus

Inferior temporal gyrus

Mamillary bodies

Base of cerebral peduncle

Fusiform (occipitotemporal) gyrus

Parahippocampal gyrus

Collateral fissure

Cingulate gyrus

Lingual gyrus

Frontal lobe

Temporal lobe

Occipital lobe

Figure 1–1. Basal view of cerebrum.

an inferior portion. The **intraparietal sulcus** is a horizontal groove that sometimes unites with the postcentral sulcus. The **superior parietal lobule** lies above the horizontal portion of the intraparietal sulcus, and the **inferior parietal lobule** lies below.

The **supramarginal gyrus** is that portion of the inferior parietal lobule which arches above the ascending end of the posterior ramus of the lateral cerebral fissure. The **angular gyrus** is that part which arches above the end of the superior temporal sulcus and becomes continuous with the middle temporal gyrus. The **posterior central gyrus** lies between the central and postcentral sulci. The **precuneus** is the posterior portion of the medial surface between the parieto-occipital fissure and the ascending end of the cingulate sulcus.

C. Occipital Lobe: The occipital lobe is the pyramid-shaped posterior lobe situated behind the parieto-occipital fissure. The **lateral occipital sulcus** extends transversely along the lateral surface, dividing the occipital lobe into a **superior** and **inferior gyrus**. The **calcarine fissure** divides the medial surface of the occipital lobe into the cuneus and the lingual gyrus. The wedge-shaped **cuneus** lies between the calcarine and parieto-occipital fissures. The **lingual gyrus** is between the calcarine fissure and the posterior part of the collateral fissure. The posterior part of the

fusiform gyrus is on the central or basal surface of the occipital lobe.

D. Temporal Lobe: The temporal lobe portion of the cerebral hemisphere lies inferior to the lateral cerebral (sylvian) fissure and extends back to the level of the parieto-occipital fissure. The **superior temporal sulcus** extends across the temporal lobe parallel to the lateral cerebral fissure. The **middle temporal sulcus** runs parallel to the superior temporal sulcus at a lower level. The **superior temporal gyrus** is the part of the lateral surface of the temporal lobe between the lateral cerebral fissure and the superior temporal sulcus. The **middle temporal gyrus** lies between the superior and middle temporal sulci. The **inferior temporal gyrus** is below the middle temporal sulcus and extends posteriorly to connect with the inferior occipital gyrus. The **transverse temporal gyrus** (Heschl's gyrus) occupies the posterior part of the superior temporal surface (the inferior border of the lateral cerebral fissure). The **inferior temporal sulcus** extends along the inferior surface of the temporal lobe from the temporal pole in front to the occipital pole behind. The **fusiform,** or **occipitotemporal, gyrus** is medial and the **inferior temporal gyrus** lateral to the inferior temporal sulcus. The **hippocampal fissure** extends along the inferomedian aspect of the temporal lobe from the area of the splenium of the corpus callosum to

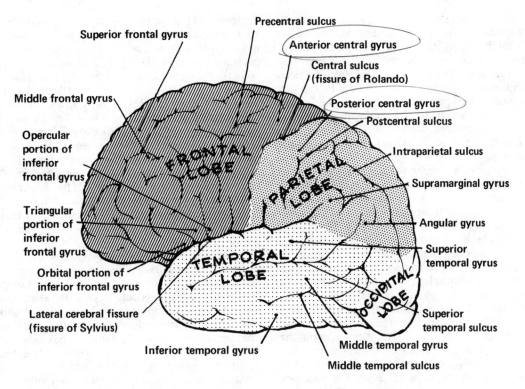

Figure 1–2. Lateral view of left cerebral hemisphere.

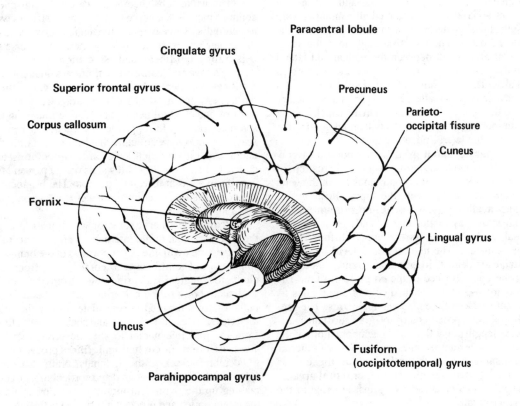

Figure 1–3. Medial view of right cerebral hemisphere.

the uncus. The **parahippocampal gyrus** lies between the hippocampal fissure and the anterior part of the collateral fissure. Its anterior part curves in the form of a hook and is known as the uncus.

E. Insula: The insula (island of Reil) lies deep within the lateral cerebral fissure and can be exposed by separating the upper and lower lips of the fissure. The deep **circular sulcus** bounds the insula. Several **short gyri,** formed by shallow sulci, occupy the anterior portion of the insula; a **long gyrus** occupies the posterior part.

The **opercula** of the insula are portions of the lips of the lateral cerebral fissure. The orbital operculum is anterior and inferior to the anterior horizontal ramus. The frontal operculum lies between the orbital operculum and the anterior ascending ramus. The parietal operculum lies between the frontal operculum and the end of the posterior ramus. The temporal operculum lies below the posterior ramus.

F. Rhinencephalon: The rhinencephalon, a phylogenetically old portion of the cerebral hemisphere, includes the portions associated with the perception of olfactory sensation. The **olfactory bulb,** an oval structure, lies on the cribriform plate of the ethmoid bone and receives the olfactory nerves that have passed upward through the cribriform plate from the olfactory zone of the nasal cavity. The **olfactory tract** lies in the olfactory sulcus on the orbital surface of the frontal lobe. As it passes posteriorly, it divides into the **lateral olfactory stria,** which passes laterally, then medially, to enter the uncus; and the **medial olfactory stria,** which passes medially and up toward the subcallosal gyrus near the inferior aspect of the corpus callosum. The **olfactory trigone** is the small triangular attachment between the medial and lateral olfactory striae, just anterior to the anterior perforated substance. The **anterior perforated substance,** a depressed area of gray matter, extends from the olfactory striae to the optic tract. The **piriform area** includes the anterior portion of the parahippocampal gyrus, the uncus, and the lateral olfactory gyrus.

The **par;aterminal gyrus** is the portion of gray matter that covers the inferior aspect of the rostrum of the corpus callosum and is continuous about the genu of the corpus callosum with the supracallosal gyrus. The **supracallosal gyrus** (indusium griseum) is the thin layer of gray matter that extends from the subcallosal gyrus and covers the upper surface of the corpus callosum. The **medial and lateral longitudinal striae** are delicate longitudinal strands that extend along the upper surface of the corpus callosum. The **dentate gyrus,** a thin crenated strip of cortex, lies on the upper surface of the hippocampal gyrus. The **hippocampus,** composed chiefly of gray substance, extends the length of the floor of the temporal horn of the lateral ventricle and becomes continuous with the supracallosal gyrus at the splenium of the corpus callosum. The **paraterminal body,** or **septal area,** is a triangular area of cortex lying just anterior to the lamina terminalis.

The **fornix** is an arched white fiber tract extending from the hippocampal formation. The **alveus** is the white layer on the ventricular surface of the hippocampus containing fibers from the dentate fascia and hippocampus. From the alveus, fibers lead to the medial aspect of the hippocampus and form the fimbria, a flat band of white fibers that ascends below the splenium of the corpus callosum and bends forward above the thalamus, forming the crus of the fornix. The **hippocampal commissure,** or **commissure of the fornix,** is the collection of transverse fibers connecting the 2 crura of the fornix. The 2 **crura** lie close to the undersurface of the corpus callosum and join anteriorly to form the body of the fornix. The 2 **columns of the fornix** bend inferiorly and posteriorly from the body to enter the anterior part of the lateral wall of the third ventricle and terminate in the **mamillary bodies of the hypothalamus.**

The **anterior commissure** is a band of white fibers that crosses the midline to join both cerebral hemispheres. It is believed to contain 2 parts: a rostral portion that joins both olfactory bulbs, and a remainder that connects the piriform areas of both cerebral hemispheres. The **septum pellucidum,** a thin-walled structure separating the lateral ventricles, is situated between the fornix and the corpus callosum. It is composed of 2 thin vertical sheets of tissue that are sometimes separated by the cavity of the septum pellucidum (cavum septi pellucidi).

White Substance

The white substance of the cerebral hemisphere contains medullated nerve fibers of many sizes as well as neuroglia. Three types of myelinated nerve make up the center of the cerebral hemisphere: transverse fibers, projection fibers, and association fibers.

Transverse (commissural) fibers interconnect the 2 cerebral hemispheres. The **corpus callosum** is the largest, and most of its fibers arise from various parts of one cerebral hemisphere and terminate in the symmetric area of the opposite cerebral hemisphere. It is a broad transverse structure that forms the roof of the lateral and third ventricles. The **anterior commissure** connects the 2 olfactory bulbs at its rostral part and the 2 piriform areas at its caudal portion. The **hippocampal commissure,** or **commissure of the fornix,** joins the 2 hippocampi.

Projection fibers, some of which pass through the corona radiata to the internal capsule, connect the cerebral cortex with the lower portions of the brain and spinal cord. The **afferent,** or **corticipetal, fibers** include the geniculocalcarine tract from the lateral geniculate body to the calcarine cortex, the auditory radiation from the medial geniculate body to the auditory cortex (Heschl's gyrus), and thalamic radiations from the thalamic nuclei to specific cerebrocortical areas. **Efferent,** or **corticifugal, fibers** proceed from the cerebral cortex to the thalamus, brain stem, and spinal cord. The corticospinal and corticobulbar tracts, making up the pyramidal motor system, originate in the motor cortex and proceed inferiorly via the internal capsule. Corticopontine tracts from the cerebral cortex to the pons include a frontopontine tract, which originates in the frontal lobe cortex and goes to the pontine nuclei; and a temporoontine tract, which terminates similarly but originates in the temporal lobe cortex. Corticothalamic fibers pass from the cerebral cortex to the thalamic nuclei. A corticorubral tract extends from the frontal lobe to the red nucleus of the midbrain. The fornix projects in part to the midbrain after originating in the hippocampus.

Association fibers connect the various portions of the same cerebral hemisphere. Short association fibers connect adjacent gyri; those located in the deeper portion of the cortex are known as intracortical fibers, whereas those just beneath the cortex are called subcortical fibers. Long association fibers connect more widely separated areas: the **uncinate fasciculus** crosses the bottom of the lateral cerebral fissure and connects the inferior frontal lobe gyri with the anterior temporal lobe. The **cingulum,** a white band lying within the cingulate gyrus, connects the anterior perforated substance and the parahippocampal gyrus. The **arcuate fasciculus** sweeps around the insula and connects the superior and middle frontal convolutions with the temporal lobe and temporal pole. The **superior longitudinal fasciculus** connects portions of the frontal lobe with occipital and temporal areas. The **inferior longitudinal fasciculus,** extending parallel to the lateral border of the inferior and posterior horns of the lateral ventricle, connects the temporal and occipital lobes. The **occipitofrontal fasciculus** extends backward from the frontal lobe, radiating into the temporal and occipital lobes. The **fornix** for the most part connects the hippocampus with the mamillary body.

Microscopic Structure of Cortex

The cortex of the cerebrum may be conveniently considered as being of 2 types: allocortex and isocortex. The **allocortex** is found predominantly in the rhinencephalon, or portions concerned with olfaction. The **isocortex** (neocortex) is the type found more commonly in most of the cerebral hemispheres. It is composed of 6 layers of cells that have their embryologic origin in the mass of gray matter surrounding the ventricles: The outermost **molecular layer (I)** contains fibers that come from within the cortex. The **external granular layer (II)** is a rather dense layer composed of small cells. The **external pyramidal layer (III)** contains pyramidal cells, frequently in row formation. The **internal granular layer (IV)** is usually a thin layer with cells similar to those in the external granular layer (II). The **ganglionic layer (V)** in most areas contains pyramidal cells that are fewer but larger than in the external pyramidal layer (III). The **fusiform layer (VI)** is composed of fusiform irregular cells whose axons enter adjacent white matter.

Medullated fiber layers between the cortical layers give the appearance of white lines. The **line of Gennari** in the striate area of the occipital lobe is quite prominent, visible to the naked eye, and forms the outer portion of the internal granular layer (IV). The same line present elsewhere in the cortex is thinner and is known as the **external line of Baillarger.** The **internal line of Baillarger** is formed by the inner portion of the ganglionic layer (V).

Division and classification of the cortex has been attempted by many investigators on the basis of cytoarchitecture, and inferences concerning its structure and function are drawn largely from observations on animals, especially monkeys and chimpanzees. The most commonly employed systems are those of von Economo and Brodmann. Von Economo differentiated 5 main types of isocortex based on the characteristics of lamination, or layering. Using numbers, Brodmann labeled individual areas that he believed were different from others (Figs 1–10 and 1–11). The areas have been used as a reference base for the localization of physiologic and pathologic processes.

Ablation and stimulation, electrically and with various chemicals, have led to functional localizations. Some of the principal areas are as follows:

(1) Frontal lobe: Area 4 is the principal motor area. Area 6 is a part of the extrapyramidal tract circuit. Area 8 is concerned with eye movements and pupillary changes. Areas 9, 10, 11, and 12 are frontal association areas.

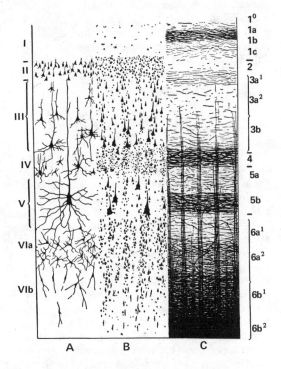

Figure 1–4. Diagram of the structure of the cerebral cortex. *A:* Golgi neuronal stain. *B:* Nissl cellular stain. *C:* Weigert myelin stain. I = molecular layer; II = external granular layer; III = layer of pyramidal cells; IV = internal granular layer; V = ganglionic layer; VI = layer of fusiform or polymorphic cells; 3a¹ = band of Bechterew; 4 = outer band of Baillarger; 5b = inner band of Baillarger. (Brodmann.) (Reproduced, with permission, from Ranson SW, Clark SL: *The Anatomy of the Nervous System,* 10th ed. Saunders, 1959.)

(2) Parietal lobe: Areas 3, 1, and 2 constitute the postcentral principal sensory area. Areas 5, 7, 39, and 40 are sensory association areas.

(3) Temporal lobe: Area 41 is the primary auditory cortex. Area 42 is the secondary, or associative, auditory cortex. Areas 38, 20, 21, and 22 are association areas.

(4) Occipital lobe: Area 17 is the striate cortex, the principal visual cortex. Areas 18 and 19 are visual association areas.

Flechsig used the myelogenetic method to make a detailed subdivision of the cerebral cortex by studying the time and pattern of myelination of fibers in white substance immediately beneath the cortex. Initially, Flechsig described 40 cortical fields; this number was later increased.

Bailey and von Bonin have made a tentative sectoral map of the human cerebral cortex (Fig 1–9); they felt that the subdivision into sectors was more logical than the customary division into lobes. The map is based principally on the distribution of corticothalamic afferents. The boundaries of the sectors are only roughly approximate, and density of radiation is not uniform throughout the sectors. The authors felt that the microscopic appearances of cortical sections from parietal, temporal, and large areas of frontal cortex were indistinguishable from each other. Their vivid color map of the cerebral cortex of humans, based on cortical cytoarchitecture, supports their statement that "the human isocortex is more remarkable for its uniformity than for multifarious differentiations."

PHYSIOLOGY & FUNCTION*

The Primary Motor Projection Cortex (Area 4)

The primary motor projection cortex is located on the anterior wall of the central sulcus and the adjacent portion of the precentral gyrus, corresponding generally to the distribution of the giant pyramidal (Betz) cells. These cells control voluntary movements of skeletal muscle on the opposite side of the body, with the impulses traveling over their axons in the corticobulbar and corticospinal tracts to the nuclei of the cerebrospinal nerves. The inverted arrangement within the motor areas appears in Figs 1–6 and 1–7. Conjugate deviation of the head and eyes occurs upon stimulation of the posterior part of the middle frontal gyrus (areas 6 and 8). Irritative lesions of the motor centers may cause convulsive seizures, beginning as focal twitchings and spreading to involve large muscle groups (jacksonian epilepsy), modification of consciousness, and postconvulsive weakness or paralysis.

Destructive lesions of the motor cortex (area 4) produce contralateral flaccid paresis or paralysis of affected muscle groups. Spasticity is more apt to occur if area 6 and also the intermediate cortex are ablated.

*Numbers in the text refer to Brodmann areas. See Figs 1–10 and 1–11.

The paralysis following ablation of area 4 is more pronounced in the distal portions of the extremities. Section of the pyramidal tract in the medulla oblongata produces a flaccid paralysis similar to that from cortical ablation of area 4. Therefore, the presence of spasticity is believed to indicate interruption of extrapyramidal pathways.

The portion of the cerebral cortex most excitable to motor stimulation is area 4. It is believed that the ganglionic layer (V), which contains the Betz cells, significantly affects the excitability of this area. Transient reduction in excitability occurs in the motor cortex on continuous stimulation; after about 15 seconds, **"extinction"** may occur, in which the motor cortex becomes temporarily unexcitable. **Facilitation** is that phenomenon by which a subthreshold stimulus becomes adequate for stimulation (as through serial repetition). **Suppression** refers to the phenomenon associated with inhibition of striated muscle responses following cerebrocortical or subcortical stimulation.

Stimulation of the "premotor area" (area 6) produces movements similar to those of the motor area (area 4). However, after ablation of area 4 or interruption of fibers between areas 4 and 6, stimulation then produces stereotyped movements accompanied by head turning and torsion of the body. Following premotor ablations in monkeys, forced grasping may become evident, best demonstrated with the subject in the lateral position and the affected side uppermost.

The Primary Sensory Projection Cortex (Areas 3, 1, 2)

The primary sensory projection cortex for the reception of general sensations is located in the postcentral gyrus and is called the somesthetic area. It receives fibers from the thalamic radiations conveying skin, muscle, joint, and tendon sense from the opposite side of the body. Irritative lesions of this area produce paresthesias—eg, numbness, formication, "electric shock," and "pins-and-needles" sensations—on the opposite side of the body. Destructive lesions produce objective impairment in sensibility—eg, inability to localize or measure the intensity of painful stimuli and impaired perception of various forms of cutaneous sensation. Complete anesthesia on a cortical basis is rare.

Experimental studies indicate that a relatively wide portion of the adjacent frontal lobe (areas 4 and 6) may also receive sensory stimuli; conversely, motor responses can be achieved by stimulation of the primary sensory areas (3, 1, 2). The primary sensorimotor area may therefore be considered capable of functioning as both motor and sensory cortex, with the portion of the cortex anterior to the central (rolandic) sulcus predominantly motor and that behind this sulcus predominantly sensory.

Topographic organization exists in both the sensory and motor areas (Figs 1–5 and 1–6). Recent findings indicate that the primary motor and primary sensory areas are arranged topographically on the cerebral cortex as contiguous mirror images.

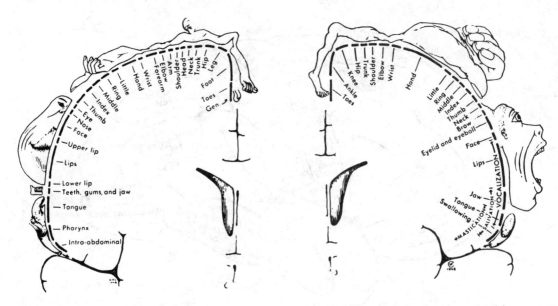

Figure 1–5. Sensory homunculus, drawn overlying a coronal section through the postcentral gyrus.

Figure 1–6. Motor homunculus, drawn overlying a coronal section through the precentral gyrus.

(*Note:* Figs 1–5 and 1–6 represent the location of cortical representation of the various parts. The size of the various parts is proportionate to the amount of cortical area devoted to them. [Reproduced, with permission, from Penfield & Rasmussen: *The Cerebral Cortex of Man: A Clinical Study of Localization of Function.* Macmillan, 1950.])

The cortical taste area is located in the facial sensory area and extends onto the opercular surface of the lateral cerebral fissure.

The Primary Visual Receptive Cortex (Area 17)

The primary visual receptive cortex is located in the occipital lobe in the cortex of the calcarine fissure and adjacent portions of the cuneus and the lingual gyrus. Irritative lesions may produce visual hallucinations, eg, flashes of light, rainbows, brilliant stars, or bright lines. Destructive lesions may cause contralateral homonymous defects in the visual fields without destruction of macular vision. Cortex containing macular representation receives overlapping blood supply from the middle and posterior cerebral arteries.

In primates, the posterior portion of the occipital pole is primarily concerned with macular vision, whereas the more anterior parts of the calcarine fissure are concerned with peripheral vision. Visual association is a function of areas 18 and 19, and injury to these areas may produce visual disorganization with defective spatial orientation in the homonymous halves of the visual field. Area 19 can receive stimuli from the entire cerebral cortex; area 18 receives stimuli mainly from area 17.

Field defects may also be caused by lesions of the parietal or temporal lobes that interfere with the optic pathways. Visual hallucinations from temporal lobe lesions may be of formed objects, people, buildings, etc. (See Figs 4–6 and 4–7.)

The Primary Auditory Receptive Area (Area 41)

The primary auditory receptive area is located in the transverse temporal gyrus (Heschl's gyrus), which lies buried in the floor of the lateral cerebral fissure. It receives the auditory radiation from the medial geniculate body, which conveys impulses from the cochlea of each ear; lesions of this area cause only mild deafness except when bilateral. Point-to-point projection of the cochlea upon the acoustic area occurs; in humans, the low tones are in the frontolateral portion and the high tones in the occipitomedial portion of area 41. In the cochlea, low tones are detected near the apex and high tones near the base.

Stimulation of the region near the primary auditory receptive area in humans causes buzzing and roaring sensations.

The Olfactory Receptive Area

The olfactory receptive area is located in the uncus and adjacent portions of the parahippocampal gyrus of the temporal lobe. Destruction of the olfactory pathways or cortex produces anosmia. Irritative lesions may cause olfactory hallucinations known as "uncinate fits," characterized by sensations of peculiar odors and tastes and often associated with a dreamy state. These may occur as an epileptic aura.

The Association Areas

The association areas are connected with the various sensory and motor areas by association fibers. They are of importance in the maintenance of higher mental activities in humans, although it is not possible to localize any specific mental faculty or fraction of conscious experience. Aphasias or speech defects resulting from cortical lesions illustrate the significance

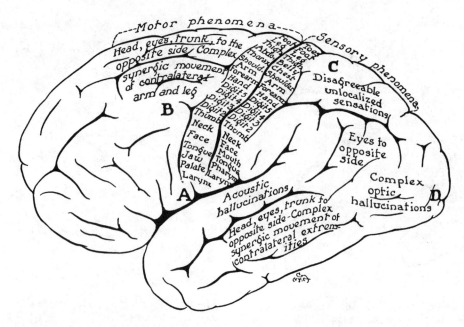

Figure 1–7. Results of electrical stimulation of the cerebral cortex. *A:* Chewing, licking, and swallowing movements. *B:* Eyes turned to the opposite side without visual aura. *C:* Sensory aura in opposite leg followed by complex synergistic movements. *D:* Unformed optical phenomena such as flames and lights. (After Foerster. Reproduced, with permission, from Bailey: *Intracranial Tumors.* Thomas, 1933.)

of association areas. In right-handed individuals, these are produced by lesions in the left hemisphere (the dominant hemisphere). Motor aphasia may result from destruction of the triangular and opercular portions of the inferior frontal gyrus (area 44). An individual can move lips and tongue but is unable to carry out the coordinated movements required in speaking. Agraphia—inability to write words—is often associated with motor aphasia. Sensory aphasia results from lesions in the posterior part of the left superior temporal gyrus (area 39). The patient may hear the spoken word but cannot comprehend its meaning. Word blindness—the inability to understand written words although vision is unimpaired—may result from lesions of the angular gyrus (area 39).

The frontal lobe, in its portions anterior to the precentral motor area, has long been known as an area concerned with higher intellectual and psychic functions. Classically, destructive lesions of this area may produce facetiousness (Witzelsucht), change in moral and social attributes, disinterest in environment and former interests, intellectual deterioration, and distractibility. The orbitofrontal area (areas 9, 10, 11, and 12) receives projections from the dorsomedial nuclei of the thalamus, which in turn has connections with the hypothalamus. Surgical procedures that affect the connections between this portion of the frontal cortex and the thalamus have been used. In general, when used they were most successful in surgical treatment of obsessions, anxiety, schizophrenic psychoses, and intractable pain. Frontal leukotomy and lobotomy severed the cortical-subcortical connections in the fron-

tal lobe, usually at about the level of the anterior limit of the lateral ventricles. Topectomy referred to the removal of cortical areas of the brain, usually areas 9 and 10 on both sides. Cortical undercutting was less commonly used; it consisted of interrupting the connections just below the cortex. Thalamotomy created a lesion, usually in the dorsomedial nucleus of the thalamus, by means of stereotaxic devices. Other methods have also been used to produce uniform subcortical destructive lesions. Radio frequency waves have been applied to stereotactically placed electrodes. In the hope of avoiding the dangers of hemorrhage and sepsis, the Bragg peak of a proton beam has been used to produce precise intracerebral lesions. Surgical section of the cingulum (anterior cingulotomy) is preferred to frontal leukotomy in some centers.

The posterior portion of the orbital surface (area 47) and the contiguous portion of the anterior half of the insula produce pronounced autonomic effects upon electrical stimulation; inhibition of respiration and alteration of blood pressure may also be readily induced. Upon stimulation of the anterior cingulate area (area 24), which lies on the medial aspect of the cerebral hemisphere, pronounced autonomic effects and inhibition of skeletal muscle tone may occur. Following ablation of this area, aggressive male monkeys become relatively tame, manageable, and less fearful and anxious.

Parietal lobe (areas 5 and 7) association centers are necessary for the correlation of cutaneous sensations, thus enabling individuals to recognize familiar objects placed in their hands (with their eyes closed), a

Table 1—1. Classification of human cerebral cortex by Bailey and von Bonin.* (See Fig 1—8.)

	Terminology of Map	Legend
Allocortex	Allocortex	
Isocortex		
Eulaminate variants		
1. Inferior parietal	Homotypical isocortex	
2. Superior parietal	Homotypical isocortex	
3. Preoccipital	Homotypical isocortex	
4. Inferior frontal	Homotypical isocortex	
5. Inferior temporal	Homotypical isocortex	
Agranular variants		
1. Simple precentral	Agranular cortex	
2. Gigantopyramidal precentral	Agranular gigantopyramidal cortex	
3. Limbic juxtallocortical	Mesocortex	
Koniose variants		
1. Occipital striate	Koniocortex	
2. Postcentral	Koniocortex	
3. Supratemporal	Koniocortex	
Limitrophic variants		
1. Occipital, postcentral, and supratemporal parakoniocortical	Parakoniocortex	
2. Temporal juxtallocortical	Juxtallocortex	
3. Frontal dysgranular	Dysgranular cortex	

*See Chusid JG: Black-and-white supplement for the color brain map of Bailey and von Bonin. *Neurology* 1964;**14**:154.

function referred to as stereognostic sense. In lesions of the parietal cortex, this ability may be lost (astereognosis).

Cerebral Dominance

Studies of patients in whom the corpus callosum has been surgically divided suggest that the major, or dominant, cerebral hemisphere is functionally distinct from the opposite, or minor, hemisphere. The dominant cerebral hemisphere (usually the left in humans) is concerned mainly with verbal, linguistic, arithmetic, calculating, and analytic functions. The minor cerebral hemisphere is concerned with nonverbal, geometric, spatial, visual, pattern, musical, and synthetic functions.

Cerebral dominance usually is not fully established until the third or fourth year of life. It may be related to structural differences between the cerebral hemispheres. Asymmetries that have been noted in the auditory region and in the lateral cerebral fissure may be related to language lateralization and hand preference. The best-defined asymmetries have been found in the upper surface of the temporal lobe in the cortical area behind Heschl's gyrus (area 41). This posterior cortical area, sometimes referred to as the planum

temporale, is reported to be larger in the left cerebral hemisphere in the majority of brains examined.

Secondary or Second Motor & Sensory Areas

These have been demonstrated in the opercular cortex (parietal lobe) forming the superior wall of the lateral cerebral fissure. These areas have extensive communications with the primary motor and sensory areas.

Supplemental Motor & Sensory Area

Electrical stimulation of a circumscribed zone of cerebral cortex situated on the medial aspect of the cerebral hemisphere, just anterior to the principal motor area for the foot, is capable of producing characteristic motor responses and, occasionally, sensory responses.

Rhinencephalon (Limbic System)

Clinical observations and animal experiments indicate that rhinencephalic structures have important functions other than those concerned with olfaction. In primates, a variety of autonomic, somatomotor, and somatosensory responses may be produced by electrical stimulation of the anterior limbic, subcallosal, and

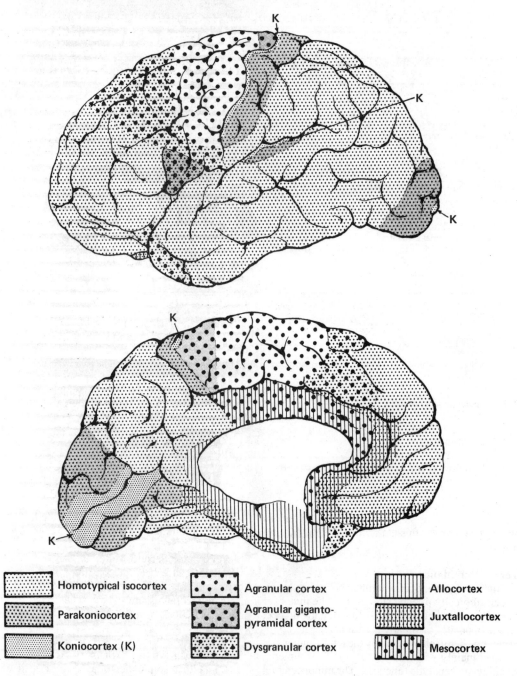

Figure 1–8. Map of human cerebral cortex based upon the original color maps of Bailey and von Bonin. Transitions from one field to another, as well as the lack of sharp boundaries, are indicated in the original maps by blending and shading of colors. See Table 1 –1. (Redrawn, modified, and reproduced, with permission, from Bailey & von Bonin: *The Isocortex of Man.* Univ of Illinois, 1951.)

posterior orbital regions of the frontal lobes; the anterior insula, anterior parahippocampal gyri, and anterior temporal cortex; and the amygdaloid body. Electrical stimulation may inhibit respiratory movements, spontaneous movements such as shivering and swallowing, and motor discharges initiated from the precentral motor cortex; or may produce chewing, swallowing, licking, faciovocal movements, tonic move-

ments of the trunk and extremities, pupillary changes, piloerection, salivation, and involuntary micturition and defecation. The electrical activity of the greater part of the cerebral cortex may be altered in various ways by electrical stimulation of these structures.

Rhinencephalic structures (such as the anterior limbic area and the posterior orbital surface) may exert an inhibitory effect on brain stem mechanisms con-

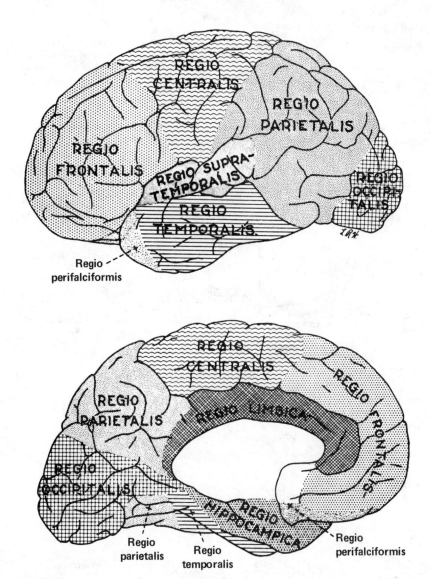

Figure 1–9. Sectoral map of the left cerebral cortex based upon distribution of fibers from thalamus to cortex. (Reproduced, with permission, from Bailey & von Bonin: *The Isocortex of Man.* Univ of Illinois, 1951.)

cerned in the expression of emotions such as anger. Restlessness and hyperactivity result from lesions affecting these structures.

The term **"visceral brain"** has been used to designate the limbic system, which includes the limbic lobe and infolded hippocampus, and subcortical cell stations: amygdala, septal nuclei, hypothalamus, anterior thalamic nuclei, parts of the basal ganglia, and probably the epithalamus. The terms limbic lobe, limbic system, and rhinencephalon are used interchangeably. The rhinencephalon has many connections with the hypothalamus and is also concerned with biologic rhythms, sexual behavior, emotions of rage and fear, and motivation. According to MacLean, the medial forebrain bundle is the major afferent and efferent communication between the limbic lobe and the brain stem, with 3 major branches to the amygdala, septum, and anterior hypothalamus.

Loss of recent memory may occur following extensive bilateral hippocampal lesions in humans.

Electrical stimulation of the cortex of the anterolateral or lateral surface of the temporal lobe of humans may produce responses that have led Penfield to label this area as the "interpretive cortex." He has reported that stimulation of the interpretive cortex in a human subject "(1) may cause the stream of former consciousness to flow again or (2) may give him an interpretation of the present that is unexpected or involuntary."

Corpus Callosum

Complete section of the corpus callosum in hu-

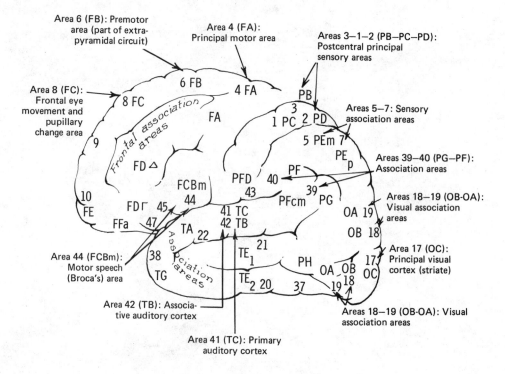

Figure 1–10. The lateral aspect of the cerebrum. The cortical areas are shown according to Brodmann (numbers) and von Economo (letters), with functional localizations.

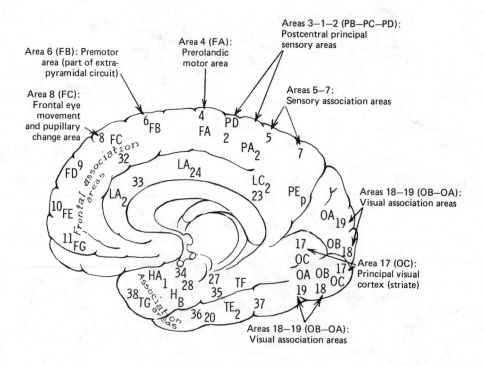

Figure 1–11. The medial aspect of the cerebrum. The cortical areas are shown according to Brodmann (numbers) and von Economo (letters), with functional localizations.

mans may produce a clinical syndrome that includes (1) inability to match an object in one hand with one placed in the other hand; (2) inability to match an object seen in one eye's visual field with one seen in the visual field of the other eye; (3) left-sided disabilities such as difficulty in carrying out verbal commands with the left hand, illegible writing with the left hand, and incorrect naming of objects placed in the left hand; and (4) constructional apraxia.

BASAL GANGLIA

Anatomy

The basal ganglia are masses of gray matter situated deep within the cerebral hemispheres. The **corpus striatum** presents a striped appearance because of the white fascicles of the internal capsule that are situated between the gray putamen and the caudate nucleus. The **caudate nucleus,** an elongated gray masswhose pear-shaped head is continuous with the anterior perforated substance, lies adjacent to the inferior border of the anterior horn of the lateral ventricle. The slender end continues backward and downward as the tail, entering the roof of the temporal horn of the lateral ventricle to end at the level of the amygdala. The **lenticular,** or **lentiform, nucleus** is situated between the insula, the caudate nucleus, and the thalamus and is divided into 2 parts by the external medullary lamina: The **putamen** is the larger, convex gray mass lying lateral to and just beneath the insular cortex. The **globus pallidus** is the smaller, median triangular zone whose numerous myelinated fibers make it appear lighter in color. The caudate nucleus sends many fibers to the putamen, which in turn sends short fibers to the globus pallidus. The putamen and globus pallidus receive some fibers from the substantia nigra, and the thalamus sends fibers to the caudate nucleus.

Efferent fibers from the corpus striatum leave via the globus pallidus. Some fibers pass through the internal capsule and, on reaching the medial side, form a bundle, the **fasciculus lenticularis.** Other fibers sweep the mesial border of the internal capsule to form a loop, the ansa lenticularis. Both of these sets of fibers give off some terminals to the subthalamic nucleus; others continue upward to the thalamus via the fasciculus thalamicus (Fig 1–22).

The **amygdaloid body** is a small, spherical gray mass located in the roof of the terminal part of the inferior horn of the lateral ventricle. The amygdalas of both cerebral hemispheres are interconnected by white commissural fibers in the anterior commissure. The **claustrum** is a thin layer of gray substance situated just beneath the insular cortex and separated from the more median putamen by the thin lamina of white matter known as the external capsule.

The **internal capsule** is a broad band of white substance separating the lenticular nucleus from the medial caudate nucleus and thalamus. In horizontal section, it presents a V appearance, with the apex, or genu, pointing medially. The anterior limb separates the lenticular from the caudate nucleus and contains (1) thalamocortical and corticothalamic fibers joining the lateral thalamic nucleus with the frontal lobe cortex; (2) frontopontine tracts from the frontal lobe to the pontine nuclei; and (3) fibers from the caudate nucleus to the putamen.

The posterior limb of the internal capsule, located between the thalamus and the lenticular nucleus, may be divided into 3 parts: lenticulothalamic, retrolenticular, and sublenticular. The anterior two-thirds of the lenticulothalamic part contains the corticobulbar tract and the corticospinal tract with the fibers to the arm anterior to the fibers to the leg; corticorubral fibers from the frontal lobe cortex to the red nucleus accompany the corticospinal tract. The retrolenticular part contains fibers from the lateral nucleus of the thalamus to the postcentral gyrus. The sublenticular part, lying below the lenticular nucleus, contains parietotemporopontine fibers from the temporal and parietal lobe cortex to the pontine nuclei; auditory radiations from the medial geniculate body to Heschl's gyrus (the transverse temporal gyrus); and optic fibers from the geniculate body to the calcarine cortex.

Physiology

The caudate and lenticular nuclei, together with the fascicles of the internal capsule that separate them, constitute the corpus striatum, an important unit of the extrapyramidal system. The corpus striatum sends efferent projections to the globus pallidus and receives fibers from the frontal lobe, thalamus, and hypothalamus. A major efferent route is from the globus pallidus via the ansa lenticularis to the cerebral nuclei and brain stem nuclei. Upon electrical stimulation of the basal ganglia, inhibition of skeletal muscle tone and cortically induced motor responses may occur. The globus pallidus and lateral nuclear groups of the thalamus appear to be focal structures upon which many pathways concerned with motor function converge. These nuclei exert important regulating and controlling influences on motor integration, in addition to relaying afferent systems to the cerebral cortex. The extrapyramidal system is a functional unit dependent upon an intact lateral corticospinal or pyramidal system.

Primary motor movements are not obtained in most animals following electrical stimulation of portions of the basal ganglia, but somatic reactions initiated by the cerebral cortex may be inhibited. In the absence of injury to the cerebral cortex, isolated lesions of the basal ganglia in primates usually give little evidence of positive symptomatology beyond a transient spasticity. When lesions of precentral motor cortical areas coexist with basal ganglia lesions, tremor and choreoathetosis or a marked increase in rigidity may occur in higher primates.

In humans, therapeutic production of lesions of

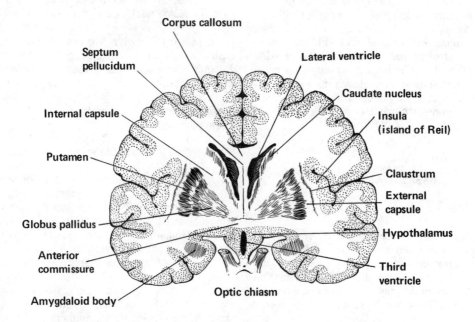

Figure 1–12. Coronal section through cerebrum at level of anterior commissure.

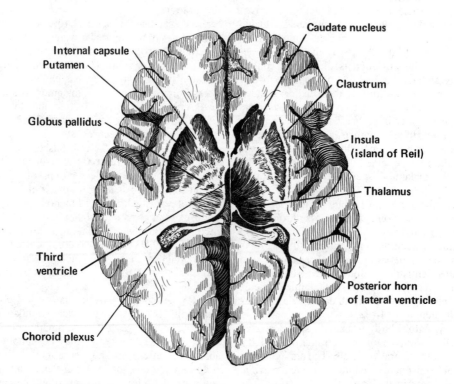

Figure 1–13. Horizontal sections through cerebrum at 2 levels to show basal ganglia.

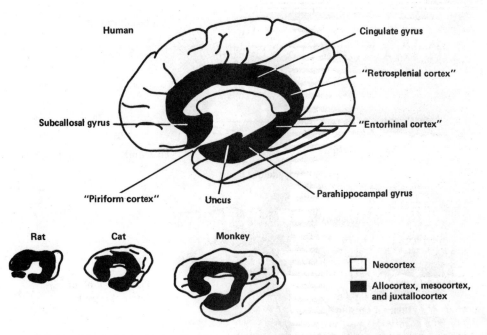

Figure 1–14. Relation of the limbic cortex in rats, cats, monkeys, and humans. (Redrawn and reproduced, with permission, from MacLean: The limbic system and its hippocampal formation. *J Neurosurg* 1954;11:29.)

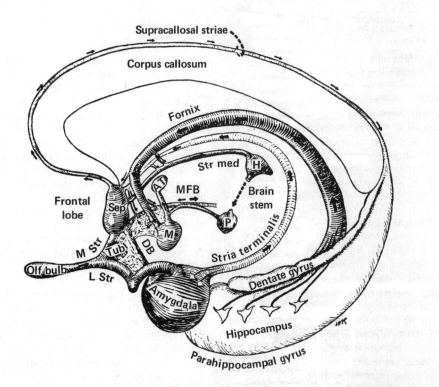

Figure 1–15. Diagram of the principal connections of the limbic system. M Str, L Str = medial and lateral olfactory striae; Str Med = stria medullaris; Tub = olfactory tubercle; DB = diagonal band of Broca; Sep = septum; AT = anterior nucleus of the thalamus; M = mamillary body; H = habenula; P = interpeduncular nucleus; MFB = medial forebrain bundle. (After Krieg. Reproduced, with permission, from MacLean: Psychosomatic disease and the visceral brain. *Psychosom Med* 1949; 11:338.)

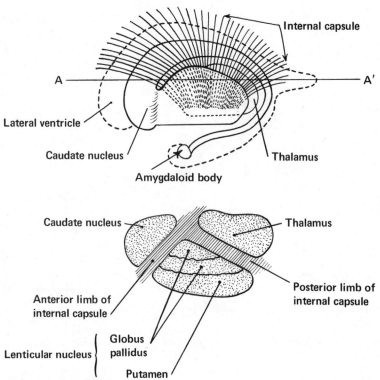

Figure 1–16. Lateral view of basal ganglia and adjacent structures with horizontal cross section at level AA′. (Reproduced, with permission, from Buchanan: *Functional Neuroanatomy,* 2nd ed. Lea & Febiger, 1951.)

the globus pallidus may reduce tremor and rigidity of patients with parkinsonism or dystonia musculorum deformans.

Secondary lesions made in the region of the globus pallidus and internal capsule may abolish tremors and alter tone of an experimental parkinsonismlike syndrome of monkeys produced by lesions made in reticular substance near the red nucleus and substantia nigra.

EXTRAPYRAMIDAL SYSTEM

The extrapyramidal system has in the past usually been assumed to consist of motor mechanisms of the CNS excluding those of the pyramidal tract. However, anatomic and physiologic separation of the extrapyramidal from the pyramidal tract system has become increasingly more difficult. The extrapyramidal system has come to be considered as a functional rather than an anatomic unit and, as such, may be said to be composed of extrapyramidal portions of cerebral cortex, thalamic nuclei connected with striatum, corpus striatum, subthalamus, and rubral and reticular systems. The extrapyramidal system, in contrast to the more direct pyramidal system, reaches segmental levels of distribution after many detours, with neuronal

chains synaptically interrupted in basal ganglia, subcortical ganglia, and reticular areas.

The extrapyramidal system may be regarded as a functional system with 3 layers of integration: cortical, striatal (basal ganglia), and tegmental (midbrain). The bulboreticular inhibitory and facilitatory area receives fibers from cerebral cortical areas, the striatum, and the anterior cerebellum. The principal functions of the extrapyramidal system are concerned with associated movements, postural adjustments, and autonomic integration. Lesions at any level may obscure or abolish voluntary movements and replace them with involuntary movements.

Clinically important syndromes caused by dysfunction of the extrapyramidal system include the following:

(1) Parkinsonism, in which resting tremors and rigidity occur. The primary disorder is frequently in the globus pallidus, its cortical projection, the substantia nigra, or the reticular substance of the midbrain.

(2) Involuntary movements: Athetosis, chorea, and torsion spasms are frequently associated with lesions of the caudate nucleus and putamen of the striate bodies and the midbrain nuclei.

(3) Involvement of the internal capsule, as frequently occurs with cerebrovascular accidents (eg, thrombosis or hemorrhage of the lenticulostriate artery), results in a spastic hemiplegia of the opposite side of the body.

The pathophysiology of diseases of the extrapyramidal system is obscure. In general, it is felt that release from suppressor circuit action may occur. Operative measures aimed at interfering with an unsuppressed, relatively overactive circuit (Brodmann area 6 and the extrapyramidal system) or the precentral motor area that this circuit in turn affects may be helpful in overcoming annoying clinical symptoms. Thus, removal of areas 6 and 4 or of area 4 alone has overcome severe hemiballism (one-sided jerking and twitching), athetosis, or tremor. Surgical or chemical destruction of the globus pallidus or the ventrolateral nucleus of the thalamus may ameliorate involuntary movements in patients with dystonias or parkinsonism.

Connection between the gamma loop (Fig 8–6) and the extrapyramidal system seems quite likely, since extrapyramidal system disease may result in hypokinetic or rigid syndromes, as well as hyperkinetic, dystonic syndromes, including choreic, athetoid, ballistic, and myotonic syndromes. Muscle innervation may be considered to be directed by either alpha or gamma fiber routes, and alterations between these systems may feature extrapyramidal system disease.

DIENCEPHALON

Enclosing the third ventricle is the diencephalon, which includes the thalamus with the geniculate bodies, epithalamus, subthalamus, and hypothalamus.

THALAMUS

Anatomy

Each cerebral hemisphere contains a thalamus—a large, ovoid gray mass located on either side of the third ventricle and situated obliquely across the rostral end of the cerebral peduncle. The rostral end (the anterior tubercle) of the thalamus is rather narrow, lies close to the midline, and forms the posterior limit of the interventricular foramen. The posterior end is broader; its prominent medial portion is known as the **pulvinar,** whereas the lateral oval swelling is called the **lateral geniculate body.** The dorsal surface is separated from the more laterally placed caudate nucleus by the **stria terminalis** and the **terminal vein.** The medial surface forms the lateral wall of the third ventricle and is connected with the corresponding surface of the opposite thalamus by the **massa intermedia,** or **interthalamic adhesion,** a short communicating bar of gray matter.

The **thalamic radiation** refers to the tracts emerging from the lateral surface of the thalamus that then enter the internal capsule and terminate in the cerebral cortex. The **external medullary lamina** is the layer of myelinated fibers on the lateral surface of the thalamus next to the internal capsule. The **internal medullary lamina** is a vertical sheet of white matter that bifurcates in its anterior portion and thus divides the gray matter of the thalamus into a lateral, medial, and anterior portion.

Five groups of thalamic nuclei have been described by A.E. Walker:

(1) Anterior nuclear group: This makes up the tubercle of the thalamus and is separated from the rest

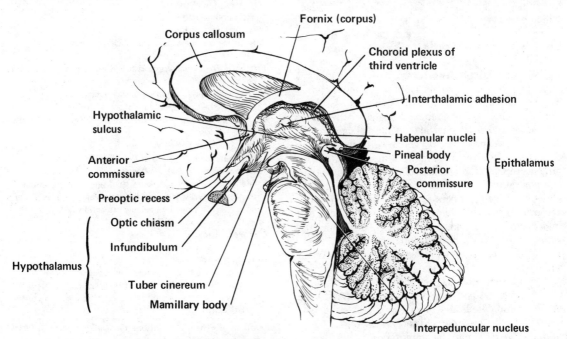

Corpus callosum

Fornix (corpus)

Choroid plexus of third ventricle

Interthalamic adhesion

Hypothalamic sulcus

Habenular nuclei
Pineal body
Posterior commissure

Epithalamus

Anterior commissure

Preoptic recess

Optic chiasm

Infundibulum

Hypothalamus

Tuber cinereum

Mamillary body

Interpeduncular nucleus

Figure 1–17. Sagittal section through brain showing the diencephalon.

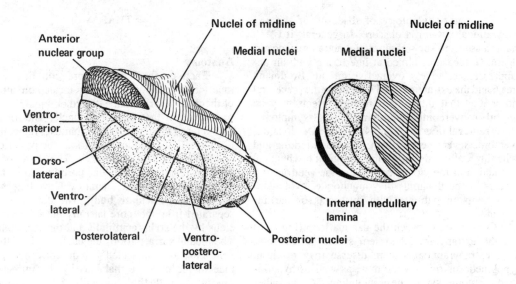

Figure 1–18. Diagrams of thalamus. Superior surface view and coronal section through posterior third. (Modified after Netter.)

of the thalamus by the limbs of the internal medullary lamina. It receives fibers from the mamillary bodies by way of the mamillothalamic tract and projects to the cingulate cortex of the cerebrum.

(2) Nuclei of the midline: These are groups of cells located just beneath the lining of the third ventricle and in the massa intermedia and are believed to connect with the hypothalamus and central periaqueductal gray matter.

(3) Medial nuclei: These include most gray substance medial to the internal medullary lamina (intralaminar nuclei) as well as the dorsal medial nucleus, which projects to the frontal cortex of the frontal pole anterior to the motor cortex; and the nucleus of the centrum medianum, which is believed to connect with the corpus striatum.

(4) Lateral nuclear mass: This constitutes a large part of the thalamus anterior to the pulvinar between the internal and external medullary laminas. This mass includes (a) a reticular nucleus between the external medullary lamina and the internal capsule; (b) an anterior ventral nucleus, which connects with the corpus striatum; (c) a lateral ventral nucleus, which projects to the cerebral motor cortex; (d) a posterolateral ventral nucleus, which projects to the postcentral gyrus and receives fibers from the medial lemniscus and from the spinothalamic and trigeminal tracts; and (e) a dorsolateral nucleus and a posterolateral nucleus, which project to the parietal lobe cortex.

(5) Posterior nuclei: These include the pulvinar and the medial and lateral geniculate bodies, including (a) the **pulvinar nucleus,** a large nucleus that connects with the parietal and temporal lobe cortices; (b) the **medial geniculate body,** which lies lateral to the midbrain under the pulvinar and receives acoustic fibers from the lateral lemniscus and inferior colliculus and projects fibers via the acoustic radiation to the tem-

poral lobe cortex (Heschl's gyrus); and (c) the **lateral geniculate body,** which receives most of the fibers of the optic tract and projects via the geniculocalcarine radiation to the visual cortex around the calcarine fis-

Table 1–2. Functional classification of the nuclei of the thalamus.*

Association nuclei
  Pulvinar
  Dorsomedial nucleus
  Dorsolateral nucleus
  Posterolateral nucleus
  Afferents: From other thalamic nuclei; no subcortical connections
  Efferents: These nuclei project to various parts of the cerebral cortex, particularly to the large association areas
Specific projection nuclei (cortical relay nuclei)
  Nucleus ventralis posteromedialis (sensation from face)
  Nucleus ventralis posterolateralis (sensation from trunk and limbs)
  Medial geniculate body (audition)
  Lateral geniculate body (vision)
  Afferents: From medial and lateral lemnisci, optic tracts, etc
  Efferents: These nuclei project specifically to points in the postcentral gyrus, temporal lobe, and calcarine area of the occipital lobe (specific thalamic projection system)
Nonspecific projection nuclei
  Nuclei of the midline
  Central medial nucleus
  Anteroventral nucleus
  Afferents: Fibers from the ascending reticular system
  Efferents: These nuclei project diffusely by a polysynaptic pathway to all the neocortex (nonspecific thalamic projection system)

*Modified from Ruch and Fulton: *Medical Physiology and Biophysics.* Saunders, 1960. Reproduced, with permission, from Ganong WF: *Review of Medical Physiology,* 7th ed. Lange, 1975.

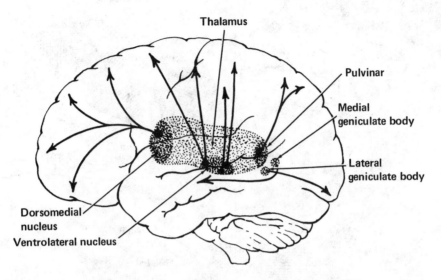

Figure 1–19. Diagram of principal thalamocortical projections.

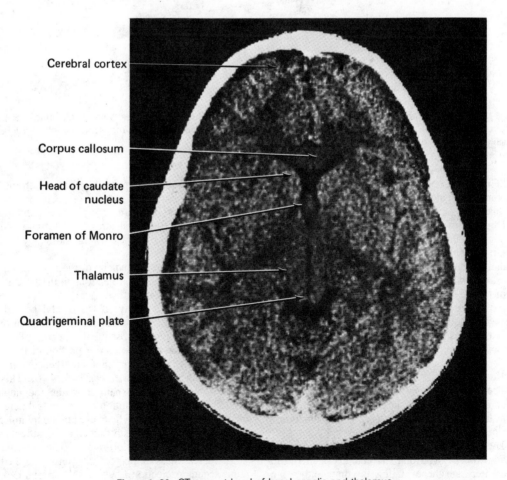

Figure 1–20. CT scan at level of basal ganglia and thalamus.

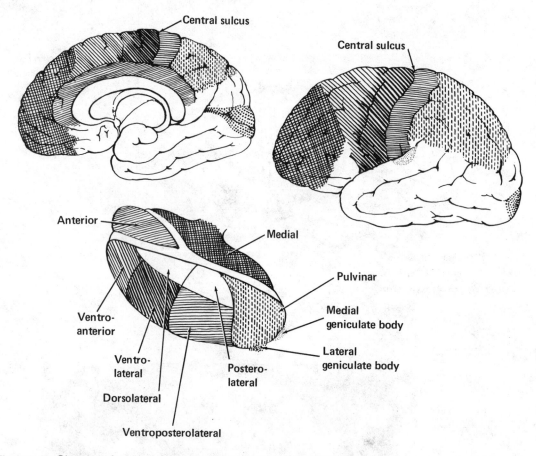

Figure 1–21. Diagrams of principal thalamocortical projections showing relation of cortical areas to thalamic nuclei. (Redrawn from original drawings by Frank H Netter, MD, that first appeared in Ciba *Clinical Symposia.* Copyright © 1950, Ciba Pharmaceutical Co. Reproduced with permission.)

sure. The lateral geniculate body appears as an oval elevation on the lateral portion of the posterior end of the thalamus.

Depending upon anatomic connections, the thalamic nuclei may be considered as nuclei with subcortical connections restricted to the thalamus, hypothalamus, basal ganglia, and subthalamus; cortical relay nuclei, which, after receiving the major sensory system fibers, send projections to the cerebral cortex primary sensory areas; or association nuclei, which project to association areas of the cerebral cortex, receive no fibers from the major sensory systems, and have connections with other diencephalic nuclei.

Function

The thalamus rather than the sensory cortex may be the crucial structure for the perception of some types of sensation, and the sensory cortex may function to give finer detail to the sensation.

The "thalamic syndrome" (thalamic apoplexy, Déjérine-Roussy syndrome) is characterized by immediate hemianesthesia. Later, the threshold to pinprick, heat, and cold is raised; when sensation is felt, it is a disagreeable and unpleasant one, sometimes referred to as thalamic hyperpathia. The syndrome usually appears during the phase of recovery from a thalamic infarct. The pains are persistent and greatly aggravated by emotional stress and fatigue and are described as distressing, burning, drawing, pulling, swelling, or "tension."

The dorsomedial nucleus of the anterior portion of the thalamus and its projections to the frontal lobe are usually the site of surgical attack in frontal lobotomy and leukotomy. If the frontal pole of the cerebral hemisphere is removed, degeneration of the dorsomedial nucleus subsequently occurs. The ventrolateral nucleus of the anterior portion of the thalamus projects to the primary motor and sensory areas of the cerebral hemispheres (areas 1, 3, 4, 6). This nucleus is a relay on the path from the red nucleus. Thalamotomy by interruption of the ventrolateral nucleus of the thalamus has been used in the treatment of patients with parkinsonism as well as in patients with dystonia musculorum deformans. The pulvinar, a large nuclear mass in the posterior portion of the thalamus, sends projection fibers to the parietal cerebral cortex; it may serve to integrate auditory, visual, and somatic impulses. The medial geniculate body is a thalamic nucleus that has been displaced downward. It projects to the primary auditory area of the temporal lobe (Brodmann area 41) and receives fibers from the lateral lemniscus. The lateral geniculate body lies lateral to the medial geniculate body and projects via the geniculocalcarine tract to the visual cortex of the occipital lobe.

Stimulation of the ventrolateral nucleus of the thalamus produces inhibition of contralateral muscle spindle discharge if the sensorimotor cortex remains intact. The muscle spindle, which is innervated by the slow, small motor fibers of the ventral motor root (gamma efferents), is believed to register differences between the main muscle mass and itself. Muscle innervation from cortical levels may be considered to be effected by either the alpha or the gamma route. The alpha route is direct or through relays to alpha anterior horn cells and thence to muscle. The gamma route is to the gamma cells of the anterior horn of the spinal cord and thence to muscle spindle. Alterations of the balance between alpha and gamma systems may produce altered muscle tone.

Thalamocortical interrelations. The spontaneous electrical activity of the cerebral cortex may be affected by stimulation of the midline nuclei of the thalamus, and a thalamic reticular system that is believed to be a continuation of the reticular systems of the brain stem has been described in this area. The "nonspecific" projection fibers from the thalamic reticular system play an important role in sustaining and regulating the normal resting rhythms of the cortex. Stimulation of the thalamic reticular system in animals via implanted electrodes may result in transient maintenance of the posture at the time of stimulation. Although thalamocortical circuits that influence the electrical activity of the thalamus and cortex are believed to exist, it must be borne in mind that both the thalamus and the cerebral cortex may show rhythmic electrical activity after interruption of the interconnecting fibers; however, this activity is usually depressed or of abnormal form. Corticifugal projections to the thalamus also assist in regulation of the thalamic reticular system activity. Local self-sustained epileptic discharges of the thalamus may be projected to the local cortical area, simulating focal cortical epilepsy.

SUBTHALAMUS

The subthalamus is the zone of brain tissue that lies between the tegmentum of the midbrain and the dorsal thalamus. The hypothalamus lies medial and rostral to it; lateral to it lies the internal capsule. The **red nucleus** and **substantia nigra** extend into its caudal part from the midbrain. The **subthalamic nucleus,** or body of Luys, is a cylindrical mass of gray substance dorsolateral to the upper end of the substantia nigra and extending posteriorly as far as the lateral aspect of the red nucleus. It receives fibers from the globus pallidus, forming a part of the efferent descending path from the corpus striatum.

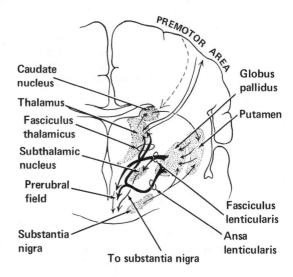

Figure 1–22. Chief connections of the corpus striatum and the subthalamus. (Reproduced, with permission, from Gatz: *Manter's Essentials of Clinical Neuroanatomy and Neurophysiology,* 4th ed. Davis, 1970.)

Anterior to the red nucleus are the **fields of Forel,** containing cells that may be a rostral extension of reticular nuclei. Fibers from the globus pallidus occupy these fields. The ventromedial portion is usually designated as field H, the dorsomedial portion as field H_1, and the ventrolateral portion as field H_2. From the globus pallidus, the **fasciculus lenticularis** (field H_2) runs medially. It is joined by the **ansa lenticularis** bending acutely in field H. The **thalamic fasciculus** extends through field H_1 to the anterior ventral nucleus of the thalamus. The **zona incerta** is a thin zone of gray substance above the fasciculus lenticularis. (See Fig 1–22.)

EPITHALAMUS

The epithalamus consists of the pineal body, the posterior commissure, and the habenular trigone. The **habenular trigone**—a small depressed triangular area anterior to the superior colliculus—contains the **habenular nuclei,** which receive fibers from the stria medullaris and are joined via the habenular commissure; and the **habenulopeduncular tract** (retroflex tract of Meynert), extending from the habenular nucleus to the interpeduncular ganglion in the midbrain.

The **pineal body** is a small mass lying in the depression between the superior colliculi. Its base is attached by a stalk. The ventral lamina of the stalk is continuous with the posterior commissure and the dorsal lamina with the habenular commissure. At their proximal ends the laminas of the stalk are separated, forming the **pineal recess** of the third ventricle.

The **posterior commissure** is a cylindrical band of white fibers that crosses the median plane on the dorsal aspect of the rostral end of the cerebral aqueduct. Some of its fibers connect the 2 superior colliculi.

HYPOTHALAMUS

The hypothalamus lies below or ventral to the thalamus and forms the floor and part of the inferior lateral walls of the third ventricle. It includes the fol-

lowing: (1) the **mamillary bodies,** 2 adjacent pea-sized white masses inferior to the gray matter of the floor of the third ventricle and rostral to the posterior perforated space; (2) the **tuber cinereum,** an eminence rostral to the mamillary bodies; (3) the **infun-**

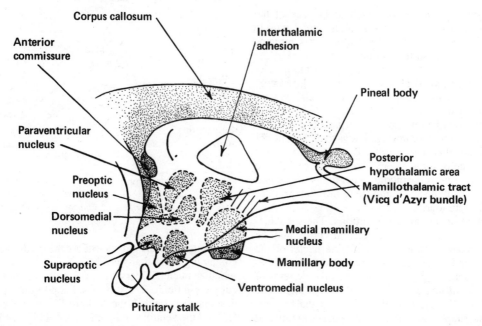

Figure 1–23. Diagram showing the hypothalamic nuclei projected onto the lateral wall of the third ventricle. (Reproduced, with permission, from Le Gros Clark WE: The topography and homologies of the hypothalamic nuclei in man. *J Anat* 1936; 70:204.)

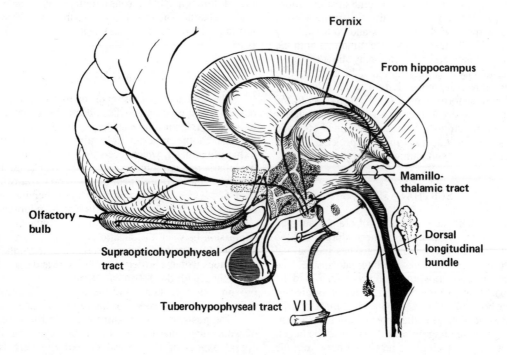

Figure 1–24. Diagram to illustrate some hypothalamic connections. (Redrawn from original drawings by Frank H Netter, MD, that first appeared in Ciba *Clinical Symposia.* Copyright © 1950, Ciba Pharmaceutical Co. Reproduced with permission.)

dibulum, a hollow process extending downward from the undersurface of the tuber cinereum to the posterior lobe of the hypophysis; and (4) the **optic chiasm.**

The lower portion of the infundibulum is continuous with the neural lobe of the hypophysis. The enlarged upper portion of the infundibulum, the median eminence, the infundibular stem, and the neural lobe of the hypophysis constitute the **neurohypophysis.**

Each half of the hypothalamus may be divided into a supraoptic, a tuberal, and a mamillary portion. The **supraoptic** portion is farthest anterior; the **tuberal** portion lies immediately behind the supraoptic portion; and the **mamillary** portion is farthest posterior. Anterior to the hypothalamus, between the optic chiasm and the anterior commissure, is a region referred to as the **preoptic area.**

The nuclei of the hypothalamus may be classified as follows:

(1) Anterior: The **paraventricular nucleus** is a flat sheet of cells lying close to the lining of the third ventricle. The **supraoptic nucleus** lies above the optic chiasm and extends along the anterior part of the tuber cinereum. It contains an especially rich network of capillaries. The supraoptic nucleus gives rise to the supraopticohypophyseal tract, which extends to the neurohypophysis by way of the pituitary stalk.

(2) Lateral: The lateral nucleus includes the lateral part of the tuber cinereum.

(3) Middle: The **ventromedial hypothalamic nucleus** is an oval mass of cells anterior to the mamillary bodies and posterior to the supraoptic nucleus. The dorsomedial hypothalamic nucleus is a mass lying above the ventromedial hypothalamic nucleus.

(4) Posterior: The cells of the posterior hypothalamic area lie above and immediately anterior to the mamillary bodies. Nuclei of the mamillary body include the **medial mamillary nucleus,** which makes up the protuberance of the mamillary body; and the **lateral mamillary nucleus,** located between the lateral border of the medial nucleus and the base of the brain. The nucleus intercalatus lies in the dorsal portion.

Afferent connections to the hypothalamus that have been described include (1) the **medial forebrain bundle,** which sends fibers to the hypothalamus from nuclei in the parolfactory area and corpus striatum; (2) **thalamohypothalamic fibers** from the medial and midline thalamic nuclei; (3) the **fornix,** which brings fibers from the hippocampus to the mamillary bodies; (4) the **stria terminalis,** which brings fibers from the amygdala; (5) **pallidohypothalamic fibers,** which lead from the lenticular nucleus to the ventromedial hypothalamic nucleus; and (6) the **inferior mamillary peduncle,** which sends fibers from the tegmentum of the midbrain.

Efferent tracts from the hypothalamus include

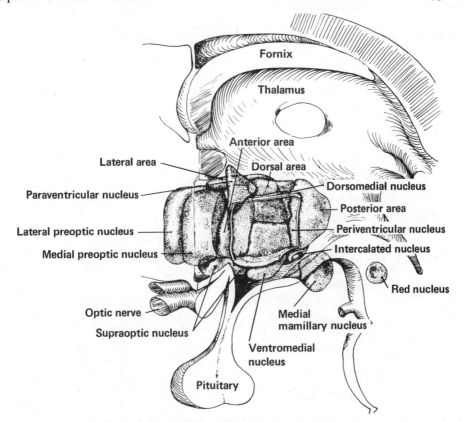

Figure 1–25. The human hypothalamus. (Redrawn from an original drawing by Frank H Netter, MD, in Ciba *Clinical Symposia.* Copyright © 1956, Ciba Pharmaceutical Co. Redrawn with permission.)

Table 1–3. Summary of hypothalamic regulatory mechanisms.*

Function	Afferents From	Integrating Areas
Temperature regulation	Cutaneous cold receptors; temperature-sensitive cells in hypothalamus	Anterior hypothalamus, response to heat; posterior hypothalamus, response to cold
Neuroendocrine control of:		
Catecholamines	Emotional stimuli, probably via limbic system	Dorsomedial and posterior hypothalamus
Vasopressin	Osmoreceptors, "volume receptors," others	Supraoptic and paraventricular nuclei
Oxytocin	Touch receptors in breast, uterus, genitalia	Supraoptic and paraventricular nuclei
Thyroid-stimulating hormone (TSH)	Temperature receptors, perhaps others (?)	Anterior median eminence and anterior hypothalamus
Adrenocorticotropic hormone (ACTH)	Limbic system (emotional stimuli); reticular formation ("systemic" stimuli); hypothalamic or anterior pituitary cells sensitive to circulating blood cortisol level; others (?)	Ventral hypothalamus
Follicle-stimulating hormone (FSH) and luteinizing hormone (LH)	Hypothalamic cells sensitive to estrogens; eyes, touch receptors in skin and genitalia of reflex ovulating species	Anterior hypothalamus, other areas
Prolactin	Touch receptors in breasts, other unknown receptors	Arcuate nucleus, median eminence (hypothalamus inhibits secretion)
Growth hormone	Unknown receptors	Anterior median eminence
"Appetitive" behavior		
Thirst	Osmoreceptors	Lateral superior hypothalamus
Hunger	"Glucostat" cells sensitive to rate of glucose utilization	Ventromedial satiety center, lateral hunger center, also limbic components
Sexual behavior	Cells sensitive to circulating estrogen and androgen, others	Anterior ventral hypothalamus, plus, in the male, piriform cortex
Defensive reactions		
Fear, rage	Sense organs and neocortex, paths unknown	Diffuse, in limbic system and hypothalamus
Control of various endocrine and activity rhythms	Retina via retinohypothalamic fibers	Suprachiasmatic nuclei

*Reproduced, with permission, from Ganong WF: *Review of Medical Physiology*, 10th ed. Lange 1981.

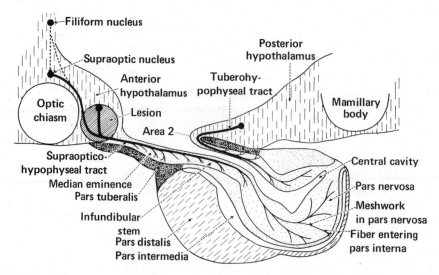

Figure 1–26. Diagram of a midsagittal section through the hypothalamus of the cat, showing the supraopticohypophyseal tract, whose interruption causes diabetes insipidus. (Modified and reproduced, with permission, from Fisher, Ingram, & Ranson: *Diabetes Insipidus and the Neurohormonal Control of Water Balance.* Edwards, 1938.)

(1) the **hypothalamicohypophyseal tract,** from the supraoptic nuclei to the neurohypophysis; (2) the **mamillotegmental tract** to the tegmentum; (3) **hypothalamic-thalamic tracts,** including the tract of Vicq d'Azyr from the mamillary nuclei to the anterior thalamic nuclei; (4) the **periventricular system,** including the dorsal fasciculus of Schütz to the lower brain levels; and (5) the **tuberohypophyseal tract,** from the tuberal portion of the hypothalamus to the posterior pituitary.

Function

The hypothalamus is believed to have diversified activities. Lesions of the hypothalamic region may produce a variety of symptoms, including diabetes insipidus, obesity, sexual dystrophy, somnolence, loss of sexual appetite, and loss of temperature control. A visual defect such as bitemporal hemianopsia frequently is present also as a result of involvement of the nearby optic chiasm.

Animals whose cerebral hemispheres have been removed may exhibit "sham rage," in which struggling, piloerection, dilatation of pupils, and increase in blood pressure occur on slight provocation. If only the posterior hypothalamus is removed, this reaction does not appear.

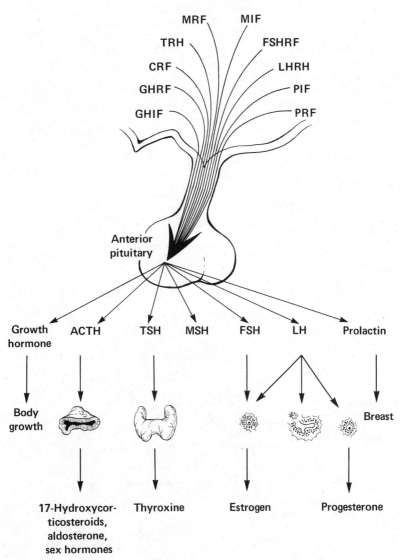

Figure 1–27. Hypothalamic releasing factors and actions of anterior pituitary hormones. GHRF = growth hormone–releasing factor; GHIF (somatostatin); CRF = corticotropin-releasing factor; TRH = thyrotropin-releasing factor; MRF = melanocyte-releasing factor; MIF = melanocyte-inhibiting factor; FSHRF = follicle-stimulating hormone–releasing factor; LHRH = luteinizing hormone– releasing factor; PIF = prolactin-inhibiting factor; and PRF = prolactin-releasing factor. (Reproduced, with permission, from Meyers FH, Jawetz E, Goldfien A: *Review of Medical Pharmacology,* 7th ed. Lange, 1980.)

Somnolence may be caused regularly by bilateral lesions of the lateral hypothalamic area. Temperature regulation disorders may be associated with hypothalamic lesions. Experimental lesions of the anterior hypothalamus may cause hyperthermia; lesions of the posterior nuclei are associated with hypothermia.

Diabetes insipidus may be caused by destruction of the neurohypophysis, the supraoptic nuclei, or the tract connecting these structures. Production of antidiuretic hormone ceases, and the patient passes excessive quantities of sugar-free urine of low specific gravity. Specialized vesicular bodies in the supraoptic nuclei have been described. These are believed to be sensitive to small changes in the osmotic pressure of blood from the internal carotid artery.

Disturbances of fat metabolism as a result of hypothalamic lesions are known to occur in rats and probably occur in other animals as well as humans.

Proposed mechanism of emotion. J.W. Papez suggested that the hypothalamus, the anterior thalamic nuclei, the cingulate gyrus, the hippocampus, and their interconnections may serve as a structural and functional unit for emotion (Papez circuit).

THE MIDBRAIN
(Mesencephalon)

Anatomy

The midbrain is the short portion of the brain between the pons and the cerebral hemispheres. The dorsal portion of the midbrain (the tectum) contains the 4 corpora quadrigemina; the ventrolateral portions contain the 2 cerebral peduncles. The **corpora quadrigemina** consist of 4 rounded eminences arranged in pairs, the superior and inferior colliculi, which are separated from each other by a cruciate sulcus. The **superior colliculi** are larger and darker than the inferior colliculi and are associated with the optic system. The superior quadrigeminal brachium extends laterally from them and connects with the **lateral geniculate body.** The **inferior colliculi** are more prominent than the superior colliculi and are associated with the auditory system. The inferior quadrigeminal brachium extends laterally to the **medial geniculate body.**

The **cerebral peduncles** converge from the lower surface of the cerebral hemispheres toward the mid-

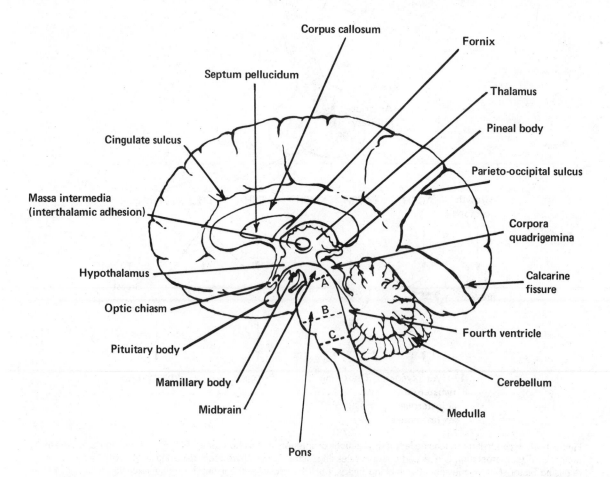

Figure 1–28. Midsagittal section of the brain. (Dotted lines do not indicate lines of demarcation of divisions of the brain but the levels at which sections are cut, as shown in Figs 1–31, 1–33, and 1–35.)

line, entering the pons on its upper surface. The interpeduncular fossa is the depressed area between the peduncles that contains in its lower portion the **interpeduncular ganglion,** the terminus for the retroflex bundle of Meynert from the habenular ganglion. The ventral portion of each peduncle is known as the **base**—a broad, compact crescentic structure. The corticospinal tract occupies the middle three-fifths of the base, the frontopontine tract is located in the medial fifth, and the temporopontine tract is in the lateral fifth. Corticobulbar fibers accompany the corticospinal tract. The **substantia nigra** is a broad layer of pigmented gray substance separating the ventral portion, or base, from the tegmentum and extending from the upper surface of the pons to the hypothalamus. It projects to and receives fibers from the corpus striatum; other connections with cerebral peduncles, thalamus, subthalamic nucleus, superior colliculi, and reticular substance also exist.

The **tegmentum** is the dorsal portion of the cerebral peduncle. It contains the lateral lemniscus, whose fibers turn laterally and lead to the inferior colliculus and the medial geniculate body. Just ventral to the lateral lemniscus is a group of fibers containing the **spinothalamic** and **spinotectal tracts.** The **medial lemniscus** forms, with the trigeminal lemniscus, a triangular bundle medial to the spinothalamic tract. The **medial longitudinal fasciculus** is in the dorsomedian part close to the central gray substance. The **red nucleus** is a large oval mass of gray substance located in the rostral part of the tegmentum in the path of the superior cerebellar peduncle. The **rubrospinal tract** arises in the posterior portion of the red nucleus and decussates early in the ventral tegmental decussation (decussation of Forel). The **superior cerebellar peduncles** enter the tegmentum and decussate beneath the central gray matter at the level of the inferior colliculus. The **tectospinal** and **tectobulbar tracts** decussate ventral to the oculomotor nucleus in the dorsal tegmental decussation (fountain decussation of Meynert). **Reticulothalamic bundles** run lateral to the medial lemniscus.

The **nucleus of the trochlear nerve** is situated in the ventral part of the central gray substance at the level of the inferior colliculus. The **nucleus of the oculomotor nerve** lies rostral to the nucleus of the trochlear nerve in the ventral part of the central gray substance beneath the superior colliculus. The **nucleus of the mesencephalic root of the trigeminal nerve** lies in the dorsolateral surface of the central gray substance. The central **periaqueductal gray matter** is continuous posteriorly with the gray substance of the third ventricle. The nucleus of Darkschewitsch lies in the ventrolateral section of this area. The **reticular formation of the midbrain** is continuous with that of the pons and the reticular nucleus of the thalamus, zona incerta, and the lateral hypothalamic area. The **red nucleus,** an ovoid large mass in the anterior part of the tegmentum at the level of the superior colliculus, extends upward into the posterior portion of the subthalamic area. Fibers leave this nucleus to go to the reticular formation nuclei, the lateroventral nucleus of the thalamus, and the rubrospinal tract. Afferents to the nucleus proceed chiefly from the superior cerebellar peduncle, globus pallidus, and frontal cortex.

Clinical Findings of Disturbed Mesencephalic Function

Symptoms that may arise from **destructive lesions** of the midbrain are usually a reflection of the

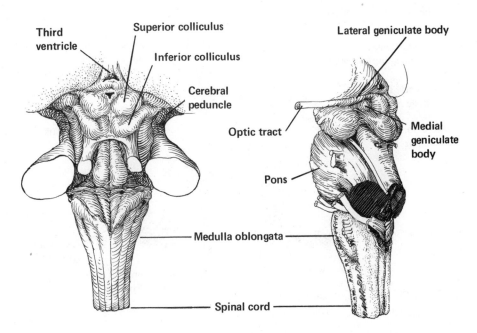

Figure 1–29. External anatomy of the brain stem.

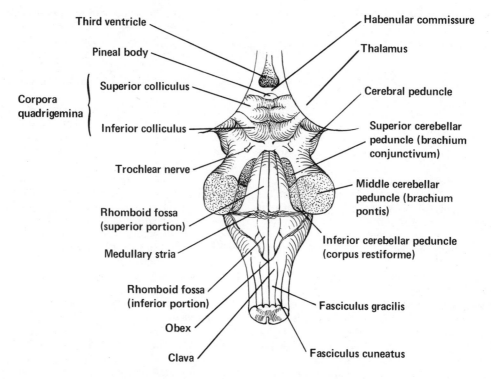

Third ventricle

Pineal body

Corpora
quadrigemina

Superior colliculus

Inferior colliculus

Trochlear nerve

Rhomboid fossa
(superior portion)

Medullary stria

Rhomboid fossa
(inferior portion)

Obex

Clava

Habenular commissure

Thalamus

Cerebral peduncle

Superior cerebellar
peduncle (brachium
conjunctivum)

Middle cerebellar
peduncle (brachium
pontis)

Inferior cerebellar peduncle
(corpus restiforme)

Fasciculus gracilis

Fasciculus cuneatus

Figure 1–30. Dorsal aspect of the brain stem.

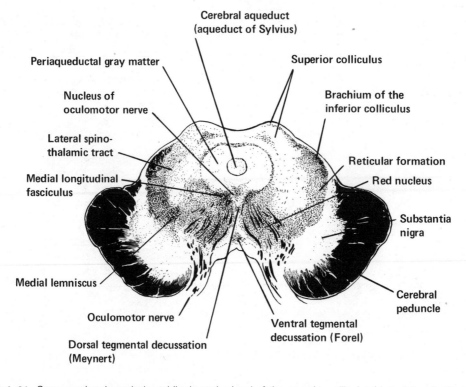

Cerebral aqueduct
(aqueduct of Sylvius)

Periaqueductal gray matter

Nucleus of
oculomotor nerve

Lateral spino-
thalamic tract

Medial longitudinal
fasciculus

Medial lemniscus

Oculomotor nerve

Dorsal tegmental decussation
(Meynert)

Superior colliculus

Brachium of the
inferior colliculus

Reticular formation

Red nucleus

Substantia
nigra

Cerebral
peduncle

Ventral tegmental
decussation (Forel)

Figure 1–31. Cross section through the midbrain at the level of the superior colliculus (dotted line A, Fig 1–28).

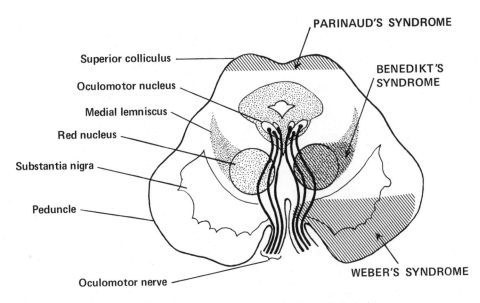

Superior colliculus

Oculomotor nucleus

Medial lemniscus

Red nucleus

Substantia nigra

Peduncle

Oculomotor nerve

PARINAUD'S SYNDROME

BENEDIKT'S SYNDROME

WEBER'S SYNDROME

Figure 1–32. Clinical syndromes associated with midbrain lesions.

structure involved. Destruction of the corpora quadrigemina causes paralysis of upward movements of the eyes. Destruction of the third and fourth cranial nerve nuclei gives rise to the classic syndromes of paralysis of these nerves (see Chapter 4). Destruction of the red nucleus, the substantia nigra, or reticular substance (as occurs in encephalitic states) may give rise to involuntary movements and rigidity (see Chapter 8). Destruction of the cerebral peduncle gives rise to spastic paralysis of the contralateral side resulting from destruction of the corticospinal tract. Cats with experimentally produced lesions of the periaqueductal gray substance resemble in behavior humans with akinetic mutism. A cataleptic state comparable to flexibilitas cerea may occur following destruction of portions of the tegmentum of the midbrain in cats. A syndrome of "obstinate progression" occurs in cats with destructive lesions of the interpeduncular area. These animals continue to push and attempt to walk against interposed resistance, such as a restraint or wall.

Irritative lesions may conceivably occur but are not well recognized. In animals, electrical stimulation produces definite reactions: stimulation of the quadrigeminal region may produce dilatation of pupils and conjugate movement of the eyes to the opposite side. Stimulation of the ventral surface may give rise to slow tonic movements of the extremities. Stimulation of the red nucleus may cause involuntary movements of the extremities in decorticate primates. Clinical syndromes may be correlated to the portions of the midbrain involved. Lesions of the ventral portion of the midbrain may produce clinical features of Weber's syndrome; lesions of tegmentum may produce the clinical picture of Benedikt's syndrome. Disorders or lesions involving the superior colliculi of the tectum, or roof, of the midbrain may produce Parinaud's syndrome.

Weber's syndrome is characterized by ipsilateral ophthalmoplegia and contralateral hemiplegia. The ophthalmoplegia results from oculomotor nerve or nucleus interruption; the hemiparesis results from involvement of the cerebral peduncle and its corticospinal tract.

Benedikt's syndrome is characterized by ipsilateral ophthalmoplegia and contralateral hyperkinesia such as tremor, chorea, and athetosis. It results from a lesion of tegmentum that destroys the oculomotor nerve and the red nucleus on one side of the midbrain.

Parinaud's syndrome consists of conjugate ocular paralysis in the vertical plane, resulting in paralysis of upward gaze. It is associated with lesions or disorders of the quadrigeminal plate of the midbrain, especially the superior colliculi, as occurs when this area is compressed by pineal body tumor. Section of the posterior commissure can produce Parinaud's syndrome.

THE PONS

Anatomy of the Pons

The pons lies ventral to the cerebellum and anterior to the medulla, from which it is separated by a groove through which the abducens, facial, and acoustic nerves emerge.

A. External Structure: The anterior limits of the pons are marked by the 2 cerebral peduncles that appear on both sides of the midline. The **brachium pontis,** also known as the **middle cerebellar peduncle,** connects the bulging ventral portion with the cerebellum. The triangular posterior or dorsal surface is concealed by the cerebellum.

B. Internal Structure: The basilar or ventral portion of the pons contains a thick superficial layer, the **superficial transverse fibers,** which give rise to

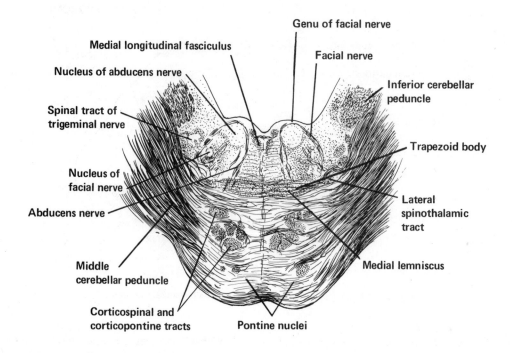

Figure 1–33. Cross section through the pons at the level of the facial colliculus (dotted line B, Fig 1–28).

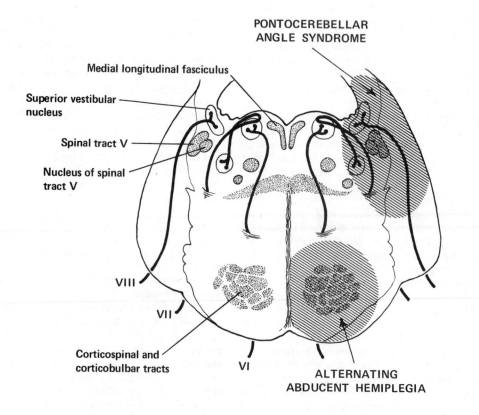

Figure 1–34. Clinical syndromes associated with pontine lesions.

the brachium pontis; **deep transverse fibers,** which lie dorsal to the corticospinal tract and also contribute to the brachium pontis; and **longitudinal fasciculi,** which lead from the cerebral peduncles into the pons.

The longitudinal fasciculi consist of (1) the **corticospinal tract,** which occupies the middle three-fifths of the cerebral peduncle, enters the pons and breaks up into small bundles, and then becomes relatively compact again as it leaves the pons; (2) the **corticobulbar fibers,** which originate in the medial portion of the cerebral peduncle, enter the pons, and pass dorsally toward the cranial nerve nuclei; (3) the **frontopontine tract** (Arnold's bundle), which originates from Brodmann area 6 of the cerebral cortex and then traverses the anterior limb of the internal capsule and the medial fifth of the cerebral peduncle to terminate in ipsilateral pontine nuclei; and (4) the **parietotemporopontine tract** (Türck's bundle), which leads from the parietal and temporal cortexes through the posterior limb of the internal capsule and the lateral fifth of the cerebral peduncle, terminating in the ipsilateral pontine nuclei.

The pontine nuclei are small collections of nerve cells profusely scattered among the transverse fiber bundles.

The dorsal, or tegmental, portion of the pons consists mainly of the rostral continuation of the gray substance and the reticular formation of the medulla. The **trapezoid body** is the group of transverse fibers in the caudal portion of the tegmentum pontis, continuous with the lateral lemniscus. The **medial lemniscus** lies along the midline of the medulla and shifts ventrally and then laterally in the pons, where it courses through the ventral portion of the reticular formation and then crosses the trapezoid body at right angles.

The **ventral spinocerebellar tract** turns dorsolaterally near the rostral end of the pons, winds about the superior cerebellar peduncle, and enters the vermis of the cerebellum. The **medial longitudinal fasciculus** receives many of its fibers from vestibular nuclei and lies in the middorsal portion of the reticular formation.

Cranial nerve nuclei in the pons. The **nucleus of the abducens nerve** lies in the dorsomedial area just beneath the floor of the fourth ventricle. Its fibers pass ventrally between lateral bundles of the corticospinal fibers to exit at the groove separating the pons and the medulla. The **nucleus of the facial nerve** is dorsal to the superior olivary nucleus. Its fibers run dorsomedially toward the floor of the fourth ventricle, make an acute compact bend at the medial side of the abducens nucleus, and then turn laterally through the pons to exit at the lower border between the olive and the inferior cerebellar peduncle. The **motor nucleus of the trigeminal nerve** and the **main sensory nucleus of the trigeminal nerve** are located close together in the dorsolateral portion of the reticular formation. The sensory nucleus is located more laterally, and the tracts that arise from it are functionally comparable to the posterior columns of the spinal cord. The **nucleus of the descending spinal tract of the trigeminal nerve**

is a continuation of the substantia gelatinosa rolandi of the spinal cord, and the spinal tract is functionally similar to the spinothalamic tract.

The **nuclei of the vestibular nerve** make up a diamond-shaped mass of gray matter in the floor and lateral wall of the fourth ventricle in the pons and the medulla. The **superior vestibular nucleus** (nucleus of Bechterew) is situated in the angle of the floor and lateral wall of the fourth ventricle just behind the trigeminal motor nucleus. The **medial vestibular nucleus** (nucleus of Schwalbe), the largest of the vestibular nuclei, occupies part of the area acoustica of the rhomboid fossa. Fibers pass from it to the medial longitudinal fasciculus, cranial nerve nuclei, and cerebellum. The **lateral vestibular nucleus** (nucleus of Deiters) is next to the inferior cerebellar peduncle at the level of the vestibular nerve entrance and gives rise to the fibers of the vestibulospinal tract. The **inferior vestibular nucleus,** or nucleus of the descending tract of the vestibular nerve, extends from the lateral nucleus to the cuneate nucleus in the medulla and lies medial to the inferior cerebellar peduncle and dorsal to the spinal trigeminal tract.

Nuclei of the cochlear nerve (acoustic nuclei) include the **dorsal cochlear nucleus,** located on the dorsolateral surface of the inferior cerebellar peduncle, and the **ventral cochlear nucleus,** located in the ventrolateral region of the inferior cerebellar peduncle at the level of the entrance of the auditory fibers.

The **reticular formation** of the pons is similar to that of the medulla.

Clinical Syndromes of the Pons

Certain clinical syndromes may be characteristically associated with lesions of the pons. Lesions of the more ventral portion of the inferior pons may produce alternating abducent hemiplegia, Millard-Gubler syndrome, or Foville's syndrome. Lesions of the lateral pons, so often associated with tumors in the pontocerebellar angle, may produce a characteristic picture. Lesions of the ventral portion of the mid pons may produce alternating trigeminal hemiplegia. More extensive lesions of the inferior pons may produce the clinical features of Raymond-Cestan syndrome.

A. Raymond's Syndrome: Alternating abducent hemiplegia characterized by ipsilateral lateral rectus muscle paresis and contralateral hemiplegia. It may occur with softening of the paramedian area of pons resulting from involvement of the abducens nerve and corticospinal tract.

B. Millard-Gubler Syndrome: A form of crossed paralysis (facial hemiplegia alternans) produced by a pontine lesion and characterized by contralateral hemiplegia and ipsilateral facial palsy. In many cases the sixth nerve is also involved, producing an internal strabismus.

C. Foville's Syndrome: A form of crossed hemiplegia from a pontine lesion. Consists of contralateral hemiplegia with ipsilateral palsy of the seventh cranial nerve and ipsilateral paralysis of lateral conjugate gaze.

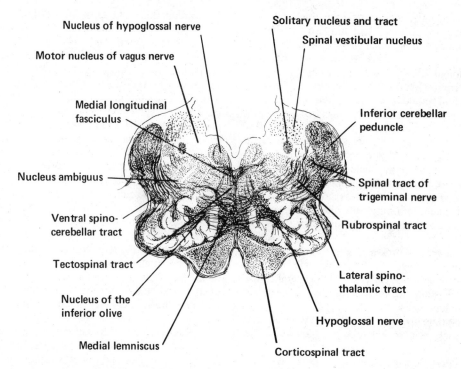

Figure 1–35. Cross section through medulla at the level of the inferior olive (dotted line C, Fig 1–28).

D. Raymond-Cestan or Cestan-Chenais Syndrome: Quadriplegia, anesthesia, and nystagmus due to softening in the pons resulting from thrombosis of twigs of the basilar artery supplying this region and involving the pyramidal tracts, medial lemnisci, and medial longitudinal fasciculus.

E. Pontocerebellar Angle Tumor Syndrome: Caused by acoustic neurinomas that involve primarily the fifth and eighth cranial nerves but may also affect cranial nerves VI, VII, IX, X, and XII.

1. Cranial nerve symptoms–VIII, persistent tinnitus, progressive deafness, and vertigo; V, ipsilateral facial anesthesia with loss of corneal and sneeze reflexes; VI, internal squint; VII, ipsilateral facial weakness; IX, dysphagia; X, syncope; XII, ipsilateral paralysis of the tongue, with thick speech.

2. Cerebellar and peduncular symptoms– Ipsilateral ataxia with staggering, vertigo, and hypotonia of the leg and arm.

3. Motor and sensory symptoms–Contralateral hemiplegia and slight hemianesthesia from pressure on the pathways in the pons.

4. General symptoms of brain tumor–Signs of increased intracranial pressure (papilledema, etc) develop sooner or later.

F. Alternating Trigeminal Hemiplegia: This may result from a lesion of the ventral pons involving the corticospinal tract and fibers of the adjacent trigeminal nerve. Clinically, there may be contralateral hemiplegia and ipsilateral paralysis of jaw muscles and loss of sensation over the same side of the face in the distribution of the trigeminal nerve.

THE MEDULLA OBLONGATA

Anatomy of the Medulla Oblongata

The medulla oblongata is the pyramid-shaped portion of the brain stem between the spinal cord and the pons. The lower half contains a central canal; the dorsal portion of the upper half forms the floor of the body of the fourth ventricle.

A. External Structure: The **anterior median fissure** extends along the ventral surface to terminate at the pontine border in the **foramen cecum.** In its lower portion, the anterior median fissure is crossed by the obliquely decussating pyramidal tracts. The **posterior median fissure,** a shallow groove along the dorsal lower half of the medulla, ends at the posterior limit of the fourth ventricle. The **median sulcus** is a longitudinal groove in the midsagittal portion of the floor of the fourth ventricle. The **anterior lateral sulcus** is a shallow furrow on the anterolateral surface; the fibers of the hypoglossal nerve emerge from the medulla in this furrow. The **posterior lateral sulcus** is a furrow on the posterolateral surface; the spinal accessory, vagus, and glossopharyngeal nerves emerge from the medulla in this furrow.

The following subdivisions of the medulla may be made: (1) The anterior (ventral) section (between the anterior median fissure and the anterior lateral sulcus) contains the pyramid, formed by the corticospinal tract. The pyramidal decussation is the area where the majority of the fibers from one pyramid cross to the opposite side. The medial longitudinal fasciculus lies anteriorly in the lower portion of the medulla. (2) The lateral (middle) section (between the anterior and posterior lateral sulci) contains a prominent mass, the olive, in its upper portion. (3) The posterior (dorsal) section (between the posterior lateral sulcus and the posterior median fissure or median sulcus) contains, in its lower portion, the **funiculus gracilis** and **funiculus cuneatus.** At the lower end of the fourth ventricle, these columns diverge from the midline and present elongated swellings; that on the funiculus gracilis is the **clava,** and that on the funiculus cuneatus is the **cuneate tubercle.** The upper portion of the posterior section is occupied by the inferior cerebellar peduncle (restiform body), which forms the floor of the lateral recess of the fourth ventricle. The striae medullares cross the floor of the fourth ventricle transversely, extending across the inferior peduncle.

B. Internal Structure: Within the substance of the medulla are situated certain gray nuclear areas. The **hypoglossal nucleus** is located near the ventrolateral portion of the central canal in the lower half of the medulla; its upper part lies a short distance from the midline under an eminence called the hypoglossal trigone. The nerve roots of the hypoglossal nerve pass ventrally to emerge at the anterior lateral sulcus. The **nucleus ambiguus,** the somatic motor nucleus of the glossopharyngeal, vagus, and spinal accessory nerves, lies in the reticular formation ventromedial to the nucleus of the spinal tract of the trigeminal nerve. Fibers from it pass toward the floor of the fourth ventricle and then turn sharply ventrolaterally to join the fibers of the dorsal nucleus of the vagus nerve. The **dorsal motor nucleus of the vagus** lies dorsolateral to the hypoglossal nucleus and gives rise to fibers that join the motor roots of the vagus and spinal accessory nerves. The **nucleus salivatorius** is located in the reticular formation near the junction of the medulla oblongata and the pons. The **nucleus of the tractus solitarius** lies ventrolateral to the dorsal motor nucleus of the vagus and extends the length of the medulla. The **sensory nucleus of the vagus** is dorsomedial to the nucleus of the tractus solitarius and lateral to the dorsal motor nucleus of the vagus. The **dorsal and ventral cochlear nuclei** are located at the dorsal and ventral borders of the inferior cerebellar peduncle near the pontine border.

The **reticular formation,** containing scattered groups of cells, is a continuation of the reticular substance of the spinal cord that extends upward through the midbrain and thalamus. The **inferior olivary nucleus** is located within the olive; olivocerebellar fibers extend through the hilum of the olive, decussate, and enter the opposite inferior cerebellar peduncle as the **internal arcuate fibers.** The **medial accessory olivary nucleus** lies between the inferior olivary nucleus and the pyramid. The **dorsal accessory olivary nucleus** is a small nucleus dorsal to the inferior nucleus. The **nucleus gracilis** and **nucleus cuneatus** are large masses of gray substance located in the posterior funiculi of the posterior portion of the medulla. Within the brain stem, a central system called the centrencephalic system has been postulated that may be involved in integration of the functions of both cerebral hemispheres or of different functions from various portions of the same hemisphere.

Fiber tracts. Fibers from the nucleus gracilis and nucleus cuneatus, known as **internal arcuate fibers,** cross in the **decussation of the lemniscus** and continue thereafter in the **medial lemniscus,** which is identified as a broad band dorsomedial to the pyramids. The **dorsal spinocerebellar tract** and the more ventromedial **ventral spinocerebellar tract** lie close to the lateral surface. The **spinal tract of the trigeminal nerve,** superficial and lateral to the **nucleus of the spinal tract of the trigeminal nerve,** lies in the dorsolateral portion of the medulla.

Clinical Findings in Lesions of the Medulla

Lesions of the brain stem produce symptoms referable to involvement of the motor and sensory pathways passing through it and particularly to involvement of the nuclei of the cranial nerves that lie within it. The symptoms are discussed under the headings of the individual cranial nerves in Chapter 4 and under Bulbar & Radicular Syndromes on p 110.

Clinical syndromes may be related to the portion of the medulla oblongata involved. Lesions of the ventral portion of the upper medulla may produce hypoglossal hemiplegia alternans (alternating hypoglossal hemiplegia), whereas lesions of the dorsolateral area of the upper medulla may produce Wallenberg's syndrome, so often associated with posterior inferior cerebellar artery disease. Involvement of the more central area of the upper medulla may produce a variety of clinical pictures depending upon the cranial nuclei and other structures involved, such as the syndromes of Jackson, Avellis, Schmidt, etc. (See p 110 for details of bulbar syndromes involving the last 4 cranial nerves.)

A. Decerebrate Rigidity: Decerebrate rigidity, in which there is an exaggerated posture with continuous spasm of muscles, especially the extensors, was first produced by Sherrington in animals by transection of the brain at a prepontine level. Since it was shown that intact vestibular nuclei were necessary for decerebrate rigidity to persist, the disorder was believed to be caused by release of vestibular nuclei from higher extrapyramidal control. Experimental studies have suggested the presence of a **facilitatory and inhibitory center** in the reticular substance extending from the medulla to the midbrain. The interplay of various pathways on these centers is considered to play an important part in reflex postural mechanisms. Experimental destruction of the inhibitory center causes decerebrate rigidity, which implies that an exaggeration or abundance of stimuli from the cortex and higher levels reaches the spinal cord and produces hyperactive extension reflexes and spasticity. In contrast, experimental destruction of the facilitatory center produces an opposite effect: decreased tone and limp, relaxed muscles.

In decerebrate rigidity the extensor muscles exhibit **lengthening** and **shortening reactions.** These

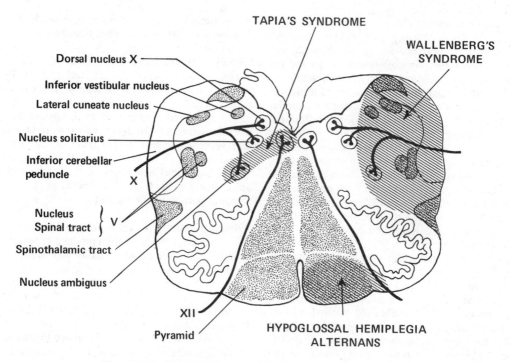

Figure 1–36. Clinical syndromes associated with medullary lesions.

reactions require intact posterior roots. The **shortening reaction** refers to the behavior of an extensor muscle that resists subsequent attempts at lengthening after its ends have been passively approximated. It is believed to depend upon the stretch reflex. The **lengthening reaction** is a phenomenon in which there is at first great resistance to passive lengthening of an extensor muscle, then sudden overcoming of resistance (clasp-knife phenomenon); the lengthened muscle then remains lengthened. **Plasticity** results from combined shortening and lengthening reactions.

In primates, decerebration produced at a high level (cortical) is associated with strong semiflexion of the upper extremities; in low decerebrations, the typical decerebrate rigidity is produced, with extension of upper as well as lower extremities.

B. Integration of Reflexes: Integration of reflexes concerned with swallowing, vomiting, respiration, and cardiovascular control occurs in the medulla oblongata. The respiratory center in the medulla is composed of an inspiratory and an expiratory portion. Electrical stimulation of the ventral reticular portion of the medulla in animals produces forced, fixed deep inspiration. Similar stimulation of the reticular formation lying more dorsally and rostrally may produce expiration. Cardiovascular reflexes essential for maintenance of blood pressure, vasopressor and vasodilator reflexes, and some cardiac reflexes require an intact medulla. Cheyne-Stokes respiration, with periodic breathing characterized by intense hyperventilation alternating with apnea, is believed to be due to increased respiratory sensitivity to CO_2 (resulting from bilateral descending motor system dysfunc-

tion at higher levels) and moderate arterial oxygen desaturation.

Animal studies indicate that the integrating mechanism for vomiting lies in the lateral reticular formation of the medulla. Two anatomically close but functionally distinct units are recognized: (1) an **emetic center** in the region of the fasciculus solitarius and the underlying reticular formation, which may be activated directly by visceral afferent stimulation from the gastrointestinal tract and which is close to areas concerned with spasmodic respiration, salivation, inspiration and expiration, vasomotor control, postural tone control, and the vestibular nuclei; and (2) a **chemoreceptor trigger zone,** which lies superficially in the floor of the fourth ventricle and is sensitive to drugs such as apomorphine and intravenous copper sulfate but requires an intact emetic center to produce vomiting.

The medulla is concerned functionally with cranial nerves VIII–XII, whose nuclei lie therein (see Chapter 4).

C. Postural Reactions: Some basic postural reactions require an intact medulla (vestibular nuclei). **Postural reflexes** of several types are recognized: (1) Local static reflexes affect single extremities and are exemplified by the positive and negative supporting reactions. In the **positive supporting reaction,** stimulation of the animal's foot causes the toes to separate and the limb to become rigidly fixed to support weight. The **negative supporting reaction** refers to the inhibition of the weight-supporting posture by flexion of distal parts of the extremity. (2) Segmental static reflexes are those in which a stimulus in one extremity

Table 1—4. Principal postural reflexes.*

Reflex	Stimulus	Response	Receptor	Integrated In
Stretch reflexes	Stretch	Contraction of muscle	Muscle spindles	Spinal cord, medulla
Positive supporting (magnet) reaction	Contact with sole or palm	Foot extended to support body	Proprioceptors in distal flexors	Spinal cord
Negative supporting reaction	Stretch	Release of positive supporting reaction	Proprioceptors in extensors	Spinal cord
Tonic labyrinthine reflexes	Gravity	Extensor rigidity	Otolithic organs	Medulla
Tonic neck reflexes	Head turned: (1) To side (2) Up (3) Down	Change in pattern of rigidity (1) Extension of limbs on side to which head is turned (2) Hind legs flex (3) Forelegs flex	Neck proprioceptors	Medulla
Labyrinthine righting reflexes	Gravity	Head kept level	Otolithic organs	Midbrain
Neck righting reflexes	Stretch of neck muscles	Righting of thorax and shoulders, then pelvis	Muscle spindles	Midbrain
Body on head righting reflexes	Pressure on side of body	Righting of head	Exteroceptors	Midbrain
Body on body righting reflexes	Pressure on side of body	Righting of body even when head held sideways	Exteroceptors	Midbrain
Optical righting reflexes	Visual cues	Righting of head	Eyes	Cerebral cortex
Placing reactions	Various visual, exteroceptive, and proprioceptive cues	Foot placed on supporting surface in position to support body	Various	Cerebral cortex
Hopping reactions	Lateral displacement while standing	Hops, maintaining limbs in position to support body	Muscle spindles	Cerebral cortex

*Modified slightly and reproduced, with permission, from Ganong WF: *Review of Medical Physiology*, 10th ed. Lange, 1981.

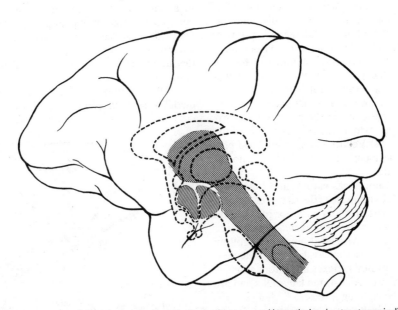

Figure 1–37. Phantom drawing of the monkey brain with the brain stem and hypothalamic structures indicated by hatching. A bulbar zone that yields generalized inhibition of motor responses throughout the neuraxis is indicated by the lines at right angles to the axis of the brain stem. The more cephalad parts of the brain stem augment motor responses generally. An anterior (mainly parasympathetic) zone of the hypothalamus and a posterior (mainly sympathetic) zone are suggested as being in intimate relation with the anterior brain stem; in fact, their anatomic separation is artificial. Jointly, these regions constitute an ascending reticular activating system that provides the background of neuronal activity essential to movement, visceral or somatic. (Reproduced, with permission, from Livingston: Some brain stem mechanisms relating to psychosomatic function. *Psychosom Med* 1955; **17**:347.)

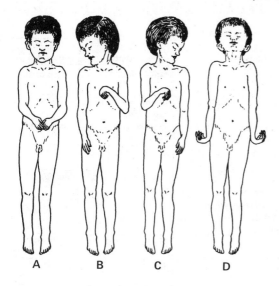

Figure 1–38. Decorticate rigidity *(A –C)* and true decerebrate rigidity *(D)* in humans. In *A,* the patient is lying supine with head unturned. In *B* and *C,* the tonic neck reflex patterns produced by turning of the head to the right or left are shown. (Reproduced, with permission, from Fulton JF [editor]: *Textbook of Physiology,* 17th ed. Saunders, 1955.)

affects the homologous opposite extremity. (3) General static reflexes originate in one segment and affect motor responses in other segments.

D. Tonic Neck Reflexes (Magnus-de Kleijn): After destruction of both labyrinths, the following reactions may be obtained in decerebrate dogs and cats (sectioned at the level of the medulla) and in primates (sectioned at the level of the midbrain): (1) Rotation of the head causes extension of the extremities on the jaw side and flexion of the opposite extremities. (2) Deviation of the head without rotation also causes extension of extremities on the jaw side and contralateral extremity flexion. (3) Dorsiflexion of the head produces extension of the upper extremities and relaxation of the lower extremities. (4) Ventroflexion of the head produces flexion of the upper extremities and extension of the lower extremities.

E. Labyrinthine, Acceleratory, and Positional Reflexes: Tonic labyrinthine reflexes can be elicited in decerebrate animals in whom posterior root section of the upper cervical nerves (to exclude tonic neck reflexes) has been done. **Acceleratory reflexes** follow stimulation of the semicircular canals, with production of nystagmus. **Positional reflexes** arise from stimulation of the otolithic maculas of the labyrinths and are concerned with the righting reflexes.

F. Righting Reflexes: The righting reflexes function to maintain the top side uppermost: (1) Labyrinthine righting reflexes maintain the head's orientation in space and require an intact midbrain. (2) Body righting reflexes acting upon the head keep the head oriented with respect to the body and require an intact midbrain. (3) Body righting reflexes arising from receptors on the body surfaces act on the body

and tend to keep it oriented in space. They require an intact midbrain. (4) Neck righting reflexes arising in the neck keep the body oriented with respect to the head and require an intact medulla. (5) Optic righting reflexes keep the head in proper orientation and depend upon an intact occipital cortex.

The Reticular Activating System

A portion of the central cephalic brain stem and adjacent areas composed of reticular formation, subthalamus, hypothalamus, and medial thalamus has been shown in animal experiments to be essential for initiation and maintenance of alert wakefulness. The reticular activating system may be considered to be essential for arousal from sleep, wakefulness, alerting or focusing of attention, perceptual association, and directed introspection; its impaired function may be associated with anesthesia and comatose states. This system can be stimulated en masse by stimulation of all peripheral sense organs. Upon excitation, a sleeping animal arouses, and electrocortical tracings change from a sleeping to a waking pattern. Corticifugal impulses of wide range, especially those from orbital, cingulate, sensorimotor, and cortical eye fields (Brodmann areas 8 and 18) may similarly excite the reticular activating system.

Hypnotic drugs selectively block transmission of impulses in the reticular activating system; awakening from the induced anesthetic state is associated with normal conductivity. Electrolytic destruction of the area containing the reticular activating system results in a state similar to that encountered in permanent coma in humans. In human patients rendered permanently unconscious by injury to or disease of the brain, the lesions responsible may be so situated as to destroy the functional capacity of the reticular activating system.

The **reticular formation** of the tegmentum of the medulla and pons refers to the diffuse primitive system

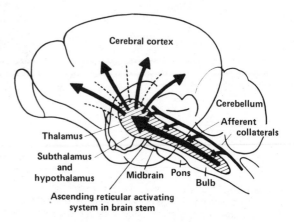

Figure 1–39. Diagram of ascending reticular system projected on a sagittal section of the cat brain. (Reproduced, with permission, from Starzl et al: Collateral afferent excitation of reticular formation of brain stem. *J Neurophysiol* 1951; **14**:479.)

of interlacing fibers and nerve cells forming the central core of the brain stem. It is bordered by the nuclei of origin or termination of the fifth to 12th cranial nerves, whose many connections add to its reticular structure. According to Papez, ascending paths from this reticular formation of the brain stem include the reticulothalamic tract, the tegmentothalamic tract, and the tectothalamic tract, which terminate in thalamic intralaminar nuclei (along the internal medullary lamina of the dorsal thalamus). Intralaminar nuclei include parafascicular, limitans, centrum medianum, central, paracentral, and central lateral nuclei. Fibers from these nuclei go to the reticular nucleus on the outer surface of the thalamus. From the reticular nucleus of the thalamus, "nonspecific" fibers project to all parts of the cerebral cortex. These fibers and pathways from the reticular nucleus of the thalamus can activate the cerebral cortex independently of the specific sensory or other neural systems that can activate cortex.

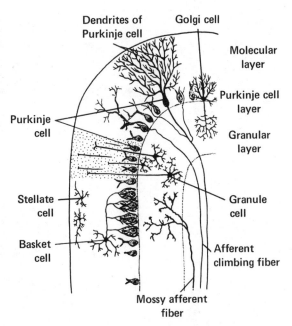

Figure 1–40. Cross section of a folium of the cerebellum. (Modified from Wyburn: *The Nervous System*. Academic Press, 1960.)

THE CEREBELLUM

The cerebellum, located in the posterior fossa of the skull behind the pons and medulla, is separated from the overlying cerebrum by an extension of dura mater, the **tentorium cerebelli.** It is oval in form, with its widest diameter along the transverse axis.

Anatomy

A. Surface: The surface of the cerebellum contains many sulci and furrows, giving it a laminated appearance which is accentuated by several deep fissures that divide the cerebellum into several lobes. The numerous shallower sulci within each lobe separate the individual folia from each other.

B. Lobes: The cerebellum is composed of a small unpaired median portion, the vermis, and 2 large lateral masses, the cerebellar hemispheres. The **flocculonodular lobe** includes the nodulus of the posterior vermis and the attached flocculi and is sometimes referred to as the **archicerebellum.**

The body of the cerebellum, or corpus cerebelli, is anterior to the flocculonodular lobe and separated from it by the **posterolateral fissure.** The body may be

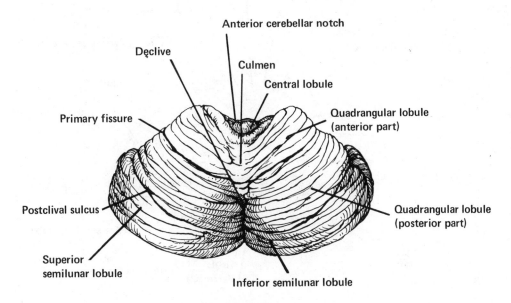

Figure 1–41. Superior surface of cerebellum.

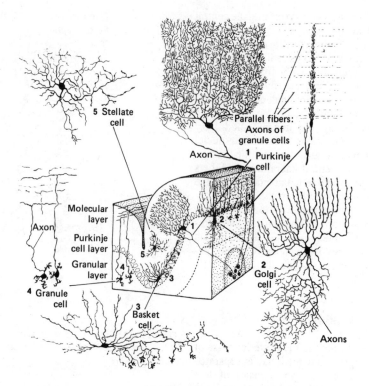

Figure 1–42. Location and structure of neurons in the cerebellar cortex. (Reproduced, with permission, from Kuffler & Nicholls: *From Neuron to Brain.* Sinauer Associates, 1976.)

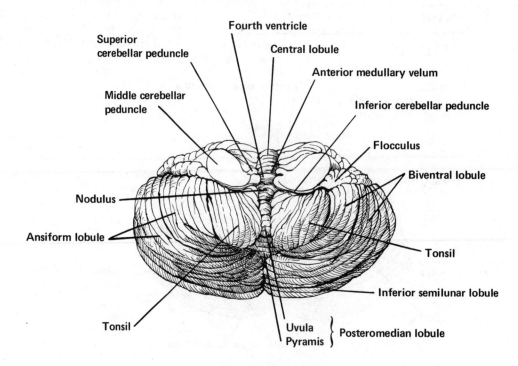

Figure 1–43. Inferior surface of cerebellum.

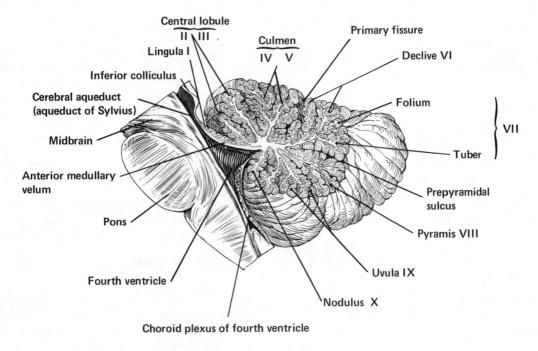

Figure 1–44. Midsagittal section through cerebellum.

subdivided into an **anterior lobe** and a **posterior lobe** with respect to the deepest fissure, the **primary fissure,** or fissura prima. The anterior lobe, which contains the **lingula, central lobule,** and **culmen monticuli,** is the paleocerebellum.

The posterior lobe makes up the greater part of the cerebellum. It may be considered to be **neocerebellum.** The neocerebellum includes the **simplex lobe** just behind the primary fissure; the **medial lobe,** made up of the tuber and folium of the vermis; and the **ansiform lobules,** which include the remainder of the cerebellar hemispheres and the tonsil.

According to Larsell's comparative studies, the vermis of the cerebellum may be divided into 10 primary lobules numbered from I to X from anterior to posterior (Fig 1–44).

C. Internal Structure: The internal structure of the cerebellum is characterized by a layer of cortex and an internal mass of white matter in which are located a group of nuclei. The **dentate nucleus** is located slightly medial to the center of the white substance of each cerebellar hemisphere. It is a serrated, purselike lamina with an open anteromedian hilum. It receives fibers from the neocerebellar portion of the posterior lobe and some from the anterior lobe. It sends fibers by the superior cerebellar peduncle to the red nucleus and the ventrolateral nucleus of the thalamus. The **emboliform nucleus** is an elongated mass just anteromedian to the hilum of the dentate nucleus. It receives fibers from the paleocerebellum and sends fibers by way of the superior cerebellar peduncle to the red nucleus. The **globose nucleus** is composed of small groups of cells between the emboliform and fastigial nuclei. Its connections are similar to those of the em-

boliform nucleus, and these 2 nuclei are referred to together as the **nucleus interpositus.** The **fastigial nucleus** lies close to the midline just over the roof of the fourth ventricle in the anterior portion of the vermis and is larger than the globose or emboliform nuclei. It receives fibers from the flocculonodular lobe and sends fibers to the vestibular and reticular nuclei via the hook bundle of Russell (uncinate fasciculus).

D. Microscopic Appearance: The cortex of the cerebellum has a rather characteristic appearance. Microscopic examination reveals an outermost molecular layer and an innermost granular layer. The molecular layer contains few nerve cells and, in transverse section, presents a finely punctate appearance. The cells are small and arranged in an outer and an inner section. Basket cells in the inner section run through the molecular layer in a plane at right angles to the long axis of the folium, giving off many collaterals with arborizations about the Purkinje cells. Stellate cells are similar but are more superficial in location. The cells of Purkinje form a single layer of large cells at the junction of the molecular and granular layers. Climbing fibers are afferent nerve fibers from inferior olivary nuclei that terminate in the molecular layer near the Purkinje cells. The granular layer is characterized by many small granule cells. Each granule cell sends an axon to the molecular layer, where it bifurcates to form a T whose arms (parallel fibers) run straight and long, making synaptic contact with many Purkinje cell dendritic trees.

Golgi cells in the granule cell layer project dendrites into the molecular layer, thus receiving input from parallel fibers, while their cell bodies receive input from collaterals of climbing fibers and Purkinje cells. Their axons project to the dendrites of granule cells. Mossy fibers are afferent fibers from brain stem and spinal cord nuclei with mosslike appendages that terminate profusely in the granular layer. Mossy fibers end on dendrites of granule cells in complex synaptic junctions called glomeruli, which also receive inhibitory endings of Golgi cells.

Climbing fibers exert a strong excitatory effect on single Purkinje cells, whereas mossy fibers exert a weak excitatory effect on many Purkinje cells by way of granule cells. Basket and stellate cells are excited by granule cell parallel fibers and inhibit Purkinje cell discharge. Golgi cells are excited by mossy fiber collaterals, Purkinje cell collaterals, and parallel fibers and inhibit transmission from mossy fibers to granule cells.

The deep cerebellar nuclei are inhibited by Purkinje cells and excited by collaterals from mossy and climbing fibers and other circuits.

E. White Matter: The cerebellum contains 3 pairs of major projection bundles, the cerebellar peduncles. The **superior cerebellar peduncle** (brachium conjunctivum) proceeds from the upper medial white substance of the cerebellar hemisphere to enter the lateral wall of the fourth ventricle. Thereaf-

ter, most of the fiber bundle ascends, going deeper into the tegmentum and decussating completely in the midbrain below the cerebral aqueduct at the level of the inferior colliculi. It contains (1) **dentatorubral and dentatothalamic fibers,** from the dentate nucleus to the opposite red nucleus and the thalamus; (2) the **ventral spinocerebellar tract,** which enters the cerebellum from the spinal cord to terminate in the cortex of the paleocerebellum; and (3) the **uncinate fasciculus** (hook bundle of Russell), by means of which fibers from the fastigial nucleus wind about the superior cerebellar peduncle to terminate in the lateral vestibular nucleus.

The **middle cerebellar peduncle** (brachium pontis) is the largest of the cerebellar peduncles. Fibers from the pontine nuclei pass to the opposite neocerebellum by means of this peduncle.

The **inferior cerebellar peduncle** (restiform body) ascends laterally from the lateral walls of the fourth ventricle and enters the cerebellum between the superior and middle cerebellar peduncles. It contains (1) the **olivocerebellar tract,** with fibers mostly from the contralateral inferior olivary nucleus to the cortex of the cerebellar hemisphere and vermis; (2) the **dorsal spinocerebellar tract,** containing fibers from the spi-

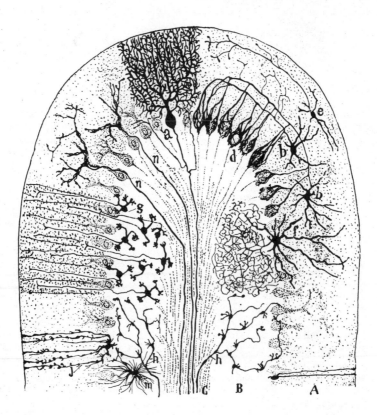

Figure 1–45. Semidiagrammatic transverse section of a cerebellar convolution of a mammal. A = molecular zone, B = granular zone, C = zone of the white substances, a = Purkinje cell seen from the side, b = small stellate cells of the molecular zone, d = final descending arborizations that surround the cells of Purkinje, e = superficial stellate cell, g = pyramidal cells with their ascending axis cylinders bifurcating, h = mossy fibers, j = neuroglia cell with a tuft, n = climbing fibers, m = neuroglia cell in the nuclear zone, f = large stellate cells of the nuclear zone. (Reproduced, with permission, from Cajal: *Recollections of My Life.* Vol 8 of: *Memoirs of the American Philosophical Society,* 1937.)

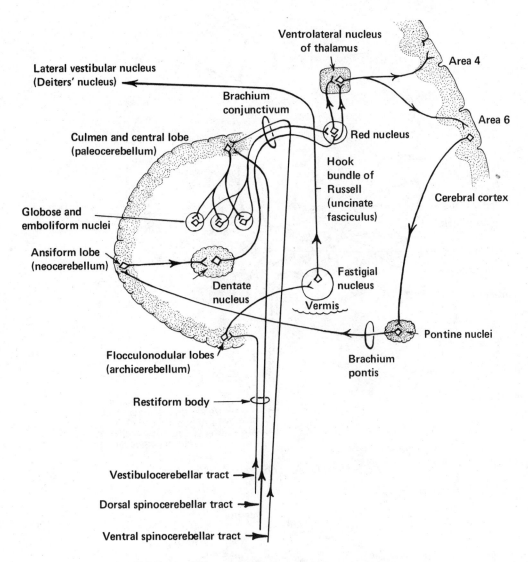

Figure 1–46. Diagram of principal cerebellar connections.

Table 1–5. Summary of levels of integration of various neural functions.*
(0 = absent; + = present; ++ = accentuated.)

| | Preparation | | | | | | |
Functions	Normal	Decorticate	Midbrain	Hindbrain (Decerebrate)	Spinal	Decerebellate	Level of Integration
Initiative, memory, etc	+	0	0	0	0	+	Cerebral cortex
Conditioned reflexes	+	+†	0	0	0	+	Cerebral cortex
Emotional responses	+	++	0	0	0	+	Hypothalamus, limbic system
Locomotor reflexes	+	++	+	0	0	Incoordinate	Midbrain, thalamus
Righting reflexes	+	+	++	0	0	Incoordinate	Midbrain
Antigravity reflexes	+	+	+	++	0	Incoordinate	Medulla
Respiration	+	+	+	+	0	+	Lower medulla
Spinal reflexes	+	+	+	+	+	+	Spinal cord

*Modified from Cobb: *Foundations of Neuropsychiatry,* 6th ed. Williams & Wilkins, 1958.
†Conditioned reflexes can be established in decorticate animals, but special techniques are required.

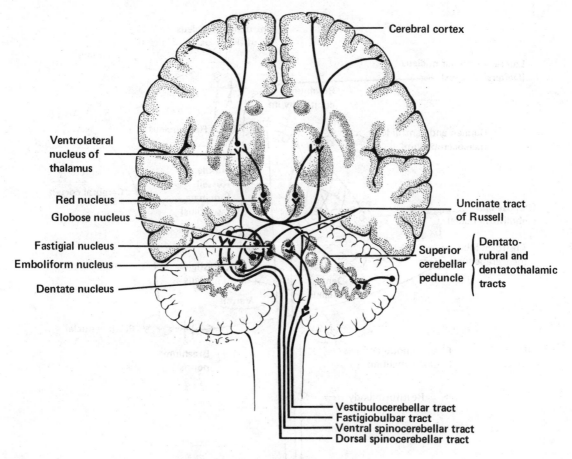

Figure 1–47. Cerebellar nuclei and connections.

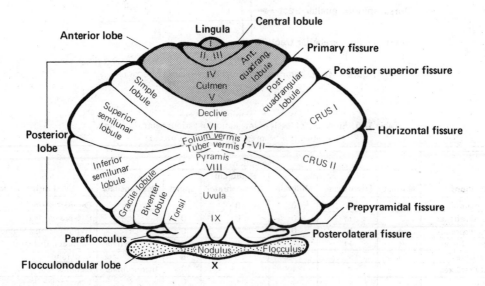

Figure 1–48. Schematic diagram of the fissures and lobules of the cerebellum. (Larsell, 1951; Jansen & Brodal, 1958; Angevine et al, 1961.) Portions of the cerebellum caudal to the posterolateral fissure (dotted) represent the flocculonodular lobule (archicerebellum), whereas portions of the cerebellum rostral to the primary fissure (dark) constitute the anterior lobe (paleocerebellum). The neocerebellum lies between the primary and posterolateral fissures. Roman numerals refer to portions of the cerebellar vermis only. (Redrawn and reproduced, with permission, from Truex & Carpenter: *Human Neuroanatomy,* 6th ed. Williams & Wilkins, 1969.)

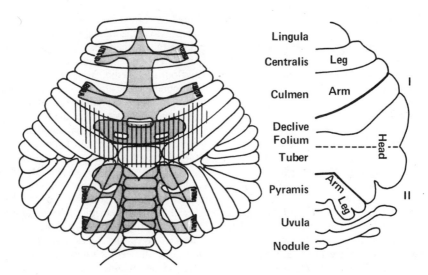

Figure 1–49. *Left:* Cerebellar homunculi. Proprioceptive and tactile stimuli are projected as shown in the figure above and the split figure below. The striped area represents the region from which evoked responses to auditory and visual stimuli are observed. (Redrawn and reproduced, with permission, from Snider: The cerebellum. *Sci Am* [Aug] 1958;**199**:84. Copyright © 1958 by Scientific American, Inc. All rights reserved.) *Right:* Projection of the body on the cerebellum. Areas I and II (above and below the dotted line) are the 2 areas where auditory and visual stimuli are projected. (Redrawn and reproduced, with permission, from Hampson et al: Cerebro-cerebellar projections and the somatotopic localization of motor function in the cerebellum. *Res Publ Assoc Res Nerv Ment Dis* 1950;**30**:299.)

nal cord that proceed to the cerebellar cortex of the anterior lobe and to the pyramis portion of the paleocerebellum; (3) the **dorsal external arcuate fibers** from the nuclei of the funiculus gracilis and cuneatus; (4) the **ventral external arcuate fibers** from the arcuate and lateral reticular nuclei of the medulla; and (5) the **vestibulocerebellar tract** from the vestibular nuclei to the cortex of the flocculonodular lobe.

Function

The functions of various portions of the cerebellum may be grossly localized on the basis of clinical observations and comparative anatomic and embryologic studies. The **archicerebellum,** the oldest portion, has the function of keeping the individual oriented in space. Lesions in this area cause trunk ataxia, swaying, and staggering that are not made worse by closing the eyes, and diminished or absent response on thermal or rotational stimulation of the labyrinths. Ablation of the nodulus produces protection against induced motion sickness in animals. Impulses from the labyrinths arrive via the vestibulocerebellar pathways to the flocculonodular lobe cerebellar cortex, pass to the roof nuclei (fastigial nucleus) of the cerebellum, and finally emerge by way of the uncinate fasciculus (hook bundle of Russell) to the lateral vestibular nucleus (Deiters' nucleus).

The **paleocerebellum,** the next oldest portion, controls the antigravity muscles of the body. In animals, stimulation causes inhibition of antigravity posture on the side stimulated; destruction causes increased stretch reflexes of the muscles of support. Studies indicate that when higher frequencies of elec-

trical stimulation are employed, facilitation rather than inhibition of cortically induced muscle contractions may occur. Impulses from antigravity muscles pass via the spinocerebellar tracts to the culmen and centralis portions of the cerebellar cortex, thence to the globose and emboliform nuclei of the cerebellum, and finally via the brachium conjunctivum to the red nucleus. Topographic orientation is believed to occur in the ipsilateral portion of the anterior cerebellum, caudal portions of the body being represented most anteriorly and the cephalic portion of the body most posteriorly. Stimulation of the anterior lobe of the cerebellum has an inhibitory effect on the blood pressure rise that usually follows sensory nerve stimulation.

The **neocerebellum,** the youngest portion, acts as a brake on volitional movements, especially those requiring checking or halting activity and fine movements of the hands. Lesions of the neocerebellum produce dysmetrias, intention tremors, and inability to perform rapidly changing movements. Impulses arrive from the premotor and motor cortex (Brodmann areas 4 and 6) via the pontocerebellar tracts and reach the ansiformis portion of the cortex of the cerebellar hemisphere, whence they are relayed to the dentate nucleus. Via the brachium conjunctivum they pass on to the red nucleus and thalamus, ultimately to return to Brodmann areas 4 and 6 of the cerebral cortex. In the higher primates, ablation of the cerebellar cortex causes transient ipsilateral awkwardness, hypotonia, and alteration in gait. With additional ablation of the dentate nucleus, more prolonged signs result, with the additional finding of intention tremor.

THE VENTRICLES

Within the brain substance is a communicating system of 4 cavities filled with cerebrospinal fluid. These are designated as the 2 lateral, the third, and the fourth ventricles.

The Lateral Ventricles

The 2 lateral ventricles are the largest of the ventricles. They are irregular in shape and are lined with ependyma, which is continuous with the ependyma of the third ventricle. The **anterior horn** is anterior to the interventricular foramen. Its roof and anterior border are formed by the corpus callosum; its vertical medial wall by the septum pellucidum; and the floor and lateral wall by the bulging head of the caudate nucleus. The central part, or body, is the long, narrow portion extending from the interventricular foramen to a point opposite the splenium of the corpus callosum. Its roof is formed by the corpus callosum and the medial wall by the septum pellucidum. The floor contains (from medial to lateral side) the following structures: the fornix, the choroid plexus, the lateral part of the dorsal surface of the thalamus, the stria terminalis, the vena terminalis, and the caudate nucleus. The **posterior horn** extends into the occipital lobe. Its roof is formed by fibers of the corpus callosum. On its medial wall is an elevation of the ventricular wall produced by the calcarine fissure, and known as the calcar avis. A more dorsally situated longitudinal elevation of the medial wall formed by the occipital portion of the corpus callosum radiation is known as the bulb of the posterior horn. The **inferior horn** (temporal horn) traverses the temporal lobe. Its roof is

formed by the white substance of the cerebral hemisphere. Along the medial border are the stria terminalis and the tail of the caudate nucleus. The amygdaloid body bulges into the terminal part of the inferior horn. The floor and medial wall are formed by the fimbria, the hippocampus, and the collateral eminence.

The **interventricular foramen** is an oval aperture between the column of the fornix and the anterior end of the thalamus through which the lateral ventricle communicates with the third ventricle. It is frequently referred to as the **foramen of Monro.**

The **choroid plexus of the lateral ventricle** is a vascular, fringelike process of pia mater projecting into the ventricular cavity and covered by an epithelial layer of ependymal origin. A triangular process of pia mater projecting upward into the body of the lateral ventricle covers the lateral edge of the fornix and is known as the **tela choroidea.** The choroid plexus extends from the interventricular foramen (where it is joined with the plexus of the opposite lateral ventricle) to the end of the inferior horn. The arteries to the plexus consist of the **anterior choroidal artery,** a branch of the internal carotid artery, which enters the plexus at the inferior horn of the ventricle; and the **posterior choroidal artery,** a branch of the posterior cerebral artery.

The Third Ventricle

The third ventricle is a narrow vertical cleft between the 2 lateral ventricles. The roof of the third ventricle is formed by a thin layer of ependyma. The lateral walls are formed mainly by the medial surfaces of the 2 thalami. The lower lateral wall and the floor of the ventricle are formed by the hypothalamus and

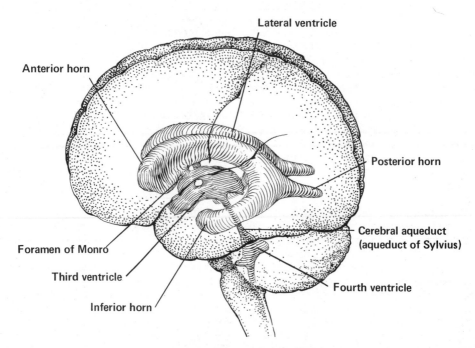

Lateral ventricle

Anterior horn

Posterior horn

Foramen of Monro

Cerebral aqueduct (aqueduct of Sylvius)

Third ventricle

Fourth ventricle

Inferior horn

Figure 1–50. The ventricular system.

subthalamus. The anterior commissure and the lamina terminalis form the rostral limit of the third ventricle. The optic recess is an extension of the third ventricle between the lamina terminalis and the optic chiasm. A small **pineal recess** projects into the stalk of the pineal body. The funnel-shaped infundibular recess is a downward extension at whose apex the hypophysis is attached. The **massa intermedia** is a band of gray matter that crosses the cavity of the ventricle, joining the external walls. The following structures may be found in the floor of the third ventricle (from anterior to posterior end): optic chiasm, infundibulum, tuber cinereum, mamillary bodies, and subthalamus.

Three openings communicate with the third ventricle: the 2 interventricular foramens at the anterior end communicate with the lateral ventricles, and the cerebral aqueduct opens into the caudal end of the third ventricle.

Two choroid plexuses extend side by side from the tela choroidea in the roof of the third ventricle from the interventricular foramens to the caudal extremity of the roof.

The Fourth Ventricle

The fourth ventricle is a cavity bounded ventrally by the pons and medulla oblongata and dorsally by the cerebellum. It is continuous with the cerebral aqueduct above and the central canal of the medulla below. The lateral recess extends as a narrow, curved extension of the cavity on the dorsal surface of the inferior cerebellar peduncle. The floor of the fourth ventricle, also known as the **rhomboid fossa,** is formed by the dorsal surfaces of the pons and medulla oblongata. The lateral boundaries of the floor of the fourth ventricle are formed by the superior cerebellar peduncles, the middle cerebellar peduncles, the inferior cerebellar peduncles, the cuneate tubercles, and the clavas. The **calamus scriptorius** is the inferior portion of the rhomboid fossa.

The **roof of the fourth ventricle** is formed by the anterior and posterior medullary vela. The **anterior medullary velum** extends between the dorsomedial borders of the superior cerebellar peduncles from the quadrigeminal plate to the middle of the cerebellum. Its dorsal surface is covered by the adherent lingula of the cerebellum. The **posterior medullary velum** extends caudally from the cerebellum. The point at which the fourth ventricle passes up into the cerebellum is called the apex, or peak.

The communications of the fourth ventricle include the cerebral aqueduct, the lateral aperture, and the medial aperture. The **cerebral aqueduct** (aqueduct of Sylvius) is a narrow canal in the midline connecting the third and fourth ventricles. It is about 1.5 cm long and 1–2 mm in diameter. Its floor is formed by the tegmentum of the midbrain. Its roof consists of the quadrigeminal plate of the midbrain and the posterior commissure. The **lateral aperture** (foramen of Luschka) is the opening of the lateral recess into the subarachnoid space near the flocculus of the cerebellum. The **medial aperture** (foramen of Magendie) is

an opening in the caudal portion of the roof of the ventricle.

The **tela choroidea** is a layer of pia mater of great vascularity that invaginates close to the median plane into the cavity of the fourth ventricle to form the **choroid plexus of the fourth ventricle.** The right and left halves of the choroid plexus diverge at right angles and run toward the lateral recesses. Modern anatomic findings indicate that the average normal ventricular system has a capacity of less than 20 mL, probably about 16 mL. There would appear to be no lower limit; but in practice about 7 mL is the smallest volume, and about 30 mL may be considered the upper limit of normal.

THE MENINGES

The Dura Mater

The dura mater, or pachymeninx, is a dense fibrous structure with an inner meningeal and an outer periosteal layer. The dural layers over the brain are generally fused, except where they separate to provide space for the venous sinuses and where the inner layer forms septa between brain portions. The outer layer attaches firmly to the inner surface of the cranial bones and sends vascular and fibrous extensions into the bone itself. The inner layer encloses some of the venous sinuses and forms partitions within the brain.

One of these partitions, the **falx cerebri,** extends down into the longitudinal fissure between the 2 cerebral hemispheres and attaches to the inner surface of the skull bones along the midline from the crista galli to the internal occipital protuberance, where it becomes continuous with the tentorium cerebelli.

The **tentorium cerebelli** separates the occipital lobes from the cerebellum. This transverse membrane attaches posteriorly and laterally to the transverse sinuses and anteriorly to the petrous portion of the temporal bone and to the posterior clinoid processes of the sphenoid bone. Toward the midline, it slopes up and continues on as the falx cerebri. The free border curves laterally to leave a large oval opening, the **incisura tentorii,** for passage of the cerebral peduncles.

The **falx cerebelli** projects into the posterior cerebellar notch between the cerebellar hemispheres from the inner surface of the occipital bone to form a small triangular dural process.

The **diaphragma sellae** forms a ceiling on the hypophyses in the sella turcica by connecting the clinoid attachments of the 2 sides of the tentorium cerebelli.

The Pia Mater

The pia mater is a thin connective tissue membrane close to the brain that carries the blood vessels supplying the nervous tissue. It covers the brain surface and extends into the sulci and fissures throughout the brain. It extends into the transverse cerebral fissure, where it forms the tela choroidea of the third ventricle and combines with the ependyma to form the choroid plexuses of the lateral and third ventricles. The pia mater passes over the roof of the fourth ventricle and forms its tela choroidea and choroid plexus.

The Arachnoid

The arachnoid is a delicate avascular membrane between the dura mater and the pia mater. It is separated from the overlying dura by the subdural space and from the underlying pia mater by the subarachnoid space, which contains cerebrospinal fluid.

The arachnoid and the pia mater are known as the **leptomeninges.** The inner surface of the arachnoid is connected to the pia mater by arachnoid trabeculae. The cranial arachnoid closely covers the inner surface of the dura mater but is separated from it in the subdural space by a thin film of fluid. The arachnoid does not dip into the sulci or fissures except to follow the falx and the tentorium. The subarachnoid space is narrow over the surface of the cerebral hemisphere, while at the base of the brain, the arachnoid is thicker and in places leaves wide intervals of space called the **subarachnoid cisterns,** which are named from their positions.

The **cisterna magna** results from the bridging of the arachnoid over the space between the medulla and the cerebellar hemispheres. It is continuous with the spinal subarachnoid space. The **cisterna pontis,** on the ventral aspect of the pons, contains the basilar artery. The **basal cistern** is the wide cavity between the 2 temporal lobes that includes the interpeduncular fossa. It extends rostrally over the optic chiasm, forming the **cisterna chiasmatis.**

Arachnoid granulations or villi are berrylike types of arachnoid that protrude into the superior sagittal sinus or its associated venous lacunae. With advancing age, they increase in size and number, sometimes pushing against the dura and causing bone absorption and depressions into the inner table of the calvaria.

BRAIN CIRCULATION

The blood transports oxygen, nutrients, and other substances that are necessary for proper functioning of living tissue. The needs of the brain are critical and vital, and a constant flow of blood must be maintained.

Arterial Circulation (See Chapters 19 and 25.)

The **circle of Willis** at the base of the brain is the principal arterial anastomotic trunk of the brain. Blood reaches it mainly via the vertebral and internal carotid arteries (Fig 1–53). Some anastomoses occur between

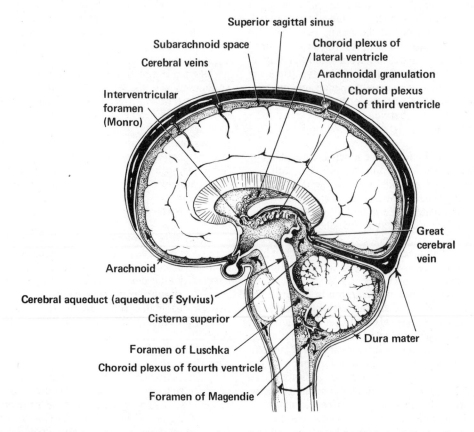

Figure 1–51. Circulation of cerebrospinal fluid. (Redrawn from original drawings by Frank H Netter, MD, that first appeared in Ciba *Clinical Symposia,* Copyright © 1950, Ciba Pharmaceutical Co. Reproduced with permission.)

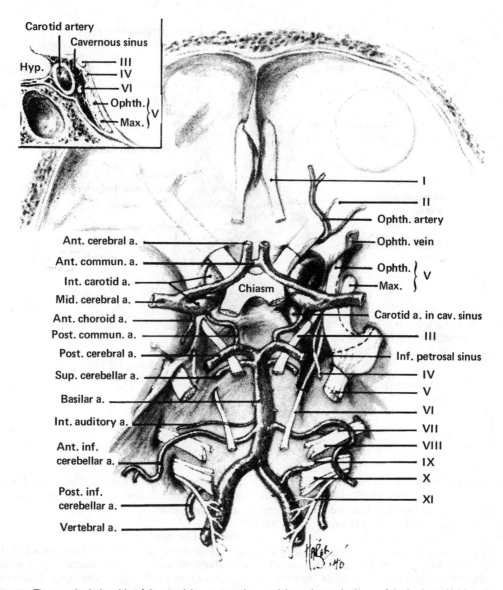

Figure 1–52. The usual relationship of the cranial nerves to the cranial arteries at the base of the brain and in the cavernous sinus. Composite drawing of the regional anatomy of the base of the skull, cranial nerves, circle of Willis, and cavernous sinus. (Reproduced, with permission, from Walsh: *Arch Ophthalmol* 1942:**27**:1.)

arteriolar branches of the circle of Willis in the subcortical white matter.

The circle of Willis is formed by the junction of the internal carotid, basilar, anterior cerebral, anterior communicating, posterior cerebral, and posterior communicating arteries.

The internal carotid artery terminates in the anterior cerebral and middle cerebral arteries. Near its termination, the internal carotid artery gives rise to the posterior communicating artery, which joins caudally with the posterior cerebral artery. The anterior cerebral arteries connect via the anterior communicating artery.

The blood supply to the cerebral cortex is mainly via cortical branches of the anterior cerebral, middle cerebral, and posterior cerebral arteries, which reach the cortex in the pia mater. The lateral surface of each cerebral hemisphere is supplied mainly by the middle cerebral artery. The medial and inferior surfaces of the cerebral hemisphere are supplied by the anterior cerebral and posterior cerebral arteries.

The middle cerebral artery, a terminal branch of the internal carotid artery, enters the lateral cerebral fissure and divides into cortical branches that supply the adjacent frontal, temporal, parietal, and occipital lobes. Small penetrating arteries, the lenticulostriate arteries, arise from the basal portion of the middle cerebral artery to supply the internal capsule and adjacent structures.

The anterior cerebral artery extends medially from its origin from the internal carotid artery into the

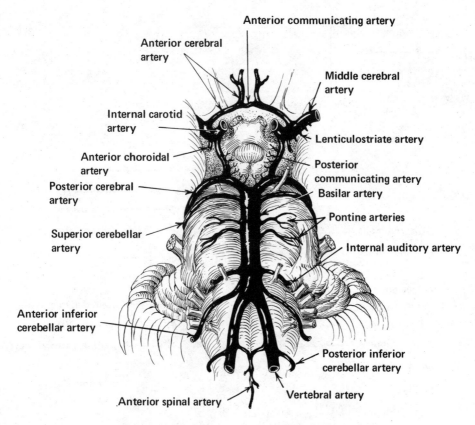

Figure 1—53. Circle of Willis and principal arteries of the brain.

longitudinal cerebral fissure to the genu of the corpus callosum, where it turns posteriorly close to the corpus callosum. It gives branches to the medial frontal and parietal lobes and to the adjacent cortex along the medial lateral surface of these lobes.

The posterior cerebral artery arises from the basilar artery at its rostral pontine border, curves dorsally around the cerebral peduncle, and sends branches to the medial and inferior surfaces of the temporal lobe and to the medial occipital lobe. Branches include the calcarine artery and perforating branches to the posterior thalamus and subthalamus.

The basilar artery is formed by the junction of the vertebral arteries. It supplies the upper brain stem via short paramedian, short circumferential, and long circumferential branches.

The midbrain is supplied by the basilar, posterior cerebral, and superior cerebellar arteries. The pons is supplied by the basilar, anterior cerebellar, inferior cerebellar, and superior cerebellar arteries. The medulla oblongata is supplied by the vertebral, anterior spinal, posterior spinal, posterior inferior cerebellar, and basilar arteries. The cerebellum is supplied by the cerebellar arteries (superior cerebellar, anterior inferior cerebellar, and posterior inferior cerebellar arteries).

The choroid plexuses of the third and lateral ventricles are supplied by branches of the internal carotid and posterior cerebral arteries. The choroid plexus of the fourth ventricle is supplied by the posterior inferior cerebellar arteries.

Venous Circulation

The venous drainage from the brain is chiefly into the **dural sinuses,** vascular channels lying within the tough structure of the dura. The dural sinuses contain no valves and, for the most part, are triangular in shape.

Superficial cortical veins drain largely into the medially situated superior longitudinal sinus. The 2 major cortical veins are the **great anastomotic vein** (vein of Trolard), which drains into the superior longitudinal sinus, and the **small anastomotic vein** (vein of Labbé), which drains into the transverse sinus. The deep cerebral veins drain the basal ganglia. The **internal cerebral vein** drains the **basal vein** of Rosenthal. The junction of the 2 internal cerebral veins forms the **great cerebral vein** of Galen, a short midline vein that enters the straight sinus.

In the falx cerebri is the **superior longitudinal sinus.** The **straight sinus,** a posterior continuation of the great cerebral vein, joins the superior longitudinal sinus to form the **confluence of sinuses.** The **transverse sinuses** conduct blood received from the superior longitudinal sinus and straight sinus to the internal jugular veins. The 2 **cavernous sinuses** receive blood from the middle cerebral veins and drain into the internal jugular veins and the transverse sinuses. The cavernous sinuses are joined across the midline by 2 **intercavernous sinuses,** one of which is anterior and the other posterior to the hypophysis, thus forming a venous circle about the hypophysis, the **circular sinus.** The **inferior petrosal sinus** drains from the cavernous sinus into the internal jugular vein. The **superior petrosal sinus** drains from the cavernous sinus into the transverse sinus. **Emissary veins** connecting extracranial veins with the venous sinuses are common.

Physiology of Cerebral Circulation

The vital need of brain tissue for oxygen is reflected in the experimental findings of workers who found severe permanent lesions in the cortex of the cat after the circulation was stopped for almost 3 minutes. It has been estimated that brain metabolism accounts for about 18% of the total oxygen consumption of the body. In a large measure the oxygen is used for the oxidation of glucose; and in the brain, carbohydrate metabolism is the chief source of energy. It can be demonstrated that protein and fat metabolism play little, if any, part in energy production. The rate at which oxygen is used is controlled to some degree by the level of high-energy phosphate derived from glucose. In humans, at any one time, the brain probably contains about 7 mL of total oxygen, which at normal rates of utilization would last about 10 seconds. It is not surprising, therefore, that the survival time of CNS tissue in the face of oxygen deficit is quite short.

The oxygen supply is maintained by means of controls upon the cerebral circulation. In general, all factors that affect systemic blood pressure indirectly affect the cerebral circulation. The well-recognized role of the carotid sinus receptors, the aortic receptors, and the vasomotor centers in the reflex regulation of blood flow depends upon cortical sensitivity to blood pressure and metabolic changes. Relatively local circulatory changes may occur within the brain as a result of metabolic or autonomic nervous stimulation. Vasoconstriction, when it can be achieved experimentally, is more prominent in pial vessels. Relatively little vasoconstriction of intracerebral arteries occurs. Vasodilatation of more pronounced degree can be obtained experimentally by stimulation of vasodilator autonomic fibers. Clinically, CO_2 inhalations, nitroglycerin, and ingestion of alcohol are believed to induce vasodilatation within the brain.

It is believed that under normal circumstances each internal carotid artery supplies the ipsilateral cerebral hemisphere, whereas the basilar artery carries blood to structures within the posterior fossa. The circle of Willis may function as an anastomotic pathway when occlusion of a major artery occurs. In arteries distal to an occluded internal carotid artery, a pressure of about half that of normal can be maintained through collaterals. Immediately following ligation of an internal carotid artery, no significant change in the EEG may occur provided there is no pronounced drop in systemic blood pressure.

Circulation of the brain has been studied by various techniques, including observations of retinal circulation, determination of difference in oxygen content of internal jugular and carotid blood, thermoelectric studies upon exposed brain surface, cerebrospinal fluid displacement upon occlusion of both internal jugular veins, and the use of diffusible indicators such as gases and radioactive nuclides (nitrous oxide, [85]Kr, ^{133}Xe, and ^{131}I-labeled iodoantipyrine) or nondiffusible indicators such as iodine-131–labeled albumin or polyvinylpyrrolidone. The nitrous oxide method, developed and applied by Kety and Schmidt and their co-workers, has provided quantitative data on human brain circulation. This method is based on the Fick principle, which states essentially that the quantity of a given substance taken up by an organ in a given time from arterial blood equals the amount of the substance carried to the organ by the arterial blood minus the amount removed by the venous blood during the same time.

The nitrous oxide method has its limitations, however. Localized changes in blood flow or in oxygen consumption are not identified as such, since the method measures overall blood flow and overall oxygen consumption. Furthermore, blood flow or metabolic changes that occur in a short period of time cannot be measured, since the nitrous oxide method requires blood sampling through a period of 10 minutes. Studies of local brain area circulation by other techniques have been reported, and estimates of the local blood flow in various areas indicate less flow in white matter than in gray matter. Anesthesia tends to reduce differences in blood flow between various areas of gray matter in the brain. Determination of rapid changes in cerebral blood flow by use of gamma-emitted ^{131}I-labeled iodoantipyrine has been reported. A steady intravenous infusion over periods of 5–25 minutes allows direct estimation of brain antipyrine content in a sensitive and instantly responsive manner; this, coupled with cerebral arteriovenous antipyrine difference, permits the determination of rapid cerebral blood flow changes.

Dye dilution techniques such as injection of radioactive diatrizoate (Hypaque) into the internal carotid arteries bilaterally with collection at both jugular bulbs have also been used. In normal controls, cerebral blood flow by this method averages 750 mL/min, with a mean circulation time averaging 8 seconds from the internal carotid artery to the jugular bulb.

The use of the electromagnetic flowmeter method allows a selective study of the blood flow through a particular artery. The amount of blood flowing through the different branches of the carotid system in humans may be calculated after measurements made on exposed but intact neck vessels. The values reported are claimed to be in good agreement with those obtained by the nitrous oxide method for total cerebral circulation. Blood flow through the common carotid artery as determined by this method is reported to be about 500 mL/min, with about 350 mL passing through the inter-

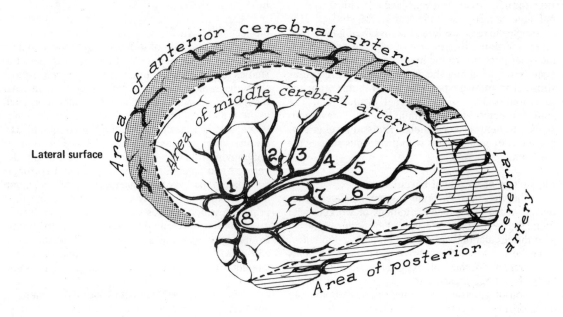

Lateral surface

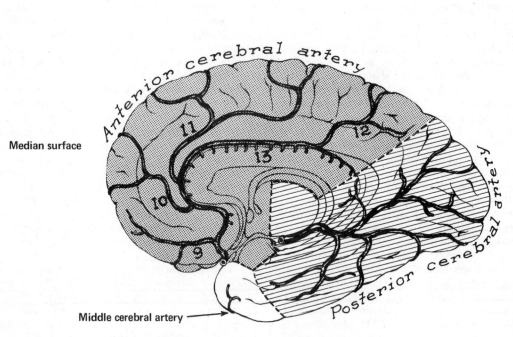

Median surface

Middle cerebral artery →

1. Orbitofrontal artery.
2. Prerolandic artery.
3. Rolandic artery.
4. Anterior parietal artery.
5. Posterior parietal artery.
6. Angular artery.
7. Posterior temporal artery.

8. Anterior temporal artery.
9. Orbital artery.
10. Frontopolar artery.
11. Callosomarginal artery.
12. Posterior internal frontal artery.
13. Pericallosal artery.

Figure 1–54. Scheme of the arterial supply of the cerebral cortex. (Redrawn and reproduced, with permission, from Bailey: *Intracranial Tumors,* 2nd ed. Thomas, 1948.)

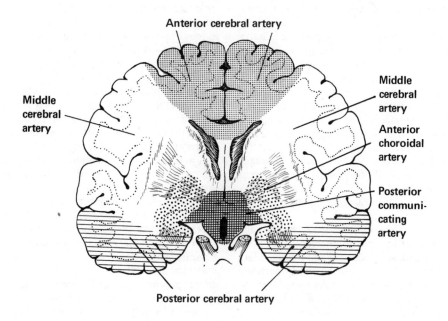

Figure 1–55. Coronal section through cerebrum at level of anterior commissure to show major arterial supply.

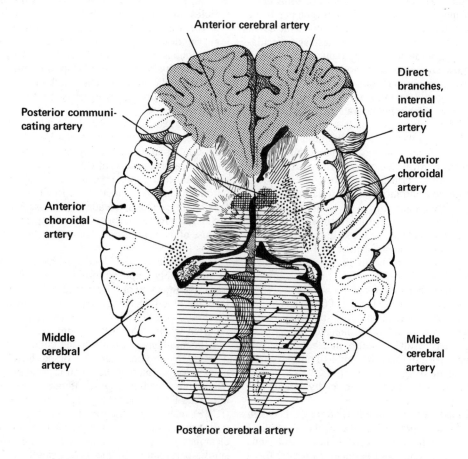

Figure 1–56. Horizontal sections through cerebrum at 2 levels to show arterial supply.

nal carotid artery and 150 mL through the external carotid artery.

The appearance of substances such as radioactive hippuric acid in each cerebral hemisphere may be monitored by scintillation detector units following intravenous injection of the substances. The amount of isotope in each hemisphere is plotted as a function of time; as the isotope arrives in the head, the curve rises rapidly for 5–10 seconds beginning about 10 seconds after its release from a mechanically obstructed arm vein. The relative rates of rise represent the relative blood flow within the 2 cerebral hemispheres. Average brain transit time is usually 6–8 seconds for the most active portion of the bolus. Because of rapid urinary excretion (usually within one hour), patient radiation is negligible.

Alterations in flow through the vertebral and carotid arteries may occur with different head positions. Studies on cadavers indicated that a great reduction of flow could occur in simultaneously perfused carotid and vertebral arteries in certain positions. At operation it has been found that turning the head may reduce carotid blood flow significantly.

According to the nitrous oxide method, blood flow in healthy young men is 54 mL per 100 g of brain per minute. A brain of average weight has 740 mL of blood circulating through it per minute. A normal brain consumes approximately 3.3 mL of oxygen per 100 g of brain per minute. It would therefore consume about 46 mL of oxygen per minute. In advanced age, circulation and oxygen consumption are reduced to as much as 30% below average levels in young adults. In sleep, blood flow through the brain is said to increase, whereas oxygen consumption is essentially unchanged. Considerably higher values are obtained in normal children: blood flow of 104 mL per 100 g of brain per minute and oxygen consumption of 5.1 mL per 100 g of brain per minute. Continuous quantitative measurements of local changes in cortical pH, oxygen and CO_2 tensions, cortical blood flow, alveolar oxygen and CO_2 concentrations, and arterial oxygen saturation have been made. Increased local cerebral metabolism results in increased local blood flow, since oxygen tension becomes reduced and CO_2 tension becomes increased in areas of increased cerebral metabolism. When cerebral metabolism is reduced, local oxygen utilization and CO_2 production also are reduced. Severe ischemia and anoxia produce cerebral metabolic paralysis, with reduction of CO_2 and oxygen metabolism before infarction. This state may be reversible if severe anoxia is not prolonged. Milder ischemic anoxia may result in a state of metabolic paralysis for prolonged periods that is reversible if normal circulation and tissue oxygen are restored.

Brain circulation may be affected by various factors:

(1) **Blood pressure head:** (Difference between arterial and venous pressures at the level of the brain.) Homeostatic mechanisms (such as the carotid sinus reflex and central control of peripheral vascular tone) tend to maintain a normal arterial blood pressure. A mean arterial blood pressure of about 70 mm Hg is believed to be critical or essential; below this level, serious limitation in brain circulation may occur. The hypersensitive carotid sinus syndrome, surgical shock, and orthostatic hypotension represent clinical states of impaired brain circulation on such a basis. When a person assumes the erect posture, effective arterial pressure at the level of the head may be significantly reduced without a compensatory reduction in brain blood flow. Venous pressure presumably tends to combat the influence of gravity upon brain circulation, and, in the preceding situation, an appropriate head of pressure could be maintained by a concomitant drop in venous pressure.

(2) **Cerebrovascular resistance,** the resistance to flow of arterial blood through the brain, may be affected by such factors as the following:

(a) **Intracranial cerebrospinal fluid pressure:** A parallel increase in resistance to blood flow occurs with increased intracranial cerebrospinal fluid pressure; at pressures of over 500 mm of water, a moderate to severe restriction in circulation occurs.

(b) **Viscosity of blood:** Circulation may be reduced over 50% in polycythemia, whereas a significant increase in brain circulation may occur in severe anemia.

(c) **Status of cerebral vessels, especially arterioles:** Stellate ganglion block may fail to influence "cerebrovascular tone" or brain blood flow in pathologic conditions. Animal experiments (cerebral embolization) and human angiographic studies suggest the possibility of brain vascular spasm. Cerebrovascular tone is believed to correlate well with CO_2 tension of arterial blood as well as with the degree of anoxemia.

Significant changes in brain blood flow may, however, occur without much change in oxygen consumption, as in the case of hyperventilation, cerebral angioma, and inhalation of 100% oxygen. Conversely, significant changes in oxygen uptake may occur without much change in blood flow. In vitro studies show that the oxygen uptake tends to decrease with increasing size of animal species; for many species, the oxygen use of the brain is of the same order as that of other organs (or even less).

Regional cerebral blood flow has been measured in operatively exposed brain areas following intracarotid injection of ^{85}Kr, based on its disappearance from the blood. Relatively easy measurement of local cerebral blood flow through the intact skull has been reported when ^{133}Xe was substituted.

Focal change in brain tissue circulation may be detected by regional cerebral blood flow measurements. An estimate of the location, severity, and extent of presumed damage or alteration in brain tissue may thus be obtained. Regional cerebral blood flow (rCBF) may be assessed by intracarotid injection of radioxenon and processing by computers of the ^{133}Xe clearance curves. Data thus derived are now under study, particularly in the investigation of vascular disorders of the brain. Measurement of local cerebral

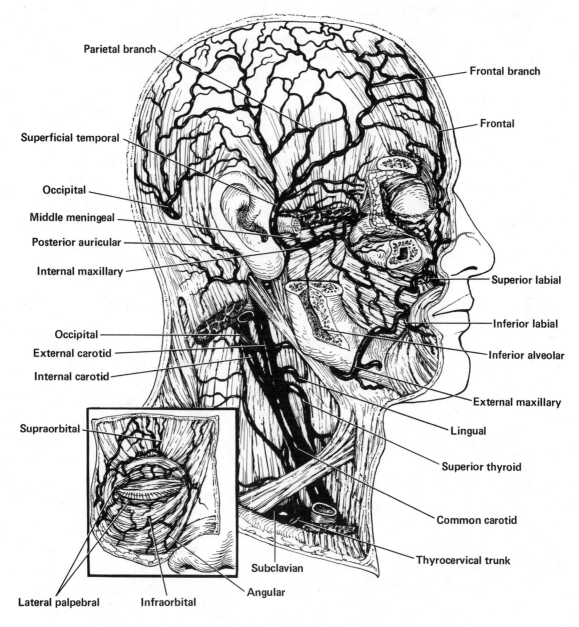

Parietal branch

Frontal branch

Frontal

Superficial temporal

Occipital

Middle meningeal

Posterior auricular

Internal maxillary

Superior labial

Inferior labial

Inferior alveolar

Occipital

External carotid

Internal carotid

External maxillary

Lingual

Superior thyroid

Supraorbital

Common carotid

Thyrocervical trunk

Subclavian

Angular

Lateral palpebral   Infraorbital

Figure 1–57. Principal arteries of the head and neck.

blood flow and metabolism in humans has been reported recently with positron emission tomography (PET). This computer-based nuclear medicine imaging technique permits in vivo measurement of local tissue concentration of radiopharmaceuticals labeled with positron-emitting radionuclides.

Estimates of retinal arterial pressure may be made by application of a measurable amount of external force to the sclera. Obstruction of an internal carotid artery proximal to the ophthalmic artery may lower the ipsilateral diastolic and systolic retinal arterial pressure, although the finding of normal retinal arterial pressure does not necessarily exclude impairment of internal carotid artery flow. While the ophthalmodynamometer applies pressure to the lateral sclera, the retinal arteries are observed with an ophthalmoscope. At diastolic pressure, main retinal arteries pulsate; with additional increase in pressure, retinal arterial systolic pressure is determined by blanching of the arteries.

A mechanical device using the principle of the plethysmograph may also be used to give repeated information. The ophthalmic artery "pulsensor" closes the anterior aspect of the orbit with a rigid artificial wall containing a sensitive pressure transducer. By applying sufficient pressure, systolic and

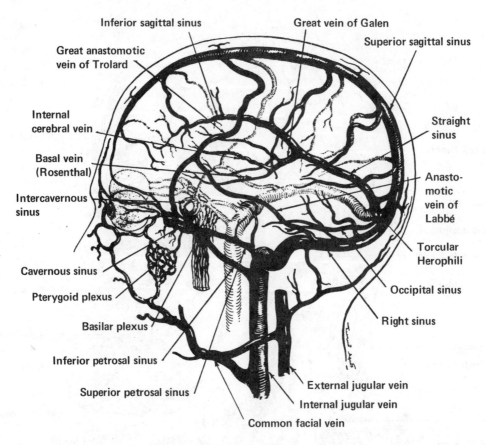

Figure 1–58. The venous drainage of the brain (semidiagrammatic). (Reproduced, with permission, from Shenkin, Harmel, & Kety: *Arch Neurol Psychiatry* 1948; **60**:245.)

diastolic pressure may be read from a manometer.

Determination of retinal artery pressure by ophthalmodynamometry with the patient in the reclining and upright positions indicates that a large majority of those with unilateral stenosis or occlusion of the carotid arterial system show an increased difference between the 2 eyes when the patient is upright.

Arm-to-retina circulation time has been measured following antecubital intravenous injection of fluorescein, with the end point being the appearance of greenish-yellow fluorescence detected in the retina by an ophthalmoscope with a blue filter. Circulation time in normal persons ranges from 8 to 18 seconds, with difference between the 2 sides usually less than 0.5 second. Compression, thrombosis, or ligation of a carotid artery causes delay in appearance of fluorescence in the ipsilateral eye.

Clinical studies with the nitrous oxide method have demonstrated that certain pathologic states have definite effects upon the cerebrovascular system.

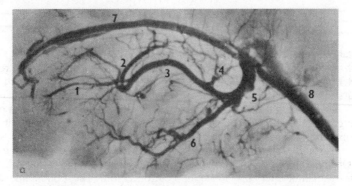

Figure 1–59. Deep cerebral veins (autopsy specimen, lateral view). 1. Septal vein. 2. Thalamostriate vein. 3. Internal cerebral vein. 4. Vein of the posterior horn. 5. Great cerebral vein (Galen). 6. Basal vein (Rosenthal). 7. Inferior longitudinal sinus. 8. Straight sinus. (Reproduced, with permission, from Johanson: *Acta Radiol* [*Suppl*] 1954; **107**:54.)

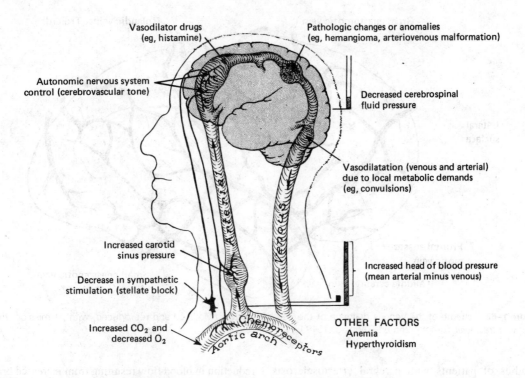

Figure 1–60. Factors that tend to increase brain blood flow.

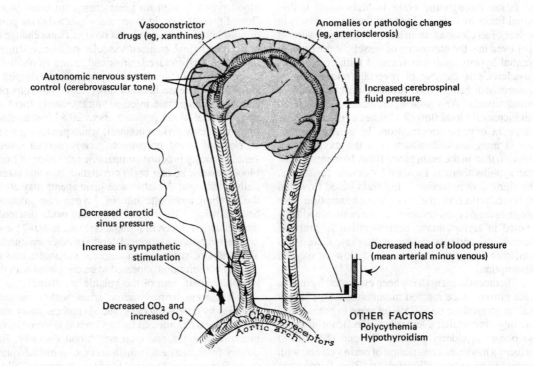

Figure 1–61. Factors that tend to decrease brain blood flow. (Modified from drawings in the Pfizer Spectrum. Reproduced with permission.)

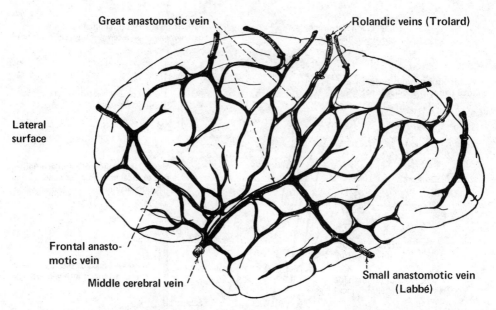

Figure 1–62. Scheme of the venous drainage of the cerebral cortex. (Modified and reproduced, with permission, from Bailey: *Intracranial Tumors,* 2nd ed. Thomas, 1948.)

Studies of patients with cerebral arteriosclerosis suggest that a decrease in brain circulation of up to 30% may occur with aging. In essential hypertension, circulation through the brain is maintained within normal limits by increased tone of the brain vessels in the face of an elevated mean arterial blood pressure. It is believed that the narrowing of vessels of the brain in essential hypertension unassociated with cerebral arteriosclerosis is capable of reversal (relaxation) by measures that bring blood pressure nearer to that of normal vessels. Angioma of the brain is associated with increased blood flow (2–3 times normal) with no change in oxygen consumption. In general paresis there is more marked reduction in the oxygen consumption than in the brain blood flow. In meningovascular syphilis there is increased vascular resistance, with significant reduction in the brain blood flow and lesser reduction in the oxygen consumption. No change in the oxygen consumption or brain blood flow is noted in asymptomatic neurosyphilis. In multiple sclerosis and epilepsy (between attacks), there is no significant alteration in brain blood flow or oxygen consumption.

Therapeutic agents have been evaluated by means of the nitrous oxide method in humans. CO_2 (5–7%) inhalations produce up to 75% increase in brain blood flow in young adults; a lesser but significant increase also occurs in elderly patients. Oxygen (85–100%) produces a moderate constriction of brain vessels, with decrease in brain blood flow (about 12%). Papaverine administered intravenously produces moderate relaxation of brain vessels and slight increase in brain circulation. Xanthine drugs consistently produce a significant brain vasoconstriction. Aminophylline and caffeine given intravenously are usually followed by marked

reduction in blood flow resulting from increased brain vascular resistance. Histamine administered intravenously dilates brain vessels and produces a decrease in blood pressure with no great change in brain blood flow. Ethyl alcohol, intravenously injected to the point of mild intoxication, produces no significant change in brain blood flow or brain vascular resistance. In patients with self-induced, profound, acute alcoholism, depression of oxygen consumption occurs despite a significant increase in brain blood flow. Norepinephrine and epinephrine injected intravenously increase mean arterial blood pressure about 20%. Hexamethonium and tetraethylammonium, while producing a fall in elevated blood pressure to nearly normal levels, simultaneously produce comparable relaxation of brain blood vessels, so that brain circulation remains essentially unchanged. Volatile anesthetic agents may affect the cerebral metabolic rate of oxygen consumption. Studies using [85]Kr instead of nitrous oxide disclosed that reduction in cerebral metabolic rate to 60–75% of normal may occur at surgical depths of ether anesthesia. The onset of reduction in cerebral metabolic rate of oxygen consumption appeared to be correlated with the solubility coefficient of the volatile anesthetic.

Recurrent hemodynamic crisis within the area supplied by a stenosed or occluded cerebral artery may depend upon extraneural factors such as lowered blood pressure, anemia, and increased blood viscosity. Recovery from transient insufficiency requires adequate systolic tension and arterial blood oxygenation; failure of compensation may be due to stenosis of multiple arteries, hypertensive effects on anastomotic vessels, vascular anomalies, or unsuspected damage to other brain vessels. Denny-Brown suggested that effects similar to those of cerebrovascular insufficiency may result from repeated embolization of cerebral vessels from platelet thrombi formed in diseased vessels. In monkey brains whose oxygen content was studied by polarographic electrodes and circulation by stereoscopic microscopy, occlusion of carotid or cerebral arteries caused an immediate drop in blood supplies to the area, with resulting decrease in oxygen levels. Although oxygen loss in normal animals was great at first, it tended to rise slowly and to reach a high or moderate recovery level. Following carotid occlusion, when the monkey's blood pressure was lowered by withdrawal of blood, small collateral vessels at first dilated but quickly became constricted. The slow flow of blood resulted in "venous microstasis," characterized by red cell clumping and stoppage of blood (stasis) in very small venules. Although venous microstasis could be reversed by an increase in blood pressure, it resulted, if untreated, in microscopic intracortical hemorrhages with a related death of affected nerve tissues.

Experimental animals after a fatty meal may show increased aggregation of red blood cells in pial vessels, beginning in small arterioles and venules and proceeding to slowing of blood flow and segmentation of blood columns. These effects are greater in areas of relative ischemia or after occlusion of a cerebral vessel. In the presence of endothelial damage, localized hemocon-centration, erythremia, and hyperproteinemia tend to produce local aggregation, segmentation, and stasis of red blood cells. Intravenous injection of high-molecular-weight substances may result in aggregation of red blood cells in small pial blood vessels, especially in areas of ischemia, where segmentation and stasis of blood may lead to infarction. These changes appear to be unrelated to increase in blood coagulability.

Cerebral vessels of various species may differ in their reactions to intra-arterial injection of noxious agents; in the same species, the same noxious agent may produce increased permeability to one substance but not to another. Thus, whereas healthy cerebral vessels of cats and rabbits are not permeable to radioactive iodinated bovine albumin and trypan blue, air embolism may produce a transient effect on cerebrovascular permeability. In the cat, following air embolization, increased permeability of the affected vessel area reaches its maximum within the first hour, declines rapidly thereafter, and disappears almost entirely after 24 hours.

BLOOD–BRAIN BARRIER

The blood-brain barrier may influence brain function by determining the level of metabolism and

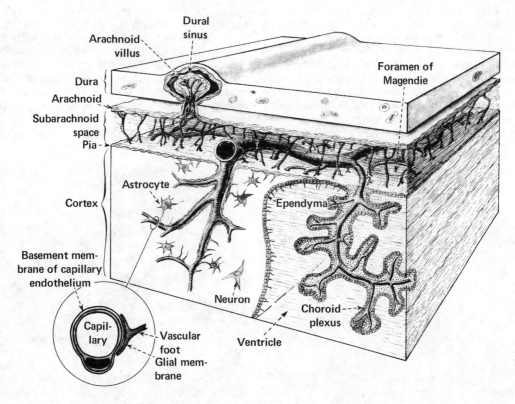

Figure 1–63. Section of the brain and investing membranes. *Inset:* Detail of the barriers between blood in a capillary and cerebral tissue. (Reproduced, with permission, from Tschirgi: Pages 1865–1890 in: *Handbook of Physiology.* Section 1. Field J, Magoun HW [editors]. The American Physiological Society, 1960.)

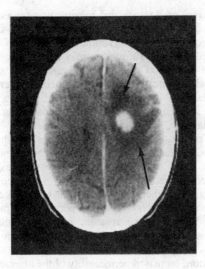

Figure 1–64. CT scan showing area of cerebral edema surrounding tumor metastatic from carcinoma of the kidney.

the ionic composition of tissue fluids. Certain types of abnormal brain function could conceivably result from an abnormal blood-brain barrier. The function of the blood-brain barrier may be influenced by the metabolism of brain cells as well as by the composition of the circulating blood, and it may hinder the free passage of many metabolites into the brain, thus protecting the brain from variations of blood composition and from the entry of toxic compounds. As the brain matures, changes occur in the relative ease with which substances can enter it. Thus, the brain of the premature human infant is quite permeable to bilirubin; kernicterus develops readily in these infants, but not at all in adults with greatly increased blood bilirubin levels. Trypan blue (an azo dye) and ferricyanide both penetrate freely into the brains of very young but not of

mature laboratory animals following intravenous injection. Radioactive phosphorus (^{32}P) enters more readily and in greater amounts into the brains of newborn and very young animals.

The blood-brain barrier may help maintain the environment of CNS neurons that may be sensitive to ionic changes. Five small areas (the circumventricular organs) stain selectively when an acidic dye is injected in an animal. Because of their permeability, these areas may be considered to be functionally outside of the blood-brain barrier. They are (1) the pineal and adjacent subcommissural organ, (2) the neurohypophysis, (3) the area postrema, (4) the supraoptic crest, and (5) the subfornical organ.

The rate of uptake of dyes, anions, and cations from the circulating blood by the intact adult CNS is slow compared with the uptake by other organs. This applies to inorganic substances (potassium, sodium, etc) as well as to organic substances (eg, glutamic acid). There is a relatively rapid gas exchange and uptake of lipid-soluble compounds and of glucose. Glutamic acid and its amide, glutamine, are present in the brain in large amounts, comprising almost half of the nonprotein nitrogen.

Following repeated electroshocks, increased cerebrovascular permeability of brain occurs in rabbits and cats, a phenomenon that does not occur in anesthetized animals. In rabbits, "water intoxication" produced by intravenous infusion of hypotonic glucose and vasopressin results in reduced responsiveness and impaired reflex activity. Convulsive seizures occur in about one-fourth of animals. During induction of water intoxication, progressive reduction in concentration of serum sodium, chloride, bicarbonate, and total effective solute occurs, with expansion of intracellular and extracellular volumes. Water intoxication relates more directly to reduction of serum osmolality than to decrease in serum sodium and chloride, since recovery follows intravenous infusion of mannitol and urea,

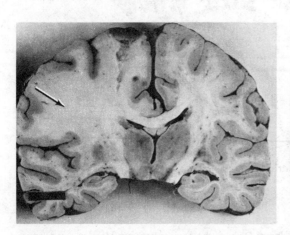

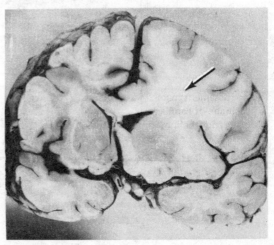

Figure 1–65. Cerebral edema of frontal lobe associated with local brain tumor (glioblastoma multiforme) *(left)* and cerebral abscess *(right)*.

which further lower the concentration of serum sodium and chloride.

There is some space between the various cellular components of the CNS. Electron microscopy suggests that in adult CNS tissue, cellular processes and vascular elements are tightly packed, leaving little extracellular space. Within the CNS, the capillaries are completely invested by glial or neural processes, so that no perivascular space is present. In cerebral edema there is definite and often rapid increase in the bulk of the brain. Cerebral edema tends to involve the white matter selectively. A vasogenic type of cerebral edema (primarily extracellular) and a cytotoxic type (primarily intracellular) may be recognized. Electron micrographs may reveal massive expansion of cytoplasm and of glial processes surrounding capillaries. Alteration in volume of the brain in cerebral edema may be not only a change in the interstitial fluid but also a change in the volume of cells and in their processes — an intracellular alteration. In experiments leading to increase of general extracellular space of other tissues and in water intoxication, the CNS water content and structure may remain unaltered. A relationship of the blood-brain barrier to the membrane of the astrocyte or oligodendroglia has been suggested by swelling of the glia when the membrane is altered or when other parts of the cell surface are exposed to fluid medium. Oligodendroglia are engaged in formation of myelin as well as in its disposal in some pathologic conditions that lead to degeneration of nerve fibers, so that synthesis, maintenance, and disposal of myelin may be considered a function of oligodendroglia.

The immature CNS, in comparison with that of the adult, has incomplete glial development, so that myelin formation is scant or incomplete, neurons may contact the capillary surface, direct neuron-to-neuron contact is common, and spaces may occasionally occur between cells and around capillaries. The lack of glial development in the immature CNS may be related to the incomplete blood-brain barrier of the newborn animal. The glial investment becomes complete at about the time the blood-brain barrier develops.

COMPOSITION OF NEURAL TISSUE

There is a high percentage of **water** in neural tissue. The adult brain is about 78% water; the spinal cord, about 75%. Gray matter has a higher water content than white matter. The water, most of which is intracellular (about 15% is extracellular), appears to be freely and rapidly diffusible, serving as a solvent for metabolites and nutrients and contributing to the osmotic and hydraulic regulation of the nervous system.

The **solids** of neural tissue are made up for the most part of proteins and lipids, with smaller fractions of inorganic salts and organic extractives. **Proteins** constitute up to 40% of the total solids. Most brain protein is linked with lipids in the form of lipoproteins, compounds that resemble living protoplasm much more closely than either free proteins or free lipids.

Water-soluble liponucleoproteins (nucleoproteins combined with lipids) are present in brain. The trypsin-resistant and pepsin-resistant protein fraction is known as neurokeratin. Globulin and albumin are present. A large fraction of brain protein is insoluble in water or saline solution but (unlike neurokeratin) is digestible by proteolytic enzyme.

Lipids make up a large part of the solid content of neural tissue (variously estimated at 40–75%). Very little simple lipid is found. The lipids of the CNS are highly complex and different from lipids of the remainder of the body. Neutral fats and cholesterol esters, common to most body tissues, are not normally present in the CNS; in general, CNS lipids are units built upon glycerol, sphingosine, or inositol, with added phosphate or hexose groups plus fatty acids and, frequently, amino acids. Compound lipids are abundant and include phospholipids (lecithins, cephalins, and sphingomyelin), cholesterol, cerebrosides or galactolipids (glycolipids), sulfur-containing lipids, and amino lipids. Lipids present in brain are synthesized there rather than transported to the brain from other sources. The white matter contains more cholesterol, sphingomyelin, and cerebrosides than the gray matter. Neural tissue lipids may be unique in that certain of their important component fatty acids (eg, 24-carbon fatty acids) have not been demonstrated elsewhere in the body. Lipids are metabolized faster during early development of brain than later; in adult brain there is a slow turnover of fatty acids that penetrate into the brain very slowly if at all. The rate of exchange of brain lipids is slow compared with that of liver lipids.

Inorganic salts are found in the combustion products (1% ash) of neural tissue. The principal inorganic salts found are potassium phosphate and chloride. Sodium and other alkaline elements are found in lesser amounts. There are high potassium and magnesium concentrations intracellularly but little or no sodium or chloride, which are found extracellularly.

The **Nissl bodies** of cytoplasm are considered to be centers of protein production. Portions of the endoplasmic reticulum supply various enzymes and substrates, and the fine granular component of the cytoplasm supplies some of the requirements for protein synthesis. Oxidative and synthetic activities of the mitochondria and glycolytic activities of the fluid matrix may be coordinated by structural alterations within the cytoplasm (mitochondrial movements, cytoplasmic streaming, and sol-gel changes in the matrix). Microsomes (particulates obtained from nerve cytoplasm by differential centrifugation) are rich in phospholipids and contain most of the ribonucleic acid of the cytoplasm.

The **nuclei** of nerve cells are rich in nucleic acids. Two general types of nucleotides are found in nucleic acids: RNA and DNA. The tissue of the CNS contains about twice as much RNA as DNA. The DNA is confined to the nuclei of nerve and glial cells, with a considerable part of the nuclear DNA in the chromo-

Table 1–6. Chemical structure and functions of the neuron.

Organelle	Structure	Function
Cell membrane	Glycolipoprotein complex	Excitation and transport
Nucleus	DNA, histones	Genetic information
Nucleolus	RNA	Protein synthesis
Nissl substance	RNA-membrane complex	Protein synthesis
Mitochondria	Enzyme-membrane complex	Energy metabolism
Lysosomes	Hydrolytic enzymes	Degradative reactions
Golgi body	Membranous	Secretory
Neurofibrils	Protein	. . .
Soluble fraction	Many enzymes	Glycolysis, etc
Myelin	Glycolipoprotein complex	Insulation
Synaptic vesicles	Transmitter substances	Synaptic transmission

somes. RNA is found both in the nucleus (mainly in the nucleolus) and in the cytoplasm. RNA may be identified histologically by the orcinol green reactions for pentoses; DNA, by the color reaction of Feulgen. Quantitative spectrophotometry can be performed on various cellular constituents with the use of the quartz microscope, which is capable of transmitting ultraviolet light. Nucleic acids absorb ultraviolet light strongly at a wavelength of 260 nm.

Histologic studies of neural tissue may permit the identification of various pigments and substances. **Melanin** is the deep black pigment found in the nerve cells of the substantia nigra, of the locus ceruleus, in some of the cerebrospinal and sympathetic ganglion cells, and in the chromatophore cells of the leptomeninges. Melanin is usually not present in the new-

Table 1–7. Fine chemical anatomy of neurons.*

Subdivision	Ultrastructure	% Water	Solids % Lipid	Solids % Protein	Solids % Nucleic Acids†
1. Nucleolus	Chains or threads of 10–30 nm diameter granules.	25	?	(96)	3.5 (P)
2. Nucleolus-associated chromatin	(a) Nucleolar caps 0.5–2 µm diameter, numbering 2–4.	. . .	. . .	. . .	. . . (D)
	(b) Satellite (sex chromatin) 1 µm diameter in females.	. . .	. . .	. . .	. . . (P)
	(c) Chromocenter area–? more prominent in females.	. . .	. . .	. . .	. . . (P)
3. Nucleus	Possesses double membrane, outer showing cytoplasmic projections and discontinuities up to 30 nm wide.	77	25	74	0.5 P/D 2/1
4. Cytoplasm (perikaryon)	(a) Nissl bodies: (1) "Endoplasmic reticulum" of parallel tubules or vesicles 100–200 nm in diameter with walls 7–8 nm thick in continuous system of lacunae. (2) Fine granules 10–30 nm in diameter in patterned rows and clusters along tubules (?microsomal fraction–no succinoxidase, 50% of pentose type nucleic acid). (b) Fibrillar network: 6–10 nm in diameter and 200+ nm long, separating Nissl bodies. (c) Mitochondria: 80% succinoxidase activity; 20% of pentose type nucleic acid. (d) Lipid droplets and yellow pigment. (e) Cell membrane: single, smooth.	60	25	73	1.5 (P)
5. Dendrites	Similar appearance to perikaryon. Synaptic bulbs or end-feet on dendrites resemble simplified version of motor end-plate of Couteaux.	. . .	. . .	. . .	. . .
6. Axon hillock		85	?	± 100	0
7. Axon: Axoplasm	(a) Extension of Nissl "endoplasmic reticulum." (b) Fibrillar network. (c) Axoplasmic migration or flow.	90	0 (?)	± 100	0
Sheath	Complex of concentric layers of protein interspersed with radially oriented bimolecular layers of lipid, each lamella separated by water spaces.	65	55	45	?

*Reproduced, with permission, from Harlow and Woolsey: *Biological and Biochemical Bases of Behavior,* University of Wisconsin, 1958.

† Nucleic acids: P = pentose type, D = deoxypentose type.

born but appears toward the end of the first year, increases in amount until puberty, and remains more or less constant thereafter. Depigmentation of the substantia nigra is a frequent finding in parkinsonism. **Lipochrome**, or **lipofuscin**, a yellow pigment, appears in spinal ganglia neurons about the sixth year; a few years later it appears in the spinal cord, and after the 20th year it is found in cerebrocortical neurons. It increases with advancing age and is quite marked in old age. It appears as droplets around the nerve cell nucleus, stains deeply with osmic acid and Sudan III, and is insoluble in the usual fat solvents.

Hemoglobin derivatives are sometimes found in the CNS. Yellow-brown granules of **hemosiderin**, an iron-containing pigment, appear following extravasations of blood and in hemochromatosis. **Hemofuscin**, a light yellow granular substance containing no iron, is found in excessive quantities in hemochromatosis. **Hematoidin**, a decomposition product of heme, forms biliverdin, a green pigment that imparts a light green color to white matter surrounding a hemorrhagic site.

Calcification occurs normally within the pineal body during adult life. Small granules or large masses of calcium phosphate and carbonate occur pathologically in the CNS. Calcification of the cerebral cortex occurs in Sturge-Weber syndrome; within the vascular tree, meninges, and the choroid plexuses as a degenerative process; and in some brain tumors such as meningiomas, oligodendrogliomas, and craniopharyngiomas. **Iron compounds** are normally present in the globus pallidus and substantia nigra. Some of the brain iron has been identified as ferritin, a crystallizable protein containing 23% iron. The tissue iron of brain probably is a product of iron metabolism, although it can also arise from extravasated red blood cells.

METABOLIC FEATURES

Embryonic Brain

The metabolism of the embryonic brain is characterized by a great capacity to synthesize the proteins and lipids needed for growth. Oxidative mechanisms are deficient, but the brain is highly capable of utilizing carbohydrates by glycolysis. During fetal life, glucose oxidation systems become more active, extending progressively from the lower to the higher centers and continuing after birth. As development proceeds, successive changes in the activity of individual enzymes take place, with new enzymes appearing, increasing in activity, and then declining.

Among the studies made in an attempt to correlate functional brain status and enzymatic findings are those of Flexner on the guinea pig. In early fetal life, the cerebral cortex of the guinea pig has been found to contain low, constant concentrations of respiratory enzymes, cytochrome c, succinic dehydrogenase, and adenylpyrophosphatase (apyrase). The concentrations of these enzymes increase sharply at the time of morphologic differentiation and the onset of electrical activity in nerve cells. The adult level is reached or approximated at birth. A similar close relationship in other vertebrate species has been noted between functional development and brain enzyme concentrations of cholinesterase and carbonic anhydrase.

Increased knowledge of the metabolic characteristics of mammalian embryonal tissues has resulted from the studies of Hicks and others on experimental induction of brain malformations of small laboratory animals. Developing cells change their response to metabolic injury as they grow, and the organism changes metabolically as it develops. Although developmental patterns are primarily genetically determined and latent genetic abnormalities may be precipitated by injurious agents, different agents may produce different types of malformation at the same stage of development. In general, the rat embryo is resistant to anoxia and hypoglycemia, but interference with nucleic acid metabolism of primitive differentiating cells causes their destruction. In late fetal and neonatal life, resistance to anoxia persists, but the interruption of some phases of glucose metabolism has serious consequences. At this stage, the brain is able to utilize glucose either aerobically or anaerobically for sustained periods. The capacity for anaerobic survival is lost at about the second or third week, when embryonal cells have generally grown to their mature forms. The cerebrum becomes dependent upon an immediate supply of glucose and oxygen, although parts of the brain stem and midbrain may be less dependent than other tissues. Some drugs (cyanide, azide, and malononitrile) can cause damage to the neurons of cortex and striatum similar to that caused by anoxia and may also damage white matter. Certain parts of the hypothalamus, brain stem, and peripheral ganglia may be damaged by acetylpyridine, and this effect can be prevented by its analog, nicotinamide. Adult neurons of the brain are relatively radioresistant.

Different types of metabolic toxins or inhibitors can selectively damage primitive, differentiating embryonal cells. Radiation attacks such primitive cells in stages at which they are apparently engaged in the synthesis of nucleic acid and protein and in rapid growth from an embryonal stage to a more adult phase. Oxidizing compounds produced in water by radiation seem to affect enzymes with sulfhydryl groups, and this type of enzyme seems to be important at this early stage of cell differentiation. Effects similar to those produced by ionizing radiation may be produced by chemicals that react with sulfhydryl groups (nitrogen mustard, iodosobenzoate) or interfere with certain phases of nucleic acid metabolism (aminopterin and certain corticosteroids).

Adult Brain

In the adult brain, the ability to synthesize certain proteins and lipids is greatly reduced, but the dependence upon carbohydrate as its main fuel persists. The brain is characterized by a high overall oxygen consumption, with metabolic activity generally highest in the cortex and cerebellum. The high energy require-

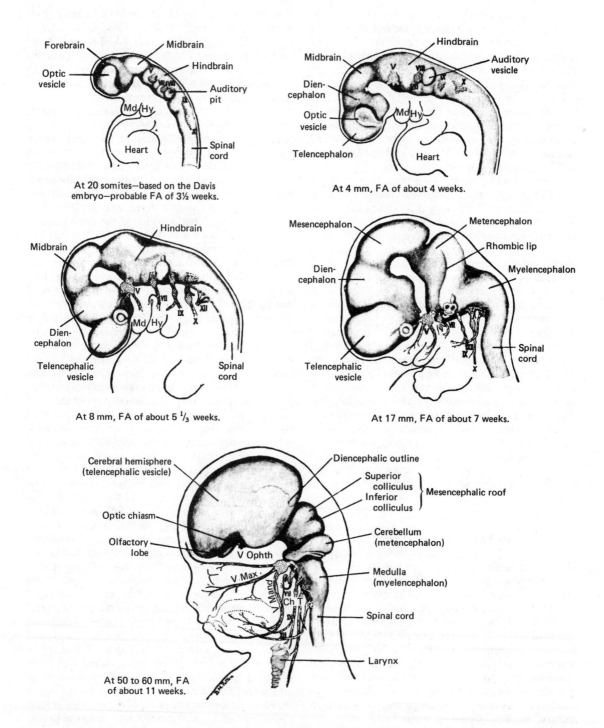

Figure 1–66. Five stages in early development of brain and cranial nerves. (Adapted from various sources, primarily figures by Streeter and reconstructions in the Carnegie Collection.) The cranial nerves shown are indicated by the appropriate roman numerals: V, trigeminal; VII, facial; VIII, acoustic; IX, glossopharyngeal; X, vagus; XI, accessory; XII, hypoglossal. FA = fertilization age; Ch T = chorda tympani branch of seventh nerve; Hy = hyoid arch; Md = mandibular arch; V Mand = mandibular branch of trigeminal nerve; V Max = maxillary branch; V Ophth = ophthalmic branch. (Reproduced, with permission, from Patten: *Human Embryology,* 2nd ed. Blakiston, 1953.)

ment of most portions of the brain is related to the transport of ions, the synthesis of acetylcholine, and the metabolism of glutamic acid. Concomitant changes affecting phospholipids and nucleoproteins occur, but the metabolic processes associated with functional activity of the brain are poorly understood.

Carbohydrate, in the form of glucose, is the principal source of energy for tissue cells of the CNS; it serves as a major contributor in the building of amino acids and fatty acids and is a source of CO_2, which helps regulate pH. Carbohydrate metabolism of nerve tissue is similar to that of muscle. Lactic acid and pyruvic acid appear under anaerobic conditions; they disappear very slowly, and oxygen does not accelerate this process. Very little storage of glycogen occurs in neural tissue, and brain extracts react more readily with glucose than with glycogen. The respiratory quotient of neural tissue is 1.0, which suggests that ordinarily the tissues of the CNS utilize carbohydrate almost exclusively, burning sugar with oxygen and introducing energy into cells via high-energy phosphate esters. In some circumstances, however, the brain can apparently remain active without the use of extrinsic or intrinsic carbohydrates.

There is no evidence that high blood glucose levels affect nervous system function directly. The effects of low blood glucose, however, are better established. Prolonged hypoglycemia depresses total brain metabolism. Patients may show confusion, excitement, combativeness, automatism, drowsiness, ataxia, incoordination, dysarthria, and diplopia. Symptoms often are preceded by marked sweating and sometimes by hunger, and some patients pass rapidly into coma and convulsions.

A constant rather than a rich supply of oxygen is considered essential for normal brain function. Quantitatively, the most important substance utilized in brain for oxygen activation is probably cytochrome oxidase. Brain has a markedly high anaerobic glycolytic rate, but its rate of aerobic glycolysis is small. Energy for the metabolic activities of the brain presumably comes largely from oxidative breakdown of glucose. Two enzymes of major importance in degradation of glucose in brain are (1) hexokinase, probably responsible for initiating the metabolic reactions of glucose; and (2) triosephosphate dehydrogenase, which controls the rate of energy production from glucose-6-phosphate.

Glutamate, aspartate, gamma-aminobutyric acid (GABA), and glutamine form about 70% of brain amino acid nitrogen. These substances are normally formed by transaminases in the brain acting on alpha-ketoglutaric acid and oxaloacetic acid, formed during carbohydrate breakdown. Subsequent enzymatic operations on glutamate produce glutamine (in the presence of adenosine triphosphate) or gamma-aminobutyric acid. Glutamine passes readily into the brain from blood and may be important in peptide synthesis or as a means of transporting ammonia. Amino acids are taken up by brain in vitro, as is easily shown by the use of radioactive compounds. However, free entry of amino acids into the brain in vivo is often hindered by the blood-brain barrier.

L-Glutamic and L-aspartic acid act as excitatory agents on the postsynaptic membranes of many neurons. Gamma-aminobutyric acid and glycine mimic natural inhibitory transmitters in the cerebral cortex, brain stem, and spinal cord.

Serotonin (5-hydroxytryptamine) may be one of the important regulatory amines of the body, similar in this respect to histamine, epinephrine, and norepinephrine. It is present in high concentration in the hypothalamus, midbrain, and caudate nucleus. It is probably synthesized from the amino acid tryptophan, although by a different metabolic pathway from that which leads to nicotinic acid, and is disposed of through deamination to 5-hydroxyindoleacetic acid (5-HIAA). It has vasoconstrictor and pressor effects and may also be found in the mammalian gastrointestinal tract and blood platelets. Some drugs, such as reserpine, may act by releasing bound serotonin in the brain. A structural analog of serotonin is lysergic acid diethylamide (LSD), which in small doses is capable of evoking mental symptoms similar to those of schizophrenia. The vasoconstrictive action of LSD is inhibited by serotonin.

The tissue enzyme **monoamine oxidase (MAO)** is responsible for the metabolism of serotonin and its excretion as 5-HIAA. Iproniazid and phenelzine increase the stores of serotonin by inhibiting MAO, whereas reserpine decreases storage of serotonin by inactivating binding sites and allowing free serotonin to be metabolized by MAO. An enzyme capable of attaching methyl groups to the amine nitrogen of tryptamine and serotonin has been found in mammalian tissues. A number of indolic substances that occur in plants are known to produce depersonalization, delusions, and hallucinations. Abnormalities of indole metabolism have been reported in schizophrenia, and some investigators believe that mammalian tissues can produce indolic hallucinogens. Serotonin injected into newly hatched chicks with incompletely developed blood-brain barriers has produced ataxia, decreased muscle tone and motor activity, and stupor. After high doses, 14 Hz and 6 Hz positive spike potentials were noted in the EEG; with sufficiently high doses, clonic convulsions occurred, followed by death.

GABA (gamma-aminobutyric acid) is present in relatively large amounts in the gray matter of brain and may regulate portions of available energy, thereby influencing the functional activity of the brain. GABA and the enzyme that forms it from L-glutamic acid, glutamic acid decarboxylase (GAD), occur uniquely in the CNS. GABA-alpha-ketoglutarate transaminase (GABA-T) catalyzes the reversible transamination of GABA with alpha-ketoglutarate. Convulsant hydrazides can lower GABA in brain by preferential inhibition of GAD, and hydroxylamine can increase the content of GABA by preferential inhibition of GABA-T.

The **catecholamines**—norepinephrine, epinephrine, and dopamine—are formed by hydroxylation

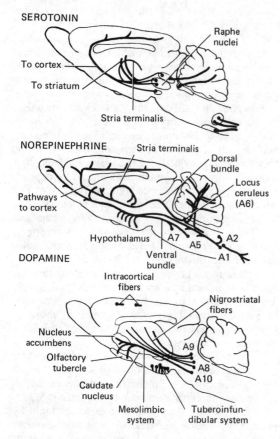

SEROTONIN

Raphe
nuclei

To cortex

To striatum

Stria terminalis

NOREPINEPHRINE   Stria terminalis

Dorsal
bundle

Locus
ceruleus
(A6)

Pathways
to cortex

Hypothalamus   A7   A2

A5

Ventral   A1
bundle

DOPAMINE

Intracortical
fibers

Nigrostriatal
fibers

Nucleus
accumbens

A9

Olfactory
tubercle   A8
A10

Caudate
nucleus

Mesolimbic   Tuberoinfun-
system   dibular system

Figure 1–67. Aminergic pathways in a rat's brain. The numbers and letters (A1, A2, etc) refer to specific groups of catecholamine-containing cell bodies. The pathways in humans are similar. (Modified and reproduced, with permission, from Ungerstedt: Stereotaxic mapping of the monoamine pathways in the rat brain. *Acta Physiol Scand* [*Suppl*] 1971;**367**:1.)

and decarboxylation of the essential amino acid phenylalanine. The enzyme responsible for conversion of norepinephrine to epinephrine is found in high concentration only in the adrenal medulla. Dopamine is the immediate precursor of norepinephrine, and its distribution in brain parallels that of norepinephrine. However, there is a very high concentration of dopamine and a low concentration of norepinephrine in the caudate nucleus and putamen. Dopamine, like norepinephrine, is inactivated by monoamine oxidase and by catechol-O-methyltransferase (COMT). In parkinsonism, the dopamine content of the caudate and putamen is reduced greatly; this may be related to secondary degeneration of nerve endings arising from degenerating cells in the substantia nigra.

Endorphins is a general term used for some endogenous morphinelike substances whose activity has been defined by their ability to bind to opiate receptors in the brain. These brain polypeptides (endorphins) with actions like opiates may act as synaptic transmitters or modulators. When injected into animals, en-

dorphins may be analgesic and tranquilizing.

Two closely related polypeptides (pentapeptides) found in brain that also bind to opiate receptors are **methionine enkephalin (met-enkephalin)** and **leucine enkephalin (leu-enkephalin).** The amino acid sequence of met-enkephalin has been found in alpha-endorphin and beta-endorphin. The amino acid sequence of beta-endorphin has been noted in the polypeptide β-lipotropin of the anterior pituitary gland.

A polypeptide formed of 11 amino acids, **substance P,** is found in the hypothalamus, substantia nigra, and dorsal roots of the spinal nerves. There is evidence that substance P is a transmitter in primary sensory afferent neurons ending in the dorsal horn of the spinal cord. Peptides such as cholecystokinin and vasoactive intestinal polypeptide, which were first known as intestinal hormones, have been found in the brain. In some cases it appears that a peptide may occur together with a classic transmitter in the same neuron. Almost 30 small peptides have been found in neurons in the mammalian CNS.

Histamine in large amounts has been found in the pituitary and adjacent median eminence of the hypothalamus.

EMBRYOLOGIC FEATURES

Early Differentiation

A thickened plate of ectoderm, the **neural plate,** develops along the middorsal line of the embryo and is transformed by invagination into a neural tube. The **neural tube** detaches from the overlying ectoderm and thickens to develop into the spinal cord and brain. The rostral end of the neural tube, which ultimately forms the brain, differentiates into 3 primary brain vesicles: (1) the **prosencephalon,** or forebrain, which lies closest to the rostrum; (2) the **mesencephalon,** or midbrain, which lies behind the prosencephalon; and (3) the **rhombencephalon,** or hindbrain, which lies most caudad.

Development of the Brain

From the prosencephalon are formed the telencephalon and diencephalon. The telencephalon forms the cerebral cortex, the striate bodies, the rhinencephalon, the lateral ventricles, and the anterior portion of the third ventricle. The diencephalon gives rise to the epithalamus, thalamus, metathalamus, hypothalamus, optic chiasm, tuber cinereum, posterior lobe of the hypophysis, mamillary bodies, and most of the third ventricle.

From the mesencephalon develop the quadrigeminal plate, the cerebral peduncles, and the cerebral aqueduct.

The rhombencephalon gives rise to the metencephalon and the myelencephalon. The metencephalon forms the cerebellum, pons, and part of the fourth ventricle. The myelencephalon forms the medulla oblongata and part of the fourth ventricle.

Table 1—8. Subdivisions of the neural tube and their derivatives.[*]

	Primary Vesicles	Subdivisions	Derivatives	Lumen
Brain	Prosencephalon	Telencephalon	Cerebral cortex Corpora striata Rhinencephalon	Lateral ventricles Rostral portion of the third ventricle

		Diencephalon	Epithalamus
			Thalamus
			Metathalamus
			Hypothalamus
			  Optic chiasm
			  Tuber cinereum
			  Posterior lobe of hypophysis
			  Mammillary bodies
				Greater part of the
				third ventricle

	Mesencephalon	Mesencephalon	Corpora quadrigemina Crura cerebri	Cerebral aqueduct
	Rhombencephalon	Metencephalon	Cerebellum Pons	Fourth ventricle
		Myelencephalon	Medulla oblongata	
Spinal cord			Spinal cord	

[*]Reproduced, with permission, from Ranson SW, Clark SL: *Anatomy of the Nervous System*, 10th ed. Saunders, 1959.

Development of the Spinal Cord

The spinal cord develops from the caudal portion of the neural tube. The earliest tracts of nerve fibers appear in the marginal zone at about the second month. Long association tracts appear about the third month and pyramidal tracts about the fifth month of fetal life. Myelination of nerve fibers of the spinal cord begins about the middle of fetal life and is not completed in some tracts for 20 years. The oldest tracts myelinate first; the pyramidal tracts myelinate later, largely during the first and second years after birth.

Cellular Developmental Changes

Initially, the neural plate consists of a single layer of cells. These divide and proliferate and their cell bodies become indistinct, so that by the time of the formation of the neural tube the wall is formed of several layers of cells with a syncytial appearance. Three layers may be differentiated early: (1) a marginal or nonnuclear outer layer, which in the spinal cord develops into the white substance; (2) a mantle layer with many nuclei, which in the spinal cord differentiates into the gray matter; and (3) an innermost ependymal layer in which may be found large mitotic nuclei of germinal cells. Neuroblasts form, which differentiate into neurons; and spongioblasts, which differentiate into neuroglial and ependymal cells.

The neural crest, a ridge of ectodermal cells at the junction of the neural groove and the overlying superficial ectoderm, gives rise to the neuroblasts that form the sensory (afferent) fibers and the sensory ganglia. Some ectodermal cells migrate from the neural tube and neural crest along the course of the ventral or dorsal roots. From these is derived the neurilemma, or nucleated sheath, of the peripheral nerve fiber. Ectodermal cells of similar origin give rise to sympathetic ganglia. The chromaffin tissue and all of the nerve cells outside of the CNS, with the exception of those arising from the neural placodes (ectodermal thickenings), come from the neural tube and neural crests. The placodes give rise to olfactory neuroepithelium, epithelium of the otocyst, and the lens of the eye and contribute to formation of the trigeminal, facial, glossopharyngeal, and vagus nerves.

2 | The Spinal Cord

ANATOMY

The spinal cord is an elongated cylindrical mass of nerve tissue that occupies the upper two-thirds of the vertebral canal and usually measures 42–45 cm in length in adults. It extends from the superior border of the atlas (first cervical vertebra) to the upper border of the second lumbar vertebra. It is continuous with the medulla oblongata at its rostral end.

The conus medullaris is the conical distal, or inferior, end of the spinal cord, from the apex of which a delicate filament, the filum terminale, extends and attaches to the first segment of the coccyx.

Until the third month of fetal life, the spinal cord is as long as the vertebral canal. Thereafter, the vertebral column elongates faster than the spinal cord, until by the end of the fifth month of fetal life the end of the cord is at the level of the base of the sacrum. At about the time of birth, the cord extends to about the third lumbar level.

Investing Membranes

Three membranes surround the spinal cord: dura mater, arachnoid, and pia mater. The **dura mater,** the outermost membrane, is a tough, fibrous, tubular sheath that extends downward to the level of the second sacral vertebra, where it ends as a blind sac. The **epidural space** separates the dura mater from the bony vertebral column and contains loose areolar tissue and venous plexuses. The **subdural space** is a thin space between the dura mater and the underlying arachnoid.

The **arachnoid** is a thin, transparent sheath separated from the underlying pia mater by the **subarachnoid space,** which contains collections of cerebrospinal fluid. The **pia mater** closely surrounds the spinal cord and sends septa into the substance of the cord.

The **filum terminale** is composed mainly of fibrous tissue and is continuous with the pia mater. The proximal three-quarters of the filum terminale, which is surrounded by the cauda equina, is known as the

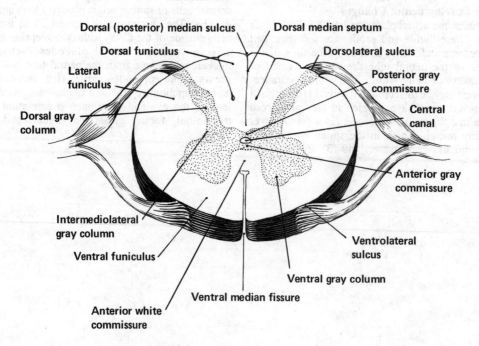

Figure 2–1. Anatomy of the spinal cord.

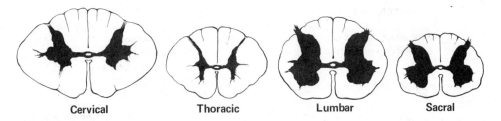

Figure 2–2. Transverse sections of the spinal cord at various levels.

internal filum terminale. The remaining portion, which is closely invested by dura mater, is known as the external filum terminale and is attached to the back of the first segment of the coccyx.

The denticulate ligament extends from each lateral surface of the pia mater and is attached by a series of processes to the inner surface of the dura mater.

Divisions of the Spinal Cord

The spinal cord contains an **anterior median fissure** and a **posterior median sulcus,** which may be considered to divide the cord into symmetric right and left halves that are joined in the central midportions. The anterior median fissure is relatively deep and contains a fold of pia mater; its floor is formed by white matter, the **anterior white commissure.** The posterior median sulcus is a shallow groove. In the cervical and upper thoracic regions, the **posterior intermediate sulcus** appears on the dorsal surface of the spinal cord between the posterior median sulcus and the posterolateral sulcus. The posterior nerve roots are attached to the spinal cord along a vertical furrow, the **posterolateral sulcus,** which lies a short distance anterior to the posterior median sulcus.

Each lateral half of the spinal cord may be divided into **columns,** or **funiculi.** The posterior column, or funiculus, lies between the posterior median sulcus and the posterolateral sulcus. In the cervical and upper thoracic region, the posterior column is divided by the posterior intermediate sulcus into a medial portion, the **fasciculus gracilis,** and a lateral portion, the **fasciculus cuneatus.** The lateral column lies between the posterolateral sulcus and the anterolateral sulcus, the line of origin of the anterior roots. The anterior column lies between the anterolateral sulcus and the anterior median fissure.

The **central canal** extends the length of the spinal cord. It is lined with ependymal cells and filled with cerebrospinal fluid and continues upward to open into the posterior portion of the fourth ventricle in the medulla oblongata.

Segments of the Spinal Cord

The spinal cord segments are referred to as cervical, thoracic, lumbar, or sacral to correspond with attachments of groups of nerves. Individual segments vary in length, being about twice as long in the midthoracic region as in the cervical or upper lumbar areas.

The spinal cord is considerably enlarged in 2 regions. The **cervical** enlargement corresponds to the area of the nerves to the upper limbs and extends from about the third cervical to the second thoracic vertebral level. The **lumbar** enlargement extends from about the level of the ninth thoracic to the 12th thoracic vertebra and tapers thereafter to form the **conus medullaris.** The 2 enlargements of the cord correspond to the origin of the nerves of the upper and lower extremities. The cervical enlargement gives origin to the nerves of the brachial plexus; the lumbar enlargement, which is not as extensive, corresponds to the origin of the nerves of the lumbosacral plexus.

Because of the different growth rates of the cord and spine, the cord segments are displaced upward from their corresponding vertebrae, the discrepancy becoming greater as one passes downward along the cord. Thus, the lower the nerve root, the greater the distance between its origin in the segment of the cord and its point of exit from the spinal canal. This relationship between cord segments and the vertebral bodies and spines is of clinical importance in locating the level of a lesion of the cord and in approaching it surgically. (See Table 2–1 and also Fig 5–2.)

Gray Matter

In transverse section the spinal cord is seen to contain an H-shaped internal mass of gray substance surrounded by white matter. The gray matter is made up of 2 symmetric halves joined across the midline by a transverse connection (commissure) of gray substance through which runs the minute central canal. The **anterior gray column** (anterior horn) is anterior to the central canal. It contains the cells of origin of the fibers of the ventral roots. The **lateral column** is the lateral triangular projection of gray matter that is prominent in the upper cervical, thoracic, and midsacral regions. It contains preganglionic cells for the autonomic nervous

Table 2–1. Anatomic relationships of spinal cord and bony spine in adults.

Cord Segments	Vertebral Bodies	Spinous Processes
C8	Lower C6 and upper C7	C6
T6	Lower T3 and upper T4	T3
T12	T9	T8
L5	T11	T10
S	T12 and L1	T12 and L1

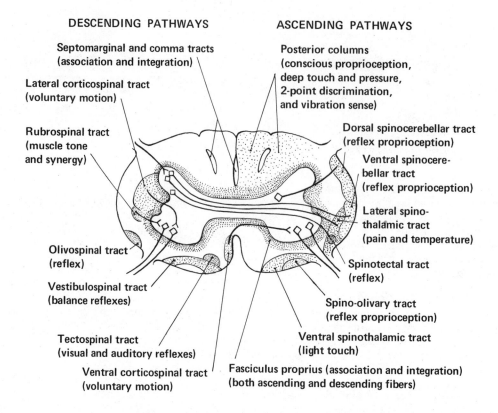

DESCENDING PATHWAYS

Septomarginal and comma tracts
(association and integration)

Lateral corticospinal tract
(voluntary motion)

Rubrospinal tract
(muscle tone
and synergy)

Olivospinal tract
(reflex)

Vestibulospinal tract
(balance reflexes)

Tectospinal tract
(visual and auditory reflexes)

Ventral corticospinal tract
(voluntary motion)

ASCENDING PATHWAYS

Posterior columns
(conscious proprioception,
deep touch and pressure,
2-point discrimination,
and vibration sense)

Dorsal spinocerebellar tract
(reflex proprioception)

Ventral spinocere-
bellar tract
(reflex proprioception)

Lateral spino-
thalamic tract
(pain and temperature)

Spinotectal tract
(reflex)

Spino-olivary tract
(reflex proprioception)

Ventral spinothalamic tract
(light touch)

Fasciculus proprius (association and integration)
(both ascending and descending fibers)

Figure 2–3. Pathways in spinal cord (lower cervical region).

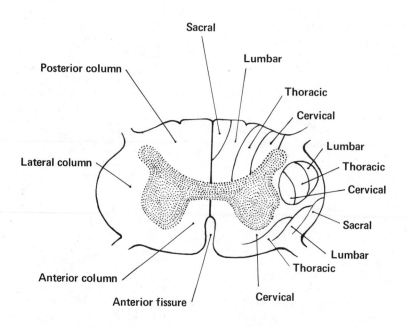

Sacral

Lumbar

Thoracic

Cervical

Posterior column

Lumbar

Thoracic

Cervical

Lateral column

Sacral

Anterior column

Lumbar

Thoracic

Anterior fissure

Cervical

Figure 2–4. Segmental arrangement in the spinal cord. (Modified after Walker.)

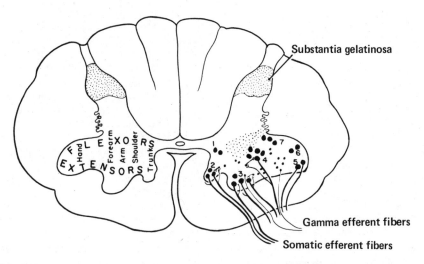

Substantia gelatinosa

Gamma efferent fibers

Somatic efferent fibers

Figure 2–5. Diagram of motor nuclei in anterior gray horn of lower cervical segment of spinal cord. On the left is shown the general location of anterior horn cells that send motor axons to specific muscle groups of the upper extremity. Motor nuclei indicated on the right are as follows: 1, posteromedial; 2, anteromedial; 3, anterior; 4, central; 5, anterolateral; 6, posterolateral; 7, retroposterolateral. Smaller anterior horn cells send axons (gamma efferents) to supply small muscle fibers of neuromuscular spindle. Note the collaterals from somatic efferent axons that return to gray matter and synapse on small medially placed "Renshaw cells." Smaller cells appearing as the dotted zone in the intermediate gray matter indicate the area of the internuncial neuron pool. (Reproduced, with permission, from Truex & Carpenter: *Human Neuroanatomy,* 6th ed. Williams & Wilkins, 1969.)

system. The **posterior gray column** (posterior horn) is a long slender column that reaches almost to the posterolateral sulcus. It is capped by a crescentic mass of translucent tissue containing nerve cells, the **substantia gelatinosa** of Rolando. The **reticular formation** is a network of processes extending into the lateral funiculus between the anterior and posterior columns. The central canal divides the transverse commissure into anterior and posterior gray commissures.

The form, quantity, and appearance of the gray substance vary at different levels. The greatest proportion of gray matter to white matter is in the lumbar and cervical enlargements. In the cervical region, the posterior gray column is comparatively narrow and the anterior column is broad and expansive. In the thoracic region, the posterior and anterior columns are narrow and a lateral column is evident. In the lumbar region, the posterior and anterior columns are broad and expanded. In the conus medullaris, the gray matter looks like 2 oval masses, one in each half of the cord, connected by a wide gray commissure.

The gray substance of the spinal cord may be divided into 2 major components: motor and receptor. The motor part consists of the anterior and lateral columns and gives rise to the anterior roots. It contains the anterior horn, or motor, cells that supply voluntary striated muscle. The lateral column cells give rise to the preganglionic fibers of the thoracic and lumbosacral autonomic systems, which leave the spinal cord via the anterior roots. Cell groups within the anterior columns may be named, according to their location, as anteromedial, posteromedial, anterolateral, postero-

lateral, retroposterolateral, and central.

The receptor part of the spinal cord consists of posterior columns. Most of the fibers from the cells of this column divide in the shape of a T in entering the white matter, giviing rise to ascending and descending branches that in turn give off branches to reenter the gray matter. The cells within the posterior column are generally not arranged in definite groups except for the **nucleus dorsalis** (Clarke's column). The medial part of the base of the posterior column is occupied by the nucleus dorsalis, which sends fibers to the ipsilateral dorsal spinocerebellar tract.

Rexed subdivided the gray matter of the spinal cord into 10 layers, or laminas, on the basis of cytoarchitecture and longitudinal organization of neurons. The posterior horn contains laminas I–VI. These are concerned with the sensory, or afferent, input into the spinal cord and may also be influenced by descending motor pathways. Lamina II corresponds to the substantia gelatinosa.

Lamina VII is in the intermediate gray area and extends into the lateral part of the anterior horn. It contains the nucleus dorsalis and the intermediolateral gray column.

The anterior horn contains lamina VIII, which has some neurons that send axons to the opposite side. Lamina IX is in the anterior horn, where it is broken into groups of cells. It includes the alpha and gamma motor neurons, which send efferent fibers via the ventral roots of the spinal cord to muscles.

Lamina X is located around the central canal of the spinal cord.

White Matter

The white matter of the spinal cord consists of nerve fibers in a network of neuroglia. These nerve fibers are myelinated or nonmyelinated and serve to link different segments of the spinal cord and to connect the spinal cord with the brain. The fasciculi proprii immediately surrounding the gray columns contain short ascending and descending fibers that terminate within the spinal cord. Three white columns are formed by the posterior roots and the most lateral of the anterior nerve roots.

A. Anterior White Column: The anterior white column extends between the anteromedian fissure and the anterolateral sulcus.

1. Descending tracts–The **ventral corticospinal tract** (direct pyramidal tract, anterior cerebrospinal tract) lies close to the anterior median fissure and ends in the midthoracic region. Its cells of origin are in the large pyramidal cells of the ipsilateral prerolandic motor cortex. The **vestibulospinal tract** is located in the marginal portion and extends from the vestibular nerve nuclei to the sacral segments. The **tectospinal tract** lies immediately posterior to the vestibulospinal tract and takes its origin from the contralateral superior colliculus of the midbrain, crossing in the fountain decussation of Meynert in the midbrain. The **reticulospinal tract** in the sulcomarginal zone comes from reticular substance of medulla and midbrain. The vestibulospinal and reticulospinal tracts tend to facilitate extensor activity and to inhibit flexor activity.

2. Ascending tracts–The **ventral spinothalamic tract** is located in the marginal portion of the anterior column and is derived from cells of the opposite posterior column. The **spino-olivary tract** is located in the anterior marginal zone and contains fibers going to the inferior olivary nucleus of the medulla oblongata.

B. Lateral White Column: The lateral white column extends between the anterolateral and posterolateral sulci.

1. Descending tracts–The **lateral corticospinal tract** (crossed pyramidal tract, lateral cerebrospinal tract) extends throughout the length of the spinal cord between the dorsal spinocerebellar tract and the fasciculus proprius. Its fibers arise from the large pyramidal cells of the contralateral precentral motor cortex and are so arranged that the fibers to the upper extremity are situated medially and those to the lower extremity peripherally. The **rubrospinal tract** (tract of Monakow) is situated just anterior to the lateral corticospinal tract and is small in humans. Its fibers originate in the red nucleus of the midbrain, cross the median plane, and then descend in the spinal cord. The olivospinal tract (Helweg's bundle) lies close to the most lateral of the anterior nerve roots in the cervical cord region and originates in the medulla oblongata in the vicinity of the inferior olivary nucleus. The lateral corticospinal tract and the rubrospinal tract tend to facilitate flexor activity and to inhibit extensor activity.

2. Ascending tracts–The **dorsal spinocerebellar tract** (tract of Flechsig, cerebellospinal tract) lies at the periphery of the posterior part of the lateral column just ventral to the posterolateral sulcus. Its fibers arise from cells of the ipsilateral dorsal nucleus (Clarke's column) and proceed to the cerebellum via the inferior cerebellar peduncle. The **ventral spinocerebellar tract** (tract of Gowers) is located at the periphery of the lateral column anterior to the dorsal spinocerebellar tract. Its fibers arise from cells of the posterior gray column and intermediate gray substance of both sides and enter the cerebellum via the superior cerebellar peduncle. The **lateral spinothalamic tract** lies on the medial and anterior side of the ventral spinocerebellar tract. Its fibers arise from cells of the opposite dorsal column and cross via the anterior white commissure shortly after their origin to end in the thalamus. The **spinotectal tract** passes ventrally to the lateral spinothalamic tract; its fibers arise from the opposite posterior gray column to end in the tectum, or roof, of the midbrain.

C. Posterior White Column: The posterior white column extends between the posterolateral and posteromedian sulci.

1. Descending tracts–The **fasciculus interfascicularis** (comma tract of Schultze) is situated between the fasciculus gracilis and fasciculus cuneatus. Its fibers are of intraspinal and dorsal root origin. The septomarginal fasciculus is located near the posteromedian septum.

Table 2–2. Important ascending and descending tracts of spinal cord.

Anterior Column	Lateral Column	Posterior Column
Ascending Tracts		
Ventral spinothalamic (light touch) Spino-olivary (reflex proprioception)	Dorsal and ventral spinocerebellar (reflex proprioception) Lateral spinothalamic (pain and temperature) Spinotectal (reflex)	Fasciculus gracilis and fasciculus cuneatus (vibration, passive motion, joint and 2-point discrimination)
Descending Tracts		
Ventral corticospinal (voluntary motion) Vestibulospinal (balance reflex) Tectospinal (audiovisual reflex) Reticulospinal (muscle tone)	Lateral corticospinal (voluntary motion) Rubrospinal (muscle tone and synergy) Olivospinal (reflex)	Fasciculus interfascicularis and septomarginal fasciculus (association and integration)

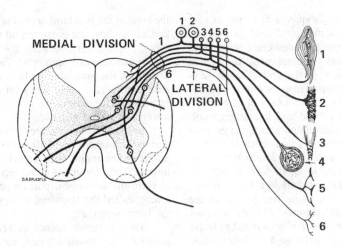

MEDIAL DIVISION

LATERAL DIVISION

Figure 2–6. Diagrammatic cross section of spinal cord showing principal sites of termination of dorsal root fibers. 1 and 2 represent large medullated fibers having large dorsal root ganglion cells and passing to the dorsal columns; they arise from pacinian (1) and muscle spindle (2) endings. 3 and 4 terminate on dorsal horn cells that give rise to spinothalamic and spinocerebellar tracts. 5 = a similar cell terminating on a neuron that gives rise to ventral spinothalamic tract. 6 = a small-fibered neuron (pain) terminating in substantia gelatinosa of Rolando giving rise to fiber of ascending spinothalamic tract of opposite side. (Reproduced, with permission, from Fulton: *Physiology of the Nervous System,* 3rd ed. Oxford Univ Press, 1949.)

2. Ascending tracts–The **fasciculus gracilis** (tract of Goll) is located next to the posteromedian septum, beginning in the lowest portion of the spinal cord and increasing in size from below upward. It receives fibers from the medial group of nerve fibers of the posterior roots and terminates in the nucleus of the funiculus gracilis in the medulla. The **fasciculus cuneatus** (tract of Burdach) lies between the fasciculus gracilis and the posterior gray column and is similarly derived from the posterior nerve roots of the thoracocervical region. It terminates in the nucleus of the funiculus cuneatus in the medulla.

The **fasciculus proprius** (juxtagriseal area), located immediately adjacent to the gray matter, is composed of a mixture of fiber pathways: short fibers running in both directions and serving to integrate the functions of the cord through intersegmental and intrasegmental association connections; fibers of the **medial longitudinal fasciculus,** descending from the medulla in the anterior portion of the fasciculus proprius and conveying impulses from the vestibular, oculomotor, trochlear, and abducens nuclei concerned with equilibratory reflexes; and fibers of the **reticulospinal tract,** conveying part of the extrapyramidal flow for the regulation of muscle tone.

Spinal Roots & Nerves

Thirty-one pairs of spinal nerves arise from the spinal cord. Each nerve has an anterior, or ventral, root and a posterior, or dorsal, root. The **spinal ganglion,** or **dorsal root ganglion,** is a swelling containing cells in the dorsal root of each nerve. Each root contains bundles of nerve fibers. The groups of spinal nerves are divided into 8 cervical, 12 thoracic, 5 lumbar, 5 sacral, and one coccygeal nerve. The nerve roots be-

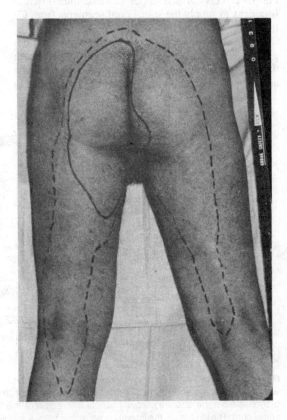

Figure 2–7. Sensory impairment in man with cauda equina syndrome after fracture of L1 vertebra. (Solid line = touch; dotted line = pain.)

come increasingly more oblique in direction at progressively lower levels of the spinal cord. In the lumbosacral region, the nerve roots descend almost vertically to exit from the bony vertebral canal. Because of their length and appearance, the collection of lumbosacral nerve roots is referred to as the **cauda equina.**

The **anterior nerve root** consists of efferent fibers originating in the ventral and lateral gray columns. These become medullated shortly after their origin and emerge from the spinal cord in 2 or 3 irregular rows over an area about 3 mm wide. The **posterior nerve root,** made up of 6–8 rootlets attached in the posterolateral sulcus in a linear series, contains afferent fibers from the nerve cells in the spinal ganglion. In general, the most medial fibers pass to the fasciculus cuneatus; most of the remaining fibers terminate in the substantia gelatinosa of Rolando and the dorsal gray column.

Spinal Cord Circulation

The **anterior spinal artery,** formed by the midline union of paired branches of the vertebral arteries, extends along the anterior surface of the cervical spinal cord, narrowing somewhat near the upper (fourth) thoracic segments.

The **lateral spinal arteries** arise as a single set of branches from the vertebral arteries and pass through the lower cervical and upper thoracic intervertebral foramens to supply the spinal cord segments from C7 to T2.

The **anterior medial spinal artery** is the prolongation of the anterior spinal artery below the fourth thoracic cord segment. Intercostal arteries from the aorta supply segmental branches to the spinal cord to the level of the first lumbar cord segment; the largest of these branches, the great ventral radicular artery, enters the spinal cord between the eighth thoracic and fourth lumbar cord segments. This large artery, also known as the arteria radicularis magna, or artery of Adamkiewicz, usually arises on the left and may be responsible for most of the arterial blood supply of the lower half of the spinal cord in some cases.

In the lumbosacral area, **radicular arteries** are derived from the lumbar, iliolumbar, and lateral sacral arteries. The major such vessel appears to enter the intervertebral foramens at the second lumbar vertebra to form the lowermost portion of the anterior spinal artery, called the **terminal artery,** which runs along the filum terminale.

The **posterior spinal arteries,** also known as posterolateral spinal arteries, receive branches from the posterolateral arterial plexus at various levels; they are paired and are considerably smaller than the single large anterior spinal artery.

Anterior sulcal arteries arise from the anterior spinal artery at various levels along the cervical and thoracic cord within the anterior sulcus and supply the anterior and lateral columns on either side of the spinal cord. At any given cord segment, only one side of the cord is supplied by this vessel. The posterior spinal arteries supply the posterior white columns and the more posterior part of the posterior gray columns.

Segmentally, arteries that enter the intervertebral foramens are given off from the intercostal vessels and lateral sacral arteries; arteries are also given off from the dorsal and ventral radicular arteries, which accompany the posterior and anterior nerve roots, respectively. These unite directly with the posterior and an-

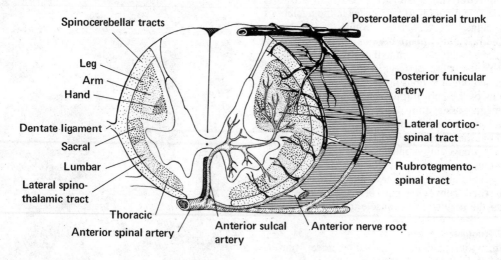

Figure 2–8. Cross section of cervical spinal cord. The diagram shows the anterior spinal artery with its anterior sulcal branch, which supplies the anteromedial two-thirds of one-half of the cervical spinal cord at any given segment. The peripheral branches from the arteriae coronae supply the region of the lateral spinothalamic tract of the anterolateral portion of the spinal cord. The leg area in the lateral corticospinal tract is supplied by the posterior funicular artery. The arm and hand portion of this tract and the rubrotegmentospinal tract are supplied by the anterior sulcal vessel. There are numerous variations in this vascular supply. (Redrawn and reproduced, with permission, from Schneider & Crosby: Vascular insufficiency of brain stem and spinal cord in spinal trauma. *Neurology* 1959; 9:643.)

terior spinal arteries and then are joined together segmentally along the periphery of the spinal cord as the **arteriae coronae.**

Vertebral Column (Spinal Column)

The vertebral (spinal) column contains 33 vertebrae joined together by ligaments and cartilage. The upper 24 vertebrae are discrete and movable; the lower 9 are fixed, with 5 vertebrae fused to form the sacrum and the terminal 4 fused to form the coccyx. The normal vertebral column may be considered to have 7 cervical, 12 thoracic, 5 lumbar, 5 sacral, and 4 coccygeal vertebrae. Mobility of the vertebrae in the cervical, thoracic, and lumbar regions is relatively free compared with the fused vertebrae of the sacrum and coccyx. The spinal column in the male is 10–12 cm longer than in the female.

The typical **vertebra** has a body and a neural arch surrounding the vertebral canal. The neural arch is composed of a pedicle on each side supporting a lamina extending posteriorly to the midline. The pedicle has a notch above and below that forms the intervertebral foramen. The arch has a posterior midline spinous process or spine, lateral transverse processes, and upper and lower articular facets. The bodies of the vertebrae gradually increase in width from the second cervical to the first thoracic vertebrae, decrease in width over the next 2 or 3 vertebrae, and then increase in width as far down as the lumbosacral angle.

The oval-shaped **intervertebral foramens,** through which pass the spinal nerves, are smallest in the cervical region and gradually increase in size as they approach the lowest lumbar vertebrae. Spinal nerves C1–C7 pass over the superior aspect of their corresponding cervical vertebrae. Spinal nerve C8 passes below the body of vertebra C7. All the subsequent spinal nerves pass below the inferior aspect of the corresponding vertebrae.

The midline **spinous processes** of the cervical vertebrae are bifid (C2–C6) and almost horizontal. The spinous processes of the thoracic and lumbar vertebrae are single. The laminas on both sides of the spinous processes form shallow grooves for muscle layers. The articular facets are lateral to the laminas, and the transverse processes are more lateral and somewhat anterior. The vertebral canal extends the length of the vertebral column and generally conforms with the size and shape of the vertebrae. It is triangular and large in the cervical region, smaller and circular in the thoracic region, and triangular and larger in the lumbar area.

The individual vertebrae of the vertebral column articulate body to body by articular facets. Movement between adjacent vertebrae is slight, but the additive effect can be large. Range of motion is greatest in the cervicothoracic and thoracicolumbar junctions, which are common sites of vertebral injury.

A series of overlapping ligaments enclose the vertebral column and aid in protection of the spinal cord. The **anterior longitudinal ligament** is a continuation of the atlantoaxial ligament and extends from the axis down the entire front end of the vertebral bodies to the sacrum. It is thickest in the thoracic region and intimately attached to the margins of the vertebral bodies. The **posterior longitudinal ligament** extends centrally down the entire length close to the vertebral margins, starting at the posterior edge of the body of the axis. It fans out at the intervertebral margins and is thinnest in the cervical and lumbar regions.

Intervertebral disks of fibrocartilage lie between contiguous vertebral surfaces from the axis to the upper sacral border. In general, they conform to the vertebral surfaces where they lie and may vary considerably in size, shape, and thickness. The intervertebral disks make up about one-fourth of the length of the vertebral column. They are thicker in the cervical and lumbar areas than in the thoracic region. Each disk is enveloped by a thick capsule, the **annulus fibrosus,** which adheres to the thin cartilage plate on the vertebral body above and below and surrounds the gelatinous, semifluid **nucleus pulposus.** The intervertebral disks are thicker anteriorly and are intimately attached to the hyaline cartilage of adjacent superior and inferior vertebrae. They permit great mobility in the cervical and lumbar regions and help absorb stress and strain transmitted to the vertebral column.

The **ligamentum flavum** is on either side of the spinous process, extends laterally to the articular facets, and attaches to the posterior margins of the lamina below and to the undersurface of the lamina above. The **supraspinous ligament** joins the spinous process tips from vertebra C7 to the sacrum. It is a continuation of the ligamentum nuchae and fuses with the interspinal ligaments. The **interspinal ligaments** connect adjacent spinous processes from their tips to their roots. They fuse with the supraspinous ligaments posteriorly and with the ligamentum flavum anteriorly.

PHYSIOLOGY

Three types of nerve fibers have been described according to their fiber diameters, conduction velocities, and physiologic characteristics (see Table 2–3). **A fibers** are large, somatic, and myelinated and conduct rapidly. They are most susceptible to injury by mechanical pressure or oxygen lack. **B fibers** are smaller, autonomic, and myelinated and conduct slowly. **C fibers** are the smallest, autonomic, non-myelinated, and slowest in conduction.

A nerve fiber may be excited from its own cell body or by a variety of mechanical, thermal, chemical, or electrical stimuli applied anywhere along its course; the energy for transmission is derived from the substance of the nerve fiber or its ensheathing tissue. The current generated is not continuous but appears to be built up in successive waves by each segment of nerve fiber acting as a metabolic unit. In a nerve trunk, the number of stimulated fibers will increase with the size of the stimulus, but in the single nerve fiber, the only

Table 2–3. Nerve fiber types in mammalian nerve.*

Fiber Type		Function	Fiber Diameter (μm)	Conduction Velocity (μm)	Spike Duration (ms)	Absolute Refractory Period (ms)
A	α	Proprioception; somatic motor sense	12–20	70–120		
	β	Touch, pressure	5–12	30–70	0.4–0.5	0.4–1
	γ	Motor to muscle spindles	3–6	15–30		
	δ	Pain, temperature, touch	2–5	12–30		
B		Preganglionic sympathetics	<3	3–15	1.2	1.2
C	dr†	Pain, reflex responses	0.4–1.2	0.5–2	2	2
	S‡	Postganglionic sympathetics	0.3–1.3	0.7–2.3	2	2

*Reproduced, with permission, from Ganong WF: *Review of Medical Physiology,* 10th ed. Lange, 1981.
†Dorsal root fibers.
‡Sympathetic C fibers.

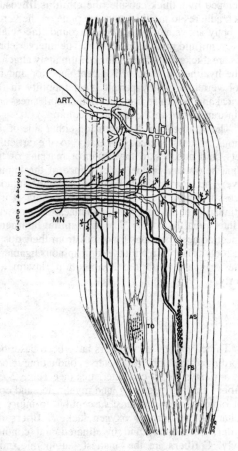

Figure 2–9. Distribution of nerve fibers to a striped muscle. MN = muscular nerve. 1 = small sensory fibers, often nonmedullated in peripheral portion, to perivascular tissue. 2 = fibers from sympathetic nervous system to arteriolar muscle coats. 3 = medium-sized fibers to motor end-plates. 4 = small fibers to end-plates of muscle spindles. 5, 6, 7 = large sensory nerve fibers to muscle spindles. AS = annulospiral ending. FS = flower-spray ending. TO = tendon organ. ART = arteriole. (Original drawing by Professor Derek Denny-Brown, MD. Reproduced, with permission, from Adams, Denny-Brown, & Pearson: *Diseases of Muscle.* Hoeber, 1953.)

gradation with intensity is the frequency of the recurrent impulses in the fiber. The velocity at which a nerve impulse is conducted is independent of the strength of the stimulus, and the impulse set up by a strong stimulus travels no faster than that from a weak stimulus. The all-or-none principle refers to the fact that if the impulse is strong enough to be propagated, the size of the response and the spread of its conduction will be independent of the size of the stimulus, so that the response obtained is all that the nerve can give at that moment.

A great deal of data on voltage, conduction velocity, frequency, refractoriness, spike potentials, and negative and positive afterpotentials is now available. During the resting state, the interior of the nerve fiber remains electrically negative with respect to the outer surface, and this gives rise to a membrane potential. The nerve impulse itself is associated with a characteristic action potential, the intact longitudinal nerve surface becoming less positive as the impulse passes. The spread of the action potential along the surface of the nerve fiber is associated with the local passage of sodium ions into the fiber during the rising phase of the action potential.

The primary function of a nerve cell, or neuron, is to conduct an impulse. When a living neuron is at rest, there is a membrane potential, or resting potential, consisting of the difference in the potential between the outer and inner surfaces of the cell membrane. The outside of the membrane at rest is normally positively charged, whereas the inside is negatively charged, and because of this disposition of electric charges the membrane is said to be polarized. Depolarization refers to a diminution of the difference in charge, whereas hyperpolarization refers to an increase in the charges normally present at the membrane surface. The conduction of the nerve impulse is associated with a characteristic electrical change known as the action potential. The passage of the nerve impulse is associated with a transient reversible depolarization of the membrane associated with membrane permeability changes. Sodium ions enter the nerve fiber during the rise of the action potential, and potassium ions leave.

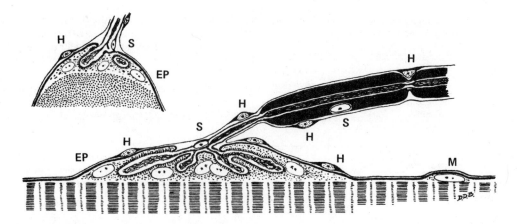

Figure 2–10. Motor end-plate, showing the relationship between the various structures in nerve and muscle. EP = end-plate nuclei. H = nuclei of Henle's sheath. M = sarcolemmal nuclei. S = nuclei of Schwann's sheath. (Original drawing by Professor Derek Denny-Brown, MD. Reproduced, with permission, from Adams, Denny-Brown, & Pearson: *Diseases of Muscle.* Hoeber, 1953.)

Although a definite threshold must be exceeded before a nerve impulse can be initiated by electric current stimulation, the impulse, once started, is independent of the stimulus needed for its evocation. The current of intensity just sufficient to excite the nerve is called the **rheobase,** and the time required by twice the rheobasic current to excite a nerve fiber is known as the **chronaxie.** The excitability of a nerve may be considered to be the reciprocal of its stimulation threshold. The absolute refractory period is the period during which no stimulus, however strong, will excite the fiber, whereas the relative refractory period is the period when the nerve can be excited only if the stimulus is of more than normal threshold strength. The period of absolute refractoriness coincides approximately with the rise of the spike potential and with its decline to the point where the negative afterpotential distorts its falling curve, at which point the nerve becomes relatively refractory, coincident with the period of transition from the spike potential to the negative afterpotential. When the relative refractory period dies out, the nerve next enters the supernormal period, when it is more excitable than normally. Following this there is a period of less excitability of the nerve fiber, referred to as the subnormal period. The supernormal period corresponds to the period of the negative afterpotential, and the subnormal period to the period of the positive afterpotential.

The action potential in mammalian nerve fibers (A type) characteristically consists of 3 components: (1) the spike potential, (2) the negative afterpotential, and (3) the positive afterpotential. The spike potential has by far the greatest magnitude and shortest duration and follows the "all-or-none" principle. The negative afterpotential, a period of heightened excitability, is quite variable; its greatest size is only 1/20 that of the spike potential, and it lasts only for about 0.015 s. The positive afterpotential that follows is of very low amplitude, but it lasts the longest (about 0.07 s).

Nerve Function

Electrolytes may influence nerve function. High external potassium and low external calcium concentrations decrease the resting potential of peripheral nerve, presumably increasing its excitability. Nerves lose calcium in low-calcium solutions and gain potassium when exposed to high concentrations of external potassium. Excessive magnesium has a general depressant effect on nervous system function.

Neural activity, such as occurs in nerve conduction, may lead to altered inorganic ion concentrations. A loss of potassium due to activity has been demonstrated in ganglia and unmyelinated nerve. According to the membrane theory of nerve action, the surface of a nerve is permeable to potassium but relatively im-

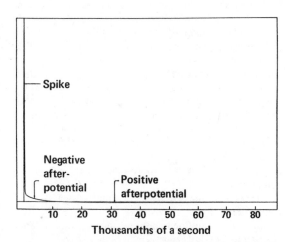

Figure 2–11. Diagram of the potentials in a mammalian nerve fiber in their normal relationship in a single response. (Reproduced, with permission, from Gasser: *The Control of Excitation in the Nervous System.* Harvey Lectures, 1936–1937.)

Table 2—4. Numerical classification sometimes used for sensory neurons and equivalents in the Erlanger and Gasser letter system.*

Number		Origin	Letter Equivalent
I	a	Muscle spindle, annulospiral ending	A α
	b	Golgi tendon organ	A α
II		Muscle spindle, flower-spray ending; touch, pressure	A β and γ
III		Pain and temperature receptors	A δ
IV		Pain and other receptors	dr C

*Reproduced, with permission, from Ganong WF: *Review of Medical Physiology,* 10th ed. Lange, 1981.

permeable to sodium; upon excitation there is an alteration in permeability of the membrane, permitting sodium and perhaps other ions to enter. When a nerve conducts an impulse following stimulation, a small amount of heat is produced. The rapidly released initial heat may represent energy associated with transmission of the impulse; the recovery, or delayed, heat (up to 45 minutes) may be related to the mechanisms of energy restoration. Under anaerobic conditions (nitrogen atmosphere), a nerve may conduct impulses and develop heat; recovery, however, depends upon oxygen utilization.

Chemical mediators may be elaborated at synaptic junctions in association with the action of a nerve impulse. **Acetylcholine** is produced in parasympathetic and voluntary nerves to skeletal muscles. **Norepinephrine** results from some sympathetic nerve stimulation, and its effects are opposite to those of acetylcholine. Norepinephrine resembles epinephrine in its activity; sympathetic nerve stimulation may cause release of epinephrine from the adrenal medulla.

The adrenal medulla is a derivative of the sympathetic portion of the autonomic nervous system; in general, the hormone of the adrenal medulla (epinephrine) duplicates the effect of sympathetic stimulation of an organ. About 80% of the hormonal activity of the adrenal medulla is due to epinephrine and the remainder to norepinephrine (arterenol), a closely related hormone that is a precursor of epinephrine. Epinephrine produces vasodilatation of the blood vessels of the skeletal muscle and vasoconstriction of the arterioles of the skin, mucosa, and splanchnic viscera; norepinephrine exerts an overall vasoconstrictor effect. Both epinephrine and norepinephrine produce elevation of blood pressure, which is more marked in the case of norepinephrine.

Acetylcholine esterase (cholinesterase), found within nerve fibers and at nerve endings, readily hydrolyzes acetylcholine to choline and acetic acid. The inactivating hydrolyzing effect of acetylcholine esterase is believed to control the action of acetylcholine in the body. This substance must be distinguished from pseudocholinesterase, found in blood serum, which hydrolyzes other esters. For resynthesis of acetylcholine, energy is required. Active acetate (coenzyme

A acetate) serves as acetate donor for acetylation of choline. Choline acetylase, activated by potassium and magnesium ions, catalyzes the transfer of acetyl from coenzyme A acetate to choline. Regeneration of adenosine triphosphate (ATP) from adenosine diphosphate (ADP) is accomplished by phosphocreatine, which is resynthesized from creatine and free phosphate with the aid of energy produced in glycolysis.

$$\begin{array}{c} + \text{ Water} \\ (\text{Acetylcholine esterase}) \end{array}$$

$$\text{Acetylcholine} \rightleftharpoons \text{Choline} + \text{Acetic acid}$$

$$(\text{Choline acetylase} + \text{Coenzyme A acetate})$$

$$(\text{ATP} \rightarrow \text{ADP})$$

Physostigmine inhibits acetylcholine esterase, thus prolonging parasympathetic activity. Neostigmine (Prostigmin), an alkaloid, is believed to act similarly. Diisopropyl fluorophosphate (DFP) is a synthetic substance that irreversibly inhibits acetylcholine esterase. This compound is believed to be one of the most powerful and specific enzyme inhibitors known. The toxic properties of some ''nerve gases'' and insecticides (such as Parathion) depend upon their action as anticholinesterases. A highly effective antidote for certain nerve gases and insecticides is pralidoxime (2-PAM), which is especially effective with atropine.

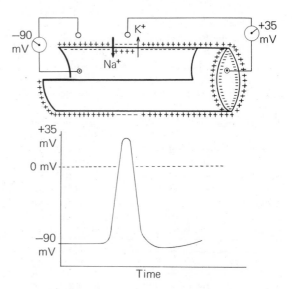

Figure 2–12. Conduction of the nerve impulse through an unmyelinated nerve fiber. In the resting axon there is a difference of −90 mV between the interior of the axon and the outer surface of its membrane (resting potential). During the impulse passage, Na⁺ (thick arrow) passes into the axon interior, while K⁺ (thin arrow) migrates in the opposite direction. The amount of Na⁺ that enters the axon is larger than the amount of K⁺ that leaves it. In consequence, there is a change in membrane polarity. It becomes relatively positive on its inner surface. The resting potential is thus replaced by an action potential, which in the example given above is equal to +35 mV. (Reproduced, with permission, from Junqueira LC, Carneiro J: *Basic Histology,* 3rd ed. Lange, 1980.)

Synaptic Transmission

Individual nerve cells are in close contact at synapses, where functional connections occur. Synaptic characteristics such as synaptic delay, facilitation, fatigue, and blockage are well recognized. By means of microelectrode techniques, an excitatory or inhibitory postsynaptic potential can be detected in association with the depolarization or hyperpolarization of the postsynaptic membrane. This potential can be clearly differentiated from the signal reaching the synapse and the all-or-none impulse originating in the postsynaptic element and thence conducted through the axon.

The excitatory postsynaptic potential (EPSP) is associated with depolarization of the postsynaptic cell membrane immediately under the active synaptic knob. The current sink thus created is too small to drain off enough positive charges to depolarize the whole membrane, and an EPSP is inscribed instead. As a result of increased permeability of the cell membrane to sodium, potassium, and chloride ions, sodium ions move into the cell. If more excitatory knobs are excited, more sodium ions enter; this increases the depolarizing potential, which may become great enough to reach the firing level and result in a propagated action potential.

Stimulation of presynaptic fibers may initiate a hyperpolarizing response in spinal motor neurons. During this potential, the excitability of the neuron to other stimuli is decreased, so that this potential is referred to as an inhibitory postsynaptic potential (IPSP). It is associated with localized increased membrane permeability to potassium and chloride ions but not to sodium ions. Increased efflux of potassium and influx of chloride ions occur in the cell, with a net effect of increasing the membrane potential and moving it farther from the firing level.

Stimulation of some sensory nerve fibers may produce EPSPs in some motor neurons and IPSPs in others. Usually, EPSPs are produced in motor neurons to which the sensory fibers pass directly and IPSPs in motor neurons separated by a single interneuron (Golgi bottle neuron). Thus, excitatory stimuli may be converted into inhibitory stimuli by interposing a single Golgi bottle type neuron between the excitatory ending and the spinal motor neuron.

In the neuromuscular junction, spontaneous miniature end-plate potentials exist, possibly related to the emission of units of acetylcholine. In this special type of synapse, the postsynaptic membrane is electrically unexcitable. The 2 essential types of synaptic actions, excitatory and inhibitory, are believed to be produced by a flux of ions across the synaptic cleft that leads, respectively, to depolarization or hyperpolarization of the postsynaptic membrane. This ionic flux is preceded by discharge of a chemical transmitter at the synaptic cleft. It has been hypothesized that the synaptic vesicles (special vesicular submicroscopic structures in synapses at presynaptic endings) represent the quantal unit of transmitter substance. Acetylcholine or other chemical mediators may be synthesized at the endings and segregated into packets surrounded by a membrane. It has been suggested that these vesicles can flow toward the presynaptic membrane, perforate it, and discharge their contents into the intermembranal cleft of the synapse.

Dendrites of neurons are believed to produce graded electrical responses, in contrast to the all-or-none responses of the axon or cell body. Such graded responses characteristically have no absolute refractory period, so that a second response may overlie the

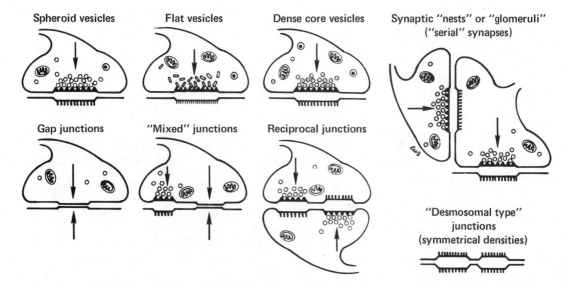

Figure 2–13. Major types of synaptic junctions. At synapses where there are vesicles, conduction is chemical, whereas conduction at gap junctions is electrical. Flattened vesicles appear to contain inhibitory mediator, whereas dense core vesicles contain catecholamines. The "desmosomal type" junctions occur in sympathetic ganglia, but their function is unknown. (Reproduced, with permission, from Bodian: Neuron junctions: A revolutionary decade. *Anat Rec* 1972;**174**:73.)

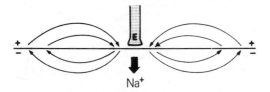

Excitatory transmitter → increased permeability of postsynaptic cell membrane to all small ions (Na⁺, K⁺, Cl⁻)

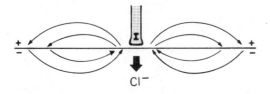

Inhibitory transmitter → increased permeability of postsynaptic cell membrane to K⁺ and Cl⁻, not to Na⁺

Figure 2–14. Summary of events occurring at synapses in mammals. (Reproduced, with permission, from Ganong WF: *Review of Medical Physiology,* 10th ed. Lange, 1981.)

first. The intensity and time course of such graded responses of dendrites are directly related to the stimulus, and the graded response is essentially a local response of postsynaptic membrane.

In contrast to peripheral nerve and muscle, CNS synapses appear to be chemically but not electrically excitable. Depending upon the type or nature of the synaptic membrane, depolarizing or hyperpolarizing electrogenesis may occur. Postsynaptic potentials generated in dendrites may be standing potentials that are not propagated except perhaps by passive electrotonic spread.

Theoretically, the cortical neuron axon may consist of membrane that responds in all-or-none fashion, is electrically excitable, and appears to transmit the impulse it receives from its somatic end unaltered to the distal end. The membrane of the cell body, or soma, may also share the all-or-none response property and is also electrically excitable. It may be that portions of the cell body covered by synaptic boutons contain "graded response" postsynaptic membrane. The dendrite at the other end of the neuron is largely made up of graded response membrane and is electrically unexcitable; its membrane responds to chemical transmitter substances liberated by the synaptic boutons that cover essentially all the dendritic surface. It may be that the very terminal axonal segment leading up to the synaptic bouton of the presynaptic axon also consists of graded response membrane. Thus, follow-

ing chemical stimulation at its synaptic end, the dendritic membrane produces standing postsynaptic potentials that can in turn affect the electrically excitable membrane of the cell body by electrotonic spread from the dendrite. Dendrites, therefore, may integrate incoming information and control the firing of the cell body and its axon. Larger, slower dendrites may help adjust the central excitatory state, whereas the smaller number of somatic synaptic knobs may rapidly trigger reflex discharge.

Dermatomes

The skin areas supplied by the dorsal (posterior) roots of a single segment have been studied by many techniques. Foerster severed 3 roots above and below the dermatome studied (in humans) (see Fig 11–11). Other techniques, such as pilomotor response and vasodilatation, generally indicate smaller though similarly located dermatomes. Kellgren made diagrams of the segmental innervation of the deep tissues based on the area of induced pain following injection of 6% saline into a muscle (see Fig 11–12). Inman and Saunders attempted to show the nerve supply of superficial and deep muscles and the skeleton ("sclerotome") based upon injections of irritant solutions into various deep somatic structures of volunteers (see Figs 11–6 to 11–9).

Motor Unit

The motor unit is made up of the anterior horn cell of the spinal cord and the muscle group it innervates. The **anterior horn cell** has a cell body, dendrites, axon, and end-plates. The **cell body** contains, in addition to its nucleus and nucleolus, specialized cytoplasmic elements such as Nissl bodies, neurofibrils, and pigment. The **dendrites** receive impulses from many posterior roots and many levels of the spinal cord and brain. The **axon** begins at the axon hillock and extends via the anterior (ventral) nerve root to the peripheral nerve and muscle. The proportion of nerve fiber to muscle fiber in motor units is designated as the innervation ratio. In some diseases, such as poliomyelitis, disorders and degeneration occur that affect motor units rather than individual muscle fibers.

Spinal Reflexes

The **segmental spinal reflex** involves the afferent neuron and a motor unit at the same level. Motor units of many spinal segments, however, may be excited by one afferent neuron. Patterns of movement rather than specific muscle contractions are concerned in the simplest reflex reactions. The junction between 2 neurons is known as a **synapse.** The bouton, or terminal knob, is intimately concerned in the synapses in the CNS; upon injury or severing of the axon, early degeneration is found in the enlarged terminals, and within a week these may fragment and disappear without altering the structure of the cell upon which they terminate. A time interval (usually between 0.001 and 0.0005 s) is required for an impulse to pass across a synapse in mammalian spinal cord. The delay, or latency, in reflexes is caused principally by a number of synaptic delays. Motor nerve fiber axons terminate at a specialized portion of the muscle fiber called the end-plate, which represents localized specialization of the sarcolemma. Transmission of the nerve impulse to the muscle occurs across the neuromuscular synapse, and it is at this junction that the muscle action current which stimulates contraction originates. The end-plate potential is the prolonged negative potential at the end-plate, which is not propagated but localized to the myoneural junction and is produced by the passage of the nerve impulse. The end-plate potential generates a muscle spike potential by depolarizing to a critical level the muscle membrane around the junction. The end-plate potential itself can be as large as the muscle action potential.

Spatial summation, in which a recipient neuron receives almost simultaneous impulses from many afferent neurons, is believed to play an important role in synaptic transmission of impulses. **Temporal summation,** which refers to the repeated stimuli occurring within a short excitable period of the synapse, is not believed to be significant in synaptic transmission.

CNS neurons may exhibit spike action potentials as well as negative and positive afterpotentials. Negative potentials of large amplitude following the spike potential are usually associated with increased excitability. A large positive potential is usually associated with depressed excitability. The action potentials of nerves are believed to be intimately related to the release of acetylcholine, especially in the transmission of nerve impulses across synapses. Cholinesterase, an enzyme that splits acetylcholine, is concentrated at

synaptic terminals and at the surface of nerve fibers. Anticholinesterases, such as DFP (diisopropyl fluorophosphate), hinder conduction in proportion to their concentration in the axon.

Inhibition, which refers to the prevention or diminution of a reflex muscle contraction, is believed to be produced in or near anterior horn cells. Humoral mechanisms, inhibitory fibers, and specialized electrical behavior have been invoked to explain the phenomenon of inhibition. Two types of central inhibition have been recognized: indirect inhibition refers to inhibition consequent to a subnormal period of recovery in nerve; direct inhibition is said to be due to polarization of adjacent neurons essential to the transmission of the reflex that is inhibited.

Various forms of indirect inhibition may occur. The postsynaptic cell may be refractory to excitation because it is in its refractory period after just having fired. The positive afterpotential (afterhyperpolarization) may be large or prolonged in spinal neurons. Fatigue may also make repeatedly fired cells refractory to further stimulation.

Presynaptic inhibition reduces the amount of synaptic mediator liberated by action potentials arriving at excitatory synaptic knobs. Neurons producing presynaptic inhibition end on the excitatory endings and, in discharging, produce a partial depolarization of the excitatory ending and reduce the size of the action potential produced by an amount equal to the amount of depolarization. Although the chemical mediator for presynaptic inhibition is not known, GABA (gamma-aminobutyric acid) is believed to play a role in presynaptic inhibition.

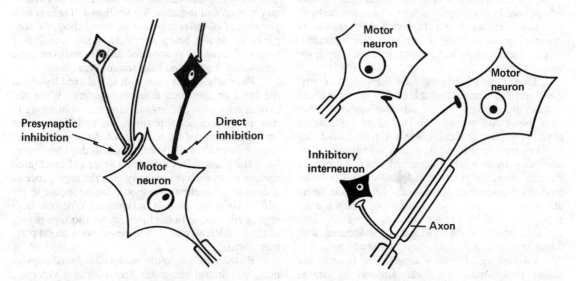

Figure 2-15. *Left:* Two types of inhibition demonstrated in the spinal cord. Direct inhibition: A chemical mediator released from an inhibitory neuron acts to cause hyperpolarization (inhibitory postsynaptic potential) of motor neuron. Strychnine blocks the action of the inhibitory mediator; tetanus toxin prevents its release. Presynaptic inhibition: A second chemical mediator is released onto the ending, or axon, of an excitatory neuron. The size of the postsynaptic excitatory potential is reduced. Picrotoxin blocks the action of this inhibitory mediator. *Right:* Diagram of a specific inhibitory system involving an inhibitory interneuron, or Renshaw cell. (Reproduced, with permission, from Ganong WF: *Review of Medical Physiology,* 9th ed. Lange, 1979.)

The **flexion reflex** represents a withdrawal mechanism by means of which an extremity may be removed from a harmful stimulus. "Spinal" animals exhibit prominent flexion responses. Several segments are involved. A single afferent nerve may stimulate many motor units; in general, the smaller nerve branches to the skin are more effective than the deep sensory nerves in exciting flexor motor units. **Occlusion** is the phenomenon that occurs when 2 sensory nerves are stimulated together, in which case the response of a given flexor muscle is little greater than that produced by stimulation of each nerve singly. It is felt that under these circumstances the 2 sensory nerves activate a certain number of the same motor neurons.

Continued discharge of motor neurons after cessation of the afferent stimulus in the simple spinal reflex is designated as **afterdischarge** and is presumably due to continued discharge among internuncial reflex circuits.

The responses seen in some forms of prolonged irritation are believed to be caused by **flexor reflexes.** Retraction of the neck and flexor hip responses (Kernig's sign) occur in meningitis; the patient with peritonitis assumes a doubled-up, frozen attitude; chronic semiflexed postures, with atrophy of the relaxed, reciprocally innervated extensors, may be observed in arthritis of the knee joint.

Extensor reflexes are concerned with resisting the action of gravity upon body posture. The stretch, or myotatic, reflex, whose receptors are in muscle, is the basis for the extensor reflex. During intervals of constant stretch, stretch reflexes may produce continued prolonged muscle tension without alteration or fatigue. Upon increased stretch, more motor units are brought into action. Posterior or anterior root section destroys the stretch reflex reaction. In stretch reflexes, slowly contracting red muscle motor units are activated. When extensor muscles contract, antagonistic flexor muscles relax.

Three types of receptors have been noted in muscle. Sherrington stated that at least 40% of nerve fibers innervating a given muscle subserve sensory rather than motor end organs: (1) The muscle spindle, a stretch receptor, which is highly differentiated and contains intrafusal fibers that receive ventral root innervation from small myelinated fibers known as gamma fibers, originating in spinal cord. (2) Golgi tendon organs, which lie in series with muscle fibers and may theoretically serve to inhibit contractile responses evoked by muscle spindles. (3) Fine nerve endings, which for the most part are associated with blood vessels and probably convey muscle pain.

Two routes of muscle innervation from motor cortex, designated as the alpha route and the gamma route, have been proposed. The alpha route is direct or through relays to the alpha anterior horn cells and so to muscles. The gamma route is composed of both rapid and slow pathways to small gamma cells of the anterior horn of the cord. Excitation of gamma elements results in contraction of muscle spindles, which in turn triggers off a barrage of afferent impulses coming back to the spinal cord and ending monosynaptically on the alpha motor neuron.

By integration of elementary reflexes, the spinal cord can produce movement patterns with apparent purpose. The **final common pathway** refers to motor units upon which there is convergence from many afferent sources. Thus, sensory impulses from many segments, involving many types of receptors, may influence the anterior horn cells for a time.

When reflexes produce the same pattern of movement, they may be classed as **allied reflexes.** Such reflexes may be active simultaneously or successively. The stretch reflex and the positive supporting reaction, both of which produce sustained extensor muscle contraction, are allied reflexes. **Antagonistic reflexes** are those that produce opposite effects. When stimuli act that would produce different or opposing reflexes, the resultant response depends upon which stimulus is the more powerful. In general, **nociceptive reflexes** are dominant.

Some patterns of intersegmental reflexes are relatively fixed. Lower extremity stimulation produces extension of the ipsilateral upper extremity and flexion of the contralateral upper extremity in spinal animals.

Spinal shock refers to the depression of reflexes that follows soon after spinal cord transection and is believed to be due to loss of stimulation from higher levels. In primates and humans, interruption of the corticospinal tracts is believed to be related to the onset of spinal shock. Spinal shock is usually transient and is followed by a period of increased reflex response.

Spinal shock occurs irrespective of the level of injury. All body segments below the level of transection become paralyzed and anesthetic, so that voluntary motion and sensation are abolished. There is suppression of all reflexes below the transection, the suppression usually being complete during the first 2 weeks after injury. Autonomic reflexes are even more completely suppressed than somatic reactions.

Beevor's sign is seen with spinal cord lesions at the level of the tenth thoracic segment. When the patient tenses the abdominal muscles, as in trying to rise from a recumbent position, the umbilicus moves upward because of the paralysis of the lower abdominal segments. Normally the umbilicus does not move.

The **mass reflex** refers to a spread of reaction to include many reflexes and may give the appearance of a stereotyped pattern of response inappropriate to the stimulus in spinal animals and humans. When the thigh is pressed, flexion of the limbs, defecation, emptying of the bladder, sweating, and elevation of blood pressure occur.

By the third and fourth weeks after spinal transection, withdrawal responses become more vigorous; and the toes, especially the great toe, tend to extend during the response (Babinski's sign). Several months after spinal transection, withdrawal reflexes tend to become quite exaggerated and spread to include visceral and autonomic outflow (mass reflex). Mass reflexes may be evoked unintentionally and at times appear spontaneously without obvious stimulation.

The peripheral nerves constitute an intricate conduction system that serves as the mediator of neural impulses traveling in both directions between the CNS and other tissues of the body and through which many important bodily functions are regulated. For descriptive purposes, the peripheral nerves may be classified according to their function and site of origin in the CNS: **cranial nerves** emerge from the base of the brain; **spinal nerves** originate in the spinal cord; and the **autonomic system** is intricately associated with the cranial and spinal nerves but differs in function and in the details of structure and distribution.

Structure of a Nerve Fiber

Each fiber represents the greatly elongated process of a nerve cell, whose cell body lies within the CNS or one of the outlying ganglia. The nerve cell, or neuron, consisting of a cell body and all of its processes, constitutes the structural and functional unit of the nervous system (the neuron doctrine). The cell body, which contains the nucleus, is the vital center controlling metabolic activity of the cell; any injury that severs a nerve fiber will result in degeneration of the distal segment.

A typical spinal motor neuron (Fig 3–1) has many processes called dendrites that extend out from the cell body and arborize greatly. It also has a long fibrous axon that originates from an area of the cell body called the axon hillock. Near its origin, the axon acquires a sheath of myelin, a protein-lipid complex made up of many layers of unit membrane. This myelin sheath envelops the axon except at its ending and at periodic constrictions about 1 mm apart known as the nodes of Ranvier. Some mammalian neurons and most neurons in invertebrates are unmyelinated, although the axons are covered by Schwann cells.

The dendritic zone refers to the receptor membrane of a neuron. The axon is a single elongated protoplasmic neuronal process with the specialized function of conducting impulses away from the dendritic zone and ends in a number of terminal buttons, or axon telodendria. Although the cell body usually is located at the dendritic zone, it may lie within the axon (eg, auditory neurons) or be attached to the side of the axon (eg, bipolar neuron). The size of the neurons and the length of their processes vary greatly in different parts of the nervous system.

Bodian suggested that the site of impulse origin

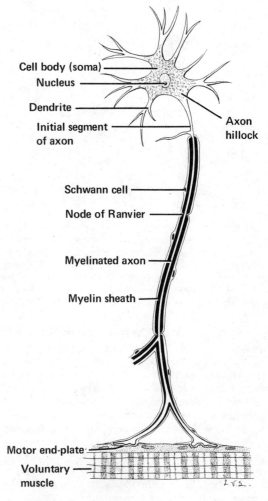

Figure 3–1. Motor neuron with myelinated axon.

rather than the cell body location be used for analyzing neuron structure (Fig 3–2). He proposed the term "dendritic zone" for the receptor membrane of a neuron, including the dendrites that receive synaptic endings of other neurons. The cell body (perikaryon) may be part of the dendritic zone or quite distant from the receptor arborizations. The impulse origin, or the physiologic "spike," occurs near the origin of the axon, which then conducts the nerve impulse away

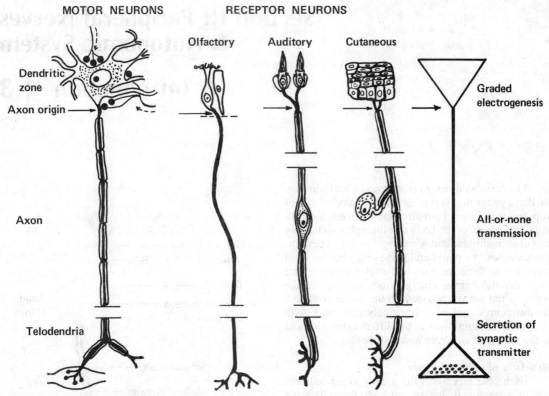

Figure 3–2. A variety of mammalian receptor and effector neurons. The neurons are arranged to illustrate the concept that impulse origin (indicated in each case by the arrow) rather than location of the cell body is the logical point of departure for analyzing neuronal structure in functional terms. Thus the dendritic zone, the area where the activity that generates the impulses occurs, may be dendrites or cell body. The axon conducts the impulses to the axon telodendria. The location of the cell body varies; it has no direct effect on impulse generation or transmission. (Modified after Grundfest and reproduced, with permission, from Bodian: The generalized vertebrate neuron. *Science* 1962;**137**:323. © 1962 by American Association for the Advancement of Science.)

from the dendritic zone. The speed of impulse conduction along the axon is related to its diameter and sheath differentiation. The telodendria are the branched differentiated terminals of axons that may show membrane and cytoplasmic changes related to synaptic transmission or neurosecretory activity. Mitochondrial concentrations, secretory granules, or synaptic vesicles are often present in the bulblike terminals of the telodendria. The telodendria transmit electrical or chemical signals capable of producing generator potentials in the dendritic zones of other neurons and in muscle. They also can stimulate innervated gland cells or even distant cells via a neurohumoral route.

When a nerve fiber has been transected or destroyed, the distal portion degenerates and may lose its myelin sheath. Degenerated fibers can be studied histologically by using Weigert or Weil stains, which stain normal myelin dark blue or black. The Marchi staining procedure, which consists of impregnation with osmium tetroxide, is effective only when the myelin is partly decomposed (6–12 days after injury), when the injured myelin stains black. For several weeks after injury, the Nissl bodies of the cell may undergo chromatolysis, with disintegration of affected cells in severe cases.

Components of a Peripheral Nerve Trunk

A peripheral nerve trunk is composed of many nerve fibers bound together by supporting connective tissue. Functionally, 3 main groups of fibers occur in peripheral nerves: (1) Motor (efferent) fibers deliver impulses from the CNS to skeletal muscles for the control of voluntary muscular activity. Their cell bodies are located in the gray matter of the spinal cord and brain stem. (2) Sensory (afferent) fibers carry impulses arising from various receptors in the skin, muscles, special sense organs, etc, to the CNS, where they are interpreted as sensations. The cell bodies lie in special ganglia located along the roots of origin of the sensory nerves. (3) Autonomic fibers (efferent in function) are concerned with the control of smooth muscle, glandular activities, and probably certain trophic functions of the body. Anatomic details are described in the section on the autonomic system (Chapter 6).

The cell body maintains the functional and anatomic integrity of the axon. If the axon is cut, the part distal to the cut degenerates (wallerian degeneration). Materials for maintaining the axon, mostly proteins, are formed in the cell body and are transported down the axon (axoplasmic transport). Proteins associated with synaptic transmitters are also synthesized in the

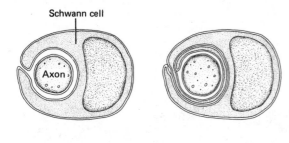

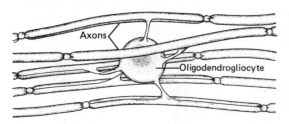

Figure 3–3. *Top:* Relation of Schwann cells to axons in peripheral nerves. *Left:* Unmyelinated axon. *Right:* Myelinated axon. Note that the cell membrane of the Schwann cell has wrapped itself around and around the axon. *Bottom:* Myelination of axons in the central nervous system by oligodendrogliocytes. One oligodendrogliocyte sends processes to up to 40 axons. (Reproduced, with permission, from Ganong WF: *Review of Medical Physiology,* 10th ed. Lange, 1981.)

endoplasmic reticulum of the cell body and are transported to the axon terminals via fast (400 mm/d) and slow (200 mm/d) transport. Fast transport relies on oxidative metabolism of the neuron and ATP. It appears to depend on microtubules, and transported material may be attached to filaments formed in the cell body and slide along the microtubules.

Lesions of the Peripheral Nerves

Lesions of the peripheral nerves include the various types of pathologic disturbances that affect other tissues of the body: congenital defects; neoplasms; inflammatory, traumatic, vascular, toxic, and degenerative lesions; and functional disorders.

The abolition of conductivity in a nerve results in impairment of neurologic function in the motor, sensory, and trophic spheres. **Motor** loss is manifested by paralysis or weakness of muscles. **Sensory** involvement may be subjective or objective. Subjective sensory findings include pain and paresthesias (numbness, tingling, crawling sensations, etc). These usually indicate partial or irritative lesions. The pain of peripheral nerve lesions is frequently worse at night. Objective findings include the loss of various sensibilities (analgesia, anesthesia, etc). **Trophic** disturbances are related to impaired nutritional and metabolic activities in tissues that are partially under neurogenic control. Signs are most marked in the cutaneous tissues, eg, dryness, cyanosis, loss of hair, brittleness of the nails, ulcerations, and slow wound healing.

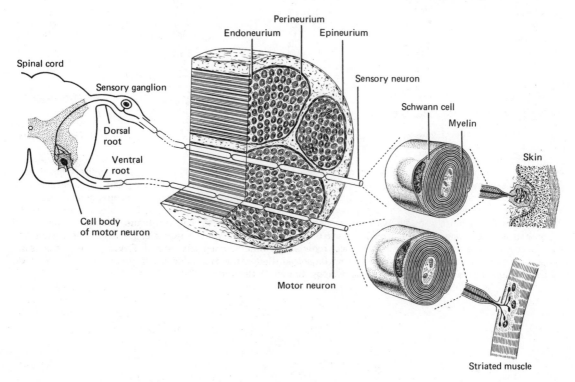

Figure 3–4. Schematic representation of a nerve and also of the simplest reflex arc. In this example, the sensory stimulus starts in the skin and the motor fiber innervates a striated skeletal muscle. (Reproduced, with permission, from Junqueira LC, Carneiro J: *Basic Histology,* 3rd ed. Lange, 1980.)

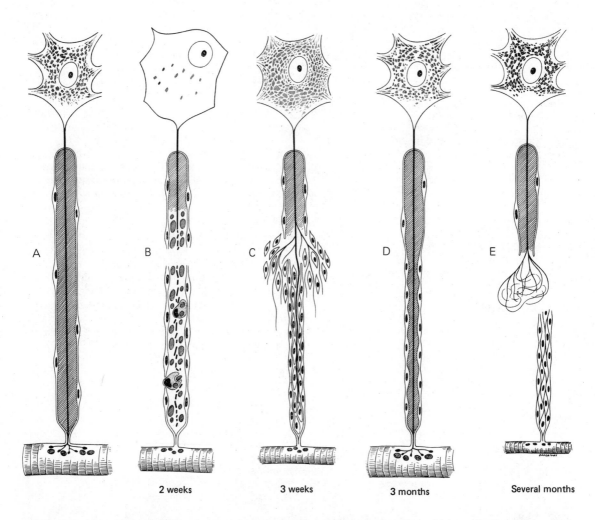

A   B   C   D   E

           2 weeks   3 weeks   3 months   Several months

Figure 3–5. Main changes that take place in an injured nerve fiber. *A:* Normal nerve fiber, with its perikaryon and the effector cell (striated skeletal muscle). Note the position of the neuron nucleus and the amount and distribution of Nissl bodies. *B:* When the fiber is injured, the neuronal nucleus moves to the cell periphery and Nissl bodies become greatly reduced in number. The nerve fiber distal to the injury degenerates along with its myelin sheath. Debris is phagocytosed by macrophages. *C:* The muscle fiber shows a pronounced disuse atrophy. Schwann cells proliferate, forming a compact cord penetrated by the growing axon. The axon grows at a rate of 0.5–3 mm/d. *D:* In this example, the nerve fiber regeneration was successful. Note that the muscle fiber was also regenerated after receiving nerve stimuli. *E:* When the axon does not penetrate the cord of Schwann cells, its growth is not organized. (Redrawn and reproduced, with permission, from Willis RA, Willis AT: *The Principles of Pathology and Bacteriology,* 3rd ed. Butterworth, 1972.)

The Cranial Nerves | 4

The cranial nerves are customarily described as comprising 12 pairs, which are referred to by numbers. Nerves I (olfactory) and II (optic) are not true nerves but fiber tracts of the brain. Except for a part of nerve XI (accessory), which is derived from the upper cervical segments of the spinal cord, the caudal 10 pairs emerge from the brain stem, in which lie their nuclei of origin.

The superficial origin of a cranial nerve is that area of the brain where the nerve appears or attaches. Those cranial nerves which have motor function take their origin from collections of cells deep within the brain stem (motor nuclei) which are analogous to the anterior horn cells of the spinal cord. The sensory cranial nerves originate from collections of cells outside the brain stem, usually in ganglia that may be considered analogous to the dorsal root ganglia of the spinal nerves.

Anatomic Relations

A. Cranial Nerve I (Olfactory): This term commonly refers to the olfactory tract, which arises from the olfactory bulb on the ventral portion of the frontal lobe and continues posteriorly to end just lateral to the optic chiasm, where it penetrates the cerebrum.

B. Cranial Nerve II (Optic): The optic nerve contains nerve fibers arising from the inner layer of the retina and proceeding posteriorly to enter the cranial cavity via the optic foramen, some crossing to the opposite side via the optic chiasm.

C. Cranial Nerve III (Oculomotor): The oculomotor nerve leaves the brain on the medial side of the cerebral peduncle, where it lies posterior to the posterior cerebral artery, anterior to the superior cerebellar artery, and lateral to the basilar artery. It then passes anteriorly, lateral to the internal carotid artery, in the cavernous sinus, to leave the skull by way of the superior orbital fissure.

D. Cranial Nerve IV (Trochlear): The trochlear nerve takes its superficial origin on the dorsal surface of the brain stem, then curves ventrally between the posterior cerebral and superior cerebellar arteries (lateral to the oculomotor nerve). It continues anteriorly in the lateral wall of the cavernous sinus, between the oculomotor nerve and the ophthalmic branch of the trigeminal nerve, to enter the orbit via the superior orbital fissure.

E. Cranial Nerve V (Trigeminal): The trigeminal nerve contains a large sensory root and a smaller motor root. The sensory, or main, portion arises from cells in the large semilunar (gasserian) ganglion in the lateral portion of the cavernous sinus, passes posteriorly between the superior petrosal sinus and the tentorium, and penetrates the middle cerebellar peduncle to enter the pons. Fibers of the **ophthalmic division** enter the skull via the superior orbital fissure. Fibers of the **maxillary branch** penetrate the foramen rotundum. Sensory fibers of the **mandibular division** of the nerve, joined by the motor or masticator portion (which leaves the pons ventromedial to the sensory rootlets), leave the cranial cavity through the foramen ovale.

F. Cranial Nerve VI (Abducens): The abducens nerve emerges from the ventral surface of the brain stem in the groove between the pyramid of the medulla and the caudal end of the pons and then passes through the cavernous sinus to exit from the cranial cavity via the superior orbital fissure.

G. Cranial Nerve VII (Facial): The motor root of the facial nerve emerges from the posterior border of the pons just lateral to the inferior olive through the medial side of the cerebellopontine angle and leaves the cranium by way of the internal acoustic meatus. The sensory root takes its origin in cells of the geniculate ganglion and passes through the internal acoustic meatus via the dorsally situated portion (nerve of Wrisberg) to penetrate the medulla.

H. Cranial Nerve VIII (Acoustic): The acoustic, or statoacoustic, nerve enters the cranial cavity via the internal acoustic meatus and enters the brain stem behind the posterior edge of the middle cerebellar peduncle. The vestibular portion arises from cells of the vestibular ganglion (ganglion of Scarpa) located in the dorsal portion of the internal auditory meatus. The cochlear portion arises from the spiral ganglion.

I. Cranial Nerve IX (Glossopharyngeal): The glossopharyngeal nerve contains sensory fibers that originate in cells in the superior and petrous ganglia, pass through the jugular foramen, and enter the medulla on the lateral side of the inferior olive just behind the facial nerve. The motor part arises in the nucleus ambiguus and leaves the lateral medulla to join the sensory part of the nerve.

J. Cranial Nerve X (Vagus): The vagus nerve contains afferent fibers that originate in cells in the jugular and nodose ganglia just below the jugular foramen and pass through the jugular foramen to enter the medulla just behind the glossopharyngeal nerve.

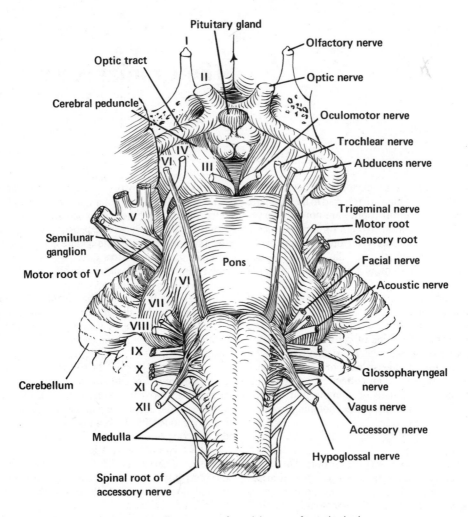

Figure 4–1. Emergence of cranial nerves from the brain.

Motor fibers leave the medulla to join the sensory part of the nerve.

K. Cranial Nerve XI (Accessory): The accessory nerve arises superficially from a series of filaments located behind the root filaments of the vagus nerve, from the lateral surface of the medulla and upper cervical spinal cord, and leaves the cranial cavity by way of the jugular foramen.

L. Cranial Nerve XII (Hypoglossal): The hypoglossal nerve takes its superficial origin by way of several filaments in the ventrolateral sulcus of the medulla between the inferior olive and pyramid; these filaments then fuse and leave the posterior fossa of the skull by way of the hypoglossal canal.

Cranial Nerve Nuclei

The nuclei of the cranial nerves lie chiefly in the brain stem. The sensory nuclei develop within the dorsal or alar plate of the neural tube; the motor nuclei within the basal plate. In the hindbrain, the alar plate lies lateral to the basal plate in the floor of the fourth ventricle.

A. Motor Nuclei:

1. Edinger-Westphal nucleus; nucleus of oculomotor nerve at level of superior colliculus.

2. Nucleus of trochlear nerve in midbrain at level of inferior colliculus.

3. Motor nucleus of trigeminal nerve at level of mid pons.

4. Nucleus of abducens nerve in dorsal pons.

5. Motor nucleus of facial nerve near caudal border of pons.

6. Nucleus salivatorius superior (facial nerve) and inferior (glossopharyngeal nerve) at border of pons and medulla.

7. Dorsal motor nucleus of vagus nerve in dorsal medulla.

8. Nucleus ambiguus (glossopharyngeal, vagus, and accessory nerves) in dorsal medulla.

9. Nucleus of hypoglossal nerve in medulla beneath fourth ventricle.

B. Sensory Nuclei:

1. Mesencephalic nucleus of trigeminal nerve in midbrain.

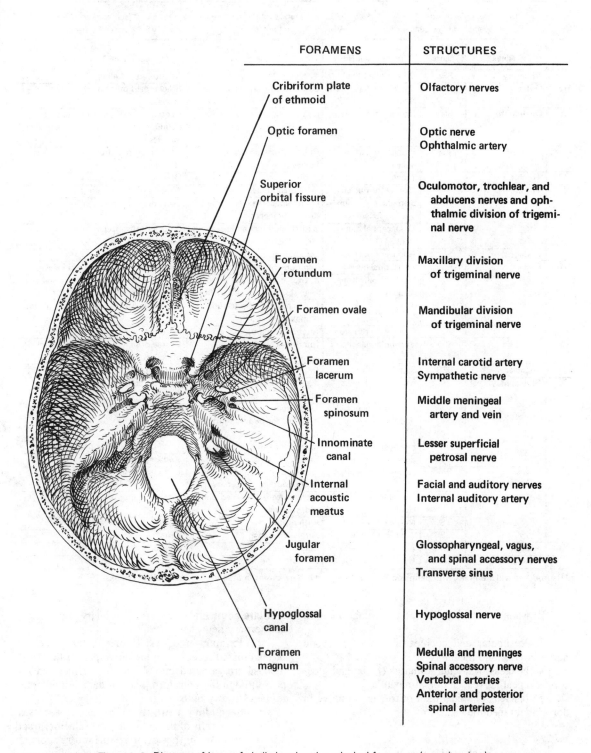

FORAMENS	STRUCTURES
Cribriform plate of ethmoid	Olfactory nerves
Optic foramen	Optic nerve Ophthalmic artery
Superior orbital fissure	Oculomotor, trochlear, and abducens nerves and ophthalmic division of trigeminal nerve
Foramen rotundum	Maxillary division of trigeminal nerve
Foramen ovale	Mandibular division of trigeminal nerve
Foramen lacerum	Internal carotid artery Sympathetic nerve
Foramen spinosum	Middle meningeal artery and vein
Innominate canal	Lesser superficial petrosal nerve
Internal acoustic meatus	Facial and auditory nerves Internal auditory artery
Jugular foramen	Glossopharyngeal, vagus, and spinal accessory nerves Transverse sinus
Hypoglossal canal	Hypoglossal nerve
Foramen magnum	Medulla and meninges Spinal accessory nerve Vertebral arteries Anterior and posterior spinal arteries

Figure 4–2. Diagram of base of skull showing the principal foramens (superior view).

Table 4—1. Components of human cranial nerves.*

BM = branchial motor	GSS = general somatic sensory	SM = somatic motor
SSS = special somatic sensory	VM = visceral motor	VS = visceral sensory

	Nerve	Compo-nents	Primary Cell Body	Course	Peripheral Termination
I	Olfactory	SSS	Olfactory epithelium	Through roof of nasal cavity	Olfactory epithelium
II	Optic	SSS	Ganglionic layer of retina	Orbit → optic chiasm → optic tracts	Bipolar cells of retina → rods and cones
III	Oculomotor	SM	Oculomotor nucleus	Orbit	Rectus superior, inferior, medial; obliquus inferior, levator palpebrae muscles
		VM	Edinger-Westphal nucleus	Ciliary ganglion → ciliary nerves	Constrictor pupillae and ciliary muscles of eyeball
IV	Trochlear	SM	Trochlear nucleus	Orbit	Obliquus superior muscle
V	Trigeminal	BM	Masticator nucleus	With mandibular	Muscles of mastication
		GSS	Semilunar ganglion	Ophthalmic, maxillary, mandibular branches	Face, nose, mouth
		GSS	Mesencephalic nucleus	With mandibular and maxillary branches	Proprioceptive to jaw muscles and tooth sockets
VI	Abducens	SM	Abducens nucleus	Under pons, into orbit	Rectus lateralis
VII	Facial	BM	Facial nucleus	Temporal bone, side of face	Muscles of expression, hyoid elevators
		VM	Superior salivatory nucleus	a. Greater superficial petrosal to sphenopalatine ganglion	a. Glands of nose, palate, lacrimal gland
				b. Chorda tympani to submaxillary ganglion	b. Submaxillary and sublingual glands
		VS	Geniculate ganglion	Chorda tympani	Anterior taste buds
VIII	Vestibular	SSS	Vestibular ganglion	Internal acoustic meatus	Cristae of semicircular canals, maculae of utricle and saccule
	Cochlear	SSS	Spiral ganglion	Internal acoustic meatus	Organ of Corti
IX	Glossopharyngeal	BM	Nucleus ambiguus	Jugular foramen → side of pharynx	Superior constrictor, stylopharyngeus muscles
		VM	Inferior salivatory nucleus	Lesser superficial petrosal → otic ganglion → auriculotemporal nerve	Parotid gland
		VS	Petrous ganglion	Side of pharynx	Taste buds of vallate papillae
		GSS	Superior ganglion	Side of pharynx	Auditory tube
X	Vagus	BM	Nucleus ambiguus	Recurrent and external branch of superior laryngeal nerve	Pharyngeal and laryngeal muscles
		VM	Dorsal motor nucleus	Along carotid artery, eosphagus, stomach	Viscera of thorax and abdomen
		VS	Nodose ganglion	With motor	Viscera of thorax and abdomen
		GSS	Jugular ganglion	Auricular branch	Pinna of ear
XI	Accessory	BM	Accessory nucleus	Side of neck	Sternocleidomastoid
XII	Hypoglossal	SM	Hypoglossal nucleus	Side of tongue	Muscles of tongue

*Reproduced and modified, with permission, from Krieg: *Brain Mechanisms in Diachrome,* 2nd ed. Brain Books, 1957.

2. Main sensory nucleus of trigeminal nerve in pons.

3. Vestibular and cochlear nuclei of acoustic nerve in pons and medulla.

4. Nucleus of tractus solitarius (facial and glossopharyngeal nerves) in dorsal medulla.

5. Nucleus of spinal tract of trigeminal nerve in dorsolateral medulla.

Cranial Nerve I:
OLFACTORY NERVE & TRACT
(Sensory Nerve)

Structurally, cranial nerve I is not a true nerve but a fiber tract of the brain. Its **peripheral and inter-** **mediate connections** consist of primary, secondary, and tertiary neurons.

(1) Primary neurons: Unmyelinated processes of the ciliated receptors in the upper part of the nasal mucosa are gathered into about 20 branches, which pass through the cribriform plate of the ethmoid bone to the olfactory bulb.

(2) Secondary neurons: Myelinated processes of the bipolar cells of the bulb form the olfactory tract and terminate in the primary olfactory cortex (periamygdaloid area and prepiriform cortex).

(3) Tertiary neurons: Neurons extend from the primary olfactory cortex to the entorhinal cortex (area 28), lateral preoptic area, amygdaloid body, and medial forebrain bundle. (See Fig 1–15.)

The **central connections** of the olfactory nerve

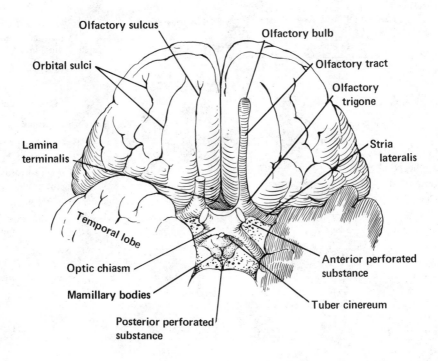

Olfactory sulcus

Orbital sulci

Olfactory bulb

Olfactory tract

Olfactory trigone

Lamina terminalis

Stria lateralis

Temporal lobe

Optic chiasm

Anterior perforated substance

Mamillary bodies

Tuber cinereum

Posterior perforated substance

Figure 4–3. The olfactory nerve (inferior view).

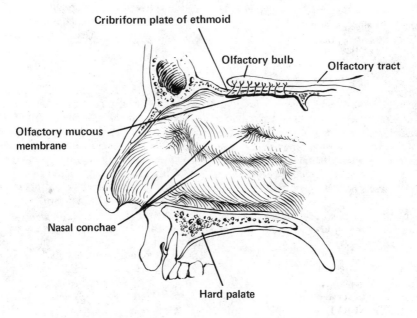

Cribriform plate of ethmoid

Olfactory bulb

Olfactory tract

Olfactory mucous membrane

Nasal conchae

Hard palate

Figure 4–4. The olfactory nerve (lateral view).

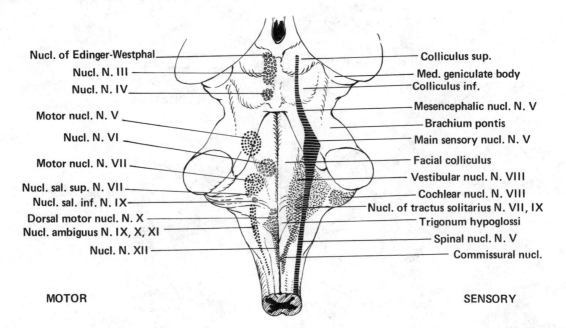

Figure 4–5. Cranial nerve nuclei. Dorsal view of the human brain stem with the positions of the cranial nerve nuclei projected upon the surface. Sensory nuclei on the right side, motor nuclei on the left. (After Herrick. Redrawn and reproduced, with permission, from Ranson SM, Clark SL: *The Anatomy of the Nervous System,* 9th ed. Saunders, 1953.)

are complex. Association fibers to the tegmentum and pons pass directly as third-order neurons from the anterior perforated substance and indirectly from the hippocampus via the fornix and olfactory projection tracts through the mamillary bodies and anterior nuclei of the thalamus. Reflex connections thus established with nuclei of the other cranial and spinal nerves may be functionally significant in swallowing and digestion.

The olfactory nerve may serve as a portal of entry for cryptogenic infections of the brain and meninges, eg, poliomyelitis, epidemic meningitis, and encephalitis.

Disorders of the sense of smell may be caused by inflammatory and other lesions of the nasal cavity, fracture of the anterior fossa of the skull, tumors of the frontal lobe and pituitary region, meningitis, hydrocephalus, posttraumatic cerebral syndrome, arteriosclerosis, cerebrovascular accidents, certain drug intoxications, psychoses, neuroses, and congenital defects.

Special syndromes involving the olfactory nerve include the Foster Kennedy syndrome and the aura of epilepsy.

Symptoms of First Nerve Involvement

A. Disorders of Sense of Smell: Anosmia (loss of sense of smell) may be of great significance. Bilateral anosmia commonly occurs with colds, rhinitis, etc. Unilateral anosmia may be of diagnostic significance in locating brain lesions such as tumors at the base of the frontal lobe. **Hyperosmia** (abnormally acute sense of smell) is present in some hysterias and is

sometimes noted in cocaine addicts. **Parosmia** (perverted sense of smell) occurs in some cases of schizophrenia, uncinate gyrus lesions, and hysterias. **Cacosmia** (unpleasant odors) is usually due to decomposition of tissues and is noticed by the patient on expiration.

B. Olfactory Hallucinations: Hallucinations of smell are present in some psychoses and in uncinate gyrus fits that are caused by lesions of the uncus and hippocampus.

Tests

Each nostril must be tested separately by occluding one nostril and holding the mouth of a small bottle containing the test substance under the other nostril.

Familiar nonirritating odors are best (volatile oils). Oil of cloves, turpentine, citron, camphor, or oil of wintergreen may be used. Avoid the use of irritant substances such as ammonia or vinegar.

The odors correctly or incorrectly identified should be noted for each nostril. A record should also be made of whether the nasal airway is clear and whether nasal catarrh is present. Although the patient may be unable to name the test substance, awareness of an odor excludes anosmia.

Cranial Nerve II:
OPTIC NERVE & TRACT
(Sensory Nerve)

Structurally, cranial nerve II is not a true nerve but a fiber tract of the brain. Its **peripheral and intermediate connections** are as follows:

(1) Rods and cones of the retina are the first-order neurons that connect with bipolar cells.

(2) Bipolar cells of the retina in turn synapse with ganglion cells near the surface of the retina.

(3) Ganglion cells are third-order neurons whose myelinated axons form the optic nerve fibers. At the optic chiasm, the nerve fibers from the nasal half of each retina cross; the nerve fibers from the temporal half of each retina are uncrossed. Thus, fibers from the ipsilateral halves of the retinas form the optic tract, passing to the lateral geniculate bodies, superior colliculi, and pretectal region.

(4) The geniculocalcarine tract contains the fourth-order neurons from the lateral geniculate bodies and passes to the occipital (calcarine) cortex. **Meyer's loop** is the fanlike radiating portion that curves around the inferior horn of the lateral ventricle.

The **central connections** of the optic nerve (see Fig 21–1) include the following: (1) from the pretectal region to the Edinger-Westphal nucleus via the posterior commissure; (2) from the superior colliculi via the tectobulbar and tectospinal tracts to other cranial and spinal nuclei; and (3) from the occipital cortex to other cortical and subcortical areas. Fibers from the pretectal region are responsible for the simple and consensual light reflexes; those from the superior colliculi for involuntary oculoskeletal reflexes. The lateral geniculate body gives rise to the geniculocalcarine tract, which is concerned with visual perception. The pretectal area is concerned with the light reflex and the superior colliculi with reflex movement of the eyes and head after optic stimulation. Association and reflex fibers pass from the occipital cortex to other cortical centers (related to higher functions, eg, reading, speech) and to the superior colliculi and thus through the tectobulbar and tectospinal tracts to (1) cranial and spinal nuclei, for involuntary reflexes (eg, accommodation); and (2) the pontine nuclei, via the corticopontine tract, for postural reflexes.

The retinal area for central vision is the macula; the remainder of the retina is concerned with paracentral and peripheral vision. The inner layers of the retina in the macular area are pushed apart, forming the fovea centralis, a small central pit composed of closely packed cones, where vision is sharpest and color discrimination most acute.

The rods and cones of the retina react specifically to physical light. The cones are stimulated by relatively high-intensity light and are responsible for sharp vision and color discrimination. The more numerous rods react to low-intensity light and function in twilight and night vision.

The portion of the spectrum that stimulates the retina to produce sight ranges from 400 to 800 nm. Stimulation of the normal eye by this entire range of wavelengths simultaneously or by mixtures from certain different parts of this range produces the sensation of white light. Monochromatic radiation from one part of the spectrum is perceived as having a specific color or hue. The Young-Helmholtz theory postulates that the retina contains 3 receptor groups, each with its own absorption property. However, later studies suggest that conversion of light to an impression of color may involve 3 or more identical photochemical receptors.

Binocular fusion of color can occur, so that if one eye is exposed to red light and the other to green light, a subjective sensation of yellow occurs. Land believes that sensation of color is produced by interplay of longer and shorter wavelengths rather than by stimulation of the eye by any particular wavelength.

In normal color (trichromatic) vision, the eye can perceive 3 light primaries (red, blue, and green) and can mix these in suitable portions so that white or any color of the spectrum can be matched. Color blindness can result from a lessened capacity to match 3 primary colors, or it can be dichromatic vision, in which only one pair of primary colors is perceived, the 2 colors being complementary to each other. Most dichromats are red-green blind and confuse red, yellow, and green.

In primates, the majority of neurons in the central retina and lateral geniculate nucleus are sensitive to both form and color. In the striate cortex (area 17), many cells are sensitive only to form, and a small fraction are sensitive to color and form; some cells respond only to properly oriented contour, color, and length.

Lesions of the Visual Apparatus

Retrobulbar neuritis involves the optic nerve or tract. Involvement may be axial, peripheral, or diffuse. The most common cause is multiple sclerosis.

Optic or bulbar neuritis includes various forms of retinitis, eg, simple, proteinuric, syphilitic, diabetic, hemorrhagic, and hereditary.

Papilledema (choked disk) is usually a symptom of increased intracranial pressure due to brain tumors, abscesses, hemorrhage, hypertension, and other causes.

Optic atrophy is associated with decreased visual acuity and a change in color of the optic disk to light pink, white, or gray. Primary optic atrophy is caused by processes that involve the optic nerve and do not produce papilledema; secondary optic atrophy is a sequel of papilledema. Primary (simple) optic atrophy may be due to tabes dorsalis, multiple sclerosis, or heredity. Secondary optic atrophy may be due to neuritis, glaucoma, or increased intracranial pressure. Opacities of the lens, corneal scars, and arteriosclerotic changes in the retina may occur. Tumors and other lesions may interrupt the optic pathways.

Syndromes

Syndromes involving the optic apparatus include the Foster Kennedy syndrome, amaurotic familial idiocy, Argyll Robertson pupil, and Holmes-Adie syndrome.

Foster Kennedy syndrome may be caused by tumors at the base of the frontal lobe and is characterized by ipsilateral blindness and anosmia (with atrophy of the optic and olfactory nerves) and contralateral papilledema.

Amaurotic familial idiocy (Tay-Sachs disease, cerebromacular degeneration) is a severe mental deficiency occurring in Jewish families and is associated with blindness, optic atrophy, and a dark cherry-red spot in place of the macula lutea.

Holmes-Adie syndrome is characterized by a tonic pupillary reaction and the absence of one or more tendon reflexes. The pupil is said to be "myotonic," with a very slow, almost imperceptible contraction to light and in near vision, a slower dilatation upon removal of the stimulus. Abnormal sensitivity to weak solutions (2.5%) of methacholine (Mecholyl) instilled into the conjunctival sac is demonstrable in affected eyes: tonic pupils constrict, whereas pupils of normal eyes remain unaffected (Adler-Scheie test).

Visual Defects (See also Chapter 21.)

A. Scotomas: Scotomas are abnormal blind spots in the visual fields. Positive scotomas are apparent to the patient as dark spots; negative scotomas may exist without the patient's knowledge. Motile scotomas result from opacities floating in the vitreous. In absolute scotoma, perception of light is entirely lost over the defective area; in relative scotoma, it is not.

Central scotomas (loss of macular vision) are due to axial neuritis. The point of fixation is involved, and central visual acuity is correspondingly impaired.

Other scotomas are due to patchy lesions, as in hemorrhage and glaucoma. Paracentral scotomas are adjacent to the point of fixation. Cecocentral scotomas involve the point of fixation and extend to the normal blind spot. Ring, or annular, scotomas encircle the point of fixation. Scintillating scotomas are subjective experiences of bright colorless or colored lights in the line of vision.

B. Amblyopia: Amblyopia (dim vision) is a defect of visual acuity.

C. Amaurosis: Amaurosis (complete blindness) may be hereditary or acquired. The use of the term is sometimes restricted to blindness occurring without

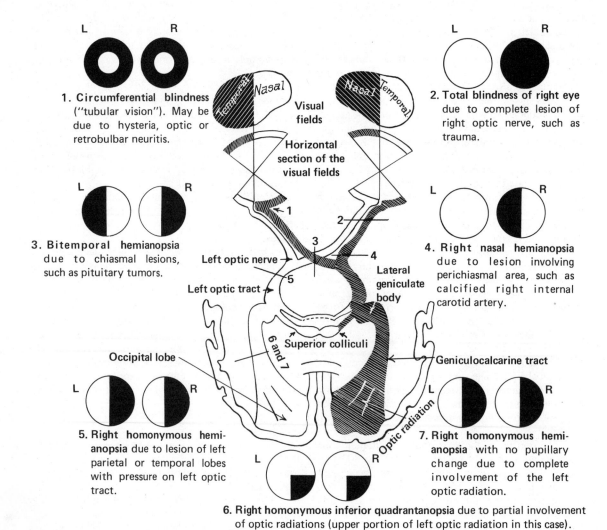

1. **Circumferential blindness** ("tubular vision"). May be due to hysteria, optic or retrobulbar neuritis.

2. **Total blindness of right eye** due to complete lesion of right optic nerve, such as trauma.

3. **Bitemporal hemianopsia** due to chiasmal lesions, such as pituitary tumors.

4. **Right nasal hemianopsia** due to lesion involving perichiasmal area, such as calcified right internal carotid artery.

5. **Right homonymous hemianopsia** due to lesion of left parietal or temporal lobes with pressure on left optic tract.

7. **Right homonymous hemianopsia** with no pupillary change due to complete involvement of the left optic radiation.

6. **Right homonymous inferior quadrantanopsia** due to partial involvement of optic radiations (upper portion of left optic radiation in this case).

Figure 4–6. Visual field defects associated with lesions of visual system.

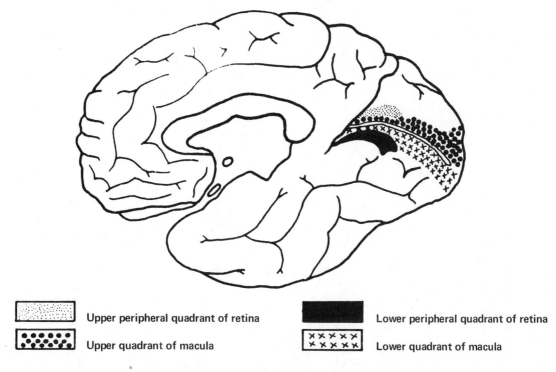

Upper peripheral quadrant of retina	Lower peripheral quadrant of retina
Upper quadrant of macula	Lower quadrant of macula

Figure 4–7. Medial view of cerebral hemisphere showing projection of the retina on the calcarine fissure in humans. (Redrawn and reproduced, with permission, from Brouwer: Projection of the retina on the cortex in man. *Res Publ Assoc Res Nerv Ment Dis* 1934; **13**:529.)

apparent ocular lesions, eg, due to disease of the brain, retina, or optic nerve.

D. Field Defects: Field defects are diagrammed in Fig 4–6. Contraction of the field of vision is a common defect that often has psychogenic causes. In severe cases it may result in tubular or gun-barrel vision. The tendency for the fields to remain small rather than to enlarge appropriately when the patient is moved away from the screen is characteristic of psychogenic field defects.

Visual acuity is not affected in papilledema, or choked disk, unless secondary atrophy occurs, after which the visual fields become contracted. Most lesions of the retina or optic nerve characteristically produce a central scotoma, although contractions of visual field or even blindness may occur.

E. Other Disorders:

1. Hemeralopia (day blindness) is a fatigue syndrome; vision is best in dim light.

2. Nyctalopia (night blindness) is sometimes associated with vitamin A deficiency.

3. Color blindness may be hereditary or acquired. Hereditary types are transmitted as recessive characteristics, sometimes X-linked. These include achromatopsia (total color blindness); monochromatism (partial color blindness, ability to recognize one of the 3 basic colors); and dichromatism (ability to recognize 2 of the 3 basic colors).

Tests (See Chapter 21.)

A. Visual Acuity: Snellen card test for persons with fairly normal vision; finger counting and finger movement tests for subnormal cases; light perception and light projection for markedly subnormal cases. (Cataracts are not removed if light perception is gone.) Near vision is tested with standard reading cards.

B. Perimetry: Plotting fields of vision for determining presence of scotomas and field defects. For equal-sized targets, the visual field for white is most extensive; visual fields for blue, red, yellow, and green follow in that order.

C. Color Blindness Tests: Using colored wools or special cards.

D. Fundus Examination: With ophthalmoscope.

Cranial Nerves III, IV, VI:
OCULOMOTOR, TROCHLEAR, ABDUCENS
(Motor to Muscles of the Eye,
Including Levator Palpebrae)

Peripheral & Intermediate Connections

(1) Oculomotor (III): Motor fibers arise from a group of nuclei in the central gray matter ventral to the cerebral aqueduct at the level of the superior colliculus. Crossed and mainly uncrossed fibers course through the red nucleus and the inner side of the substantia nigra to emerge on the sella turcica in the outer wall of the cavernous sinus and through the superior orbital fissure to supply the medial, superior, and inferior rectus muscles and the inferior oblique and levator palpebrae muscles. **Parasympathetic fibers**

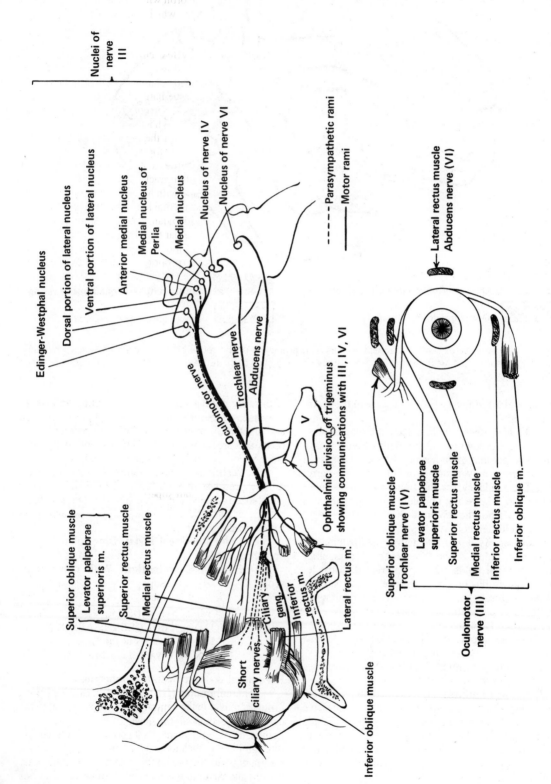

Figure 4–8. The oculomotor, trochlear, and abducens nerves.

arise (1) from the Edinger-Westphal nucleus, just rostrad to the motor nucleus of III, passing via the nasociliary branch of III to the ciliary ganglion, whence short ciliary nerves are distributed to the sphincter muscle of the iris; and (2) from the upper portion of the medial nucleus of III, passing via the ciliary ganglion and short ciliary nerves to the ciliary muscle, which on contraction thickens the lens. (See Fig 6–3.)

(2) Trochlear (IV): Motor (entirely crossed) fibers arise from the trochlear nucleus just caudad to III at the level of the inferior colliculus, run posteriorly, decussate in the anterior medullary velum, and wind around the cerebral peduncles. The nerve then follows III along the cavernous sinus to the orbit, where it supplies the superior oblique muscle, which moves the axis of vision downward and inward.

(3) Abducens (VI): Motor (entirely uncrossed) fibers arise from the nucleus in the floor of the fourth ventricle in the lower portion of the pons near the internal genu of the facial nerve. The fibers pierce the pons and emerge anteriorly, the nerve running a long course over the tip of the petrous portion of the temporal bone to the outer wall of the cavernous sinus. The nerve then enters the orbit with III and IV to supply the lateral rectus muscle, which rotates the eyeball outward.

The **central reflex connections** from these nerves include the following: (1) from the pretectal region via the posterior commissure to the Edinger-Westphal nucleus for mediation of ipsilateral and consensual light reflexes (interruption of this pathway is believed to cause the Argyll Robertson pupil); (2) from the superior colliculi via the tectobulbar tract to the nuclei of III, IV, and VI for the mediation of accommodation and other reflexes; (3) from the inferior colliculi via the tectobulbar tract to the eye muscle nuclei for reflexes correlated with hearing, and from the vestibular nuclei via the medial longitudinal fasciculus for reflex correlation with balance; and (4) from the cortex through the corticobulbar tract for mediation of voluntary and conditioned movements of the eyes.

A few sensory (proprioceptive) fibers from the muscles of the eye are present for each of these nerves. The central terminations of these fibers are not known.

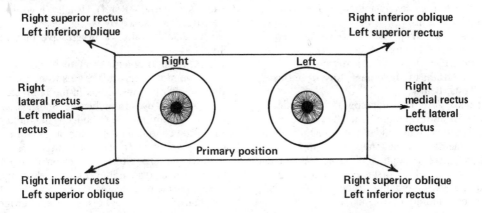

Figure 4–9. Muscles used in conjugate ocular movements in the 6 cardinal directions of gaze.

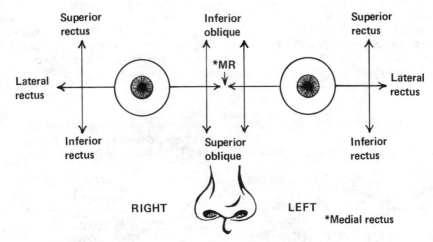

Figure 4–10. Diagram of eye muscle action.

Among the disorders that may involve these nerves are the following: syphilis, meningitis, encephalitis, diphtheria, botulism, cavernous sinus thrombosis, polioencephalitis hemorrhagica superior, suppuration of the accessory nasal sinuses, tumors of the orbit and brain, cerebral hemorrhage, aneurysm of the internal carotid artery of the circle of Willis, multiple sclerosis, skull fracture, hysterias, and certain drug intoxications.

Symptoms & Signs (See Chapter 21.)

A. Squint or Strabismus: Deviation of either eye or both. In internal strabismus, the visual axes cross each other; in external strabismus, the visual axes diverge from each other.

B. Diplopia (Double Vision): A subjective phenomenon present usually when looking with both eyes. (Monocular diplopia is usually a hysterical phenomenon.)

C. Tilting of Head: To compensate for diplopia.

D. Conjugate Deviation: Both eyes turned to same side; may be spasmodic or paralytic. Usually caused by central lesions.

E. Nystagmus: Rhythmic or undulating movements of the eyes may be physiologic or due to central or labyrinthine lesions.

F. Ptosis (Lid Drop): Due to weakness or paralysis of the superior levator muscle.

G. Dizziness: Often associated with diplopia.

H. Limitations of Movement, Loss of Reflexes, Etc: See Tests, below.

I. Hippus: Alternate dilatation and contraction of the pupil under uniform illumination can be observed in normal persons only under high magnification. These movements are exaggerated in hysteria.

J. Oscillopsia: An optical illusion of movement of a fixed stationary object that may be associated with drug intoxications or organic lesions of the visual, vestibular, or oculomotor systems.

Classification of Disorders of Nerves III, IV, & VI

A. Ophthalmoplegias (Paralyses): Lesions causing these may be acute, chronic, or progressive, and central or peripheral.

1. Oculomotor paralysis (III)–

a. External ophthalmoplegia–Divergent strabismus, diplopia, and ptosis of lid.

b. Internal ophthalmoplegia–Dilated pupil, loss of light and accommodation reflexes.

c. Paralysis of individual muscles–See Table 4–2.

d. Paralysis of levator palpebrae–Ptosis (common in myasthenia gravis).

e. Argyll Robertson pupil–Miosis with loss of light and ciliospinal reflexes. Accommodation is retained.

f. Paralysis of convergence (central lesion)–Internal recti are normal except that they cannot converge the eyes. Double vision for near but not for distant objects may be present. Associated pupil contraction is lost also.

2. Trochlear paralysis (IV)–(Rare.) Slight convergent strabismus and diplopia on looking downward. The patient cannot look down and in and hence has difficulty in descending stairs. The head is tilted as a compensatory adjustment, and this may be the first indication of a trochlear lesion.

3. Abducens paralysis (VI)–(Fig 4–11.) (Most common of eye palsies; due to long course of nerve.) Convergent strabismus and diplopia; especially common in late syphilis, basilar diseases, and trauma.

4. Chronic progressive ophthalmoplegia (Graefe's disease)–(Rare.) Usually involves all 3 nerves together; caused by nuclear lesion, eg, bulbar paralysis, late syphilis, or progressive muscular atrophy.

5. Ophthalmoplegia internuclearis–A dissociation of eye movements that results from injury to the medial longitudinal fasciculus in the brain stem. Efforts to move the eyes from the side of the lesion result in partial outward movement plus nystagmoid movements of the contralateral eye; the ipsilateral eye fails to move beyond the position of central fixation.

B. Myasthenic States: An effort is required to keep the visual axes parallel. Functional, congenital, and neurasthenic weaknesses are also present. Muscular weakness causes visual disturbances, vertigo, migraine, paresthesia, and pains in the head, especially in the occipital and cervical regions.

C. Supranuclear Lesions: Lesions of the frontal or occipital lobes may produce paralysis of the conjugate gaze to the opposite side, with deviation of the eyes to the side of the lesion. Spontaneous recovery usually occurs in a few days. Irritative lesions usually produce conjugate deviation of the eyes to the opposite side.

Table 4–2. Chart of paralyses of individual eye muscles.*

Muscle	Nerve	Deviation of Eyeball	Diplopia Present When Looking*	Direction of Image
Medial rectus	III	Outward (external squint)	Toward nose	Vertical
Superior rectus	III	Downward and inward	Upward and outward	Oblique
Inferior rectus	III	Upward and inward	Downward and outward	Oblique
Inferior oblique	III	Downward and outward	Upward and inward	Oblique
Superior oblique	IV	Upward and outward	Downward and inward	Oblique
Lateral rectus	VI	Inward (internal squint)	Toward temple	Vertical

*Diplopia is noted only when the affected eye attempts these movements.

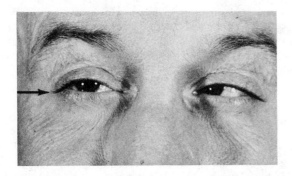

Figure 4–11. Right abducens paralysis. Right eye fails to abduct on right lateral gaze.

D. Nystagmus: Nystagmus is an involuntary back-and-forth, up-and-down, or rotating movement of the eyeballs. It usually results from lesions affecting the neural mechanism, which tends to keep the eyes in a constant relation to their environment and which is concerned with equilibrium. Physiologic nystagmus may be elicited by turning the eyes far to one side and is characterized by rapid jerks with a quick component in the direction of gaze. Peripheral vestibular nystagmus results from stimulation of the peripheral vestibular apparatus and is always accompanied by vertigo. CNS nystagmus seldom is associated with vertigo and occurs with lesions in the region of the fourth ventricle. Optokinetic (railway) nystagmus occurs when there is continuous movement of the visual field past the eyes. Pendular nystagmus has no quick or slow component and is of either ocular origin, due to poor vision, or hereditary, associated with good vision. Toxic nystagmus may follow treatment with certain drugs, eg, phenytoin (Dilantin), bromides, barbiturates, and alcohol.

Syndromes Involving Nerves III, IV, & VI

Benedikt's syndrome, bulbar palsy, Gradenigo's syndrome, Graefe's disease (see above), Foville's syndrome, Korsakoff's syndrome, Nothnagel's syndrome, Weber's syndrome, Argyll Robertson pupil (see above), Millard-Gubler syndrome, syndrome of the superior colliculus, and Wernicke's syndrome.

Duane's retraction syndrome may follow paralysis of the lateral rectus muscle and is characterized by retraction of the eyeball on adduction of the eye, with oblique upward movement of the eyeball and narrowing of the palpebral fissure.

Gradenigo's syndrome may be produced by meningitis at the tip of the petrous bone, is characterized by pain in the face (from irritation of the semilunar ganglion) and lateral rectus palsy (from paralysis of the sixth cranial nerve), and results in internal strabismus and diplopia. It is usually a complication of purulent otitis media.

Tolosa-Hunt syndrome (painful ophthalmoplegia) is characterized by recurrent unilateral retro-orbital pain with extraocular palsies, usually involving the third, fourth, fifth, and sixth cranial nerves. Initially, it was attributed to inflammation of the cavernous sinus. It may last for several months and is often very responsive to corticosteroid therapy.

Tests (See Chapter 21.)

A. Finger Following: For ocular movements.

B. Accommodation: By noting convergence and pupillary change when patient follows objects brought from a distance up close to the eyes.

C. Light Reflex: By shining light into the eye from side (also depends on optic nerves).

D. Consensual Light Reflex: By shining light into one eye and noting change in opposite eye.

E. Prism Tests: For ability of medial and lateral recti to coalesce images. Normally, the lateral rectus muscles should overcome a prism of 8 degrees or more; the medial rectus muscles should overcome a prism of 23–25 degrees or more.

F. Diplopia Testing: May be performed by using red glass or a Maddox rod to determine the relative positions of false and true images for various portions of the visual fields. The false image commonly appears in the direction in which the paralyzed muscle usually should pull the eye.

Table 4–3. Local effects of drugs on the eye.

Parasympathomimetic Used as miotics (constrict pupil) for control of intraocular pressure in glaucoma	Parasympatholytic Used as mydriatics (dilate pupil) to aid in eye examination or as cycloplegics (relax ciliary muscles)	Sympathomimetic Used for mydriasis; do not cause cycloplegia

A. Act on Myoneural Junction:
  1. Pilocarpine
  2. Carbachol (Doryl)
  3. Methacholine (Mecholyl)
B. Cholinesterase Inhibitors:
  1. Physostigmine (eserine)
  2. Isoflurophate (Floropryl, DFP)
	A. Mydriatic: Eucatropine (Euphthalmine)
	B. Cytoplegic and Mydriatic:
	  1. Homatropine
	  2. Scopolamine (hyoscine)
	  3. Atropine
	  4. Cyclopentolate (Cyclogyl)
		1. Phenylephrine (Neo-Synephrine)
		2. Hydroxyamphetamine (Paredrine)
		3. Epinephrine
		4. Cocaine

Cranial Nerve V:
TRIGEMINAL
(Mixed Nerve)

Peripheral & Intermediate Connections

Sensory fibers arise from unipolar cells in the semilunar (gasserian) ganglion. Peripherally, they supply sensation (1) via the **ophthalmic division,** from the forehead, eyes, nose, temples, meninges, paranasal sinuses, and part of the nasal mucosa; (2) via the **maxillary division,** from the upper jaw, teeth, lip, cheeks, hard palate, maxillary sinuses, and nasal mucosa; and (3) via the **mandibular division,** from the lower jaw, teeth, lip, buccal mucosa, tongue, and part of the external ear, auditory meatus, and meninges. Centrally, the fibers pass as the portio major and split into (1) short ascending rami ending in the main sensory nucleus of V (just lateral to the motor nucleus) and subserving mainly touch; and (2) long descending rami subserving touch, pain, and temperature and giving off collaterals to the spinal nucleus of V, which extends through the medulla to overlap with Lissauer's tract.

Sensory proprioceptive fibers arise from unipolar cells within the mesencephalic nucleus of V; the peripheral processes pass via the motor root to nerve spindles in the muscles of mastication, and possibly also to the extraocular muscles.

Motor fibers from the motor nucleus of V (at the level of the mid pons) pass (1) as the motor root (portio minor) from the ventral surface of the pons through the foramen ovale to supply the muscles of mastication (the masseter, temporal, internal and external pterygoids); (2) via the otic ganglion to supply the tensor tympani and tensor veli palatini; and (3) via the mylohyoid nerve to the mylohyoid muscle and the anterior belly of the digastric muscle.

Central Connections

The motor nucleus receives bilateral (mainly crossed) cerebral connections from the corticobulbar tracts and reflex connections from the spinal tract of V and extrapyramidal tracts. From the main sensory nucleus of V, touch pathways pass to the thalamus and higher centers via the dorsal secondary tract of V. From the spinal nucleus of V, touch, pain, and temperature pathways pass to the thalamus via the ventral

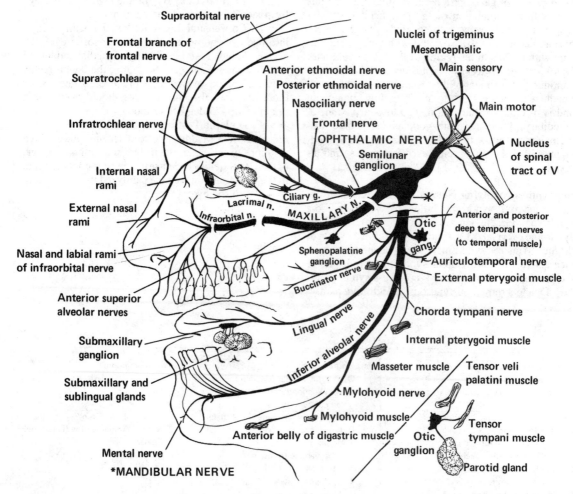

Figure 4–12. The trigeminal nerve.

secondary tract of V, and reflex connections pass to the motor nuclei of cranial nerves V, VII, and IX. Pain and temperature fibers whose cell bodies lie within the semilunar ganglion run caudally to form the spinal root of the trigeminal nerve, with terminal branches to the spinal root of the trigeminal nerve descending through the pons and medulla. New fibers arise from cells of the spinal root and cross to the opposite side of the brain stem in a diffuse pattern and then ascend via the trigeminal lemniscus to the posterior ventral nucleus of the thalamus. Central connections of the mesencephalic nucleus are obscure.

Disorders

Disorders that may affect the trigeminal nerve include neuralgias and neuritis, syphilis, tuberculosis, syringobulbia, tumors of the brain, basilar meningitis, pontine diseases, skull fracture, aneurysm of the carotid artery or circle of Willis, psychoneuroses, and cavernous sinus thrombosis.

Syndromes Involving the Trigeminal Nerve

Tic douloureux (trifacial neuralgia, prosopalgia, Fothergill's neuralgia, chronic paroxysmal trigeminal neuralgia) is characterized by severe pains in the distribution of one or more branches of the trigeminal nerve. Individual pains are abrupt in onset and brief in duration, usually lasting a fraction of a second to several seconds. The pain has a lightninglike or electric shock–like quality. Between paroxysms, the patient may be quite comfortable. Excruciating, paroxysmal pain of short duration may follow irritation of the "trigger zone," a point on the lip, face, gum, or tongue that is frequently sensitive to cold, pressure, or a blast of air. Involvement is usually unilateral and confined to one division of the nerve. The disorder occurs in adults over age 40 years. Although the cause is unknown and little or no pathologic change has been noted, trigeminal neuralgia is sometimes associated with dental or sinus disease. Treatments used for tic doulourex include analgesics, anticonvulsants, neurotomy, alcohol injection, trichloroethylene inhalations, intramedullary and mesencephalic tractotomy, and decompression of the posterior root (see p 392).

The **paratrigeminal syndrome** (Raeder's syndrome) is a rare disorder produced by tumors arising in the semilunar ganglion and characterized by trigeminal neuralgia at the onset, followed by facial anesthesias on the affected side. The muscles of mastication are weakened or paralyzed, and the adjacent third nerve may be paralyzed. Ipsilateral Horner's syndrome may occur from involvement of the carotid sympathetic plexus.

The **auriculotemporal nerve syndrome** (Frey's syndrome) consists of flushing and sweating of the ipsilateral face in the distribution of the auriculotemporal nerve upon eating or tasting. It is occasionally seen following injury or infection of the parotid gland area.

Bonnier's syndrome is discussed on p 111.

Symptoms of Trigeminal Involvement

A. Pain: Marked if gasserian ganglion or peripheral branches are involved.

B. Loss of Sensation: Over sensory distribution; corneal anesthesia early.

C. Dissociate Anesthesia: Loss of pain but not touch may be noted when the spinal tract of the fifth nerve is involved (eg, in syringobulbia).

D. Paresthesia: Occasionally seen in anemia and in nervous and hysterical patients.

E. Paralysis: Paralysis of muscles of mastication, with deviation of jaw to affected side.

F. Reflexes: Loss of jaw jerk, sneeze, and lid, conjunctival, and corneal reflexes.

G. Hearing: Impaired hearing due to paralysis of tensor tympani.

H. Trismus (Lockjaw): Tonic spasm of muscles of mastication in rabies, tetany, tetanus, epilepsy, and hysteria.

I. Trophic and Secretory Disturbances: Herpes simplex, neurokeratitis, dryness of nose (causes anosmia, as moisture is necessary to smell), ulcerations of face, and loss of teeth.

Tests

A. Sensation: With wisps of cotton, pinpricks, and warm or cold objects.

B. Reflexes: Corneal (wink), conjunctival, jaw jerk, sneeze.

C. Motor Status: Ability to chew; palpation of masseter and temporal muscles when the jaws are clamped tightly together. Wasting of the masseter muscles and deviation of the mandible to one side on attempting to lower the jaw against resistance are noted when present.

Cranial Nerve VII:
FACIAL
(Mixed Nerve; Mainly Motor)

Peripheral & Intermediate Connections

Motor fibers from the motor nucleus of VII in the caudal portion of the pons loop around the nucleus of VI (internal genu) and leave the skull by a long course through the petrous portion of the temporal bone. These fibers supply the stapedius muscle of the middle ear, the superficial musculature of the face and scalp, the platysma, the posterior belly of the digastric muscle, and the stylohyoid muscle.

Parasympathetic fibers from the superior salivatory nucleus pass via the nervus intermedius (glossopalatinus, or nerve of Wrisberg) to the glands and mucous membranes of the pharynx, palate, nasal cavity, and paranasal sinuses via the great superficial petrosal and the sphenopalatine ganglion; and to the submaxillary and sublingual glands via the chorda tympani and lingual nerves and the submaxillary ganglion.

Sensory fibers arise from unipolar cells in the geniculate ganglion. Peripheral branches carry taste

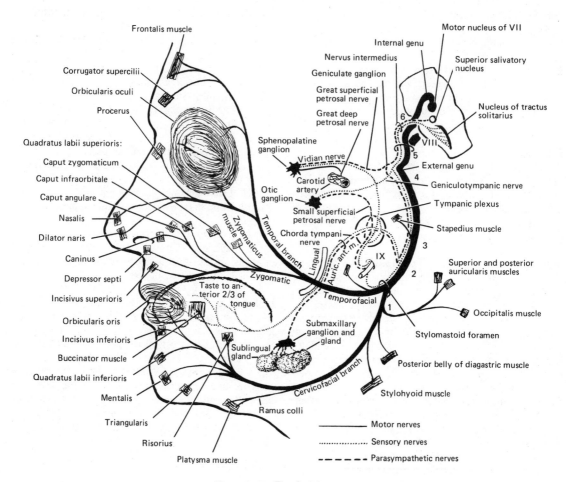

Figure 4–13. The facial nerve.

from the anterior two-thirds of the tongue via the lingual and chorda tympani nerves and sensation from the parotid gland via the otic ganglion and the geniculotympanic nerve. Central branches pass via the nervus intermedius to the nucleus of the tractus solitarius. (There are also some proprioceptive fibers carrying deep pressure and position sense from the facial muscles via the facial nerve.)

Central Connections

The motor nucleus receives crossed and uncrossed fibers from the corticobulbar tract, extrapyramidal tracts, and tectospinal tract and reflex connections from the nucleus of the tractus solitarius and the nucleus of the spinal tract of the trigeminus. The facial muscles below the forehead receive contralateral cortical innervation (crossed corticobulbar fibers); however, the frontalis muscle receives bilateral cortical innervation and is therefore not paralyzed by lesions involving one motor cortex or its pathways.

The superior salivatory nucleus receives cortical impulses via the dorsal longitudinal tract and reflex connections from the nucleus of the tractus solitarius.

The sensory fibers are connected with the cortex via the medial lemnisci and thalamus; with the salivatory nuclei and motor nuclei of VII by reflex neurons.

The cortical taste area is located in the inferior central (face) region and is believed to extend onto the opercular surface of the parietal lobe.

Lesions of the Facial Nerve

A. Bell's Palsy: (Peripheral facial paralysis, prosopoplegia.) May be caused by chilling of the face, middle ear infections, tumors, fractures, meningitis, hemorrhage, infectious diseases, and other less commonly encountered disorders. Seventy-five percent of all facial nerve lesions fall into this group. Bell's palsy may occur at any age but is slightly more common in the age group from 20 to 50. When an attempt is made to close the eyelids, the eyeball on the affected side may be seen to turn upward (Bell's phenomenon).

1. Symptoms and signs–These depend upon the

location of the lesions, as follows: (Numbers in the text refer to numbers in Fig 4–13.)

a. Lesion (1) outside the stylomastoid foramen (signs are on affected side)–The mouth droops and may draw to the other side, food collects between cheeks and gums, and deep facial sensation is lost. Patients cannot whistle, wink or close their eyes, or wrinkle their foreheads. Tearing occurs if the eye is unprotected. Paralysis is of the flaccid lower motor neuron (LMN) type. The reaction of degeneration (see p 248) appears in 10–14 days, depending upon the extent of damage.

b. Lesion (2) in facial canal and involving the chorda tympani nerve–All the above signs are present, as well as loss of taste in the anterior two-thirds of the tongue and reduced salivation on the affected side.

c. Lesion (3) higher in the facial canal and involving the stapedius muscle–Signs of (a) and (b) plus hyperacusis.

d. Higher lesion (4) involving the geniculate ganglion–Onset is often acute, with pain behind and within the ear. Herpes of the tympanum and concha may precede the palsy. Ramsay Hunt syndrome is Bell's palsy associated with herpes zoster of the geniculate ganglion, herpetic lesions being visible on the tympanic membrane, external auditory canal, and on the pinna.

e. Lesion (5) in the internal auditory meatus–Signs of Bell's palsy and deafness from eighth nerve involvement.

f. Lesions (6) at the emergence of the facial nerve from the pons (eg, meningitis)–Bell's palsy with involvement of other nerves as well, eg, V and VIII and, at times, VI, XI, and XII. In the Marcus Gunn (jaw-winking) phenomenon, seen in congenital ptosis, elevation of a ptotic eyelid occurs on movement of the jaw to the contralateral side. Marin-Amat syndrome is usually observed after peripheral facial paralysis and is referred to as an inverted Marcus Gunn phenomenon. Closing of the eyes occurs when patients open their mouths forcefully and maximally.

2. Treatment and prognosis–Reassure the patient that recovery may occur in 2–8 weeks (or up to 1–2 years in older patients). Keep the face warm and avoid further exposure, especially to wind and dust. Protect the eye with a patch if necessary. Support the face with tape or wire anchored at the angle of the mouth and looped about the ear. Electrical stimulation (every other day after the 14th day) may be used to help prevent muscle atrophy. Gentle upward massage of the involved muscles for 5–10 minutes 2–3 times daily may help to maintain muscle tone. Heat from an infrared lamp may hasten recovery.

In the vast majority of cases, partial or complete recovery occurs. When recovery is partial, contractures may develop on the paralyzed side. Recurrence on the same or the opposite side is occasionally reported.

B. Nuclear Type of Facial Palsy: Signs of Bell's palsy plus contralateral hemiplegia (from pyramidal involvement) with paralysis of the sixth and sometimes the eighth nerve. Millard-Gubler syndrome is a form of crossed paralysis (facial hemiplegia alternans) produced by a pontile lesion and characterized by contralateral hemiplegia and ipsilateral facial palsy. In many cases the sixth nerve is also involved, producing an internal strabismus. Foville's syndrome is a form of crossed hemiplegia from a pontile lesion. It consists of contralateral hemiplegia with ipsilateral palsy of the seventh cranial nerve and ipsilateral paralysis of conjugate gaze.

C. Supranuclear Type of Facial Palsy: Often associated with ipsilateral hemiplegia or monoplegia. The facial paralysis is of the spastic type. Taste and salivation are not affected, and the frontalis muscle is spared (owing to bilateral cortical innervation). Reflexes and emotional responses are retained, and there is no reaction of degeneration.

D. Geniculate Neuralgia: (Rare.) Pain behind and within the ear and loss of the taste sense. It is usually a transient accompaniment of Bell's palsy, type (d) (see above) but may appear with herpes of the tympanum and concha with or without facial palsy (Hunt's syndrome).

E. Crocodile Tears Syndrome: Paroxysmal lacrimation during eating, occurring usually as a result of injury to the facial nerve proximal to the geniculate ganglion.

F. Facial Spasm: (Paroxysmal hyperkinesia of the facial muscles.) Begins with twitching, is usually unilateral, and cannot be inhibited at will. During an attack, voluntary movements are impossible. Facial spasm commonly occurs after suture of a divided seventh nerve.

G. Bilateral Facial Palsy: (Facial diplegia.) (Rare.) Causes a flat, expressionless, drooling facies. It occurs with bulbar lesions, polyneuritis, and myasthenia gravis.

H. Striatum Lesions: Cause grimaces, choreiform movements, etc.

I. Möbius' Syndrome: (Congenital oculofacial paralysis, congenital facial diplegia, infantile nuclear aplasia.) A congenital disorder characterized by paresis or paralysis of both lateral rectus muscles and face muscles and sometimes associated with other musculoskeletal anomalies.

Tests

A. Motor Status: Ability to smile, whistle, etc. Electrical testing of the facial nerve and facial muscles and electromyography may provide valuable prognostic information.

B. Reflexes: Corneal (wink), conjunctival, and lid reflexes should be examined.

C. Sensory Status: Taste is tested as follows: sweet with sugar, sour with citric acid, bitter with quinine, and salty with salt.

D. Facial Symmetry: Asymmetry of the face at rest or during voluntary facial movement should be noted.

Cranial Nerve VIII:
ACOUSTIC
(Composite Sensory Nerve)

The acoustic, or statoacoustic, nerve consists of 2 separate parts known as the cochlear and vestibular nerves.

Peripheral & Intermediate Connections

A. Cochlear Nerve (for Hearing): Fibers from bipolar cells in the spiral ganglion consist of peripheral branches that end in the spiral organ (organ of Corti) and central branches that terminate in the ventral and dorsal cochlear nuclei.

B. Vestibular Nerve: Fibers from bipolar cells in the vestibular ganglion (ganglion of Scarpa) consist of peripheral branches that pass to the neuroepithelium in the ampullae of the semicircular canals and in the maculas of the utricle and saccule, and central branches that enter the brain stem median to the restiform body and end in the vestibular nuclei. Some central branches pass without interruption to the cerebellum.

Central Connections

From the cochlear nuclei, fibers pass by second-order neurons through the trapezoid body and lateral lemnisci to the medial geniculate bodies. From this area, auditory radiations are projected to the auditory cortex, and reflex connections pass to eye muscle nuclei and other motor nuclei of the cranial and spinal nerves via tectobulbar and tectospinal tracts.

Vestibular connections are from the superior and lateral vestibular nuclei to the cerebellum; from the lateral nuclei to ipsilateral spinal centers via the direct vestibulospinal tracts; and from the superior and medial nuclei to eye muscle nuclei and other motor nuclei of the cranial and spinal nerves via the medial longitudinal fasciculi of the same and opposite sides.

Diseases & Lesions That May Involve the Acoustic Nerve

Peripheral lesions usually involve both the cochlear and vestibular nerves. Examples include otitis media, meningitis, skull fractures, otosclerosis, basal tumors, infectious diseases, degenerative diseases, and Meniere's syndrome. **Central lesions** may involve either of the nerves independently and include syphilis, multiple sclerosis, congenital defects, brain tumors, hysterias and other psychogenic disorders, and degenerative diseases of the brain and blood vessels. Certain drugs (eg, quinine, cinchophen, and salicylates) may affect the cochlear nerve. Streptomycin sometimes causes vestibular nuclear degeneration. Seasickness (due to continuous movement of the endolymph in susceptible individuals) is characterized by vertigo and disturbances in equilibrium, nausea and vomiting (not related to diet), and occasionally pallor, sweating, tachycardia, dyspnea, tremor, and faintness. Seasickness can be treated by using hypnotics, antihistamines, or tranquilizing drugs or by having the patient lie down and vary the position of the head.

Other syndromes and diseases affecting the eighth nerve are Meniere's syndrome (paroxysmal vertigo), syndrome of pontocerebellar angle tumors, Bonnier's syndrome (from a lesion of Deiters' nucleus), Lermoyez's syndrome (paroxysmal deafness), and Costen's syndrome. Lermoyez's syndrome consists of attacks of decreased auditory acuity followed by vertigo, at which time the hearing returns to normal. The cause and mechanism are not known. Costen's syndrome is said to result from pressure or distortion changes of the temporomandibular joints and is characterized by pains in the head, neck, ear, tongue, nose, and eyes as well as tinnitus, impaired hearing, and dizziness. Cogan's syndrome consists of keratitis and deafness of sudden onset and unknown cause in nonsyphilitic patients. It occurs predominantly in young adults.

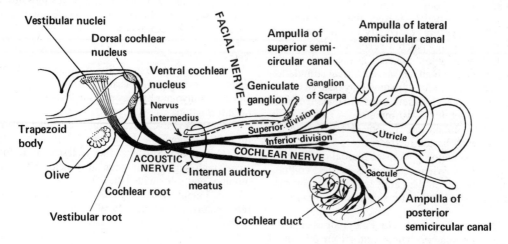

Figure 4–14. The acoustic nerve.

Symptoms of Acoustic Nerve Involvement

A. Cochlear:

1. Tinnitus–Ringing, buzzing, hissing, singing, or roaring noises in the ear are a frequent sign of early peripheral cochlear disease. Central tinnitus is rare and more complex and takes the form of music, etc. Noises from sclerotic cerebral vessels and aneurysms are transmitted to the eighth nerve. In organic cochlear lesions, tinnitus is usually followed by deafness.

2. Deafness–Nerve deafness is due to interruption of the nerve pathway; conduction deafness is due to middle or external ear disease. Cortical lesions do not cause deafness unless bilateral.

3. Hearing scotomas–Deafness to certain pitches and noises is not infrequent in hysterias, multiple sclerosis, paresis, and schizophrenia.

4. Supranuclear disorders–Sensory aphasia (word deafness; ability to hear but not to comprehend words) is associated with lesions of the posterior portion of the superior temporal gyrus of the dominant cerebral hemisphere. Auditory hallucinations may occur in psychoses or drug intoxications. Epileptic auras occur in the auditory sphere.

B. Vestibular:

1. Vertigo–A feeling of giddiness with disorientation in space, usually resulting in a disturbance of equilibrium, is often a sign of labyrinthine disease of middle or internal ear origin. It may also result from lesions of the eighth nerve (eg, tumors) or from reflex phenomena (eg, seasickness). Vertigo is often relieved or induced by placing the head in certain positions.

2. Nystagmus–A rhythmic to-and-fro ocular movement with a slow pull and a rapid return jerk usually accompanies vertigo in vestibular disease. It represents a disturbance in the reflex control of the ocular muscles, which is mainly a function of the semicircular canals. Nystagmus is named for the quick component, which is a compensatory adjustment to the slow reflex movement. There are various types: vertical, horizontal, rotatory, etc. Other forms of nystagmus occur in central, cerebellar, and cerebral lesions.

3. General symptoms–Labyrinthine disease may be associated with general symptoms such as diaphoresis, tachycardia, nausea and vomiting, and lowered blood pressure.

Tests (See Chapter 22.)

A. Cochlear:

1. Hearing acuity–Cover the other ear and test with a watch, whisper, or audiometer.

2. Weber's test–No lateralization of sound to either ear normally occurs when the stem of a vibrating tuning fork is held against the midline vertex of the skull. If sound is referred to a poorer hearing ear, loss of hearing is due to impaired conduction in the external or internal ear. If sound is referred to a better hearing ear, loss of hearing is attributable to impaired function of the auditory nerve or cochlea.

3. Rinne's test–A tuning fork is placed on the mastoid bone, and when sound is no longer heard, placed in front of the ear. If sound is not heard in front

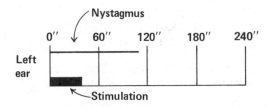

Figure 4–15. Hallpike caloric test (normal example). Stimulation of left ear for 40 seconds with cold water (30 °C) produces nystagmus lasting 110 seconds.

of the ear, suspect middle ear disease. (Normally, air conduction is greater than bone conduction.) As a rule, no sound is heard in either case in severe nerve deafness.

4. Bing's test–Place a tuning fork (C = 256 Hz) on the vertex and cover one ear. Normally, the closed ear hears sound best by bone conduction. If no sound is heard in the closed ear, nerve deafness is suspected.

5. Otoscopic examination–The ear should be examined with an otoscope for foreign bodies, congenital malformations, etc.

6. Audiometry–See Chapter 22.

B. Vestibular:

1. Caloric test–Following irrigation of the right ear with cold water (up to 10 °C), with the subject seated and the head tilted back 60 degrees, nausea, horizontal nystagmus with slow component to the right, past-pointing to the left, and falling to the right normally occur. (With warm water, the quick component is to the right.) Complete interruption of vestibular nerve function is characterized by absence of reaction to irrigation; partial interruption of vestibular nerve function produces diminished responses.

In the Hallpike caloric test, at least 250 mL of water at 30 °C (7 degrees below normal) is applied to the external auditory canal for 40 seconds. The test is repeated with water at 44 °C (7 degrees above normal). The vestibule receives equal and opposite standard and repeatable stimuli. Normal afternystagmus is 90–140 seconds.

2. Electrical test–The amount of galvanic current (in milliamperes) necessary to produce nystagmus, past-pointing, and inclination of the head when the current is passed between 2 saline-soaked pads placed over each ear is noted. The comparative effect of placing the cathode (the stimulating electrode) on the right and left ear is determined.

Cranial Nerve IX:
GLOSSOPHARYNGEAL
(Mixed Nerve)

Cranial nerve IX leaves the skull via the jugular foramen with X and XI and lies anterolateral to X.

Peripheral & Intermediate Connections

Motor fibers from the nucleus ambiguus pass to the stylopharyngeus muscle.

Parasympathetic fibers from the inferior salivatory nucleus pass via the nerve of Jacobson, tympanic plexus, and small superficial petrosal nerve to the otic ganglion, from which the postganglionic fibers pass to the parotid gland.

Sensory fibers arise from unipolar cells in the petrous and jugular ganglia. Centrally, they terminate in the tractus solitarius and its nucleus. Peripherally, they supply general sensation to the pharynx, soft palate, posterior third of the tongue, fauces, tonsils, auditory tube, and tympanic cavity. Through the sinus nerve, they supply special receptors in the carotid body and carotid sinus concerned with reflex control of respiration, blood pressure, and heart rate. Special visceral afferents supply taste buds of the posterior third of the tongue. A few fibers join the auricular branch of the vagus nerve and pass to the external auditory meatus.

Central Connections

The nucleus ambiguus receives cortical connections via the corticobulbar tract and reflex connections from the extrapyramidal and tectobulbar tracts and from the nucleus of the tractus solitarius.

The inferior salivatory nucleus receives cortical impulses via the dorsal longitudinal tract and reflexes from the nucleus of the tractus solitarius.

The sensory fibers are connected with the cortex via the medial lemnisci and thalamus and reflexly with the salivatory nuclei, nucleus ambiguus, and the motor nucleus of VII.

The glossopharyngeal nerve is rarely involved alone (eg, by neuralgia) but generally together with the vagus and accessory nerves by compression, inflammation, or trauma. Lesions that may involve the ninth nerve include bulbar diseases, syphilis, tuberculosis, basal tumors, jugular vein thrombosis, trauma in the retroparotid space, aneurysm of the circle of Willis, and diphtheritic neuritis.

Syndromes Involving the Glossopharyngeal Nerve

Syndromes involving the ninth nerve include the following: (1) Bonnier's syndrome. (2) Vernet's syndrome. (3) **Glossopharyngeal neuralgia,** characterized by paroxysmal pain similar in type to that of trigeminal neuralgia, which starts in the throat, radiates to the auditory tube and behind the ear, and is often initiated by coughing, swallowing, or clearing the throat. (4) Neuralgia of the tympanic branch (Jacobson's nerve), characterized by pain limited to the ear and auditory tube.

The pain of glossopharyngeal neuralgia usually starts in the tonsillar fossa and extends to the ipsilateral ear. Paroxysms of pain of increasing intensity last 20–30 seconds and are often followed by a burning sensation for 2–3 minutes.

Reichert's syndrome is an "incomplete" neuralgia affecting the tympanic branch of the glossopharyngeal nerve. It may be relieved by intracranial section of the glossopharyngeal nerve.

Tests

The pharyngeal (gag) reflex depends on the ninth nerve for its sensory component; stroking of the affected side does not produce gagging if the nerve is injured.

Vernet's rideau phenomenon (constriction of the posterior pharyngeal wall in saying, "ah") is absent when the ninth nerve is involved.

The carotid sinus reflex depends on the ninth nerve for its sensory component. Pressure over the sinus normally produces slowing of the heart and a fall in blood pressure.

Taste tests on the posterior third of the tongue are discussed on p 101.

Symptoms of Ninth Nerve Involvement

(1) Loss of the gag (pharyngeal) reflex.

(2) Slight dysphagia.

(3) Loss of taste in the posterior third of the tongue.

(4) Deviation of the uvula to the well side.

(5) Loss of sensation in the pharynx, tonsils, fauces, and back of the tongue.

(6) Loss of constriction of the posterior pharyngeal wall when saying, "ah."

(7) Increased salivation from involvement of the tympanic plexus in middle ear lesions.

(8) Rarely, "nystagmus" of the uvula in central inflammatory and vascular lesions.

(9) Tachycardia in some ninth nerve lesions, probably from disturbance of the carotid sinus reflex.

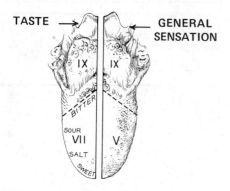

Figure 4–16. Sensory innervation of the tongue.

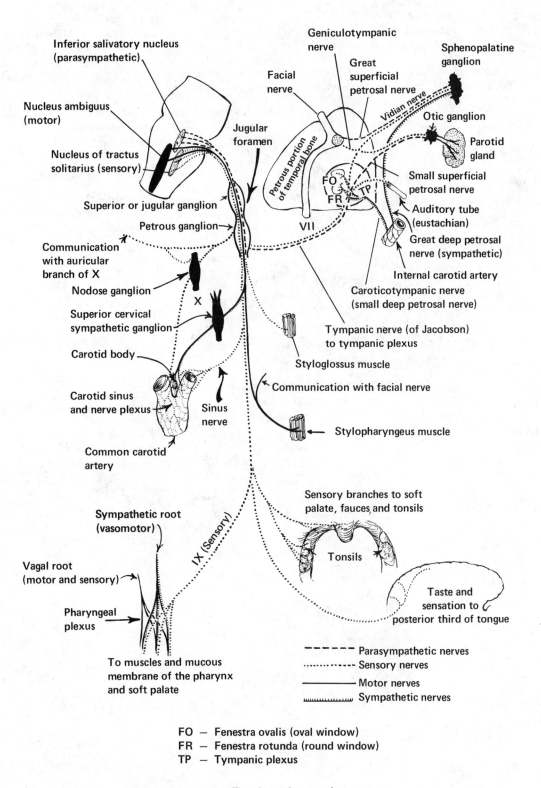

Figure 4–17. The glossopharyngeal nerve.

FO — Fenestra ovalis (oval window)
FR — Fenestra rotunda (round window)
TP — Tympanic plexus

Cranial Nerve X:
VAGUS
(Mixed Nerve)

Peripheral & Intermediate Connections

Motor fibers from the nucleus ambiguus contrib-

ute to the rootlets of the glossopharyngeal nerve, vagus, and the internal ramus of the accessory nerve (XI). Those of the vagus nerve pass to the muscles of the soft palate and pharynx. Those to the accessory nerve join the vagus outside the skull and pass via the recurrent laryngeal nerve to the intrinsic muscles of the larynx.

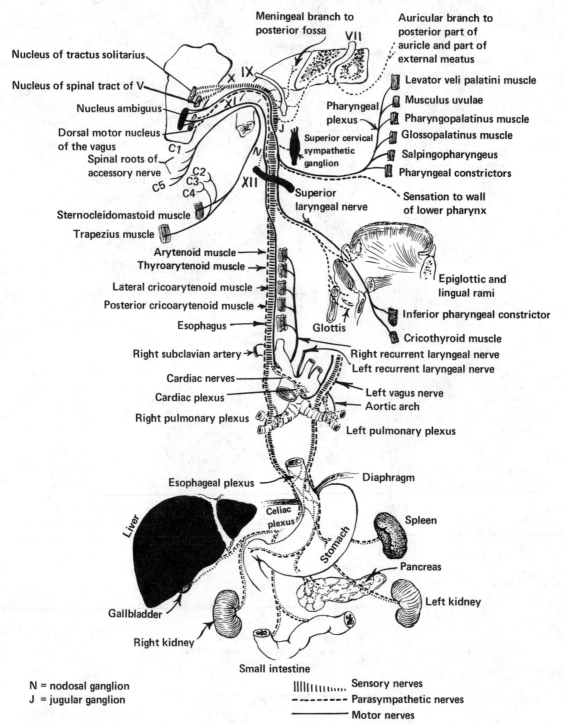

Figure 4–18. The vagus nerve.

Parasympathetic fibers from the dorsal motor nucleus of the vagus are distributed to the thoracic and abdominal viscera. Their postganglionic fibers arise in the terminal ganglia of the viscera. They inhibit heart rate and suprarenal secretion and stimulate gastrointestinal peristalsis and gastric, hepatic, and pancreatic glandular activity. (See Fig 6–2.)

Somatic sensory fibers of unipolar cells in the jugular ganglion send peripheral branches via the auricular branch to the external auditory meatus and part of the ear and, via the recurrent meningeal branch, to the dura of the posterior fossa, and central branches to the spinal tract of the trigeminus and its nucleus.

Visceral sensory fibers of unipolar cells in the ganglion nodosum send peripheral branches to the pharynx, larynx, trachea, esophagus, and the thoracic and abdominal viscera and a few special afferents to taste buds in the epiglottic region. Central branches run to the tractus solitarius and terminate in its nucleus. The visceral afferents of the vagus nerve carry the sensation of abdominal distention and nausea and impulses concerned with regulation of the depth of respiration and the control of blood pressure.

Central Connections

For central connections of the nucleus of the tractus solitarius and nucleus ambiguus, see p 104. For central connections of the nucleus of the spinal tract of the trigeminus, see p 98. The central connections of the **dorsal motor nucleus** of the vagus include reflex neurons from the nucleus of the tractus solitarius and the nucleus of the spinal tract of the trigeminal nerve.

Lesions of the Vagus Nerve

Intramedullary lesions include hemorrhage, thrombosis, tumors, multiple sclerosis, syphilis, syringobulbia, and amyotrophic lateral sclerosis. Basilar disease is caused by spirochetal and other types of meningitis, hemorrhage, tumors, and aneurysms.

Peripheral lesions include primary neuritis (alcoholic, diphtheritic, lead, arsenic), tumors (eg, goiter), adenopathies of the retroparotid space, trauma to the retroparotid space, and aortic aneurysms.

Vagus nerve lesions often involve the glossopharyngeal, accessory, and hypoglossal nerves also.

Diseases & Syndromes Involving the Vagus Nerve (See also p 110.)

A. Complete Bilateral Vagal Paralysis: (Rapidly fatal.) Complete laryngeal paralysis, aphonia and vomiting, dyspnea or pseudoasthma, dilatation and pain in the stomach, cardiac arrhythmia, and death.

B. Unilateral Vagal Paralysis From Peripheral Lesions: Unilateral paralysis of soft palate, unilateral paralysis and anesthesia of pharynx and larynx, hoarseness and nasal speech, dyspnea and dysphagia, paralysis of one vocal cord.

C. Unilateral Vagal Paralysis From Nuclear Lesions: Symptoms of (B), plus contralateral loss of pain and temperature senses from interruption of the spinothalamic tract (see Avellis' syndrome).

D. Unilateral Paralysis of Recurrent Laryngeal Nerve: The voice is weakened. Aortic aneurysms are a frequent cause of left-sided palsies.

E. Unilateral Paralysis of Superior Laryngeal Nerve: (Rare; usually traumatic.) Anesthesia of larynx, hoarseness, voice tires easily.

F. Superior Laryngeal Neuralgia: Pain radiating from the side of the thyroid to the ear.

G. Hysterical Aphonia: From laryngospasm.

Symptoms & Signs Suggestive of Vagus Nerve Involvement

A. Motor Disturbances:

1. Aphonia–Loss of voice (from paralysis of vocal cords or hysteria).

2. Dysphonia–Impairment of voice; may occur with unilateral lesions.

3. Altered position of vocal cords–Examination may reveal objective changes in the position of the vocal cords.

4. Dysphagia–Difficulty in swallowing; may be associated with regurgitation of fluids through the nose, as in pharyngeal and laryngeal spasms (occurs in some hysterias and in rabies).

5. Spasm–Esophageal, cardiac, or pyloric spasm not due to local causes may be of vagal origin.

6. Paralysis of soft palate–With loss of the gag reflex.

B. Sensory Disturbances: Pain or paresthesias in the pharynx, larynx, and external auditory meatus occur with irritative lesions. Anesthesia of the lower pharynx and larynx occurs in complete lesions. Cough is a constant symptom of vagal irritation. Dyspnea and pseudoasthma are due to interruption of the reflex vagal control of respiration. Temporary salivary hypersecretion occurs with irritative lesions, and hyposecretion with palsies.

C. Vegetative (Parasympathetic) Disturbances: Bradycardia with irritative lesions, tachycardia with palsies of the vagus, and dilatation of the stomach.

Tests

(1) Laryngoscopic examination.

(2) Sensory status of pharynx and larynx.

(3) Pharyngeal (gag) reflex.

(4) Oculocardiac reflex: Press over orbit.

(5) Carotid sinus reflex: Press on carotid sinus to produce cardiac slowing.

Cranial Nerve XI:
ACCESSORY
(Motor Nerve)

Two separate branches of cranial nerve XI leave the skull together through the jugular foramen.

Peripheral & Intermediate Connections

A. Internal, or Medullary, Branch: Motor fi-

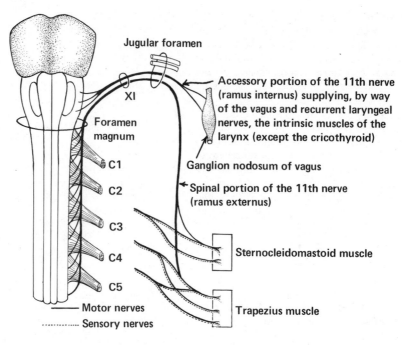

Figure 4-19. The accessory nerve.

bers from the nucleus ambiguus to the intrinsic muscles of the larynx (and possibly a few parasympathetic fibers) join the vagus outside the skull. These have been described with the vagus nerve on p 106.

B. External, or Spinal, Branch: Motor fibers from the lateral part of the anterior horns of the first 5 or 6 cervical cord segments ascend as the spinal root of the accessory nerve through the foramen magnum to leave the skull via the jugular foramen and supply part of the trapezius and sternocleidomastoid muscles.

Central Connections

For the central connections of the internal branch, see p 107. The central connections of the spinal, or external, branch are those of the typical lower motor neuron: voluntary impulses via the corticospinal tracts, postural impulses via the extrapyramidal tracts, reflexes through the vestibulospinal and tectospinal tracts, and intersegmental and intrasegmental arcs.

Lesions That May Affect the Accessory Nerve

Cerebral disorders (certain epilepsies, multiple sclerosis, CNS syphilis, tumors, etc) cause irregular and spasmodic contractions. Nuclear affections are rare and involve other cranial nerve nuclei as well (see p 110). Peripheral palsies may be due to diseases of the base of the skull (meningitis, syphilis, osteitis, etc) or to trauma (bullets, stab wounds, operations on tuberculous nodes, etc). Torticollis (wryneck) is discussed on p 369.

Syndromes Involving the Accessory Nerve (See also p 110.)

Avellis' (X and internal ramus of XI) (nuclear

lesion), Schmidt's (X and XI) and Jackson's (X, XI, and XII) (nuclear or radicular lesions), Vernet's (IX, X, and XI) (peripheral lesion), and Villaret's and Collet's (IX, X, XI, and XII) (peripheral lesion).

Signs of Eleventh Nerve Paralysis

A. Unilateral, From Peripheral Lesions: Cannot rotate head to healthy side; atrophy of sternocleidomastoid and reaction of degeneration; cannot shrug affected shoulder; drooping of affected shoulder; scapula displaced downward; depression of shoulder contour from atrophy of trapezius.

B. Bilateral, From Nuclear or Peripheral Lesion: Difficulty in rotating head or raising chin (sternocleidomastoid muscle). Head drops forward; atrophy of trapezius causes squareness of shoulders.

C. Central Paralysis: Produces similar limitations of movement but no muscle atrophy or reaction of degeneration. The muscles are spastic, and if the lesion is unilateral, torticollis results.

Tests

(1) Ability to shrug shoulders and rotate head against resistance.

(2) Deviation on bending chin downward against resistance indicates paralyzed side.

(3) Objective examination for muscle atrophy, shoulder drop, etc.

(4) Electrical examination of affected nerves and muscles; electromyography, etc.

Cranial Nerve XII:
HYPOGLOSSAL
(Motor Nerve)

Peripheral & Intermediate Connections

Motor fibers from the hypoglossal nucleus in the ventromedian portion of the gray matter of the medulla emerge from the anterolateral sulcus between the pyramid and the olive to form the hypoglossal nerve. The nerve leaves the skull through the hypoglossal canal and passes to the muscles of the tongue.

A few proprioceptive fibers from the tongue probably course in the hypoglossal nerve. With fibers derived from communications with the first cervical nerve, the hypoglossal distributes motor branches to the geniohyoid and infrahyoid muscles and a sensory recurrent meningeal branch to the posterior fossa of the skull.

Central Connections

Central connections of the hypoglossal nucleus include the corticobulbar (crossed), extrapyramidal, and tectobulbar tracts, and reflex neurons from the sensory nuclei of the trigeminal nerve and the nucleus of the tractus solitarius.

Lesions That May Affect the Hypoglossal Nerve

A. Peripheral (Usually From Mechanical Causes): Basal skull fractures, dislocations of upper cervical vertebrae, tuberculosis, aneurysm of the circle of Willis, cerebral syphilis, and lead, alcohol, arsenic, and carbon monoxide poisonings.

B. Nuclear and Supranuclear Lesions: Medullary hemorrhage, poliomyelitis, bulbar paralysis and pseudobulbar palsy, syphilis, tumors, brain abscess, arteriosclerosis, multiple sclerosis, syringobulbia, and amyotrophic lateral sclerosis (bulbar form). Psy-

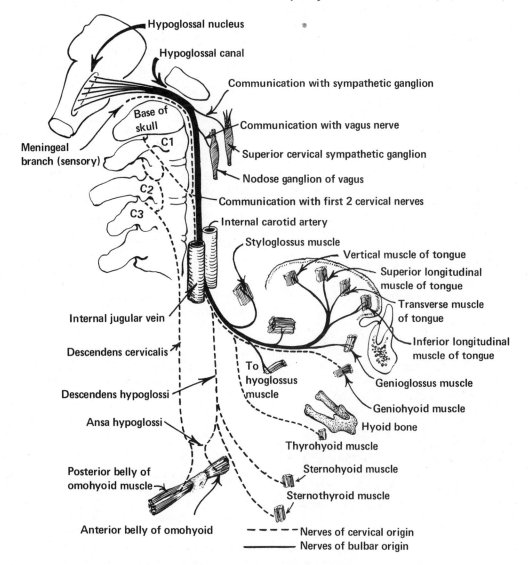

Figure 4–20. The hypoglossal nerve.

chogenic disturbances (eg, hysterical paralysis, stammering, and tics) must be differentiated.

Syndromes Involving the Hypoglossal Nerve

Syndromes involving the hypoglossal nerve include (see below and p 111) Jackson's (X, XI, and XII) (nuclear or radicular lesions), Tapia's (X and XII) (nuclear or radicular lesions), and Villaret's and Collet's (IX, X, XI, and XII) (peripheral lesion); and hypoglossal hemiplegia alternans, a bulbar lesion involving the pyramid near the decussation and hypoglossal roots near their point of emergence and causing contralateral hemiplegia and ipsilateral paralysis of the tongue.

Symptoms & Signs of Hypoglossal Nerve Involvement

A. Supranuclear (Spastic Paralysis): Contralateral hemiplegia and paralysis of tongue; no atrophy or fibrillation of tongue. On protrusion, the tongue deviates to the side opposite the lesion.

B. Peripheral (Flaccid Paralysis): Reaction of degeneration, ipsilateral paralysis of the tongue, atrophy on the side of the lesion. On protrusion, the tongue deviates to the side of the lesion (Fig 4–21). Fasciculations of the tongue may be present.

C. Nuclear or Medullary Lesion (Flaccid Paralysis): Signs of peripheral involvement are present in addition to the following:

1. Fasciculation accompanies or precedes atrophy. Other nerves and structures are affected also.

2. Sensory disturbances are apparent, eg, loss of deep sensation or of pain and temperature sense of half of the face or body, or bilaterally in midline lesions.

3. If lesion is bilateral, the tongue is completely paralyzed, and dysphagia, dysarthria, and difficulty in chewing food occur.

D. Cortical Lesions: May cause dysarthria and ataxia of the tongue.

E. Striatum Lesions: Striatum lesions (eg, chorea) cause irregular arrhythmic movements of the tongue.

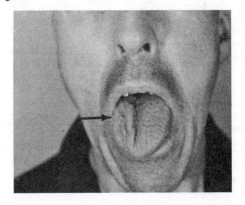

Figure 4–21. Right hypoglossal paralysis. Atrophy of the right side of the tongue and deviation of the tongue to the right following surgical section of the right hypoglossal nerve.

F. Psychogenic: Psychogenic disturbances include tongue tics, stammering, stuttering, and lisping. Hysterical paralysis shows resistance to passive movement and no reaction of degeneration or atrophy.

Tests

(1) Strength of the tongue is tested by having the patient push the tip of the tongue against the cheek on each side against the resistance of the examiner's finger.

(2) Note the deviation of the tongue on protrusion.

(3) Note atrophy or tremors of the tongue.

(4) Electrical examination of the tongue muscles may be performed.

SYNDROMES DUE TO LESIONS OF THE LAST FOUR CRANIAL NERVES

Bulbar & Radicular Syndromes

Lesions of the medulla oblongata (bulb) produce characteristic symptoms which are referable to involvement of the motor and sensory pathways passing through the bulb and particularly to the involvement of the nuclei of the last 4 cranial nerves which lie within it. Lesions of the posterior fossa (tumors, syphilis, inflammations) may involve the roots of the last 4 cranial nerves between their emergence from the medulla and their exit from the skull. (See Fig 1–36.)

A. Avellis' Syndrome (X and Bulbar XI): Caused by a lesion of the nucleus ambiguus, tractus solitarius, and the adjacent spinothalamic tract, thus affecting the vagus, the internal branch of the accessory nerve, and the ascending sensory tracts:

1. Ipsilateral paralysis of the soft palate, pharynx, and larynx, with dysarthria, dysphagia, and anesthesia of the pharynx and larynx (X and bulbar portion of XI).

2. Contralateral dissociate hemianesthesia, with loss of pain and temperature sense but not of the touch and pressure senses (spinothalamic tract).

B. Schmidt's Syndrome (X and all of XI): From a lesion of the vagal nuclei and both bulbar and spinal nuclei of the accessory or their radicular fibers:

1. Ipsilateral paralysis of the soft palate, pharynx, and larynx, with anesthesia of the pharynx and larynx (X and bulbar portion of XI).

2. Ipsilateral sternocleidomastoid muscle paralysis and, at times, paralysis of part of the trapezius muscle, resulting in inability to rotate the head to the side opposite the lesion and inability to shrug the shoulder (spinal portion of XI).

C. Jackson's Syndrome (X, XI, and XII): Produced by a nuclear or radicular lesion of the vagus, accessory, and hypoglossal nerves:

1. Ipsilateral paralysis of the soft palate, pharynx, and larynx (X).

2. Ipsilateral paralysis of the sternocleidomastoid and trapezius muscles (XI).

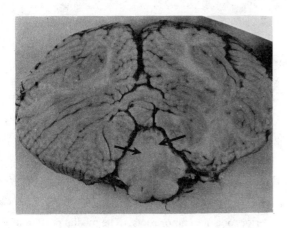

Figure 4–22. Astrocytoma of medulla.

3. Ipsilateral paralysis and atrophy of the tongue (XII). (See Fig 1–36.)

D. Tapia's Syndrome (X and XII): Produced by a lesion affecting the motor nuclei or rootlets of the vagus and hypoglossal nerves:

1. Ipsilateral paralysis of the pharynx and larynx (X).

2. Ipsilateral paralysis and atrophy of the tongue (XII).

E. Babinski-Nageotte Bulbar Syndrome (IX, X, Bulbar Portion of XI, and Part of V): Produced by scattered lesions of the nucleus ambiguus, tractus solitarius, spinal tract of V, hypoglossal nucleus, restiform body, and reticular formation:

1. Ipsilateral paralysis of the tongue, pharynx, and larynx.

2. Ipsilateral loss of taste on the posterior third of the tongue.

3. Ipsilateral Horner's syndrome (miosis, ptosis, and enophthalmos).

4. Ipsilateral loss of pain and temperature sense on the face.

5. Ipsilateral asynergia and ataxia and a tendency to fall to the side of the lesion.

6. Contralateral hemiplegia (of arm and leg) with contralateral dissociate hemianesthesia (loss of pain and temperature sense).

F. Syndrome of Thrombosis of the Posterior Inferior Cerebellar Artery (Wallenberg's Syndrome): Resembles that of Babinski-Nageotte but without the hemiplegia. (See Fig 1–36.)

G. Cestan-Chenais Syndrome: (Thrombosis of the vertebral artery before it gives off the posterior inferior cerebellar and anterior spinal branches.) Structures involved include the restiform body, spinothalamic tract, sympathetics, nuclei of X and XI, descending tract of V, and sometimes the pyramid; the corresponding symptoms are extensive and variable.

H. Bonnier's Syndrome (VIII, IX, and X): From a lesion of the lateral vestibular (Deiters') nucleus and adjacent pathways:

1. Symptoms of Meniere's disease (paroxysmal vertigo).

2. Symptoms of involvement of IX, X, and sometimes III and V.

3. Contralateral hemiplegia.

4. Somnolence at times.

5. Apprehension, tachycardia, and weakness.

I. Hypoglossal Hemiplegia Alternans (XII): From a lesion of the pyramid near the decussation involving the emerging hypoglossal roots:

1. Contralateral hemiplegia.

2. Ipsilateral paralysis of the tongue. (See Fig 1–36.)

Syndromes Caused by Peripheral Lesions

During World Wars I and II, many cases of lesions of the last 4 cranial nerves were reported. Because of the proximity of the last 4 cranial nerves to each other, many combined lesions were found:

A. Vernet's Syndrome (of the Jugular Foramen), Involving IX, X, and XI: Usually the result of a basilar skull fracture involving the jugular foramen:

1. Ipsilateral glossopharyngeal paralysis.

2. Ipsilateral vagus paralysis.

3. Ipsilateral accessory paralysis.

B. Villaret's, Collet's, or Sicard's Syndrome (of Retroparotid Space Injury): Ipsilateral paralysis of the last 4 cranial nerves. (Villaret's case also involved the sympathetics, thus adding Horner's syndrome.)

5 | The Spinal Nerves

The spinal nerves consist of 31 symmetrically arranged pairs, each derived from the spinal cord by 2 roots: a sensory (dorsal) root and a motor (ventral) root. They are divided topographically into 8 cervical pairs (C1–8), 12 thoracic (T1–12), 5 lumbar (L1–5), 5 sacral (S1–5), and one coccygeal (C).

Each nerve contains several kinds of fibers. **Motor fibers** originate in large cells in the anterior gray column of the spinal cord. These form the ventral root and pass to the skeletal muscles. **Sensory fibers** originate in unipolar cells in the spinal ganglia that are interposed in the course of the dorsal roots. Peripheral branches of these ganglion cells are distributed to both visceral and somatic structures as mediators of sensory impulses to the CNS. The central branches convey these impulses through dorsal roots into the dorsal gray column and the ascending tracts of the spinal cord. **Sympathetic fibers** from the thoracic and lumbar cord segments are distributed throughout the body to the viscera, blood vessels, glands, and smooth muscle. **Parasympathetic fibers,** which are present in the middle 3 sacral nerves, pass to the pelvic and lower abdominal viscera. (For details on sympathetic and parasympathetic distribution, see Figs 6–1 and 6–2 and p 140.)

Spinal Nerve Roots

The Bell-Magendie law states that the posterior (sensory) roots convey impulses to the CNS. (The anterior roots are motor roots.) The medial portion of the posterior roots consists of thick myelinated fibers; the lateral part consists mostly of unmyelinated and small myelinated fibers. Cathode ray oscillographic studies have made possible a classification into 3 groups of fibers, as follows: **A group** (myelinated) fibers are largest and convey impulses most rapidly. **B group** fibers are next largest and consist of the smaller myelinated fibers. **C group** fibers are smallest and convey impulses most slowly (Table 2–3). These fibers are mostly unmyelinated fibers carrying pain.

The **central connections** of motor and sensory roots of spinal nerves are diagrammed in Chapters 8 and 10.

Branches of Typical Spinal Nerves

The **posterior primary** divisions usually consist of a medial branch, which is in most instances largely sensory, and a lateral branch, which is mainly motor. **Anterior primary** divisions are usually larger than the posterior primary divisions. They form the cervical, brachial, and lumbosacral plexuses. In the thoracic

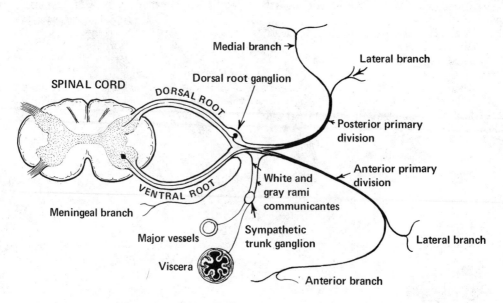

Figure 5–1. Schematic illustration of a typical spinal nerve.

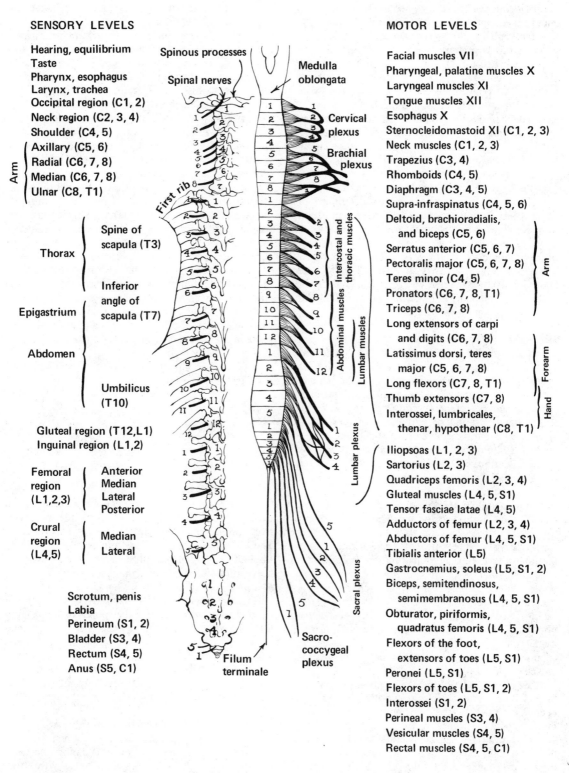

SENSORY LEVELS

Hearing, equilibrium
Taste
Pharynx, esophagus
Larynx, trachea
Occipital region (C1, 2)
Neck region (C2, 3, 4)
Shoulder (C4, 5)

Arm
{
Axillary (C5, 6)
Radial (C6, 7, 8)
Median (C6, 7, 8)
Ulnar (C8, T1)
}

Thorax — Spine of scapula (T3)

Epigastrium — Inferior angle of scapula (T7)

Abdomen

Umbilicus (T10)

Gluteal region (T12, L1)
Inguinal region (L1, 2)

Femoral region (L1, 2, 3) — Anterior Median Lateral Posterior

Crural region (L4, 5) — Median Lateral

Scrotum, penis
Labia
Perineum (S1, 2)
Bladder (S3, 4)
Rectum (S4, 5)
Anus (S5, C1)

Spinous processes
Spinal nerves
First rib
Medulla oblongata
Cervical plexus
Brachial plexus
Intercostal and thoracic muscles
Abdominal muscles
Lumbar muscles
Lumbar plexus
Sacral plexus
Filum terminale
Sacro-coccygeal plexus

MOTOR LEVELS

Facial muscles VII
Pharyngeal, palatine muscles X
Laryngeal muscles XI
Tongue muscles XII
Esophagus X
Sternocleidomastoid XI (C1, 2, 3)
Neck muscles (C1, 2, 3)
Trapezius (C3, 4)
Rhomboids (C4, 5)
Diaphragm (C3, 4, 5)
Supra-infraspinatus (C4, 5, 6)
Deltoid, brachioradialis, and biceps (C5, 6)
Serratus anterior (C5, 6, 7)
Pectoralis major (C5, 6, 7, 8)
Teres minor (C4, 5)
Pronators (C6, 7, 8, T1)
Triceps (C6, 7, 8)
Long extensors of carpi and digits (C6, 7, 8)
Latissimus dorsi, teres major (C5, 6, 7, 8)
Long flexors (C7, 8, T1)
Thumb extensors (C7, 8)
Interossei, lumbricales, thenar, hypothenar (C8, T1)

Arm
Forearm
Hand

Iliopsoas (L1, 2, 3)
Sartorius (L2, 3)
Quadriceps femoris (L2, 3, 4)
Gluteal muscles (L4, 5, S1)
Tensor fasciae latae (L4, 5)
Adductors of femur (L2, 3, 4)
Abductors of femur (L4, 5, S1)
Tibialis anterior (L5)
Gastrocnemius, soleus (L5, S1, 2)
Biceps, semitendinosus, semimembranosus (L4, 5, S1)
Obturator, piriformis, quadratus femoris (L4, 5, S1)
Flexors of the foot, extensors of toes (L5, S1)
Peronei (L5, S1)
Flexors of toes (L5, S1, 2)
Interossei (S1, 2)
Perineal muscles (S3, 4)
Vesicular muscles (S4, 5)
Rectal muscles (S4, 5, C1)

Figure 5–2. Motor and sensory levels of the spinal cord.

region they remain segmental, as intercostal nerves, dividing into the lateral cutaneous branch (sensory) and a mixed anterior branch. **Rami communicantes** join the spinal nerves to the sympathetic trunk. The white ramus is present only in the thoracic and upper lumbar nerves. The gray ramus is present in all spinal nerves. **Meningeal, or recurrent meningeal,** branches are quite small, carrying sensory and vasomotor innervation to the spinal meninges.

The distribution and clinical aspects of the various spinal nerves are presented in detail on the following pages. Segmental and peripheral cutaneous distribution is diagrammed in Figs 11–1 to 11–5.

Lesions of the Spinal Nerves

The spinal nerves are subject to the various types of disorders outlined for peripheral nerves in general on p 83. Traumatic lesions, however, constitute the majority of peripheral nerve lesions. Most of the cases in the literature are from war records. The 1020 cases of peripheral nerve injuries compiled by Pollock and Davis included 165 radial, 160 sciatic, 136 ulnar, 120 peroneal, 93 median, 71 brachial plexus, and 58 combined median and ulnar nerve lesions.

Diagnosis of Peripheral Nerve Lesions

The diagnosis of peripheral nerve lesions depends upon a careful history and physical examination. The examination should be performed with the patient's clothes removed and should take particular note of the site of the injury, obvious deformities, gait, etc. Post-surgical regeneration of peripheral nerves may be aided by wrapping the area of nerve sutured in Millipore or Silastic.

A. Motion: Motion is studied to determine muscle weakness or paralysis. The physician should observe active (voluntary) movements, taking care to rule out modifying factors such as pain, swelling, fractures, dislocations, adhesions, ankylosis, and contractures. Passive movements may be reserved for further study of the range of motion where active motion seems to be abnormally limited. Posture of the limb is important, eg, wristdrop, footdrop, clawhand, or ape hand. Supplementary or trick movements should be sought, since they may mask a true paralysis. Joint changes and contractures must be noted as possible factors in limitations of motion. Careful dynamometric examination will demonstrate the distribution and degree of weakness in involvement of the muscles of the fingers.

B. Muscle Atrophy: Muscle atrophy and loss of tone of the affected muscles occur after the nerve has been interrupted, and they are often an obvious sign of the distribution of the disorder.

C. Subjective Sensory Changes: Pain, hyperesthesia, paresthesias, etc are uncommon after nerve injuries except in partial lesions. **Causalgia,** however, may occur with incomplete median, sciatic, or tibial nerve injuries, although it may not appear until several weeks after the injury. It is characterized by severe pain in the affected part, brought on by the slightest

exposure or jarring, and may be partially relieved by wet compresses. Trophic skin and nail changes are usually associated with it.

D. Objective Sensory Disturbances: The degree and distribution of pain, temperature sense, deep touch and pressure, vibration, and joint sense can be evaluated with the aid of an esthesiometer or algesimeter. The patient's cooperation must be obtained. Nerve overlap must be kept in mind in evaluating sensory loss.

E. Vasomotor, Trophic, and Secretory Disturbances: Cyanosis, swelling, edema, discoloration, hypertrichosis or hypotrichosis, nail changes, trophic ulcers, etc, should be noted.

F. Electrical Examination: Stimulation of the affected muscles at their respective motor points with electrical currents may serve as an aid in diagnosis and prognosis of nerve injury. The electrical resistance of denervated skin is usually higher than that of the surrounding normal skin because of the absence of the normal skin fluids and electrolytes. An accurate assay of functional status may be made with stimulation studies using needle electrodes placed directly in nerves or branches of nerves. Electromyographic studies of affected muscles may be of assistance in evaluating their functional status (see Chapter 17).

G. Reflex Changes: These are specifically related to the nerve injured.

THE CERVICAL NERVES
(See Fig 5–4.)

The 8 pairs of cervical nerves are derived from cord segments between the level of the foramen magnum and the middle of the seventh cervical vertebra. The cervical nerves emerge from the spinal column through laterally placed intervertebral foramens. Each nerve joins with a gray communicating ramus from the sympathetic trunk (through which it receives vasomotor fibers). It also sends a small recurrent meningeal branch back into the spinal canal to supply the dura with sensory and vasomotor innervation and branches into anterior and posterior primary divisions, which are mixed nerves that pass to their respective peripheral distributions. The motor branches carry a few sensory fibers that convey proprioceptive impulses from the neck muscles.

Posterior Primary Divisions (See Table 5–1.)

C1 (suboccipital nerve) is the only branch of the first posterior primary division; it is a motor nerve to the muscles of the suboccipital triangle, with a few sensory fibers.

Anterior Primary Divisions

The anterior primary divisions of the first 4 cervical nerves collectively form the cervical plexus. Those of the second 4 together with the first thoracic nerve form the brachial plexus.

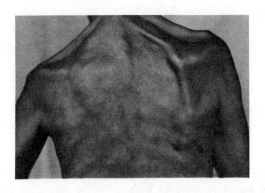

Figure 5–3. Atrophy of shoulder and neck muscles secondary to neurinomas of the cervical nerves in a 51-year-old man with Recklinghausen's disease.

THE CERVICAL PLEXUS
(C1–4)
(See Fig 5–4.)

Sensory Branches

The **small occipital nerve** (C2, 3) supplies the skin of the lateral occipital portion of the scalp, the upper median part of the auricle, and the area over the mastoid process. The **great auricular nerve** (C2, 3)

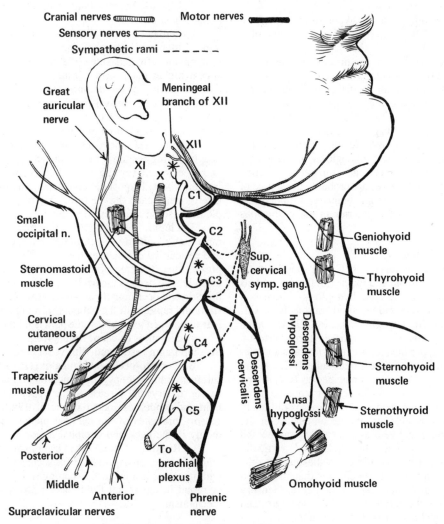

Figure 5–4. The cervical plexus.

Table 5–1. Course of the posterior primary divisions of C2–8.

Medial Branches	Lateral Branches
C2: Great occipital nerve. Sensory to the occipital portions of the scalp and neck.	**C2:** Motor twigs to the obliquus capitis inferior, splenius, and longissimus capitis muscles.
C3: Third occipital nerve. Sensory to a small portion of the scalp and neck.	**C3:** Motor twig to the semispinalis capitis muscle.
C4, 5: Sensory to skin of back of neck.	**C4–8:** Motor to the longissimus capitis and cervicis, semispinalis capitis and cervicis, and iliocostalis cervicis muscles.
C6–8: Motor to the multifidi and adjacent muscles.	

supplies the skin of the back of the ear and the area over the mastoid process and parotid gland. The cervical cutaneous nerve (cutaneus colli) (C2, 3) supplies the skin over the anterior portion of the neck. Supraclavicular branches (C3, 4) supply the skin over the clavicle and the upper deltoid and pectoral regions as low as the third rib.

Communicating Branches

Communication with the hypoglossal nerve from C1, 2 carries motor fibers to the geniohyoid and thyrohyoid muscles and to the sternohyoid and sternothyroid muscles by way of the descendens hypoglossi; and sensory fibers are carried to the dura of the posterior fossa of the skull via the recurrent meningeal branch of the hypoglossal nerve. The communication with the vagus nerve from C1 is of undetermined function, although the vagus occasionally distributes fibers to the infrahyoid muscles that are usually distributed by the descendens hypoglossi. Communications from the superior cervical sympathetic ganglion to the first 4 cervical nerves are probably the source of vasomotor fibers. (These are branches to the spinal nerves rather than to the anterior primary divisions alone.)

Muscular Branches

The descendens cervicalis (C2, 3) supplies the 2 bellies of the omohyoid and joins with the descendens hypoglossi to form the ansa hypoglossi. There is a branch to the sternocleidomastoid muscle from C2, and branches to the trapezius muscles (C3, 4) via the subtrapezial plexus. Twigs to the adjacent vertebral musculature supply the rectus capitis lateralis and rectus capitis anterior (C1), the longus capitis (C2, 4) and longus colli (C1–4), the scalenus medius (C3, 4) and scalenus anterior (C4), and the levator scapulae (from C3–5). The **phrenic nerve** (C3–5) passes obliquely over the scalenus anterior muscle and between the subclavian artery and vein to enter the thorax behind the sternoclavicular joint, where it descends vertically through the superior and middle mediastinum to the diaphragm. Motor branches supply the diaphragm and constitute the principal respiratory nerve. Sensory branches supply the pericardium, the diaphragm, and part of the costal and mediastinal pleurae.

Lesions of the First Four Cervical Nerves

Meningitis or high cord tumors may cause cervico-occipital neuralgia. Peripheral lesions are rare in the cervical region because of the protection afforded by surrounding muscles. They occasionally occur in deep wounds, operative trauma, fractures, dislocations, infections, multiple neuritis, and other diseases of the cervical vertebrae.

Clinical Features of Upper Cervical Lesions

A. Phrenic Involvement: The most important of cervical lesions.

1. Unilateral paralysis causes few or no symptoms. Litten's (diaphragm) phenomenon may be absent on the affected side. The liver or spleen may appear higher than normal. Fluoroscopy shows relative immobility of the diaphragm on one side.

2. Bilateral paralysis is characterized by dyspnea upon the slightest exertion; a scaphoid abdomen not protruded on expiration; overactivity of accessory respiratory muscles, the chest and shoulders heaving deeply during respiration; and difficulty in coughing and sneezing. X-ray shows the diaphragm drawn high into the chest. Hypostatic congestion and pneumonia often complicate the picture. (Diaphragmatic and pleural disease must be ruled out.)

3. Phrenic neuralgia (diaphragmatic neuralgia; rare) may result from neck tumors, aortic aneurysm, and pericardial or other mediastinal affections. Pain is present near the free border of the ribs, beneath the clavicle, and deep in the neck; it may extend as high as the chin and occasionally down the arm. Respiration is short and rapid, as if the patient is afraid to breathe for fear of pain. In most cases, the pain is on the left side.

4. Singultus (hiccup) results from brief spasm of the diaphragm associated with vocal cord adduction.

B. Cervico-occipital Neuralgia (Rare): May result from traumatic, psychogenic, infectious, neoplastic, or aneurysmal disease of the upper neck region. Pain and tenderness occur in the distribution of the sensory branches of the cervical plexus, most commonly in the neck and occipital regions.

C. Rigidity of the Neck: Occurs with neuralgia, other neck lesions, posterior fossa masses, and also with irritative lesions of the meninges, eg, meningitis or blood in the spinal fluid. It is a protective reflex mechanism.

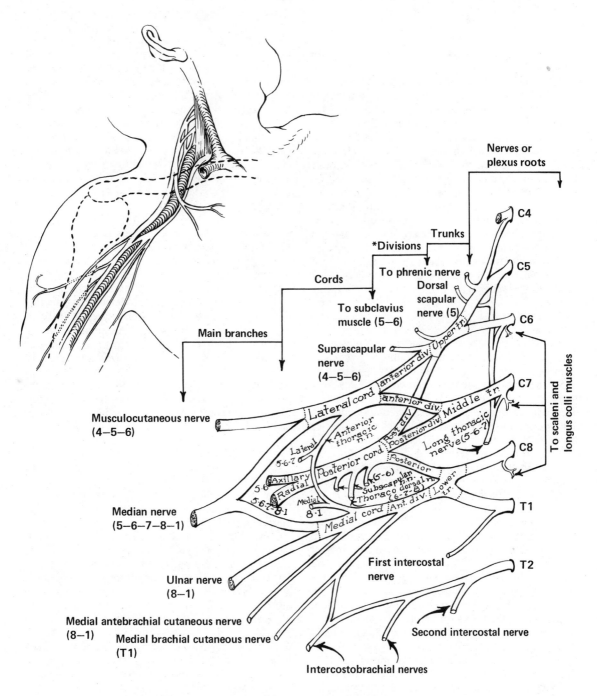

*Splitting of the plexus into anterior and posterior divisions is one of the most significant features in the redistribution of nerve fibers, since it is here that fibers supplying the flexor and extensor groups of muscles of the upper extremity are separated. Similar splitting is noted in the lumbar and sacral plexuses for the supply of muscles of the lower extremity.

Figure 5–5. The brachial plexus (formed from the anterior primary divisions of C5–8 and T1, 2)

THE BRACHIAL PLEXUS
(See Figs 5–5 and 5–6.)

The brachial plexus is formed by the anterior primary divisions of the last 4 cervical and the first thoracic nerves. The roots of the plexus consist of C5 and C6, which unite to form the upper trunk; C7, which becomes the middle trunk; and C8 and T1, which unite to form the lower trunk. Each of the 3 trunks divides into anterior and posterior divisions. The anterior divisions of the upper and middle trunk form the lateral cord; the anterior division of the lower trunk forms the medial cord; and all 3 posterior divisions unite to form the posterior cord. The 3 cords (named for their relationship to the axillary artery) split to form the main branches of the plexus: branches from the medial and lateral cords form the **median nerve;** the remainder of the lateral cord becomes the **musculocutaneous nerve;** the remainder of the medial cord becomes the **ulnar nerve;** and the posterior cord splits to become the **radial** and **axillary nerves.**

Numerous smaller nerves arise from various parts of the plexus:

(1) Branches from the roots of the plexus: A twig passes to the phrenic nerve from C5. The posterior thoracic nerves consist of the dorsal scapular nerve (C5), motor to the rhomboid muscles, and the long thoracic nerve (of Bell) (C5–7), which descends by a deep course to supply the serratus anterior muscle. Twigs extend to the scaleni and longus colli muscles from C6–8. The first intercostal nerve extends from T1 (see under Thoracic Nerves).

(2) Branches from the trunks: A nerve extends to the subclavius muscle (C5–6) from the upper trunk or fifth root. The suprascapular nerve (C5–6) arises from the upper trunk or its anterior division and supplies the supraspinatus and infraspinatus muscles.

(3) Branches from the cords: The medial and lateral anterior thoracic nerves extend from the medial (C8, T1) and lateral (C5–7) cords, respectively, and are usually united by a loop. They supply the pectoralis major and pectoralis minor muscles.

The 3 subscapular nerves from the posterior cord consist of (1) the upper (or short) subscapular nerve (C5, 6) to the subscapularis muscle; (2) the middle (long) subscapular or thoracodorsal nerve (C7, 8), which innervates the latissimus dorsi muscle; and (3) the lower subscapular nerve (C5, 6) to the teres major and part of the subscapularis muscle. Sensory branches of the medial cord (C8, T1) comprise the medial antebrachial cutaneous nerve to the medial surface of the forearm and the medial brachial cutaneous nerve to the medial surface of the arm.

Lesions of the Brachial Plexus & Its Nerves

Spinal cord lesions may involve these nerves also, as in traumatic lesions of the lower cervical spine area. Peripheral lesions are more common in wartime but are not infrequently seen in civilian practice. Peripheral nerve injury may follow violent pulling or wrenching of the arms; blows to or weight upon the neck; operative trauma in the neck or axilla; or childbirth injuries (from pulling on or compressing nerves); gunshot wounds, stab wounds, automobile accidents, etc; fractures and dislocations of the neck, shoulder, or neck of the humerus; tumors of the neck and aneurysms of the subclavian artery; infectious, toxic, and multiple neuritis; the scalenus anticus syndrome, cervical rib (a congenital anomaly), and certain sleeping postures ("neurovascular syndrome" or "hyperabduction syndrome"). Bikeles' sign (of brachial plexus neuritis or meningitis) may be present, ie, extension at the elbow when the arm is upward and backward meets with resistance because of the stretch put on the brachial plexus.

Classification of Brachial Plexus Injuries

Attempts have been made to classify the numerous possible types of brachial plexus injuries as radicular, trunk, and cord lesions; upper, middle, and lower types; incomplete and complete types; supraclavicular and infraclavicular lesions, etc. Meige's diagram (Fig 5–6) illustrates some of the difficulties of these attempts at classification. Meige's technique is to systematically test the muscles by electrical stimulation and record the results opposite their names on the chart—"W" for weak and "P" for paralyzed muscles. The lesion can be localized by noting in the plexus the point where the fibers to the affected muscles are most concentrated. The distribution of sensory and trophic disturbances is also considered.

Symptoms & Signs of Brachial Plexus Injuries

Brachial plexus injuries are most commonly seen in children and are usually caused by birth injuries. There are 2 classic types: the upper plexus type (Erb-Duchenne paralysis) and the less common lower plexus type (Klumpke's paralysis).

A. Upper Plexus Type (Erb-Duchenne): This is the most common type. It is caused by compression or tearing of the fifth and sixth plexus roots or upper trunk. There is paralysis and atrophy of the deltoid, biceps, brachialis, and brachioradialis muscles, with loss of abduction and external rotation of the arm and weak forearm flexion and supination. The arm and hand assume the "waiter's tip" position. The supraspinatus, infraspinatus, subscapularis, serratus, and rhomboid muscles are occasionally affected (see below). Sensation is lost over the deltoid and radial surfaces of the forearm and hand.

B. Lower Plexus Type (Klumpke): This may result from injury to the eighth cervical and first thoracic plexus roots or lower trunk. Compression of the lower plexus roots or trunk by a cervical rib may be responsible for a lower plexus type of palsy. Prognosis of this type is more favorable. Klumpke's paralysis is characterized by paralysis and atrophy of the small hand muscles and flexors of the wrist ("clawhand") and an ulnar type of sensory loss (see p 127), edema of the skin, cyanosis, and perhaps trophic nail changes. It

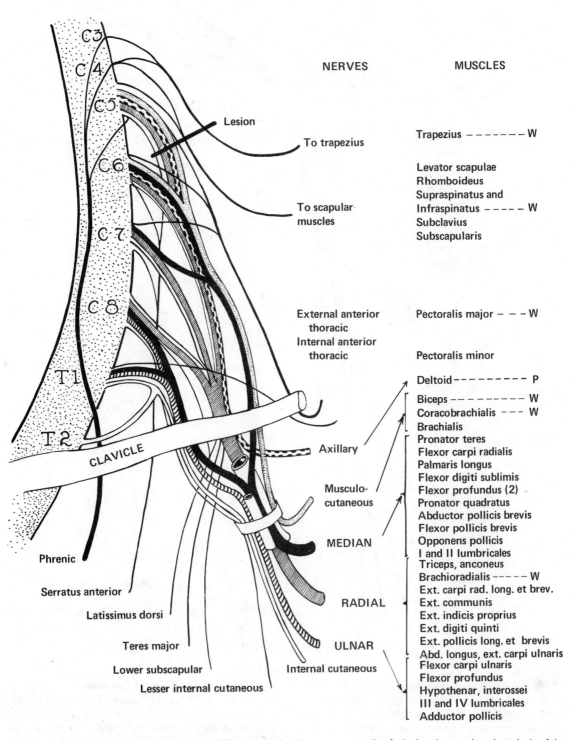

Figure 5—6. The brachial plexus (after Meige). The illustration shows an example of a lesion that produced paralysis of the deltoid and weakness in the supraspinatus and infraspinatus, trapezius, pectoral, biceps, coracobrachialis, and brachioradialis muscles.

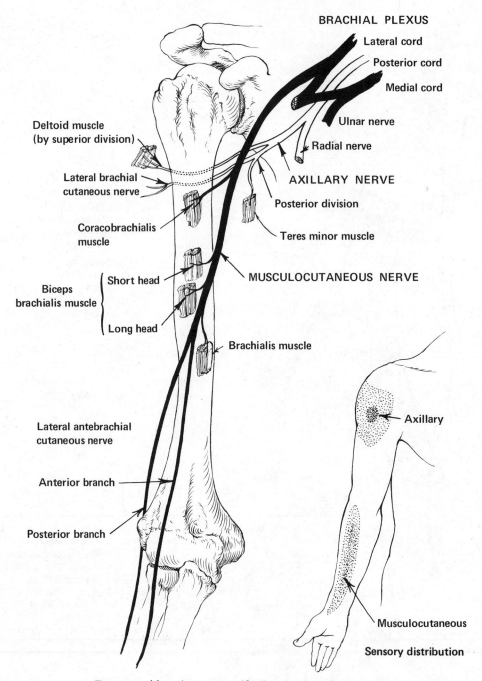

Figure 5–7. Musculocutaneous (C5,6) and axillary (C5,6) nerves.

may also cause **Horner's syndrome** (when the sympathetic rami of T1 are involved): ipsilateral miosis, narrowed palpebral fissure, enophthalmos, absence of sweating, and increased temperature over the face and neck.

C. Middle Plexus Type: Involvement of the middle trunk (C7), although rarely seen by itself, is occasionally associated with one of the above types. Symptoms are triceps paralysis and weakening of the extensors of the wrist and fingers.

Signs According to Nerves Involved

A. Long Thoracic Nerve (C5–7): Although rarely injured alone, it may be involved in supraclavicular and axillary wounds, neck blows, or injuries resulting from carrying weights on the shoulders. Paralysis of the serratus anterior (magnus) causes "winging" of the scapula when the arm is extended and pressed against a fixed object in front of the patient (Fig 5–8). There is difficulty in raising the arm above the horizontal.

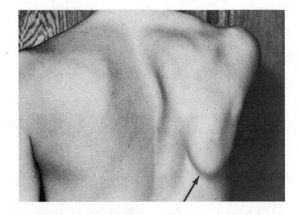

Figure 5–8. Long thoracic nerve paralysis. Winging of right scapula after trauma to right long thoracic nerve.

B. Suprascapular Nerve (C5, 6): Isolated paralysis is rare but may occur as a result of carrying heavy weights on the shoulder, severe blows, etc. Symptoms are paralysis of the supraspinatus and infraspinatus muscles, with loss of fixation at the head of the humerus (subluxation), causing difficulty in lifting heavy weights. Atrophy occurs above and below the spine of the scapula.

C. Dorsal Scapular Nerve (C5, 6): Injury results in paralysis of the rhomboids; the scapula becomes slightly winged and cannot be drawn close to the vertebral column.

D. Thoracodorsal Nerve (C7, 8): Injury results in paralysis and atrophy of the latissimus dorsi. Adduction and internal rotation of the arm are weakened.

E. Anterior Thoracic Nerves (C5–8, T1): These nerves are rarely involved alone; lesions result in atrophy of the pectoralis muscles, apparent below the clavicle and in the anterior axillary fold. Adduction power of the upper arm is lost, and the patient is unable to touch the opposite shoulder.

F. Medial Brachial and Antebrachial Cutaneous Nerves (C8, T1): Although injury of these nerves is unimportant, pain in their distribution and in that of the ulnar nerve, particularly on the left side, is often indicative of cardiac disease.

Tests

A. Motor Status: Limitations of movement, electromyography, electrical stimulation of muscles at their motor points, reflexes, and reaction of degeneration. These are all helpful in determining the prognosis.

B. Sensory Status: Pain, tenderness, hyperesthesias; loss of pain, touch, heat and cold, vibration, and temperature senses.

C. Trophic Changes: Muscle atrophy, nail changes, etc.

THE MUSCULOCUTANEOUS NERVE
(C5, 6)
(See Fig 5–7.)

The musculocutaneous nerve arises from the lateral cord of the brachial plexus and is composed of fibers from the fifth and sixth cervical segments. At first lying lateral to the axillary artery, it pierces the coracobrachialis muscle and descends obliquely and laterally between the biceps and brachialis muscles. It terminates as the lateral antebrachial cutaneous nerve, which divides into anterior and posterior branches.

Motor branches supply the coracobrachialis, biceps, and brachialis muscles. The **sensory terminal branch** supplies the anterolateral surface of the forearm.

The musculocutaneous nerve is rarely affected alone, but it may be involved in spinal cord or brachial plexus lesions, fractures of the humerus, aneurysms of the axillary artery, bullet wounds, stab wounds, etc. It may be injured by pressure on the arm during sleep. Musculocutaneous neuritis (toxic, diabetic, infectious, etc) is rare.

The clinical features of musculocutaneous involvement include paralysis of the coracobrachialis, biceps, and brachialis muscles, causing inability to flex the forearm when it is supinated; weakened supination; loss of biceps jerk; muscle atrophy; reaction of degeneration (in complete peripheral lesions); and loss of sensation to the anterolateral surface of the forearm.

THE AXILLARY (CIRCUMFLEX) NERVE
(C5, 6)
(See Fig 5–7.)

The axillary nerve is derived from the posterior cord of the brachial plexus and is composed of fibers from the fifth and sixth cervical segments. Passing dorsally, it accompanies the posterior circumflex artery around the neck of the humerus and through the quadrilateral space, dividing into a small superior and a larger inferior division. **Motor branches** supply the deltoid (from the superior division) and teres minor (from the inferior division) muscles. **Sensory branches,** mainly from the inferior division, supply the skin over the lower portion of the deltoid muscle.

The axillary nerve is rarely affected alone, but it may be involved in spinal cord and brachial plexus lesions; fractures and dislocations of the head of the humerus; violent blows on the shoulder; bullet, stab, and other wounds; pressure or stretching of the shoulder during sleep or anesthesia; and, rarely, tumors. Axillary neuritis (toxic, diabetic, infectious, etc) is rare. Isolated paralysis occasionally occurs with carbon monoxide poisoning, malaria, and infections.

Deltoid paralysis causes inability to protract or retract the arm or raise it to the horizontal position.

After some time, supplementary movements may partially take over these functions. Teres minor paralysis causes weakness of external rotation. Atrophy of affected muscles occurs in severe or complete peripheral lesions. Sensation is lost over the deltoid prominence. Pain is present in neuritis.

THE RADIAL (MUSCULOSPIRAL) NERVE
(C6–8 and T1)
(See Fig 5–9.)

The radial nerve is the largest branch of the brachial plexus. It begins at the lower border of the pectoralis minor as the direct continuation of the posterior cord and derives fibers from the last 3 cervical and first thoracic segments of the spinal cord. During its descent in the arm, it accompanies the profunda artery behind and around the humerus and in the musculospiral groove. It pierces the lateral intermuscular septum and reaches the lower anterior side of the forearm, where its terminal branches arise.

Motor branches in the arm supply the triceps, anconeus, and the upper portion of the extensor-supinator group of forearm muscles. Motor branches in the forearm supplied by the deep radial nerve pass to the rest of the extensor-supinator group of muscles. **Sensory branches** supplying innervation to skin areas include the posterior brachial cutaneous nerve, to the dorsal aspect of the arm; the posterior antebrachial cutaneous nerve, to the dorsal surface of the forearm; and the superficial radial nerve, to the dorsal aspect of the radial half of the hand. The isolated area of supply is a small patch of skin over the dorsum of the first interosseous space.

Lesions Affecting the Radial Nerve
The radial nerve is the most commonly injured peripheral nerve. It may be involved in cervical cord and brachial plexus lesions. Peripheral injuries may affect the trunk or some of the branches of the nerve, as in dislocations of the shoulder; fractures of the humerus; callus formation around a fracture; pressure incurred from a crutch or during sleep, anesthesia, or drunkenness ("Saturday night palsy"); violent blows on the arm; tuberculosis of the bone; tumors; syphilis (rare); or fractures of the neck of the radius. Toxic (alcohol, lead, arsenic) or infectious neuritis and polyneuritis involving the radial nerve also occur.

Clinical Features of Peripheral Radial Nerve Lesions
A. Motor Signs of Complete Radial Nerve Palsy: Extensor paralysis: inability to extend the thumb, proximal phalanges, wrist, and elbow; pronation of the hand, with the wrist and fingers flexed in a position termed "wristdrop"; adduction of the thumb, which may interfere with flexion of the index finger; and inability to grasp objects adequately or to make a fist because of the wristdrop, which interferes with the action of the flexors. Triceps, radial, and periosteal-radial reflexes are absent. (Supplementary movements may partially mask a radial palsy; energetic contraction of finger flexors and occasionally the pronator teres may extend the wrist.)

B. Sensory Disturbances: Sensory loss is slight (owing to overlapping innervation), being most marked on the dorsal radial surface of the hand. Pain is rare.

C. Vasomotor and Secretory Disturbances: These are absent or very slight.

D. Muscle Atrophy: Muscle atrophy develops in 2–3 months and may be very marked on the dorsum of the forearm. Palsies due to pressure do not show atrophy.

E. Radial Nerve Lesions That Occur:

1. Below the triceps innervation–Power to extend elbow retained.

2. Below the brachioradialis branch–Some supination ability retained.

3. In the forearm–May affect branches to small muscle groups: extensors of the thumb, extensors of the index finger, extensors of the other fingers, and extensor carpi ulnaris.

4. On the dorsum of the wrist–Only sensory loss on the hand shown.

F. Partial Lesions: Partial lesions of the radial nerve in the arm occasionally affect fascicles to small muscle groups like those cited above.

THE MEDIAN NERVE
(C6–8, T1)
(See Fig 5–10.)

The median nerve arises from the brachial plexus by 2 heads: a medial head from the medial cord and a lateral head from the lateral cord. The 2 heads unite at the lower margin of the pectoralis minor muscle. The trunk thus derives its fibers from the lower 3 (sometimes 4) cervical and the first thoracic segments of the spinal cord. In the arm it has no branches; the trunk descends along the course of the brachial artery and passes onto the volar side of the forearm, where it gives off muscular branches, and enters the hand, where it terminates with muscular and cutaneous branches. **Motor branches** pass to most of the flexor-pronator muscles of the forearm, supplying all of the superficial volar muscles except the flexor carpi ulnaris and all of the deep volar muscles except the ulnar half of the flexor digitorum profundus. In the hand the motor branches supply the first 2 lumbricales and the thenar muscles that lie superficial to the tendon of the flexor pollicis longus. **Sensory branches** supply the skin of the palmar aspect of the thumb and the lateral 2½ fingers and the distal ends of the same fingers. Many **vasomotor** and **trophic** fibers are also distributed by the median nerve.

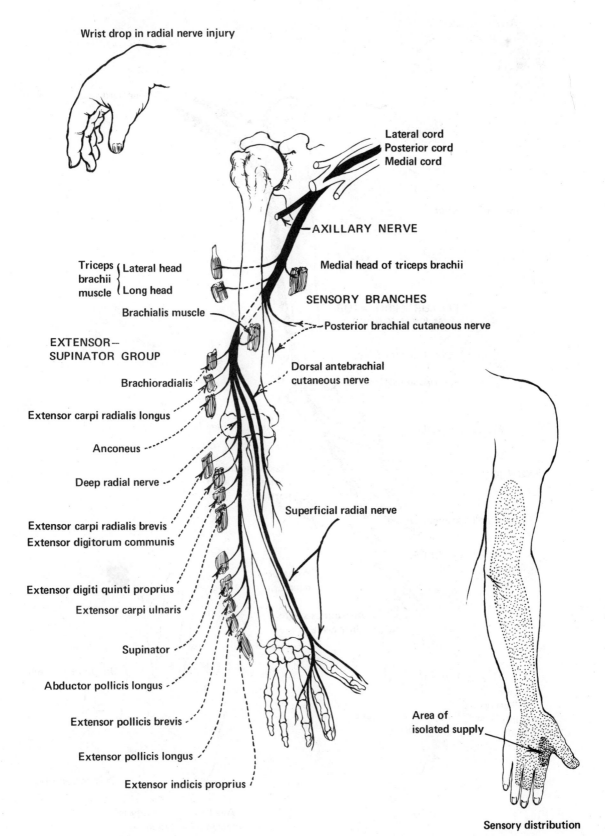

Figure 5–9. The radial (musculospiral) nerve (C6–8 and T1).

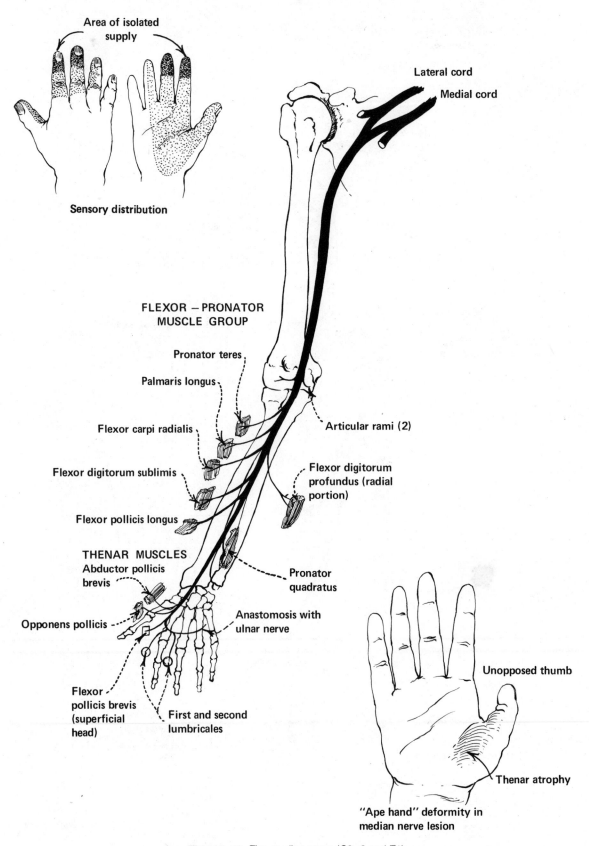

Figure 5–10. The median nerve (C6–8 and T1).

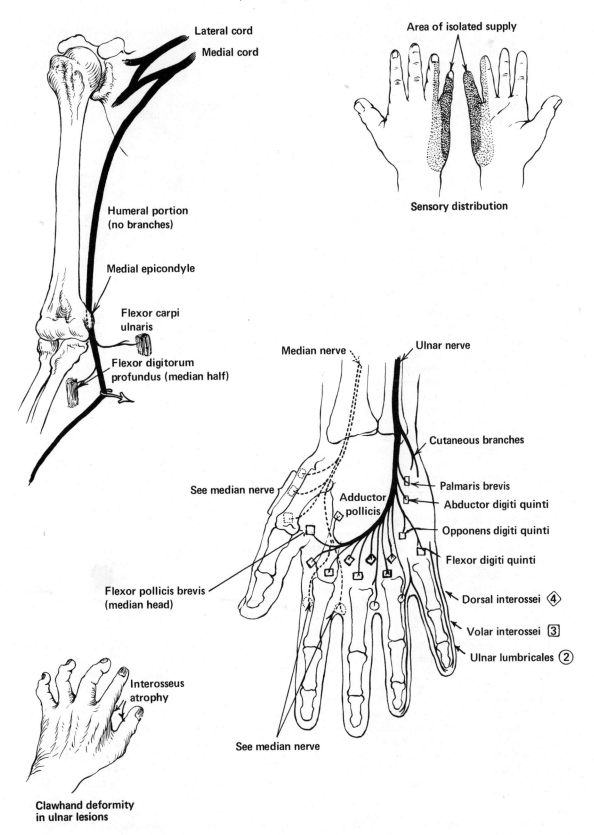

Lateral cord

Medial cord

Area of isolated supply

Sensory distribution

Humeral portion
(no branches)

Medial epicondyle

Flexor carpi
ulnaris

Flexor digitorum
profundus (median half)

Median nerve

Ulnar nerve

Cutaneous branches

See median nerve

Adductor
pollicis

Palmaris brevis

Abductor digiti quinti

Opponens digiti quinti

Flexor digiti quinti

Flexor pollicis brevis
(median head)

Dorsal interossei ④

Volar interossei ③

Ulnar lumbricales ②

Interosseus
atrophy

See median nerve

Clawhand deformity
in ulnar lesions

Figure 5–11. The ulnar nerve (C8, T1).

Lesions Affecting the Median Nerve

Cervical cord and brachial plexus lesions may involve the median nerve. Peripheral nerve injuries may occur in lacerations of the arm, forearm, wrist, or hand caused by automobile accidents, stab wounds, bullets, broken water faucets, suicide attempts, etc. Such injuries may also occur following prolonged compression incurred in sleep, anesthesia, or, rarely, cervical rib syndrome; or after dislocations of the ulna or fractures of the elbow joint and lower radius. Toxic or infectious neuritis or polyneuritis involving the median nerve also occurs.

Clinical Features of Peripheral Median Nerve Lesions

A. Motor Signs (of Complete Lesions): Paralysis of the flexor-pronator and thenar muscles. In the forearm, pronation is weak or lost and is supplemented by flexing the forearm and holding the elbow out. At the wrist, weak flexion and abduction; hand inclining to ulnar side. In the hand, "ape hand" deformity (thumb in plane of hand and thenar atrophy): inability to oppose or flex the thumb or abduct it in its own plane; weakened grip, especially in thumb and index finger, with tendency for these digits to become hyperextended and the thumb adducted; inability to flex the distal phalanx of the thumb and index finger (never supplemented), tested by patient clasping hands as in prayer or attempting to make a fist. Flexion of middle finger is weakened.

B. Supplementary Movements: In addition to pronation as above, flexion of the middle and proximal phalanges of the first 2 fingers may be affected by action of the deep flexor through its pull on the inert lumbricales and by the influence of flexion of the ring finger on the second finger.

C. Sensory Disturbances: Loss of sensation to a variable degree over the cutaneous distribution of the median nerve, most constantly over the distal phalanges of the first 2 fingers. Pain is present in many median nerve lesions, particularly partial injuries, and may be extreme. These cases, together with similar sciatic nerve injuries, are described under the name of causalgia.

D. Atrophic Lesions: Atrophy of the thenar eminence is seen early; atrophy of the flexor-pronator group of muscles in the forearm is seen after a few months.

E. Vasomotor and Trophic Signs: The skin of the palm is frequently dry, cold, discolored, chapped, and at times keratotic. Nails are often ridged and brittle. Once injured, the skin in these areas heals slowly.

F. Partial Lesions: Partial lesions of the median nerve are not uncommon and may produce weakness or paralysis in all or part of the motor distribution and in small groups of muscles. Sensory loss is usually less than in complete lesions; pain is more frequently present.

G. Carpal Tunnel Constriction: Progressive partial paralysis and atrophy of the thenar muscles and sensory disturbances involving the radial half of the

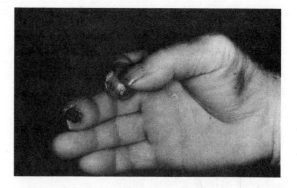

Figure 5–12. Carpal tunnel syndrome with median nerve paralysis. Thenar atrophy and paralysis, trophic changes of fingertips, and sensory disturbance of first 3 fingers relieved subsequently by section of transverse carpal ligament at the wrist.

palm and the palmar aspect of the first 3 fingers may follow compression of the median nerve in the carpal tunnel at the wrist. Decompression of the nerve by section of the transverse carpal ligament may be required for relief.

THE ULNAR NERVE
(C8, T1)
(See Fig 5–11.)

The ulnar nerve is the largest branch of the medial cord of the brachial plexus. It is composed of fibers from the eighth cervical and first thoracic segments. It originates at the lower border of the pectoralis minor, descends on the medial side of the arm, and pierces the medial intermuscular septum to continue its descent in a groove on the medial head of the triceps. From there it passes behind the medial epicondyle of the humerus and down the ulnar side of the forearm into the hand. **Motor branches** in the forearm supply the flexor carpi ulnaris and the ulnar head of the flexor digitorum profundus. Motor branches in the hand supply all of the small muscles deep and medial to the long flexor tendon of the thumb except the first 2 lumbricales. **Sensory branches** supply the skin of the little finger and the medial half of the hand and the ring finger.

Lesions Affecting the Ulnar Nerve

Cervical cord and brachial plexus lesions may involve the fibers of the ulnar nerve. Peripheral injuries include fractures and dislocations of the head of the humerus and at the elbow; direct trauma in lacerating wounds, eg, knife stabs or automobile accidents; pressure on the nerve during sleep, drunkenness, or general anesthesia; and, less commonly, cervical rib, callus formation, and neurinoma. Mononeuritis may occur with lead poisoning or as a complication of typhus fever, malaria, or influenza.

Clinical Features of Peripheral Ulnar Nerve Lesions

A. Motor Signs (of Complete Lesions):

1. Clawhand results from unopposed action of the extensor digitorum communis in the fourth and fifth digits (associated with interosseous atrophy). The patient is unable to flex the proximal or distal phalanges of the fourth and fifth digits. The first phalanges of these fingers remain hyperextended, the distal 2 flexed. The fifth finger is abducted.

2. Inability to extend the second and distal phalanges of any of the fingers.

3. Inability to adduct or abduct the fingers or to oppose all the fingertips, as in making a cone with the fingers and thumb.

4. Inability to adduct the thumb. In holding a paper between the thumb and index finger, the patient substitutes flexion of the thumb to compensate for paralysis of the adductor pollicis (Froment's sign).

5. At the wrist, flexion is weak and ulnar abduction lost. The ulnar reflex is lost.

B. Atrophic Lesions:
Atrophy of the interosseous spaces (especially the first) and of the hypothenar eminence.

C. Supplementary Movements:
Slight flexion of the ring finger and sometimes of the fifth finger may occur with violent contraction of the flexor digitorum sublimis. Adduction of the thumb is supplemented by the extensor pollicis longus. Abduction of the first 2 fingers is produced by forced extension and in some cases possibly by their interossei receiving dual innervation. Slight extension of the distal phalanges may occur with contraction of the common extensor by its pull on tendons of the inert interossei.

D. Sensory Disturbances:
Loss of sensation on the ulnar side of the hand and ring finger and most markedly over the entire little finger. Subjective pain is uncommon except with neuritis and partial lesions. Referred pain in the ulnar distribution may occur in coronary disease.

E. Vasomotor and Trophic Changes:
The skin of the hypothenar eminence and little finger is cold and dry and at times discolored. The nail of the little finger may be deformed. Ulcerations may occur on the little finger from cigarette burns, etc (healing is poor).

F. Partial Lesions:
Partial lesions may produce only motor weakness or paralysis of a few of the muscles supplied by the ulnar nerve. Lesions low in the forearm or at the wrist spare the deep flexor and the flexor carpi ulnaris.

COMBINED MEDIAN & ULNAR NERVE LESIONS
(See Figs 5–10 and 5–11.)

The median and ulnar nerves are frequently injured together. If the lesion is complete, the functional disturbances are constant, but if one or both nerves are only partially involved, the symptoms differ widely and are classified according to the varied appearance and functions of the hand.

Clinical Features

A. Motor Symptoms (in Total Paralysis of Both Nerves):
The wrist is slightly hyperextended and inclined to the radial side. "Ape hand" deformity is present, with the thumb in the plane of the hand and slightly abducted. The first phalanges are moderately extended, the last 2 slightly flexed. Flexor movements are not possible except with supplementary movements. The patient cannot abduct or adduct the fingers.

B. Atrophic Lesions:
Atrophy is marked in the dorsal interosseous spaces and in the thenar and hypothenar eminences; the flexor tendons ridge the palm.

C. Supplementary Movements:
Slight passive flexion of the wrist or fingers is produced by sudden relaxation following hyperextension of the hand or fingers. Slight abduction of the fingers is produced by energetic contraction of the extensors.

D. Sensory Symptoms:
The sense of touch is lost over the combined distribution of both nerves. Pain and temperature senses are lost to a lesser degree, corresponding to the overlap of the radial and musculocutaneous nerves.

E. Vasomotor and Trophic Changes:
These are common in the sensory distribution and include deformities of the nails; dryness, coldness, and discoloration of the skin; and, when associated with a vascular lesion (which is common), marked vasomotor changes, with cyanosis, glossy skin, or edema.

F. Partial Lesions:
Partial lesions may produce many types of dissociated paralysis, eg, paralysis of the small hand muscles and flexors of the fingers or paralysis of the small hand muscles and weakness of the deep flexors, resulting in a marked clawing of the proximal phalanges.

Tests

Careful dynamometric studies of the motor power of the various phalanges are useful in determining the exact distribution of muscle weakness and paralysis.

THE THORACIC NERVES
(See Fig 5–1.)

The thoracic nerves consist of 12 pairs of spinal nerves derived from cord segments located between the seventh cervical and ninth thoracic vertebrae. In general, they retain their segmental relationship throughout their distribution, each one branching into posterior primary and anterior primary divisions, a small recurrent meningeal branch to the spinal dura, and gray and white communicating branches to the sympathetic trunk. The **posterior primary division** divides into a medial branch, distributed to short, medially placed back muscles and the skin of the back as far as the midscapular line, and a lateral branch, supplying twigs to the sacrospinalis muscles. The lower 6 thoracic nerves also send sensory branches to the skin of the lower lateral part of the back. The **anterior primary division** becomes an intercostal nerve having a lateral branch sensory to the skin of the lateral aspect of the trunk and an anterior branch supplying the intercostal muscles, parietal pleura, and the skin over the anterior aspect of the thorax and abdomen. The lower 6 nerves also innervate the muscles of the abdominal wall.

Anatomic Variations

The major portion of the first thoracic nerve enters the brachial plexus. T2 and T3 contribute sensory branches to the axilla and the medial side of the arm. T12 contributes to the lumbar plexus, and the rest of its anterior division becomes a subcostal rather than an intercostal nerve. The lower 3 or 4 thoracic nerves supply a variable number of twigs to the periphery of the diaphragm and to the serratus posterior inferior muscle.

Clinical Aspects

The thoracic nerves may be involved by the same types of lesions that affect other peripheral nerves. However, loss of function of one or even several thoracic nerves is not in itself of great importance, although this information may be of diagnostic aid in localizing spinal cord lesions.

Involvement of the first thoracic segments may produce **Horner's syndrome,** characterized by enophthalmos, miosis, and ptosis and caused by interruption of sympathetic nerves to the face and eye. Paralysis of the intercostal muscles is often difficult to diagnose, but if 2 or more thoracic nerves are involved, the segmental sensory loss is characteristic.

Lesions of the lower thoracic nerves may produce partial or complete paralysis of the abdominal muscles. The abdominal reflexes are lost in the affected quadrants, and in unilateral lesions the umbilicus is usually drawn toward the unaffected side. Upward movement of the umbilicus when the patient tenses the abdomen (as in trying to sit up from a reclining position) is known as **Beevor's sign** and indicates paralysis of the lower abdominal muscles owing to a lesion at the level of the tenth thoracic segment.

Girdlelike root pains occurring with injuries to the midthoracic vertebrae demonstrate the segmental distribution of the thoracic nerves. The segmental arrangement of these nerves is again illustrated by the distribution of vesicles in herpes zoster (shingles), a disease of the posterior root ganglia caused by a virus.

Thoracic cord levels that should be kept in mind include the anterior aspect of the chest (T1–6), the nipple line (T4), the upper abdomen (T7–9), the umbilicus (T10), and the lower abdomen (T11, 12 and L1).

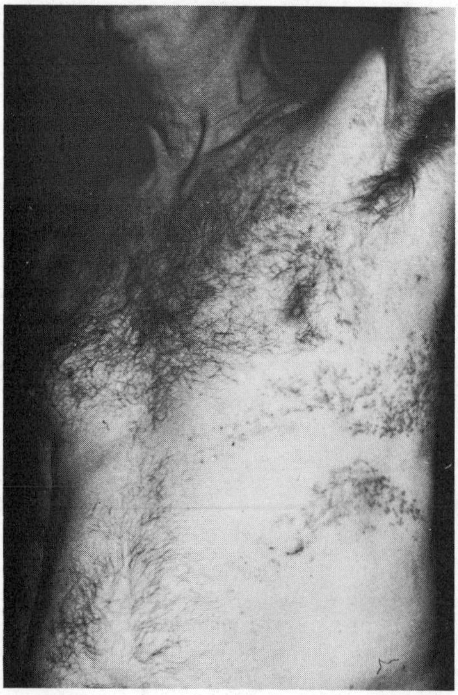

THE LUMBAR NERVES
(See Fig 5–14.)

The lumbar nerves are 5 pairs of spinal nerves derived from cord segments located between the ninth and the lower portion of the eleventh thoracic vertebrae. Each follows the division of a typical spinal nerve. **Posterior primary divisions** split into (1) medial branches, which supply the multifidus spinae muscles (the lower 3 also send small sensory rami to the skin of the sacral region); and (2) lateral branches, the upper 3 of which give twigs to the adjacent sacrospinal muscles and become cutaneous as the **superior clunial nerves.** The lower 2 lateral branches are small and end in the sacrospinal muscles. **Anterior primary divisions** of the lumbar nerves, together with those of the sacral and coccygeal nerves, form the lumbosacral plexus, from which the major nerves of the pelvic girdle and lower extremity are derived. A variable number of **communicating rami** join the lumbar nerves to the sympathetic trunk. Small **recurrent branches** supply the spinal dura.

Figure 5–13. Herpes zoster, thoracic. Vesicular eruption of herpes zoster in left thoracic area (T6, 8).

THE LUMBAR PLEXUS
(See Fig 5–14.)

The lumbar plexus, located in the substance of the psoas muscle, is the upper portion of the lumbosacral plexus. It is ordinarily formed by the anterior primary divisions of the first 3 lumbar nerves and part of the fourth, and in 50% of cases it receives a contribution from the last thoracic nerve.

L1, L2, and L4 divide into upper and lower branches. The upper branch of L1 forms the **iliohypogastric** and **ilioinguinal nerves.** The lower branch of L1 joins the upper branch of L2 to form the **genitofemoral nerve.** The lower branch of L4 joins L5 to form the lumbosacral trunk.

The lower branch of L2, all of L3, and the upper branch of L4 split into a smaller anterior and a large posterior division each. The 3 anterior divisions unite to form the **obturator nerve.** The 3 posterior divisions unite to form the **femoral nerve,** and the upper 2 give

off twigs that form the **lateral femoral cutaneous nerve.**

Collateral muscular branches supply the quadratus lumborum and intertransversarii from L1 and L4 and the psoas muscle from L2 and L3.

Distribution of Terminal Branches

The **iliohypogastric nerve** (T12, L1) passes laterally around the iliac crest between the transversus and internal oblique muscles and divides into an iliac (lateral) branch to the skin of the upper lateral part of the thigh and a hypogastric (anterior) branch descending anteriorly to the skin over the symphysis. The **ilioinguinal nerve** (L1) follows a course slightly inferior to the iliohypogastric, with which it may anastomose, and is distributed to the skin of the upper medial part of the thigh and the root of the penis and scrotum or mons pubis and labium majus. The **genitofemoral nerve** (L1, 2) emerges from the anterior surface of the psoas, runs obliquely downward on the surface of this muscle, and divides into the **external spermatic nerve** to the cremasteric muscle

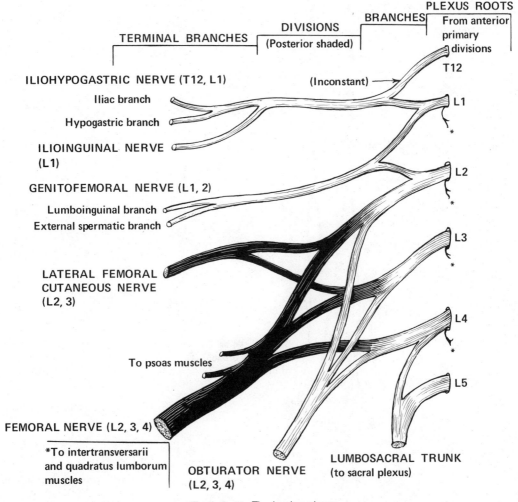

Figure 5–14. The lumbar plexus.

Labels in figure:

PLEXUS ROOTS — From anterior primary divisions

BRANCHES

DIVISIONS (Posterior shaded)

TERMINAL BRANCHES

ILIOHYPOGASTRIC NERVE (T12, L1)
Iliac branch
Hypogastric branch

ILIOINGUINAL NERVE (L1)

GENITOFEMORAL NERVE (L1, 2)
Lumboinguinal branch
External spermatic branch

LATERAL FEMORAL CUTANEOUS NERVE (L2, 3)

To psoas muscles

FEMORAL NERVE (L2, 3, 4)
*To intertransversarii and quadratus lumborum muscles

OBTURATOR NERVE (L2, 3, 4)

LUMBOSACRAL TRUNK (to sacral plexus)

(Inconstant)

T12
L1
L2
L3
L4
L5

and the skin of the scrotum or labia and the **lumboinguinal nerve** to the skin of the middle upper part of the thigh. The **lateral femoral cutaneous nerve** (L2, 3) passes obliquely across the iliacus muscle and under Poupart's ligament to divide into several rami distributed to the skin of the anterolateral side of the thigh. The **lumbosacral trunk** (L4, 5) descends into the pelvis, where it enters the formation of the sacral plexus. The **femoral** and **obturator nerves** are described in Fig 5–15 and on p 131.

Lesions of the Lumbar Plexus

Spinal cord and cauda equina lesions may involve fibers of these nerves. Nonfatal injuries to the lumbar plexus are rare because of its deep location, but the following may occur: fractures, dislocations, bullet wounds, and tuberculosis of the vertebrae; psoas abscess; and pressure from pelvic tumors (including the gravid uterus).

Clinical Features According to Nerves Involved*

A. Ilioinguinal, Iliohypogastric, and Genitofemoral Nerves: Injury to these nerves in itself is of little importance; however, sensory loss or pain in their distribution may be of value in locating spinal cord and

*Femoral and obturator nerves; see Fig 5–15 and p 131.

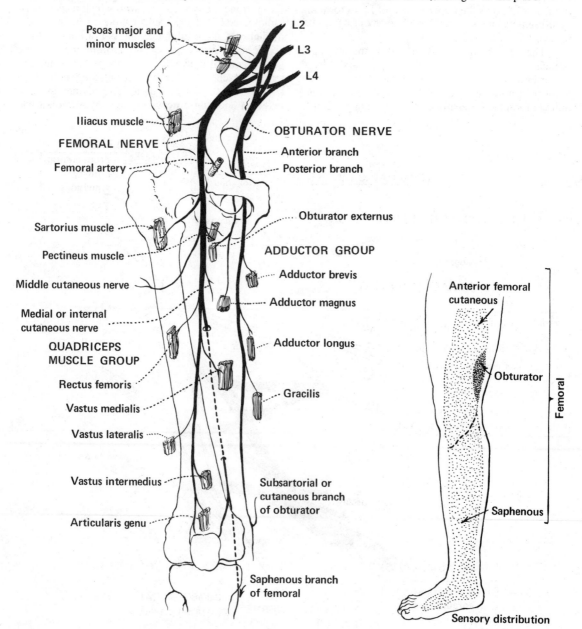

Figure 5–15. The femoral (L2–4) and obturator (L2–4) nerves.

root lesions. Referred pain in their distribution occurs with diseases of the renal pelvis and ureter.

B. Lateral Femoral Cutaneous Nerve: Injury is of clinical significance because this nerve is frequently the seat of paresthesias and occasionally pain (meralgia paresthetica of Roth). Symptoms include numbness, tingling, and pain over the outer aspect and front of the thigh, most marked on walking and standing. The cause is not known, though various pathologic entities have been incriminated, eg, neuritis, angulation of the nerve as it leaves the pelvis, fascial pressure, flat feet, obesity, spondylitis, and pressure from tight clothing. It is most common in middle-aged men and may occur as the first sign of a lumbar cord tumor.

THE FEMORAL (ANTERIOR CRURAL) NERVE (L2–4)
(See Fig 5–15.)

The femoral nerve is the largest branch of the lumbar plexus. It arises from the 3 posterior divisions of the plexus, which are derived from the second, third, and fourth lumbar nerves; emerges from the lateral border of the psoas just above Poupart's ligament; and descends beneath this ligament to enter the femoral trigone on the lateral side of the femoral artery, where it divides into terminal branches. **Motor branches** above the inguinal ligament supply the iliopsoas muscle. Motor branches in the thigh supply the sartorius, pectineus, and quadriceps femoris muscles. **Sensory branches** include the anterior femoral cutaneous branches to the anterior and medial surfaces of the thigh and the saphenous nerve to the medial side of the leg and foot.

Lesions Affecting the Femoral Nerve
Lesions of the femoral nerve frequently involve the obturator nerve also. Spinal cord, cauda equina, and lumbar plexus lesions must be considered. Peripheral injuries may result from pelvic tumors, psoas abscess, fractures of the pelvis and upper femur, forceps injury during labor, injury during reduction of congenital dislocation of the hips, pressure during prolonged operations when the thighs are strongly abducted, bullet and stab wounds, aneurysms of the femoral artery (especially in wartime), and neuritis, particularly in diabetes mellitus.

Clinical Features
These depend upon the level of the involvement.

A. Motor Symptoms: Paralysis of the iliopsoas causes inability to flex the thigh on the trunk. If the iliacus alone is paralyzed, flexion of the thigh is weakened. In paralysis of the quadriceps, both extension of the leg and the knee jerk are lost. Walking forward is difficult (impossible in bilateral involvement), and patients use a pseudosteppage gait, often steadying their thighs with their hands. Walking backward is often easier.

B. Atrophic Lesions: Atrophy develops over the anterior aspect of the thigh.

C. Sensory Disturbances: Sensation is lost in the cutaneous distribution of the femoral nerve. Pain occurs with irritative lesions and is often most marked in the knee.

D. Partial Lesions: Injuries in the thigh may involve only single branches of the femoral nerve, eg, the saphenous nerve alone or the branches to the quadriceps.

THE OBTURATOR NERVE (L2–4)
(See Fig 5–15.)

The obturator nerve arises from the lumbar plexus by a fusion of the 3 anterior divisions of the plexus, which are derived from the second, third, and fourth lumbar nerves. Emerging from the medial border of the psoas near the brim of the pelvis, it passes on the lateral side of the hypogastric vessels and ureter and descends through the obturator canal in the upper part of the obturator foramen to the medial side of the thigh. In the canal, the obturator nerve splits into anterior and posterior branches. **Motor rami** from the posterior branch supply the obturator externus and adductor magnus muscles. Motor rami from the anterior branch supply the adductors longus and brevis and the gracilis muscles. **Sensory rami** from the anterior branch of the nerve supply the hip joint and a small area of skin on the middle internal part of the thigh.

Lesions Affecting the Obturator Nerve
The obturator nerve may be involved by the same processes that affect the femoral nerve; isolated paralysis is rare. Pressure from a gravid uterus and damage in severe labor are not uncommon. External rotation and adduction of the thigh are impaired, and crossing of the legs is difficult. Sensory loss is usually not significant. Howship-Romberg syndrome is caused by pressure on the obturator nerve by obturator hernia (rare). The chief symptom is pain, which radiates down the inner side of the thigh and is usually most marked at the knee.

THE SACRAL NERVES
(See Fig 5–16.)

The sacral nerves are 5 pairs of spinal nerves derived from cord segments located opposite the bodies of the twelfth thoracic and first lumbar vertebrae. The upper 4 **posterior primary divisions** pass through the posterior sacral foramens, the fifth emerg-

ing between the sacrum and the coccyx. The upper 3
divide into 2 sets of branches: the medial branches,
which are distributed to the multifidi muscles, and the
lateral branches, which become the medial clunial
nerves and supply the skin over the medial part of the
gluteus maximus. The lower 2 posterior primary divisions, with the posterior division of the coccygeal
nerve, supply the skin over the coccyx.

The anterior primary divisions appear at the an-

terior sacral foramens and contribute to part of the
lumbosacral plexus. This is described below.

White rami (parasympathetic in this instance)
pass from the second, third, and fourth sacral nerves to
the pelvic and lower abdominal viscera via the
hypogastric plexus. **Gray rami** (sympathetic) join
each sacral nerve from the sympathetic trunk.

Small **recurrent meningeal branches** pass back
to the spinal dura.

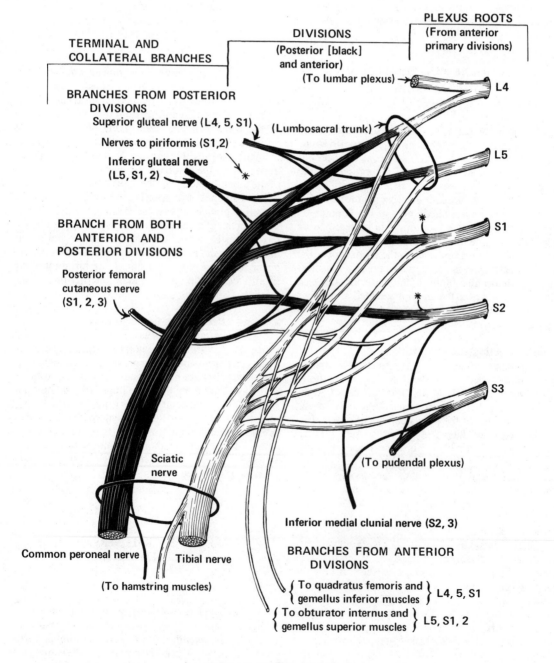

Figure 5–16. The sacral plexus.

THE SACRAL PLEXUS
(See Fig 5–16.)

The sacral portion of the lumbosacral plexus lies against the piriformis muscle on the posterior wall of the pelvis. In front of it are the pelvic colon, the hypogastric vessels, and the ureter. It ordinarily arises by 5 plexus roots formed by the anterior primary divisions of the fifth and part of the fourth lumbar nerves (lumbosacral trunk) and the first and parts of the second and third sacral nerves. One main terminal branch, the **sciatic nerve,** and several collateral branches are formed by the plexus.

Each of the 5 plexus roots splits into an **anterior** and a **posterior division.** The upper 4 posterior divisions (L4, 5 and S1, 2) join to form the **common peroneal nerve.** All 5 of the anterior divisions (L4, 5 and S1, 2, 3) join to form the **tibial nerve.** (In the thigh the peroneal and tibial nerves are fused as the **sciatic nerve.**) The posterior division of S3, together with twigs from the anterior divisions of S2 and S3, contributes to the pudendal plexus (see p 139).

Collateral Branches From the Posterior Divisions

The **superior gluteal nerve** (L4, 5 and S1) passes above the piriformis muscle through the greater sciatic foramen into the buttock, where it supplies the gluteus medius and minimus and the tensor fasciae latae muscles. The **inferior gluteal nerve** (L5 and S1, 2) passes below the piriformis muscle through the greater sciatic foramen to the gluteus maximus muscle. Nerves to the piriformis consist of short twigs from S1 and S2. The **inferior medial clunial** (perforating cutaneous) nerve (S2, 3) perforates the sacrotuberous ligament and is distributed to the lower medial gluteal region.

The **posterior femoral cutaneous** (small sciatic) nerve constitutes a collateral branch, with roots from both anterior and posterior divisions of S1, 2 and the anterior divisions of S2, 3. Perineal branches pass to the skin of the upper medial aspect of the thigh and the skin of the scrotum or labium majus. **Inferior clunial nerves** extend to the lower lateral gluteal region; and femoral cutaneous branches to the back of the thigh toward the medial side. **Collateral branches** from the anterior divisions extend to the quadratus femoris and gemellus inferior muscles (from L4, 5 and S1) and to the obturator internus and gemellus superior muscles (from L5 and S1, 2).

Lesions of the Sacral Plexus

Spinal cord and cauda equina lesions may involve these nerves. Injury to the plexus itself is infrequent but may result from pelvic fractures, dislocations, stab and gunshot wounds, tuberculosis and malignant tumors of the pelvis, pressure from the fetal head or trauma from forceps during childbirth, or toxic or infectious neuritis.

Clinical Features According to the Nerves Involved

The sciatic nerve is discussed separately.

A. Superior Gluteal Nerve (L4, 5 and S1): Rarely injured alone. Paralysis of the gluteus medius and minimus weakens abduction of the leg, which interferes with walking and causes inclination of the pelvis to the opposite side when the patient stands on the affected limb. One can test abductor power against passive adduction.

B. Inferior Gluteal Nerve (L5 and S1, 2): Injured more frequently than the superior gluteal, though rarely alone. Paralysis of the gluteus maximus and the consequent weakened extensor power at the hip make it difficult for the patient to rise from a seated position or to run and jump or climb stairs. In unilateral lesions, the contracted buttocks will be asymmetric.

C. Posterior Femoral Cutaneous (Small Sciatic) Nerve (S1–3): Pain in its distribution may occur in partial and irritative plexus or root lesions. Complete interruption is followed by sensory loss in its distribution.

THE SCIATIC NERVE
(L4, 5 and S1–3)
(See Fig 5–17.)

The sciatic nerve is the largest nerve in the body. It consists of 2 separate nerves in one sheath: the **common peroneal nerve,** formed by the upper 4 posterior divisions of the sacral plexus, and the **tibial nerve,** from all 5 anterior divisions. The nerve leaves the pelvis through the greater sciatic foramen, usually below the piriformis muscle, and descends between the greater trochanter of the femur and the ischial tuberosity along the posterior surface of the thigh to the popliteal space, where it terminates by dividing into the tibial and common peroneal nerves. Branches in the thigh supply the hamstring muscles. Rami from the tibial trunk pass to the semitendinosus and semimembranosus muscles, the long head of the biceps, and the adductor magnus muscle. A ramus from the common peroneal trunk supplies the short head of the biceps. (See also discussion under peroneal and tibial nerves, pp 135 and 138.)

Lesions Affecting the Sciatic Nerve

Injury to the sciatic nerve may result from herniated intervertebral disk (protruded nucleus pulposus); dislocations of the hip or attempts at reducing them; childbirth injury to the infant by traction on the legs, or injury to the mother from compression by the fetus or from forceps; pelvis fractures, tumors, or stab or gunshot wounds; or injections of drugs into or near the nerve. Alcoholic, lead, arsenic, or infectious polyneuritis may occur, as well as mononeuritis due to osteoarthritis of the spine or sacroiliac joint.

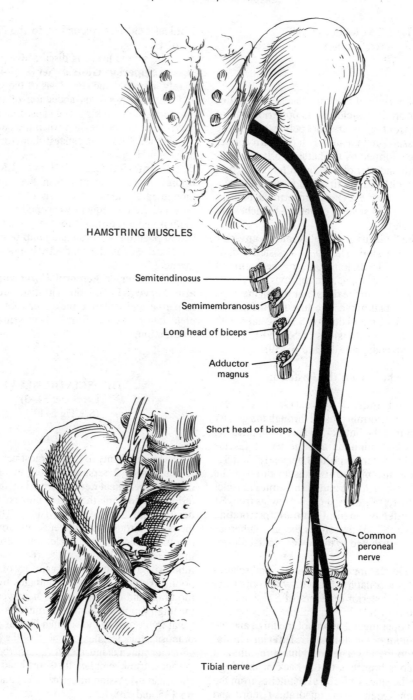

HAMSTRING MUSCLES

Semitendinosus

Semimembranosus

Long head of biceps

Adductor
magnus

Short head of biceps

Common
peroneal
nerve

Tibial nerve

Figure 5–17. The sciatic nerve (L4, 5 and S1–3).

Clinical Features

A. Motor Signs:

1. Hamstring paralysis–Flexion of the leg is lost (or weakened in partial lesions, which often spare the semitendinosus and semimembranosus).

2. Paralysis of all the muscles of the leg and foot, causing a steppage gait and inability to stand on the heels or toes. Running is impossible.

3. Loss of Achilles jerk and plantar reflex.

B. Supplementary Movements: These do not occur in complete sciatic lesions.

C. Sensory Disturbances: Sensibility is lost on the outer side of the leg and the entire foot except for the instep and internal malleolus. Causalgic pain is often present with irritative or partial lesions, particularly of the tibial trunk.

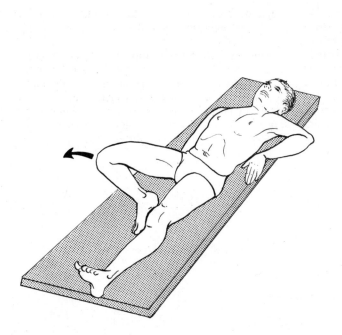

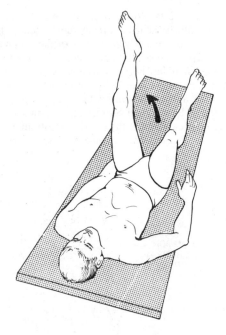

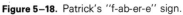

Figure 5–18. Patrick's "f-ab-er-e" sign.

Figure 5–19. Lasègue's sign.

D. Atrophic Lesions: Atrophy of the involved muscles occurs, but it may be masked by edema.

E. Vasomotor and Trophic Changes: Edema of the leg and foot is common, the skin being dry or discolored. Plantar hyperkeratosis is often seen. Slight injuries to the sole may cause ulcerations that heal slowly.

F. Partial Lesions: Partial lesions produce dissociated paralysis from greater damage to either the tibial or common peroneal trunks, or from partial injury of both. The common peroneal usually suffers the greater damage.

G. Patrick's "F-ab-er-e" Sign (of Hip Joint Disease): With the heel of the painful extremity placed on the opposite knee, the affected knee remains elevated and cannot be depressed toward the bed without pain. In short, there is pain upon attempting *f*lexion, *ab*duction, and *e*xternal *r*otation and *e*xtension simultaneously (f-ab-er-e). In sciatica, the knee of the affected side is only slightly elevated and can be depressed to the bed without pain or rotation of the pelvis. (See Fig 5–18.)

H. Lasègue's Sign (of Sciatic Nerve Disease): Pain is present along the course of the sciatic nerve when it is put on the stretch by flexing the thigh on the abdomen and extending the leg at the knee. When sitting in a chair, the patient may be unable to fully extend the knee because of pain. (See Fig 5–19.)

THE COMMON PERONEAL (EXTERNAL POPLITEAL) NERVE
(L4, 5 and S1, 2)
(See Fig 5–20.)

The common peroneal nerve is formed by a fusion of the upper 4 posterior divisions of the sacral plexus and thus derives its fibers from the lower 2 lumbar and the upper 2 sacral cord segments. In the thigh it is a component of the sciatic nerve as far as the upper part of the popliteal space. Here it begins its independent course, descending along the posterior border of the biceps femoris, diagonally across the dorsum of the knee joint to the upper external portion of the leg near the head of the fibula, where it turns forward between the peroneus longus and the bone and divides into 3 terminal rami.

Branches given off in the popliteal space are **sensory** and include the superior and inferior articular branches to the knee joint, and the **lateral sural cutaneous nerve,** which joins the medial sural cutaneous nerve (from the tibial nerve) to form the sural nerve, supplying the skin of the lower dorsal aspect of the leg, the external malleolus, and the lateral side of the foot and fifth toe.

The 3 terminal branches are the recurrent articular and the superficial and deep peroneal nerves. The **recurrent articular nerve** accompanies the anterior tibial recurrent artery, supplying the tibiofibular and knee joints and a twig to the tibialis anterior muscle. The **superficial peroneal nerve** descends along the intermuscular septum to supply muscular branches to the peroneus longus and brevis muscles, cutaneous branches to the lower front of the leg, and terminal cutaneous branches to the dorsum of the foot, part of the big toe, and adjacent sides of the second to fifth toes up to the second phalanges. The **deep peroneal** (anterior tibial) nerve descends in the anterior compartment of the leg. Muscular branches extend to the tibialis anterior, extensor digitorum longus, extensor hallucis longus, and peroneus tertius muscles. Articular filaments supply the inferior tibiofibular and ankle joints. Terminal branches extend to the skin of the

adjacent sides of the first 2 toes and to the extensor digitorum brevis muscle and adjacent joints.

Lesions Affecting the Common Peroneal Nerve

Sacral plexus and sciatic nerve lesions may involve fibers of the common peroneal nerve. Peripheral injury may result from direct trauma (especially in the region of the neck of the fibula) or from fractures of the leg or compression from prolonged kneeling, prolonged sitting with crossed knees, or compression of

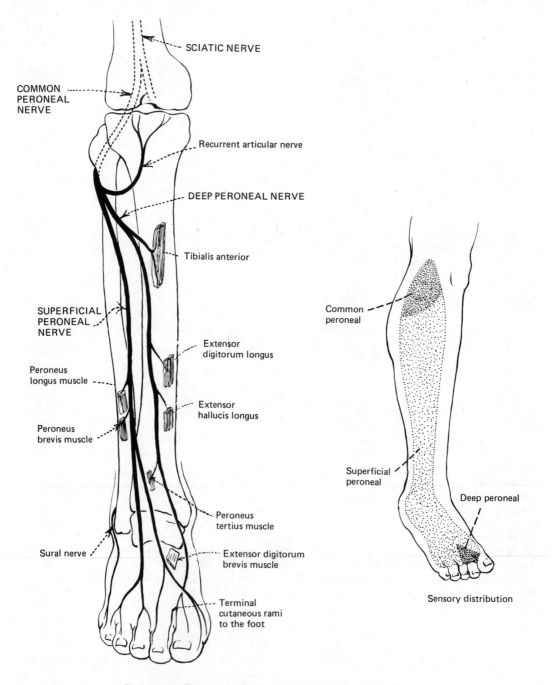

Figure 5–20. The common peroneal nerve (L4, 5 and S1, 2).

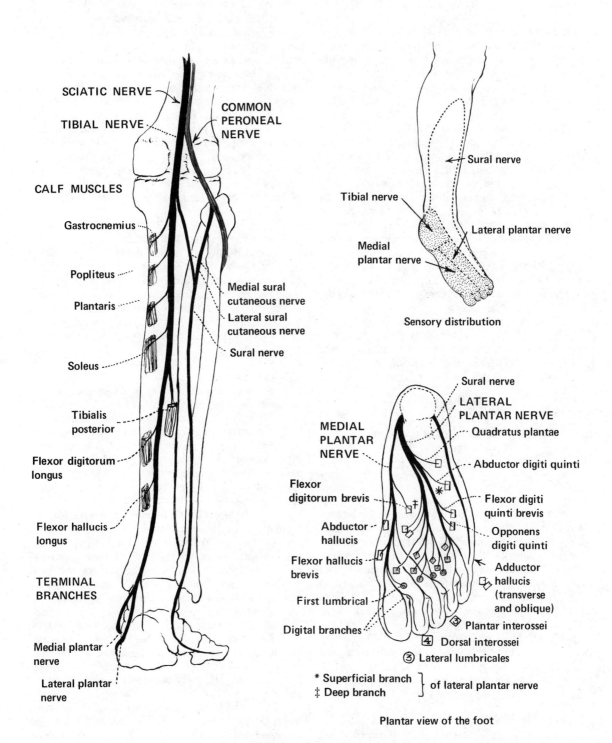

SCIATIC NERVE

TIBIAL NERVE

COMMON PERONEAL NERVE

CALF MUSCLES

Gastrocnemius

Popliteus

Plantaris

Soleus

Tibialis posterior

Flexor digitorum longus

Flexor hallucis longus

TERMINAL BRANCHES

Medial plantar nerve

Lateral plantar nerve

Medial sural cutaneous nerve

Lateral sural cutaneous nerve

Sural nerve

Sural nerve

Tibial nerve

Medial plantar nerve

Lateral plantar nerve

Sensory distribution

Sural nerve

LATERAL PLANTAR NERVE

Quadratus plantae

Abductor digiti quinti

Flexor digiti quinti brevis

Opponens digiti quinti

Adductor hallucis (transverse and oblique)

Plantar interossei

Dorsal interossei

Lateral lumbricales

MEDIAL PLANTAR NERVE

Flexor digitorum brevis

Abductor hallucis

Flexor hallucis brevis

First lumbrical

Digital branches

* Superficial branch
‡ Deep branch } of lateral plantar nerve

Plantar view of the foot

Figure 5–21. The tibial nerve (L4, 5 and S1–3).

the legs in a lying position. Primary neuritis has a special predilection for this nerve.

Clinical Features

A. Motor Disturbances: Paralysis of the extensor-abductor muscles of the foot causes inability to extend (dorsiflex) the foot or proximal phalanges of the toes, resulting in a "footdrop" deformity; inability to abduct and evert the foot or to stand on the affected heel; and steppage gait (patient raises the knee high, and the foot hangs flexed and adducted).

B. Supplementary Movements: Slight extension of the foot may accompany vigorous flexion of the toes. Slight extension of the toes may occur upon sudden relaxation of the flexors.

C. Sensory Disturbances: Sensibility is lost over the dorsum of the foot and outer side of the leg. Pain is rarely present and, if so, is usually mild.

D. Atrophic Lesions: Vasomotor and trophic changes are not marked; the involved muscles atrophy.

E. Partial Lesions: These are infrequent; they produce dissociated paralysis, eg, loss of activity of the tibialis anterior alone or of only the extensors of the toes.

F. Biopsy: Sural nerve biopsy may be performed under local anesthesia about 1 cm above the lateral malleolus. The sural nerve is a suitable sensory nerve for biopsy to determine pathologic diagnosis in patients with neuropathies and neural atrophies.

THE TIBIAL (INTERNAL POPLITEAL) NERVE
(L4, 5 and S1–3)
(See Fig 5–21.)

The tibial nerve is formed by all 5 of the anterior divisions of the sacral plexus, thus receiving fibers from the lower 2 lumbar and the upper 3 sacral cord segments. The tibial nerve forms the largest component of the sciatic nerve in the thigh. It begins its own course in the upper part of the popliteal space and descends vertically through this space and the dorsum of the leg to the dorsomedial aspect of the ankle, from which point its terminal branches, the medial and lateral plantar nerves, continue into the foot. The portion of the tibial trunk below the popliteal space was formerly called the posterior tibial nerve; that portion within the space was called the internal popliteal nerve.

Branches From the Tibial Nerve Proper

Motor branches extend to the gastrocnemius, plantaris, soleus, popliteus, tibialis posterior, flexor digitorum longus pedis, and flexor hallucis longus muscles. A **sensory branch,** the medial sural cutaneous nerve, joins the lateral sural cutaneous nerve from the common peroneal to form the sural nerve (external saphenous), which supplies the skin of the dorsolateral

part of the leg and the lateral side of the foot. Articular branches pass to the knee and ankle joints.

There are 2 **terminal branches** (as well as numerous small articular rami not listed). The **medial plantar nerve** (comparable to the median nerve in the hand) sends motor branches to the flexor digitorum brevis, abductor hallucis, flexor hallucis brevis, and first lumbrical muscles; and sensory branches to the medial side of the sole, the plantar surfaces of the medial 3½ toes, and the ungual phalanges of the same toes. The **lateral plantar nerve** (comparable to the ulnar nerve in the arm and hand) sends motor branches to all of the small muscles of the foot except those innervated by the medial plantar nerve (Fig 5–21); and sensory branches to the lateral portions of the sole, the plantar surface of the lateral 1½ toes, and the ungual phalanges of these toes.

Lesions Affecting the Tibial Nerve

Sacral plexus and sciatic nerve injuries usually involve fibers of the tibial nerve. Isolated tibial paralysis is usually due to an injury in or below the popliteal space, eg, from gunshot or stab wounds, automobile accidents, or fractures of the leg. Injury to the tibial nerve is much less common than injury to the peroneal nerve because of its deeper location and more protected course.

Clinical Features

A. Motor Signs: Inability to plantarflex, adduct, or invert the foot; elevation of the foot often results from contracture of the tibialis anterior; inability to flex, abduct (separate), or adduct the toes; and inability to stand on tiptoe. Walking is difficult, fatiguing, and often painful. The foot may become deformed from fibrosis of the tibiotarsal articulation, and unopposed action of the dorsal flexors may produce a "clawfoot." The ankle jerk reflex is absent.

B. Supplementary Movements: Feeble plantar flexion by the peroneus longus.

C. Sensory Disturbances: Sensibility is lost over the sole (except inner border), the lateral surfaces of the heel, and the plantar surfaces of the toes and ungual phalanges. Pain of severe causalgic nature is common with incomplete and irritative lesions.

D. Atrophic Lesions: Atrophy of the calf and foot muscles occurs. It may be masked by edema.

E. Vasomotor and Trophic Changes: These are common. The foot becomes edematous, discolored, and cold. Nail changes and hypotrichosis are often seen. Trophic ulcers may occur on the malleoli, heel, and toes.

F. Partial Lesions: In partial lesions, dissociated paralysis may occur. Injuries in the calf spare the innervation of the calf muscles, so that the motor loss is limited to the muscles of the foot. Pain is usually present.

G. Tarsal Tunnel Syndrome: Pain and sensory loss involving the medial anterior foot and adjacent great toe may be due to compression of the medial plantar nerve. Tapping of the medial malleolus just

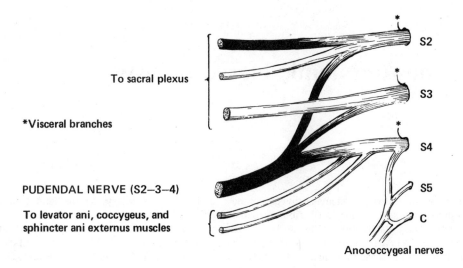

To sacral plexus

*Visceral branches

PUDENDAL NERVE (S2–3–4)

To levator ani, coccygeus, and
sphincter ani externus muscles

S2

S3

S4

S5

C

Anococcygeal nerves

Figure 5–22. The pudendal and coccygeal plexuses.

above the margin of the flexor retinaculum may produce paresthesias in the affected area. Operative section of the flexor retinaculum and mobilization of the
compressed nerve may be required for satisfactory
symptomatic relief.

THE PUDENDAL & COCCYGEAL
PLEXUSES
(See Fig 5–22.)

The pudendal and coccygeal plexuses are the
most caudal portions of the lumbosacral plexus and
supply nerves to the perineal structures. The plexus
roots are from the anterior primary divisions of the
lower 4 sacral and coccygeal nerves. The fourth sacral
nerve is the chief component, as most of S2, 3 passes to
the sacral plexus, and the last 2 spinal nerves are quite
small.

Branches of the Pudendal Plexus

Muscular rami extend from the fourth sacral
nerve to the coccygeus, levator ani, and sphincter ani
externus muscles. The **pudendal** (pudic) nerve from
S2–4 accompanies the internal pudic artery through
the greater sciatic foramen below the piriformis muscle
and across the ischial spine, where it reenters the lower
portion of the pelvis via the small sciatic foramen and
Alcock's canal in the lateral wall of the ischiorectal
fossa. At this point it divides into (1) the **inferior
hemorrhoidal nerves** to the external anal sphincter
and adjacent skin; (2) the **perineal nerve;** and (3) the
dorsal nerve of the penis. The perineal nerve has a
deep branch, which pierces the urogenital diaphragm
(after giving twigs to the levator and sphincter ani) to

supply the muscles of the perineal compartments and a
few sensory twigs to the urethra; and a superficial
branch, which divides into the posterior scrotal or
labial nerves. The dorsal nerve of the penis runs
obliquely through the urogenital diaphragm, gives a
branch to the corpus cavernosum penis, and passes
forward to supply the skin of the dorsum of the penis
and the glans. In the female, this nerve is small and
supplies the clitoris.

Branches of the Coccygeal Plexus

These are the small sensory anococcygeal nerves
derived from the last 3 segments (S4, 5, C). They
pierce the sacrotuberous ligament and supply the skin
in the region of the coccyx.

Visceral Rami

Visceral rami from S2–4 are parasympathetic
(Fig 6–2). They are primary branches of these spinal
nerves rather than plexus branches.

Lesions of the Pudendal & Coccygeal Plexuses

Lesions of the pudendal and coccygeal plexuses
are usually part of a sacral plexus involvement.

Clinical Features

A. Motor Signs: Motor signs of rare pudendal
nerve involvement include partial incontinence of
urine and feces, tenesmus, and difficulty on urination.

B. Sensory Disturbances: Subjective sensory
disturbances seen with partial or irritative lesions are
usually spoken of as neuralgia of the pudendal plexus,
which is characterized by pain in the anus, perineum,
scrotum, penis, or vagina; difficulty and burning on
urination and defecation; and occasionally priapism or
even ejaculation.

C. Coccygeal Neuralgia: Practically limited to
women. There is severe pain and tenderness limited to
the tip of the coccyx.

6 | The Autonomic Nervous System

The autonomic nervous system is a division of the peripheral nervous system that is distributed to the smooth muscle and glands throughout the body. By definition it is entirely a motor (efferent) system, and it is "automatic" in the sense that most of its functions are carried out below the conscious level. It is, however, highly integrated in structure and function with the rest of the nervous system. Anatomically, the autonomic system is divided into 2 divisions according to the location of the preganglionic cell bodies: the sympathetic and parasympathetic nervous systems.

Structure of Autonomic Nerves

A 2-neuron chain characterizes the structure of the autonomic nerves. The cell body of the primary (presynaptic or preganglionic) neuron, located within the CNS, sends its axon out to synapse with the secondary (postsynaptic or postganglionic) neuron located in one of the outlying autonomic ganglia, whence the postganglionic axon passes to its terminal distribution.

Since the postganglionic outnumber the preganglionic neurons by a ratio of about 32:1, a single primary neuron may serve to discharge a number of ganglion cells; thus, the autonomic functions of a rather extensive terminal area may be controlled by relatively few central connections.

The autonomic nervous system helps maintain the constancy of the internal environment of the body (homeostasis).

The Sympathetic (or Thoracolumbar) Division (See Fig 6–1.)

The sympathetic division of the autonomic nervous system arises from preganglionic cell bodies located in the intermediolateral cell column of the 12 thoracic and upper 3 or 4 lumbar segments of the spinal cord. The axons of these cells (preganglionic fibers) are mostly myelinated fibers. After traversing the ventral roots, they form the **white communicating rami** of the thoracic and lumbar nerves, through which they reach the trunk ganglia of the sympathetic chain. These lie on the lateral sides of the bodies of the thoracic and lumbar vertebrae. Upon entering the trunk ganglia, these fibers may synapse with a nest of ganglion cells, pass up or down the sympathetic trunk to synapse with ganglion cells at a higher or lower level, or pass through the trunk ganglia and out to one of the collat-

eral, or intermediary, sympathetic ganglia (eg, the celiac ganglion).

Branches from the sympathetic trunk may be classified as follows: (1) Those composed of postsynaptic fibers* (mainly unmyelinated). The **gray communicating rami** join all of the spinal nerves. Through these rami, vasomotor, pilomotor, and sweat gland innervation is distributed throughout the somatic areas. Branches of the **superior cervical sympathetic ganglion** enter into the formation of the sympathetic plexuses about the internal and external carotid arteries for distribution of sympathetics to the head. The **superior cardiac nerves** from the 3 pairs of cervical sympathetic ganglia pass to the cardiac plexus at the base of the heart and distribute accelerator fibers to the myocardium. Branches from the **upper 5 thoracic ganglia** pass to the thoracic aorta (vasomotor) and the posterior pulmonary plexus, through which dilator fibers reach the bronchi. (2) Those composed of presynaptic fibers* (mainly myelinated). The **splanchnic nerves** arising from the lower 7 thoracic ganglia pass to the celiac and superior mesenteric ganglia, where synaptic connections occur with ganglion cells whose axons then pass to the abdominal viscera via the celiac plexus. The **lumbar splanchnic nerves** arising from trunk ganglia in the lumbar region convey fibers to synaptic stations in the inferior mesenteric ganglion and small ganglia associated with the hypogastric plexus, through which postsynaptic fibers are distributed to the lower abdominal and pelvic viscera.

The Parasympathetic (or Craniosacral) Division (See Fig 6–2.)

The parasympathetic division of the autonomic nervous system arises from preganglionic cell bodies in the gray matter of the brain stem and the middle 3 segments of the sacral cord. The parasympathetic distribution, in contrast to that of the sympathetics, is confined entirely to visceral structures. Most of its preganglionic neurons run without interruption from their central origin to the wall of the viscus they supply or to where they synapse with terminal ganglion cells associated with the plexuses of Meissner and Auerbach in the intestinal tract. (The parasympathetic supply in

---

*These nerves also carry some visceral afferent fibers, which convey sensory impulses. By definition, however, these do not belong to the autonomic system.

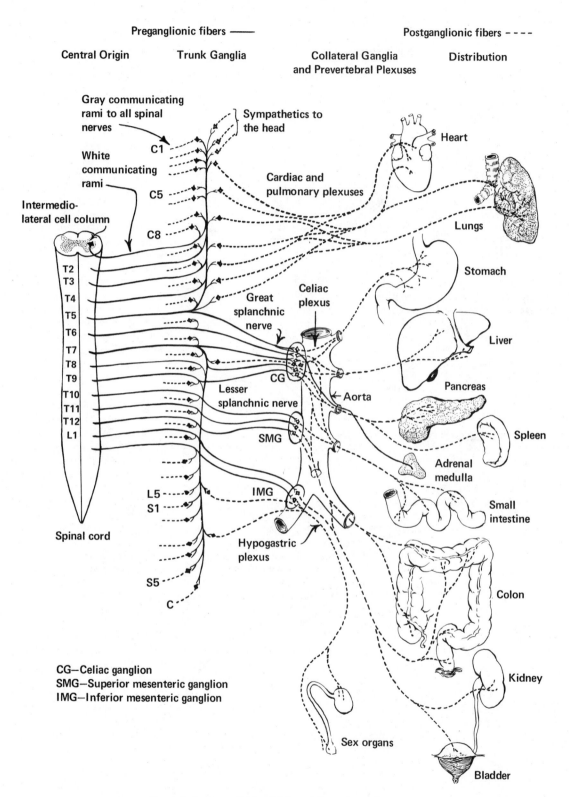

Figure 6–1. Sympathetic division of the autonomic system.

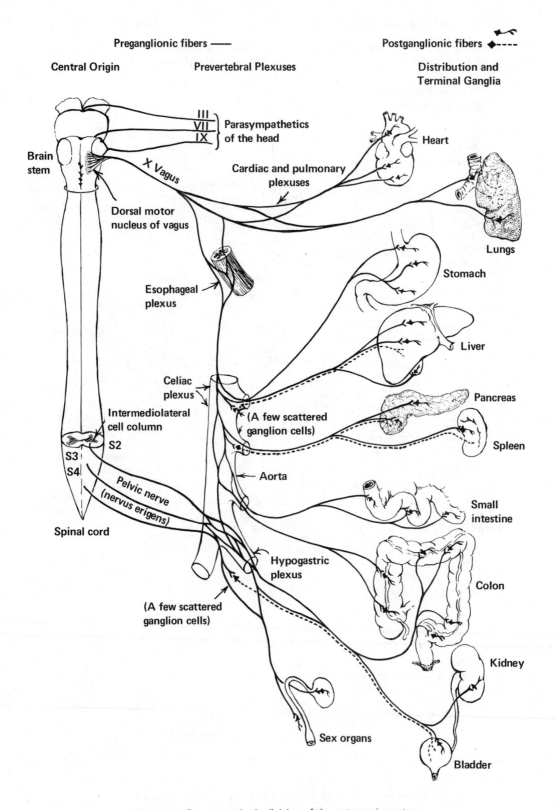

Figure 6–2. Parasympathetic division of the autonomic system.

the head follows a unique pattern outlined below.)

Nerves conveying parasympathetic fibers (preganglionic) consist of the **vagus nerve** (cranial nerve X), which distributes its autonomic fibers to the thoracic and abdominal viscera via the prevertebral plexuses; the **pelvic nerve** (nervus erigens), which distributes parasympathetics to most of the large intestine and to the pelvic viscera and genitalia via the hypogastric plexus; and **cranial nerves III, VII,** and **IX,** which distribute parasympathetics to the head.

The Great Prevertebral Plexuses of the Autonomic System (See Fig 6–2.)

These are large networks of nerves which serve as areas of redistribution for the sympathetic and parasympathetic (and sensory) fibers which enter into their formation. The cardiac plexus is located about the bifurcation of the trachea and roots of the great vessels at the base of the heart. It is divided into superficial and deep parts. It is formed from the cardiac sympathetic nerves and cardiac branches of the vagus nerve, which it distributes to the myocardium and walls of the vessels leaving the heart. The **right** and **left pulmonary plexuses** are intimately joined with the cardiac plexus and are located about the primary bronchi and pulmonary arteries at the roots of the lungs. They are formed from both the vagus and the upper thoracic sympathetic nerves and are distributed mainly to the vessels and bronchi of the lung.

The **celiac** (or **solar**) **plexus** is located in the epigastric region of the abdomen over the abdominal aorta near the origin of the celiac and superior mesenteric arteries. It is formed from vagal fibers reaching it via the esophageal plexus and sympathetic fibers arising from the associated celiac ganglia that are located on the sides of the celiac axis, together with some sympathetic fibers continued down from the thoracic aortic plexus. Its distribution includes most of the abdominal viscera, which it reaches by numerous subplexuses continued out along the various visceral branches of the aorta. These plexuses include the phrenic plexuses, the hepatic plexus, the splenic plexus, the superior gastric plexus, the suprarenal plexuses, the renal plexuses, the spermatic or ovarian plexuses, the superior and inferior mesenteric plexuses, and the abdominal aortic plexus.

The **hypogastric plexus** is located in front of the fifth lumbar vertebra and the promontory of the sacrum. It receives sympathetic fibers from the aortic plexus and lumbar trunk ganglia and parasympathetic fibers from the pelvic nerve. Its 2 lateral portions, the pelvic plexuses, lie on either side of the rectum. Distribution to the pelvic viscera and genitalia is effected by subplexuses extending out along the visceral branches of the hypogastric artery. These include the middle hemorrhoidal plexus, to the rectum; the vesical plexus, to the bladder, seminal vesicles, and ductus deferens; the prostatic plexus, to the prostate, seminal vesicles, and penis; the vaginal plexus, to the vagina and clitoris; and the uterine plexus, to the uterus and uterine tubes.

AUTONOMIC NERVES TO THE HEAD
(See Fig 6–3.)

The autonomic supply to the head deserves special consideration. The skin of the face and scalp receives sympathetic innervation from the superior cervical ganglion via plexuses extending along the branches of the external carotid artery. The intrinsic muscles of the eye, salivary glands, and mucous membranes of the nose and pharynx, however, receive a dual autonomic supply. This is mediated via 4 pairs of cranial autonomic ganglia, each of which receives a sympathetic, a parasympathetic, and a sensory root. Only the parasympathetic fibers effect synaptic connections within these ganglia, which contain the cell bodies of the postganglionic parasympathetic fibers. The sympathetic and sensory fibers pass through these ganglia without interruption.

The **ciliary ganglion** is located between the optic nerve and the lateral rectus muscle in the posterior part of the orbit. It is composed of a **parasympathetic root,** which originates from cells of the Edinger-Westphal nucleus and the upper medial oculomotor nucleus, fibers of which reach the ganglion via the inferior division of the oculomotor nerve; a **sympathetic root,** consisting of postsynaptic fibers from the superior cervical sympathetic ganglion via the carotid plexus about the internal carotid artery; and a **sensory root** from the nasociliary branch of the ophthalmic nerve. Distribution is via 12–15 short ciliary nerves, which supply the ciliary muscle of the lens and the muscles of the iris.

The **sphenopalatine ganglion** is located deep in the pterygopalatine fossa and is associated with the maxillary nerve. It is composed of a **parasympathetic root** from cells of the superior salivatory nucleus via the glossopalatine nerve, great superficial petrosal nerve, and vidian nerve through the pterygoid (vidian) canal (Fig 6–3); a **sympathetic root** from the internal carotid plexus via the great deep petrosal nerve, which joins the great superficial petrosal nerve to form the vidian nerve; and **sensory fibers,** most of which originate in the maxillary nerve but a few of which arise in cranial nerves VII and IX via the tympanic plexus and vidian nerve. Distribution is via pharyngeal rami to the mucous membranes of the roof of the pharynx; via nasal and palatine rami to the mucous membranes of the nasal cavity, uvula, palatine tonsil, and hard and soft palates; and via orbital rami to the periosteum of the orbit and the lacrimal glands. **Vail's syndrome** consists of severe attacks of unilateral, often nocturnal neuralgic pains of nose, face, eye, neck, and shoulder, attributed to neuralgia of the vidian nerve.

The **otic ganglion** is located medial to the mandibular nerve just below the foramen ovale in the infratemporal fossa. It is composed of **parasympathetic root** fibers arising in the inferior salivatory nucleus in the medulla, which course via the ninth cranial nerve, the tympanic plexus, and the lesser

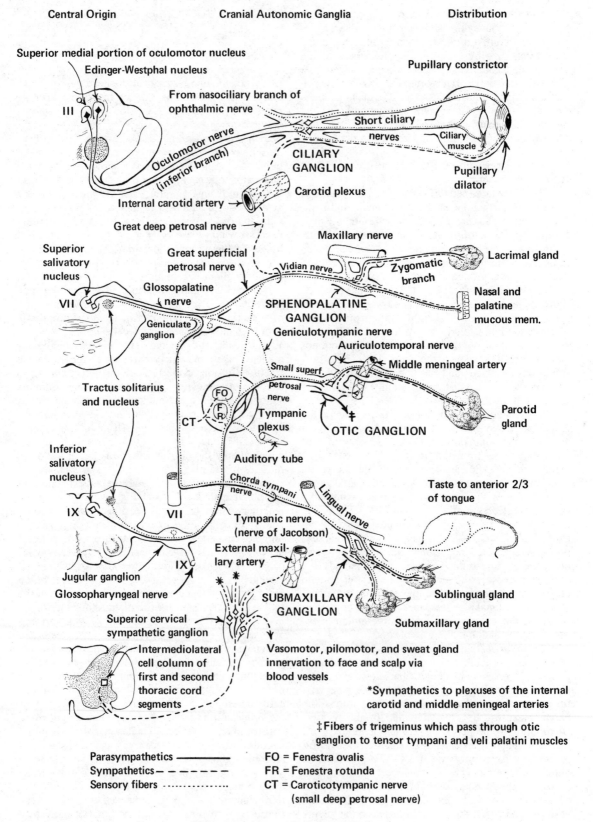

Figure 6–3. Autonomic nerves to the head.

superficial petrosal nerve (Fig 6–3); a **sympathetic root** from the superior cervical sympathetic ganglion via the plexus on the middle meningeal artery; and a **sensory root,** which probably includes fibers from the ninth cranial nerve and from the geniculate ganglion of the seventh cranial nerve via the tympanic plexus and the lesser superficial petrosal nerve. The otic ganglion supplies secretory and sensory fibers to the parotid gland. A few somatic motor fibers from the trigeminal nerve pass through the otic ganglion and supply the tensor tympani and tensor veli palatini muscles.

The **submaxillary ganglion** is located on the medial side of the mandible between the lingual nerve and the submaxillary duct. It is composed of **para-sympathetic root** fibers from the superior salivatory nucleus via the glossopalatine, chorda tympani, and lingual nerves; a **sympathetic root** from the plexus of the external maxillary artery; and a **sensory root** from the geniculate ganglion via the glossopalatine, chorda tympani, and lingual nerves. It is distributed to the submaxillary and sublingual glands.

AUTONOMIC NERVES TO THE UROGENITAL ORGANS & RECTUM

URINARY BLADDER
(See Fig 6–4.)

The urinary bladder and sphincters are under the control of the autonomic nervous sytem. Major integrating centers are in the spinal cord, and these may be considered to be both sympathetic and parasympathetic in type.

Sympathetic Innervation
A. Afferent: Afferent fibers are believed to pass from their origin in the body of the bladder (detrusor muscle) through the hypogastric plexus to the upper lumbar sympathetic ganglia, then through the posterior upper lumbar and lower thoracic nerve roots to terminate in the intermediolateral cells of the T9–L2 segments of the spinal cord. Pain and proprioceptive sensation from the bladder may be conveyed along this route.

B. Efferent: Efferent fibers are said to then proceed via the anterior T11–L2 nerve roots as white rami through the sympathetic ganglia to the hypogastric plexus, whence gray rami then innervate the detrusor muscle and internal sphincter. This system may be concerned with bladder filling. The efferent fibers may be inhibitory to the bladder detrusor and motor to the internal sphincter.

Parasympathetic Innervation
A. Afferent: Afferent fibers pass via the pudendal nerve to the second to fourth sacral posterior nerve roots, entering and terminating in the anterolateral gray matter of the sacral spinal cord at this level. These fibers are assumed to convey pain, touch, temperature, and muscle stretch sensation from the bladder and internal sphincter.

B. Efferent: Efferent fibers pass from the second to fourth sacral segments of the spinal cord as preganglionic fibers to the hypogastric plexus, whence postganglionic fibers emerge to innervate the detrusor of the bladder and the internal sphincter. These fibers are motor to the detrusor and may be inhibitory to the internal sphincter. Their action in emptying the bladder is mainly upon the detrusor.

The **external sphincter** is innervated by pudendal nerve branches which arise in the anterior horns of S2–4 segments of the spinal cord and which leave via the corresponding anterior roots (pudendal plexus). These fibers are felt to be motor for the external sphincter (and perineal musculature), which are under predominantly voluntary control. Afferent fibers within the pudendal nerve convey sensation from the external sphincter and the posterior urethra.

Suprasegmental Innervation
Cortical representation of the bladder is present in the paracentral lobule, whose stimulation may evoke bladder contractions. This system may play a part in initiating voluntary micturition and in stopping micturition by initiating contraction of the external sphincter. Other higher level representation is believed to occur also, but the specific participating structures remain obscure.

Physiology of Bladder Function
The ability to voluntarily relax the perineal muscles is essential to initiate urination, and normal tone of the pelvic diaphragm is useful for urinary continence. Cinefluorographic studies indicate that the voluntary muscles of micturition are the levator and the sphincter urethrae and the bulbocavernosus (in the male). As voiding is initiated, a progressive descent of the pelvic diaphragm occurs, and the posterior urethra fills. As the diaphragm reaches its most inferior level, there occurs a wavelike detrusor contraction that continues uninterrupted until the bladder is emptied. If the urinary stream is voluntarily interrupted, the contraction of the external sphincter interrupts the urethral stream; simultaneously, the pelvic diaphragm rapidly elevates the bladder. The distal urethra in the female then empties immediately; in the male, contraction of the bulbourethral muscle occurs to empty the distal urethra.

The bladder wall musculature, through variation in muscle tone, tends to maintain a relatively constant intravesical pressure despite varying volumes of urine. The desire to urinate usually occurs when intravesical pressure reaches about 7–8 cm of water.

Voluntary micturition may be initiated even when the bladder contains only a small amount of urine. Suprasegmental stimulation, presumably arising from the paracentral lobe of the cerebral hemisphere, activates contraction of the detrusor, with relaxation of the

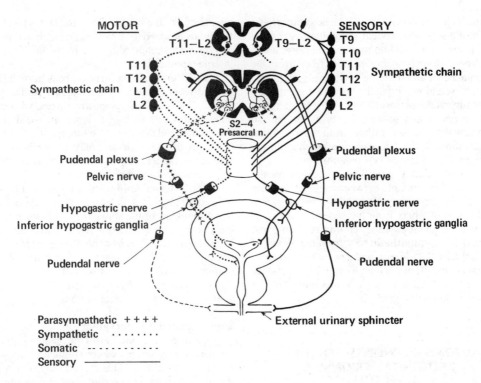

Figure 6–4. Segmental and peripheral innervation of the urinary bladder. (Reproduced, with permission, from Bors: *J Nerv Ment Dis* 1952; 116:572.)

internal and external sphincters. Associated voluntary contraction of the abdominal wall muscles plus contraction of the diaphragm with closure of the glottis, thus raising the intra-abdominal pressure, may also occur.

Following urination, voluntary contraction of the ischiocavernosus and bulbocavernosus muscles and the external sphincter closes off the bladder. Strong voluntary contractions of these muscles are required to interrupt the act of urination.

Suprasegmental, higher level inhibition may be overcome involuntarily when intravesical pressure reaches a very high level, the detrusor muscle contracting and the external sphincter relaxing. Involuntary urination in response to smaller quantities of urine may occur in a pathologically affected bladder or under emotional stress.

Disorders of Bladder Function

After acute transection of the spinal cord, control of micturition by higher centers is abolished. Complete retention occurs as a result of paralysis of the detrusor muscle and the tonic status of the internal sphincter. Overflow incontinence results from the rise of intravesical pressure overcoming the tone of the internal sphincter. Days or weeks later, a **reflex bladder** occurs, with automatic evacuation of the bladder taking place (sometimes aided by increased intra-abdominal extravesical pressure). A mass reflex may precipitate or assist emptying of the bladder by increased extravesical pressure resulting from abdominal muscle spasm.

A **flaccid neurogenic bladder** may occur when innervation from segmental spinal connections is interrupted, as in the cauda equina syndromes.

In diseases involving the afferent pathways to the CNS (such as tabes dorsalis), distention of the bladder with accumulation of urine may result, presumably because of interruption of the sensory path leading from the bladder. Involuntary automatic urinary expulsion and subsequent dribbling of urine may then occur as a result of the reaction of the bladder wall musculature and a rise in intravesical pressure above that of the internal sphincter. Disorders involving the sympathetic pathway may give rise to dilatation of ureteral orifices, relaxation of internal sphincters, and frequency of urination.

Impaired sacral parasympathetic action at the spinal cord level may cause **flaccid paralysis** of the bladder wall. If this is incomplete, difficult and inadequate evacuation may result, and residual urine will collect in the bladder. Automatic periodic expulsion of urine may occur later. Hypesthesia or anesthesia, with partial retention and overflow incontinence, may occur in congenital spinal cord disorders associated with lumbosacral spina bifida.

In children, urinary control is self-taught. Enuresis can often be stopped when the bladder can hold 300–350 mL. The ability to initiate or stop micturition develops when the child learns how to control abdominal pressure by coordination of the levator ani, the abdominal muscles, and the diaphragm. The bladder enlarges in children and is usually sufficient to hold the nightly output of urine by the time a child is 4½ years old. The ability to initiate micturition comes between age 3½ and 6 years. Contraction of the diaphragm and abdominal musculature and relaxation of the pubococcygeus muscle depress the vesical neck and initiate detrusor contraction, which expels urine. Treatment of enuresis by increasing bladder capacity by means of forcing fluids and instructing the child to hold the urine as long as possible may be effective. Drugs such as atropine sulfate, imipramine (Tofranil), methantheline (Banthine), etc, given during the daytime and at night, may help relax the bladder detrusor and promote bladder distention.

DEFECATION

The mechanisms involved in defecation are believed to be more or less similar to those of micturition. The afferent fibers enter the S3–5 segments of the spinal cord. The external anal sphincter is under voluntary control; its action is less important than that of the internal anal sphincter. Distention of the walls of the rectum is felt to be an adequate stimulus for defecation, producing contraction of the rectal muscles and relaxation of the internal anal sphincter. Stimulation of lower sacral dermatomes and bladder activity facilitate more complete response.

Abdominal wall muscular action (sixth to 12th thoracic spinal cord segments) is under voluntary control and may act as a detrusor mechanism. Transverse lesions of the spinal cord may not affect internal anal sphincter tone, but the resultant impaired contraction of the rectal wall may lead to fecal retention. Intermittent rectal incontinence may also be encountered with lesions of the spinal cord above the lower sacral level. With lesions of the third, fourth, and fifth sacral spinal cord segments, fecal incontinence is apt to occur, especially if the stool is soft or fluid. Anesthesia of the anal area may occur with lesions of the conus medullaris or with tabes dorsalis, resulting in loss of internal sphincter tone and reflex activity, with incontinence. Automatic rectal activity, like automatic bladder activity, may occur independently of CNS connections of the terminal bowel.

SEXUAL FUNCTION

The male sexual organs are innervated by 2 sets of fibers. **Parasympathetic** fibers, originating in intermediolateral cells of the second, third, and fourth sacral spinal segments, pass via the pelvic nerves to form perivesicular, prostatic, and cavernous plexuses. Vasodilator fibers pass to the corpora cavernosa. The ischiocavernosus and bulbocavernosus muscles, which are concerned in erection and ejaculation, are innervated by the perineal branch of the pudendal nerve (S2–4). **Sympathetic** nerves to the sexual organs come from the lumbar spinal cord via the hypogastric plexus. Fibers from the hypogastric plexus

and fibers from the pelvic nerves form the perivesicular plexuses. The dorsal nerves of the penis are believed to carry sympathetic fibers causing vasoconstriction in the corpora cavernosa and resultant relaxation of the penis.

Erection results from parasympathetic stimulation and is effected by engorgement of the corpora cavernosa. A purely spinal reflex erection may follow stimulation of the glans penis. Erections presumably upon a purely hormonal basis without spinal cord or higher level participation may occur. Relaxation of the penis following ejaculation is believed to be due to decreased stimulation via the pelvic nerves and contraction of the smooth muscle of the corpora cavernosa, innervated by sympathetic fibers. Emotional changes such as anger or fear, or the application of cold to the skin of the trunk, may lead to relaxation of the erect penis.

Ejaculation involves reflex patterns originating in the genital corpuscles of the glans. By way of the dorsal nerve of the penis and the common pudendal nerves, impulses enter the posterior roots of the S2–4 spinal cord segments, also traveling in part to the upper lumbar spinal cord. From the upper lumbar spinal cord, the rami communicantes pass via the hypogastric nerves to the perivesicular and prostatic plexuses, from which the unstriated musculature of the ductus deferens, the seminal vesicles, and the prostate is innervated. It is felt that soon after activation of the upper lumbar reflex mechanisms, sacral spinal cord stimulation of muscle fibers of the bulbocavernosus and ischiocavernosus muscles leads to their clonic contraction. **Nocturnal ejaculations** presumably do not require the same stimuli as do ejaculations in the waking state. Sleep probably depresses the inhibitory effects of higher centers on spinal cord reflex mechanisms.ᵗ

Orgasm is made up of the associated reactions and sensations occurring with ejaculation of semen in men and with rhythmic contraction of muscles of the distended vagina in women. Autonomic nervous system effects such as increase in heart rate and blood pressure and altered respiratory patterns may occur. Tonic contraction of the thigh muscles may accompany orgasm.

PHYSIOLOGY OF THE AUTONOMIC SYSTEM

The Sympathetic Division

The sympathetic division of the autonomic nervous system is thrown into activity in preparation of the organism for "flight or fight." It gives rise to mass responses as a possible consequence of the existence of sympathetic ganglion chains or plexuses where the preganglionic synapses occur. In action it tends to produce vasoconstriction of the skin and viscera, shifting more blood to the brain, skeletal muscles, and heart. Removal of the sympathetic chain in animals and humans may lower blood pressure and body temperature.

The Parasympathetic Division

The parasympathetic division, on the other hand, tends to give more localized reactions, and this may be related to the anatomic fact that the preganglionic synapse is usually embedded in the organ to be affected.

Functional Antagonism of the Two Systems

The viscera receive a dual autonomic supply. In

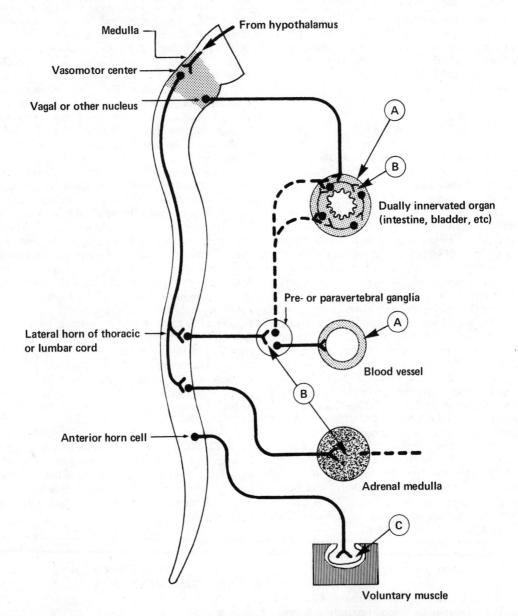

Figure 6–5. Functional organization and chemical transmission in autonomic and somatic efferent nerves. Fibers of cholinergic neurons are shown by solid lines, and the presence of a myelin sheath may be indicated. Fibers of adrenergic neurons are shown by dashed lines. Cholinomimetic drugs act at the following sites: *A:* On muscarinic receptors on the effector tissue to contract nonvascular smooth muscle and stimulate exocrine glands but to relax vascular smooth muscle. *B:* On nicotinic receptors at ganglionic synapses where acetylcholine is also the mediator. Postganglionic sympathetic activity is increased, which constricts blood vessels and stimulates the heart. The adrenal medulla is also activated by agents that mimic the effect of preganglionic activity, and epinephrine is released into the circulation. *C:* On receptors on the motor end-plate of voluntary muscle to initiate contraction of single units. Cholinesterase inhibitors act at *A*, *B*, and *C* by allowing the accumulation of acetylcholine, but not at *A* in blood vessels, since no acetylcholine is liberated that can be protected from hydrolysis. (Reproduced, with permission, from Meyers FH, Jawetz E, Goldfien A: *Review of Medical Pharmacology,* 7th ed. Lange, 1980.)

most cases, the 2 sets of nerves function antagonistically to one another. However, some autonomic effectors appear to have a sympathetic nerve supply only. In some cases where there is a dual nerve supply, the action of the 2 divisions (sympathetic and parasympathetic) may not be antagonistic. Classification of autonomic postganglionic neurons as adrenergic or cholinergic may be more useful clinically and functionally than their classification as sympathetic or parasympathetic. Most (but not all) sympathetic postganglionic elements are adrenergic. Most (but probably not all) parasympathetic postganglionic elements are cholinergic.

Autonomic Representation of the Cerebral Cortex (See Figs 1–10 and 1–11.)

Autonomic representation also takes place within the cerebral cortex and indicates that higher integration may occur. Autonomic and motor cortical overlapping often occurs, as demonstrated by lacrimation and pupillary changes on stimulation of the eye field area of the cortex (Brodmann area 8) and the production of conjugate ocular movements. Blood pressure changes, inhibition of respiration, vasoconstriction and vasodilatation, gastrointestinal hypermotility, salivation, and abnormalities of sweating have been produced by cortical stimulation. Cardiovascular reactions may occur after stimulation of Brodmann areas 4 and 6; elevation or depression of blood pressure, alteration of heart rate, and vasoconstriction and vasodilatation of the blood vessels of the extremities have been described. Respiration may be inhibited by stimulation of the orbital surface (area 47), cingulate gyrus (area 24), the anterior portion of the insula, and the tip of the temporal lobe (area 38). Sweat secretion is altered by area 6 stimulation. Gastrointestinal function may be affected by cortical stimulation. Increased peristaltic movement and gastric secretion may follow stimulation of area 8, and inhibition of the gastric musculature may follow stimulation of area 47. Evidence of marked hunger is evident in animals with premotor ablation. Salivation may occur following stimulation of the motor area of the tongue and face (area 4). Urinary incontinence may follow bilateral lesions of the portions of areas 4 and 6 lying on the medial surface of the cerebral hemispheres.

Integration of autonomic activity at other suprasegmental levels can occur. The medulla oblongata integrates sweating reflexes and blood pressure alterations. The hypothalamus affects heat regulation (peripheral vasoconstriction, vasodilatation, and sweating).

PHARMACOLOGY OF THE AUTONOMIC SYSTEM

Acetylcholine and norepinephrine are the principal transmitter agents involved in transmission at synaptic junctions between pre- and postganglionic neurons and between postganglionic neurons and autonomic effectors.

Acetylcholine is liberated at all preganglionic endings. High concentrations of acetylcholine, choline acetylase, and specific cholinesterase are found only in cholinergic nerve endings.

Norepinephrine (levarterenol) is the chemical transmitter at most sympathetic postganglionic endings. Norepinephrine and its methyl derivative, epinephrine, are secreted by the adrenal medulla. Epinephrine, however, is not considered to be a mediator at sympathetic endings. Although many viscera contain both norepinephrine and epinephrine, only the norepinephrine content can be related to the number of sympathetic nerve endings in the organ. Some sympathetically innervated organs contain only norepinephrine. Drugs that block the effects of epinephrine but not norepinephrine have little effect on the response of most organs to stimulation of their adrenergic nerve supply.

The autonomic nervous system may be divided into cholinergic and adrenergic divisions based on the chemical mediator released. Cholinergic neurons include the following: (1) all preganglionic neurons, (2) anatomically parasympathetic postganglionic neurons, (3) anatomically sympathetic postganglionic neurons to sweat glands, and (4) anatomically sympathetic vasodilator neurons to skeletal muscle blood vessels. In the adrenal medulla, the postganglionic cells have lost their axons and have become specialized for secretion directly into the blood; the cholinergic preganglionic neurons to these cells act as the secretomotor nerve supply to the gland.

Postganglionic sympathetic neurons are generally considered to be adrenergic except for the sympathetic vasodilator neurons and the sweat gland neurons. Some secretion of norepinephrine by adrenergic neurons may be preceded by liberation of acetylcholine in these neurons.

The effectors on which epinephrine and norepinephrine act can be separated into 2 categories based on their different sensitivities to certain drugs. This is felt to be related to the existence of 2 types of catecholamine receptors in the effector organs: the alpha (α) and beta (β) receptors. The α receptors mediate vasoconstriction, whereas the β receptors mediate such actions as increase in cardiac rate and strength of cardiac contraction. Two subtypes of α receptors (α_1 and α_2) and 2 subtypes of β receptors (β_1 and β_2) have been described. Alpha and beta receptors occur in presynaptic endings as well as in postsynaptic membranes. The presynaptic α-adrenergic endings are of the α_2 type, and the postsynaptic receptors are of the α_1 and α_2 types.

There is usually no acetylcholine in circulating blood, and the effects of localized cholinergic discharge are generally discrete and short because of high concentrations of cholinesterase at cholinergic nerve endings. Norepinephrine has a more prolonged and wider action than acetylcholine.

Table 6–1. Responses of effector organs to autonomic nerve impulses and circulating catecholamines.*

Effector Organs	Cholinergic Impulses Response	Noradrenergic Impulses Receptor Type	Noradrenergic Impulses Response
Eye			
Radial muscle of iris	...	a	Contraction (mydriasis)
Sphincter muscle of iris	Contraction (miosis)		...
Ciliary muscle	Contraction for near vision	β	Relaxation for far vision
Heart			
S-A node	Decrease in heart rate; vagal arrest	β_1	Increase in heart rate
Atria	Decrease in contractility and (usually) increase in conduction velocity	β_1	Increase in contractility and conduction velocity
A-V node and conduction system	Decrease in conduction velocity; A-V block	β_1	Increase in conduction velocity
Ventricles	...	β_1	Increase in contractility and conduction velocity
Arterioles			
Coronary, skeletal muscle, pulmonary, abdominal viscera, renal	Dilatation	a β_2	Constriction Dilatation
Skin and mucosa, cerebral, salivary glands	...	a	Constriction
Systemic veins	...	a β_2	Constriction Dilatation
Lung			
Bronchial muscle	Contraction	β_2	Relaxation
Bronchial glands	Stimulation	?	Inhibition (?)
Stomach			
Motility and tone	Increase	a, β_2	Decrease (usually)
Sphincters	Relaxation (usually)	a	Contraction (usually)
Secretion	Stimulation		Inhibition (?)
Intestine			
Motility and tone	Increase	a, β_2	Decrease
Sphincters	Relaxation (usually)	a	Contraction (usually)
Secretion	Stimulation		Inhibition(?)
Gallbladder and ducts	Contraction		Relaxation
Urinary bladder			
Detrusor	Contraction	β	Relaxation (usually)
Trigone and sphincter	Relaxation	a	Contraction
Ureter			
Motility and tone	Increase (?)	a	Increase (usually)
Uterus	Variable†	a, β_2	Variable†
Male sex organs	Erection	a	Ejaculation
Skin			
Pilomotor muscles	...	a	Contraction
Sweat glands	Generalized secretion	a	Slight, localized secretion‡
Spleen capsule	...	a β_2	Contraction Relaxation
Adrenal medulla	Secretion of epinephrine and norepinephrine		...
Liver	...	a, β_2	Glycogenolysis
Pancreas			
Acini	Secretion	a	Decreased secretion
Islets	Insulin and glucagon secretion	a β_2	Inhibition of insulin and glucagon secretion Insulin and glucagon secretion
Salivary glands	Profuse, watery secretion	a β_2	Thick, viscous secretion Amylase secretion
Lacrimal glands	Secretion		...
Nasopharyngeal glands	Secretion		...
Adipose tissue	...	β	Lipolysis
Juxtaglomerular cells	...	$\beta (\beta_1 ?)$	Renin secretion
Pineal gland	...	β	Melatonin synthesis and secretion

*Modified from Gilman AG, Goodman LS, Gilman A (editors): *The Pharmacological Basis of Therapeutics,* 6th ed. Macmillan, 1980.
†Depends on stage of menstrual cycle, amount of circulating estrogen and progesterone, and other factors. Responses of pregnant uterus different from those of nonpregnant.
‡On palms of hands and in some other locations ("adrenergic sweating").

Table 6–2. Some drugs that affect sympathetic activity. Only the principal actions of the drugs are listed. Note that guanethidine is believed to have 2 principal actions.*

Site of Action	Drugs That Augment Sympathetic Activity	Drugs That Depress Sympathetic Activity
Sympathetic ganglia	**Stimulate postganglionic neurons** Nicotine Dimethphenylpiperazinium **Inhibit acetylcholinesterase** DFP (diisopropyl fluorophosphate) Physostigmine (eserine) Neostigmine (Prostigmin) Parathion	**Block conduction** Chlorisondamine (Ecolid) Hexamethonium (Bistrium, C-6) Mecamylamine (Inversine) Pentolinium (Ansolysen) Tetraethylammonium (Etamon, TEA) Trimethaphan (Arfonad) High concentrations of acetylcholine, anticholinesterase drugs
Endings of postganglionic neurons	**Release norepinephrine** Tyramine Ephedrine Amphetamine	**Block norepinephrine synthesis** a-Methyl-p-tyrosine **Interfere with norepinephrine storage** Reserpine Guanethidine (Ismelin) **Prevent norepinephrine release** Bretylium tosylate (Darenthin) Guanethidine (Ismelin) **Form false transmitters** a-Methyldopa (Aldomet)
a Receptors	**Stimulate a_1 receptors** Methoxamine (Vasoxyl) Phenylephrine (Neo-Synephrine) **Stimulates a_2 receptors** Clonidine	**Block a receptors** Phenoxybenzamine (Dibenzyline) Phentolamine (Regitine) Prazosin (blocks a_1) Yohimbine (blocks a_2)
β Receptors	**Stimulates β receptors** Isoproterenol (Isuprel)	**Block β receptors** Propranolol (Inderal) Practolol (blocks β_1) Butoxamine (blocks β_2)

*Reproduced, with permission, from Ganong WF: *Review of Medical Physiology,* 10th ed. Lange, 1981.

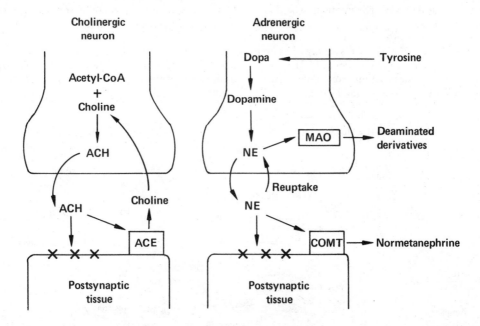

Figure 6–6. Comparison of the biochemical events at cholinergic endings with those at adrenergic endings. ACH = acetylcholine; ACE = acetylcholinesterase; NE = norepinephrine; X = receptor. Note that monoamine oxidase (MAO) is intracellular, so that some norepinephrine is being constantly deaminated in adrenergic endings. Catechol-O-methyltransferase (COMT) acts on norepinephrine after it is secreted. (Reproduced, with permission, from Ganong WF: *Review of Medical Physiology,* 10th ed. Lange, 1981.)

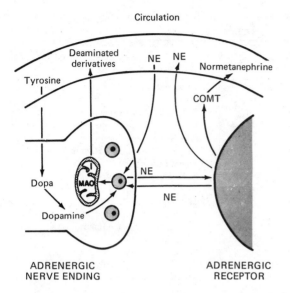

Figure 6–7. Formation, uptake, and metabolism of norepinephrine at adrenergic nerve endings. Norepinephrine in the granulated vesicles is mainly released from the endings by action potentials in the sympathetic nerves. However, some of the norepinephrine constantly diffuses from the granules to the mitochondria, where it is oxidized to deaminated derivatives. Norepinephrine in the vesicles is formed from dopamine, taken up from the circulation, and taken up again after it is released from the endings (reuptake). (Reproduced, with permission, from Ganong WF: *Review of Medical Physiology,* 5th ed. Lange, 1971.)

Autonomic drugs may act by mimicking or blocking cholinergic or adrenergic discharges. Drugs may also produce specific effects within the stages of transmitter effect: (1) synthesis, (2) storage in nerve endings, (3) release near effector cells, (4) action on effector cells, and (5) destruction. Sometimes, a drug action may release 2 mediators rather than one.

Despite apparent similarities in the transmitter chemistry of preganglionic and postganglionic cholinergic neurons, drugs may act at these sites differently. **Muscarine** has little effect on autonomic ganglia but stimulates visceral cholinergic postganglionic neurons. Drugs with muscarinelike action include acetylcholine, congeners of acetylcholine, and inhibitors of cholinesterase (DFP, nerve gases, etc). Atropine, belladonna, and other natural and synthetic belladonnalike drugs block the muscarinic effects of acetylcholine by preventing the mediator from acting on visceral effector organs.

Although small doses of acetylcholine stimulate postganglionic cells, large doses block the transmission of impulses from pre- to postganglionic neurons. These actions are not affected by atropine. **Nicotine** has the same actions, and the actions of acetylcholine in the presence of atropine are called its nicotinic effects.

Curariform agents act by blocking transmission principally at cholinergic motor neuron endings on skeletal muscle fibers.

Drugs that block the effects of norepinephrine on visceral effectors are often called adrenergic blocking agents, adrenolytic agents, and sympatholytic agents.

When autonomic effectors (smooth muscle, cardiac muscle, or glands) are partially or completely separated from their normal nerve connections, they may become more sensitive to the action of chemical substances. This effect is more pronounced after postganglionic as opposed to preganglionic interruption. This denervation sensitization was labeled by Cannon a "law of denervation."

A protein **nerve growth factor** has been found in the salivary glands of some laboratory mammals that stimulates neuron growth, particularly in the autonomic nervous system. Injection of antiserum to this nerve growth factor in newborn animals leads to severe destruction of the sympathetic ganglia, producing an "immunosympathectomy" in these animals.

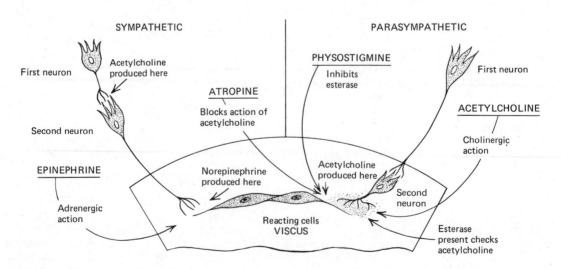

Figure 6–8. Sites of action of drugs on a viscus.

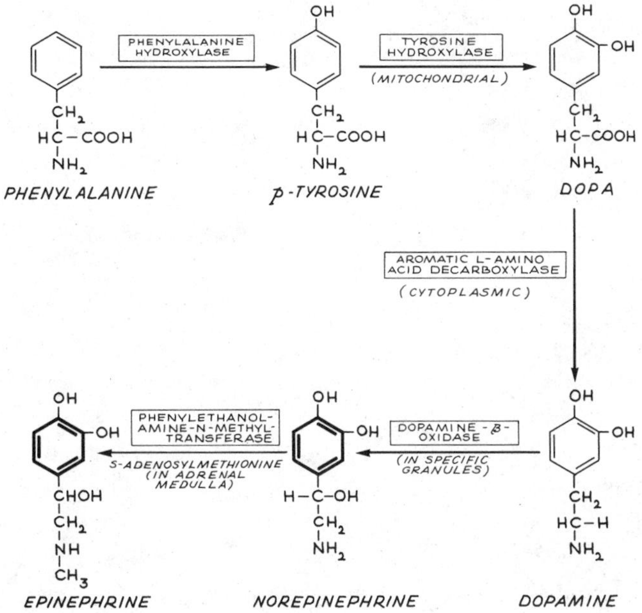

Figure 6–9. Biosynthesis of catecholamines. Dopa = dihydroxyphenylalanine; dopamine = dihydroxyphenylethylamine. (Reproduced, with permission, from Meyers FH, Jawetz E, Goldfien A: *Review of Medical Pharmacology,* 7th ed. Lange, 1980.)

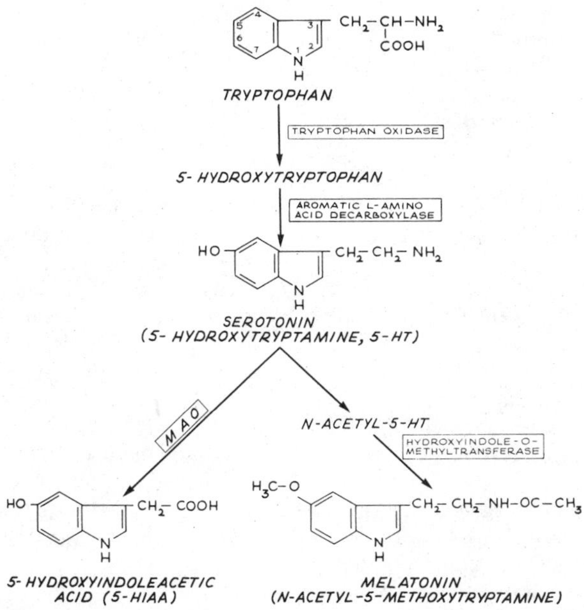

Figure 6–10. Synthesis and metabolism of serotonin. Note that the same enzyme catalyzes the decarboxylation of 5-hydroxytryptophan to serotonin and dopa to dopamine. (Reproduced, with permission, from Meyers FH, Jawetz E, Goldfien A: *Review of Medical Pharmacology,* 7th ed. Lange, 1980.)

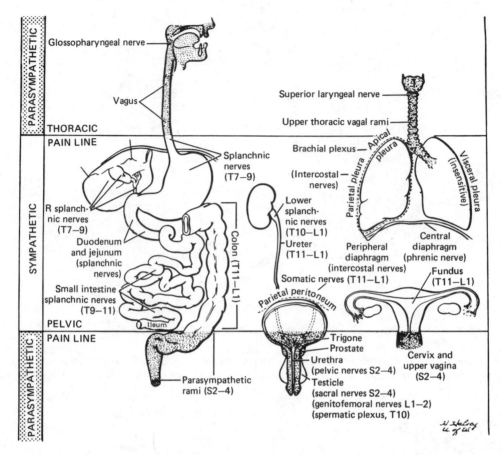

Figure 6–11. Pain innervation of the viscera. Pain afferents from structures above the thoracic pain line and below the pelvic pain line traverse parasympathetic pathways. (After White. Reproduced, with permission, from Ruch TC, in: *Physiology and Biophysics,* 19th ed. Ruch TC, Patton HD [editors]. Saunders, 1965.)

DISORDERS OF
THE AUTONOMIC SYSTEM

Disturbances Clearly Related to Autonomic Involvement

Horner's syndrome (Fig 6–12) is a unilateral enophthalmos, ptosis, miosis, and flushing of the face often caused by an ipsilateral involvement of the sympathetic fibers in the cervical sympathetic chain or upper thoracic cord.

Hirschsprung's disease (megacolon) consists of a tremendous dilatation of the colon, with chronic constipation. It is associated with congenital lack of parasympathetic ganglia and the existence of abnormal nerve fibrils in an apparently normal segment of large bowel wall.

Spinal shock, or **diaschisis,** is a type of vascular failure possibly due to sudden release of sympathetic vasomotor tone resulting from transection of or severe injury to the spinal cord or from an overdose of spinal anesthetic.

Vasomotor, Trophic, & Secretory Disturbances

Disturbances occurring in the affected tissues in various central and peripheral nerve injuries may be partly the result of interruption of the sympathetic fibers, but the importance of concomitant circulatory disturbances and disuse must not be overlooked. Included in this group are muscle atrophy, skin and nail changes, etc, which are described in Chapter 14.

Trophoneuroses

These are probably related to autonomic dysfunction. **Acroparesthesia** is a slowly progressive disorder most commonly found in women of middle age and

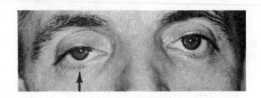

Figure 6–12. Horner's syndrome. Right Horner's syndrome associated with right superior sulcus lung tumor.

characterized by crawling and tingling sensations, usually of the hands, and often associated with pain, hyperesthesia, hyperalgesia, and coldness of the hands. Some claim it is a mild form of Raynaud's disease (see below). **Erythromelalgia** (Weir Mitchell's disease) is a rare condition of middle life characterized by periodic reddening of the skin and severe pain in one or more extremities. Attacks seldom last more than a few hours and are associated with marked hyperalgesia and sweating of the affected parts. Trophic changes usually develop in the skin and nails.

Raynaud's disease is a disease of young women that affects the toes, the fingers, the edges of the ears, and the tip of the nose and spreads to involve large areas. Beginning with local changes, when the parts are pale and cold, it may progress to local asphyxia characterized by a blue-gray cyanosis and, finally, symmetric dry gangrene. It is a disorder of the peripheral vascular innervation. **Scleroderma** is a diffuse or circumscribed thickening of the skin that may be accompanied by or follow Raynaud's disease or other vasomotor-trophic disturbances.

Angioneurotic edema (Quincke's disease) consists of attacks of acute circumscribed nonpitting edema occurring on the arms or face and preceded by general malaise, chills, and slight fever. It may be precipitated by emotional stress but lasts only a few hours. In rare cases, death has resulted from involvement of the respiratory passages.

Hereditary trophedema (Milroy's disease) is a rare, chronic, familial, nonpitting edema of one or more extremities, producing local elephantiasis.

Lipodystrophy is a rare affliction, more common in women, characterized by wasting of the fatty tissues of the upper part of the body and excessive obesity of the hips and lower extremities.

Progressive facial hemiatrophy (Romberg's disease) is a rare disorder of early life characterized by marked wasting of one side of the face. Total hemiatrophy, an allied condition, is even less common.

Morvan's disease is a term applied to the atrophic changes of the bones, skin, and muscles of the hand in syringomyelia.

Adiposis dolorosa (Dercum's disease) is characterized by large painful lumps or layers of fat over the shoulders, arms, and legs, usually in women. The cause is not known.

Hemiedema is a unilateral edema associated with hemiplegia.

Causalgia is a painful condition of the hands or feet caused by irritation of the median or sciatic nerve by injury and characterized by severe burning pain, glossy skin, swelling, redness, sweating, and trophic nail changes. Causalgia may frequently be relieved by sympathetic blocks or sympathectomy of the involved areas.

Riley-Day syndrome (familial dysautonomia) is characterized by defective lacrimation, absence of tears on crying, excessive sweating, sialorrhea, emotional lability, symmetric blotchy erythema upon emotional stress or eating, relative indifference to pain, poor motor coordination, hyporeflexia, postural hypotension, and behavioral difficulties. This congenital condition is seen most often in children of Jewish ancestry. Response to intradermal histamine (1:1000) may serve as a diagnostic test, since the usual zone of erythema ("flare") is absent in affected subjects.

7 | Muscle

COMPOSITION OF MUSCLE

The chemical composition of muscle has been most completely studied in striated muscle, where it consists of 75% water, 20% protein, and 5% inorganic material, organic "extractives," and carbohydrates (glycogen and its derivatives).

Muscle Proteins

The muscle fibrils are mainly protein, and these fibrillar proteins are characterized by their elasticity, or contractile power.

A. Myosin: Myosin is the most abundant protein in muscle. Myosin is a globulin, soluble in dilute salt solution and insoluble in water. In the presence of ATP (adenosine triphosphate), a complex of actin and myosin (actomyosin) dissociates into actin and myosin A, accompanied by muscular contraction. The energy for the contraction is supplied by the breakdown of ATP to ADP (adenosine diphosphate), a reaction catalyzed by adenosine triphosphatase (ATPase).

B. Actin: Actin is a globulin (MW about 45,000) that binds one ATP per mole. If actin is prepared by extraction with dilute salt solutions, the protein can be obtained in the form of G- (globular) actin. G-actin polymerizes to F- (fibrous) actin in the presence of Mg^{2+} or when the ionic strength of G-actin is increased.

C. Tropomyosin and Troponin: Tropomyosin is a protein (MW about 70,000) located in the thin filaments between 2 strands of actin. Troponin is a complex of 3 polypeptide chains (TpT, TpI, and TpC), also located in the actin filaments. The troponin molecules are small globular units located at intervals along the tropomyosin molecule. The effect of calcium ion on the interaction of myosin and actin is mediated by tropomyosin and troponin. Troponin T (TpT) binds the other troponin components to tropomyosin; troponin I (TpI) inhibits the interaction of actin and myosin; and troponin C (TpC) contains the binding sites for ionic calcium, which initiates contraction.

D. Myoglobin: This conjugated protein, often called muscle hemoglobin, is similar to hemoglobin and may function as an oxygen carrier. The molecular weight of myoglobin is one-fourth that of hemoglobin. In crush injuries and some muscle disorders, myoglobin appears in the urine. It may precipitate in the renal tubules, causing obstruction of the tubules and anuria.

Muscle Extractives

A variety of compounds can be easily extracted from muscle with water, alcohol, or ether. Those containing nitrogen include creatine and phosphocreatine; the purines adenine, guanine, xanthine, hypoxanthine, uric acid, and adenylic acid (from ATP); carnosine and anserine; and the betaine carnitine.

Other extractives of muscle (nonnitrogenous) are mainly glycogen and its derivatives formed in glycolysis.

Inorganic Constituents of Muscle

The cations of muscle include potassium, sodium, magnesium, and calcium, with potassium characteristically high. The anions include phosphate, chloride, and small amounts of sulfate.

Intracellular potassium is important in muscle metabolism. A considerable amount of potassium is incorporated into tissue when glycogen is deposited in muscle and when protein is being synthesized. Muscle weakness is often associated with potassium deficiency. Calcium and magnesium of muscle appear to function as activators or inhibitors of intramuscular enzyme systems.

STRUCTURE OF MUSCLE
(See Fig 7–1.)

Muscles usually are classified as striated or smooth, depending upon their appearance under an ordinary light microscope. **Striated muscle** is made up of muscle fibers that may run the whole length of the muscle and join with tendons at its ends. Around each fiber is an electrically polarized membrane, the inside of which is about 100 mV negative with respect to the outside. If this membrane is temporarily depolarized, the muscle fiber contracts. The nerve impulse traveling down the motor nerve is transmitted at the motor endplate, and a wave of depolarization (**"action potential"**) then sweeps down the muscle fiber and in some way causes a single twitch.

The great mass of somatic musculature is striated. It has well-developed cross-striations, usually does not contract in the absence of nervous stimulation, lacks anatomic and functional connections between individual muscle fibers, and is generally under voluntary control. Cardiac muscle also has cross-striations but

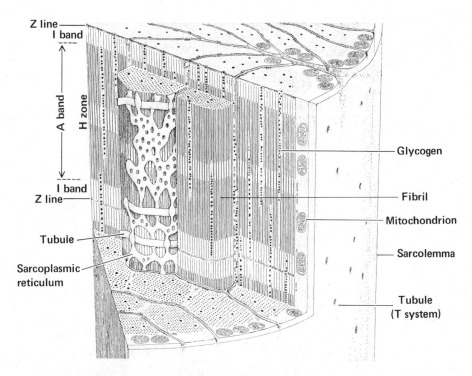

Figure 7–1. Structure of skeletal muscle fiber. The fiber is made up of a number of fibrils and surrounded by a membrane, the sarcolemma. Each fibril is surrounded by sarcoplasmic reticulum and by the T system of tubules, which opens to the exterior of the fiber. (Reproduced, with permission, from Hoyle: How is muscle turned on and off? *Scientific American* [April] 1970; **222**:84. Copyright © 1970 by Scientific American, Inc. All rights reserved.)

appears functionally to be syncytial and contracts rhythmically even when denervated. **Smooth muscle,** present in walls of blood vessels and most hollow viscera, is sometimes syncytial and has inherent rhythmic contractile activity.

Striated muscle in humans may also be classified grossly as red or white. The red, or "slow," muscles contain more myoglobin, have less evident striations, respond more slowly, and have a longer latency than the white. They are adapted for long, slow posture-maintaining contractures. (The long muscles of the back are typical examples.) White muscles are "fast," have fewer muscle fibers per motor unit and short twitch durations, and are specialized for fine skilled movements. Extraocular muscles and hand muscles

belong to the white muscle group. Eccles has found that in kittens the muscle changes from slow to fast when single nerve fibers are crossed from fast to slow muscles, suggesting that a nerve cell affects the properties of the muscle it innervates.

In mammalian skeletal muscle, at least 2 different histologic and morphologic types of striated muscle fibers occur. These are known as type I and type II fibers, and histochemical differences between the 2 types of fibers are being established. Differences between the 2 fiber types in their glycogen, phosphorylase, cytochrome oxidase, several dehydrogenases, etc, have been noted through the use of histochemical methods.

The chemical reactions that are the source of

Table 7–1. Five major cellular compartments in muscle and their functional significance.*

Compartment	Pertinent Biochemical Constituents	Function
Sarcoplasm	Numerous enzymes	Glycolysis
Mitochondria	Enzymes of oxidation and phosphorylation	Steady-state aerobic activity or recovery from oxygen debt
Fibrils	Actin and myosin	Contraction
Sarcotubular system	Active concentration and release of calcium ions	On-and-off control of active state
Membrane	Lipoprotein structure with variable selective permeability for ions	Excitation and impulse conduction

*Reproduced, with permission, from Pearson et al: Skeletal muscle: Basic and chemical aspects and illustrative new diseases. *Ann Intern Med* 1967;**67**:614.

Table 7—2. Significant muscle fiber characteristics.*

Special Features	Histochemical Type I Fibers	Histochemical Type II Fibers
Anatomic location		
Extremities	Deep muscles and axial portions of surface muscles	Superficial portions of surface muscles
Contraction characteristics	Slow contraction, tension sustained	Rapid strong contraction, short duration
Metabolic characteristics		
Energy source	Oxidative phosphorylation	Glycolysis
Metabolites	Fatty acids, glucose	Glycogen
Enzymatic characteristics†		
Mitochondrial enzymes	Rich	Low
Cytochrome oxidase		
DPNH diaphorase		
Beta-hydroxybutyric dehydrogenase		
Succinate dehydrogenase		
Krebs cycle enzymes		
Glycolytic enzymes	Low	Rich
Phosphorylase		
Lactic dehydrogenase		
Myosin ATPase	Low	Rich
Predominant isozymes of lactic dehydrogenase	LD_1, LD_2, LD_3	LD_4, LD_5

*Reproduced, with permission, from Pearson et al: Skeletal muscle: Basic and chemical aspects and illustrative new diseases. *Ann Intern Med* 1967;**67**:614.
†DPNH = reduced diphosphopyridine nucleotide; ATPase = adenosine triphosphatase.

energy for muscle contraction must be controlled not only by the changes in length of the muscle but also by the tension placed on the muscle during the change. The contractile structure of muscle consists mostly of protein (myosin, actin, and tropomyosin). Myosin is especially abundant and can catalyze the removal of a phosphate group from ATP, a reaction closely associated with the events of contraction. Myosin and actin in solution can combine to form a complex known as actomyosin, and threads of actomyosin contract in the presence of ATP.

The striated appearance of skeletal muscle arises from a repeating variation in the density, ie, the concentration of protein along the myofibril. There is a regular alternation of dense bands (A bands) and light bands (I bands). The central region of the A band, known as the H zone, is often less dense than the rest of this band. The Z membrane, or Z line, is a dense narrow line that bisects the I band. The area between 2 adjacent Z lines is called a sarcomere.

Electron microscopy indicates that myofibrils contain 2 types of filament, one twice as thick as the other. The thick filaments are believed to be myosin (MW about 500,000) and the thin filaments actin (MW about 45,000). Overlapping of filaments is believed to

give rise to the striations, or cross-bands, of the myofibril. Changes in pattern occur during contraction, when it is believed that the 2 sets of filaments (thick and thin) slide past each other.

The sarcotubular system, made up of a T system and a sarcoplasmic reticulum, surrounds the muscle fibrils and appears as vesicles and tubules in electron photomicrographs. The T system, which is continuous with the membrane of the muscle fiber, forms a grid perforated by individual muscle fibrils, and the space between the 2 layers of the T system is an extension of the extracellular space. The sarcoplasmic reticulum forms an irregular curtain around each of the fibrils between its contacts with the T system, which is at the junction of the A and I bands. The juxtaposition of the central T system with sarcoplasmic reticulum has led to the use of the term "triads" to describe the system at these junctions. The T system appears to aid the rapid transmission of action potentials from the cell membrane to all the fibrils of muscle. The sarcoplasmic

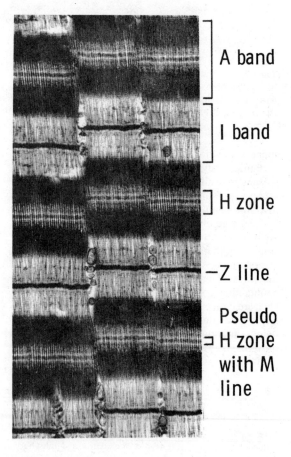

Figure 7—2. Electron micrograph of skeletal muscle of rabbit (× 24,000), showing lines, bands, and zones. (Photograph reproduced, with permission, from Huxley: The contraction of muscle. *Scientific American* [Nov], 1958;**199**:66. Copyright © 1958 by Scientific American, Inc. All rights reserved.)

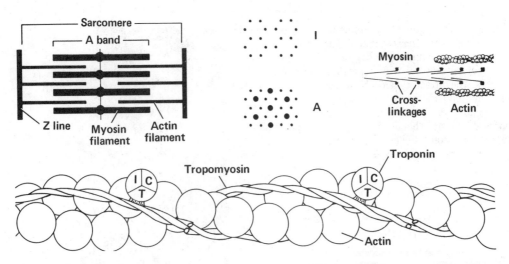

Figure 7-3. *Top left:* Arrangement of actin and myosin filaments in skeletal muscle. I and A represent a cross section through the I band and the lateral portion of the A band, respectively. *Top right:* Detail of structure of myosin and actin. *Bottom:* Diagrammatic representation of the arrangement of actin, tropomyosin, and the 3 subunits of troponin. (Reproduced, with permission, from Ganong WF: *Review of Medical Physiology,* 10th ed. Lange, 1981.)

reticulum is concerned with calcium movement and muscle metabolism.

In the absence of calcium ions, troponin and tropomyosin inhibit the interaction of actin and myosin. Release of calcium ions from the sarcolemma occurs after excitation of the motor nerve to muscle, whereupon binding of calcium to troponin C then occurs, leading to changes in tropomyosin and thence in actin. Actin then reacts with myosin, resulting in associated muscular contraction that persists until the calcium ion is removed or inactivated.

FUNCTION OF MUSCLE

Upon effective stimulation, several almost instantaneous transformations occur in muscle. The muscle shortens or attempts to shorten, and electrical, structural, chemical, and thermal changes occur that are reversible and can repeat themselves after very brief intervals, resulting in cycles of contraction and relaxation. Contraction of muscle under a constant load is called isotonic. Contraction at a constant length of muscle is called isometric.

One of the factors determining muscle tension is the number of fibers or motor units activated by a given stimulus. A twitch is the response of skeletal muscle to a single nerve impulse. With a maximal single stimulus, all motor units are activated and maximal twitch tension or shortening is developed. If 2 maximal stimuli are delivered in quick enough succession so that the second stimulus arrives before the contraction cycle is over, the response is greater than that elicited by a single maximal stimulus to the single muscle fiber, motor unit, or whole muscle. There is thus a mechanical fusion, or summation, of contractions. The degree of fusion is greatest when the stimulus

interval is shortest; the degree of summation decreases as the interval between the stimuli approaches the duration of the single mechanical response.

When a series of repetitive stimuli is applied at a rate high enough to cause summation of contraction, it may be possible to cause complete mechanical fusion and a sustained smooth response, known as **tetanus.** The critical fusion rate (the frequency of stimulus necessary to produce a complete tetanus) is higher for "fast" muscle, with relatively brief contraction time, and lower for "slow" muscle, with longer contraction time.

Gradation of muscular activity may be affected also by such factors as the number of motor units activated, variations in stimulus frequency, and the arrival of impulses at various motor units nonsimultaneously.

Neuromuscular transmission refers to the process by which a nerve impulse is converted into a muscle action current. Each nerve fiber terminates at a specialized region of the muscle fiber, a delicate and intricate arborization called the **end-plate.** The end-plate represents a localized specialization of the sarcolemma. Transmission of the nerve impulse to the muscle is across the neuromuscular, or myoneural, junction. This junction is the point of origin of the muscle action current that stimulates contraction.

A nerve impulse produces a prolonged negative potential at the end-plate that is not propagated but is localized at the myoneural junction. This end-plate potential generates the muscle spike potential by depolarizing, to a critical level, the muscle membrane around the junction. The end-plate potential itself can be as large as the muscle spike potential. Neuromuscular delay refers to the time interval between the arrival of the nerve impulse at the terminals and the beginning of the end-plate potential.

Muscle action potentials resemble those of nerve (spike potentials and afterpotentials). The muscle action potential is a conducted process, normally all-or-none in skeletal muscle, with a propagation rate of about 3 m/s. The refractory period is related to the time necessary for repolarization of membrane. The muscle action potential serves as the trigger to an additional response of muscle, the mechanical response. The energy of the isotonic twitch may be 1000 times the energy of the muscle spike potential.

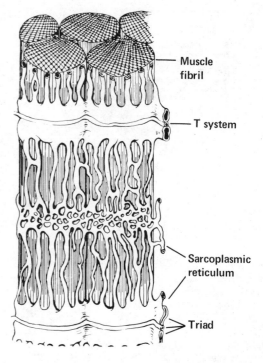

Figure 7–5. Cutaway drawing showing the relations of the sarcotubular system to muscle fibrils. (Modified and reproduced, with permission, from Peachey: The sarcoplasmic reticulum and transverse tubules of the frog's sartorius. *J Cell Biol* 1965; **25**:209.)

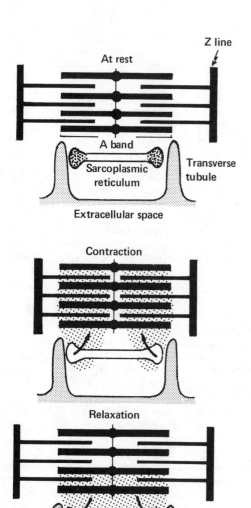

Figure 7–4. Muscle contraction. Calcium ions (represented by black dots) are normally stored in the cisterns of the sarcoplasmic reticulum. The action potential spreads via the transverse tubules and releases Ca²⁺. The actin filaments (thin lines) slide on the myosin filaments, and the Z lines move closer together. Ca²⁺ is then pumped into the sarcoplasmic reticulum and the muscle relaxes. (Modified from Layzer & Rowland: Cramps. *N Engl J Med* 1971;**285**:31.)

METABOLISM OF MUSCLE

The nerve impulse to the muscle initiates muscle contraction, and breakdown of ATP to ADP supplies the energy for this contraction. The resynthesis of ATP from ADP and phosphate (as well as that of phosphocreatine) is accomplished with the aid of energy from glycolytic mechanisms. The hydrolysis of phosphocreatine can also be used for prompt resynthesis of ATP. Maintenance of the activity of the muscle is dependent upon a steady supply of high-energy phosphate as ATP or phosphocreatine.

Resting muscle does not require breakdown of glycogen to secure energy. Sixty percent of the energy required for maintenance of resting muscle can be obtained by direct use of carbohydrates diffusing into tissues from the blood. Other metabolites from the blood supply the remainder. Preformed stores of ATP and phosphocreatine in the muscle may also be called upon.

MUSCLE RECEPTORS

A large number of the nerve fibers of muscles are sensory in function. Sherrington estimated that at least 40% of nerve fibers innervating a given muscle subserve sensory rather than motor end organs. Three major groups or types of receptors in muscle have been recognized.

Muscle Spindles (Intrafusal Fibers) (See p 167.)

The regular contractile units of muscle are known as **extrafusal fibers.** In contrast, the term **intrafusal fibers** refers to muscle spindles, which are more embryonal in character and have less striations than the remaining muscle fibers. The intrafusal fibers (muscle spindles) are in parallel with the rest of the muscle fibers, with the ends of their capsules attached to tendons at either end of the muscle or to the sides of adjacent extrafusal fibers.

The 2 ends of each intrafusal fiber (muscle spindle) are contractile, but the middle portion (nuclear bag region) is considered to be noncontractile. In this region are located the annulospiral endings, continuous with rapidly conducting afferent nerves (8–12 μm in diameter). These are wrapped around the intrafusal fibers (muscle spindles) in a complex manner and serve as receptors for the stretch reflex.

On either side of the annulospiral endings are **flower-spray endings,** which are receptors of smaller myelinated fibers and are also responsive to stretch, producing increased flexor and decreased extensor motor neuron activity.

The gamma efferents (small motor nerve system) are the motor supply to the muscle spindle, distributed

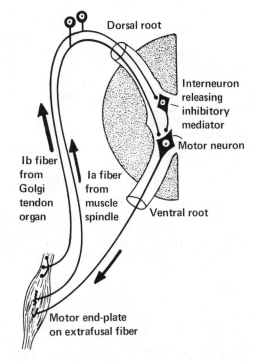

Figure 7–7. Diagram illustrating the pathways responsible for the stretch reflex and the inverse stretch reflex. Stretch stimulates the spindle and impulses pass up the Ia fiber to excite the motor neuron. It also stimulates the Golgi tendon organ, and impulses passing up the Ib fiber activate the interneuron to release inhibitory mediator. With strong stretch, the resulting hyperpolarization of the motor neuron is so great that it stops discharging. (Reproduced, with permission, from Ganong WF: *Review of Medical Physiology,* 10th ed. Lange, 1981.)

to the motor end-plate on the contractile ends of the intrafusal fibers.

Golgi Tendon Organs

These lie in series with muscle fibers and may serve to inhibit contractile responses evoked by the muscle spindle (intrafusal fiber). When the tension developed at a tendon becomes of dangerous magnitude, active muscle contraction is automatically inhibited, so that the interaction of these 2 groups (Golgi tendon organs and muscle spindles) assures smoothness of muscle performance. The threshold of Golgi tendon organs is considerably higher than that of muscle spindles. The Golgi tendon organs are netlike collections of knobby nerve endings among fascicles of a tendon. These nerve fibers are myelinated and rapidly conducting and are believed to end in the spinal cord on inhibitory interneurons (Renshaw cells) that terminate directly on motor neurons to the same muscle.

Free Nerve Endings

These have long been recognized in muscles, for the most part associated with blood vessels. Muscle pain can be evoked by deep palpation of the muscle mass or by squeezing the tendon.

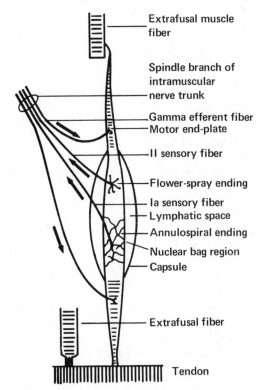

Figure 7–6. Muscle spindle, nuclear bag fiber type (highly diagrammatic). (Reproduced, with permission, from Ganong WF: *Review of Medical Physiology,* 6th ed. Lange, 1973.)

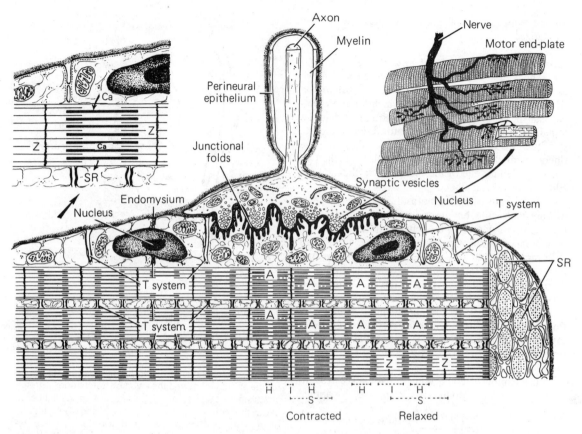

Figure 7–8. Diagram illustrating the ultrastructure of the motor end-plate and the mechanism of muscle contraction. The upper right drawing shows the branching of a small nerve with a motor end-plate for each muscle fiber. The aspect of one of the bulbs of an end-plate is seen highly enlarged in the central drawing. The axon loses its myelin sheath and dilates, establishing close, irregular contact with the muscle fiber. Muscle contraction begins with the release of acetylcholine from the synaptic vesicles of the end-plate. This substance promotes a local increase in the permeability of the sarcolemma. This process is propagated to the rest of the sarcolemma, including its invaginations, all of which constitute the T system, and is transferred to the sarcoplasmic reticulum (SR). The increase of permeability in this organelle liberates calcium ions that will in turn trigger the sliding mechanism of muscle contraction. Consequently, the thin filaments slide between the thick filaments and thus reduce the distance between the Z lines. This promotes a reduction in the size of all bands with the exception of the A band. This drawing represents the structure of amphibian muscle. One should bear in mind that mammalian muscle actually has 2 triads per sarcomere (S) located in the transition between the A and I bands. (Reproduced, with permission, from Junqueira LC, Carneiro J: *Basic Histology,* 3rd ed. Lange, 1980.)

LMN *UMN* *spasticity*
paresis
↑DTR's **Motion** | **8**
Abn. reflexes

flacidity
atrophy
↓, absent DTR's
absent Abn. reflexes

Motion is a fundamental property of most animal life. In the simple unicellular animals, motion and locomotion depend upon the contractility of protoplasm and the action of accessory organs such as cilia, flagella, etc. The lowest multicellular animals possess rudimentary neuromuscular mechanisms; in higher forms, motion is based upon the transmission of impulses from a receptor through an afferent neuron and ganglion cell to muscle. This same principle is found in the reflex arc of higher animals, including humans, in whom the anterior spinal cord has developed into a central regulating mechanism, the brain, which is concerned with initiating and integrating movements.

DISTURBANCES IN MOTOR POWER

Motor disturbances include weakness and paralysis, which may result from lesions of the voluntary motor pathways or of the muscles themselves. Impaired motor functioning may result from involvement of muscle, myoneural junction, peripheral nerve, or CNS.

The **lower motor neuron** (final common pathway) consists of a cell body located in the anterior gray column of the spinal cord or brain stem and an axon passing by way of the peripheral nerves to the motor end-plates of the muscles. It is the essential motor cell concerned with skeletal activity. It is called the "final common pathway" because it is acted upon by the corticospinal, rubrospinal, olivospinal, vestibulospinal, reticulospinal, and tectospinal tracts as well as by intersegmental and intrasegmental reflex neurons and because it is the ultimate pathway through which neural impulses reach the muscle.

Lesions of the lower motor neurons may be located in the cells of the ventral gray column of the spinal cord or brain stem or in their axons, which constitute the ventral roots of the spinal nerves or the cranial nerves. Lesions may result from trauma, toxins, infections, vascular disorders, degenerative processes, neoplasms, or congenital malformations. Signs of lower motor neuron lesions include flaccid paralysis of the involved muscles, muscle atrophy (with degeneration of muscle fibers), and reaction of degeneration (10–14 days after injury). Reflexes of the

DTR's

involved muscle are diminished or absent, and no pathologic reflexes are obtainable.

The **upper motor neuron** conveys impulses from the motor area of the cerebrum and is essential to voluntary muscular activity. It is the nerve cell of the motor cortex with its process that passes through the internal capsule, brain stem, and spinal cord by way of the corticobulbar or corticospinal tract to the lower motor neuron.

Lesions of the upper motor neuron may be located in the cerebral cortex, the internal capsule, the cerebral peduncles, the brain stem, or the spinal cord. These may be due to birth injuries, neoplasms, inflammation, hemorrhage, thrombosis, degenerative processes, or trauma. Signs of upper motor neuron lesions include spastic paralysis or paresis of the involved muscles, little or no muscle atrophy (probably atrophy of disuse), and hyperactive deep reflexes, diminished or absent superficial reflexes, and pathologic reflexes and signs.

Muscle may be unable to react normally to stimuli conveyed to it by the lower motor neuron, manifesting weakness, paralysis, or tetanic contraction due to disturbances in the muscle itself or at the myoneural junction. Myasthenia gravis, myotonia congenita, and progressive muscular dystrophy are typical disorders characterized by muscular dysfunction in the presence of apparently normal nerve tissue.

According to Yakovlev, the vertebrate neuraxis may be considered to contain 3 longitudinal effector systems of neuronal assemblies arranged from within outward (Fig 8–1). The **innermost system** is diffuse and reticulate in its neuronal pattern. This arrangement is suited for slow propagation of neuronal activity in all directions and for long-term maintenance of excitatory and inhibitory states in the neuraxis. It is related to physiologic activities in the sphere of "visceration." The **intermediate system,** which is nucleate in its pattern of neuronal collections, contains units arranged in series. Such a type of arrangement is suited to the instantaneous activation or modification of the activities of diverse neuronal fields in distant areas of the neuraxis. It is concerned with external expression of internal (visceral) states through the activities of the body wall (skeletal musculature). The **outermost system** is stratilaminate in its pattern of neuronal assembly and contains cell collections arranged in parallel. This variety is especially well suited to patterns of

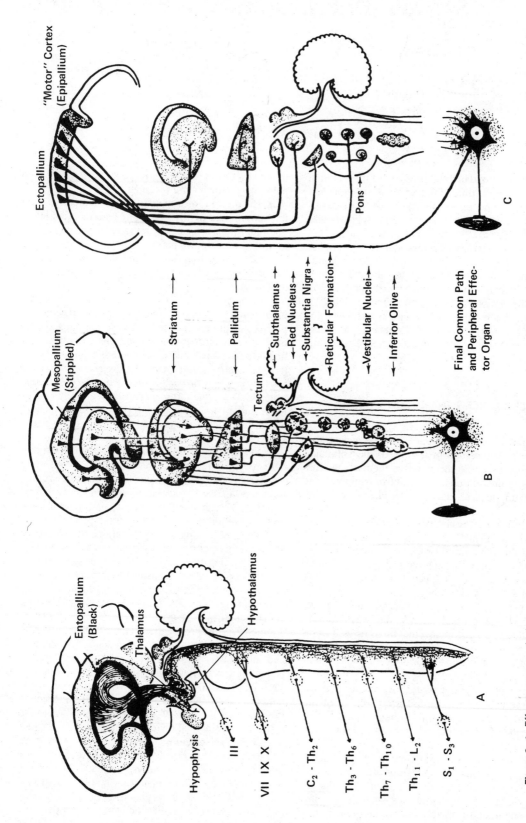

Figure 8-1. Effector systems in the neuraxis. *A*: Innermost system of visceration (reticulate system). *B*: Intermediate system of outward expression of internal states (nucleate system in series). *C*: Outermost system of effective transaction with the world about (stratilaminate system in parallel). (Reproduced, with permission, from Yakovlev: Motility behavior and the brain. *J Nerv Ment Dis* 1948; 107:313.)

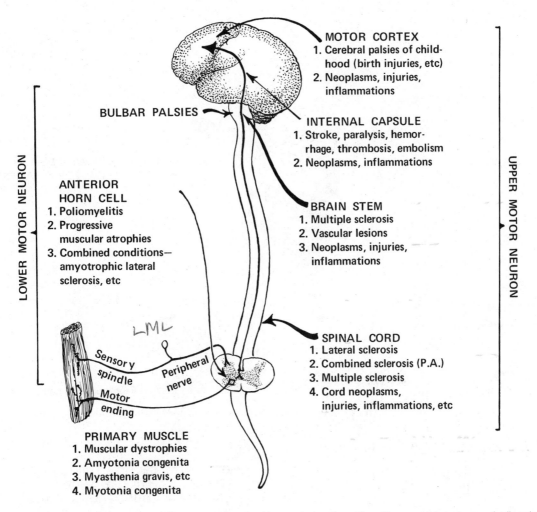

Figure 8–2. Motor pathways. (Modified and reproduced, with permission, from Chor: Some problems in muscle disorders. *Physiother Rev* 1936; **16:**2.)

organismal behavior whose ends are constantly changing, requiring the widest possible opportunities for recombination of available patterns of behavior to meet the unpredictable needs of adaptation. The cerebral cortex is representative of this type.

Types of Paralysis or Paresis Based on Location

Hemiplegia is a spastic or flaccid paralysis of one side of the body and extremities limited by the median line in front and in back. **Monoplegia** is a paralysis of one extremity only. **Diplegia** is a paralysis of any 2 corresponding extremities, usually both lower extremities (but may be both upper). **Paraplegia** is a symmetric paralysis of both lower extremities. **Quadriplegia,** or **tetraplegia,** is a paralysis of all 4 extremities. **Hemiplegia alternans** (crossed paralysis) is a paralysis of one or more ipsilateral cranial nerves and contralateral paralysis of the arm and leg.

INCREASED MOVEMENTS & DISTURBANCES IN TONUS

With a few exceptions, hyperkinesias and hypertonic states (rigidity) are due to involvement of the **extrapyramidal system.** In general, the extrapyramidal system includes all descending pathways exclusive of the pyramidal tract that act directly or through internuncial neurons on primary motor neurons.

Muscle **tonus** is a state of continuous mild contraction of muscle dependent upon the integrity of nerves and their central connections and the complex properties of muscles such as contractility, elasticity, ductility, and extensibility. Atonic muscles are soft and flabby; hypertonic muscles are rigid and spastic. Normal muscle at rest has a certain resilience rather than absolute flabbiness; when muscle is passively stretched by a joint movement, a certain amount of involuntary resistance is encountered. These features are considered clinical manifestations of muscle tonus.

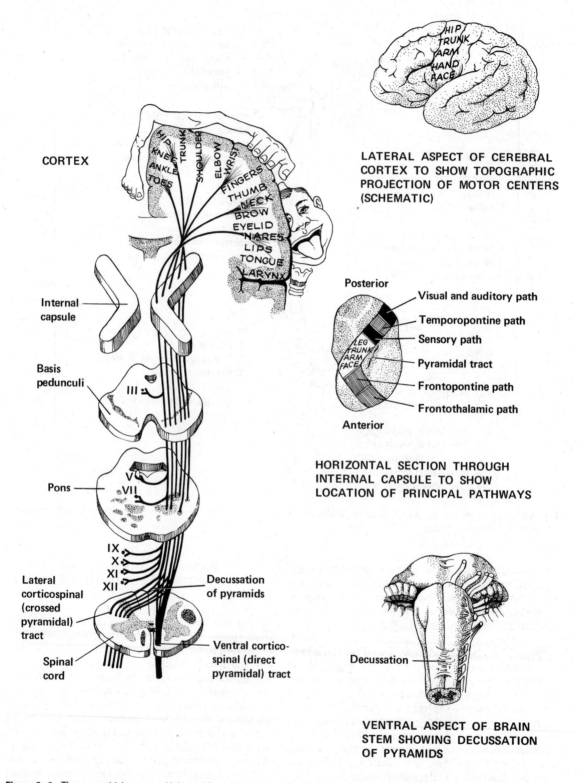

CORTEX

Internal capsule

Basis pedunculi

Pons

Lateral corticospinal (crossed pyramidal) tract

Spinal cord

Decussation of pyramids

Ventral cortico-spinal (direct pyramidal) tract

LATERAL ASPECT OF CEREBRAL CORTEX TO SHOW TOPOGRAPHIC PROJECTION OF MOTOR CENTERS (SCHEMATIC)

Posterior

Visual and auditory path
Temporopontine path
Sensory path
Pyramidal tract
Frontopontine path
Frontothalamic path

Anterior

HORIZONTAL SECTION THROUGH INTERNAL CAPSULE TO SHOW LOCATION OF PRINCIPAL PATHWAYS

Decussation

VENTRAL ASPECT OF BRAIN STEM SHOWING DECUSSATION OF PYRAMIDS

Figure 8–3. The pyramidal system. (Adapted from Netter FH: *The Ciba Collection of Medical Illustrations.* Copyright © Ciba Pharmaceutical Co. Reproduced with permission.)

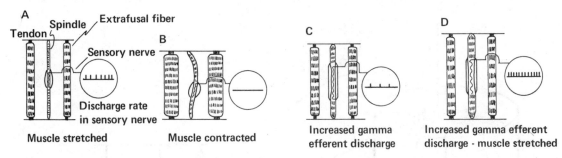

Figure 8–4. Effect of various conditions on muscle spindle discharge. In *A* the spindle is stretched the same amount as the extrafusal fibers. In *B* it is relaxed and hence longer than the contracted extrafusal fibers. In *C* the contractile portions of the spindle are shortened, and the pull on the nuclear bag portion causes sensory nerve discharge. In *D* the nuclear bag region, already stretched because of the γ efferent discharge, is stretched farther, causing the very high rate of discharge in the sensory nerve. (Drawn in part from Patton, in: *Physiology and Biophysics,* 19th ed. Ruch TC, Patton HD [editors]. Saunders, 1965.)

Tonus is usually greatly diminished or abolished by section of the motor nerve fibers to the muscle or of the sensory fibers from the muscle.

The stretch reflex is considered essential in maintaining muscle tonus and can produce increased tension of certain muscle groups so as to provide a background of postural muscle tonus against which voluntary movements can occur (Fig 7–7). Although most reflex arcs include at least one internuncial neuron between the afferent and efferent fibers, the stretch reflex has no such internuncial, or intermediary, neuron; and the afferent neuron makes direct contact with the efferent neuron across a single synapse in the spinal cord.

Mammalian muscle may contain 2 types of intrafusal fibers, or muscle spindles. The first type has a dilated central area with many nuclei and is known as a **nuclear bag fiber.** The second type, which is thinner, shorter, and without a bag, is a **nuclear chain fiber;** it is attached at its ends to the sides of the nuclear bag fibers.

Two kinds of sensory endings occur in each spindle. The primary, or **annulospiral, endings** are rapidly conducting Ia afferent fibers that wrap around the center of the nuclear bag fiber and nuclear chain fiber. The secondary, or **flower-spray, endings** are group II sensory fibers near the ends of the intrafusal fibers, mainly on nuclear chain fibers.

The motor supply of these muscle spindles is via gamma efferents, or the small motor nerve system. These nerve fibers are 3–6 μm in diameter and belong to the A γ group (see Table 2–3). There is also sparse innervation of muscle spindles by motor fibers of intermediate size (beta efferents), whose function is unknown.

Stretching a muscle stimulates its muscle spindles, specialized receptors that lie parallel with and interspersed among muscle fibers (Fig 7–6). Afferent nerve fibers from muscle spindles enter the spinal cord through dorsal root nerves and go anteriorly through the gray matter of the spinal cord to reach the anterior horn, where synapses with motor cells are made.

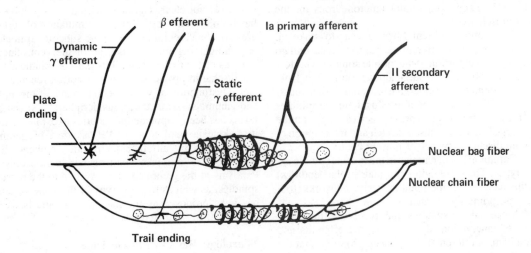

Figure 8–5. Diagram of muscle spindle. (Modified and reproduced, with permission, from Stein RB: Peripheral control of movement. *Physiol Rev* 1974; **54:**215.)

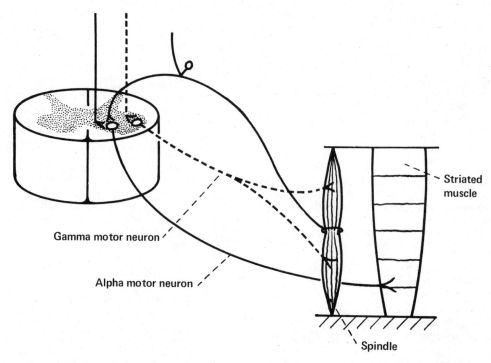

Figure 8–6. Gamma loop showing parallel alignment of muscle spindle and striated fiber. Gamma efferent fiber (broken line) to contractile portion of muscle spindle; sensory afferent fiber from spindle (solid line). (Reproduced, with permission, from Stern & Ward: *Arch Neurol* 1960;**3**:193.)

Higher supraspinal motor centers are believed to send impulses to skeletal muscle by 2 routes—one involving large alpha motoneuron cells and the other small gamma motoneurons.

The gamma neuron may be stimulated by afferent dorsal root fibers coming from the muscle spindles so as to cause contraction of intrafusal muscle fibers via a stretch reflex. Although this is a relatively minor change, it appears adequate to activate the main muscle mass, so that gamma innervation may serve as a "starter" for activation of alpha motoneurons and the main muscle mass.

The gamma efferent fibers appear to make up almost a third of the efferent ventral root fibers and go to the muscular portion of the muscle spindles via slow small motor fibers. The large alpha motor fibers from the anterior horn cells innervate the main muscle mass. The parallel arrangement of intrafusal muscle spindles and the main muscle mass provide activation of spindle discharge by passive muscle stretch and interruption of spindle discharge by active muscle contraction.

Gamma efferent endings in the muscle spindle are of 2 types. There are motor end-plates (plate endings) on the nuclear bag fibers and extensive networks (trail endings) primarily on nuclear chain fibers.

Since muscle spindles may receive 2 functional types of innervation (dynamic gamma efferents and static gamma efferents), it has been proposed that the dynamic gamma efferents terminate at the plate endings and that the static gamma efferents terminate at trail endings.

The "gamma loop" refers to the circuits to and from the spinal cord involving the muscle spindle with its gamma efferent fibers. The muscle spindle may be considered the sensing element of a reflex system that registers differences in length between itself and the main muscle mass and acts to reduce this difference. Steady voluntary or postural contraction may be considered a result of tonic innervation and facilitation of alpha motoneurons via this loop.

The role of supraspinal controls on the gamma system is not clear. Gamma facilitation or inhibition has been obtained by electrical stimulation of certain areas of the cerebral cortex, some subcortical nuclei, and the cerebellum. Stimulation of the ventrolateral nucleus of the thalamus inhibits muscle spindle afferent discharge provided the motor cortex remains intact. Dysfunction of various components of the alpha and gamma systems at various peripheral and central levels has been implicated in theories to explain rigidity, akinesia, and tremor. "Blockade" of gamma motoneurons by intrathecal procaine or phenol has been reported to improve patients with parkinsonism. Paralysis of the gamma efferent system to the muscle spindles, as well as hyperactivity of the same system, has been proposed as the pathophysiologic basis of parkinsonism by different investigators.

Neurologic Basis of Muscle Tone

The maintenance and control of muscle tone is dependent upon normal function at 6 levels: (1) the precentral motor cortex (Brodmann areas 4 and 6), (2)

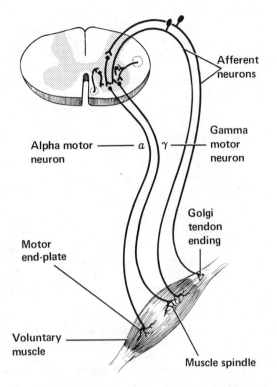

Figure 8–7. Alpha and gamma efferent motor neuron loops. (See Figs 7–6 and 7–7.)

the basal ganglia, (3) the midbrain, (4) the vestibulum, (5) the spine, and (6) the neuromuscular system.

The reticular formation of the brain stem contains an "inhibitory" area caudad and inferior to a "facilitatory" area. Appropriate stimulation of the inhibitory area decreases muscle tonus; similar excitation of the facilitatory area increases muscle tonus. Conversely, destruction of the inhibitory area or inhibitory afferents gives rise to increased tone (such as decerebrate rigidity), and destruction of the facilitatory area or facilitatory efferents gives rise to decreased tone. Experimental studies indicate that the so-called suppressor strips of the cerebral cortex, the basal ganglia, and the anterior lobe of the cerebellum connect with the bulbar inhibitory areas.

Normal muscle tone may be increased (hypertonia) or decreased (hypotonia). Hypertonic muscles are noted in spasticity, rigidity, and flexor spasms. In **spasticity,** there is increased resistance to sudden passive movements, and after the initial resistance there may be muscle relaxation (clasp-knife phenomenon). In **rigidity,** there is increased resistance on passive motion in any direction, usually unrelated to speed or direction of movement, due to steady contraction of flexors and extensors. Marked mass flexor spasms leading to permanent contracture of flexor muscles may occur in complete lesions of the spinal cord.

Hypotonic muscles feel soft and flabby and may offer less than normal resistance to passive movement; in marked hypotonia, the joints may be hyperextended when the extremity is shaken. Hypotonia may occur with impaired muscle proprioceptive or motor innervation, cerebellar disease, or muscular disease.

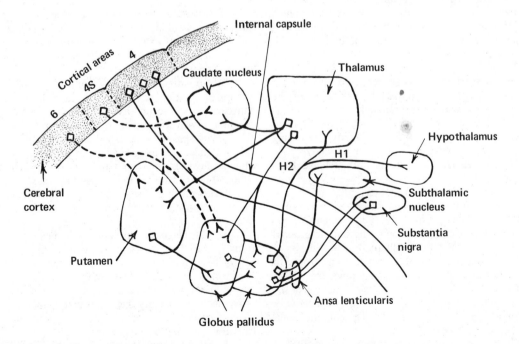

Figure 8–8. Connections between basal ganglia and cortex. (Reproduced, with permission, from Kennard: Experimental analysis of the functions of the basal ganglia in monkeys and chimpanzees. *J Neurophysiol* 1944; **7**:142.)

The **spinal cord** is the seat of the stretch (myotatic) reflex that functions in the maintenance of tone, or "static activity." The impulses pass through the simple reflex arc, which includes the neuromuscular spindles, afferent nerves, and spinal cord connections, to the anterior horn cells and the efferent nerves. **Neuromuscular** or **idiomuscular activity** depends upon the contractility, elasticity, irritability, ductility, and extensibility of the muscle itself.

Lesions Affecting Tonus & Causing Increased Movements

Extrapyramidal involvement, especially in the region of the basal ganglia, produces spasms and excessive movements by a mechanism known as the "release phenomenon." Since normally these centers may inhibit spontaneous rhythmic movements initiated by the cortex, disease results in the "release" of such movements, which manifest themselves as tremors, choreiform or athetoid movements, etc. Degenerative diseases, encephalitis, and tumors are the most common lesions affecting the extrapyramidal system.

Involvement of the spinal level and reflex arc may be manifest in fascicular movements that may result from progressive lesions of the anterior horn cells or motor nuclei of the cranial nerves. Reflex rigidity may be due to sensory irritation, eg, stiff neck with meningitis, boardlike abdomen with peritonitis. Tone is lost or diminished when the reflex arc is interrupted.

Neuromuscular or idiomuscular activity is frequently manifest in the late stages of chronic wasting diseases as a local hyperirritability of the muscles known as myoedema: pinching or tapping a muscle produces a local contraction lasting several seconds.

Psychogenic causes are the basis of many tics; bizarre forms of increased movement are seen in certain hysterias.

Signs of Disturbed Tonus & Increased Movements

A. Rigidity: Generalized hypertonicity of the muscles occurs with extrapyramidal lesions, as in parkinsonism caused by encephalitis, which has an affinity for the basal ganglia. Local reflex rigidity occurs with peripheral irritative lesions as cited above.

B. Increased Movements and Release Phenomena:

1. Tremors–The distribution, rate, and rhythm of tremors and the effects of movement and rest should be noted. Tremors are involuntary movements resulting from the contraction of opposing muscle groups, which produces rhythmic or alternating movements of a joint or group of joints. Slow tremors range from 3 to 6 per second, and rapid tremors may range from 10 to 20 per second. Resting tremors may disappear or diminish with action; intention tremors may appear only on voluntary movement of a limb. The amplitude of a tremor may be coarse or fine.

In parkinsonism, a coarse tremor may be noted at rest, with a rate of 3–6/s. The tremor is "pill-rolling," ie, the affected fingers show less tremor on movement. There is usually greater shaking of the distal than the proximal portions of the extremities. Associated increased muscle tone is noted, together with other signs of parkinsonism.

Senile tremor may resemble the tremors of parkinsonism in degree, amplitude, rate, and occurrence at rest. It most commonly affects the head, jaws, and lips, and the head may nod to and fro or from side to side. Increased muscle tone and other evidences of parkinsonism are not present.

Cerebellar tremor, sometimes referred to as intention tremor, occurs during movement and is intensified at the termination of the movement. It may be noted in multiple sclerosis.

Familial, or essential, tremor is absent at rest and appears when muscles act to move or support an extremity. This tremor is not intensified toward the end of movement and is not associated with other evidence of neurologic disease. It may be lessened by alcohol or sedatives but is not affected by drugs of the belladonna group.

Toxic tremors are associated with endogenous disorders (thyrotoxicosis, uremia) or exogenous toxic disorders (alcohol, tobacco). Usually these are fine and rapid.

Physiologic tremors are usually transient and may occur in normal people under emotional stress, extreme fright, and exposure to cold.

In Wilson's disease, a resting tremor similar to that of parkinsonism may be noted; however, it becomes aggravated by motion of the extremity. Violent up-and-down movements of the upper extremities, resembling wing-beating movements in birds, may occur.

In advanced hepatic disease, coarse flapping movements resulting from alternate flexion and extension of the wrists of the outstretched arms have been noted and are referred to as "wrist-flapping." Tremors of the fingers may also occur.

2. Spasms–Involuntary contraction of large groups of muscles may involve the arm, leg, or neck muscles (spastic torticollis). Causes include extrapyramidal involvement and hypoparathyroid tetany. Oculogyric spasm (or crisis), characterized by a fixed upward gaze, is usually a sequel of encephalitis, and attacks may last from several minutes to several hours. These tonic spasms of the extraocular muscles may sometimes result in forced conjugate movements in other directions, rarely in fixation of gaze in the eyes-centered position.

3. Choreiform movements–These are extremely variable, purposeless, coarse, quick, and jerky; they begin suddenly and show no rhythmicity. When the movement is over, the part remains at rest and is atonic until the next one begins. Choreiform movements are usually due to an involvement of the basal ganglia. These movements are of variable distribution and may occur in sleep.

4. Athetoid movements–These are continuous, arrhythmic, slow, and wormlike; they are always the

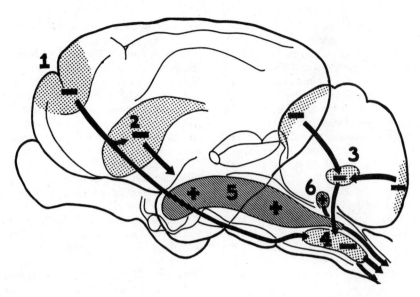

Figure 8–9. Spasticity. Suppressor pathways are as follows: (1) corticobulboreticular, (2) caudatospinal, (3) cerebelloreticular, and (4) reticulospinal. Facilitatory pathways are (5) reticulospinal and (6) vestibulospinal. (Reproduced, with permission, from Lindsley, Schreiner, & Magoun: An electromyographic study of spasticity. *J Neurophysiol* 1949; **12**:188.)

same in the same patient and cease only during sleep. The muscles are always hypertonic and may show transient stages of spasms.

5. Dystonia–Dystonia is characterized by bizarre twisting movements of the body and trunk, some of the muscles being hypertonic. Dystonia usually refers to mobile spasms of the axial and proximal muscles of the extremities. Torsion spasm, with resulting twisting or turning movements, is included; and spasmodic torticollis is the most commonly encountered torsion spasm. Dystonic movements tend to involve large portions of the body and have an undulant, sinuous character that may produce grotesque posturing and bizarre writhing movements.

6. Tics, or habit spasms–These are brief, recurrent, inappropriate, stereotyped, compulsive movements involving a relatively small segment of the body, frequently on a psychogenic basis. Tics may be briefly controlled voluntarily but are apt to be followed then by more intense contractions. Tics in young people must be distinguished from chorea. **Gilles de la Tourette syndrome** is a childhood disorder characterized by bizarre tics, imitative gestures, coprolalia, and behavioral changes.

7. Myoclonus–This refers to abrupt, sudden, isolated muscle contractions that occur irregularly, especially in the limbs, and frequently produce no associated movement. A sudden jerk or series of jerks may occur with rates as fast as 50–60/min or as slow as 5–10/min. They are apt to occur in the muscles of the limbs, face, and oral cavity and disappear during sleep. If large groups of muscles are affected, they may produce joint movements that may be of sufficient violence to jar patients or throw them to the ground. Palatal myoclonus usually results from lesions in the pathways connecting the red nucleus, the olivary

bodies of the medulla, and the dentate nucleus of the cerebellum.

8. Hemiballism–Hemiballism is a rare symptom characterized by continuous coordinated activity of the axial and proximal extremity musculature, sometimes to such a degree that the limbs fly about. It is usually confined to one side of the body and sometimes resembles hemichorea. In most cases, lesions of the opposite subthalamic nucleus are noted, particularly vascular lesions (hemorrhagic softening). Onset of hemiballism is usually sudden, with involvement principally of the leg and relative sparing of the face. Mental symptoms (confusion, disorientation, or dementia) are often associated. Medical therapy is usually ineffective.

DISTURBANCES IN SYNERGY

Lesions of the cerebellum or its pathways may be characterized by dyssynergia, a failure in the integrated, coordinated action between muscle groups. The mechanism of synergy (the regulation of reciprocal innervation) is as follows: The unpaired vermis of the cerebellum regulates bilaterally innervated muscles of the head, neck, and trunk. The right and left cerebellar hemispheres regulate antagonistic muscular activity on their ipsilateral sides as extension and flexion. The spinal cord is important in controlling bilaterally innervated muscular activity of the extremities, as in walking.

Anatomy of the Cerebellum (See p 37.)

The cerebellum is the highest proprioceptive ganglion. **Afferent tracts** enter the cerebellum from the cortex, brain stem, and cord. Impulses from the cerebral cortex pass via the corticopontocerebellar tracts entering through the brachium pontis (middle cerebellar peduncle). Impulses from the spinal cord pass via the dorsal spinocerebellar tract, spino-olivocerebellar tract, and external arcuate fibers to enter the cerebellum through the restiform body (inferior cerebellar peduncle); and via the ventral spinocerebellar tract and brachium conjunctivum (superior cerebellar peduncle) to the cerebellum. Impulses from the vestibular labyrinth and vestibular nuclei enter via the vestibulocerebellar tract located medial to the restiform body. **Efferent tracts** from the cerebellum pass to the lower motor neurons via the brachium conjunctivum, red nucleus, and rubrospinal tract. Impulses from the cerebellar hemisphere pass via the dentate nucleus or the globose and emboliform nuclei to the opposite red nucleus and thalamus. Impulses from the vermis pass via the fastigial (roof) nuclei to vestibular nuclei.

Diseases of the Cerebellum

The cerebellum, like other organs, may be involved in hereditary or congenital anomalies or in inflammatory, traumatic, neoplastic, vascular, degenerative, functional, toxic, or metabolic disorders. Symptoms and signs are essentially the same regardless of the cause.

Cerebellar Symptoms & Signs

The following clinical findings suggest cerebellar disorders:

Ataxia, a reeling, drunken, unsteady gait with a wide base and a tendency to fall toward the side of the lesion. **Vertigo** may accompany the ataxia.

Adiadokokinesia, inability to perform rapidly alternating movements such as supination and pronation.

Dysmetria (past-pointing phenomenon), inability to estimate the range of voluntary movement. In the finger-to-nose test, the finger shoots past the nose onto the cheek.

In **decomposition of movement** ("by-the-numbers" phenomenon), voluntary movements are jerky and broken up; a coarse **tremor** precipitated by movement and disappearing at rest may be associated.

In the **rebound phenomenon of Holmes** (lack of check reflex), when a patient's arm is flexed against resistance of the examiner and is suddenly released, it will strike the patient's body or face.

Nystagmus is often present in cerebellar lesions but occurs usually when the eyes move away from a central fixation or rest point. It is most marked when the patient is looking to the side of the lesion.

Dysarthria, explosive, slurred speech.

Pleurothotonos, a tendency to lean and fall to the side of the lesion. **Hypotonia,** noted by "floppiness" of the limbs and decreased resistance to passive movement. **Skew deviation of the eyes,** a condition in which one eyeball is deviated upward and outward, the other downward and inward, occurring particularly with lesions of the middle cerebellar peduncle brachium pontis). **Cerebellar fit** is a rigid tonic convulsion that is sometimes seen in cerebellar disease.

GAITS

Tabetic or Ataxic Gait

Tabetic or ataxic gait is characteristic of posterior column disease and results from the loss of proprioceptive sense in the extremities. Such patients walk on a wide base, slapping their feet, and usually watch their legs so they will know where they are. In the dark or with the eyes closed, the ataxia is much worse. Clumsiness and uncertainty are characteristic. The feet are placed too widely apart, and in taking a step the subject will lift the advancing leg abruptly and too high and then stamp or slap the foot solidly to the ground. Uneven spacing of steps, tottering, and swaying occur, usually with deviation to one side or the other.

Hemiplegic Gait

The affected leg is rigid and is swung from the hip in a semicircle by movements of the trunk; the patient leans to the affected side, and the arm on that side is held in a rigid, semiflexed position. A somewhat similar gait occurs with any disorder producing an immobile hip or knee. The affected spastic limb is moved forward with difficulty because of impaired joint mobility. The toes of hemiplegic lower limbs tend to be forced down, so that abduction and circumduction of the limb are necessary to move it forward.

Scissors Gait

Scissors gait is characteristic of spastic paraplegia. The legs are adducted, crossing alternately in front of one another with the knees scraping together. The resulting steps are short and progression slow. Both

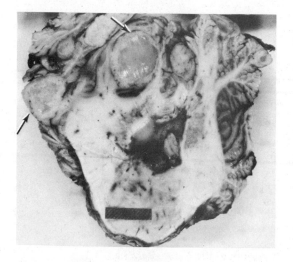

Figure 8–10. Cerebellar metastases from carcinoma of the lung.

lower limbs are spastic. The lower extremities are moved forward in a stiff, jerky manner, often accompanied by pronounced compensatory motions of the trunk and upper extremities.

Drunken or Staggering Gait

Drunken or staggering gait as seen in acute alcoholism may also result from drug poisoning, multiple neuritis, brain tumors, multiple sclerosis, or general paresis.

Waddling or Clumsy Gait

Waddling or clumsy gait results from dislocated hips or muscular dystrophies with weakness of the hips. In either case, the trunk muscles are drawn into play, so that the patient rolls from side to side. Weakness of trunk and pelvic girdle muscles produces pelvic tilt. The waddle results from difficulty in maintaining the pelvis at a proper angle to the weight-bearing extremity, with slump of the pelvis toward the non-weight-bearing side, which in turn produces exaggerated compensatory sway of the trunk toward the weight-bearing side. Muscular dystrophy is characterized by weakness of trunk and pelvic girdle muscles, producing a swaybacked, potbellied posture and waddling gait.

Steppage Gait

Steppage gait (or footdrop gait) is characterized by high knee action and flopping of the feet (or foot). Even when the leg is raised, the toes tend to drag along the floor. It occurs with paralysis of the anterior tibial group of muscles, as in alcoholic neuritis, peroneal nerve injuries, poliomyelitis, and progressive muscular atrophy. With bilateral footdrop, the gait may resemble that of a high-stepping horse.

Cerebellar Gait or Ataxia

Cerebellar gait or ataxia is characterized by marked irregularity and unsteadiness associated with vertigo and a tendency to reel to one side. The lower extremities appear loose; movement of the advancing limb starts slowly, but the limb is unexpectedly, erratically, and vigorously flung forward and lands with a stamp on the floor. The gait is wide-based, irregular, reeling, or deviated, with staggering on turning.

Propulsion or Festination Gait

Propulsion or festination gait of paralysis agitans is characterized by a forward-leaning posture and short shuffling steps, beginning slowly at first and becoming more rapid ("marche à petits pas"). Patients with the classic features of parkinsonism have a stooped posture, take short steps, and frequently accelerate rapidly, so that they appear to be chasing their center of gravity.

Hysterical Gaits

Hysterical gaits simulate various paralyses (eg, monoplegias, hemiplegias, or paraplegias) but differ from the organic forms in being more pronounced and

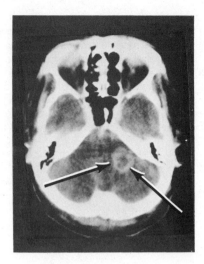

Figure 8–11. CT scan showing cerebellar metastasis from carcinoma of the lung in a 78-year-old man with gait disturbance.

complete, with the ability to use the limb in emergencies. The gait is apt to be bizarre or fantastic, characterized by exaggerated balancing motions and inconsistency between the gait shown and the patient's actual ability to move the limbs voluntarily. There may be lurching, wildly weaving, irregular bobbing movements or exaggerated, very slow, hesitant, slow-motion action.

Astasia-Abasia

Astasia-abasia is a hysterical ataxia with such bizarre incoordination that the patient is unable to stand or walk, yet all leg movements can be performed normally while the patient is sitting or is in bed.

Limping Gait

When pain is produced by weight-bearing on a lower extremity, the patient puts the affected extremity down carefully and takes a short step to get the weight off the painful limb as soon as possible. The good limb is brought forward rapidly and lands vigorously on the floor. Limping may be associated with a variety of conditions, including shortening of the lower extremity and deformity of the foot.

DEFORMITIES & POSTURES

Deformities of the **spine** (lordosis, scoliosis, or kyphosis) are often seen with muscular dystrophies, syringomyelia, and Friedreich's ataxia. **Clubfoot** is usually present in cases of Friedreich's ataxia. Dangling and swinging of the **hands** suggest lower motor neuron paralysis, eg, poliomyelitis or polyneuritis. **Accoucheur's hand** or "waiter's tip" position occurs with Erb's upper arm type of brachial plexus (birth) palsy. **Opisthotonos** (stiff extended neck and spine) suggests meningeal irritation. **Sardonic smile** is associated with facial muscle spasms of tetanus. **Potbelly** in children may be due to muscular dystrophy. **Hemiplegic arm** is adducted, flexed at the elbow and fingers, and maintained in this position by muscle rigidity. Inability of the patient to **lower an arm** is a characteristic of a lesion at the level of the seventh cervical cord segment. An arm may be raised by the patient when the examiner attempts to place it at the patient's side. During sleep, the affected arm lies on the pillow beside the patient's head (Jolly's position).

Various peripheral nerve injuries produce characteristic postural changes (eg, wristdrop, footdrop, clawhand, ape hand, winged scapula, shoulderdrop). These are described in Chapter 5.

Posture in paralysis agitans is stooped, with the head forward and elbows flexed.

Table 9—1. Segmental motor innervation: Upper extremity.

	C4	C5	C6	C7	C8	T1
Shoulder	- - - - - - - Supraspinatus- - - - - - - -					
	- - - - - - -Teres minor- - - - - - -					
		- - - - - - - - Deltoid - - - - - - - -				
	- - - - - - - Infraspinatus - - - - - - - -					
		- - - - - - - - Subscapularis - - - - - -				
		- - - - - - - Teres major - - - - - -				
Arm		- - - - - - - - Biceps - - - - -				
		- - - - - - - Brachialis- - - - - -				
		- - - - - - - - Coracobrachialis - - - - - - - - - -				
			- - - - - - - - - -Triceps brachialis- - - - - - - - - - -			
			- - - - - - - Anconeus- - - - - - - -			
Forearm		- - - - - Supinator longus - - - - -				
		- - - - - - - -Supinator brevis - - - - - - -				
			- - - - - - Extensor carpi radialis- - - - -			
			- - - - - - Pronator teres - - - - - -			
			- - - - Flexor carpi radialis- - - -			
				- - - - - -Flexor pollicis longus- - - - -		
				- - -Abductor pollicis longus- - -		
				- - - Extensor pollicis brevis- -		
			- - - - - -Extensor pollicis longus - - - - -			
			- - - - -Extensor digitorum longus - - - -			
			- - - - - Extensor indicis proprius- - - -			
			- - - - - -Extensor carpi ulnaris- - - - - -			
			- - - - - - Extensor digit quinti - - - - -			
Hand				- - - - - - - - Flexor digitorum sublimis - - - - - - -		
				- - - - - - - - Flexor digitorum profundus- - - - - - -		
				- - - - - - - - - Pronator quadratus - - - - - - - - - -		
				- - - - - - - - Flexor carpi ulnaris - - - - - - - - - -		
				- - - - - -Palmaris longus- - - - -		
			- - - - - - - -Abductor pollicis brevis - - - - - - - -		
				- - - - Flexor pollicis brevis - - -		
				- - - - - Opponens pollicis- - - -		
				- - - - -Flexor digiti quinti - - - -		
				- - - Opponens digiti quinti - - -		
					- - - - - Adductor pollicis - - - - -	
					- - - - - - Palmaris brevis - - - - - -	
					- - - Abductor digiti quinti - - -	
					- - - - - - - Lumbricales - - - - - - -	
					- - - - - - - Interossei - - - - - - -	

Table 9–2. Segmental motor innervation: Lower extremity.

	L1	L2	L3	L4	L5	S1	S2
Hip	·········· Iliopsoas ···········						
				···· Tensor fasciae latae ····			
				··········· Gluteus medius ···········			
				··········· Gluteus minimus ···········			
				··········· Quadratus femoris ···········			
				··········· Gemellus inferior ···········			
				········ Gemellus superior ·······			
				··········· Gluteus maximus ···········		
				····· Obturator internus ····		
				········ Piriformis ········		
Thigh		········ Sartorius ········					
		········ Pectineus ········					
		····· Adductor longus ·····					
		······· Quadriceps femoris ······				
		········· Gracilis ··········				
		·········· Adductor brevis ··········				
			···· Obturator externus ····			
			····· Adductor magnus ····			
			····· Adductor minimus ····			
				··········· Semitendinosus ···········		
				··········· Semimembranosus ···········		
				········ Biceps femoris ···········		
Leg				··· Tibialis anticus ···			
				····· Extensor hallucis longus ·····			
				········· Popliteus ··········		
				·········· Plantaris ··········		
				········ Extensor digitorum longus ······		
				·········· Soleus ···········		
				·········· Gastrocnemius ··········	
				····· Peroneus longus ·····		
				····· Peroneus brevis ·····		
				····· Tibialis posterior ·····		
				········ Flexor digitorum longus ········		
				········ Flexor hallucis longus ········	
Foot				····· Extensor hallucis brevis ·····			
				········ Extensor digitorum brevis ·······		
				··· Flexor digitorum brevis ··		
				····· Abductor hallucis ·····		
				·········· Flexor hallucis brevis ··········	
				··········· Lumbricales ··········	
						····· Adductor hallucis ·····
						····Abductor digiti quinti ···
						···· Flexor digiti quinti ····
						··· Opponens digiti quinti ···
						···· Quadratus plantaris ····
						········ Interossei ········

Table 9—3. Muscle innervation listed by individual nerves.

Upper Extremity		Lower Extremity	
Suprascapular nerve	**Radial nerve**	**Superior gluteal nerve**	**Sciatic nerve, tibial**
Shoulder girdle	Arm	Buttock	**division (cont'd)**
Supraspinatus	Triceps (long head, lateral	Gluteus medius	Leg
Infraspinatus	head, medial head)	Gluteus minimus	Tibialis posterior
Long thoracic nerve	Anconeus	Tensor fasciae latae	Flexor digitorum longus
Shoulder girdle	Brachioradialis	**Inferior gluteal nerve**	Flexor hallucis longus
Serratus anterior	Extensor carpi radialis	Buttock	Foot
Axillary nerve	Forearm	Gluteus maximus	Abductor hallucis
Shoulder girdle	Extensor carpi radialis	**Femoral nerve**	Abductor digiti minimi
Teres minor	brevis	Thigh	Dorsal interossei
Deltoid	Supinator longus	Pectineus	**Sciatic nerve, peroneal division**
Musculocutaneous nerve	Extensor digitorum com-	Sartorius	Thigh
Arm	munis	Quadriceps femoris (rectus	Biceps (short head)
Biceps brachii	Extensor digiti quinti	femoris, vastus lateralis,	Leg (deep peroneal nerve)
Coracobrachialis	Extensor carpi ulnaris	vastus intermedius, vastus	Tibialis anterior
Brachialis	Abductor pollicis longus	medialis)	Extensor hallucis longus
Median nerve	Extensor pollicis longus	**Obturator nerve**	Extensor digitorum longus
Forearm	Extensor pollicis brevis	Thigh	Peroneus tertius
Pronator teres	Extensor indicis proprius	Adductor longus	Foot
Flexor carpi radialis	**Ulnar nerve**	Gracilis	Extensor digitorum brevis
Palmaris longus	Forearm	Adductor brevis	Leg (superficial peroneal nerve)
Flexor digitorum sublimis	Flexor carpi ulnaris	Obturator externus	Peroneus longus
Flexor digitorum pro-	Flexor digitorum profundus	Adductor magnus	Peroneus brevis
fundus	(medial half)	**Sciatic nerve, tibial division**	
Flexor pollicis longus	Hand	Thigh	
Pronator quadratus	Flexor digiti quinti brevis	Semitendinosus	
Hand	Abductor digiti quinti	Biceps (long head)	
Abductor pollicis brevis	Opponens digiti quinti	Semimembranosus	
Opponens pollicis	Interossei	Popliteal space (tibial nerve)	
Flexor pollicis brevis	Lumbricales III and IV	Gastrocnemius	
Lumbricales I and II	Adductor pollicis	Plantaris	
	Flexor pollicis brevis (deep	Popliteus	
	part)	Soleus	

Table 9—4. Muscle strength grading.

Normal	N	5	Complete range of motion against gravity with full resistance.
Good	G	4	Complete range of motion against gravity with some resistance.
Fair	F	3	Complete range of motion against gravity.
Poor	P	2	Complete range of motion with gravity eliminated.
Trace	T	1	Evidence of slight contractility. No joint motion.
Zero	0	0	No evidence of contractility.

Table 9–5. Motor function chart.*

Action to Be Tested	Muscles	Cord Segment	Nerves	Plexus
Shoulder Girdle and Upper Extremity				
Flexion of neck	Deep neck muscles (sterno-	C1—4	Cervical	Cervical
Extension of neck	mastoid and trapezius also			
Rotation of neck	participate)			
Lateral bending of neck				
Elevation of upper thorax	Scaleni	C3—5	Phrenic	
Inspiration	Diaphragm			
Adduction of arm from behind to front	Pectoralis major and minor	C5—8, T1	Thoracic anterior (from medial and lateral cords of plexus)	Brachial
Forward thrust of shoulder	Serratus anterior	C5—7	Long thoracic	
Elevation of scapula	Levator scapulae	C5 (3, 4)	Dorsal scapular	
Medial adduction and elevation of scapula	Rhomboids	C4, 5		
Abduction of arm	Supraspinatus	C4—6	Suprascapular	
Lateral rotation of arm	Infraspinatus	C4—6		
Medial rotation of arm	Latissimus dorsi, teres major, and subscapularis	C5—8	Subscapular (from posterior cord of plexus)	
Adduction of arm from front to back				
Abduction of arm	Deltoid	C5, 6	Axillary (from posterior cord of plexus)	
Lateral rotation of arm	Teres minor	C4, 5		
Flexion of forearm	Biceps brachii	C5, 6	Musculocutaneous (from lateral cord of plexus)	
Supination of forearm				
Adduction of arm	Coracobrachialis	C5—7		
Flexion of forearm				
Flexion of forearm	Brachialis	C5, 6		
Ulnar flexion of hand	Flexor carpi ulnaris	C7, 8, T1	Ulnar (from medial cord of plexus)	
Flexion of terminal phalanx of { ring finger, little finger	Flexor digitorum profundus (ulnar portion)	C7, 8, T1		
Flexion of hand				
Adduction of metacarpal of thumb	Adductor pollicis	C8, T1		
Abduction of little finger	Abductor digiti quinti	C8, T1		
Opposition of little finger	Opponens digiti quinti	C7, 8, T1		
Flexion of little finger	Flexor digiti quinti brevis	C7, 8, T1		
Flexion of proximal phalanx, extension of 2 distal phalanges, adduction and abduction of fingers	Interossei	C8, T1		
Pronation of forearm	Pronator teres	C6, 7	Median (C6, 7 from lateral cord of plexus; C8, T1 from medial cord of plexus)	
Radial flexion of hand	Flexor carpi radialis	C6, 7		
Flexion of hand	Palmaris longus	C7, 8, T1		
Flexion of middle phalanx of { index finger, middle finger, ring finger, little finger	Flexor digitorum sublimis	C7, 8, T1		
Flexion of hand				
Flexion of terminal phalanx of thumb	Flexor pollicis longus	C7, 8, T1		
Flexion of terminal phalanx of { index finger, middle finger	Flexor digitorum profundus (radial portion)	C7, 8, T1		
Flexion of hand				
Abduction of metacarpal of thumb	Abductor pollicis brevis	C7, 8, T1	Median (C6, 7 from lateral cord of plexus; C8, T1 from medial cord of plexus)	
Flexion of proximal phalanx of thumb	Flexor pollicis brevis	C7, 8, T1		
Opposition of metacarpal of thumb	Opponens pollicis	C8, T1		
Flexion of proximal phalanx and extension of the 2 distal phalanges of { index finger, middle finger	Lumbricals (the 2 lateral)	C8, T1		
{ ring finger, little finger	Lumbricals (the 2 medial)	C8, T1	Ulnar	
Extension of forearm	Triceps brachii and anconeus	C6—8	Radial (from posterior cord of plexus)	
Flexion of forearm	Brachioradialis	C5, 6		
Radial extension of hand	Extensor carpi radialis	C6—8		
Extension of phalanges of { index finger, middle finger, ring finger, little finger	Extensor digitorum communis	C6—8		
Extension of hand				
Extension of phalanges of little finger	Extensor digiti quinti proprius	C6—8		
Extension of hand				
Ulnar extension of hand	Extensor carpi ulnaris	C6—8		

*Modified from JC McKinley. Reproduced with permission.

Table 9–5 (cont'd). Motor function chart.

Action to Be Tested	Muscles	Cord Segment	Nerves	Plexus
Shoulder Girdle and Upper Extremity (cont'd)				
Supination of forearm	Supinator	C5–7	Radial (from posterior cord of plexus)	Brachial
Abduction of metacarpal of thumb	Abductor pollicis longus	C7, 8		
Radial extension of hand				
Extension of thumb	Extensor pollicis brevis and longus	C7, 8		
Radial extension of hand		C6–8		
Extension of index finger	Extensor indicis proprius	C6–8		
Extension of hand				
Trunk and Thorax				
Elevation of ribs	Thoracic, abdominal, and back		Thoracic and posterior lumbosacral branches	Brachial
Depression of ribs				
Contraction of abdomen				
Anteroflexion of trunk				
Lateral flexion of trunk				
Hip Girdle and Lower Extremity				
Flexion of hip	Iliopsoas	L1–3	Femoral	Lumbar
Flexion of hip (and eversion of thigh)	Sartorius	L2, 3		
Extension of leg	Quadriceps femoris	L2–4		
Adduction of thigh	Pectineus	L2, 3	Obturator	
	Adductor longus	L2, 3		
	Adductor brevis	L2–4		
	Adductor magnus	L3, 4		
	Gracilis	L2–4		
Adduction of thigh	Obturator externus	L3, 4		
Lateral rotation of thigh				
Abduction of thigh	Gluteus medius and minimus	L4, 5, S1	Superior gluteal	Sacral
Medial rotation of thigh				
Flexion of thigh	Tensor fasciae latae	L4, 5		
Lateral rotation of thigh	Piriformis	L5, S1		
Abduction of thigh	Gluteus maximus	L4, 5, S1, 2	Inferior gluteal	
Lateral rotation of thigh	Obturator internus	L5, S1	Muscular branches from sacral plexus	
	Gemelli	L4, 5, S1		
	Quadratus femoris	L4, 5, S1		
Flexion of leg (assist in extension of thigh)	Biceps femoris	L4, 5, S1, 2	Sciatic (trunk)	
	Semitendinosus	L4, 5, S1		
	Semimembranosus	L4, 5, S1		
Dorsal flexion of foot	Tibialis anterior	L4, 5	Deep peroneal	
Supination of foot				
Extension of toes II–V	Extensor digitorum longus	L4, 5, S1		
Dorsal flexion of foot				
Extension of great toe	Extensor hallucis longus	L4, 5, S1		
Dorsal flexion of foot				
Extension of great toe and the 3 medial toes	Extensor digitorum brevis	L4, 5, S1		
Plantar flexion of foot in pronation	Peronei	L5, S1	Superficial peroneal	
Plantar flexion of foot in supination	Tibialis posterior and triceps surae	L5, S1, 2	Tibial	
Plantar flexion of foot in supination	Flexor digitorum longus	L5, S1, 2		
Flexion of terminal phalanx of toes II–V				
Plantar flexion of foot in supination	Flexor hallucis longus	L5, S1, 2		
Flexion of terminal phalanx of great toe				
Flexion of middle phalanx of toes II–V	Flexor digitorum brevis	L5, S1		
Flexion of proximal phalanx of great toe	Flexor hallucis brevis	L5, S1, 2		
Spreading and closing of toes	Small muscles of foot	S1, 2		
Flexion of proximal phalanx of toes				
Voluntary control of pelvic floor	Perineal and sphincters	S2–4	Pudendal	

FUNCTIONAL TESTS FOR THE PRINCIPAL MUSCLES

Muscle testing depends upon a thorough understanding of which muscles are used in performing certain movements. Testing is best performed when the subject is warm, rested, comfortable, attentive, and alone with the examiner. Since several muscles may function similarly, it is not always easy for the patient to contract a single muscle upon request. By positioning or fixation of parts, the contraction of a particular muscle can be emphasized while other muscles of similar function are inhibited. The effect of gravity must be considered, since it may enhance or reduce certain movements. Individual muscle testing is useful in evaluation of peripheral nerve and muscle function and disorders.

Two techniques of testing may be used: active motion against the examiner's resistance, and resistance against a movement performed by the examiner. The degree of impairment of muscle function may be difficult to estimate by inspection. It is helpful to palpate the body or tendon of a muscle for evidence of contraction or movement. The normal or least affected muscles should be tested first to gain the cooperation and confidence of the subject. The strength of the muscle tested should always be compared with that of its contralateral analog.

Grading of Strength of Muscle

The strength of various muscles should be graded and charted periodically (Fig 9–55). Grading scales of various types are used, eg, minus to 4+, 0 to 100%, and letter codes such as "N" for normal, "G" for good, "F" for fair, "P" for poor, "T" for trace, and "O" for zero.

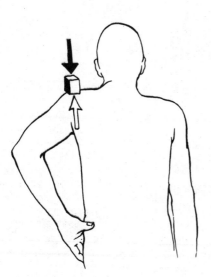

Figure 9–1. Trapezius, upper portion (C3, 4; spinal accessory nerve). The shoulder is elevated against resistance.

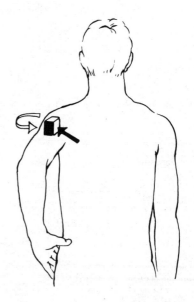

Figure 9–2. Trapezius, lower portion (C3, 4; spinal accessory nerve). The shoulder is thrust backward against resistance.

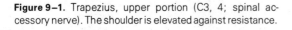

White arrows indicate the direction of movement in testing in a given muscle. Black arrows show the direction of resistance. The blocks show the site of application of resistance.

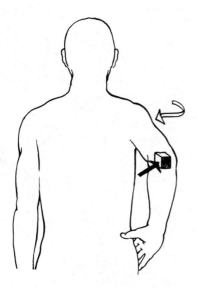

Figure 9–3. Rhomboids (C4, 5; dorsal scapular nerve). The shoulder is thrust backward against resistance.

Figure 9–4. Serratus anterior (C5–7; long thoracic nerve). The subject pushes hard with outstretched arms; the inner edge of the scapula remains against the thoracic wall. (If the trapezius is weak, the inner edge may move from chest wall.)

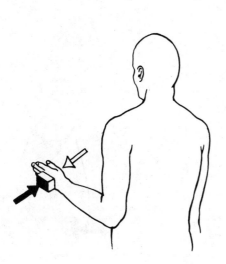

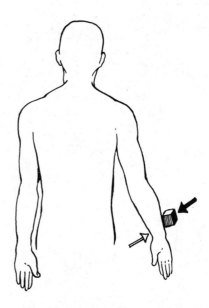

Figure 9–5. Infraspinatus (C4–6; suprascapular nerve). With the elbow flexed at the side, the arm is externally rotated against resistance on the forearm.

Figure 9–6. Supraspinatus (C4–6; suprascapular nerve). The arm is abducted from the side of the body against resistance.

White arrows indicate the direction of movement in testing in a given muscle. Black arrows show the direction of resistance. The blocks show the site of application of resistance.

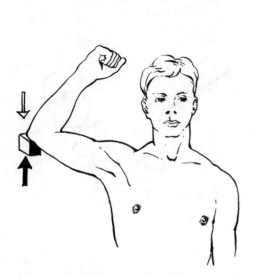

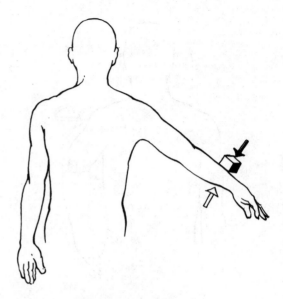

Figure 9–7. Latissimus dorsi (C6–8; subscapular nerve). The arm is adducted from a horizontal and lateral position against resistance.

Figure 9–8. Deltoid (C5, 6; axillary nerve). Abduction of laterally raised arm (30–75 degrees from body) against resistance.

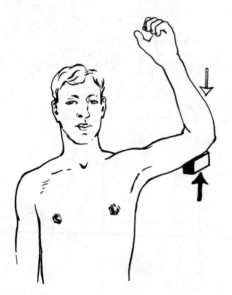

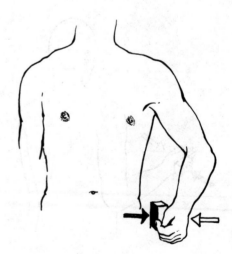

Figure 9–9. Pectoralis major, upper portion (C5–8; lateral and medial pectoral nerves). The arm is adducted from an elevated or horizontal and forward position against resistance.

Figure 9–10. Pectoralis major, lower portion (C5–8, T1; lateral and medial pectoral nerves). The arm is adducted from forward position below horizontal against resistance.

White arrows indicate the direction of movement in testing in a given muscle. Black arrows show the direction of resistance. The blocks show the site of application of resistance.

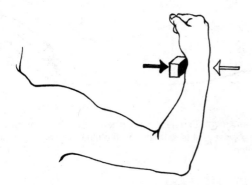

Figure 9–11. Biceps (C5, 6; musculocutaneous nerve). The supinated forearm is flexed against resistance.

Figure 9–12. Triceps (C6–8; radial nerve). The forearm, flexed at the elbow, is extended against resistance.

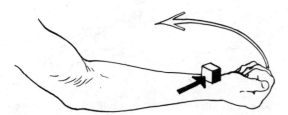

Figure 9–13. Brachioradialis (C5, 6; radial nerve). The forearm is flexed against resistance while it is in "neutral" position (neither pronated nor supinated).

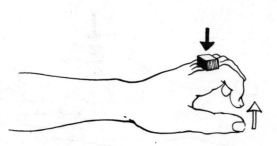

Figure 9–14. Extensor digitorum (C7, 8; radial nerve). The fingers are extended at the metacarpophalangeal joints against resistance.

Figure 9–15. Supinator (C5, 6; radial nerve). The hand is supinated against resistance, with arms extended at the side. Resistance is applied by the grip of the examiner's hand on patient's forearm near the wrist.

White arrows indicate the direction of movement in testing in a given muscle. Black arrows show the direction of resistance. The blocks show the site of application of resistance.

Figure 9–16. Extensor carpi radialis longus (C6–8; radial nerve). The wrist is extended to the radial side against resistance; fingers extended.

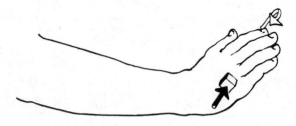

Figure 9–17. Extensor carpi ulnaris (C6–8; radial nerve). The wrist joint is extended to the ulnar side against resistance.

Figure 9–18. Extensor pollicis longus (C7,8; radial nerve). The thumb is extended against resistance.

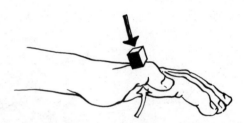

Figure 9–19. Extensor pollicis brevis (C7,8; radial nerve). The thumb is extended at the metacarpophalangeal joint against resistance.

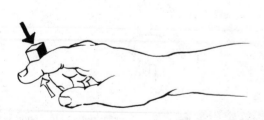

Figure 9–20. Extensor indicis proprius (C6–8; radial nerve). The index finger is extended against resistance placed on the dorsal aspect of the finger.

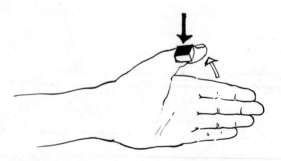

Figure 9–21. Abductor pollicis longus (C7, 8, T1; radial nerve). The thumb is abducted against resistance in a plane at right angle to the palmar surface.

White arrows indicate the direction of movement in testing in a given muscle. Black arrows show the direction of resistance. The blocks show the site of application of resistance.

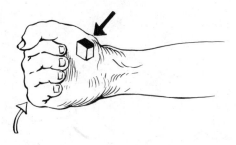

Figure 9–22. Flexor carpi radialis (C6, 7; median nerve). The wrist is flexed to the radial side against resistance.

Figure 9–23. Flexor digitorum sublimis (C7, 8, T1; median nerve). Fingers are flexed at first interphalangeal joint against resistance; proximal phalanges fixed.

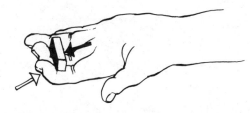

Figure 9–24. Flexor digitorum profundus I and II (C7, 8, T1; median nerve). The terminal phalanges of the index and middle fingers are flexed against resistance, the second phalanges being held in extension.

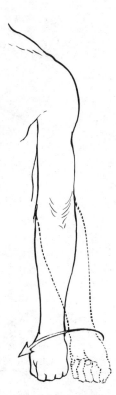

Figure 9–25. Pronator teres (C6, 7; median nerve). The extended arm is pronated against resistance. Resistance is applied by grip of examiner's hand on patient's forearm near the wrist.

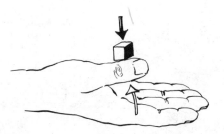

Figure 9–26. Abductor pollicis brevis (C7, 8, T1; median nerve). The thumb is abducted against resistance in a plane at a right angle to the palmar surface.

White arrows indicate the direction of movement in testing in a given muscle. Black arrows show the direction of resistance. The blocks show the site of application of resistance.

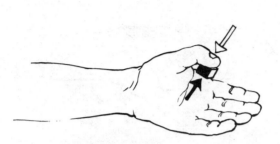

Figure 9–27. Flexor pollicis longus (C7, 8, T1; median nerve). The terminal phalanx of the thumb is flexed against resistance as the proximal phalanx is held in extension.

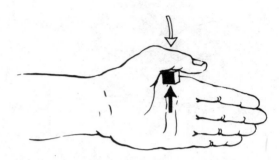

Figure 9–28. Flexor pollicis brevis (C7, 8, T1; median nerve). The proximal phalanx of the thumb is flexed against resistance placed on its palmar surface.

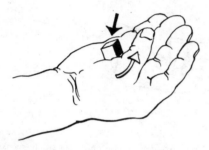

Figure 9–29. Opponens pollicis (C8, T1; median nerve). The thumb is crossed over the palm against resistance to touch the top of the little finger, with the thumbnail held parallel to the palm.

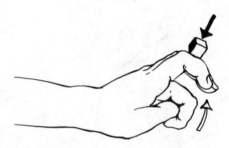

Figure 9–30. Lumbricalis-interossei (radial half) (C8, T1; median and ulnar nerves). The second and third phalanges are extended against resistance; the first phalanx is in full extension. The ulnar has the same innervation and can be tested in the same manner.

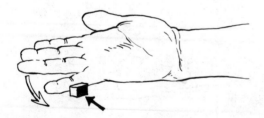

Figure 9–31. Flexor carpi ulnaris (C7, 8, T1; ulnar nerve). The little finger is abducted *strongly* against resistance as the supinated hand lies with fingers extended on table.

Figure 9–32. Flexor digiti quinti (C7, 8, T1; ulnar nerve). The proximal phalanx of the little finger is flexed against resistance.

White arrows indicate the direction of movement in testing in a given muscle. Black arrows show the direction of resistance. The blocks show the site of application of resistance.

Figure 9–33. Flexor digitorum profundus III and IV (C8, T1; ulnar nerve). The distal phalanges of the little and ring fingers are flexed against resistance; the second phalanges are held in extension.

Figure 9–34. Abductor digiti quinti (C8, T1; ulnar nerve). The little finger is abducted against resistance as the supinated hand with fingers extended lies on the table.

Figure 9–35. Opponens digiti quinti (C7, 8, T1; ulnar nerve). With fingers extended, the little finger is moved across the palm to the base of the thumb.

Figure 9–36. Adductor pollicis (C8, T1; ulnar nerve). A piece of paper grasped between the palm and the thumb is held against resistance with the thumbnail kept at a right angle to the palm.

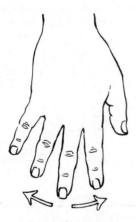

Figure 9–37. Dorsal interossei (C8, T1; ulnar nerve). The index and ring fingers are abducted from midline against resistance as the palm of the hand lies flat on the table.

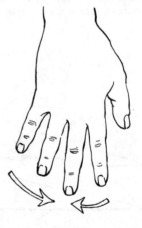

Figure 9–38. Palmar interossei (C8, T1; ulnar nerve). The abducted index, ring, and little fingers are adducted to midline against resistance as the palm of the hand lies flat on the table.

White arrows indicate the direction of movement in testing in a given muscle. Black arrows show the direction of resistance. The blocks show the site of application of resistance.

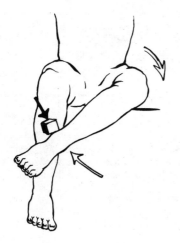

Figure 9–39. Sartorius (L2, 3; femoral nerve). With the subject sitting and the knee flexed, the thigh is rotated outward against resistance on the leg.

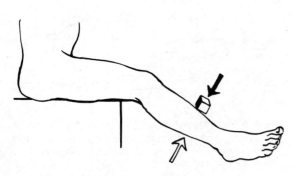

Figure 9–40. Quadriceps femoris (L2–4; femoral nerve). The knee is extended against resistance on the leg.

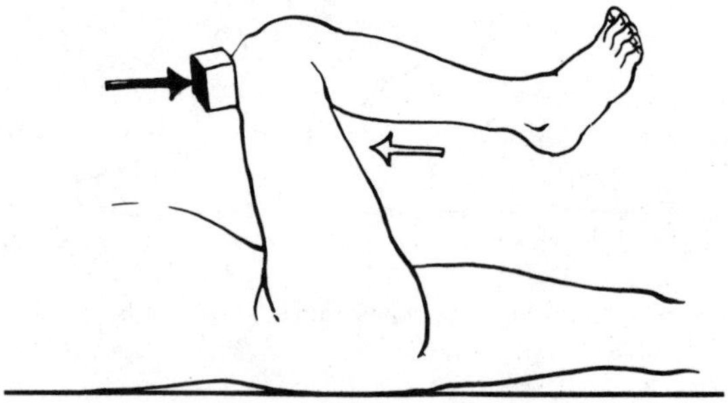

Figure 9–41. Iliopsoas (L1–3; femoral nerve). The subject lies supine with knee flexed. The flexed thigh (at about 90 degrees) is further flexed against resistance.

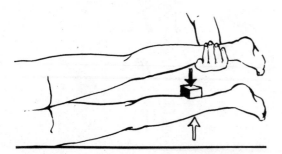

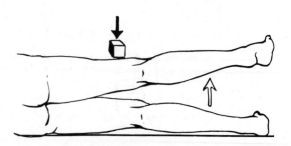

Figure 9–42. Adductors (L2–4; obturator nerve). With the subject on one side with knees extended, the lower extremity is adducted against resistance; the upper leg is supported by the examiner.

Figure 9–43. Gluteus medius and minimus; tensor fasciae latae (L4, 5, S1; superior gluteal nerve). Testing abduction: With the subject lying on one side and the thigh and leg extended, the uppermost lower extremity is abducted against resistance.

White arrows indicate the direction of movement in testing in a given muscle. Black arrows show the direction of resistance. The blocks show the site of application of resistance.

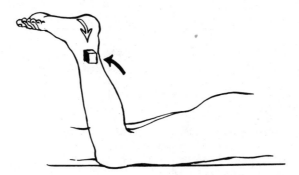

Figure 9–44. Gluteus medius and minimus; tensor fasciae latae (L4, 5, S1; superior gluteal nerve). Testing internal rotation: With the subject prone and the knee flexed, the foot is moved laterally against resistance.

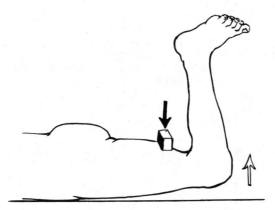

Figure 9–45. Gluteus maximus (L4, 5, S1, 2; inferior gluteal nerve). With the subject prone, the knee is lifted off the table against resistance.

Figure 9–46. "Hamstring" group (L4, 5, S1, 2; sciatic nerve). With the subject prone, the knee is flexed against resistance.

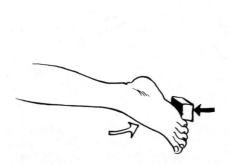

Figure 9–47. Gastrocnemius (L5, S1, 2; tibial nerve). With the subject prone, the foot is plantar-flexed against resistance.

Figure 9–48. Flexor digitorum longus (S1, 2; tibial nerve). The toe joints are plantar-flexed against resistance.

White arrows indicate the direction of movement in testing in a given muscle. Black arrows show the direction of resistance. The blocks show the site of application of resistance.

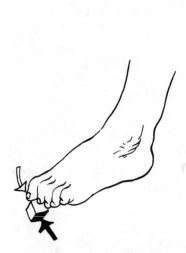

Figure 9–49. Flexor hallucis longus (L5, S1, 2; tibial nerve). The great toe is plantar-flexed against resistance. The second and third toes are also flexed.

Figure 9–50. Extensor hallucis longus (L4, 5, S1; deep peroneal nerve). The large toe is dorsiflexed against resistance.

Figure 9–51. Extensor digitorum longus (L4, 5, S1; deep peroneal nerve). The toes are dorsiflexed against resistance.

Figure 9–52. Tibialis anterior (L4, 5; deep peroneal nerve). The foot is dorsiflexed and inverted against resistance applied by gripping the foot with the examiner's hand.

Figure 9–53. Peroneus longus and brevis (L5, S1; superficial peroneal nerve). The foot is everted against resistance applied by gripping the foot with the examiner's hand.

Figure 9–54. Tibialis posterior (L5, S1; tibial nerve). The plantar-flexed foot is inverted against resistance applied by gripping the foot with the examiner's hand.

White arrows indicate the direction of movement in testing in a given muscle. Black arrows show the direction of resistance. The blocks show the site of application of resistance.

MUSCLE EXAMINATION

Patient's Name_____Chart No._____

Date of Birth_____Name of Institution_____

Date of Onset_____Attending Physician_____M. D.

Diagnosis:

LEFT						RIGHT			
				Examiner's Initials					
				Date					
				NECK Flexors	Sternocleidomastoid				
				Extensor group					
				TRUNK Flexors	Rectus abdominis				
				Rt. ext. obl.⎫ Rotators ⎧Lt. ext. obl. Lt. int. obl.⎭ ⎩Rt. int. obl.					
				Extensors	⎧Thoracic group ⎩Lumbar group				
				Pelvic elev.	Quadratus lumb.				
				HIP Flexors	Iliopsoas				
				Extensors	Gluteus maximus				
				Abductors	Gluteus medius				
				Adductor group					
				External rotator group					
				Internal rotator group					
				Sartorius					
				Tensor fasciae latae					
				KNEE Flexors	⎧Biceps femoris ⎩Inner hamstrings				
				Extensors	Quadriceps				
				ANKLE Plantar flexors	⎧Gastrocnemius ⎩Soleus				
				FOOT Invertors	⎧Tibialis anterior ⎩Tibialis posterior				
				Evertors	⎧Peroneus brevis ⎩Peroneus longus				
				TOES M. P. flexors	Lumbricales				
				I. P. flexors (1st)	Flex. digit. br.				
				I. P. flexors (2nd)	Flex. digit. l.				
				M. P. extensors	⎧Ext. digit. l. ⎩Ext. digit. br.				
				HALLUX M. P. flexor	Flex. hall. br.				
				I. P. flexor	Flex. hall. l.				
				M. P. extensor	Ext. hall. br.				
				I. P. extensor	Ext. hall. l.				

Measurements:

Cannot walk	Date	Speech	
Stands	Date	Swallowing	
Walks unaided	Date	Diaphragm	
Walks with apparatus	Date	Intercostals	

KEY

5 N	Normal	Complete range of motion against gravity with full resistance.
4 G	Good*	Complete range of motion against gravity with some resistance.
3 F	Fair*	Complete range of motion against gravity.
2 P	Poor*	Complete range of motion with gravity eliminated.
1 T	Trace	Evidence of slight contractility. No joint motion.
0 0	Zero	No evidence of contractility.

S or SS   Spasm or severe spasm.
C or CC   Contracture or severe contracture.
  * Muscle spasm or contracture may limit range of motion. A question mark should be placed after the grading of a movement that is incomplete from this cause.

Figure 9–55. Muscle examination. (Courtesy of The National Foundation for Infantile Paralysis.)

LEFT   RIGHT

				Examiner's Initials					
				Date					
				SCAPULA Abductor	Serratus anterior				
				Elevator	Upper trapezius				
				Depressor	Lower trapezius				
				Adductors	{ Middle trapezius				
					{ Rhomboids				
				SHOULDER Flexor	Anterior deltoid				
				Extensors	{ Latissimus dorsi				
					{ Teres major				
				Abductor	Middle deltoid				
				Horiz. abd.	Posterior deltoid				
				Horiz. add.	Pectoralis major				
				External rotator group					
				Internal rotator group					
				ELBOW Flexors	{ Biceps brachii				
					{ Brachioradialis				
				Extensor	Triceps				
				FOREARM Supinator group					
				Pronator group					
				WRIST Flexors	{ Flex. carpi rad.				
					{ Flex. carpi uln. ✓				
				Extensors	{ Ext. carpi rad. l. & br.				
					{ Ext. carpi uln.				
				FINGERS M. P. flexors	Lumbricales ✓				
				I. P. flexors (1st)	Flex. digit. sub. ✓				
				I. P. flexors (2nd)	Flex. digit. prof. ✓				
				M. P. extensor	Ext. digit. com.				
				Adductors	Palmar interossei ✓				
				Abductors	Dorsal interossei ✓				
				Abductor digiti quinti ✓					
				Opponens digiti quinti ✓					
				THUMB M. P. flexor	Flex. poll. br.				
				I. P. flexor	Flex. poll. l.				
				M. P. extensor	Ext. poll. br.				
				I. P. extensor	Ext. poll. l.				
				Abductors	{ Abd. poll. br.				
					{ Abd. poll. l.				
				Adductor pollicis ✓					
				Opponens pollicis					
				FACE:					

Additional data:

Figure 9–56 (cont'd). Muscle examination. (Courtesy of The National Foundation for Infantile Paralysis.)

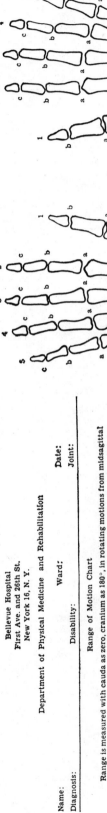

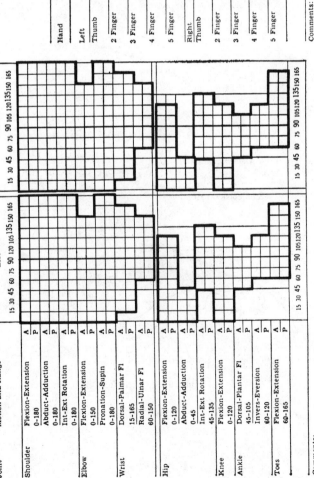

Figure 9–56. Range of motion chart. (Courtesy of Institute of Physical Medicine and Rehabilitation. New York University–Bellevue Medical Center.)

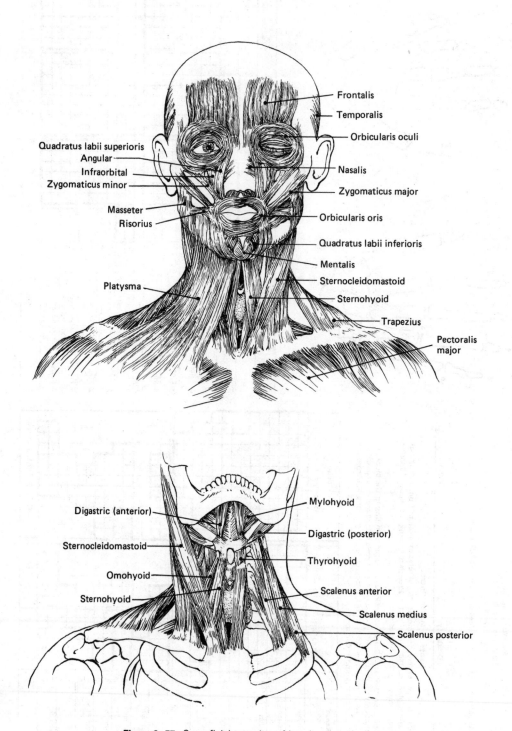

Figure 9–57. Superficial muscles of head and neck.

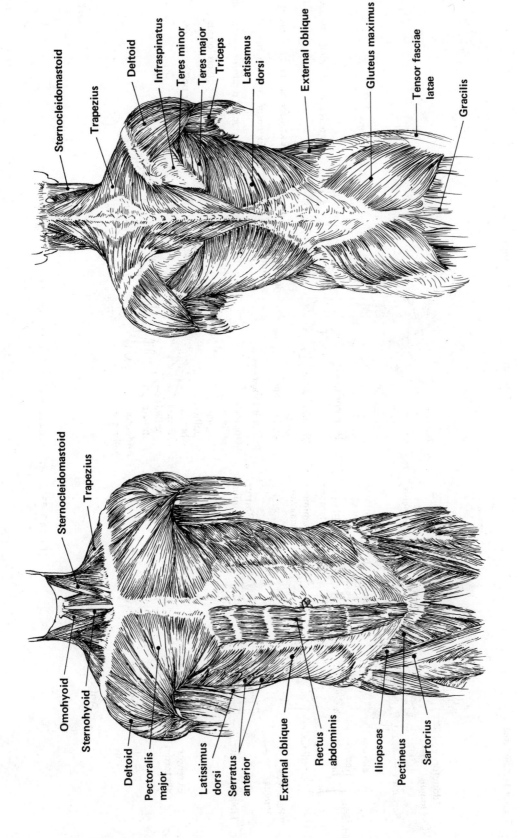

Figure 9–58. Superficial muscles of trunk.

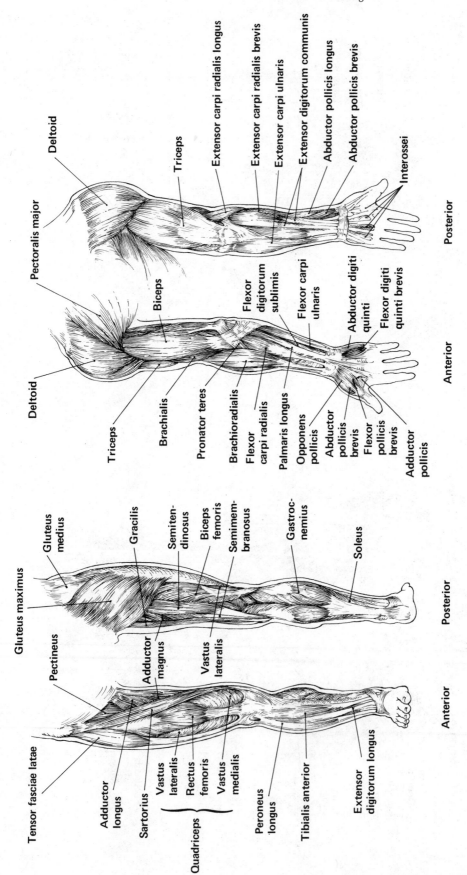

Figure 9–59. Superficial muscles of right extremities.

Sensation may be divided into 3 groups: superficial, deep, and combined. **Superficial sensation** is concerned with touch, pain, temperature, and 2-point discrimination; **deep sensation,** with muscle and joint position sense (proprioception), deep muscle pain, and vibration sense (pallesthesia). Both superficial and deep sensory mechanisms are involved in stereognosis, the recognition and naming of familiar objects placed in the hand; and topognosis, the ability to localize cutaneous stimuli. Stereognosis depends upon the integrity of the cerebral cortex.

Head's classification divides cutaneous sensibility into 2 groups, epicritic and protopathic, each served by a different type of neuron. His conclusions were based on observations of regenerating nerves following injury. Protopathic senses return rapidly (7–10 weeks), whereas epicritic senses remain impaired for 1–2 years or do not return at all. The **epicritic** senses are concerned with perception of light touch, 2-point discrimination, and small differences in temperature; the **protopathic** senses with pain and severe degrees of temperature.

Receptors

Specialized cells for detecting particular changes in the environment are called receptors. **Exteroceptors** include those receptors affected primarily by the external environment: Meissner's corpuscles, Merkel's corpuscles, and hair cells for touch; Krause's end bulbs for cold, Ruffini's cylinders for warmth, and free nerve endings for pain. **Teleceptors** are sensitive to distant stimuli. **Proprioceptors** receive impulses primarily from muscle spindles and Golgi tendon organs. **Interoceptors** are sensitive to changes within visceral tissues and blood vessels.

Each individual receptor fires completely or not at all when stimulated. The intensity of a stimulus, therefore, is reflected in the stimulation of more end organs at an increased rate of discharge over a longer period of time. **Adaptation** refers to the diminution in rate of discharge of some receptors upon constant stimulation.

Cutaneous senses for which separate receptors exist include touch, pressure, warmth, cold, and pain. Touch receptor organs adapt rapidly, are most numerous in the fingers and eyes, and are relatively scarce on the trunk. Many touch receptors are also found around hair follicles.

Two types of temperature sense organs may be found: those responding maximally to temperature slightly above and those responding maximally to temperature slightly below body temperature. Skin mapping shows discrete warmth-sensitive and more numerous cold-sensitive spots. The pain sense organs

Table 10–1. Principal sensory modalities. (The first 11 are conscious sensations.)*

Sensory Modality	Receptor	Sense Organ
Vision	Rods and cones	Eye
Hearing	Hair cells	Ear (organ of Corti)
Smell	Olfactory neurons	Olfactory mucous membrane
Taste	Taste receptor cells	Taste bud
Rotational acceleration	Hair cells	Ear (semicircular canals)
Linear acceleration	Hair cells	Ear (utricle and saccule)
Touch-pressure	Nerve endings	Various
Warmth	Nerve endings	Various
Cold	Nerve endings	Various
Pain	Naked nerve endings	. . .
Joint position and movement	Nerve endings	Various
Muscle length	Nerve endings	Muscle spindle
Muscle tension	Nerve endings	Golgi tendon organ
Arterial blood pressure	Nerve endings	Stretch receptors in carotid sinus and aortic arch
Central venous pressure	Nerve endings	Stretch receptors in walls of great veins, atria
Inflation of lung	Nerve endings	Stretch receptors in lung parenchyma
Temperature of blood in head	Neurons in hypothalamus	. . .
Arterial PO_2	Nerve endings?	Carotid and aortic bodies
pH of cerebrospinal fluid	Receptors on ventral surface of medulla oblongata	. . .
Osmotic pressure of plasma	Cells in anterior hypothalamus	. . .
Arteriovenous blood glucose difference	Cells in hypothalamus (glucostats)	. . .

*Reproduced, with permission, from Ganong WF: *Review of Medical Physiology,* 10th ed. Lange, 1981.

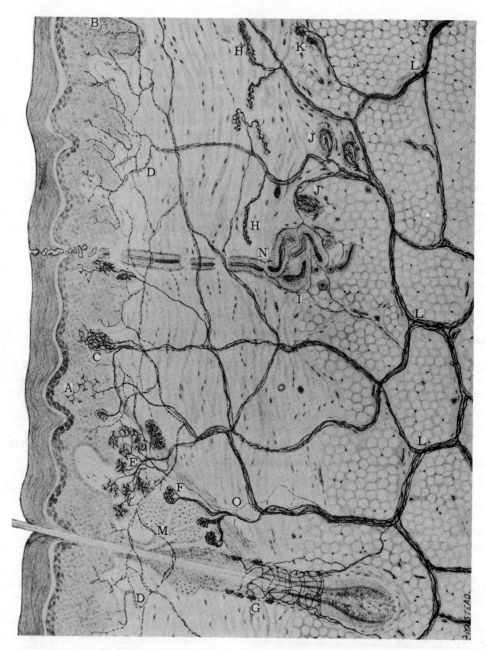

A. Merkel's corpuscles, subserving touch.
B. Free nerve endings, subserving pain.
C. Meissner's corpuscles, subserving touch.
D. Nerve fibers, subserving pain.
E. Krause's end bulbs, subserving cold.
F. Nerve endings, subserving warmth (sometimes called Ruffini's endings).
G. Nerve fibers and endings on the hair follicles, subserving touch.
H. Ruffini's endings, subserving pressure.
I. Sympathetic nerve fibers innervating sweat glands.
J. Pacini's corpuscles, subserving pressure.
K. Golgi-Mazzoni endings, subserving pressure.
L. Nerve trunks containing thick and thin fibers.
M. Sebaceous gland.
N. Sweat gland.
O. Sympathetic fibers supplying arrectores pilorum muscles.

Figure 10–1. Composite diagram showing the innervation of the human skin. (Reproduced, with permission, from Woollard, Weddell, & Harpman: *J Anat* 1940; **74**:413.)

are naked nerve endings found in almost every tissue of the body.

Impulses from muscle spindles and the Golgi tendon organs reach the cerebellum without affecting consciousness. Conscious awareness of various parts of the body depends upon impulses arising from sense organs in and around joints. The receptors involved are slowly adapting spray endings, Golgi tendon organ-like structures, and pacinian corpuscles in synovia and ligaments.

Anatomy of Sensation

The cell bodies of the peripheral sensory neurons are located in the spinal root ganglia and homologous cranial nerve ganglia. These are unipolar cells with a single process (dendraxon), which splits dichotomously into central and peripheral branches. The peripheral processes form the sensory fibers of the peripheral nerves, which end in special receptors located in the skin, muscles, tendons, etc. The central processes pass via the dorsal roots (or cranial nerve trunks) into the spinal cord and brain stem, where they make synaptic connections with second-order neurons.

Central Connections (See pp 66–73.)

Pain and temperature fibers are very closely associated anatomically. Pain fibers enter the spinal cord and synapse with internuncial neurons in the substantia gelatinosa of the same level. Fibers then cross within one or 2 spinal segments and ascend in the lateral spinothalamic tract through the spinal cord, brain stem, and midbrain to the posteroventral nucleus of the thalamus and proceed to the postcentral gyrus of the parietal lobe (Fig 10–2).

Proprioceptive fibers carrying sensory impulses from muscle, tendons, ligaments, and joints enter the posterior spinal cord. (1) Some proceed as direct fibers of the stretch reflex arc to lower motor neurons of the anterior horn of the spinal cord. (2) Other proprioceptive fibers connect with cells of the posterior gray column of the spinal cord and ascend via the spinocerebellar tracts. The dorsal spinocerebellar tract continues uncrossed via the inferior cerebellar peduncle to the cerebellum. The ventral spinocerebellar tract, containing crossed and uncrossed fibers, reaches the cerebellum via the superior cerebellar peduncle. (3) Still other proprioceptive fibers ascend in the posterior white columns via the fasciculi gracilis and cuneatus to the ipsilateral nuclei gracilis and cuneatus, cross in the decussation of the medial lemniscus, and proceed via the medial lemniscus to the posteroventral nucleus of the thalamus and then to the postcentral gyrus of the parietal lobe (Fig 10–3).

Touch sensation of 2 types may be distinguished: (1) tactile discrimination, including deep pressure sense, 2-point discrimination, vibration sense, form perception, and conscious proprioception; and (2) light touch, including light pressure and touch and crude tactile localization. Tactile discrimination fibers proceed in the posterior white columns to the ipsilateral

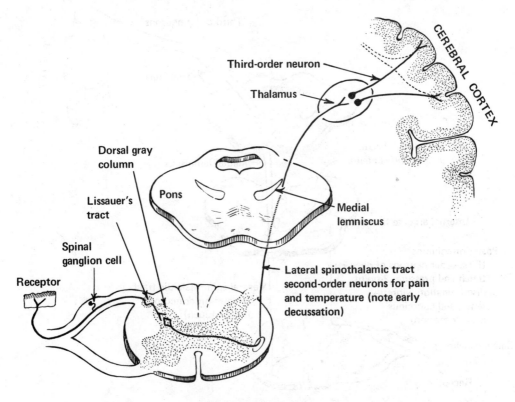

Figure 10–2. Pain and temperature.

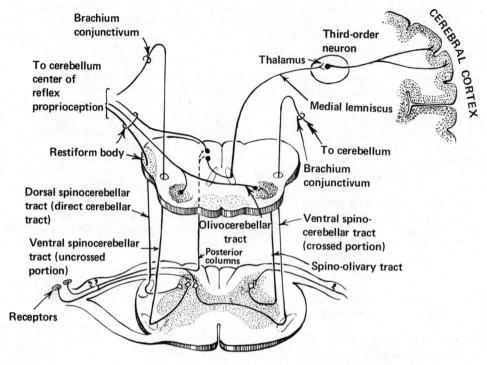

Figure 10–3. Proprioception.

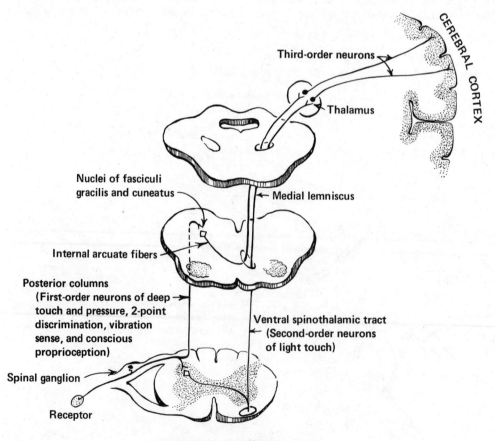

Figure 10–4. Touch and pressure.

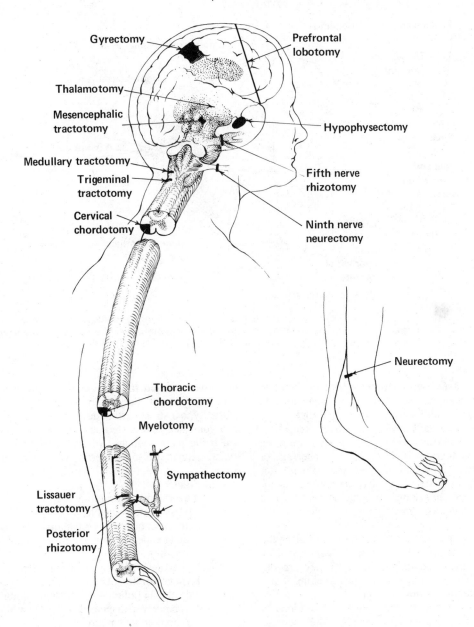

Figure 10–5. Schematic diagram illustrating various surgical procedures designed to alleviate pain. (Redrawn and reproduced, with permission, from MacCarty: *Proc Staff Meet Mayo Clin* 1956;**31**:208.)

nuclei gracilis and cuneatus and ascend like the proprioceptive fibers described above. Light touch fibers synapse with posterior gray horn cells of the spinal cord and, after decussation, cross the anterior white column and ascend in the ventral spinothalamic tract through the spinal cord, brain stem, and midbrain to the posteroventral nucleus of the thalamus and then to the postcentral gyrus of the parietal lobe (Fig 10–4).

Symptoms & Signs of Disturbances of Sensation

A. Symptoms: Pain may be local or diffuse, constant or intermittent, burning, shooting, gnawing,

sharp, dull, knifelike, etc. **Paresthesia** consists of abnormal sensations, numbness, tingling, and formication (crawling sensations). The character of the pain may reflect the underlying site of the disorder. In peripheral nerve lesions, pain is usually limited to the area supplied by the affected nerve or nerves. Pain is often burning or prickling in type, often worse at night and unrelated to position.

The pain of trigeminal and other neuralgias is limited to the tissues supplied by one or more branches of the affected nerve. Pains are usually very severe, although individual pains may be brief in duration and

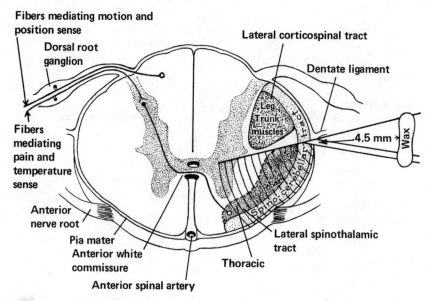

Figure 10–6. Ideal chordotomy at upper dorsal spinal cord segments. Surgical interruption of the lateral spinothalamic tract may provide relief from intractable pain of the opposite half of the body below the level of chordotomy. (Redrawn and reproduced, with permission, from Kahn & Rand: *J Neurosurg* 1952; **9**:611.)

abrupt in onset, with lightninglike or electric shock-like qualities. These are frequently precipitated by peripheral stimuli activating a trigger zone.

Root pains usually are localized to the dermatome supplied by the affected root. These pains are often produced or aggravated by coughing, sneezing, or straining, and they may awaken the patient after several hours of sleep and may be relieved within 30 minutes after sitting upright. Maneuvers that stretch the involved roots aggravate or produce the pains.

Thalamic pains affect the contralateral half of the body. Pains are persistent and readily aggravated by emotional stress and fatigue. Usually they are described as burning, drawing, pulling, swelling, tense pains of a highly distressing type.

A painful stimulus may cause 2 sensations: a sharp, localized sensation followed by a dull, aching, more diffuse response. These 2 sensations are sometimes referred to as fast and slow pain, or first and second pain. The farther from the brain the stimulus is applied, the greater is the temporal separation of these 2 components of pain.

Deep pain, unlike superficial pain, is poorly localized, unpleasant, and nauseating and may be associated with sweating and blood pressure changes. Pain produced by saline injection into periosteum or ligaments may cause reflex contraction of nearby skeletal muscles. Steadily contracting muscles may become ischemic, stimulating more pain receptors in muscles.

Pain from visceral structures is usually poorly localized, unpleasant, and associated with nausea and autonomic symptoms and often radiates to or is referred to other areas. Irritation of a viscus often pro-

duces pain not felt in the viscus but perceived in a distant somatic structure (referred pain). Referred pain is usually to a structure that developed from the same embryonic segment or dermatome as the structure in which the pain originates (dermatomal rule). Deep somatic pain may also be referred, but superficial pain is not.

B. Signs:

Anesthesia: Complete loss of sensation. Dissociated anesthesia is loss of some forms of cutaneous sensibility (usually pain and temperature) and preservation of others (tactile).

Hypesthesia: Diminished sensation.

Hyperesthesia: Increased tactile sensibility.

Allesthesia (allochiria): A single stimulation is perceived displaced across the midline to a homologous region.

Synesthesia (synchiria): With a single stimulation, 2 sensations are perceived, one well localized and the other appearing in an area in which there is dysesthesia or burning pain, or on the opposite side of the body.

Analgesia: Complete loss of pain sensibility.

Hypalgesia: Diminished sensibility to pain.

Hyperalgesia: Increased sensibility to pain (tenderness).

Astereognosis: Inability to recognize familiar objects by the sense of touch (anesthesia not being present). It usually indicates a lesion in the parietal cerebral cortex.

Atopognosis: Inability to localize tactile stimuli.

Baragnosis: Inability to distinguish between different weights.

Extinction: With 2 simultaneous stimulations, one is well localized and the other is perceived poorly or not at all.

Displacement: With 2 simultaneous stimulations, one sensation is well localized and the other is displaced toward it.

Overlap

In peripheral nerve injuries, the impairment of touch perception corresponds more nearly to the anatomic distribution of the involved nerve than does the impairment of pain perception, which is less extensive because overlap from adjacent peripheral nerves supplies many pain endings. However, in lesions of the dorsal roots, the loss of pain perception closely parallels the anatomic distribution of the root, and touch perception is largely retained because of overlap supplied by adjacent roots.

Methods of Examination

These require the cooperation of the patient.

Light touch may be tested with a wisp of cotton; pressure sense with the unsharpened end of a lead pencil; pain with a pin or a simple algesimeter;* temperature with test tubes containing hot and cold water; vibration sense with a tuning fork placed over the bone of the part tested; stereognosis with the use of familiar objects, eg, coins, pen, knife.

Position sense. As the examiner moves the patient's extremities, the blindfolded subject is asked to describe their position. Other tests of proprioception include the heel-to-knee test, finger-to-finger test, finger-to-nose test, and Romberg's test or sign.

Number writing (graphesthesia). Test ability of patient to recognize numbers traced lightly on the skin.

Two-point discrimination. Using calipers, determine the smallest area in which 2 points can be separately perceived.

Double stimulation. Two stimulations may be presented together to both sides of the body in homologous areas (simultaneous homologous) or in nonhomologous areas (simultaneous nonhomologous). Similarly, 2 stimulations of the same side of the body can be carried out.

DISORDERS CHARACTERIZED BY MARKED SENSORY DISTURBANCES

Complete Peripheral Nerve Injuries

These are characterized by loss of all forms of sensibility in the dependent areas. The loss of touch is most marked and corresponds more nearly to the anatomic distribution of the nerve than does the loss of pain, because overlap from adjacent peripheral nerves supplies many pain endings. **Incomplete**

*Made by placing a large-headed pin in the barrel of a glass syringe, allowing the point to extend through the tip, and replacing the plunger; the weight of the plunger thus assures uniform stimulation.

peripheral nerve injuries show a lesser degree of sensory loss and often show subjective symptoms such as pain.

Neuritis

Inflammation or other alteration of a peripheral nerve (toxic, traumatic, or infectious) is characterized by pain and tenderness in the distribution and along the course of the nerve. In advanced cases, there is complete loss of both motor and sensory functions of the nerve, with diminution or loss of reflexes.

Neuralgia

Neuralgia is characterized by bouts of severe pain that are often set off by accidental stimulation of a "trigger zone." Usually there is no demonstrable pathology. In trigeminal neuralgia (tic douloureux, trifacial neuralgia), the paroxysms occur in the distribution of one of the main branches of the trigeminal nerve; the bouts of pain may last only a few seconds.

Causalgia

Causalgia is characterized by disagreeable, painful, burning sensations, usually along the distribution of the median or tibial nerves, associated with trophic changes in the skin and nails. Moist applications seem to bring relief. Causalgia results from partial injuries of the median and posterior tibial or sciatic nerves. It may sometimes be relieved by sympathetic block or sympathectomy.

Acroparesthesia

Acroparesthesia is characterized by numbness and prickly or tingling sensations of the tips of the fingers and toes. This is classed as a vasomotor-trophic disorder in which the nerve endings or end organs are probably involved.

Restless Legs Syndrome

This involves paresthesias of legs, coldness of feet, and tiredness of the lower extremities of intermittent occurrence and unknown cause. Paresthesias (pins and needles, numbness, vibration, and cramps) cause the patient to seek temporary relief by keeping the legs in motion while in bed.

"Root Pains"

These are segmental in distribution and occur with various lesions of the dorsal roots of the spinal nerves, eg, cord tumors, fractures, or inflammatory diseases of the vertebrae, and meningitis. The pains are sharp and lightninglike.

Herpes Zoster

Herpes zoster (shingles) is due to a viral inflammation of the posterior root ganglia, producing pain and vesicle formation in the segmental distribution of the involved roots. The disease is self-limited, but sensation is sometimes lost after the inflammation disappears. Motor paralysis, usually transient, may also occur. Painful persistent paresthesias resistant to

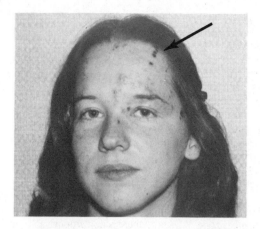

Figure 10–7. Herpes zoster in distribution of ophthalmic division of the trigeminal nerve.

treatment may occur in the later phases (postherpetic neuralgia).

Brown-Séquard Syndrome

(Caused by hemisection of the spinal cord as a result of syringomyelia, cord tumor, hematomyelia, bullet or stab wounds, etc): (1) Ipsilateral lower motor neuron paralysis in the segment of the lesion. (2) Ipsilateral upper motor neuron paralysis below the level of the lesion. (3) Ipsilateral zone of cutaneous anesthesia in the segment of the lesion. (4) Ipsilateral hyperesthesia below the anesthetic zone. (5) Ipsilateral loss of proprioceptive, vibratory, and 2-point

discrimination sense below the level of the lesion. (6) Contralateral zone of hyperesthesia in the segment of the lesion. (7) Contralateral loss of pain and temperature sense below the lesion. (See Fig 10–8.)

Tabes Dorsalis

Tabes dorsalis is characterized by marked ataxia owing to loss of the proprioceptive pathways (dorsal roots and posterior columns). Subjective sensory disturbances known as tabetic crises consist of severe, cramping pains in the stomach, larynx, or other viscera.

Syringomyelia

Syringomyelia is characterized by loss of pain and temperature sense (Fig 10–9), but the patient retains touch and pressure senses in the affected parts (dissociated anesthesia). Syringomyelia is produced by gliosis around the central canal of the spinal cord.

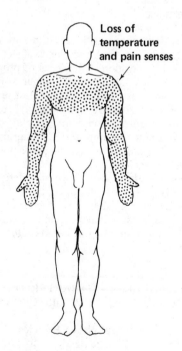

Loss of temperature and pain senses

Figure 10–9. Syringomyelia.

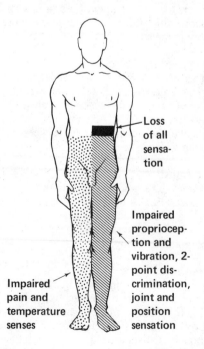

Loss of all sensation

Impaired proprioception and vibration, 2-point discrimination, joint and position sensation

Impaired pain and temperature senses

Figure 10–8. Brown-Séquard syndrome, with lesion at left tenth thoracic level.

Pernicious Anemia

Advanced cases are associated with combined degeneration of the posterior and lateral columns of the spinal cord, thus producing marked sensory and motor disturbances. Diminished vibration sense is a prominent feature of the sensory involvement (Fig 10–10).

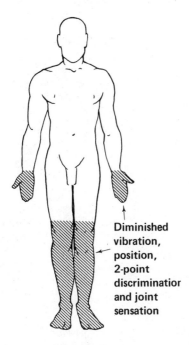

Diminished vibration, position, 2-point discrimination and joint sensation

Figure 10–10. Posterolateral sclerosis.

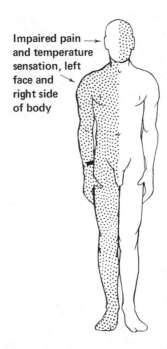

Impaired pain and temperature sensation, left face and right side of body

Figure 10–12. Left posterior inferior cerebellar artery occlusion (Wallenberg's syndrome).

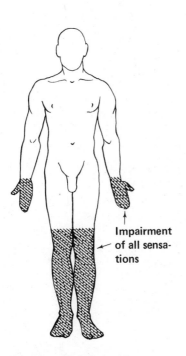

Impairment of all sensations

Figure 10–11. Polyneuritis.

Multiple Sclerosis

Numbness and paresthesia are often present in the early stages. Later there are marked sensory and motor disturbances caused by the disseminated patches of gliosis in the cord and brain.

Thalamic Lesions

Lesions of the thalamus are characterized by outbursts of severe, poorly localized pain (thalamic pain) associated with weakness, ataxia, hyperkinesia, paresthesia, and loss of ability to discriminate or localize simple crude sensations. Slight stimuli may evoke severe and disagreeable sensations.

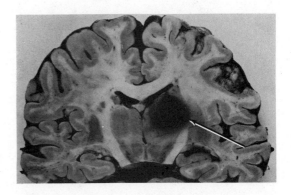

Figure 10–13. Thalamic hemorrhage. Hemorrhage in the right posterior thalamus in a 64-year-old woman.

Déjérine's Cortical Sensory Syndrome

Lesions of the sensory parietal cortex may impair the ability to make fine sensory distinctions, although the ability to recognize pain, temperature, and vibration may be unimpaired. Thus, there may be contralateral astereognosis, inability to appreciate or identify numbers or figures traced on the skin, inability to perceive passive joint motions, difficulty in distinguishing between different weights, and inability to recognize various textures by touch (Fig 10–14).

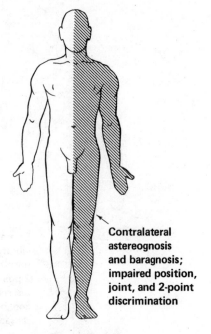

Contralateral astereognosis and baragnosis; impaired position, joint, and 2-point discrimination

Figure 10–14. Right parietal lobe cortex lesion. (See Déjérine's cortical sensory syndrome.)

Cutaneous Innervation | 11

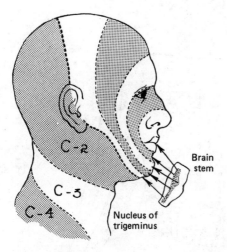

Figure 11–1. Segmental distribution to the head.

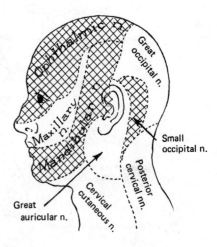

Figure 11–2. Peripheral distribution to the head.

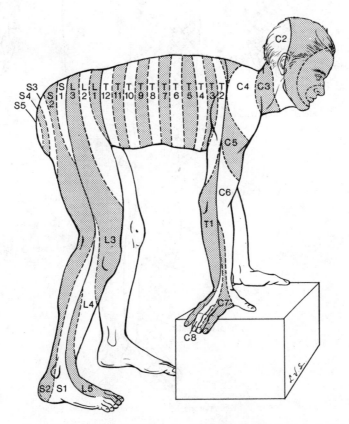

Figure 11–3. Segmental distribution viewed in the quadruped position.

PERIPHERAL DISTRIBUTION

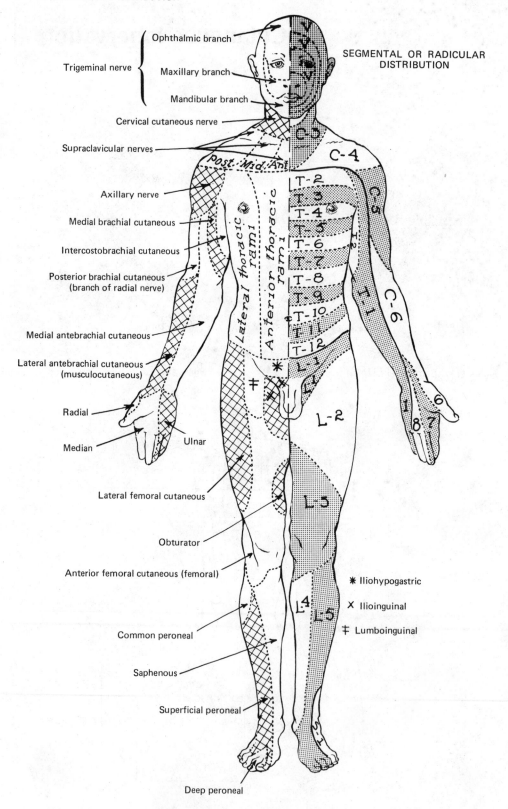

Figure 11–4. Cutaneous innervation.

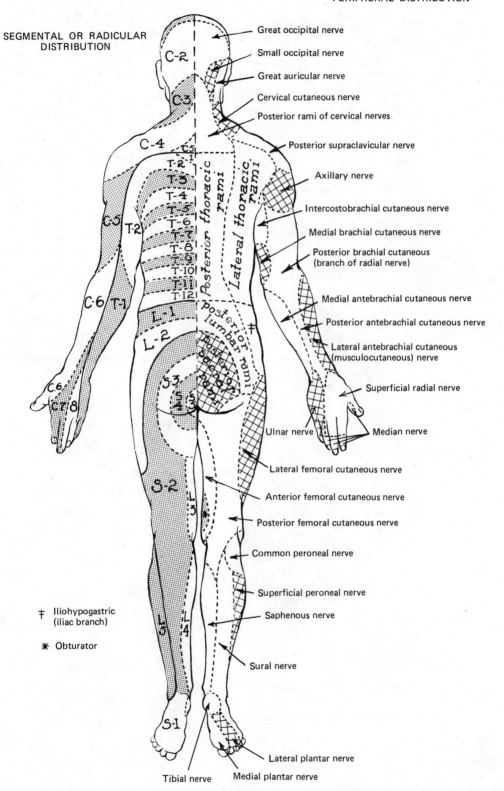

PERIPHERAL DISTRIBUTION

SEGMENTAL OR RADICULAR
DISTRIBUTION

Great occipital nerve

Small occipital nerve

Great auricular nerve

Cervical cutaneous nerve

Posterior rami of cervical nerves

Posterior supraclavicular nerve

Axillary nerve

Intercostobrachial cutaneous nerve

Medial brachial cutaneous nerve

Posterior brachial cutaneous
(branch of radial nerve)

Medial antebrachial cutaneous nerve

Posterior antebrachial cutaneous nerve

Lateral antebrachial cutaneous
(musculocutaneous) nerve

Superficial radial nerve

Ulnar nerve   Median nerve

Lateral femoral cutaneous nerve

Anterior femoral cutaneous nerve

Posterior femoral cutaneous nerve

Common peroneal nerve

Superficial peroneal nerve

Saphenous nerve

Sural nerve

Lateral plantar nerve

Tibial nerve   Medial plantar nerve

‡ Iliohypogastric
(iliac branch)

✳ Obturator

Figure 11–5. Cutaneous innervation.

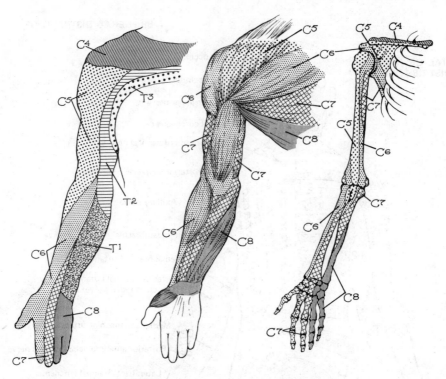

Figure 11–6. Segmental innervation of right upper extremity, anterior view. (Reproduced, with permission, from Inman VT, Saunders JBdeCM: Referred pain from skeletal structures. *J Nerv Ment Dis* 1944; **99**:660.)

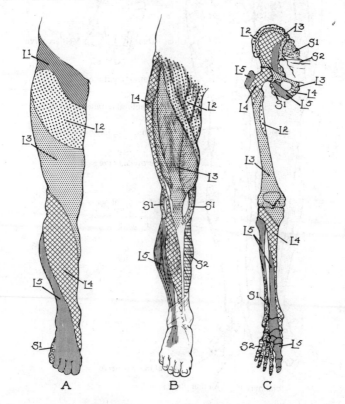

A   B   C

Figure 11–7. Segmental innervation of right lower extremity, anterior view. (Reproduced, with permission, from Inman VT, Saunders JBdeCM: Referred pain from skeletal structures. *J Nerv Ment Dis* 1944; **99**:660.)

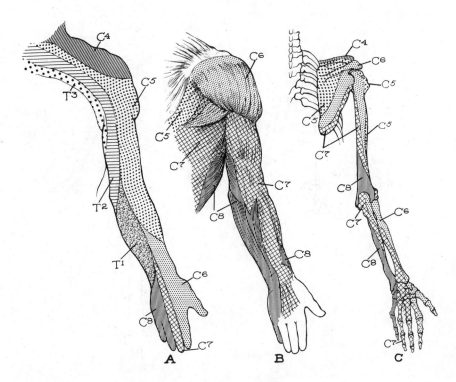

Figure 11–8. Segmental innervation of right upper extremity, posterior view. (Reproduced, with permission, from Inman VT, Saunders JBdeCM: Referred pain from skeletal structures. *J Nerv Ment Dis* 1944;99:660.)

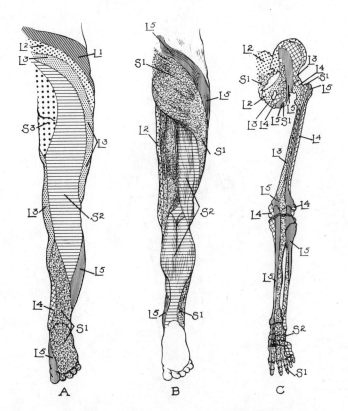

Figure 11–9. Segmental innervation of right lower extremity, posterior view. (Reproduced, with permission, from Inman VT, Saunders JBdeCM: Referred pain from skeletal structures. *J Nerv Ment Dis* 1944;99:660.)

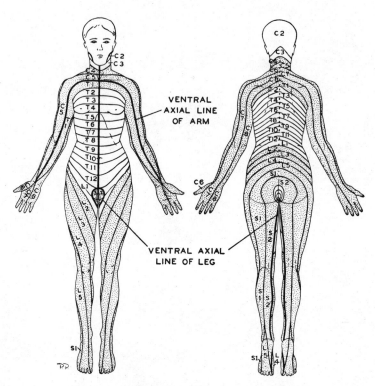

Figure 11–10. Dermatomes according to Keegan. Based upon hypalgesia from compression of single nerve roots. (Reproduced, with permission, from Keegan & Garrett: *Anat Rec* 1948; **102:**4, 409.)

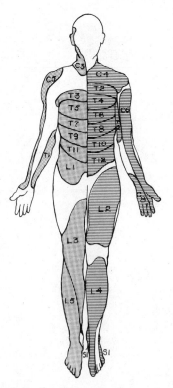

Figure 11–11. Dermatomes according to Foerster. Determined by the method of "remaining sensibility" on human cases. (See p 78.)

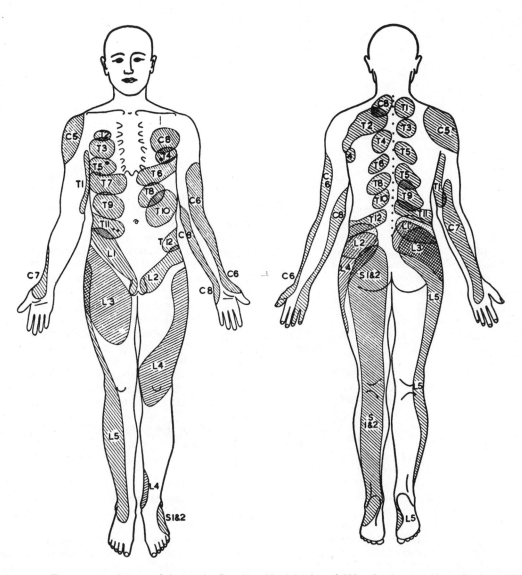

Figure 11–12. The segmental areas of deep pain. Developed by injection of 6% saline into corresponding interspinous ligaments; diagrams constructed from Kellgrren material. (Reproduced, with permission, from Lewis: *Pain.* Macmillan, 1942.)

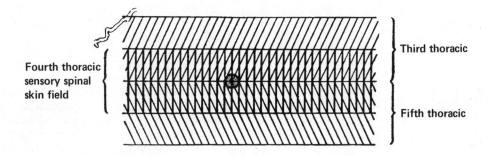

Figure 11–13. Diagram of the position of the nipple in the sensory skin fields of the third, fourth, and fifth thoracic spinal roots. The overlapping of the cutaneous areas is represented. (Sherrington.) (Reproduced, with permission, from Ranson SW, Clark SL: *The Anatomy of the Nervous System,* 10th ed. Saunders, 1959.)

12 | Reflexes

Reflexes are inborn stimulus-response mechanisms. The instinctive behavior of lower animals is governed largely by reflexes; in humans, behavior is more a matter of conditioning, and reflexes are subordinated as basic defense mechanisms. The reflexes are, however, extremely important in the diagnosis and localization of neurologic lesions.

ANATOMY OF REFLEXES
(The Reflex Arc)

The essential neural portion of a reflex includes a sensory and a motor neuron. Several structures, however, are involved: (1) A receptor, such as a special sense organ, cutaneous end organ, or neuromuscular spindle, stimulation of which initiates an impulse. (2) The afferent (or sensory) neuron, which transmits the impulse through a peripheral nerve to the CNS, where synapse occurs with an intercalated neuron. (3) An intercalated neuron, which relays the impulse to the efferent nerve. (4) The efferent (or motor) neuron, which, passing outward in the nerve trunk, delivers the impulse to an effector. (5) An effector, such as a muscle or gland that produces the response.

Interruption of the reflex arc at any point will abolish the response.

TYPES OF REFLEXES

The reflexes that are of importance to the clinical neurologist may be divided into 4 groups: (1) superficial (or skin and mucous membrane) reflexes, (2) deep (or myotatic) reflexes, (3) visceral (or organic) reflexes, and (4) pathologic (or abnormal) reflexes.

Reflexes may also be classified according to the level of their central representation, eg, as spinal, bulbar (postural and righting reflexes), midbrain, or cerebellar reflexes. Idiomuscular or neuromuscular responses, such as myoedema, are not true reflexes and so are classified as pseudoreflexes. They are responses of irritable muscle tissue to direct stimulation.

Superficial Reflexes
  A. Mucous Membrane Reflexes:
  1. Corneal (or conjunctival) reflex–Blinking of

the eye upon gentle irritation of the cornea or conjunctiva with a small piece of absorbent cotton. This reflex is lost in lesions of the fifth or seventh cranial nerves or their central connections in the pons. Corneal ulcers will often result when the reflex is not present; this is because of the absence of the protective mechanism.

2. Nasal (or sneeze) reflex–Sneezing when the nasal membrane is irritated depends upon the afferents of the fifth nerve and the central connections and motor nuclei of the fifth to tenth cranial nerves and the upper cervical nerves.

3. Pharyngeal (or gag) reflex–Retching or gagging when the pharynx is irritated is absent in lesions of the ninth or tenth cranial nerves or their nuclei and in hysteria.

4. Uvular (or palatal) reflex–Raising of the uvula in phonation or upon irritation of its mucous membrane is also dependent upon the ninth and tenth nerves.

  B. Skin Reflexes:
  1. Interscapular reflex–Drawing inward of the scapula when the skin of the interscapular space is irritated.

2. Upper and lower abdominal reflexes–(Tested on each side.) Tensing of the muscles beneath the skin area stroked usually causes the umbilicus to move in the direction of the skin area stimulated.

3. Cremasteric reflex–Elevation of the testicle upon stroking the inner aspect of the thigh.

4. Gluteal reflex–Contraction of the buttocks when the skin over them is irritated.

5. Plantar reflex–Plantar flexion of the toes upon stroking the sole of the foot. In children there is usually also a retraction of the foot.

6. Anal reflex–Contraction of the sphincter ani upon stroking the perianal area or upon inserting a gloved finger into the rectum.

  C. Significance of Abnormal Reflex Responses: Diminished or absent superficial skin reflexes are of neurologic importance when associated with exaggerated deep reflexes and positive pathologic reflexes. This combination is diagnostic of upper motor neuron involvement. The explanation offered for the absence of skin reflexes in such cases is that the reflex arc, which probably includes the cortex, is interrupted at the higher level.

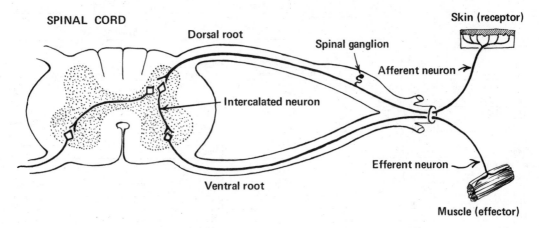

Figure 12–1. Simple reflex arc.

Deep Reflexes

A. Important Deep Reflexes:

1. Maxillary (jaw jerk) reflex–Sudden closure of the jaw upon striking the middle of the chin when the mouth is slightly open or upon tapping a pencil laid on the lower teeth or jaw.

2. Biceps reflex–Flexion at the elbow when the biceps tendon is struck.

3. Triceps reflex–Extension at the elbow when the triceps tendon is struck.

4. Periosteoradial reflex–Flexion and supination of the forearm upon striking the styloid process of the radius.

5. Periosteoulnar reflex–Extension and ulnar abduction of the wrist when the styloid process of the ulna is struck.

6. Wrist reflexes–Extension or flexion when the corresponding tendons are sharply struck.

7. Patellar (knee jerk) reflex–Extension at the knee when the patellar tendon is struck. Absence of this reflex is known as Westphal's sign. If the reflex cannot be obtained in the normal manner, the Jendrassik method of reinforcement should be tried. This is done by having patients pull on their clenched hands at the moment the test is made.

8. Achilles tendon reflex–Plantar flexion of the foot when the Achilles tendon is struck.

B. Significance of Abnormal Reflex Responses: Diminution or absence of these reflexes may result from any lesion that interrupts the reflex arc, eg, peripheral nerve disease, involvement of the posterior columns of gray matter of the spinal cord, and cerebellar disease. Since the deep reflexes are normally under partial inhibition by the higher centers, lesions of the motor cortex or pyramidal tracts (upper motor neuron) result in exaggerated deep reflexes and muscular rigidity. Hyperactive reflexes also occur in strychnine poisoning and in some functional disorders.

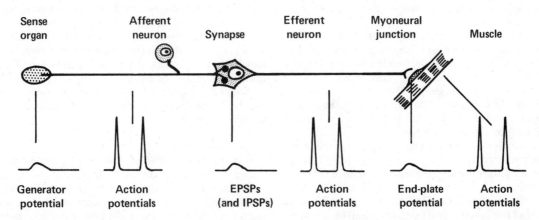

Figure 12–2. The reflex arc. Note that at the receptor and at each of the junctions in the arc, there is a nonpropagated graded response which is proportionate to the magnitude of the stimulus, whereas in the portions of the arc specialized for transmission (axons, muscle membrane) the responses are all-or-none action potentials. (Reproduced, with permission, from Ganong WF: *Review of Medical Physiology,* 10th ed. Lange, 1981.)

Table 12—1. Summary of reflexes.

Reflexes	Afferent Nerve	Center	Efferent Nerve
Superficial Reflexes			
Corneal	Cranial V	Pons	Cranial VII
Nasal (sneeze)	Cranial V	Brain stem and upper cord	Cranials V, VII, IX, X, and spinal nerves of expiration
Pharyngeal and uvular	Cranial IX	Medulla	Cranial X
Upper abdominal	T7, 8, 9, 10	T7, 8, 9, 10	T7, 8, 9, 10
Lower abdominal	T10, 11, 12	T10, 11, 12	T10, 11, 12
Cremasteric	Femoral	L1	Genitofemoral
Plantar	Tibial	S1, 2	Tibial
Anal	Pudendal	S4, 5	Pudendal
Deep Reflexes			
Jaw	Cranial V	Pons	Cranial V
Biceps	Musculocutaneous	C5, 6	Musculocutaneous
Triceps	Radial	C6, 7	Radial
Periosteoradial	Radial	C6, 7, 8	Radial
Wrist (flexion)	Median	C6, 7, 8	Median
Wrist (extension)	Radial	C7, 8	Radial
Patellar	Femoral	L2, 3, 4	Femoral
Achilles	Tibial	S1, 2	Tibial
Visceral Reflexes			
Light	Cranial II	Midbrain	Cranial III
Accommodation	Cranial II	Occipital cortex	Cranial III
Ciliospinal	A sensory nerve	T1, 2	Cervical sympathetics
Oculocardiac	Cranial V	Medulla	Cranial X
Carotid sinus	Cranial IX	Medulla	Cranial X
Bulbocavernosus	Pudendal	S2, 3, 4	Pelvic autonomic
Bladder and rectal	Pudendal	S2, 3, 4	Pudendal and autonomics

Visceral Reflexes:

A. Pupillary Reflexes:

1. Light reflex–Constriction of the pupil when light is thrown on the retina. This depends upon the integrity of cranial nerves II and III and certain of their central connections (For Argyll Robertson pupil, see p 330.)

2. Consensual light reflex–Constriction of the pupil when light is thrown into the opposite eye is dependent upon central commissural connections.

3. Accommodation reflex–Constriction of pupils when the patient looks at near objects and the eyes are converged depends upon the occipital cortex and pathways.

4. Ciliospinal reflex–Dilatation of the pupil upon painful stimulation of any sensory area, usually by pinching the neck, is dependent upon the integrity of the cervical sympathetics. This reflex is lost in Horner's syndrome (see p 154).

B. Blink Reflex of Descartes: Abrupt and unexpected approach of an object toward the eyes causes blinking or closure of eyelids.

C. Oculocardiac Reflex: Slowing of the heart rate produced by pressure over the eyeballs. This reflex is used for testing the integrity of cranial nerves V and X.

D. Carotid Sinus Reflex: Slowing of the heart and fall in blood pressure (vasodilatation) produced by pressure over the carotid sinus in the neck. This reflex is abolished by lesions of cranial nerves IX or X and is hyperactive in certain persons with marked vasomotor instability, in whom slight stimulation of this sort produces fainting (carotid sinus syncope).

E. Bulbocavernosus Reflex: Contraction of the bulbocavernosus muscle upon stroking the dorsum of the glans penis or after pinching or pricking the skin of the penis.

F. Bladder and Rectal Reflexes: The normal sphincter control of urine and feces by the pelvic autonomics is dependent upon these reflexes. Interruption of these motor fibers results in incontinence. Interruption in the afferent tract (as in tabes dorsalis) abolishes the urge to urinate or defecate, resulting in distention and dribbling.

G. Mass Reflex (of Riddoch): Sudden emptying of the bladder and bowel, flexion of the lower limbs, and sweating are present in some normal infants but in adults are under the control of the higher centers and may be released in emotional states such as fear. This reflex is released pathologically by complete severance of the spinal cord, being set off by stimulating the skin below the level of the lesion, as by scratching the sole of the foot.

Pathologic Reflexes

In this group are found certain primitive defense responses that occur only with lesions of the upper motor neuron. Normally, they are suppressed by cerebral inhibition. When the lower motor neuron is separated from the influence of the higher centers, as in pyramidal tract lesions, they are released. Not infrequently, they can be elicited in normal infants up to age 5–7 months. The principal pathologic reflexes are as follows:

A. Lower Extremity:

1. Babinski's sign–Extension of the large toe with fanning of the small toes upon stimulation of the plantar surface of the foot. Szapiro recommends forcibly flexing the second to fifth toes while eliciting Babinski's response in the usual manner.

2. Chaddock's toe sign–Babinski response obtained by stroking the lateral malleolus.

3. Gordon's leg sign–Babinski-like response upon squeezing the calf muscle.

4. Oppenheim's sign–Babinski-like response elicited by firm downward stroking of the tibia and tibialis anterior muscle.

5. Gonda reflex–Upward movement of the big toe upon pressing one of the other toes downward and releasing it with a snap.

6. Schaefer's sign–Babinski-like response upon squeezing the Achilles tendon.

7. Stransky reflex–Dorsiflexion of the great toe accompanying or following vigorous abduction of the little toe for 1–2 seconds with subsequent sudden release.

8. Rossolimo's sign–Flexion of the toes upon tapping the ball of the foot.

9. Mendel-Bechterew sign–Flexor movement of the 4 outer toes upon striking the dorsum of the foot over the cuboid bone.

10. Hirschberg's sign–Adduction and internal rotation of the foot upon stroking the inner border of the foot.

11. Ankle clonus–A continued rapid flexion and extension of the foot obtained by forcibly and quickly dorsiflexing the foot while the leg is held up by the examiner's other hand placed under the popliteal space. A rapidly exhaustible clonus may be normal.

12. Patellar clonus (trepidation sign)–A rapid up-and-down movement of the patella when it is forcibly depressed with a quick movement while the leg is in extension and relaxed.

13. Grasset and Gaussel sign–When lying supine, the patient can raise either leg separately but cannot raise both simultaneously. If the paralyzed leg is raised, it will fall back heavily when the examiner raises the unaffected leg.

14. Hoover's sign–With the hemiplegic patient recumbent, the palms of the examiner's hands are placed beneath the patient's heels, and the patient is asked to press down. Pressure will be felt only from the heel of the nonparalyzed leg. The examiner's hand is then removed from beneath the nonparalyzed heel and placed on the dorsum of this foot, and the patient instructed to raise the well leg against this resistance. If the patient has a true organic hemiplegia, no added pressure will be felt by the hand remaining beneath the heel of the paralyzed leg. However, if the patient has a hysterical paralysis, the heel of the supposedly paralyzed leg will press down against the examiner's hand as an attempt is made to raise the well leg.

15. Huntington's sign–Flexion at the hip, extension at the knee, and elevation of the affected weak lower extremity upon coughing and straining.

16. Marie and Foix retraction sign–Upon forcing the toes downward, the knee and hip are drawn into flexion.

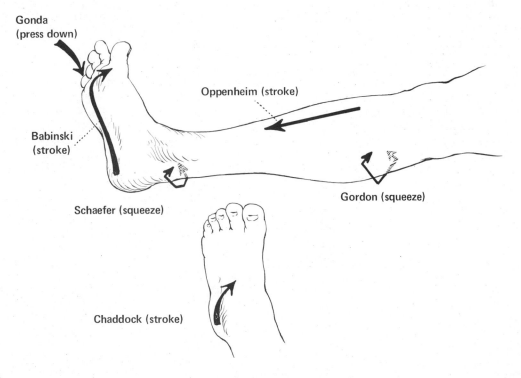

Figure 12–3. Methods of testing for extensor-plantar reflexes.

17. Neri's sign–As the patient alternately raises one leg at a time (while recumbent), the knee of the paralyzed side flexes, the other remaining straight. Forward flexion of the trunk in the standing position causes the paretic lower limb to flex while the normal one remains straight.

18. Raimiste's leg sign–With the subject in a recumbent position and the lower extremities moderately abducted, the paretic leg performs a movement similar to that attempted by a normal leg (adduction or abduction).

19. Strümpell's tibialis anterior sign–Flexion of the thigh at the hip joint results in dorsal flexion and adduction of the foot, especially if the leg movement is resisted by the examiner.

20. Crossed extension reflex–With the subject supine and both legs flexed, stimulation of the sole of the foot causes extension of the contralateral leg.

21. Extensor thrust–Extension of a flexed lower limb when the sole of the foot is pressed upward.

B. Upper Extremity:

1. Hoffmann's sign–Clawing movement of the fingers produced by flicking the distal phalanx of the index finger. The thumb is also clawed.

2. Finger flexion reflex (Trömner's sign)–A sharp tap on the palmar surface or the tips of the middle 3 fingers produces prompt flexion of the fingers.

3. Gordon's finger sign–Extension of the flexed fingers or the thumb and index finger when pressure is exerted over the pisiform bone.

4. Chaddock's wrist sign–Flexion of the wrist, with extension and fanning of the fingers upon stroking the ulnar side of the forearm near the wrist.

5. Babinski's pronation sign–The patient's hands are placed in approximation with the palms upward, and they are then jarred several times by the examiner's own hands from below. The affected hand will fall in pronation, the sound hand remaining horizontal.

6. Bechterew's sign–The patient flexes and then relaxes both forearms. The paralyzed forearm falls back more slowly and in a jerky manner, even when contractures are mild.

7. Klippel and Weil thumb sign–When the flexed fingers of the patient are quickly extended by the examiner, flexion and adduction of the patient's thumb ensues.

8. Leri's sign–Absence of normal flexion of the elbow upon forceful passive flexion of the wrist and fingers.

9. Mayer's sign–Absence of adduction and opposition of the thumb upon passive forceful flexion of the proximal phalanges, especially of the third and fourth fingers, of the supinated hand.

10. Souques' sign–In attempting to raise the paralyzed arm, the fingers spread out and remain separated.

11. Sterling's sign–Adduction of a paretic arm upon forceful active adduction, against resistance, of the unaffected normal arm.

12. Strümpell's pronation sign–Upon flexing the forearm, the dorsum of the hand instead of the palm approaches the shoulder.

13. Forced grasping–Firm radialward stroking by the examiner's fingers across the subject's palm causes a grasp reaction of the hand.

14. Kleist's hooking sign–Reactive flexion of the fingers of the affected hand upon pressure exerted by the examiner's hand against the flexor surface of the fingertips.

C. Head:

1. Babinski's platysma sign–If resistance is offered to flexion of the chin against the chest or to opening the mouth, the platysma on the sound side will contract, whereas that on the affected side will not.

2. McCarthy's sign (glabella reflex)–Percussion of the supraorbital ridge results in a reflex contraction of the orbicularis oculi muscle.

3. Snout reflex–Sharp tapping of the middle of the upper lip induces exaggerated reflex contraction of the lips.

4. Head retraction reflex–Sharp downward percussion upon the upper lip with the head inclined slightly forward produces head bending followed by brisk head retraction.

APHASIA

Aphasia, as the term is generally used, refers to those motor and sensory language disturbances caused by brain lesions but not those caused by mental defects, disturbances in the sense organs, or paralysis of the muscles essential for speech.

Lesions of certain areas of the dominant cerebral hemisphere are prone to be associated with aphasia. **Broca** concluded from his study of a pathologic specimen that the third frontal convolution was the seat of "articulated speech"; he described "aphemia" as the clinical condition resulting from a lesion involving this area. **Wernicke** felt that destruction of the first temporal gyrus (superior temporal convolution) could abolish sound images and result in lack of understanding of spoken words through impaired function of the cerebral auditory center. Plentiful, free speech characterized by errors, which Wernicke felt depended on the temporal lobe defect and loss of normal auditory control, associated with defects in writing and reading, became known as **sensory aphasia,** or Wernicke's aphasia.

Pierre Marie disagreed with Broca and demonstrated that widespread cortical and subcortical damage existed in the pathologic specimen that was used as the basis of Broca's report. Marie felt that lesions in a **quadrilateral space** of the cerebral hemisphere would destroy articulate speech. This space, referred to as a "zone of anarthria," included the island of Reil and the underlying claustrum, the internal and external capsule, and the caudate and lenticular nuclei. He felt that "true aphasia" was usually associated with a general intellectual deficiency and a special language defect. He differentiated 3 cerebral zones of disordered function: (1) **temporal zone,** associated with true aphasia in its purest form, with good articulation but great difficulty in understanding, naming, reading, and writing; (2) an **angular zone,** associated with severe alexia and moderate disturbances in other language functions; and (3) a **supramarginal zone,** associated with a "global aphasia" affecting all elements of the function of language.

Hughlings Jackson emphasized that the problem of aphasia had important psychologic aspects. He concluded that "to speak is to propositionize" and that loss of speech in aphasia entailed the loss of the power to propositionize. This power can be lost not only when the subject has lost the power to talk (propositionize aloud) but also when the patient cannot propositionize "internally." Speech responses that might occur under the influence of emotional excitement or in situations where the speech response was highly automatic were not considered true propositions in an otherwise speechless patient.

Henry Head conceived of aphasia as an impairment of the power to formulate and use symbols. Any act of external or internal verbal expression (speech or thought) that demands symbolic formulation therefore tends to be defective because of the impaired ability, and the difficulties accumulate as the propositional values of the symbols required increase. Head recognized 4 types of aphasia, as follows:

(1) **Verbal aphasia,** characterized by a defect in the power to form individual words, whether for external or internal use. In severe cases, the subject may be able to produce only one or 2 words aside from "automatic speech."

(2) **Syntactic aphasia,** characterized by disturbances of balance and rhythm of words or phrases spoken in sequence, with faulty phrases or mispronounced words. Subjects can write better than they can speak, and they understand single words well. They can obey commands except when such commands demand the precise recall of a spoken phrase.

(3) **Nominal aphasia,** characterized by impairment of the ability to name objects and to understand the nominal significance of words.

(4) **Semantic aphasia,** characterized by inability to appreciate the metaphoric significance, or "coloration," of words and phrases (connotation) apart from their immediate meaning (denotation). There is loss of the power to arrive at logical conclusions from a given sequence of ideas or series of actions. The patient can read, but the full meaning is liable to be misinterpreted or inadequately grasped. The patient has the ability to write, but the results are unsatisfactory. It is generally true that semantic defects tend to impair understanding of the connected sequence of what is written even when the individual verbal forms are sufficiently clear.

Goldstein stated that **all** disturbances of language may be designated as aphasia. He distinguished between language difficulties due to "disturbances of instrumentalities" and those due to "impairment of abstract attitude" and other nonlanguage mental phenomena. His classification of language disturbances included the following:

(1) Disturbances of the expressive side of language because of cortical lesions: **Dysarthria** is due to paresis of the muscles used in speaking. **Peripheral motor aphasia** is a defect of the learned and specialized motor speech performances. **Central motor aphasia** consists of disintegration of motor speech owing to impairment of abstract attitude and impaired function of motor modalities.

(2) Disturbances of language due to impairment of nonlanguage mental processes: These may be due to impairment of abstract attitude or of "basic functions of the brain."

(3) Disturbances of the receptive side of language because of cortical lesions: **Cortical deafness** is a disturbance of acoustic perception resulting from a cortical lesion. **Noise and musical cortical deafness** is a disturbance of perception of the characteristic sounds of noise and music, although hearing is not impaired. **Sensory aphasia** may be **peripheral** (pure sensory aphasia) or **central** (cortical sensory aphasia).

(4) **Central aphasia:** Aphasia occurring without any definite motor or perceptual changes.

(5) **Amnesic aphasia:** Lack of nouns, adjectives, verbs, and especially names for concrete objects, with impairment of abstract attitude.

(6) **Transcortical aphasias:** Characterized by better preservation of repetition than of understanding and spontaneous speech; classified as transcortical motor symptom complexes, transcortical sensory symptom complexes, and mixed.

(7) **Agraphia:** Disturbances in writing. **Primary** agraphia consists of inability to build letters, without disturbances in the spheres of speech and vision. **Secondary** agraphia is due to defects in language.

(8) **Alexia:** Disturbances in reading. **Primary** alexia is also called visual agnostic alexia. **Secondary** alexia is due to defects in language.

(9) **Echolalia:** The subject is able to repeat heard language but does not understand the words that are heard.

Nielsen believed that language or performance difficulty is related to a specific site of cerebral pathology. In right-handed persons the left cerebral hemisphere is usually dominant (major); in left-handed persons, the right hemisphere. (Exceptions to these general rules are more common among left-handed persons.) In either case, the other cerebral hemisphere is referred to as the recessive (minor) hemisphere. Nielsen's conclusions may be summarized as follows:

(1) A lesion in the isthmus of the major temporal lobe incapacitates the major language area entirely.

(2) Some varieties of aphasia have localizing value. In **motor aphasia,** the lesion affects fibers from the major convolution of Broca on their way to the ipsilateral precentral gyrus. The lesion of **Wernicke's aphasia** affects the major temporal lobe, especially the superior temporal convolution in its posterior half. **Aphasic alexia** is referable to a lesion in the major temporal lobe. **Formulation aphasia** and **jargon aphasia** are caused by lesions in the major temporal lobe at area 37.

(3) **Agraphia** has no localizing value unless it is the only symptom present, in which case it may be caused by a lesion at the border between the major

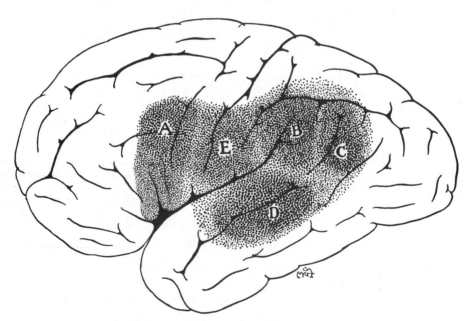

Figure 13–1. Aphasic zone of the left cerebral hemisphere. Neurologic deficits include *A.* Middle and inferior frontal gyri and lower precentral gyrus: Anarthria, alexia, contralateral facial weakness. *B.* Supramarginal gyrus: Generalized aphasia, hemianesthesia, hemianopsia. *C.* Angular gyrus: Aphasia with reading disturbance, quadrantanopia, hemiplegia, hemianesthesia. *D.* Posterior superior and middle temporal gyri: Sensory aphasia, paraphasia, jargon aphasia. *E.* Includes island of Reil: Severe aphasia, anarthria, right hemiplegia. (Modified and reproduced, with permission, from Bailey: *Intracranial Tumors.* Thomas, 1933.)

Table 13–1. Some classifications of aphasia. (After Weisenburg and McBride.)

Broca	Wernicke	Marie	Pick	Goldstein	Head
Aphemia	Motor aphasia	Anarthria		Peripheral form of motor aphasia	
		Broca's aphasia	Expressive aphasia	Transcortical form of motor aphasia	
				Central form of motor aphasia (cortical motor)	Verbal aphasia
Verbal amnesia	Sensory aphasia	Wernicke's, or the true aphasia	Impressive aphasia	"Pure" word deafness	
				Sensory aphasia (cortical sensory)	Different aspects introduced in nominal, syntactic, and semantic aphasia
	Conduction aphasia			Central aphasia / Amnesic aphasia	
			Amnesic aphasia		
	Total aphasia		Total aphasia		

angular gyrus and the occipital lobe or by a lesion of the major second frontal convolution.

(4) Certain **agnosias** (difficulties in identification or recognition) are highly specific in localization.

Studies made upon human subjects at the time of cerebral operation under local anesthesia have indicated that certain portions of the cerebral cortex of the dominant cerebral hemisphere may be intimately related to speech function. Penfield has published a cerebral map indicating those areas where electrical stimulation is highly effective in altering voluntary speech in the conscious patient (Fig 13–3).

Diagnosis

Speech function may be systematically and elabo-rately examined and detailed observations may be recorded. Abnormalities of speech associated with defective or disordered function of the muscles of phonation (as in diseases of the cerebellum, basal ganglia, medulla, or motor cortex) must be distinguished from purely aphasic disorders. In **bulbar palsy,** the speech of the patient is thick, nasal, and feeble. In **cerebellar disorders,** the speech may be explosive and intermittent. In **multiple sclerosis,** a scanning type of speech with a monotonous, sing-song quality is characteristically found. In **basal ganglia disorders,** speech may be slurred and very feeble, reduced in volume, and monotonous. **Stammering and stuttering,** which involve hesitation in the pronunciation of some words, sounds, or syllables, and involuntary repetitions last-

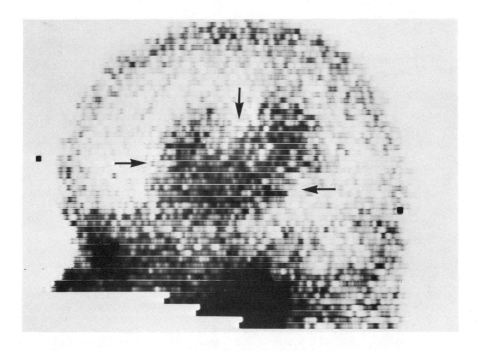

Figure 13–2. Brain scan with increased uptake in left frontoparietotemporal area 3 weeks after acute onset of global aphasia in a 56-year-old man with thrombosis of left internal carotid artery in the neck.

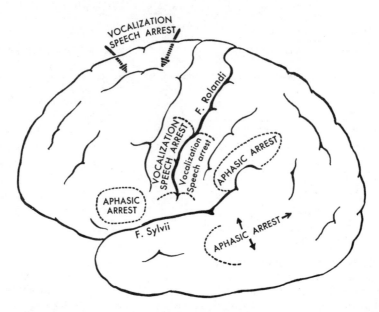

Figure 13–3. Summary of areas in which stimulation may interfere with speech or produce vocalization in the dominant hemisphere. Speech interference produced by stimulation of the superior intermediate frontal area within the longitudinal fissure has in certain cases produced evidence of aphasia rather than simple arrest, an observation that calls for further study. (Reproduced, with permission, from Penfield & Rasmussen: *The Cerebral Cortex of Man.* Macmillan, 1950.)

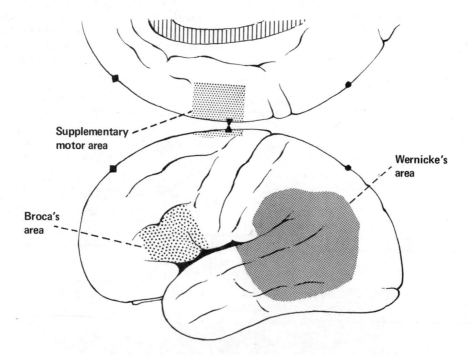

Figure 13–4. Three speech areas of dominant cerebral hemisphere. (1) The posterior, or parietotemporal, area (Wernicke's area) is most important. (2) The anterior, or Broca's, area is next most important but is dispensable in some patients at least. (3) The superior, or supplementary motor, area is dispensable but may be important after damage to other speech areas. (Redrawn and reproduced, with permission, from Penfield & Roberts: *Speech and Brain-Mechanisms.* Princeton, 1959.)

ing as long as several minutes, frequently have a psychogenic component.

Analysis of aphasic disorders involves the following types of tests:

(1) Ability to comprehend spoken language: The capacity of the patient to understand simple questions and commands is evaluated. Commands of increasing complexity, involving 3 or more separate acts, may be necessary before a defect can be suitably demonstrated.

(2) Ability to comprehend written language: A series of written commands of increasing complexity is shown to the patient and all responses are noted. The ability to read aloud and comprehend printed items in a book or newspaper is then tested. A passage should be chosen whose meaning the subject would ordinarily understand.

(3) Ability to express oneself in spoken language: The ability of the patient to speak in ordinary conversation is noted, together with the patient's associated behavior. Automatic responses, as in counting numbers, enumerating days of the week or months of the year, and recital of the alphabet may be relatively well preserved in the presence of otherwise serious difficulties with motor speech. Difficulty in writing is frequently associated with difficulty in motor speech. **Paraphasia** refers to a defect of expression in which a different word (perhaps a word of similar sound) is substituted for the exact word required.

(4) Ability to name objects: The capacity of the patient to name familiar objects such as a watch, pen, coins, buttons, or knife is tested, and note is made of the ability to explain the specific use of particular items. The ability of the patient to identify and recognize parts of the body should be verified.

(5) Ability to repeat spoken language: The repetition of digits, words, phrases, sentences, syllables, etc, of varying complexity and structure is tested.

(6) Ability to write: The patient is asked to sign his or her name and to write from dictation words, phrases, and sentences. The patient then writes a sentence describing job, home, friends, and hobbies. The examiner then presents words, figures, and designs and asks the patient to copy them.

Batteries of tests are usually required for formal testing of language function, and such tests vary widely among different clinical investigators. Among the types of tests listed by Weisenburg and McBride are the following: spontaneous speaking, naming, repeating, understanding spoken language, following directions, reading, arithmetic, language intelligence, reproduction of verbal material, nonlinguistic tests, and handedness.

In most aphasic persons, alteration of nonlanguage capacities may also be demonstrated (as in the reactions to situations of daily life, social responses, and attitudes).

Amobarbital sodium (Amytal) aphasia test. In certain cases, especially where surgery is contemplated, it may be useful to establish which cerebral hemisphere is dominant with respect to speech.

Table 13–2. Classification of clinical varieties of aphasia used by the Boston Veterans Administration Hospital Aphasia Research Unit.

Aphasia with repetition disturbance
Broca's aphasia
Wernicke's aphasia
Conduction aphasia
Aphasia without repetition disturbance
Isolation of speech area
Transcortical motor aphasia
Transcortical sensory aphasia
Anomic aphasia
Disturbance primarily affecting reading and writing
Alexia with agraphia
Total aphasia
Global aphasia
Syndromes with disturbance of a single language modality
Alexia without agraphia
Aphemia
Pure word deafness
Nonaphasic misnaming

Amobarbital is injected into a carotid artery while the patient is counting aloud and making rapidly alternating movements of the fingers of both hands. When the carotid artery of the dominant side is injected, a much greater and prolonged relative interference with speech function occurs than after injection of the other side.

APRAXIA

By apraxia is meant the inability to carry out on request a complex or skilled movement. This failure is not due to paralysis, ataxia, sensory changes, or deficiencies of understanding (confusion).

Ideational apraxia is believed to be due to loss of the power to formulate the ideational concepts necessary to the performance of the act; the subject cannot grasp or retain the idea of the desired act. Simple and isolated movements may be unaffected, but more complicated acts are impossible. Ideational apraxia occurs as a manifestation of certain diffuse brain disorders (eg, cerebral arteriosclerosis).

Motor apraxia is believed to represent the loss of the kinesthetic memory patterns necessary to the performance of the act. The purpose of the movements is usually apparent to the patient, but execution remains defective. Motor apraxia is usually associated with a lesion of the precentral gyrus.

Ideomotor apraxia is a state in which the patient cannot perform a given act correctly although old habitual motor acts can be performed spontaneously or repetitively (often with perseveration). Ideomotor apraxia is associated with lesions of the dominant cerebral hemisphere (supramarginal gyrus).

In testing for apraxia, the responses, failures, and reactions upon testing are noted. Examples of tests for apraxia include requesting the patient to show how to use a toothbrush, light a cigarette, place a letter in an envelope, pretend to drive a car, and construct a square from toothpicks.

AGNOSIA

Agnosia generally refers to the failure to recognize familiar objects perceived by the senses. It is the loss of ability to recognize objects or symbols by one sense organ with recognition of the same object or symbol by other sense organs. In tests for agnosia, identification of hands, eyes, feet, etc, of the patient or of the examiner must be made by the patient. The patient may be required to show awareness of the disease or deficit; to distinguish right from left; and to demonstrate a sense of self and an awareness of orientation in time and space. The subject may be asked to imagine performing such acts as walking, sitting, or standing. More specific tests—including numerical relationships, body scheme, and revisualization tests—may be used.

Agnosias are usually considered to be caused by disturbances in the association function of the cerebral cortex. **Astereognosis** refers to failure of tactile recognition of objects. Agnosia for body parts may occur, as well as disturbances in concepts of the patient's body scheme. **Anosognosia,** the lack of awareness of disease or denial of disease, may occur with disease of the parietal lobe in the area of the supramarginal gyrus. **Autotopagnosia,** the impaired recognition of body parts, may occur with lesions of the posteroinferior portion of the parietal lobe.

Visual agnosia may occur with or without hemianopsia on the dominant side as a result of parieto-occipital lesions, with loss of visual recognition of objects, pictures, persons, and spatial relationships.

Charcot-Wilbrand syndrome consists of visual agnosia and loss of ability to revisualize images. It may be associated with occlusion of the posterior cerebral artery of the dominant cerebral hemisphere.

Anton's syndrome is a form of anosognosia in which the patient denies blindness. The patient usually confabulates and claims to see objects in the blind field.

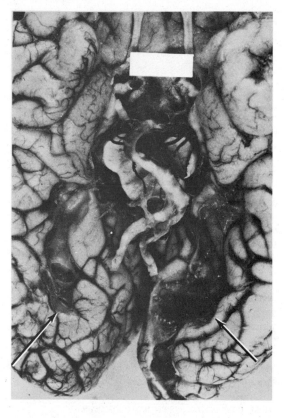

Figure 13–5. Bilateral posterior cerebral infarcts. Old cystic infarcts of the temporo-occipital lobes in a 72-year-old hypertensive man with severe atherosclerosis of vertebral and basilar arteries. Cerebellum and brain stem removed.

Gerstmann's syndrome is characterized by disability in calculation (acalculia), finger agnosia, right-left disorientation, and writing disability and is usually associated with a focal lesion of the dominant cerebral hemisphere in the region of the angular gyrus.

Trophic Changes | 14

Nutritional, or trophic, changes form an important part of the symptomatology in many neurologic disorders. They may appear in the skin, nails, subcutaneous tissues, muscles, bones, and joints.

Classification

A. Skin and Nails: Glossy, smooth skin; hyperhidrosis (excessive sweating), hypohidrosis or anhidrosis (reduced or absent sweating); white, leathery skin; cyanosis or discoloration; hypertrichosis (excess of hair), hypotrichosis (loss of hair); edema of the skin; brittle, ridged nails; and trophic ulcers, or mal perforant, which heal very slowly.

B. Musculoskeletal System: Joint changes are seen in tabes dorsalis. So-called Charcot joints are painless in spite of the marked destruction of cartilage, ligaments, and joint surfaces; bone fragments and excess fluid fill the joint cavity, and mobility is increased. The larger joints (knee, hip, and ankle) are most often affected.

Bone atrophy or osteoporosis accompanies paralysis and disuse.

Muscle atrophy is discussed below.

Causes of Trophic Change

Although a neurologic basis has usually been stressed as a prime factor in the causation of trophic changes, other factors apparently also play a role. These include activity, blood supply, diet and vitamins, lymph drainage, and endocrine disorders.

A. Inactivity: Muscle "atrophy of disuse" follows any prolonged immobilization and is characterized by a reduction in the amount of sarcoplasm without loss of striation, degeneration of muscle fibers, or change in electrical response. No degeneration of intramuscular nerves or their endings occurs. Atrophy of other tissues, including bone, also results from disuse.

B. Neurogenic Control: Denervated tissues soon lose the vitality of normal tissues; muscles, in addition to a reduction in the amount of sarcoplasm, show a loss of striation and an alteration in electrical responses. Gerard suggested that "neurogenic metabolites" are transmitted along the axons and mediate trophic functions. The **motor nerves** (from cells of the anterior gray column) are essential to normal muscle metabolism, since their degeneration is accompanied by a rapid loss of motor end-plates and muscle striations. Substances carried by axoplasmic flow of neurons may have a trophic effect. Acetylcholine, the neuromuscular transmitter, may be a mediator of neurotrophic influences. Other neurotransmitters may also exert trophic effects (see Table 14–1). The **sympathetic nerves** (from the cells of the intermediolateral cell column) affect the trophic state of tissues through their vasomotor activities and, according to the results of some workers, also exert a specific effect on the metabolism of muscles and other tissues. Poliomyelitis, which is characterized by marked trophic dysfunction in the involved tissues, shows a lesion of both motor and sympathetic neurons. There is little evidence that fibers of the **sensory nerves** (from cells of the dorsal root ganglia) have any direct trophic function. Loss of pain sensibility predisposes to ulcerations from trauma and burns, as frequently occur in analgesic extremities in syringomyelia and peripheral nerve injuries. The skin lesions in herpes zoster occur in the distribution of spinal roots involved in the inflammatory process.

C. Blood Supply: Adequate blood supply is essential to nutrition and oxygenation of tissues. Vascular disturbances, such as Volkmann's ischemic contracture, are characterized by severe damage to the affected muscles and other tissues. Trophic skin and nail changes as well as the angioneuroses are probably the result of disturbances in the innervation of blood vessels.

D. Other Factors Affecting the Trophic State of Tissues:

1. Diet–Food intake must be sufficient to balance tissue catabolism in order to prevent cachexia and general weight loss. Avitaminoses cause specific trophic changes seen in beriberi, pellagra, scurvy, xerophthalmia, etc.

2. Endocrine disorders–Thyroid deficiency results in myxedema. Pituitary dysfunction is responsible for rare growth disturbances, eg, acromegaly, pituitary cachexia, and possibly adiposis dolorosa.

3. Lymph drainage–The trophic importance of an adequate lymph supply is not well understood. Obstruction results in marked edema and skin changes, as seen in elephantiasis. Toxins of various types may act locally or systemically to produce marked atrophy or wasting of tissue, as, for example, in carcinoma and infections.

Table 14–1. Known and suspected synaptic transmitter agents and "neural hormones" in mammals.*

Substance	Locations Where Substance is Secreted	
	Known	Suspected
Acetylcholine	Myoneural junction; preganglionic autonomic endings, postganglionic parasympathetic endings, postganglionic sympathetic sweat gland and muscle vasodilator endings; many parts of the brain; endings of some amacrine cells in retina.	Primary auditory afferents.
Norepinephrine	Most postganglionic sympathetic endings, cerebral cortex, hypothalamus, brain stem, cerebellum, spinal cord.	
Dopamine	SIF cells in sympathetic ganglia; striatum, median eminence, and other parts of hypothalamus; limbic system; parts of neocortex; endings of some interneurons in retina.	
Epinephrine	Hypothalamus, thalamus, periaqueductal gray, spinal cord.	
Serotonin	Hypothalamus, limbic system, cerebellum, spinal cord.	Retina, gastrointestinal tract.
Substance P	Endings of primary afferent neurons, many other parts of brain.	Retina, gastrointestinal tract.
Histamine		Hypothalamus.
Vasopressin	Posterior pituitary.	Other parts of brain, spinal cord.
Oxytocin	Posterior pituitary.	Other parts of brain, spinal cord.
Hypothalamic hypophysiotropic hormones		
CRH	Median eminence of hypothalamus.	
TRH	Median eminence of hypothalamus.	Other parts of brain, retina, gastrointestinal tract.
GRH	Median eminence of hypothalamus.	
Somatostatin	Median eminence of hypothalamus.	Other parts of brain, substantia gelatinosa, retina, gastrointestinal gract.
LHRH	Median eminence of hypothalamus.	Circumventricular organs, preganglionic autonomic endings.
PRH	Median eminence of hypothalamus.	
Glycine	Neurons mediating direct inhibition, retina.	
Gamma-aminobutyric acid (GABA)	Cerebellum, cerebral cortex, neurons mediating presynaptic inhibition, retina.	
Glutamic acid		Cerebellum, baroreceptor afferents.
Enkephalins, β-endorphin	Substantia gelatinosa, many other parts of CNS; gastrointestinal tract.	
Cholecystokinin (CCK) octapeptide		Cerebral cortex.
Vasoactive intestinal peptide (VIP)		Hypothalamus, gastrointestinal tract, vasomotor nerves.
Neurotensin		Hypothalamus, gastrointestinal tract.
Bombesin		Hypothalamus, gastrointestinal tract.

*Reproduced, with permission, from Ganong WF: *Review of Medical Physiology*, 10th ed. Lange, 1981.

DISEASES SHOWING MARKED TROPHIC CHANGES

Neurologic Disorders

A. Syringomyelia: Syringomyelia (eg, Morvan's disease) is associated with trophic disturbances of the skin, subcutaneous tissues, and bones, usually of the upper extremity. Glossiness of the skin, deep fissures, and nail changes are common. Progressive atrophy beginning in the small muscles of the hands and gradually involving the arms and shoulders is usually seen. Perforating ulcers from trauma to the analgesic fingers and hands may occur, and joint changes are occasionally seen.

B. Tabes Dorsalis: Freely movable, swollen,

painless "Charcot" joints are often seen late in the course of tabes. Perforating ulcers of the ball of the foot are occasionally found, and the marked muscular hypotonia is accompanied by some atrophy, probably from relative disuse.

C. Herpes Zoster: Herpes zoster (shingles) is characterized by pain and vesicle formation (blisters) in the cutaneous distribution of the sensory roots involved by the viral inflammation. These areas may become anesthetic later.

D. Lower Motor Neuron Disease: Lower motor neuron disease, either in the anterior gray column of the spinal cord or in the peripheral nerves, is characterized by marked atrophy of the paralyzed muscles as well as the associated bones and skin. In this group are included poliomyelitis, amyotrophic lateral sclerosis, primary muscular atrophies, and peripheral nerve lesions. **Peripheral neuritis** is a lower motor neuron disorder in which trophic changes are usually quite marked.

E. Causalgia: Causalgia is a painful disorder of an arm or leg that is usually associated with median, sciatic, or tibial nerve injury and accompanied by trophic changes in the affected skin and nails. Osteoporosis of the bones of the affected extremity is occasionally present.

F. Neurogenic Arthropathy (Charcot's Joint): Joint destruction may result from impaired perception of proprioception, pain, and temperature. Although clinically seen in tabes dorsalis, it may also occur with diabetic neuropathy, syringomyelia, spinal cord disorders, and peripheral nerve injuries. Prolonged administration of intra-articular hydrocortisone may also cause Charcot's joint. Treatment is directed against the underlying disease, with the use of devices to assist in weight-bearing and to prevent further trauma to joints.

Vascular Disorders

Various diseases of the blood vessels such as thromboangiitis obliterans (Buerger's disease), endarteritis obliterans, arteriosclerosis, varicose veins, and Volkmann's ischemic contracture may produce trophic ulcers, skin changes, and gangrene in the dependent tissues because of the reduced blood supply to these parts.

Other Trophic Disorders

Trophic disorders associated with various skin infections, malignancies, endocrine disorders, and similar conditions are not within the scope of neurology.

Trophoneuroses

These are thought to be due to dysfunction of the sympathetic innervation and are defined on p 155. The association of trophic disorders with lesions of the hypothalamic region suggests that this part of the brain may be the central representation of the autonomic system.

SWEATING

The various types of sweating have been classified on the basis of the mechanism involved in their production. Thermoregulatory sweating is generalized and centrally induced and can be produced by ingestion of fluids or antipyretics and exposure to heat. Emotional sweating is localized. It is most commonly seen on the flexor surfaces of the hands and feet and in the axillas and may be elicited by emotional or painful stimuli. Drugs such as the cholinergic substances pilocarpine and methacholine (Mecholyl) may induce a variable amount of sweating by a presumed effect on the sweat glands or on cholinergic nerve endings. In

some normal individuals, eating spicy foods can induce localized facial sweating (gustation sweating). In pathologic circumstances, this kind of sweating may become pronounced. In subjects with transverse lesions of the spinal cord, an appropriate local stimulus applied to an area below the level of the lesion may induce automatic reflex sweating as part of a mass reflex response (spinal reflex sweating). Sweating is frequently associated with peripheral vasodilatation.

Anatomy (Fig 14–1)

Anatomic pathways involved in thermoregulatory sweating have been suggested as follows: Crossed

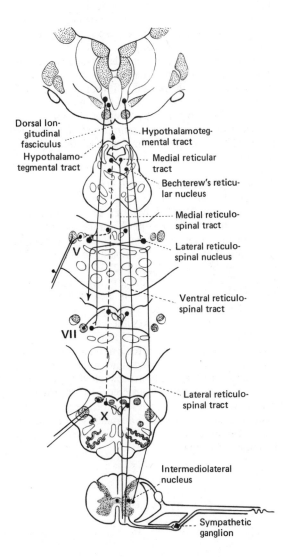

Figure 14–1. The probable pathways of thermoregulatory sweating (hypothalamotegmental and reticulospinal connections). (Reproduced, with permission, from List & Peet: Sweat secretion in man. *Arch Neurol Psychiatry* 1939; 42:1098.)

and uncrossed fibers from the hypothalamus travel via the tegmentum of the pons and the lateral reticular substance of the medulla to the lower brain stem and cervical spinal cord. They then descend farther as uncrossed fibers in the anterolateral and lateral tracts of the spinal cord to the intermediolateral gray column of the spinal cord. From here, fibers emerge via the anterior roots to join the sympathetic chain and peripheral nerves.

Two sets of cholinergic fibers have been postulated on the basis of sweat responses to injection of pilocarpine or methacholine (Mecholyl): postganglionic sympathetic and parasympathetic cholinergic fibers. Most of the cholinergic fibers to the trunk and extremities emerge via the thoracolumbar sympathetic system. Most of the cholinergic fibers to the head travel via the cranial parasympathetic nerves.

Sweat glands are believed to possess a predominantly sympathetic nerve supply. Although the sympathetic innervation of sweat glands in humans is cholinergic, species differences have been noted. In cats (as in humans), epinephrine causes little or no sweat secretion, and the secretion obtained by stimulation of the sympathetics is blocked by atropine. In horses, epinephrine evokes sweat secretion, and the secretion obtained by sympathetic stimulation is not blocked by atropine.

Tests for Lesions of the Sympathetic Nervous System

A. Sweat Test of Minor: Thermoregulatory sweating may be used to demonstrate lesions of the sympathetic nervous system, since it is dependent upon the thoracolumbar sympathetic system. The sweat test of Minor (Fig 14–2) is commonly employed. The subject takes 0.5 g of aspirin 30 minutes prior to the test and the skin is then painted with an iodine solution. After the skin dries, it is dusted with fine rice starch powder. The subject then drinks a large quantity of hot tea, is exposed to the heat of a large electric cabinet, and is covered carefully with blankets draped over a frame. The moisture of the sweat secretion facilitates the reaction between the iodine and starch, producing a blue-black color change on the skin in the sweating areas. In lesions of the sympathetic system, local loss of thermoregulatory sweating occurs. The immediately adjacent skin area may show increased sweating.

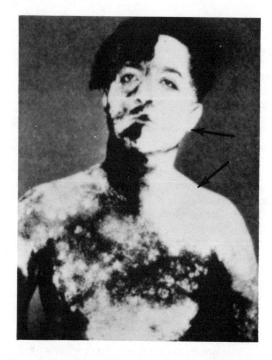

Figure 14–2. Sweat test on patient with injury to left cervical sympathetic chain. No sweating of affected left face and neck indicated by white areas. (Reproduced, with permission, from List & Peet: Sweat secretion in man. *Arch Neurol Psychiatry* 1938;**40**:27.)

B. Skin Resistance to Electric Current: The resistance of the skin to the passage of an electric current is greatly influenced by activity of the sweat glands and may be measured with a dermometer. Areas of skin with impaired or absent autonomic nerve supply show greatly increased resistance to the passage of small currents. If sweat glands are active, skin resistance is low; if sweat glands are inactive, skin resistance is high, the affected zones being similar in configuration to those demonstrated by the sweat test of Minor. A small current is passed between an ear electrode and an exploring skin electrode. Whereas dampness of normal skin permits the passage of a small current that is registered on a sensitive ammeter, a dry area has a high resistance and allows little or no current to pass.

Normal cerebrospinal fluid is clear, colorless, and odorless. Some of the more important average normal values are as follows:

> Specific gravity: 1.007
> pH: 7.35
> Chlorides (as NaCl): 120–130 mEq/L
> Glucose: 65 mg/dL
> Total base: 157 mEq/L
> Gamma globulin: 6–13% of total protein
>
> Total protein:
>   Lumbar: 15–45 mg/dL
>   Cisternal: 10–25 mg/dL
>   Ventricular: 5–15 mg/dL

The cerebrospinal fluid is present for the most part in a system that may be considered to be composed of 2 communicating portions: The **internal system** consists of the 2 lateral ventricles, their interventricular foramens (of Monro), the third ventricle, the cerebral (sylvian) aqueduct, and the fourth ventricle. The **external system** consists of the subarachnoid spaces, including the dilated portions known as cisterns. Communication of the internal and external systems occurs through the 2 lateral apertures of the fourth ventricle (foramens of Luschka) and the medial foramen of the fourth ventricle (foramen of Magendie).

Formation

The choroid plexuses are believed to be the principal sources of the cerebrospinal fluid. Fluid may also be formed by diffusion through the ependymal and pial vessels. It is estimated that 95% of the fluid is formed in the lateral ventricles. Most of the remainder is formed in the third and fourth ventricles.

It is probable that much of the cerebrospinal fluid is formed by dialysis across the walls of the choroid plexuses. Studies using tracer substances indicate that the cerebrospinal fluid may not be fully formed when it appears and that exchanges of particular constituents between the cerebrospinal fluid and the blood may occur at more or less characteristic rates. Water and electrolytes enter and leave the cerebrospinal fluid rapidly, in both the ventricular and subarachnoid spaces, and not exclusively through the choroid plexuses. Protein is absorbed largely from the arachnoid villi. The rate and site of protein reabsorption significantly affects the direction and rate of cerebrospinal

fluid flow. Although the formation of cerebrospinal fluid is predominantly in the cerebral ventricles, it may also be formed in the subarachnoid spaces. There is evidence to suggest that cerebrospinal fluid may come from the brain as well as from the choroid plexuses. Usually the cerebrospinal fluid is hypertonic to blood, and changes in cerebrospinal fluid osmotic pressure usually follow changes in blood osmotic pressure.

Wide variations in the amount of fluid formed daily are believed to occur. The overall addition of cerebrospinal fluid beyond the volumes exchanged has been estimated to be as little as 10–20 mL/d via the choroid plexuses of the ventricles. Factors influencing the bulk formation of cerebrospinal fluid may operate independently of each other and thus change in relative importance. Cerebral metabolism, hydrodynamic forces of blood flow, and changes in blood osmotic pressure influence the fluctuating rate of cerebrospinal fluid flow, although there may be an irreducible minimum of cerebrospinal fluid produced that is related to the arterial blood pressure.

Circulation

The existence of an active circulation of cerebrospinal fluid has been postulated. According to this concept, fluid is formed in the lateral ventricles, circulates through the interventricular foramens into the third ventricle, and then via the cerebral aqueduct into the fourth ventricle. Here the fluid escapes via the lateral apertures of the fourth ventricle and the medial foramen of the fourth ventricle into the subarachnoid spaces, where it diffuses over the brain and spinal cord. Respiratory and circulatory changes are believed to change the pressure within the closed system and promote the mixing and diffusion of fluid.

Absorption

The site of greatest absorption of cerebrospinal fluid is believed to be the arachnoid villi that project into the dural venous sinuses. The pacchionian bodies are relatively large arachnoid villi distributed along the superior longitudinal sinus. Absorption into the pial veins may also occur.

Functions

The cerebrospinal fluid probably acts as a cushion for the brain, preventing or diminishing the transmission of jarring or shocking forces to the brain and spinal cord. Its role in metabolism is conjectural. It

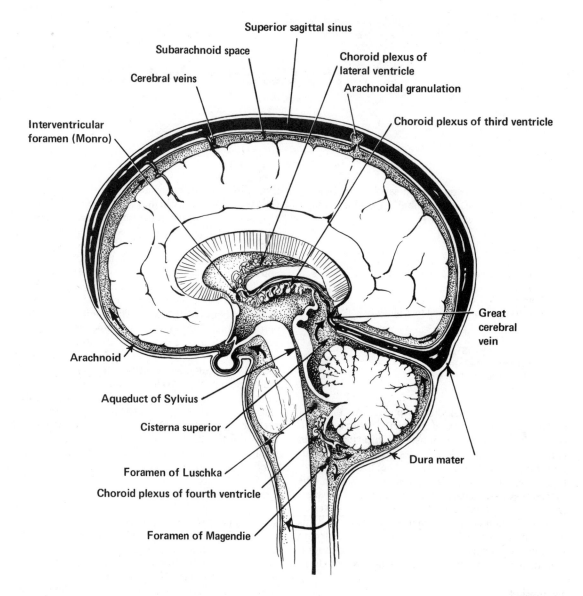

Figure 15–1. Circulation of cerebrospinal fluid. (Redrawn from original drawing by Frank H Netter, MD, which first appeared in Ciba *Clinical Symposia.* Copyright © 1950, Ciba Pharmaceutical Co. Reproduced with permission.)

might conceivably convey nutritive materials to the CNS and carry away metabolites. Changes in the intracranial volume are sometimes compensated for by the production of cerebrospinal fluid. This is apparent in destructive or postoperative lesions.

Evidence from studies with deuterium and tritium suggests that water may enter at many points other than the choroid plexus, although isotope studies with solutes suggest that most enter the cerebral ventricles via the choroid plexus. In the same way, cerebrospinal fluid may exit by routes other than the arachnoidal villi. This rapid transfer of water into and out of the cerebrospinal compartments permits the extracellular fluids of the CNS to remain isotonic with other body fluids. Experimental studies indicate that heavy water

enters the subarachnoid space faster than it enters a similar volume of ventricle. Flow out of the ventricles accounts for less than 1/25 of the total water that leaves the 4 ventricles. Most monovalent electrolyte and protein can enter the subarachnoid space as well as the ventricles directly.

Hydrodynamics

Because the cerebrospinal fluid is contained within a closed system, the bony spine and the skull, forces that tend to increase the volume of the cerebrospinal fluid are apt to increase its pressure. Increased blood circulation or blood pressure within the arterioles and capillaries of the choroid plexus tends to increase the amount of cerebrospinal fluid formed and

Table 15–1. Cerebrospinal fluid findings.

Entity	Appearance	Pressure (in mm of water)	Cells (per μL)	Protein	Miscellaneous Cerebrospinal Fluid Findings
Normal lumbar	Clear and colorless	70–200	0–5	15–45 mg/dL	Glucose 50–75 mg/dL
Normal ventricular	Clear and colorless	70–190	0–5 (lymphocytes)	5–15 mg/dL	NPN 10–35 mg/dL Kahn and Wassermann negative
Traumatic tap	Bloody; supernatant fluid clear	Normal	Red blood cells	4 mg/dL rise per 5000 red cells	Bloody; supernatant fluid clear
Cerebral hemorrhage Ventricular Subarachnoid	Bloody; supernatant fluid yellow	Slightly increased	Red blood cells	As above	Blood equal in all 3 specimens
Meningitis Acute purulent	Clear, cloudy, milky, or xanthochromic; occasional clot formation	Greatly increased (250–700)	Polymorphonuclear cells, usually over 1000	Increased	Glucose decreased early; chlorides decreased late; organisms on smear and culture
Acute tuberculous	Opalescent to turbid; faint fibrin web or pellicle formation	Moderately increased (200–450)	10–500 (lymphocytes)	Increased	Chlorides decreased early, often before decrease of glucose. Smear, culture, and guinea pig inoculation for organisms
Acute syphilitic	Clear to turbid; fibrin clot	Moderately increased (200–350)	100–1000 (mostly lymphocytes)	Slightly increased	Positive Wassermann
Syphilis Meningovascular Parenchymatous	Clear and colorless	Normal	Normal or increased	Slightly increased	Positive Wassermann
Brain tumor	Usually clear and colorless	Increased	Normal or increased	Increased	Findings depend on location and type of tumor
Brain abscess	Clear and colorless	Greatly increased	Polymorphonuclear cells normal or increased	Increased	Pressure may go as high as 600–700 mm of water
Subdural hematoma	Classically yellow, but often clear and colorless	Usually increased	Normal	Normal or slightly increased	. . .
Encephalitis	Clear and colorless	Normal	Normal or increased (mostly lymphocytes)	Normal or slightly increased	Serologic tests of value in virus infections
Uremia	Clear and colorless	Slightly increased	Normal	Normal or slightly increased	Spinal fluid NPN increased
Lead encephalopathy	Clear or slightly cloudy	Increased	Lymphocytes	Normal or slightly increased	Lead in spinal fluid
Arterial hypertension	Clear	Normal or increased	Normal	Normal or slightly increased	Choked disk may suggest brain tumor
Epilepsy (idiopathic)	Normal fluid	Normal	Normal	Normal	. . .
Multiple sclerosis	Normal fluid	Normal or low	Normal or ncreased	Normal or increased (increased gamma globulin)	Negative serology
Poliomyelitis, acute	Opalescent, may be faintly yellow; delicate fibrin web	Slightly increased	Slightly increased	Slightly increased (for a few weeks)	Preparalytic stage, 80% polymorphonuclear cells; paralytic state, mononuclears
Spinal cord tumor Partial block	Clear and colorless	Normal	Normal	Slightly increased	. . .
Complete block (Froin's syndrome)	Yellow	Normal or low	Slightly increased	Marked rise (200–600 mg/dL)	Coagulation may occur
Diabetic coma	Clear and colorless	Decreased	Normal	Normal or slightly increased	Glucose elevated; may reach 200–300 mg/dL
Acute alcoholic coma	Clear and colorless	Slightly increased	May be slightly increased	Normal	Alcohol content parallels that of blood

its pressure. Obstruction to the flow of venous blood in the sinuses blocks the free absorption of fluid and also increases the amount and pressure of the fluid. Anesthetics may produce primary or secondary changes in cerebrospinal fluid pressure. Those administered via semiclosed systems produce rises in cerebrospinal fluid pressure proportionate to CO_2 retention, and these rises can be prevented by previous hyperventilation. Rise in cerebrospinal fluid pressure also occurs with administration of anesthetics that cause excitement, cough, laryngospasm, or respiratory obstruction. Barbiturate anesthesia tends to lower cerebrospinal fluid pressure, whereas halothane raises it. Ether, trichloroethylene, nitrous oxide, and cyclopropane have no primary effect but tend to raise cerebrospinal fluid pressure because of secondary effects.

Lumbar Puncture

Lumbar puncture is usually performed with the patient lying down; in this position the pressure is normally 70–200 mm of water (average, 125 mm of water). If the puncture is done with the patient sitting upright, the fluid will normally rise to about the level of the midcervical spine. Coughing or straining will usually cause a prompt rise and subsequent fall in pressure. This is due to congestion of the spinal veins and the resultant increase of pressure on the contents of the subarachnoid space.

A. Technique: After the initial pressure has been determined and found to be normal, 3–4 specimens of 2–3 mL each are usually withdrawn in sterile tubes for laboratory examination. Cultures and special tests, such as those for sugar and chlorides, are done when indicated. Routine examination usually includes cell counts, total protein, and Wassermann reaction. The pressure is routinely measured also after the fluid is removed. In cases of spinal subarachnoid block, a normal initial pressure will suffer a profound drop after the removal of 7–10 mL of fluid.

The **Ayala index** is helpful in the diagnosis of subarachnoid block, hydrocephalus, etc:

$$\text{Ayala index} = \frac{\text{Quantity of fluid removed}}{\text{Initial pressure}} \times \text{Final pressure}$$

A normal Ayala index is 5.5–6.5. An index greater than 7.0 is interpreted to mean a large reservoir, as in hydrocephalus or serous meningitis. An index of less than 5.0 means a small reservoir, as in subarachnoid block.

B. After-Effects: Severe headache may occur following lumbar puncture. This may be due to the loss of the fluid or the leakage of fluid through the puncture site. Lumbar puncture headaches are characterized by relief on lying down and exacerbation upon raising the head. The injection of saline solution into the subarachnoid spaces may give partial or complete relief.

C. Contraindications: Contraindications to

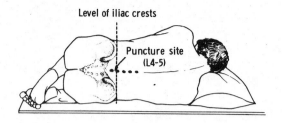

Figure 15–2. Lying position for lumbar puncture. (Reproduced, with permission, from Krupp MA et al: *Physician's Handbook,* 20th ed. Lange, 1982.)

lumbar puncture are relatively few. In cases of brain tumor, especially of the posterior fossa, spinal puncture should be done carefully, since herniation of the cerebellum and medullary compression may follow removal of fluid.

D. Queckenstedt's Test or Maneuver: Queckenstedt's test is performed by compressing the jugular veins during lumbar puncture. Normally there is a prompt rise in cerebrospinal fluid pressure that is maintained as long as compression is maintained. A moderate rise in pressure occurs if one jugular vein is compressed, and a further rise occurs when the second jugular vein is compressed. On release of compression of the jugular veins, the cerebrospinal fluid pressure promptly returns to normal levels. If the pressure fails to rise and fall promptly, a block in the system is presumed to be present between the site of the puncture and the site of the compression of the jugular vein. Absence of pressure rise on compression of one jugular vein can be caused by thrombosis of the lateral sinus on the same side. Absence of pressure rise—or a slow rise and slow fall—upon compression of both jugular veins implies a complete or partial block in the spinal subarachnoid pathway; further definitive studies, such as iophendylate (Pantopaque) myelography, are then usually indicated.

Queckenstedt's test is contraindicated if intracranial tumor or bleeding is present or suspected, since it may abruptly precipitate further bleeding or cause herniation of the cerebellar tonsils, with medullary compression.

E. Froin's Syndrome: Yellow spinal fluid (xanthochromia) which is high in globulin and practically free of cells and which clots spontaneously on standing may be associated with subarachnoid block.

F. Increased Intracranial Pressure: Increased intracranial pressure may be associated with headache, vomiting, and papilledema. In children and young infants, cranial enlargement may be the only or the most significant finding. Increased intracranial pressure may be noted in a variety of clinical disorders, including brain tumor, intracranial hemorrhage, hydrocephalus, encephalopathies, head trauma, CNS infections, sinus thrombosis, craniostenosis, pseudotumor cerebri, etc.

Electroencephalography | 16

Electroencephalography is the study of the electrical activity of the brain. Variations exist in the electrical activity of the brains of humans. By comparing records taken from standardized positions on the head, valid interpretations may be made.

The average amplitude of electrical activity in the brain is about 1% of that obtained from the heart. Sensitive but stable amplification is necessary, therefore, to produce an undistorted record of brain activity. The potentials of the brain that are recorded in an electroencephalogram (EEG) appear in wave form ranging from 1 to 100 cycles per second (cps, hertz, Hz) and an amplitude ranging from 5 to several hundred microvolts.

Electroencephalography provides useful information in organic disease of the brain; its value in nonorganic diseases is questionable. Epilepsy, brain tumor, brain abscess, cerebral trauma, subdural hematoma, meningitis, encephalitis, cerebral vascular accident, and congenital defects of the brain represent types of conditions in which electroencephalography is useful. Focal changes may furnish considerable aid in the localization of cerebral damage. The EEG is widely used as a guide in surgery of the epileptic. In posttraumatic epilepsy, a cerebral scar may be present which is electrically inactive and which is surrounded by a zone of hyperexcitable cortex. The hyperactive foci, as determined by means of spontaneous and electrically evoked activity, may be excised. Surgical extirpation of the anterior temporal lobe is sometimes performed in those patients with psychomotor epilepsy in whom a prominent spike focus in this area is demonstrable in the EEG. Depth electrography—localization of a focus by depth recording—may be advisable in certain cases.

Serial recordings are helpful in distinguishing expanding from vascular lesions and in following the clinical course after head injury, cerebrovascular accident, and inflammatory and other brain disorders.

Electroencephalography has its limitations, however, and normal-appearing records may be obtained in spite of clinical evidence of severe organic brain disease.

Technique

Records are taken simultaneously, when possible, from multiple analogous areas of the brain in order to detect changes in activity that may be of diagnostic importance. Electrodes covered with electrolyte paste or jelly are ordinarily attached by means of collodion to the scalp over the frontal, parietal, occipital, and temporal areas and are attached also to the ears.

With the subject recumbent or seated in a grounded, wire-shielded cage and with the eyes closed, a record is taken for at least a 20-minute period. Hyperventilation, during which the patient takes 40–50 deep breaths per minute for 3 minutes, is routinely employed, since it frequently accentuates abnormal findings and may disclose latent abnormalities. "Scalp to ear" and "scalp to scalp" leads are routinely used, with the addition of further electrodes as necessary in order to accurately localize abnormalities in the graph. Rhythmic light flash stimulation (1–30 Hz) is carried out for 2 or more minutes.

Interpretation (See Glossary, p 238.)

The interpretation of the EEG depends on the frequency, amplitude, form, and distribution of the wave activity present. In the **Davis system,** each record is graded from 1 to 5 on the basis of stability of the pattern. Rating 1 is given to any normal type of pattern that is stable and whose fluctuations of frequency and voltage lie within fairly narrow limits without sharp transitions. Rating 2 includes normal records which are slightly less stable or regular than those rated 1 and which may fluctuate in a somewhat atypical manner or which have an alpha rhythm that is regular but unusual in wave form. Rating 3 includes normal records in which a feature that cannot in itself be regarded as abnormal may be exaggerated. Rating 4 is given to any dysrhythmic and suspicious record in which abnormalities are clear but not diagnostic. Rating 5 is given to any record that reveals well-recognized abnormal dysrhythmias, such as those found in epilepsy.

The pattern of electrical activity is further evaluated in the Davis system as either A, B, M, MF, or MS. The A type pattern has a regular alpha rhythm with proportioned distribution over the occipital, precentral, and frontal areas when recorded simultaneously. The B type of pattern, under standard conditions and at a resting level of activity, is made up predominantly of fast frequencies of 14–30 Hz. The M type is composed of mixed frequencies, none clearly dominant, and contains slow, alpha, and fast frequencies. The MF type contains mixtures of frequencies in the alpha and fast frequency ranges. The MS type includes records whose frequencies are in the alpha and slow frequency range.

In the **Gibbs classification,** emphasis is upon the dominant frequency or significant wave form present. With one exception, all records not classified as paroxysmal, slow, or fast are normal and are classified according to the frequency of the dominant rhythm (8.5 Hz, 9, 9.5, etc, up to 12 Hz). A low-voltage record with no countable frequency is classified "low-voltage fast" and is considered normal. Records containing activity slower than 8.5 Hz and with voltages of more than 20 μV are classified as "slow" and subclassified as "moderately slow" (S1) and "very slow" (S2). If there is much activity with a frequency greater than 12 Hz and a voltage of more than 15 μV, the record is classified as "fast" and subclassified as "moderately fast" (F1) and "very fast" (F2). Records containing a mixture of fast and slow waves are classified according to which predominates, or both.

Moderately slow and fast records are considered mildly abnormal; very slow and very fast records are definitely abnormal.

Paroxysmal records are classified by Gibbs according to the type of clinical seizure with which he believes they are associated and are subclassified as petit mal variant (PMV), petit mal (PM), psychomotor (PSY), spikes (SP), and grand mal (GM) records.

Hypsarhythmia is a striking pattern consisting of high-voltage activity of the slow, sharp, and polyspike type in all regions. It is seen in infants and young children who usually have massive spasms and generalized tonic-clonic seizures that are difficult to control.

Fourteen and six positive spikes is a pattern in which positive spikes repeat at a frequency of 14 or 6 Hz. It is most pronounced in the occipitotemporal region and is believed to have its origin in the hypothalamus or thalamus. According to Gibbs, this pattern may be more frequently encountered in children and adolescents with clinical histories of autonomic or visceral manifestations, headache, or behavior disturbances.

Jasper and his co-workers have based their classification primarily on the location of abnormal wave forms. The types they recognize are as follows: **Localized unilateral:** random spike focus (L1), random sharp waves (L2), delta foci (L3), and local paroxysmal rhythm (L4) (10 Hz or more, localized to a discrete cortical area). **Diffuse:** multiple spikes (D1) (usually associated with diffuse fast rhythm, 14–25 Hz), multiple sharp waves (D2), and multiple delta (D3). **Bilaterally synchronous:** wave and spike (B3 and 1), 3 Hz (B3), 6 Hz (B4), and sharp waves (B2). Combined forms may occur.

It has been demonstrated that with the use of nasopharyngeal electrodes inserted through the nasal passages, additional information concerning the electrical activity at the base of the brain may be obtained. Such an electrode may serve also as a convenient "reference," or localizing, electrode. The use of "tympanic leads" placed in contact with the tympanic membranes, in conjunction with nasopharyngeal and other electrodes, may more conveniently demonstrate deep lesions or foci.

EEGs may be made during sleep or in circumstances simulating those most apt to precipitate clinical seizures or electrical abnormalities. Chemical activation with drugs such as pentylenetetrazol (Metrazol) may be used. Sleep records made during normal or drug-induced sleep may disclose abnormalities in patients whose patterns would otherwise be considered normal. "Photic driving" refers to the phenomenon in which some cerebral frequencies may be controlled by the intermittent illumination of the retina. This procedure may induce convulsive seizures in some epileptic patients.

Asymmetries between normal rhythms due to suppression or augmentation of the rhythm on one side may reflect cerebral pathologic changes, eg, partial or complete suppression of alpha rhythm may occur on the side of an acute destructive lesion or subdural hematoma.

Delta rhythms—complex, irregular, slow waves with little tendency to repetition of the same wave forms and usually unaffected by alerting, hyperventilation, or eye opening—are seen with tumors, vascular occlusion, and inflammations. Dysrhythmias (3–7 Hz)—more repetitive and rhythmic than normal, at times with a characteristic wave form—may be accentuated by hyperventilation and inhibited by eye opening or mental activity, with a tendency to be synchronized in different parts of the cerebral hemisphere.

A recording of electrical activity of an operatively exposed brain is designated as an **electrocorticogram.** Needle electrodes may be introduced into the brain for recording from multiple subcortical areas at operation or postoperatively. Stereotactic instruments for the more accurate placement of small needle electrodes into the human brain are available.

Frequency analyzers that depend upon mechanical or electrical devices are employed to give a quantitative measurement of the specific frequencies present and permit the recognition of frequencies whose presence otherwise might be difficult to determine.

Physiology

The activity recorded in the EEG is mainly that of the superficial layers of the cerebral cortex. Current is believed to flow between fluctuating dipoles formed of cortical cell dendrites and cell bodies. The dendrites are similarly oriented, densely packed units of the cerebral cortex. As excitatory and inhibitory endings on the cell dendrites become active, current flows into and out of these dendritic areas from the rest of the dendritic process and the cell body. The relationship between the dendrite and cell body is that of a constantly shifting dipole. When the sum of the dendritic activity is negative relative to the cell, the cell is hypopolarized and hyperexcitable; when the sum is positive, the cell is hyperpolarized and less excitable.

The activity of many of the dendritic units is synchronized to form the wave pattern of the alpha rhythm. This synchronization is affected by (1) the

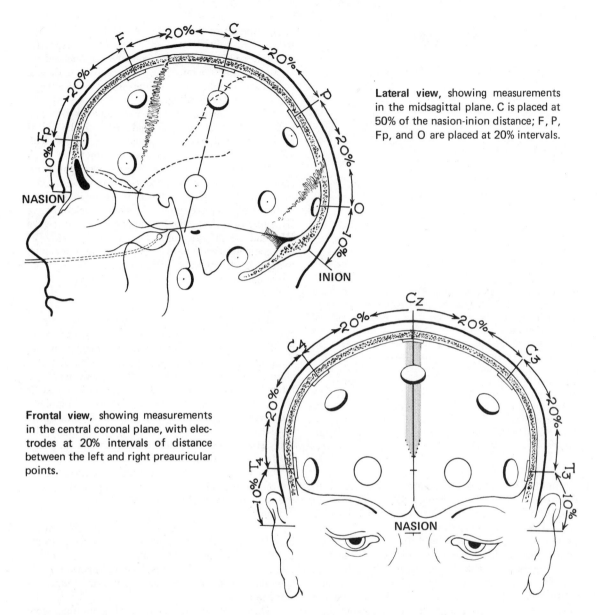

Lateral view, showing measurements in the midsagittal plane. C is placed at 50% of the nasion-inion distance; F, P, Fp, and O are placed at 20% intervals.

Frontal view, showing measurements in the central coronal plane, with electrodes at 20% intervals of distance between the left and right preauricular points.

Figure 16–1. Electrode placements in the "ten twenty" electrode system. (C = central; F = frontal; Fp = frontal pole; O = occipital; P = parietal.) (Redrawn and reproduced, with permission, from *EEG Clin Neurophysiol* 1958;10:352.)

synchronizing effect on each unit of activity in neighboring parallel fibers, and (2) the influence of impulses from the thalamus and related parts of the brain stem. Large lesions of the nonspecific projection nuclei of the thalamus disrupt the electroencephalographic synchrony on the side of the lesion. Stimulation of these nuclei at a frequency of about 8 Hz produces a characteristic 8 Hz response through most of the ipsilateral cortex, whose amplitude waxes and wanes **(recruiting response).**

Desynchronization—replacement of a rhythmic electroencephalographic pattern with irregular low-voltage activity—is produced by stimulation of the specific sensory systems up to the level of the mid-

brain. High-frequency stimulation of the reticular formation of the midbrain or of the nonspecific thalamic projection nuclei desynchronizes the EEG and arouses a sleeping animal.

When the eyes are opened, the alpha rhythm is replaced by fast, irregular low-voltage activity **(alpha block).** Other forms of sensory stimulation or mental concentration may also produce breakup of the alpha pattern (desynchronization). This is sometimes referred to as the arousal, or alerting, response, since desynchronization may be produced by sensory stimulation and is correlated with an aroused or alert state.

A characteristic response is noted in animals under light barbiturate anesthesia when a sense organ

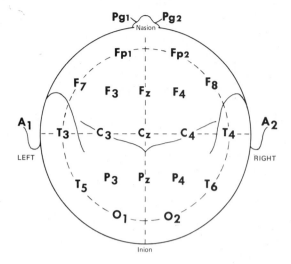

Figure 16–2. A single plane projection of the head showing all standard positions of electrode placement and the locations of the central sulcus (fissure of Rolando) and the lateral cerebral fissure (fissure of Sylvius). The outer circle is drawn at the level of the nasion and the inion. The inner circle represents the temporal line of electrodes. This diagram provides a useful stamp for the indication of electrode placement in routine recording. (A = ear; C = central; C_Z = central at zero, or midline; F = frontal; F_p = frontal pole; F_Z = frontal at zero, or midline; O = occipital; P = parietal; P_g = nasopharyngial; P_Z = parietal at zero, or midline; T = temporal.) (Reproduced, with permission, from Grass Medical Instruments Co., Quincy, Mass.)

is stimulated and the cerebral cortex is monitored with electrodes. After a latency of 5–12 ms, a surface-positive wave is seen, followed by a small negative wave **(the primary evoked potential).** A larger, more prolonged positive wave **(the diffuse secondary response)** follows thereafter with a latency of 20–80 ms.

The primary evoked potential is quite specific in location and is noted where pathways from a particular sense organ end. It has been used to map specific cortical sensory areas. The positive wave component is believed to represent activity in fibers ascending from deep to superficial layers of the cortex, whereas the small negative deflection represents activity spreading laterally in association fibers of the superficial layers of the cortex. Although the primary evoked potential is largely obscured by the spontaneous activity of the brain in unanesthetized animals, it may be demonstrated with special techniques. It is somewhat more diffuse in unanesthetized animals than in anesthetized ones but still well localized compared to the diffuse secondary response.

The diffuse secondary response is not highly localized and appears at the same time over most of the cortex and other parts of the brain. The uniform latency in different parts of the cortex and its unchanging character following circular cortical cuts indicate that the diffuse secondary response is due to activity ascending from below the cerebral cortex rather than to the

lateral spread of the primary evoked potential. The pathway involved appears to be the nonspecific thalamic projection system from the midline and related thalamic nuclei. The surface-positive diffuse secondary response is sometimes followed by a negative wave or series of waves.

Short-latency brain stem auditory evoked potentials may be averaged and analyzed with the aid of computer techniques. In a normal human subject with a vertex scalp (C_Z) electrode placement, a click stimulus presented to the ear may evoke typical responses with 7 wave components. These wave components are believed to come from the regions of the auditory nerve (wave I), dorsal cochlear nucleus (wave II), superior olive (wave III), lateral lemniscus (wave IV), and the inferior colliculus (wave V). Wave VI may indicate activity of the rostral midbrain or caudal thalamus, whereas wave VII may reflect activity from the thalamus or thalamocortical projections.

Sleep

Upon falling asleep, a normal adult shows a succession of electroencephalographic changes that may be divided into 4 stages. After fragmentation and disappearance of alpha activity, the waves diminish slightly in frequency, and their amplitude increases (stage 1). Thereafter, high-voltage notched slow waves, "K complexes," and 14 Hz "sleep spindles" are noted (stage 2). Then high-amplitude delta waves (1–2 Hz) progressively appear (stage 3). Finally, the delta activity becomes more or less continuous (stage 4). In waking, these stages may be reversed.

More recently, sleep has been considered to consist of 2 phases: (1) a sleep stage accompanied by rapid eye movements (REM sleep) and (2) a non–rapid eye movement stage (NREM sleep).

The initial period of REM sleep usually occurs 50–70 minutes after the onset of sleep and recurs every 80–90 minutes thereafter, comprising 20–25% of the night's sleep of young adults. The REM periods average about 20 minutes but usually become longer toward morning.

During REM sleep, the high-amplitude slow waves are replaced by rapid, low-voltage, irregular electroencephalographic activity resembling that seen in alert humans and animals. However, since sleep is not interrupted, this condition has also been called "paradoxic sleep." During this state, the threshold for arousal by sensory stimuli and by stimulation of the reticular formation is elevated, and there are associated rapid roving movements of the eyeballs. NREM sleep occurs during slow wave, or spindle, stages of sleep.

REM sleep is found in all species of mammals and in birds. Humans, if aroused at a time when they show the low-voltage electroencephalographic activity of REM sleep, generally report they were dreaming. Individuals awakened from NREM, or spindle, sleep usually do not report dreams. These observations suggest an association between REM sleep and dreaming. During REM sleep there is a marked reduction of skeletal muscle tone. In males, there is a high inci-

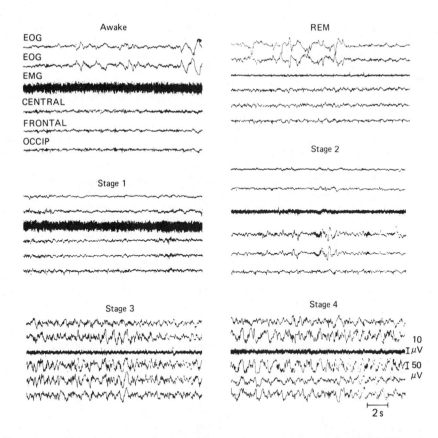

Figure 16–3. Sleep stages. Note the low muscle tone with extensive eye movements in REM. (EOG = electrooculogram registering eye movements; EMG = electromyogram registering skeletal muscle activity; central, frontal, occip = 3 EEG leads.) (Reproduced, with permission, from Kales A et al: Sleep and dreams: Recent research on clinical aspects. *Ann Intern Med* 1968; **68**:1078.)

dence of penile erections during REM sleep, and the bruxism (tooth grinding) that occurs in some individuals takes place during REM sleep. Surprisingly, REM sleep occurs in greater amounts in children and infants who are probably too young to have visual dreams.

If humans are awakened every time they show paradoxic (REM) sleep, they may become anxious and irritable and in a few days may develop a variety of mental abnormalities. If they are then permitted to sleep without interruption, they show a greater amount of paradoxic sleep for a few nights, and their symptoms disappear.

Sleepwalking (somnambulism) and bedwetting (nocturnal enuresis) are particularly apt to occur during arousal from slow wave (NREM) sleep. Episodes of sleepwalking may last several minutes; somnambulists walk with their eyes open and avoid obstacles, but when awakened they cannot recall the episode.

Excessive daytime sleepiness (hypersomnia) and recurrent apnea during sleep may occur. These patients are apt to be obese middle-aged men who snore loudly. Functional obstruction of the oropharyngeal airway in sleep has been implicated in this group, and in severe cases, symptoms may be relieved by tracheostomy.

In experiments on cats, Bremer found a waking pattern if a transection was made at the medulla-spinal cord junction *(encéphale isolé)*, whereas there was a slow wave pattern if the transection was at a higher midbrain level *(cerveau isolé)*. Jouvet's studies on cats suggest that REM sleep may be initiated from nuclei in the brain stem. He reported that the midline raphe system of the pons may be the main center responsible for bringing on sleep and that it acts by secretion of serotonin, which modifies many of the effects of the reticular activating system. He stated that paradoxic (REM) sleep follows when a second secretion (norepinephrine), produced by the locus ceruleus, supplants the raphe secretion and produces effects resembling normal wakefulness. Destruction of the rostral reticular nucleus of the pons abolishes REM sleep without usually affecting slow wave sleep or arousal. REM sleep is suppressed by dopa or monoamine oxidase inhibitors, which increase the norepinephrine concentration in the brain. Lesions of the raphe nuclei in the pons cause prolonged wakefulness. These nuclei contain appreciable amounts of serotonin, and it has been shown that treatment with p-chlorophenylalanine (which inhibits serotonin synthesis) causes wakefulness in cats. Administration of compounds that increase serotonin increases slow wave sleep in cats.

Microelectrode Studies

Fine microelectrodes inserted within animal brain may record the action potential spikes of single neurons. These unit spikes last less than 1 ms. Recorded outside of cells, they range in amplitude from 0.5 to 10 mV. With ultrafine intracellular electrodes, spikes of 40–80 mV may be recorded as well as the resting membrane potential of individual cells. Epileptic neurons are characterized by very high rates of repetitive discharge reaching 500–1000 Hz (in contrast with normal cell rates of about 10–15 Hz). These epileptic neurons are also found to have a very unsteady membrane potential, being rapidly depolarized and remaining depolarized presumably because of defective recovery processes. Under certain conditions, inhibitory effects have also been noted, a cell becoming "hyperpolarized" with arrest of its discharge.

When unit discharges measured by microelectrodes are recorded simultaneously with the surface activity measured by gross electrodes, the relationship between surface waves and cell discharges appears variable. Very active unit discharge may be recorded during a relatively flat "desynchronized" surface EEG. The surface waves are made up largely of "dendritic," or synaptic, potentials very loosely coupled to the unitary cellular activity of the cortex, except under certain conditions of massive synchronization. Some of the waves appear to have an inhibitory rather than an excitatory effect upon repetitive cell discharge during an epileptiform discharge.

A variety of patterns of neuronal hyperactivity may occur in monkeys made epileptic by alumina cream treatment of the cerebral cortex. Most frequently, rhythmically recurrent bursts of high-frequency discharges occur in the epileptic cortical neuron interseizure patterns. Random bursts with varying frequencies of soma discharge may also occur over long periods. In other cases, interseizure hyperactivity of the neurons may consist of long trains of high-frequency discharges of variable frequency. Brief bursts of high-frequency discharges of 800 Hz or more and brief silences may occur.

There is no apparent relationship between the surface electrode recording and that from within the epileptic cells. At times, surface electrode "spikes" occur either associated or unassociated with bursts of discharges of cell bodies. Surface cortical electrodes of epileptic monkeys reveal that spontaneous electrical seizures originate in the region of the cortical scar and spread to involve the ipsilateral as well as the contralateral cortex, and seizure discharges recorded in EEGs show a tonic-clonic sequence like that of humans. Microelectrode studies of single cells during seizures show that before the onset of the propagated disturbance, spontaneous activity will be increased, with very high frequency discharges at rates up to 1000 Hz. The cortical standing potential develops a negative baseline shift of about 3 mV after the seizure is started, and this direct current shift slowly progresses to a peak value. It then shifts more quickly in the positive direction toward the original value as the tonic phase of the seizure ends. The cessation of the seizure may be the result of local metabolic exhaustion, but active inhibition by involvement of inhibitory interneurons may also play a role.

Spread of a seizure discharge from an epileptic focus can occur either by local spread through the cortical feltwork, involving mechanisms similar to those of spreading depression, or by spread of seizure discharges to other portions of the cortex and subcortex via conventional neuronal pathways. "Mirror foci," cortical and subcortical, showing spontaneous paroxysmal abnormalities as well as hypersensitivity to various activating agents, may occur in association with an experimentally induced cortical epileptic focus.

GLOSSARY OF TERMS

Activity: Any sequence of waves.

Alpha rhythm: Rhythm, usually with frequency of 8–13 Hz in adults, most prominent in the posterior areas, present most markedly when the eyes are closed, and attenuated during attention, especially visual.

Alpha wave: An individual component of an alpha rhythm.

Attenuation: Decrease in amplitude of activity.

Background activity: More or less general and continuous activity, in contrast with paroxysmal and focal activities.

Beta: Used to indicate a frequency band, ie, frequencies higher than 13 Hz.

Beta rhythm: Rhythm with frequency higher than 13 Hz.

Beta wave: Wave with a duration of less than 1/13 s and usually forming part of a beta rhythm.

Burst: See Paroxysm.

Common average reference lead: The common lead is the average of potential differences at a number of electrodes.

Common reference lead: Lead that is the same in all deviations of a montage.

Complex: Group of 2 or more waves, clearly distinguished from background activity and occurring with a well-recognized form or recurring with consistent form.

Cycle: The complete series of potential changes undergone by a wave before the same series is repeated.

Delta: Used to indicate a frequency band or a period, ie, frequency of less than 4 Hz and period of more than 1/4 s.

Delta activity: Series of regular or irregular waves with durations of more than 1/4 s.

Delta rhythm: Rhythm with frequency of less than 4 Hz.

Delta wave: Wave with a duration of more than 1/4 s.

Depth EEG: EEG derived from electrodes in direct contact with subcortical structures.

Derivation: Recording from a pair of leads.

Diffuse: Occurring over large areas without constant location. Used to describe activity occurring more or less simultaneously (without necessarily being synchronous) in large areas.

Diphasic: See Phase.

Driving: Occurrence of waves phase-locked with rhythmic stimuli.

Duration of a wave: Time interval from beginning to end of wave.

Electrical silence: Absence of electrical activity.

Electrocorticogram (ECoG): Record of electrical activity derived from electrodes in direct contact with the cortex.

Electroencephalogram (EEG): Record of electrical activity of the brain.

Focus: A limited region involved by, or the point of maximum potential of, a specified wave or activity (eg, spike focus, slow wave focus).

Frequency: The number of complete cycles of a rhythm in 1 s.

Index: The percentage of time occupied by the wave specified (eg, alpha index) with larger than specified amplitude (usually 10 μV) in a given sample (usually of 1 minute's duration).

K complex: Variable combination of sharp wave, slow wave, and sigma paroxysm occurring with maximal voltage over the vertex in response to sudden stimuli, especially during sleep.

Lambda wave: Sharp wave in the occipital areas, mainly positive in relation to other areas, and usually evoked by visual exploration.

Lead: Term used to denote a single electrode placement.

Location: Refers to brain area.

Low-voltage EEG: EEG in which no activity larger than 20 μV can be recorded between any 2 points on the scalp.

Monophasic: See Phase.

Montage: Combination of a number of derivations. Lead denotes single electrode placement. Derivation denotes recording from a pair of leads.

Morphology: The shape (form) of a wave or activity.

Mu rhythm: Rhythm at 7–11 Hz in central region, often with arcade or comb form, associated with beta rhythm; attenuated by real, imagined, or intended movement or tactile stimulation, particularly of the hands.

Paroxysm: Group of waves which appears and disappears abruptly and which is clearly distinguished from background activity by different frequency, morphology, or amplitude. (Synonym: burst.)

Period: Duration of a cycle. The period is the reciprocal of the frequency of a rhythm.

Phase: Strictly: Amplitude-time relations of sinusoidal waves. Loosely: Time relations of different parts of a wave (or waves) in a single trace, or of a wave

(or waves) as recorded simultaneously in different traces.

    Monophasic (wave): Deflected to one side of the baseline.

    Diphasic (wave): Deflected to one side, then to the other, of the baseline.

    Polyphasic (wave): Deflected several times in opposite directions.

Polyspike and wave complex: See Spike and Wave.

Quantity: Amount of activity in terms of amplitude and number of waves, with respect to time.

Random: Occurring at inconstant time intervals.

Reactivity: Changeability of the EEG following change in the environment.

Rhythm: Activity of approximately constant period and morphology, but not necessarily of amplitude.

Sharp and slow wave complex: Complex of 2 waves, one having a duration of between 1/12 s and 1/5 s, the other of between 1/2 s and 1 s.

Sharp wave: Wave, distinguished from background activity, with a duration of more than 1/12 s and less than 1/5 s.

Sigma rhythm: Episode rhythm at about 14 Hz, usually diffuse, with a maximum near the vertex, usually occurring during certain stages of sleep. (Synonym: sigma spindle.)

Sigma spindle: See Sigma rhythm.

Slow wave: Wave with a duration of more than 1/8 s.

Spike: Wave distinguished from background activity and having a duration of 1/12 s or less.

Spike and wave complex: Complex of 2 waves, one with a duration of 1/12 s or less (spike) and the other with a duration of 1/5–1/2 s (wave).

    Polyspike and wave complex: Spike and wave complex with more than one spike.

Spike and wave rhythm: Bilaterally synchronous spike and wave complexes, recurring rhythmically with a frequency of 2.5–3.5 Hz, closely associated with clinical petit mal seizures.

Theta: Used to indicate a frequency band or a period, ie, frequency of 4 Hz to less than 8 Hz or a period of 1/4 s to more than 1/8 s.

Theta activity: Series of regular or irregular waves with durations of 1/4 s to more than 1/8 s.

Theta rhythm: Rhythm with frequency of 4 Hz to less than 8 Hz.

Theta wave: Wave with a duration of 1/4 s to more than 1/8 s.

Topography: Distribution of activity with respect to anatomic landmarks. (Synonym: spatial distribution.)

Transient: Any single wave (spike, sharp wave, etc) or brief complex noticeably different from background activity.

Unilateral: Occurring on one side of the head.

Vertex sharp wave: Sharp wave, maximal at the vertex and negative in relation to other areas, often associated with arousal stimuli.

Wave: Any transient change of potential difference in the EEG.

R = right	F = frontal	P = parietal	AT = anterior temporal	T = temporal
L = left	O = occipital	Pc = precentral	Pf = posterior frontal	E = ear

Calibration: 50 μV (vertical) and 1 s (horizontal).

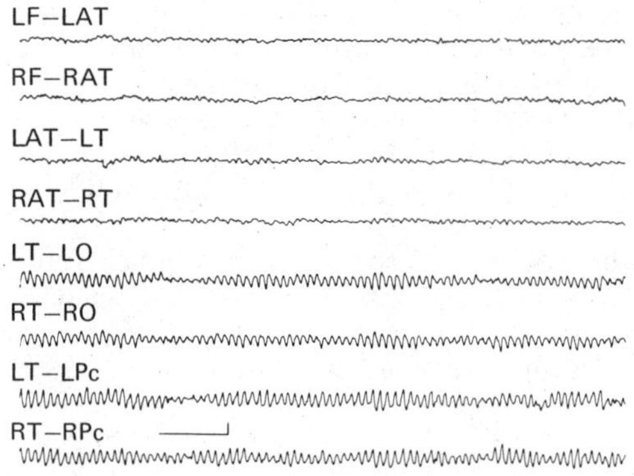

LF–LAT

RF–RAT

LAT–LT

RAT–RT

LT–LO

RT–RO

LT–LPc

RT–RPc

Normal Adult

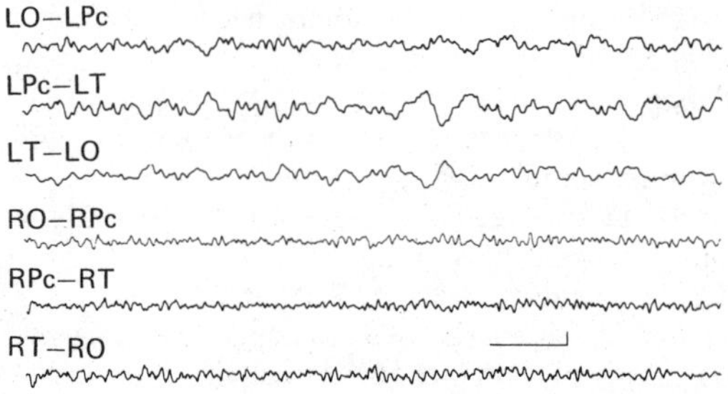

LO–LPc

RO–RPc

LPc–LT

RPc–RT

LPc–LF

RPc–RF

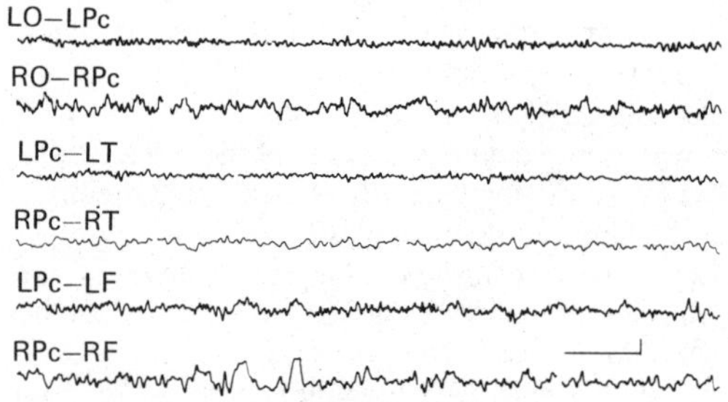

Cerebral Thrombosis. Tracing of a 71-year-old woman who showed moderate improvement 1 month after the onset of a left hemiplegia.

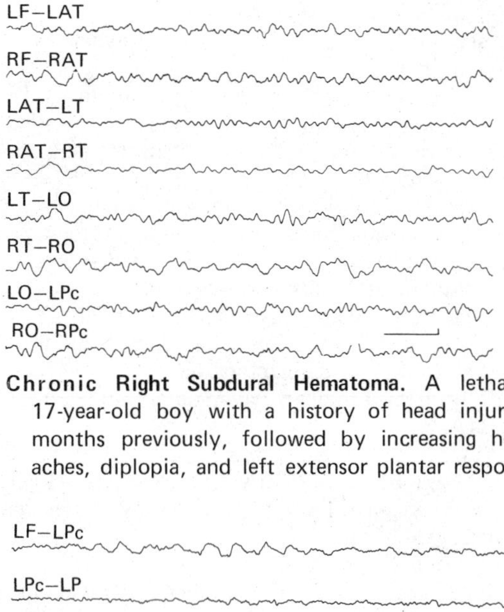

LF–LE

RF–RF

LPc–LE

RPc–RE

LAT–LE

RAT–RE

LO–LE

RO–RE

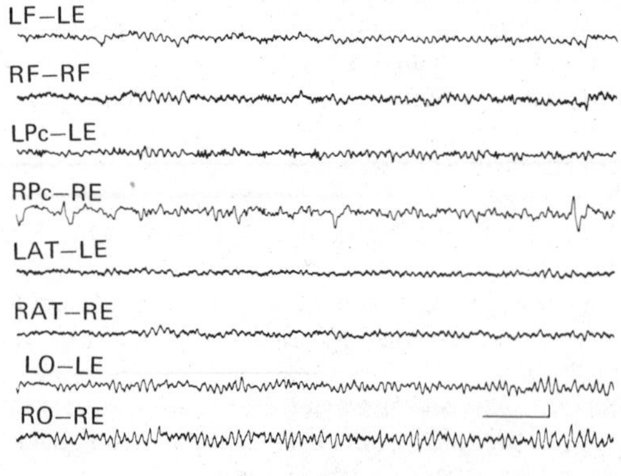

Hypertensive Encephalopathy. A 66-year-old hypertensive woman 5 days after acute onset of left hemiparesis and left focal motor seizures starting in the foot.

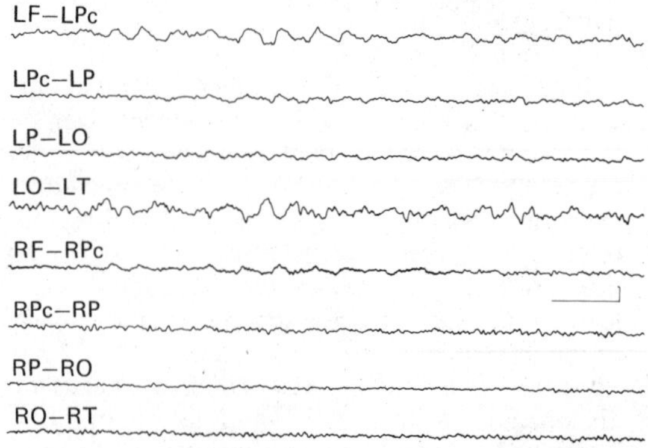

LO–LPc

LPc–LT

LT–LO

RO–RPc

RPc–RT

RT–RO

Cerebral Embolism. Record made 1 month after onset of aphasia and right hemiplegia that occurred 4 days after acute anterior myocardial infarct.

LF–LAT

RF–RAT

LAT–LT

RAT–RT

LT–LO

RT–RO

LO–LPc

RO–RPc

Chronic Right Subdural Hematoma. A lethargic 17-year-old boy with a history of head injury 3 months previously, followed by increasing headaches, diplopia, and left extensor plantar response.

LF–LPc

LPc–LP

LP–LO

LO–LT

RF–RPc

RPc–RP

RP–RO

RO–RT

Thrombosis Left Internal Carotid Artery. Disorientation, euphoria, impaired mentation, and acalculia began suddenly in this 41-year-old man 2 weeks earlier.

Figure 16–4. Representative EEGs.

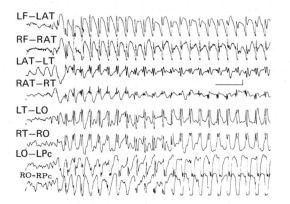

LF–LAT
RF–RAT
LAT–LT
RAT–RT
LT–LO
RT–RO
LO–LPc
RO–RPc

Petit Mal Epilepsy. This 6-year-old boy had one of his "blank spells," in which he was transiently unaware of surroundings and blinked his eyelids, during the recording.

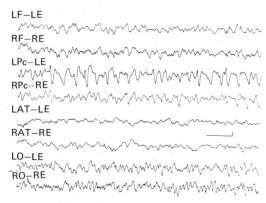

LF–LE
RF–RE
LPc–LE
RPc–RE
LAT–LE
RAT–RE
LO–LE
RO–RE

Epilepsy. Record of a 6-year-old girl with frequent nocturnal major convulsions as well as daily seizures in which she became stiff, started, and shook slightly.

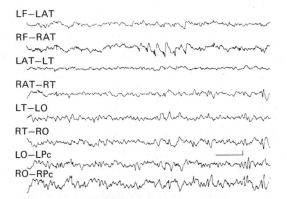

LF–LAT
RF–RAT
LAT–LT
RAT–RT
LT–LO
RT–RO
LO–LPc
RO–RPc

Epilepsy. This 6-year-old child had suffered 3 major convulsions, 2 of which appeared to start in the left extremities.

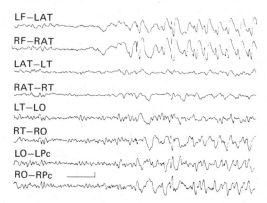

LF–LAT
RF–RAT
LAT–LT
RAT–RT
LT–LO
RT–RO
LO–LPc
RO–RPc

Epilepsy. Record of a 34-year-old man with history of recurrent nightmares and major and minor seizures since age 12 years.

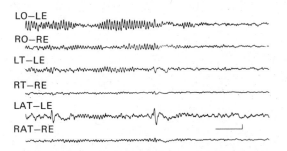

LO–LE
RO–RE
LT–LE
RT–RE
LAT–LE
RAT–RE

Psychomotor Epilepsy. This 20-year-old man had monthly episodes for the previous 6 years characterized by motor automatisms and frequently followed by generalized tonic-clonic convulsions.

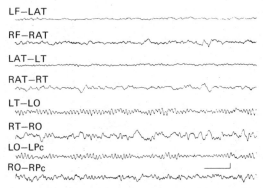

LF–LAT
RF–RAT
LAT–LT
RAT–RT
LT–LO
RT–RO
LO–LPc
RO–RPc

Focal Motor Epilepsy. This 47-year-old man with focal motor seizures beginning in the left hand stated his seizures began 20 years previously, approximately one year after a severe head injury.

Figure 16–5. Representative EEGs.

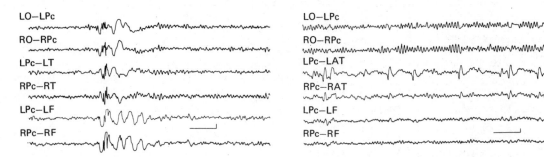

LO–LPc

RO–RPc

LPc–LT

RPc–RT

LPc–LF

RPc–RF

LO–LPc

RO–RPc

LPc–LAT

RPc–RAT

LPc–LF

RPc–RF

Epilepsy. Tracing of a 24-year-old man with generalized tonic-clonic convulsions and aura of nausea.

Epilepsy. Tracing of a 27-year-old woman with history of meningitis at age 15 months and generalized tonic-clonic seizures since age 12 years.

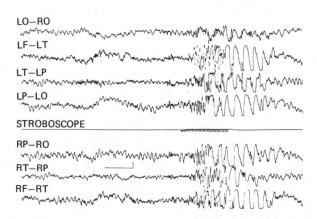

LO–RO

LF–LT

LT–LP

LP–LO

STROBOSCOPE

RP–RO

RT–RP

RF–RT

Epilepsy. This 13-year-old girl had brief episodes characterized by blinking of the eyes and absences over the past 3 years. Activation of an electrical cerebral seizure was produced by photic stimulation at a frequency of 20 Hz.

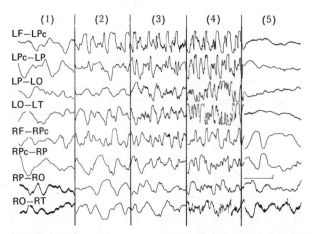

(1)   (2)   (3)   (4)   (5)

LF–LPc

LPc–LP

LP–LO

LO–LT

RF–RPc

RPc–RP

RP–RO

RO–RT

Status Epilepticus. Excerpts from the record of a 5-year-old comatose boy whose seizures began 5 days previously in association with a febrile illness: (1) Resting record. (2) Beginning of electric seizure (LF). (3) Clinical seizure apparent in right arm and face. (4) Height of clinical seizure. (5) Postconvulsive period.

Figure 16–6. Representative EEGs.

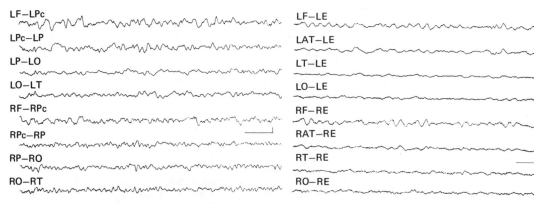

LF–LPc
LPc–LP
LP–LO
LO–LT
RF–RPc
RPc–RP
RP–RO
RO–RT

LF–LE
LAT–LE
LT–LE
LO–LE
RF–RE
RAT–RE
RT–RE
RO–RE

Left Cerebral Brain Abscess. Severe headaches, progressive right hemiparesis, and aphasia occurred in this 50-year-old woman with left temporofrontal abscess.

Skull Fracture and Brain Contusion. This 45-year-old man was found wandering on the streets in a disoriented and confused state 1 week earlier, at which time skull x-rays revealed left parietotemporal fracture and lumbar puncture disclosed xanthochromic cerebrospinal fluid under mildly increased pressure.

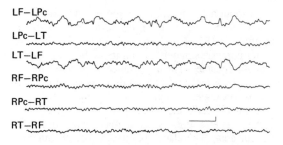

LF–LPc
LPc–LT
LT–LF
RF–RPc
RPc–RT
RT–RF

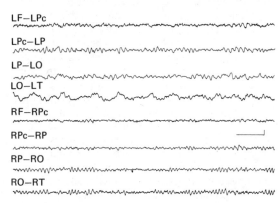

LF–LPc
LPc–LP
LP–LO
LO–LT
RF–RPc
RPc–RP
RP–RO
RO–RT

Left Frontal Tumor. A left frontal glioblastoma multiforme was found in this 58-year-old man with onset of seizures, right hemiparesis, and aphasia 2 years previously.

Left Temporal Tumor. Astrocytoma was found in this 66-year-old man with a history of headaches and aphasia of 3 weeks' duration.

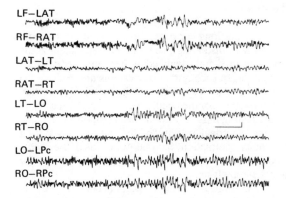

LF–LAT
RF–RAT
LAT–LT
RAT–RT
LT–LO
RT–RO
LO–LPc
RO–RPc

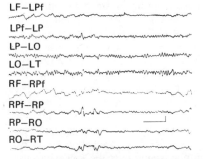

LF–LPf
LPf–LP
LP–LO
LO–LT
RF–RPf
RPf–RP
RP–RO
RO–RT

Barbiturate Intoxication. Tracing of a 32-year-old woman, a barbiturate drug addict, during a period in which she suffered intermittent confusion, amnesia, and generalized motor seizures.

Infarct, Right Posterior Cerebral. Tracing 5 weeks after acute onset of transient left hemiparesis, left homonymous hemianopsia, and left motor seizures with visual aura in a 52-year-old man with normal right carotid angiogram and pneumoencephalogram.

Figure 16–7. Representative EEGs.

17 | Electromyography

Electromyography is concerned with the study of the electrical activity arising from muscles and associated with muscle activity. Variations of potential are detected by needle electrodes inserted into skeletal muscle; the electrical activity may be displayed on a cathode ray oscilloscope and played on a loudspeaker for simultaneous visual and auditory analysis.

The striated muscle of humans is composed functionally of motor units in which the axons of single motor (anterior horn) cells innervate many muscle fibers. Hundreds of muscle fibers may be innervated by a single axon. All the fibers innervated by a single motor unit respond immediately in an "all-or-none" pattern to adequate stimulation. The interaction of many motor units can produce relatively smooth motor performance. Increased motor power results from activation of a greater number of motor units or from repeated activation of a given number of motor units. The action potential of a muscle consists of the sum of the action potentials of many motor units. The action potential of normal muscle fibers originates at the motor end-plates and is triggered by an incoming nerve impulse at the myoneural junction. It then spreads along muscle fibers, exciting contraction. The contraction itself produces no electrical activity.

Electrical potentials may be recorded, after amplification, by a cathode ray oscillograph. Ink-writing oscillographs, such as are used in electroencephalography, may be used in clinical studies and permit simultaneous recording from many muscles. However, the use of a cathode ray oscillograph recording as a control is advisable. Surface electrodes attached over the muscle with collodion may be used for recording muscle action potentials. With microelectrodes or coaxial needle electrodes, the discharges of single motor units may be recorded. The amplitude of single motor unit discharges (diphasic or triphasic waves) ranges from 20 to 2000 μV; duration of discharge is usually 0.003–0.015 s; frequency varies usually from 6 to 30 Hz. Such discharges produce a knocking or thumping sound over the loudspeaker.

Clinical studies indicate that normal muscle at rest shows no action potentials. In simple movements, the contracting muscle gives rise to action potentials while its antagonist relaxes and gives rise to no potentials. During contraction, different portions of the same muscle may discharge at different rates, and parts may appear to be transiently inactive; in strong contractions, many motor units are active, producing numerous action potentials. Passive stretching of a muscle is associated with action potentials from the stretched muscle; further stretching produces the additional finding of action potentials in the antagonistic muscle. In each area of muscle tested, observations may be made of "insertion potentials" evoked by movement of the needle, resting muscle activity, and electrical activity during voluntary muscle contraction.

Although the majority of motor unit potentials have a simple biphasic or triphasic form with an amplitude of 0.5–2 mV and a duration of 3–15 ms, smaller potentials may be found in the face and external ocular muscles. The appearance of an active motor unit may be greatly influenced by its position relative to the recording electrode. During strong contraction, a concentric needle electrode may not be suitable for following single units, since it may record from too large an area. Therefore, microelectrode techniques have been devised which indicate that in the initiation of voluntary contractions the first motor units to discharge are apparently smaller than those which follow at higher tensions.

Technique

A concentric (coaxial) needle, usually 24 gauge and 3–4 cm long, or a monopolar solid steel needle coated with insulating plastic or varnish except at the tip, is inserted and advanced by steps to several depths of muscle. In each area, observations are made of (1) the electrical activity evoked in the muscle by insertion and movement of the needle, (2) the electrical activity of the resting muscle with the needle undisturbed, and (3) the electrical activity of the motor units during voluntary contraction. Several insertions of the needle into different parts of a muscle may be necessary for adequate analysis.

Variations in electrical potential between the needle tip and a metal plate (reference electrode) on the skin surface are amplified and displayed on a cathode ray oscilloscope. Fluctuations of voltage may be converted into sound waves by connecting the output of the amplifier to a loudspeaker. Permanent records may be made by photographs of traces on the oscilloscope screen or by storage of the electrical signals on magnetic tape.

Clinical Application

Although the electromyogram does not give a

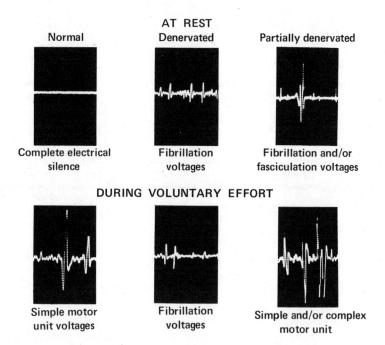

AT REST

Normal | Denervated | Partially denervated

Complete electrical silence | Fibrillation voltages | Fibrillation and/or fasciculation voltages

DURING VOLUNTARY EFFORT

Simple motor unit voltages | Fibrillation voltages | Simple and/or complex motor unit

Figure 17–1. Electromyograms showing characteristic voltages of normal and abnormal voluntary muscle. (Reproduced, with permission, from Golseth: Diagnostic contributions of the electromyogram. *Calif Med* 1950;**73**:355.)

specific clinical diagnosis, it may aid in diagnosis. Information must be integrated with results of other tests, clinical features, etc, in arriving at a final diagnosis. The electromyogram is useful to the clinician, particularly in the diagnosis of lower motor neuron disease, in the detection of defects in transmission at the neuromuscular junction, and in the diagnosis of primary muscle disease.

Insertion activity in muscle at rest may be prolonged in denervated muscle, polymyositis, myotonic disorders, and some other myopathies. In neuromuscular disorders, spontaneous potentials such as fibrillation potentials, positive sharp waves, fasciculations, myotonic discharges, and bizarre high-frequency potentials may be evident after insertion activity ceases (Fig 17–2).

The term "fibrillation" is reserved for spontaneous independent contraction of individual muscle fibers which are so minute that they cannot be observed through the intact skin. Denervated muscle may show electromyographic evidence of fibrillations 1–3 weeks after the muscle has lost its nerve supply. "Fasciculation" twitches, on the other hand, may be seen, palpated, and even heard with the aid of a stethoscope, and they represent contractions of muscle fibers of a motor unit. Spontaneous fasciculations may vary because of the length and number of muscle fibers involved. Spontaneous fasciculations may result from disorders of the lower motor neuron and may be seen in poliomyelitis, spinal cord disease, motor root and peripheral nerve disease, and amyotrophic lateral sclerosis. Benign fasciculations are fasciculations unassociated with other clinical or electrical signs of

denervation and occur in persons without recognizable neurologic or muscular disease.

In diseases where the lower motor neuron and the muscle innervated by it become atrophied, fasciculations and, later, fibrillations may occur in the muscles. Fibrillations are believed to represent the contractions of single muscle fibers and are associated with irregular potentials of low voltage and high frequency.

In **anterior poliomyelitis,** the presence of synchronous motor unit discharges in partially functioning muscles and their antagonists is interpreted to indicate a disturbance of reciprocal innervation. In clinical conditions associated with **spasticity,** the resting muscle may show no action potentials. In such cases, however, minimal stimuli may set off strong muscle contractions (associated with action potentials) in antagonistic muscle groups.

In **parkinsonism,** with rigidity, persistent simultaneous activity occurs in antagonistic muscles despite attempted relaxation. With diseases characterized by irregular involuntary movements (athetosis, dystonia), irregular, asynchronous patterns of discharge occur in the muscles.

Fibrillation potentials are simple monophasic or biphasic spikes less than 200 μV in amplitude and less than 2 ms in duration. Fibrillation potentials produce a sharp clicking sound in the loudspeaker and are clearly distinguishable from normal motor unit potentials by their small size, brief duration, and sharp sound.

In a complete nerve lesion, fibrillation potentials occur without motor unit potentials, whereas partial nerve lesions show both fibrillation and motor unit activity or voluntary muscle contraction. Diminution

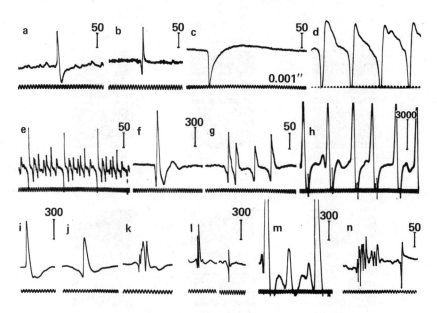

Figure 17–2. Action potentials in electromyography. *(a)* "Nerve potential" from normal muscle; *(b)* fibrillation potential and *(c)* positive wave from denervated muscle; *(d)* high-frequency discharge in myotonia; *(e)* bizarre high-frequency discharge; *(f)* fasciculation potential, single discharge; *(g)* fasciculation potential, repetitive or grouped discharge; *(h)* synchronized repetitive discharge in muscle cramp; *(i)* diphasic, *(j)* triphasic, and *(k)* polyphasic motor unit action potentials from normal muscle; *(l)* short-duration motor unit action potentials in progressive muscular dystrophy; *(m)* large motor unit action potentials in progressive muscular atrophy; *(n)* highly polyphasic motor unit action potential and short-duration motor unit action potential during reinnervation. Calibration scales are in microvolts. All time scales are 1000 Hz. An upward deflection indicates a change of potential in the negative direction at the needle electrode. (Reproduced, with permission, from *Clinical Examinations in Neurology,* 3rd ed. Members of the Sections of Neurology and Section of Physiology, Mayo Clinic and Mayo Foundation for Medical Education and Research, Graduate School, University of Minnesota, Rochester, Minnesota. Saunders, 1971.)

or cessation of fibrillation potentials and the appearance of small disintegrated motor unit action potentials occur with nerve regeneration. Fibrillations in a paretic muscle are increased by warmth, activity, and neostigmine and decreased by cold or immobilization.

After **complete section of a nerve,** denervation fibrillation potentials are evident in all areas of the muscles supplied by a peripheral nerve after about 18 days. In **partial nerve injuries,** despite the clinical appearance of complete paralysis, some motor unit discharges persist. By mapping the areas in which denervation fibrillation potentials are present, single nerve root disorders may be diagnosed. Spinal nerve root compression can be recognized with the aid of such a technique. Extramedullary **cord tumors** are characterized by the frequent associated involvement of nerve roots, with consequent local denervation fibrillation potentials.

Alterations in the electromyogram are commonly encountered in the **myopathies.** In the myotonias (myotonia congenita, atrophica, and acquisita), there is accentuation of the electromyographic response upon voluntary muscle contraction or insertion of the needle. The repetitive discharge of single muscle fibers or groups is initially high in frequency and declines rapidly, the discharge ceasing within a few seconds; this gives rise to the so-called "dive-bomber"

sound in the loudspeaker. Denervation muscle potentials are not seen. In the muscular dystrophies, voluntary muscle contraction produces electrical patterns of diminished amplitude and frequency. In myasthenia gravis, with continued muscle contraction, there is a gradual diminution in amplitude and frequency of motor unit discharges. In progressive muscular atrophy and amyotrophic lateral sclerosis, there are usually diffuse denervation fibrillation and fasciculation discharges, even in cases that upon clinical examination appear to be anatomically limited to the distal portion of the upper extremities.

The electromyogram produced after appropriate motor nerve stimulation provides a useful clinical means of studying **neuromuscular diseases and disorders.** The response to single nerve stimuli or to repeated nerve stimulation may be studied in pathologic states and under modifications produced by therapy. Thus, the effectiveness of medication in modifying the reaction of muscles in conditions like myasthenia gravis may be readily evaluated. The **conduction velocities** of motor nerves may be readily estimated by this technique. Conduction velocity may be markedly slowed in conditions affecting the peripheral nerves, as shown by increase in conduction time from the point of stimulation to the muscle and increase in duration of action potentials of the muscle. The time

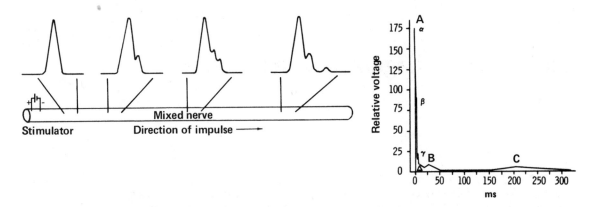

Figure 17–3. Compound action potential. *Left:* Record obtained with recording electrodes at various distances from the stimulating electrodes along a mixed nerve. *Right:* Reconstruction of a compound action potential to show relative sizes and time relationships of the components. (Redrawn and reproduced, with permission, from Erlanger & Gasser: *Electrical Signs of Nervous Activity.* Univ of Pennsylvania Press, 1937.)

and manner of reinnervation of muscles supplied by an injured or sectioned nerve can also be observed and correlated with clinically detectable movements during voluntary motion. In a functional disorder, such as hysteria, a normal pattern is demonstrable.

The electromyogram may be used in the study of physiologic phenomena and the effects of pathologic processes, drugs, etc. For example, electrical stimulation of a mixed peripheral nerve may result in characteristic responses in the electromyogram, since a mixed peripheral nerve has both afferent and efferent fibers of different diameters. Thus, when a mixed peripheral nerve such as the posterior tibial nerve is stimulated by current of low intensity, only fibers of large diameter (Ia fibers) are stimulated, since fibers of large diameter have the lowest threshold. These large Ia fibers are afferent fibers from the muscle spindle and connect monosynaptically in the spinal cord with motor neurons of the anterior horn (Fig 7–6); these neurons discharge and produce in the gastrocnemius muscle a response called the H (Hoffmann) response, which can be recorded. With a stimulus of slightly greater or medium intensity, smaller efferent fibers are also stimulated in addition to the aforementioned afferent fibers, producing a direct muscle response, the M wave, in the electromyogram, followed by an H response. With stronger stimuli, antidromic impulses in the efferent fibers may interfere with the production of the H wave, so that only an M wave is produced in the electromyogram.

The H wave is the electrical counterpart of the tendon jerk. The amplitude of the H response depends on the number of motor neurons discharged, and its variability may reflect internuncial activity. In hemiplegic extremities, large H responses may be due to release of motor neurons from suprasegmental inhibitory mechanisms. Increase in latency of the H response can occur in conditions that involve only nerve cells, spinal cord, nerve roots, or peripheral nerve fibers, but not muscle.

In humans, following electrical stimulation of a mixed nerve, 2 potentials may be recorded in muscle that have a latency greater than the direct muscle response, or M wave. In addition to the H response, an antidromic motor response (the F response) of approximately the same latency can occur when the stimulating and recording electrodes remain in the same position. The H response occurs with threshold stimulation, is blocked by supramaximal stimulation of the nerve, and is a monosynaptic response. The F response persists with supramaximal stimulation of the nerve, is present even in deafferented muscle, and is produced by antidromic activation of motor neurons. The H and F responses can be readily separated from each other by study of their recovery following prior stimulation: a preceding electrical stimulus inhibits the H response for about 150 ms, whereas the F response is depressed for a much shorter time (2–20 ms).

18 | Electrodiagnostic Examinations

Electrical stimulation of muscles and nerves is of clinical value in the diagnosis and prognosis of motor disorders. Galvanic (direct or continuous) current normally produces momentary contraction of a muscle upon "making" or "breaking" the circuit. It may be used to stimulate the nerve or the muscle directly. Faradic (induced or interrupted) current normally produces a continuous tetanic contraction owing to the rapidly repeated stimuli. It is ordinarily used in stimulating the nerve only. Interrupted currents whose component electrical pulses are measurable in terms of duration of pulse, form of pulse (square wave, sawtooth, etc), and electrical energy may also be used.

In the muscle-nerve complex, a variation is noted in the excitability of different parts. The nerve is most sensitive to stimulation; the myoneural junction is intermediate in sensitivity; and the muscle itself is the least sensitive. Clinically, stimulation is usually applied over the course of the nerve or at the **motor point** of the muscle being tested. The motor point is normally the most excitable point of a muscle and represents the greatest concentration of nerve endings. It is located on the skin over the muscle and corresponds approximately to the level at which the nerve enters the muscle belly. Since some muscle fibers may be affected differently than others, it is often necessary to test different portions of the same muscle. Muscles should always be tested at the motor point; denervated muscles should be tested at the former motor point and in the neighborhood of the motor point.

A minimum amount of time is necessary for an electrical current to produce stimulation of a nerve or muscle. This is expressed by the **chronaxie,** the time necessary for a current that is twice the rheobase to produce a response. The **rheobase** is the minimum amount of current necessary to stimulate a nerve or muscle.

Electrical skin resistance (see p 228) may be greatly increased in disorders that impair peripheral or autonomic nerve function, with associated decrease in sweat secretion.

Normal Formula of Response (NFR)

In the use of galvanic current, 2 electrodes are needed. The indifferent electrode is broad and is placed against a large flat surface, eg, the patient's back. This is necessary to afford good contact. The stimulating electrode is small and is placed over the nerve or motor point of the muscle being tested. Either electrode may be used as the anode, the other as the cathode. Ordinarily, only closing, or "make," shocks are used, since opening, or "break," shocks usually require a painful amount of current to produce a response. With the cathode as stimulating electrode, less current is needed to produce a response than when the anode is used. In other words, CCC (cathode closing contraction) exceeds ACC (anode closing contraction); the NFR, therefore, can be written CCC > ACC.

A "reversal of polarity" occurs when an injured nerve has undergone degeneration. A greater amount of current is needed to produce a response, and ACC > CCC. This polar inversion has never been satisfactorily explained.

The response of denervated muscle to galvanic current or interrupted current with pulses of long duration (0.5 s or longer) is retained but altered. In severe injuries, galvanic stimulation of the nerve produces no response, and stimulation of the muscle causes a vermicular (wormlike) contraction instead of the normal quick reaction. Furthermore, the motor point disappears, and the muscle becomes isosensitive throughout. The best response is then obtained by "longitudinal reaction," in which the lines of current are directed through the whole muscle instead of being concentrated at one point.

Degeneration of motor neurons may cause denervated muscles to fail to contract upon stimulation with interrupted current of electrical pulses of short duration (less than 0.0005 s, or faradic). This change, which occurs after a delay of 2–3 weeks, is comparable in significance to the appearance of fibrillation denervation potentials in the electromyogram.

Reaction of Degeneration (RD)

The characteristic electrical changes in lower motor neuron lesions are known as the "reaction of degeneration." This reaction may be partial or complete, depending upon the severity of the injury. It is always necessary to wait 10–14 days after the injury before testing the RD, since that much time is required for degeneration of an injured nerve to occur. Both galvanic and faradic currents are used to test the degree of RD. In **mild partial RD,** faradic stimulation of nerve requires more current than normal, and galvanic stimulation of nerve and muscle produces a normal response. In **severe partial RD,** faradic stimulation of nerve produces no contraction, and galvanic stimulation of nerve and muscle produces a normal response.

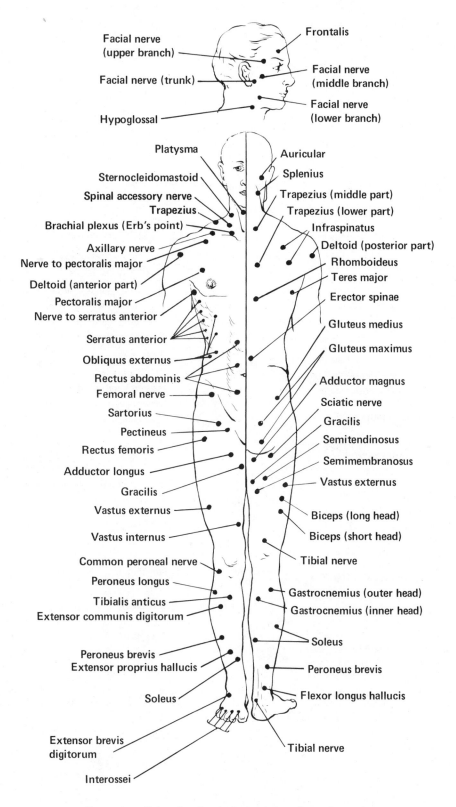

Figure 18–1. Points for electrical stimulation of muscles and nerves.

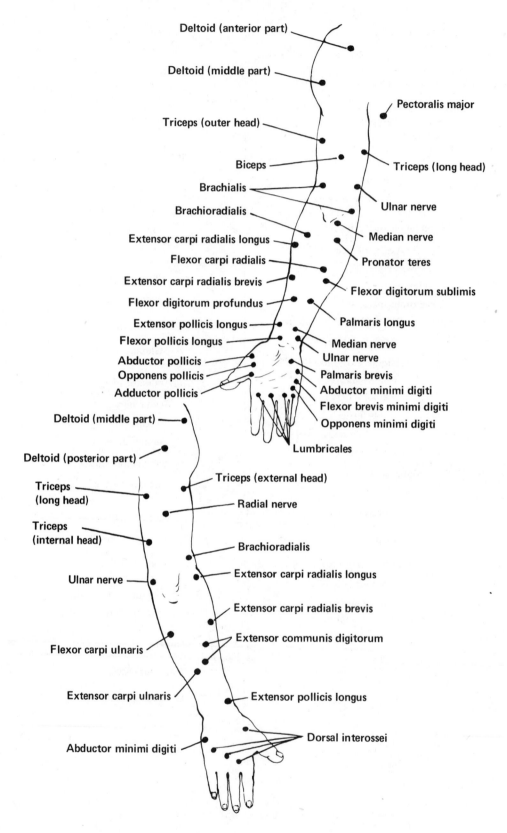

Figure 18–2. Points for electrical stimulation of muscles and nerves.

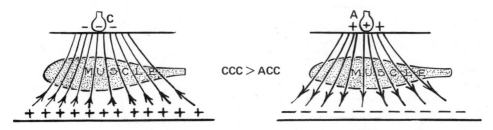

Figure 18–3. The normal formula of response (NFR).

In **complete RD,** faradic or galvanic stimulation of nerve produces no response, and galvanic stimulation of muscle produces vermicular contractions.

A. Prognostic Significance of RD: Changes in RD were at one time advocated as a prognostic guide to recovery of function. Experience has shown this to be a limited and unreliable index. Faradic excitability may return much later than the disappearance of fibrillation potentials in the electromyogram and is sometimes delayed until after the return of voluntary muscle movement.

The following claims for the prognostic significance of RD have been made: mild partial RD, recovery expected in 6 weeks; severe partial RD, recovery expected in 6 months; complete RD, recovery not expected for 1–2 years or may never occur. The time required for recovery depends somewhat upon how far the regenerating fibers must grow. The rate of growth is about 1 mm/d or 2.5 cm/mo.

B. Diagnostic Significance of RD: RD is absent in upper motor neuron lesions and functional paralysis; present in lower motor neuron lesions and true organic lower motor neuron paralysis. RD is not present in cases of motor loss resulting from cut tendons and hence is useful in differentiating such lesions from motor loss due to lower motor neuron changes.

Chronaxie

The chronaxie of denervated muscle (see p 248) may be greatly increased; the value for normal human skeletal muscle usually does not exceed 0.7 ms. After section of a motor nerve, electrical stimulation of a distal portion of the nerve and motor point chronaxie may remain normal for 2 days. On about the third day, stimulation of the distal portion of the sectioned nerve may produce no response. Motor point chronaxie may be increased, but muscle response may appear normal, with the muscle contracting and relaxing abruptly.

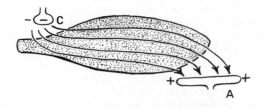

Figure 18–4. Longitudinal reaction.

Chronaxie continues to rise thereafter. In about 1 week, slowness in relaxation of muscle following electrically induced contraction may be evident. About a month after nerve section, motor point chronaxie may have increased 100 times. Upon galvanic stimulation, muscle contraction and relaxation are slowed.

With nerve regeneration and muscle reinnervation, progressive decrease in chronaxie may occur. The muscle then begins to contract rapidly on electrical stimulation of the nerve.

Galvanic Tetanus Ratio

The ratio of current strength required for a minimal visible muscle contraction to that required for a sustained contraction when long constant (galvanic) currents are used is called the galvanic tetanus ratio. In normal muscle, the ratio is 1:4; in denervated muscle, 1:1. Although the gradual change in this ratio toward normal has been described as a more sensitive index of reinnervation than the return of faradic excitability, the method has been criticized because it does not yield constant results. Increased responsiveness to constant currents may also be shown by the use of slowly rising currents that may cause tetanic contractions in denervated muscle without affecting normal muscles at comparable current strengths.

Strength-Duration Curves

The excitability of nerve and muscle may be measured with the help of stimulators that provide interrupted current with pulses varying from 0.0001 to 1 s. In general, the shorter the pulses used, the greater the strength of current required to reach the threshold of excitation. A strength-duration curve may be plotted to show the excitation time characteristics and chronaxie of a particular locus. Although this method is not as sensitive as electromyography, such curves may show evidence of denervation following nerve injury or chronic lower motor neuron disease at times when spontaneous fibrillations are difficult to detect. In normal muscle, the nerves remain the most excitable component, and the curve reflects the excitability characteristic of nerve; in denervated muscle, the curve reflects the excitability of denervated muscle fibers rather than of the nerve components.

Electrical Stimulation of Nerve Trunks

The presence, absence, or reduction of innerva-

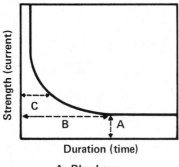

A: Rheobase
B: Utilization time
C: Chronaxie

Figure 18–5. Strength-duration curve, relating the strength of a stimulus to the time for which it must be applied to an excitable tissue to produce a response. (Reproduced, with permission, from Ganong WF: *Review of Medical Physiology,* 10th ed. Lange, 1981.)

tion may be determined by electrical stimulation of peripheral nerves. The location of a nerve block may be demonstrated. Anomalies of innervation may be detected by noting which muscles respond to nerve stimulation. Abnormal fatigability following repeated stimulation of the nerve may be noted.

In the presence of paralysis, stimulation of the peripheral nerve with a normal response of innervated muscles shows that the cause of paralysis is proximal to the stimulated point. On the other hand, an absent or

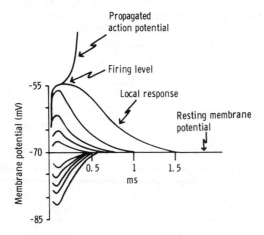

Figure 18–6. Electrotonic potentials and local response. The changes in the membrane potential of a neuron following application of stimuli of 0.2, 0.4, 0.6, 0.8, and 1.0 times threshold intensity are shown superimposed on the same time scale. The responses below the horizontal line are those recorded near the anode, and the responses above the line are those recorded near the cathode. The stimulus of threshold intensity was repeated twice. Once it caused a propagated action potential (top line), and once it did not. (Based on a diagram from Hodgkin: The subthreshold potentials in a crustacean nerve fiber. *Proc R Soc Lond [Biol]* 1938; **126**:87.)

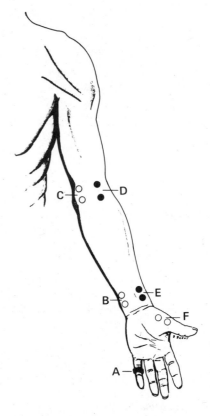

Figure 18–7. Conduction velocity studies. A–C are electrode placements for ulnar nerve evoked potentials; A is a ring stimulating electrode, and B and C are recording electrodes. D–F are electrode placements for median nerve motor conduction velocity study; D and E are points where the nerve is stimulated, and F is the recording electrode. (Reproduced, with permission, from Samaha FJ: Electrodiagnostic studies in neuromuscular disease. *N Engl J Med* 1972; **285**:1244.)

weak response suggests that further testing is desirable to detect the site and nature of the defect.

In diseases affecting peripheral nerves, there may be a reduction in conduction velocity of motor nerves. This may be evident in the increase in conduction time from the point of stimulation of the nerve to the muscle and by increase in duration of the muscle action potential. Marked slowing in conduction velocity occurs in diseases that affect peripheral nerves, as in chronic neuropathies, during regeneration following nerve injuries, and in Charcot-Marie-Tooth atrophy. No slowing in conduction occurs in progressive muscular dystrophy or polymyositis; in diseases affecting the anterior horn cells, such as amyotrophic lateral sclerosis and progressive muscular atrophy, there is no slowing or very mild slowing in conduction velocity. Conduction velocity may decrease by 2 m/s for each 1 °C (1.8 °F) drop in limb temperature.

Normal motor nerve conduction is 50–60 m/s in ulnar and median nerves and 45–55 m/s in the common peroneal nerve. Conduction rates below 40 m/s frequently occur in neuropathies.

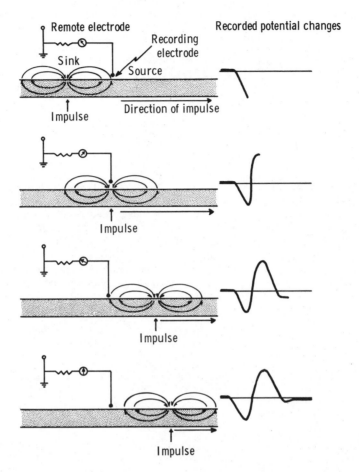

Figure 18–8. Potential changes recorded during passage of an impulse along an axon in a volume conductor. One electrode (recording electrode) is on the surface of the axon; the other (remote or indifferent electrode) is on inactive tissue at a distance in the conducting medium. (Adapted and reproduced, with permission, from Brazier: *The Electrical Activity of the Nervous System,* 3rd ed. Pitman, 1968.)

Other Clinical Applications of Electrical Examinations

A. Jolly's Myasthenic Reaction: In myasthenia gravis and in some other types of neural disorders, involved muscles show rapid fatigue upon repeated faradic stimulation and finally do not respond at all. Excitability usually returns after a rest period.

Repetitive supramaximal stimulation of a peripheral nerve may reveal abnormal fatigability of the peripheral neuromuscular system. The action potential of muscle may be recorded as a measure of the response; in myasthenia gravis, the characteristic response is most evident in severely affected muscle.

B. Myasthenic Syndrome (Eaton-Lambert Syndrome): This disorder, frequently associated with small cell carcinoma of the lung, is characterized by proximal muscle weakness, easy fatigability, and diminished deep tendon reflexes. There is a marked facilitation and increased muscle response to high rates of electrical stimulation. There is poor response to edrophonium (Tensilon), unusual sensitivity to curare, and improvement with guanidine hydrochloride.

C. Myotonic Reaction: In disorders characterized by myotonia (eg, myotonia congenita or myotonia atrophica), affected muscles may show a prolonged response to a single stimulation.

D. Tetanic Reaction: In tetany, muscles may be hyperexcitable (Erb's sign). However, the chronaxie of muscles may be significantly increased.

E. Cadaveric Reaction: In an acute attack of familial periodic paralysis, complete absence of electrical excitability may occur. Normal excitability may return after the attack.

F. Miscellaneous: Muscular dystrophy may be characterized by a disparity between the feeble muscle contraction elicited on electrical stimulation and the apparent mass of pseudohypertrophic muscle. Vascular disorders that produce impaired circulation (eg, Buerger's disease) may produce increased chronaxie in muscles of affected extremities. In atrophies of disuse and in paralysis not due to lower motor neuron disease, the chronaxie of motor points is usually normal.

19 | Radiologic Examination

ROENTGENOGRAPHY
OF THE SKULL

A complete roentgenographic study of the skull may require 6–7 different views. For most routine studies, however, a right and left lateral view, a posteroanterior view, and an oblique anteroposterior (Towne) view are adequate.

The skull is slightly asymmetric, and one half is usually slightly larger in the posteroanterior view. In this view, the frontal sinuses may appear to be of different shape and size and the septum slightly to the right or left of center. The right and left nasal cavities may also be of different shape and size.

In the lateral view, one can get a general impression of the convexity of the skull and its size and

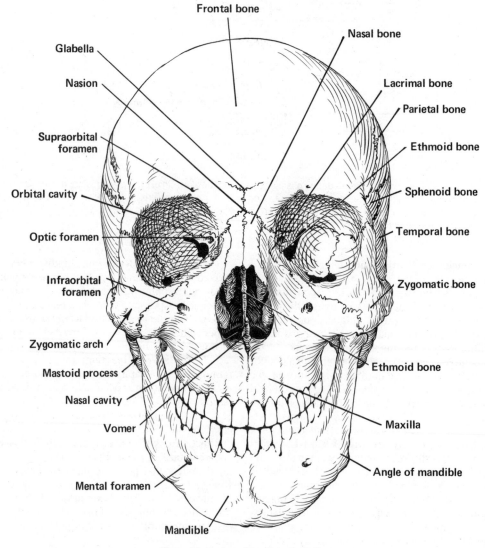

Figure 19–1. Anterior view of skull.

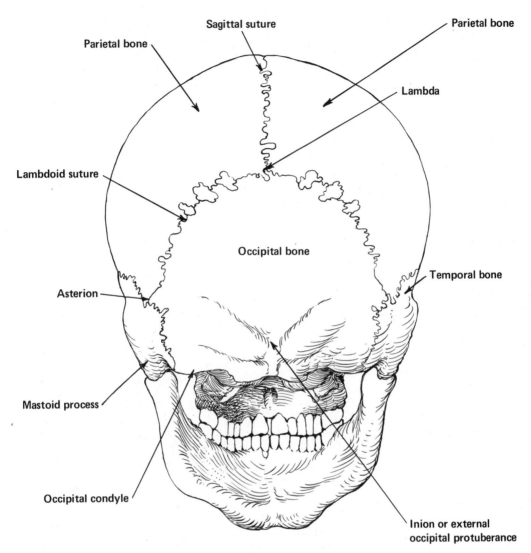

Figure 19–2. Posterior view of skull.

relationship to the facial bones (Fig 19–3). The cranial wall varies in thickness in different individuals as well as in different regions of the skull; it usually appears to be either homogeneous or granular. In elderly persons, coarse mottling or pronounced osteoporosis may occur. The cranial wall varies in thickness from 3–5 mm in the frontoparietal regions to 15 mm in the area of the occipital protuberance. The sphenoidal sinuses vary considerably in size and extension; the petrous bone is seen as a dense triangular shadow.

The cranial sutures are usually easily recognized in skull roentgenograms, particularly the coronal, lambdoid, and temporoparietal sutures. The coronal suture is especially evident near the vertex in the lateral view. Occasionally, sutures ossify in later life and may be difficult to identify. Suture lines, especially in children, may be readily mistaken for fractures. The infant skull often shows sutures and bones not seen in the adult skull.

Skull roentgenograms of normal adults frequently show dense shadows of varying size, shape, and position. These correspond to deposits of calcium in certain intracranial structures such as the pineal body, the falx cerebri, the tentorium cerebelli, the choroid plexuses, the pacchionian granulations, and the habenular commissure. **Reid's base line** (Fig 19–5) passes through the center of the external auditory meatus and the lower orbital margin. It is sometimes more convenient to use the orbitomeatal line, which joins the external auditory meatus to the outer canthus of the eye, as a line of reference.

Roentgenograms of the skull may show abnormal features in association with neurologic disorders. These include the following:

(1) Skull deformities: Congenital malformations, hydrocephalus, basilar impression.

(2) Head injuries: Skull fractures, bony skull defects, subdural hematoma.

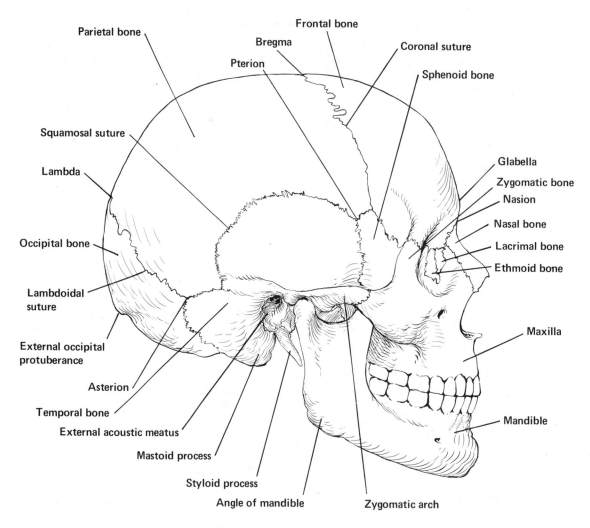

Figure 19–3. Lateral view of skull.

(3) Skull lesions: Osteitis, hyperostosis, osteomas, skull tumor, vascular lesions of the scalp.

(4) Systemic disease: Xanthomatosis, osteitis deformans, marble bones, hyperparathyroidism, rickets, chondrodystrophy, erythroblastic anemia, senile atrophy, tuberous sclerosis, cretinism, mongolism.

(5) Brain calcifications: Toxoplasmosis, Sturge-Weber syndrome, endocrine disorders.

(6) Increased intracranial pressure: Brain tumor, brain abscess, hydrocephalus, intracranial hematoma.

(7) Vascular anomalies: Cerebral aneurysm, vascular malformations of the brain.

Plain x-rays may reveal significant information in a variety of disorders and diseases of the CNS. Skull roentgenograms may disclose typical changes suggestive of an intracranial tumor. In children, these include suture diastasis or separation, sellar changes, and increased convolutional markings of the cranial vault. In adults, there may be sellar changes ranging from de-

mineralization and thinning of the dorsum sellae to actual erosion or pineal displacement.

Intracranial calcifications may occur with a variety of neurologic disorders. Among brain tumors, calcification may be seen in (1) gliomas, especially slow-growing ones such as oligodendrogliomas; (2) meningiomas, especially those that are parasagittal or along the sphenoid ridge; and (3) craniopharyngiomas, usually suprasellar and in children.

Vascular calcification commonly occurs in cerebral arteriosclerosis and is usually situated in the carotid artery (carotid siphon) as it lies in the cavernous sinus. The walls of cerebral aneurysms may show circular or arcuate calcifications. Basal ganglia calcification may occur with hypoparathyroidism or pseudohypoparathyroidism.

In Sturge-Weber syndrome (trigeminal angiomatosis), typical "railroad track" calcification (double linear) may be seen. This is due to calcification or opacification of atrophic cerebral cortex, usually in the occipital regions. Intracranial calcification in

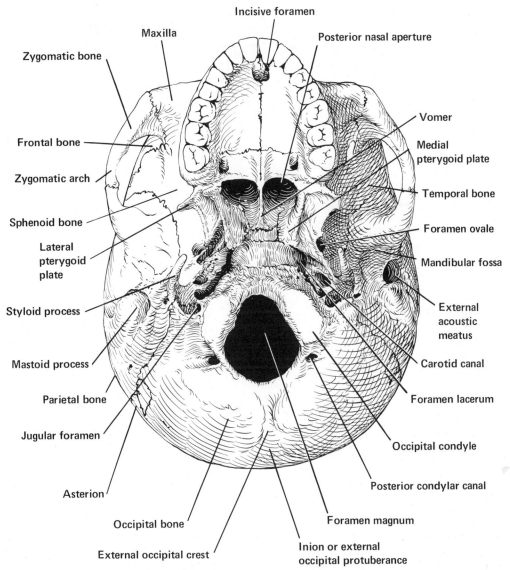

Incisive foramen
Maxilla
Posterior nasal aperture
Zygomatic bone
Vomer
Medial pterygoid plate
Frontal bone
Zygomatic arch
Temporal bone
Sphenoid bone
Foramen ovale
Lateral pterygoid plate
Mandibular fossa
Styloid process
External acoustic meatus
Mastoid process
Carotid canal
Parietal bone
Foramen lacerum
Jugular foramen
Occipital condyle
Asterion
Posterior condylar canal
Occipital bone
Foramen magnum
External occipital crest
Inion or external occipital protuberance

Figure 19-4. Basal view of skull.

tuberous sclerosis tends to be subcortical and paraventricular and is more marked after puberty.

Local erosions or enlargements of foramens occur with some intracranial masses. In acoustic neurinoma, enlargement of the internal auditory meatus, producing funnel-shaped or fish-mouth deformity, may be detected on routine x-rays. A glioma of the optic nerve may enlarge the optic foramen. The superior orbital fissure may enlarge with retro-orbital aneurysm or meningioma. Ballooning of the sella turcica is usually due to chromophobe and, more rarely, to eosinophilic adenoma of the pituitary. The foramen spinosum may be enlarged unilaterally with meningiomas because of the enlarged meningeal vessels on the affected side.

Hyperostosis of local type may be caused by meningioma. Characteristic sites of meningioma formation include the parasagittal area, the sphenoid ridge, the olfactory groove, and the base of the skull. A more benign form of hyperostosis is hyperostosis frontalis interna, which is usually bilateral, sparing the midline; it affects only the inner table of the skull and occurs with high frequency in postmenopausal women.

Increased vascular markings, if generalized, pronounced, and symmetric, may be associated with intracranial vascular malformation. Locally increased meningeal or diploic markings often occur with angioma or meningioma.

INTRACRANIAL PNEUMOGRAPHY

Intracranial pneumography has become one of the most valuable diagnostic aids at the disposal of the

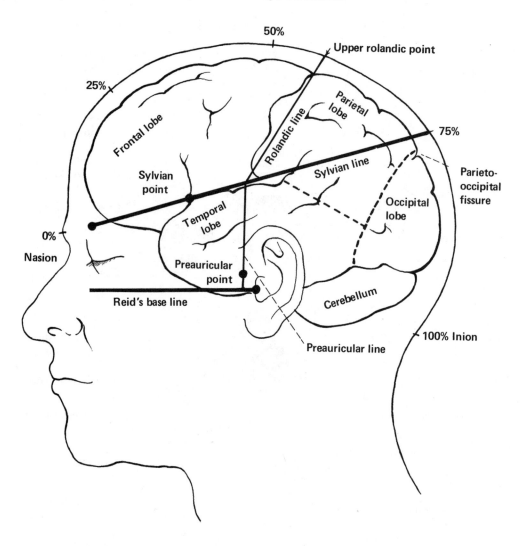

Figure 19–5. Determination of the fissure of Rolando (central cerebral sulcus) and fissure of Sylvius (lateral cerebral fissure). (Reproduced, with permission, from Taylor & Haughton: *Trans R Acad Med Ireland* 1900; **18**:511.)

neurologist or neurosurgeon. Its purpose is to localize intracranial disease. The procedure is based upon the principle that a gaseous replacement of the fluid within the ventricular and subarachnoid systems offers a contrast medium, air being much less dense than fluid to roentgen rays. In this manner, the convolutions and ventricles can be visualized.

An encephalogram is a roentgenogram of the skull following replacement of cerebrospinal fluid by air or oxygen by means of lumbar puncture. The subarachnoid spaces, including the cisterns and ventricles, can usually be visualized by this method. It is contraindicated whenever lumbar puncture is not safe.

A ventriculogram is a roentgenogram of the skull following replacement of cerebrospinal fluid by air or oxygen by means of ventricular puncture. This is an operating room procedure. Ventricular puncture drains only the ventricular system; the subarachnoid spaces and cisterns are not visible in this film. Ventriculog-

raphy is usually considered safer than encephalography in the diagnosis of expanding intracranial lesions.

In patients with posterior fossa lesions or obstructive hydrocephalus, it is sometimes desirable and helpful to perform ventriculography with a positive contrast medium. Iophendylate (Pantopaque) is usually injected into a lateral ventricle with the patient's head so positioned that the contrast medium will fall into an anterior horn. The head is then manipulated carefully so that the medium enters the third ventricle and thence the cerebral aqueduct and the fourth ventricle.

PNEUMOENCEPHALOGRAPHY

Pneumoencephalography is widely used for demonstrating cerebral structures. The technique is to replace measured quantities of cerebrospinal fluid with

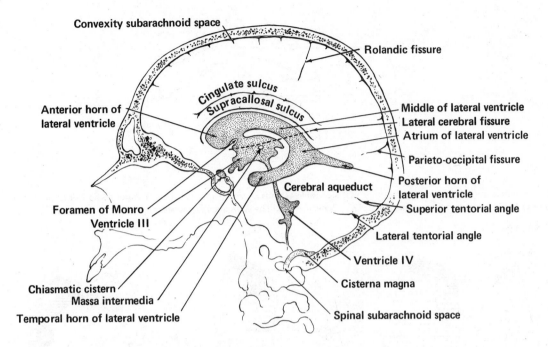

Figure 19–6. Lateral encephalogram.

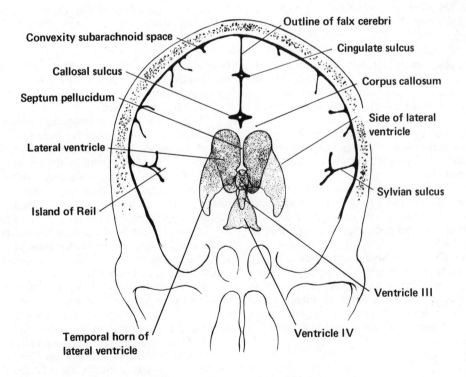

Figure 19–7. Anteroposterior encephalogram.

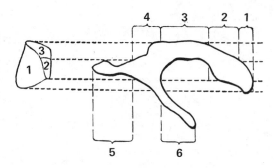

The lateral ventricle divided into 6 portions that are visible as units in anteroposterior views. The dotted horizontal lines serve to project portions 1, 2, and 3 on an imaginary plate. These lines would be approximately parallel to the base of the skull.

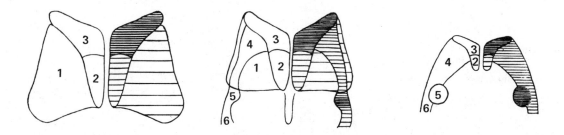

Figure 19–8. Normal anatomy of the lateral ventricle as determined by ventriculographic studies. (Rearranged and reproduced, with permission, from Peele: *The Neuroanatomical Basis for Clinical Neurology.* Blakiston, 1954.)

air or some other suitable gas introduced by means of lumbar puncture (or, more rarely, by cisternal puncture). It is used mainly in those cases in which intracranial cerebrospinal fluid pressure is not increased.

Air is believed to enter the ventricular system mainly through the medial foramen of the fourth ventricle (foramen of Magendie), situated at the top of the funnel-shaped cisterna magna.

Failure of filling of the ventricular system may be due to increased intracranial pressure, the valvelike action of the pia arachnoid at the medial foramen of the fourth ventricle, or other mechanical causes of obstruction at this site.

It is usually best to wait about 10 days after a previous lumbar puncture before attempting pneumoencephalography. This is to avoid entering a fluid-distended subdural space instead of subarachnoid space. Although air may be injected by the cisternal as well as the lumbar route, the latter is preferred for technical reasons.

Indications

Pneumoencephalography has been useful in the study of patients with epilepsy, cerebral atrophies, congenital brain lesions, and posttraumatic cerebral disorders.

Brain tumors may produce relatively characteris-

tic alterations in ventricular pattern, suggesting tumor location and type. These tumors may be classed radiographically as follows:

A. Supratentorial:

1. Lateral–These produce displacement of the septum pellucidum and third ventricle away from the side of the lesion. The physician usually can estimate the height, size, and location of the lesion.

2. Midline–These include tumors of the corpus callosum, septum pellucidum, third ventricle, and adjacent region, most of which have characteristic appearances on pneumoencephalography. Suprasellar tumors may be considered part of this group and include craniopharyngioma, extensions of pituitary adenomas, meningioma of tuberculum sellae, chiasmatic gliomas, and aneurysms.

B. Infratentorial: These can often be precisely localized, especially with the use of added techniques such as autotomography. Useful radiographic landmarks in this group include the following:

1. Twining's line–The midpoint of a line joining the tuberculum sellae to the internal occipital protuberance (in lateral view) normally lies in the fourth ventricle.

2. Lysholm's line–The cerebral aqueduct lies below the junction of the first and second thirds of a line from the clivus through the aqueduct to the skull vault.

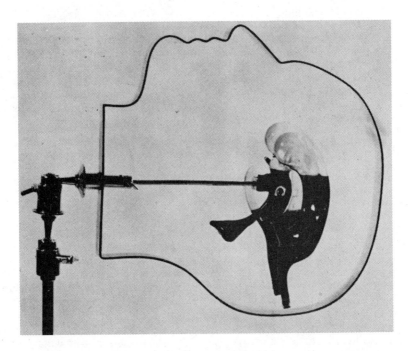

Figure 19–9. Brow-up position of a model of the ventricular system partially filled with air. (Reproduced, with permission, from De Vet: Translucent glass model of the cerebral ventricular system. *J Neurosurg* 1951;**8**:454.)

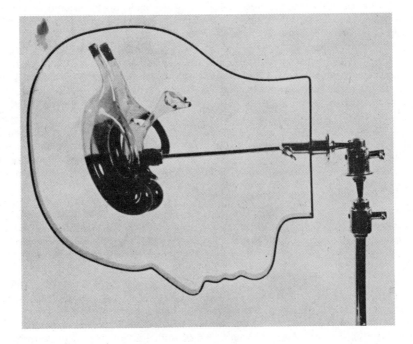

Figure 19–10. Occiput-up position of a model of the ventricular system partially filled with air. (Reproduced, with permission, from De Vet: Translucent glass model of the cerebral ventricular system. *J Neurosurg* 1951;**8**:454.)

Technique

Simple replacement of cerebrospinal fluid by air without the use of elaborate apparatus is widely used. A manometric reading of the cerebrospinal fluid pressure prior to the injection of air is always indicated. Lumbar puncture is made under local anesthesia (in children, a general anesthetic is used). When large quantities of gas are injected, about 5% less gas than the volume of cerebrospinal fluid withdrawn is injected; this is to allow for expansion of the injected gas at body temperature. Cerebrospinal fluid should not be aspirated but should be allowed to escape spontaneously. The rate of escape of fluid and injection of the gas should not exceed 5 mL in one minute. The quantity of gas injected varies. Fifty to 70 mL is usually sufficient to adequately fill the ventricles and subarachnoid spaces. The normal capacity of the ventricular system is 18–20 mL of gas. In marked hydrocephalus, 120–150 mL of gas may be required.

Modified Robertson's Technique (Fractional Encephalography)

With the subject seated and the head slightly flexed, 5 mL of filtered air are slowly injected at a rate of 1 mL/min. A posteroanterior x-ray is then taken; this usually shows air in the fourth ventricle, the aqueduct, and the third ventricle. Cerebrospinal fluid is allowed to drip slowly through the needle until the manometer indicates approximately initial pressure; another 5 mL of gas is then injected and another posteroanterior x-ray taken. After injection of another 5 mL of gas, a lateral view (with the patient still sitting) is taken; this view should show air in the fourth ventricle, the aqueduct, the posterosuperior part of the third ventricle, the posterior horns, and the posterior parts of the bodies of the lateral ventricles. Alternate introduction of air and removal of cerebrospinal fluid are continued until a satisfactory filling of the ventricles is obtained. In normal subjects, about 20 mL of air is sufficient to fill the ventricles. To outline the basal cisterns, the head and neck are slightly extended and, after introduction of a further quantity of air, a lateral x-ray taken. After removal of the needle, the patient is placed in the supine position, which brings air into the anterior parts of the lateral and third ventricles. An anteroposterior x-ray is then taken in this position. The subject then is placed in the prone position and a posteroanterior x-ray made. Supplementary views, including lateral and oblique, may then be made to complete the study.

Absorption of Air

Air is absorbed most rapidly from the subarachnoid spaces over the convexity of the cerebral hemispheres, frequently within 24 hours. Air in the cisterns may be absorbed in 48 hours. Air in the ventricles may be absorbed for the most part in 72 hours.

Complications

Headache and nausea and vomiting are relatively minor complications that may occur after pneumoen-cephalography and usually respond well to symptomatic therapy and rest flat in bed. Disturbances of intracranial pressure and beginning tentorial or medullary pressure cones may lead to grave consequences. Ventricular tap and prompt decompression may be immediately necessary in this group.

In the presence of elevated cerebrospinal fluid pressure, a pneumoencephalogram is hazardous. The risk is reduced by controlled encephalography using small quantities of air.

ANGIOGRAPHY

Iodopyracet (Diodrast) and, less frequently, Thorotrast (thorium dioxide, 25% suspension) were first used as contrast media in angiographic studies. Diodrast, when used in 35% concentration, is relatively nontoxic. Thorotrast carries the threat of delayed reactions because of its persistent radioactivity and its prolonged retention in significant amounts by the reticuloendothelial system. Contrast media such as acetrizoate (Urokon), diatrizoate (Hypaque), and meglumine diatrizoate and sodium diatrizoate injection (Renografin) have proved to be more satisfactory and are now widely used.

The injection may be made through the intact skin or following operative exposure of a suitable vessel. After injection of the selected artery, roentgenograms may be made of the arterial and venous phases of circulation through the brain and head.

Normal Findings

Internal carotid injections may disclose the arterial vessels of the cerebral hemispheres. The internal carotid artery may be visualized as it penetrates the skull, usually in a single or double S-curve. The ophthalmic artery branch is the first major branch and enters the orbit through the optic foramen. The posterior communicating artery is seldom seen. The small anterior choroidal artery is frequently seen and passes posteriorly to enter the choroid plexuses of the lateral ventricles.

The anterior cerebral artery, which passes anteriorly and medially and curves around the genu of the corpus callosum, is readily visualized. The frontopolar artery is a branch that passes toward the frontal pole. The pericallosal artery is a branch that curves posteriorly and remains adjacent to the corpus callosum. The callosomarginal artery also extends posteriorly and supplies the uppermost medial portion of the cerebral hemispheres.

The middle cerebral artery is readily seen in normal subjects and curves posteriorly into the lateral cerebral fissure. The ascending frontoparietal artery is a branch that supplies the inferior frontoparietal area. The terminal branches of the middle cerebral artery are known as the sylvian group and consist of the posterior parietal artery, which supplies the convexity of the

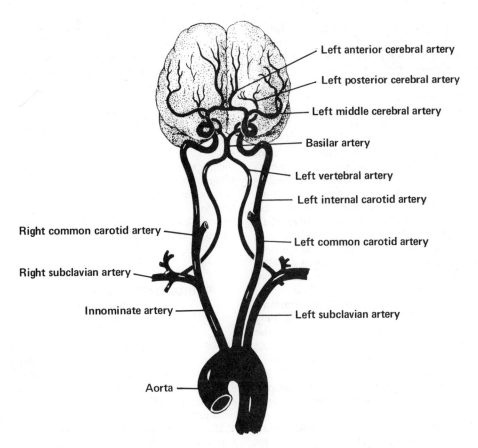

Left anterior cerebral artery

Left posterior cerebral artery

Left middle cerebral artery

Basilar artery

Left vertebral artery

Left internal carotid artery

Right common carotid artery

Left common carotid artery

Right subclavian artery

Innominate artery

Left subclavian artery

Aorta

Figure 19–11. Cerebral arteries.

parietal lobe; the angular artery, which supplies the angular gyrus and the adjacent parieto-occipital area; and the posterior temporal artery, which supplies the superoposterior portion of the temporal lobe.

Vertebral arteriograms disclose the circulation of the structures of the posterior fossa and the posterior portions of the cerebral hemispheres. The course of the vertebral artery may be seen as it passes upward. The posterior inferior cerebellar artery may be visualized as the first intracranial branch and supplies the ventrolateral portion of the cerebellum and medulla. The basilar artery is formed by the 2 vertebral arteries at the junction of the pons and medulla. The anterior inferior cerebellar and the superior cerebellar arteries, supplying the dorsum of the cerebellum and midbrain, may be visualized. The 2 posterior cerebral arteries are the terminal branches of the basilar artery; they supply the basilar portions of the temporal and occipital lobes.

Visualization of the venous passages following internal carotid artery injection demonstrates 3 major collecting systems: (1) The superficial cerebral veins are variable in number and empty into the superior longitudinal sinus and the transverse sinus. (2) The deep cerebral veins drain the basal ganglia. The internal cerebral vein (located in the tela choroidea on the dorsal surface of each thalamus) drains the basal vein of Rosenthal, which comes from the base of the brain

around the cerebral peduncle. The junction of the 2 internal cerebral veins forms the great cerebral vein of Galen, a short midline vessel that enters the straight sinus. (3) The venous sinuses include the superior longitudinal sinus, which terminates in the confluence of sinuses by joining the lateral and straight sinuses; and the inferior longitudinal sinus, located at the inferior edges of the falx cerebri, which forms the straight sinus by joining with the great cerebral vein of Galen.

Clinical Applications

Angiography is of value in demonstrating intracranial aneurysms, vascular disorders, hematomas, and tumors. **Meningiomas** usually obtain their vascular supply chiefly from branches of the external carotid artery and are most readily seen in the venous phase of the angiogram. In addition to displacing adjacent vessels, cerebral **gliomas** may present typical vascular patterns. Frontal gliomas may dislocate the anterior cerebral artery toward the opposite side and may depress the sylvian group of vessels. Parietal gliomas may push the anterior cerebral artery to the opposite side; occasionally, there may also be depression of the terminal portions of the anterior cerebral artery. Temporal gliomas characteristically displace the vessels of the sylvian group upward, especially if they are near the tip of the temporal lobe. Increased vascularity is typical of glioblastoma multiforme and metastatic carcinomas. **Hematomas** are characterized by avascular local areas with displacement of adjacent vessel trunks. Alterations may be demonstrated in intracranial and extracranial arteries to the brain and head, including occlusion, stenosis, angulation, distortion, malformation, and anomalous course and distribution.

Cerebral angiography often provides localization and clues to pathologic types of tumor. The blood supply and vascularity to a mass can thus be clearly defined. Tumors of the cerebral hemispheres usually displace the anterior cerebral artery across the midline. Local stretching of arteries near the tumor may disclose the exact site of the tumor. Characteristic deformities and displacement of deep cerebral veins may help localize tumors of the midline and the basal ganglia area. Highly vascular tumors such as glioblastoma multiforme, meningioma, and metastatic tumor may be visualized by a tumor stain, or blush.

Vascular lesions such as intracranial aneurysms and angiomatous malformations usually require study by angiography before adequate therapy can be planned. Angiography has stimulated increased efforts to decrease morbidity and mortality rates associated with bleeding aneurysms. In relatively small accessible arteriovenous malformations, angiography has led to increasing use of extirpation and allied types of therapy.

Subdural hematoma usually can be readily diagnosed by angiography. A characteristic avascular area between the brain and adjacent skull vault may be seen on anteroposterior skull x-rays.

Internal carotid artery thrombosis often occurs within 1 cm of the origin of this artery in the neck from the common carotid artery and is readily demonstrable by angiography. Anastomosis between the ophthalmic artery and the external carotid artery (via the maxillary artery) may be demonstrable, as well as increased blood supply to the affected cerebral hemisphere from occipital vertebral anastomoses.

In selected patients, the association of stenosis of the internal carotid artery in the neck has led to endarterectomy in the belief that such vessels are precursors to local internal carotid artery thrombosis. In such cases, preoperative and postoperative angiography are essential for adequate clinical management and evaluation.

Vertebral angiography by a variety of techniques may disclose evidence of expanding masses or vascular lesions of the posterior fossa. A characteristic vascular stain may occur with hemangioblastoma or meningioma of the posterior fossa; however, pneumography may be more effective in demonstrating pontine and cerebellopontine angle masses. Vascular lesions of the posterior fossa (aneurysm, angioma, stenosis, etc) usually require vertebral angiography for adequate visualization.

RADIOISOTOPIC ENCEPHALOGRAPHY
(Brain Scan)

Recent technical improvements and new radioisotopic compounds have increased the reliability and accuracy of radioisotopic encephalography.

Formerly, chlormerodrin Hg 203 and chlormerodrin Hg 197 were widely used. Currently, the most extensively used radioisotope for brain scanning studies is technetium Tc 99m, which is injected intravenously as sodium pertechnetate in doses of 10–15 mCi. Emitted gamma rays are detected on a scanner or a scintillation camera.

The patient receives an intravenous injection of technetium Tc 99m after pretreatment with Lugol's solution or potassium perchlorate to block technetium Tc 99m uptake in the choroid plexus and salivary glands. Multiple view gamma images are obtained an hour later.

For ready detection, the ratio of lesion uptake to background should exceed 3:1, and the lesion should be over 1–2 cm in diameter. Lesions near normal

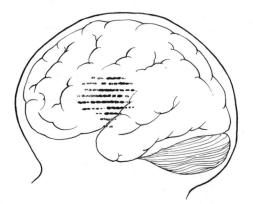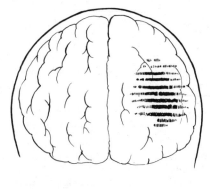

Figure 19–12. Brain scan (radioisotope encephalogram) with radioactive mercury on patient with meningioma. (Redrawn and reproduced, with permission, from Overton, Snodgrass, & Haynie: *JAMA* 1965;**192**:747.)

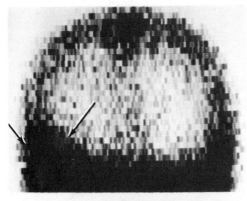

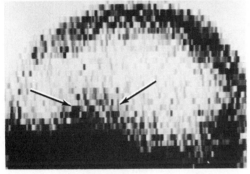

Figure 19–13. Anterior *(top)* and lateral *(bottom)* views of brain scan of a 73-year-old woman with right frontotemporal glioblastoma multiforme.

vascular structures, especially in the middle and posterior fossae, may be obscured by background radioactivity.

The patient's head is immobilized, and appropriate landmarks (vertex of skull, nasion, external auditory meatus, and glabella) are recorded before scanning. Scans are obtained in the anteroposterior, lateral, and posteroanterior positions. Suspected lesions are more readily detected when the lesion is nearer the probe.

Focal intracranial abnormalities in brain scans are believed to relate to (1) alteration in blood-brain barrier, (2) abnormal blood vessels of sufficient size, and (3) abnormal cerebrovascular filling and cerebral perfusion.

Positive brain scans (increased focal uptake) may be obtained with brain tumors, subdural hematomas, brain abscesses, and cerebral infarcts. Among neoplasms, meningiomas stand out, particularly in scans (Fig 33–1).

Delayed scanning, in which a second brain scan is done 3–4 hours following intravenous isotope injection, enhances the detection of some lesions, especially brain tumors.

RADIOISOTOPIC CISTERNOGRAPHY

Information about cerebrospinal fluid flow and reabsorption may be obtained by radioisotopic cisternography.

Intrathecal injection into the lumbar subarachnoid space of an appropriate radioisotopic compound such as 100 mCi of radioiodinated (^{131}I) albumin (RIHSA I 131) is followed by sequential imaging of the radioactivity over the spinal cord at 4, 24, and 48 hours after injection.

Normally, by 4–6 hours the activity has ascended from the lumbar level to the head, appearing in the cisterna magna, basal cisterns, and subtentorial subarachnoid spaces. A small amount of activity may be noted in the supratentorial subarachnoid space.

By 24–48 hours, most of the activity has passed over the cerebral convexities, with some midline or parasagittal accumulation. Normally, the isotope passes over the cerebral convexities without entering the ventricles.

A block in the flow of cerebrospinal fluid interferes with the movement of labeled cerebrospinal fluid at the level of the lesion. In patients with communicating or normal pressure hydrocephalus, there usually is a block of normal parasagittal reabsorption of cerebrospinal fluid, so that there is no flow of activity over the convexities and the isotope moves into the ventricles, where it remains for the duration of the study (48 hours or longer).

COMPUTERIZED TOMOGRAPHY
(CT Scan)

Computerized x-ray examination of the brain is a very useful and informative neurodiagnostic tool. The examination is relatively safe and easy to conduct, and it can be performed on an outpatient basis without difficulty.

Scanning of the head in successive layers by a narrow beam of x-rays enables the transmission of x-ray photons in each layer to be measured. A small computer is used to process the accumulated x-ray photon data.

In the EMI model of the CT scanner, a total of 160 readings of photon transmission is taken during each degree traversal of a 180-degree field. These 28,800 readings form the basis of the simultaneous equations solved by the computer that are then transformed into absorption coefficients.

Values are calculated for tissue blocks $3 \times 3 \times 13$ mm, and the results are displayed as a digital printout of the absorption coefficients of each of 6400 small blocks of tissue and also as a display on a cathode ray tube in which the brightness is proportionate to the absorption values. A picture of the internal structure of the brain in terms of shape, size, and position, with alterations of normal density indicating pathologic change, may be constructed from these data.

For clinical use of the results, the series of images

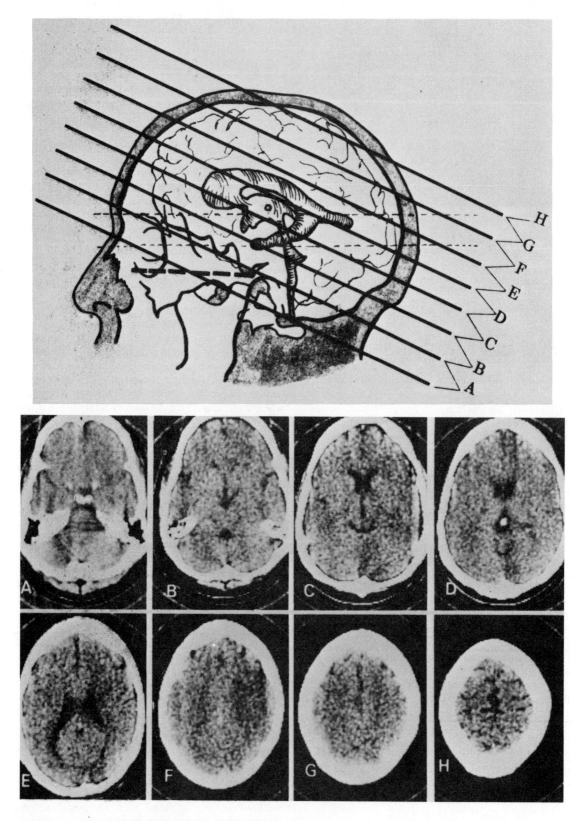

Figure 19–14. Normal CT scan. *Top:* Tomographic planes used in CT scan. Lines define the planes (perpendicular to the page) cut by the CT scanner; letters correspond to the computed projection at bottom. (Reproduced, with permission, from Taveras JM, Wood EH: *Diagnostic Neuroradiology,* 2nd ed. Williams & Wilkins, 1976.)

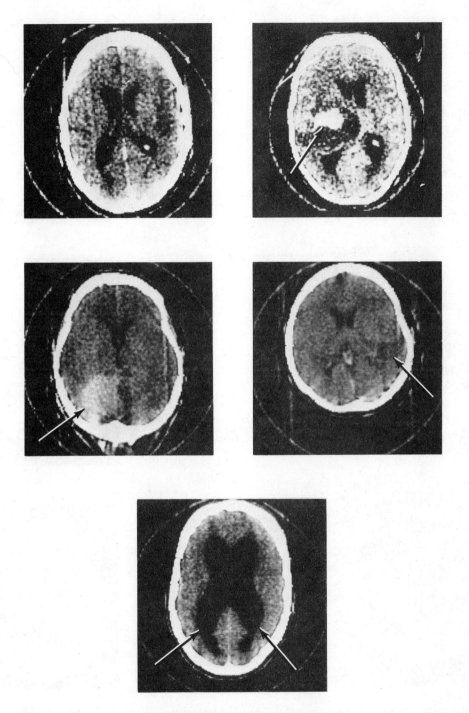

Figure 19–15. Representative examples of computerized tomograms (CT scans). *Top left:* Alzheimer's disease. Dilated ventricles and cerebral sulci in a 59-year-old man with progressive dementia. *Top right:* Brain tumor. Left cerebral glioma in a 21-year-old woman with progressive right spastic hemiparesis and right homonymous hemianopsia. *Center left:* Brain tumor. Meningioma in left posterior fossa in a 33-year-old woman with ataxia, dysmetria, headaches, and papilledema. *Center right:* Postencephalomalacic cyst. Right temporoparietal cyst in a 48-year-old hypertensive woman recovered from an old episode of acute left hemiplegia. *Bottom:* Communicating hydrocephalus. Dilated ventricles in a 44-year-old man with mild organic brain syndrome.

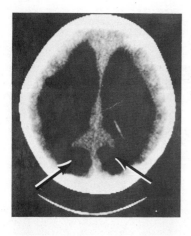

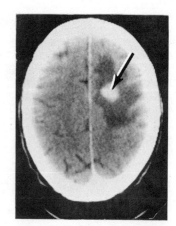

Top left: Hydrocephalus. Dilated ventricles in a 7-year-old boy who had undergone a shunting operation at age 1 year.

Top right: Brain tumor. Cerebral metastasis from carcinoma of lung in a 65-year-old man.

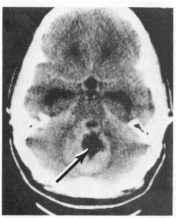

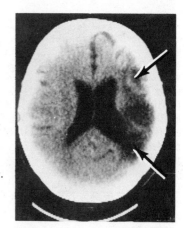

Center left: Brain tumor. Cerebellar medulloblastoma in a 16-year-old male.

Center right: Cerebral hemiatrophy. History of subarachnoid hemorrhage 5 years previously in a 48-year-old woman.

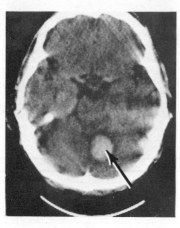

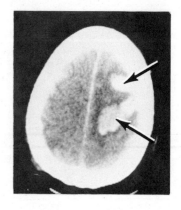

Lower left: Cerebellar hemorrhage. Eighty-one-year-old hypertensive man with acute onset of coma and quadriparesis.

Lower right: Traumatic intracerebral hemorrhage. History of a fall by an intoxicated 78-year-old man, followed by confusion and hemiplegia.

Figure 19–16. Representative examples of computerized tomograms (CT scans). (Courtesy of GP Ballweg.)

on the cathode ray tube is photographed using a Polaroid camera. The scanning examination may usually be completed in less than 30 minutes; the patient is required to lie still for a few minutes at a time during each of 4 or 5 scans.

Normal intracranial structures—such as the ventricular system, cortical gyri and sulci, corpus striatum, internal capsule, pineal body, choroid plexus, and basal cisterns—may be demonstrated. A wide variety of intracranial disorders may be demonstrated, including neoplasms, cerebral infarcts, hydrocephalus, cerebral atrophy, cerebral hemorrhage, cerebral abscess, etc. Intravenous injection of standard roentgenographic contrast media may be used to facilitate the study.

Various types of cerebral atrophy and obstructive

hydrocephalus may be identified. Many types of intra-cranial neoplasms can be recognized by their charac-teristic features. Edema associated with various intra-cerebral masses can be appreciated.

Calcification and vascularity are readily high-lighted. The effects of masses on adjacent structures and the ventricular system may be seen. Cystic lesions can be readily recognized. Although acute extracere-bral hematomas and hygromas are easily detected, some chronic subdural hematomas are more difficult to detect.

Posterior fossa examination is usually less satis-factory than scans at higher levels because of the rela-tively small size of the area and the presence of adja-cent dense bone.

ECHOENCEPHALOGRAPHY

A diagnostic technique of value in neurologic diagnosis involves the use of an ultrasound generator and receiver that display echoes on an oscilloscope with camera attachment for permanent recording. The same transducers used for generation of ultrasound (1–10 MHz) are used for reception. The region of the skull to be investigated is wet with water, mineral oil, or maple syrup, and the tip of the transducer is im-mersed in the same solution before firm application to the side of the head at right angles to the skull. Optimal detection of midline echo comes from application of the transducer 4–5 cm vertically above the external auditory meatus. For detection of tumor echoes, the transducer may be placed at right angles at any locus of the head above the level of the inion and zygoma.

The significance of a shift in the midline echo is analogous to that of a shift of the pineal in plain skull x-rays. The source of a midline echo may be pineal and midline structures such as the third ventricle, septum pellucidum, longitudinal fissure, and falx cerebri.

The "A" scan, a 2-plane time-intensity plot of the skull, indicates the position of the midline struc-tures. The "B" scan integrates many echoes in a 3-dimensional section or tomogram and may localize intracranial masses.

Intracerebral echoes have also been obtained from the lateral ventricles, the lateral cerebral fissure, and space-occupying masses.

Figure 19–17. Echoencephalogram. Normal "A" scan trac-ing.

ROENTGENOGRAPHY OF THE SPINE

Plain x-rays of the spine are often useful in evalu-ation of neurologic disorders. They should be made in suspected spinal cord and spinal root compressions. Evidence of the underlying disease may be demon-strated in congenital lesions such as spina bifida, Klippel-Feil deformity, occipitoatlantal fusion, con-genital hemivertebra, and bony dystrophies. Signs of tuberculosis of the spine, primary or secondary neo-plasms, and trauma to the spine may be readily disclosed on routine films.

Intraspinal tumor may be noted or suspected be-cause of widening or erosion of the vertebral pedicles, local erosion of the intervertebral foramen or the poste-rior surface of a vertebral body, or associated paraspi-nal mass.

Intervertebral disk disease may be noted on plain x-rays by the narrowing of the intervertebral disk space. Osteophytosis or sclerosis of adjacent vertebral margins may also occur. Disk calcification may occa-sionally be demonstrated. Local immobility or fixation of the spine associated with intervertebral disk disease may also be seen in appropriate views.

The results of trauma to the spinal column may also be seen on plain x-rays: compression of vertebral bodies, dislocation of the spine, fractures of vertebrae, alterations of normal curvature, or narrowing of inter-vertebral foramens. Evidence of coexisting narrowing of intervertebral disk space can also be seen.

MYELOGRAPHY

X-rays made after the introduction of a radi-opaque substance into the spinal subarachnoid space are sometimes helpful. Iophendylate (Pantopaque), a liquid of relatively low viscosity, is the contrast medium of choice. It should be aspirated at the termi-nation of the myelographic examination, although re-actions following its use are minimal even when it has been left in the spinal canal for prolonged periods. Metrizamide (Amipaque) is preferred in some centers and is useful in routine lumbar myelography. Me-trizamide is a water-soluble contrast medium that is rapidly absorbed into the general circulation. The puncture needle can be removed immediately follow-ing injection of the medium into the subarachnoid space, since it is not necessary to remove the metriz-amide.

Air injection into the spinal subarachnoid space was formerly used but is technically inferior to iophen-dylate myelography. However, air myelography may be very useful when used with autotomography and especially in the study of the upper cervical portion of the spinal cord.

Technique

The site of injection depends upon the suspected site of the lesion. Since artifacts may be produced by

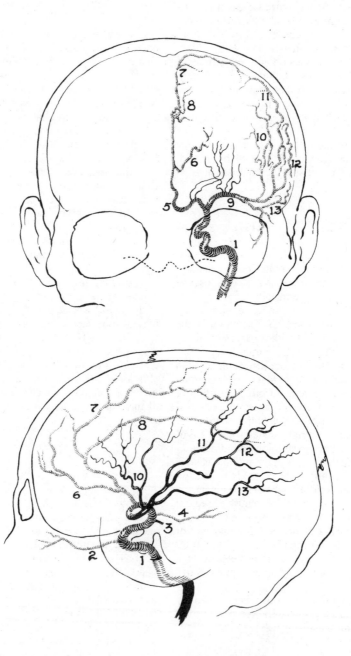

1. Internal carotid artery.
2. Ophthalmic artery.
3. Posterior communicating artery.
4. Anterior choroidal artery.
5. Anterior cerebral artery.
6. Frontopolar artery.
7. Callosomarginal artery.

8. Pericallosal artery.
9. Middle cerebral artery.
10. Ascending frontoparietal artery.
11. Posterior parietal artery.
12. Angular artery.
13. Posterior temporal artery.

Figure 19–18. Schematic drawings of normal arteriograms of the internal carotid artery. *Above:* Anteroposterior projection. *Below:* Lateral projection. (Redrawn and reproduced, with permission, from List, Burge, & Hodges: Intracranial angiography. *Radiology* 1945;**45**:1.)

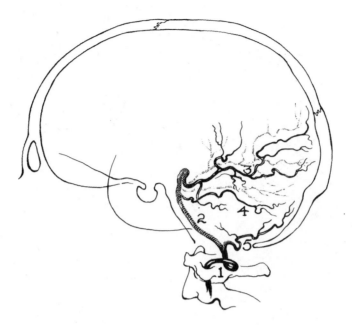

1. Vertebral artery.
2. Basilar artery.
3. Posterior cerebral artery.
4. Superior cerebellar artery.
5. Posterior inferior cerebellar artery.

Figure 19–19. Schematic drawing of a normal vertebral arteriogram in lateral projection. (Redrawn and reproduced, with permission, from List, Burge, & Hodges: Intracranial angiography. *Radiology* 1945;**45**:1.)

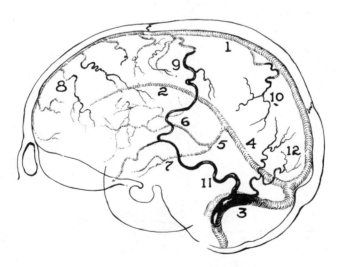

1. Superior sagittal sinus.
2. Inferior sagittal sinus.
3. Transverse sinus.
4. Straight sinus.
5. Great cerebral vein of Galen.
6. Internal cerebral vein.
7. Basal vein of Rosenthal.
8. Frontal ascending vein.
9. Rolandic vein of Trolard.
10. Parietal ascending vein.
11. Communicating temporal vein of Labbé.
12. Descending temporo-occipital vein.

Figure 19–20. Schematic drawing of normal venogram in lateral projection, obtained by carotid injection. Superficial veins are shaded more darkly than the sinuses and deep veins. (Redrawn and reproduced, with permission, from List, Burge, & Hodges: Intracranial angiography. *Radiology* 1945;**45**:1.)

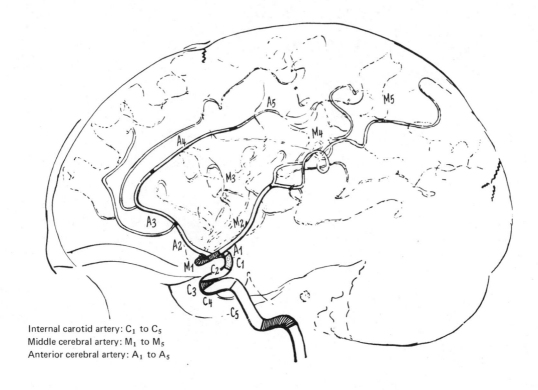

Internal carotid artery: C_1 to C_5
Middle cerebral artery: M_1 to M_5
Anterior cerebral artery: A_1 to A_5

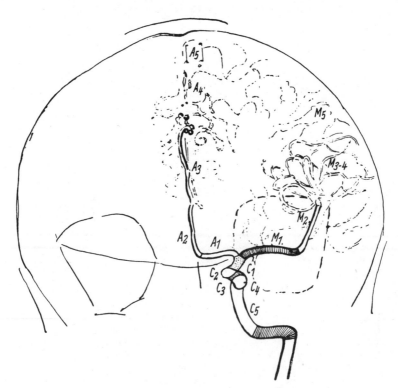

Figure 19–21. Diagrams of lateral *(above)* and anteroposterior *(below)* arteriograms. (Redrawn and reproduced, with permission, from Fischer: *Zentralbl Neurochir* 1938;**3**:300.)

the needle puncture, the spinal subarachnoid space is usually entered at other than the suspected level. Similarly, spinal dynamics (Queckenstedt's test) may be performed prior to the injection of the iophendylate to determine the existence of a partial or complete block in the spinal subarachnoid space. The cerebrospinal fluid removed prior to the injection may be useful for diagnostic tests.

Following the injection of contrast medium, fluoroscopic examination of the spine and spot x-ray films are made on a tilting table.

Clinical Applications

Myelography is used most widely for the demonstration of herniations or protrusions of the intervertebral disks. The myelogram should be interpreted in terms of the clinical findings. Minor or minimal filling defects at an appropriate level may be significant. On the other hand, "characteristic" filling defects are sometimes demonstrated in individuals who have no symptoms. The myelographic abnormalities due to herniated disks may be medially or laterally situated, usually at the level of the intervertebral disk.

A complete block in the flow of contrast medium may be due to a tumor, adhesions, mechanical con-striction as by a bony lesion, or a herniated intervertebral disk. If the presence of a block is determined, introduction of media at a higher spinal or cisternal level may define the physical extent of the block.

With spinal tumors, myelography often provides information regarding the location, nature, and anatomic features of the mass. Intramedullary tumors may show diffuse enlargement of the spinal cord on myelography, and this is characteristically noted with ependymoma and syringomyelia. Extramedullary intradural masses characteristically produce deviation or displacement of the cord by the tumor. Extramedullary extradural masses are apt to be associated with abrupt cut-off of the contrast column, with an irregular "paintbrush" border appearance.

Angiomatous lesions of the spinal cord may be suspected based on the presence of the negative shadows in the contrast column produced by the characteristic wormlike enlarged vessels.

A variety of other lesions that cause spinal cord compression may be demonstrated by myelography. These include extradural spinal abscess, scoliosis and kyphosis of the spine, meningeal adhesions, and spinal column or vertebral compression, fracture, or dislocation.

20 | Cystometry

When the urinary bladder is filled through a catheter with successive increments of fluid, the detrusor musculature of the bladder will contract, producing a measurable increase of intravesical pressure. As 50-mL increments of fluid are introduced, notations are made of the patient's responses: (1) the ability to perceive temperature and entrance of fluid; (2) the point at which "desire to void" is experienced; and (3) the stage at which pain or distress is first felt, as well as the point of severe pain beyond which no further vesical filling can be tolerated.

Urinary bladder filling and emptying are normally automatic processes dependent upon the fact that distention beyond a certain point produces bladder contractions that increase in intensity until a massive contraction empties the bladder. Normally, this reaction is postponed by the action of the higher centers. Because of the neural arrangement at the sphincter, its

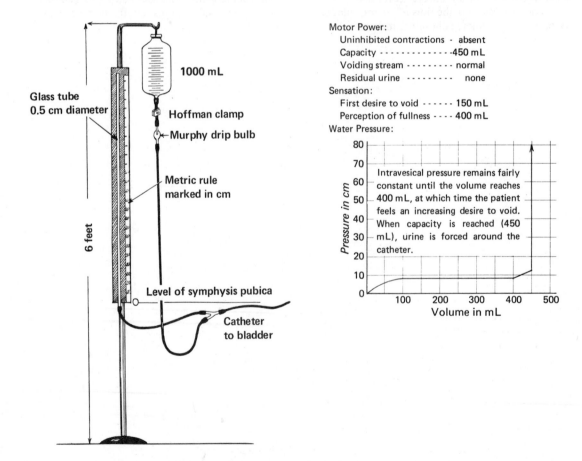

Motor Power:
   Uninhibited contractions - absent
   Capacity - - - - - - - - - - - - -450 mL
   Voiding stream - - - - - - - - normal
   Residual urine - - - - - - - - none
Sensation:
   First desire to void - - - - - - 150 mL
   Perception of fullness - - - - 400 mL
Water Pressure:

1000 mL

Glass tube 0.5 cm diameter

Hoffman clamp

Murphy drip bulb

Metric rule marked in cm

6 feet

Level of symphysis pubica

Catheter to bladder

Intravesical pressure remains fairly constant until the volume reaches 400 mL, at which time the patient feels an increasing desire to void. When capacity is reached (450 mL), urine is forced around the catheter.

Pressure in cm — *Volume in mL*

Figure 20–1. Cystometry. *Left:* A simple water manometer. *Right:* Normal cystometrogram. As fluid is slowly introduced into the bladder, the detrusor gradually relaxes to accept increasing amounts of fluid without change in intravesical pressure. At a volume of 400 mL, the patient felt an urge to void. Shortly thereafter, an involuntary contraction of the detrusor occurred that was reflected in a sharp increase in intravesical pressure. (Reproduced, with permission, from Smith DR: *General Urology,* 10th ed. Lange, 1981.)

function may be considered to be in opposition to that of the bladder muscle (detrusor).

Cystometrograms

A normal cystometrogram records little or no tone initially. As 50-mL increments of fluid are added, the intravesical pressure rises slowly until about 500 mL of solution have been introduced. At this stage, a marked contraction usually occurs, with a sharp rise of intravesical pressure to about 40–100 cm of water.

A normal bladder can usually perceive the entrance of the first fluid injected and can usually interpret temperature. The desire to void, apparently a muscle stretch phenomenon, usually occurs when the bladder is distended with about 200 mL of fluid. Distress may be felt after about 400 mL of filling and severe pain at about 500 mL.

There are 2 types of **neurogenic bladder:** (1) efferent (hypertonic bladder with small capacity, presumably due to lack of inhibition from higher levels upon lower spinal cord segments); and (2) afferent (hypotonic bladder of large capacity).

A. Efferent (Spastic) Neurogenic Bladder: Patients with efferent (spastic) neurogenic bladder may

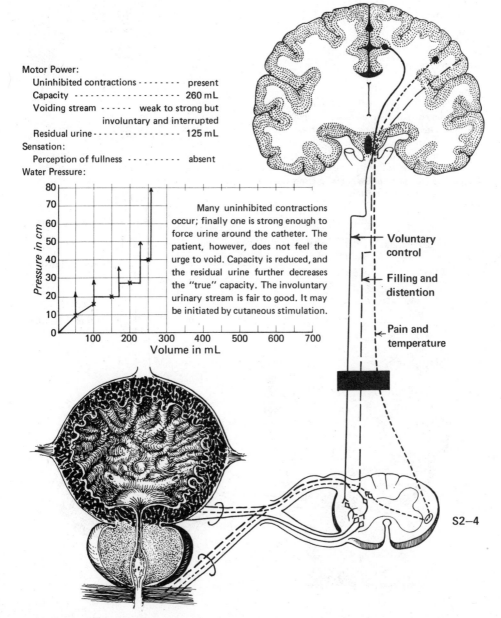

Motor Power:
  Uninhibited contractions · · · · · · · · present
  Capacity · 260 mL
  Voiding stream · · · · · · weak to strong but
                  involuntary and interrupted
  Residual urine · · · · · · · · · · · · · · · · 125 mL
Sensation:
  Perception of fullness · · · · · · · · · · absent
Water Pressure:

Many uninhibited contractions occur; finally one is strong enough to force urine around the catheter. The patient, however, does not feel the urge to void. Capacity is reduced, and the residual urine further decreases the "true" capacity. The involuntary urinary stream is fair to good. It may be initiated by cutaneous stimulation.

Voluntary control

Filling and distention

Pain and temperature

S2–4

Figure 20–2. Spastic neurogenic bladder. Caused by a more or less complete transection of the spinal cord above S2. Cystometric study of a typical case shows function after recovery from spinal shock. (Modified after Nesbit, Lapides, & Baum: *Fundamentals of Urology.* Edwards, 1953.)

show a desire to void with the first or second filling (50–100 mL of fluid), and moderate distention of the bladder causes severe pain. This type of bladder is commonly associated with disorders involving the pyramidal tracts; lesions involving a single pyramidal tract have been claimed to produce hypertonic bladders. The internal sphincter also becomes hypertonic, but not sufficiently so to withstand the effect of the hypertonic detrusor; dribbling and perhaps incontinence result.

B. Afferent (Flaccid) Neurogenic Bladder: Patients with afferent (flaccid) neurogenic bladder may tolerate up to 2 L of fluid added in 50-mL quantities. Desire to void, distress, and pain are produced only when greater than usual amounts of fluid have been added. Hyposensitivity or complete lack of sensitivity may be associated, in which case the desire to void may not occur until 500 mL have been introduced, and distress and severe pain may be delayed until up to 800 mL have been introduced. The internal sphincter pres-

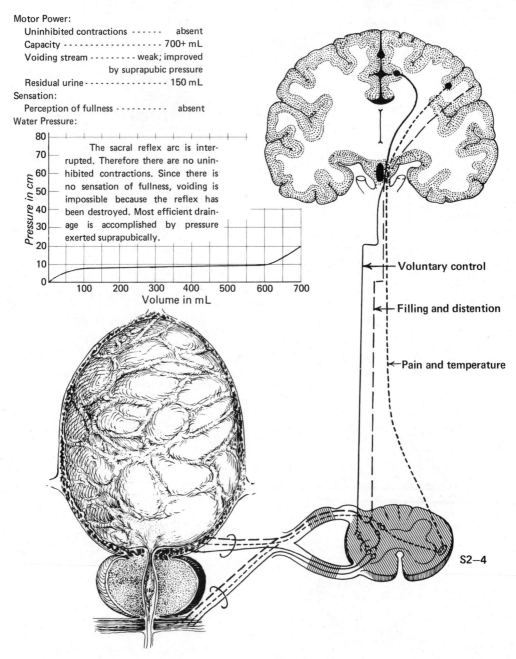

Motor Power:
    Uninhibited contractions · · · · · ·   absent
    Capacity · · · · · · · · · · · · · · · · · · 700+ mL
    Voiding stream · · · · · · · · · weak; improved
                    by suprapubic pressure
    Residual urine · · · · · · · · · · · · · · · 150 mL
Sensation:
    Perception of fullness · · · · · · · · · ·   absent
Water Pressure:

The sacral reflex arc is interrupted. Therefore there are no uninhibited contractions. Since there is no sensation of fullness, voiding is impossible because the reflex has been destroyed. Most efficient drainage is accomplished by pressure exerted suprapubically.

(graph: Pressure in cm vs Volume in mL)

Voluntary control

Filling and distention

Pain and temperature

S2–4

Figure 20–3. Flaccid neurogenic bladder. Caused by a lesion of the sacral portion of the cord or of the cauda equina. Cystometric study of a typical case shows function after recovery from spinal shock. (Modified after Nesbit, Lapides, & Baum: *Fundamentals of Urology.* Edwards, 1953.)

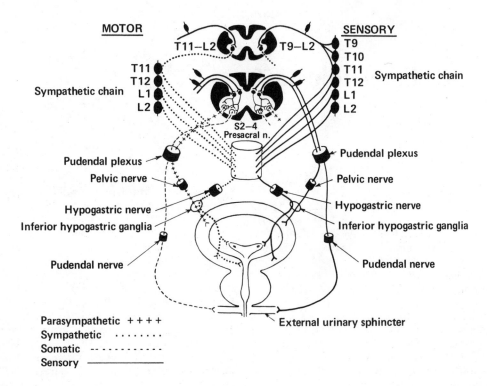

MOTOR   **SENSORY**

T11–L2   T9–L2   T9
                                 T10

T11   T11

T12   T12   **Sympathetic chain**

Sympathetic chain   L1   L1

L2   L2

S2–4
Presacral n.

Pudendal plexus   **Pudendal plexus**

Pelvic nerve   **Pelvic nerve**

Hypogastric nerve   **Hypogastric nerve**

Inferior hypogastric ganglia   **Inferior hypogastric ganglia**

Pudendal nerve   **Pudendal nerve**

Parasympathetic + + + +
Sympathetic . . . .
Somatic - - - - - - - - - - -
Sensory ——————

External urinary sphincter

Figure 20–4. Segmental and peripheral innervation of the urinary bladder. (Reproduced, with permission, from Bors: *J Nerv Ment Dis* 1952; **116**:572.)

sure remains normal despite a hypotonic detrusor muscle. The aid of the voluntary abdominal muscles is therefore frequently required in micturition. This type of bladder is associated with disorders affecting the afferent pathway (end organs, posterior roots, or posterior spinal columns). Hyposensitivity of the bladder may lead to delayed awareness of the need to empty the bladder. Atrophy of the detrusor muscle owing to prolonged overdistention plus inability of the internal sphincter to relax at the proper time may result.

Ice Water Test (Bors)

Sixty milliliters of sterile ice water are introduced into the empty urinary bladder through a 16F whistle-tip catheter. In efferent neurogenic bladder (upper motor neuron lesion), the ice water and even the catheter may be forcefully expelled in a few seconds. In afferent neurogenic bladder (lower motor neuron lesion), no response occurs.

Sphincterometry

When the detrusor muscle of the bladder contracts, the internal sphincter of the bladder relaxes from its normal tonic state. As soon as urine enters the posterior urethra, the external sphincter may relax to allow the stream to pass. The external sphincter, however, can voluntarily restrain the stream unless the urge to void is too great. Normally, internal sphincter tone is about 15 mm Hg (21 cm of water); the external sphincter tone, about 23 mm Hg (32 cm of water).

The external (dominant) sphincter is rarely affected by disease. If its fibers are surgically divided, incontinence results.

The internal sphincter is rarely paralyzed; it may be severely damaged surgically without resultant incontinence.

Incontinence of urine may be of the overflow or the hypertonic type. Normally, the detrusor does not force urine through the internal sphincter. If the detrusor is markedly hypertonic, a normal or even hypertonic sphincter may be overcome.

In overflow incontinence associated with hypotonic, hyposensitive bladders, the incontinence is not due to a defect in function of the internal sphincter. Overflow occurs when intravesical pressure exceeds internal sphincter pressure. When the atonic, atrophic bladder collects a large quantity of urine, intravesical pressure gradually rises (helped by muscle stretch reflex, elasticity of bladder, and contractions of abdominal musculature). Large amounts of residual urine may occur because the internal sphincter has not lost its tone and may close down after a portion of the urine in the bladder has been expelled.

21 | Ophthalmologic Tests

Visual Acuity

The visual acuity of each eye is usually tested separately for distant and near vision. Distant visual acuity may be measured with the aid of a visual acuity chart. A subject with normal visual acuity can read the line of letters at the indicated distances. In the Snellen chart, each line of letters is marked to show the distance at which the parts of the letters subtend 1 minute of arc.

Visual acuity is usually expressed as a fraction, with the numerator as the distance at which the test is made and the denominator the line of the smallest letters that can be read. Distances are usually measured in feet (20 feet) or meters (6 meters). A person with normal visual acuity is thus described as having 20/20 (or 6/6) vision. If the subject normally wears glasses, the test may be made without glasses (uncorrected) and then with glasses (corrected).

The Snellen test chart is commonly used at a distance of 20 feet, with the chart diffusely illuminated without glare or background contrast. A visual acuity of 20/20 usually indicates normal macular function. Relative impairment of visual acuity may be corrected or improved with the use of corrective lenses. In the USA, legal blindness is defined as visual acuity not correctable to better than 20/200.

Near visual acuity may be tested with the aid of a reading card using Jaeger test type. This card is held 14 inches from the subject, and the examiner notes what line of letters the subject can read. Normally, the subject can read the letters of the line designated 14, and the visual acuity is recorded as 14/14.

Pupillary Reactions

The pupils are examined for size, shape, equality, reaction to light stimulus, effect of accommodation, and consensual light reaction. Light directed into one pupil normally constricts the pupils of both eyes. Examination for reaction to light is best performed in a darkened room with the examiner at the side of the subject. Pupils may be markedly constricted (miotic) owing to the effects of bright illumination, CNS disorders, or narcotic or parasympathomimetic drugs.

Anisocoria (unequal pupils) is sometimes normal but may suggest organic nervous system disease (see pp 90–97).

Ophthalmoscopy

Although direct ophthalmoscopic examination is more easily performed through a dilated pupil, a satisfactory examination may be made in most cases through an undilated pupil if the media (aqueous humor, lens, vitreous humor) are clear. The illumination in the examination room should be diminished during the examination.

The gaze of the subject is fixed on a given object, the direction of gaze depending upon the portion of the fundus being examined. The right eye is inspected with the ophthalmoscope held in the right hand of the examiner, who is positioned at the right side of the subject. For examination of the left eye, the instrument is held in the left hand and the examiner is positioned at the left side of the patient. The examiner rotates a +10 or +12 convex lens into the aperture of the ophthalmoscope, directs the light beam toward the subject's eye, and brings the instrument closer to the subject so that the magnified details of the anterior segment of the eye (cornea, iris, and lens) are visualized. The strength of the plus convex lenses is gradually reduced so that the focus of observation extends posteriorly through the vitreous until the retinal details are brought into view.

Details of the optic disk structure are noted. The color of the optic disk, the sharpness of the disk edges, and the details of the physiologic cup are noted. Elevation of the disk (papilledema) may be estimated by comparing the strength of the lens through which the central vessels are seen to the strength required to focus on surrounding adjacent vessels in the same area. The depth of the optic cup, or depression, may be measured similarly. The macular area and the periphery of the retina are examined by having the patient look in the directions that are to be examined. The size and regularity of the retinal vessels, as well as the presence of hemorrhages, exudates, pigmentation, or other abnormalities, are noted.

Ocular Movements

Ocular movements may be tested by having the subject turn the eyes in the 6 cardinal directions of gaze and by having the eyes converge on a near point (see pp 90–93). Weakness or paralysis of one or several muscles, conjugate eye movements, and the presence of nystagmus are noted. The function of individual extraocular muscles is best tested by observing them in the field of their maximal or best action.

The subject is requested to look first to one side and then to the other in order to test the medial and

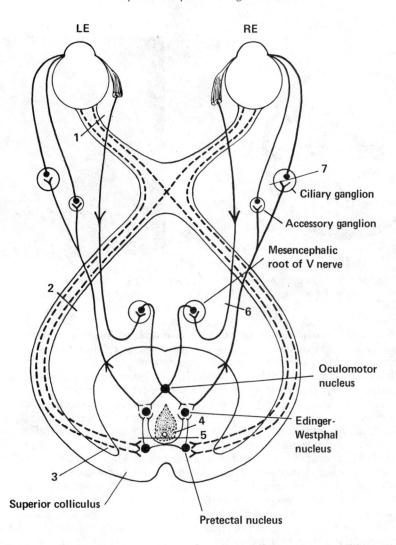

LE   RE

7 — Ciliary ganglion

Accessory ganglion

Mesencephalic
root of V nerve

6

Oculomotor
nucleus

4
5
Edinger-
Westphal
nucleus

3

Superior colliculus

Pretectal nucleus

1. Lesion at optic nerve. Loss of direct and opposite consensual reaction. Retention of near reflex.
2. Lesion at optic tract. Contralateral hemianopsic loss of reaction (Wernicke's).
3. Lesion at optic tract beyond the point at which the pupillary fibers leave optic tract. No pupillary reaction loss (right homonymous hemianopsia present).
4. Lesion between decussation and Edinger-Westphal nucleus. Loss of ipsilateral direct and consensual reaction.

Near reflex intact (unilateral Argyll Robertson pupil).
5. Lesion of all fibers from pretectal nucleus to Edinger-Westphal nucleus. Loss of all light response. Retention of near reflex (complete Argyll Robertson pupil).
6. Lesion of cranial nerve III. Absolute ipsilateral pupillary paralysis.
7. Lesion of ciliary ganglion. Ipsilateral loss of light reflex with retention of near reflex (unilateral Argyll Robertson pupil).

Figure 21–1. Pupillary pathways for light reflex and miosis of accommodation. Solid lines = efferent pathway. Dotted lines = afferent pathway. (From Vaughan D, Asbury T: *General Ophthalmology,* 9th ed. Lange, 1980. Redrawn and reproduced, with permission, from Duke-Elder S: *Textbook of Ophthalmology.* Vol 4. Mosby, 1949.)

lateral rectus muscles. While looking to one side, the subject is instructed to look up and down; in this position the abducted eye is elevated by the superior rectus muscle and depressed by the inferior rectus muscle. The adducted eye is elevated by the inferior oblique and depressed by the superior oblique muscles. The subject is then requested to look to the opposite side, and the procedure is then repeated in order to test the opposite pairs of muscles.

Each eye may be tested individually for its power of rotation. The examiner places a hand over one eye of the patient and asks the patient to follow the movement of the examiner's other hand up, down, to the right, and to the left.

If diplopia is present in the absence of a gross ocular rotation defect, a red glass or Maddox rod may be placed before an eye and the patient asked to look at a small light held at a distance of 0.5–1 m. By moving

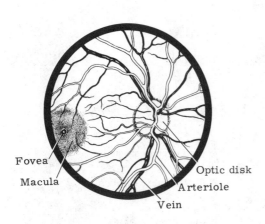 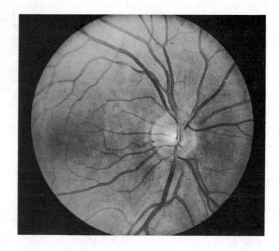

Figure 21–2. The normal fundus. Diagram at left shows landmarks of the photograph at right. (Photo by Diane Beeston. Reproduced, with permission, from Vaughan D, Asbury T: *General Ophthalmology,* 9th ed. Lange, 1980.)

the light to one side or the other into each of the quadrants of the field of vision, the position with greatest separation of the 2 images may be determined.

Diplopia fields may be plotted showing the position of the true and false images in the various portions of the field of vision. In diplopia testing, the head should be fixed or held immobile while the relative positions of the true and false images are plotted on a simple chart. Diplopia occurs in those positions of the eyes that depend upon contraction of weakened muscles. The distance between images increases as the test object is moved in the direction of action of a weak muscle. The false image is usually less distinct and is projected in the direction of action of weak muscles.

Impaired rotatory movement of the eyeballs may be caused by oculomotor, trochlear, or abducens nerve disorders, by interruption of their supranuclear connections, or by disorders of the extraocular muscle such as muscular dystrophy or myasthenia. Intraorbital masses, trauma, inflammation, etc, may also impair movement of the eyeball.

A variety of associated movements of the lids may occur in recovery from oculomotor nerve paralysis, including upper lid retraction on attempted downward movement of the eye, and elevation of a ptotic lid on adduction or elevation of the affected eye or on passive closure of the normal eye. Convergence paralysis, characterized by inability to converge the eyes on a close point without weakness of the medial rectus muscles, may occur with disease of the oculomotor nucleus (Perlia's nucleus).

Disorders of frontal or occipital cortex may disturb conjugate eye movements. Paralysis of conjugate gaze to the opposite side, with deviation of the eyes toward the side of the lesion, may occur after acute destruction of cerebral cortex and last several days. Irritative cortical lesions may produce conjugate deviation of eyes away from the side of the lesion. Conjugate deviation resulting from lateral pontine destruction produces eyeball deviation away from the

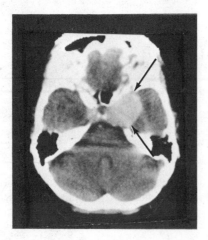

Figure 21–3. CT scan of sphenoid ridge meningioma in a 72-year-old woman with diplopia.

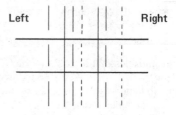

Figure 21–4. Diagram of relative positions of true and false images with paralysis of right external (lateral) rectus muscle. Solid lines indicate image from normal eye, and broken lines indicate image from paretic right eye.

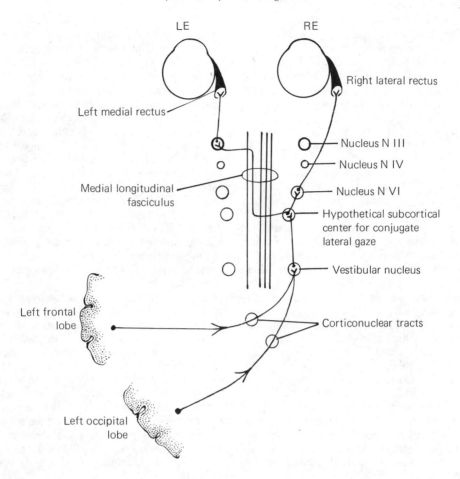

LE   RE

Left medial rectus

Right lateral rectus

Nucleus N III

Nucleus N IV

Medial longitudinal
fasciculus

Nucleus N VI

Hypothetical subcortical
center for conjugate
lateral gaze

Vestibular nucleus

Left frontal
lobe

Corticonuclear tracts

Left occipital
lobe

Figure 21–5. Conjugate right gaze. The impulses for voluntary conjugate movements in right lateral gaze are initiated in the left frontal lobe. Involuntary conjugate movements in right lateral gaze are initiated in the left occipital lobe or, according to recent reports, the ipsilateral occipital lobe. (After Spiegel and Sommer.)

side of the lesion, with paralysis of conjugate deviation toward the side of the lesion. Paralysis of upward gaze is generally due to supranuclear disease. Bilateral paralysis of upward gaze (Parinaud's syndrome) may occur with tumor of the pineal gland region and, more rarely, with cerebrovascular disease or encephalitis.

Perimetry

Visual field examination is important in the clinical study of patients with neurologic disorders. It may be possible to determine the approximate site of a lesion from the type of visual field alteration. Perimetry aids in assessing the site and degree of visual pathway involvement (see pp 90–93).

The portion of space in which objects are visible during fixation of gaze in one direction is defined as the field of vision. In clinical perimetry, the field of vision may be regarded as the inner surface of part of a hemisphere, on which the level of vision is determined at various distances from the point of fixation by use of targets of various sizes and colors. The isopter for a test target is the line drawn on the chart of a visual field indicating the limit of the area in which that target can

be recognized. The visual field chart may contain several concentric lines, each an isopter for a specific target.

A perimeter may be used to study the peripheral portions of the visual field and usually includes an arc which may be turned in various meridians and which is marked up to 90 degrees. A white test object is carried along the arc from the point of fixation until it disappears from view and is then returned into the seeing field. The point where it reappears is recorded as the edge of the field for that test object. Larger targets may be used when the subject cannot see adequately to permit the use of the usual 3-mm test object or where there is a dense defect within the visual field. At least 12 radials of each field are investigated. In addition to determination of the peripheral limits of the visual field, the visual field is explored for scotomas—areas of defective or depressed vision.

Visual field exploration with white targets of different size is known as quantitative perimetry. The use of colored targets (qualitative perimetry) may aid in distinguishing disorders of retinal reception (greater loss for blue) from interruption of conduction pathways (greater loss for red). Color test objects are also useful in mapping central scotomas.

Plotting the physiologic blind spot at the beginning of the examination is usually advisable, since this makes the subject aware of the possibility of other blind areas (scotomas). It is customary to start at the point of fixation, to move the target away until it disappears, and then to bring it back until it reappears and to record this latter position. A standard or artificial illumination of 7 foot-candles is commonly used.

Visual fields are recorded on charts so that the field is represented as the subject sees it. Thus, the field for the right eye is placed to the right on the chart with the upper portion above, the temporal portion to the right, and the nasal portion to the left. A fraction is used to indicate the size (in millimeters) of the test object used in the numerator and the distance in millimeters at which it was used in the denominator. Thus, 3/330 means that a 3-mm test object was used on the arm of a perimeter at a distance (arc radius) of 330 mm.

The boundary of a visual field for a given test object is usually drawn on the chart as a solid line. Customarily, heavy lines are used for large targets and thin or broken lines for smaller targets. Scotomas may be indicated by single-hatched lines if relative and by cross-hatched lines if dense. In mapping defects in the visual field, it is best to begin with the smallest target the subject can see, to progress to one or 2 of medium size, and finally to determine the largest test object that will disappear in any portion of the defect. Visual field defects may vary in their density depending upon the degree of interruption of involved nerve fibers. A defect so dense that light is not perceived within it is said to be absolute, whereas all other defects are designated as relative.

A tangent screen such as the Bjerrum screen permits detailed exploration of the central area of the visual field out to 30 degrees. It may be used at a distance of 1 or 2 m from the subject's eye. The various isopters may be drawn with dark-colored chalks directly on a black felt covering the tangent screen and later brushed off. A 1-mm white test object is usually visible over most of the tangent screen at 1 m except at the physiologic blind spot. A defect discovered with a small test object is rechecked with larger targets, and the largest target that can be made to disappear indicates the density of the defect. With greatly reduced central vision, fixation is frequently unsatisfactory, and the subject may be asked to fix on the center of a circle of adequate size or at the junction of a pair of crossing lines.

Interruption of the visual pathway behind the optic chiasm may produce homonymous hemianopsia—defects in the right or left halves of both visual fields—without affecting the other half-fields of vision. As commonly used, the term hemianopsia is not restricted to complete loss of the half-field of vision but also includes partial, quadrantic, and lesser losses of a half-field of vision. Defects of the visual field that are similar in both eyes are known as congruous defects and usually indicate interruption of the posterior portion of the optic radiations (geniculocalcarine tract). Slightly incongruous visual field defects result from interruptions of the anterior portion of the optic radia-

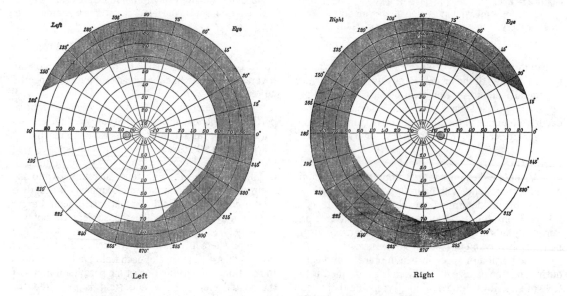

Figure 21–6. Visual field charts. In order to chart fields on the perimeter, small white objects subtending 1 degree or 0.5 degree are moved slowly. The smaller the object, the more sensitive the test. With gross error of refraction, 1 degree is reliable. State the size of object used (in degrees or millimeters) over distance in millimeters (eg, 5/2000). Red has the smallest normal field and gives the most sensitive field test. Chart central field defects on a Bjerrum screen, moving an object from the center outward until it can be seen. Make sure the patient's eye does not move or deviate while the object is being moved.

tions. Incongruous homonymous defects of the visual fields that are grossly dissimilar may result from interruption of the optic tract.

Sparing of the macula may occur in homonymous hemianopsia due to occipital lobe lesions. Lesions of a temporal lobe are likely to produce superior quadrantic homonymous defects that extend to the fixation point without macular sparing. Parietal lobe lesions may produce inferior quadrantic homonymous defects without macular sparing.

Bitemporal hemianopsia, loss of vision in the temporal parts of the visual fields of each eye, may result from a lesion at the optic chiasm. With masses involving the optic chiasm, the bitemporal hemianopsia may be augmented by a central scotoma due to optic nerve interruption; or one eye may be blind, leaving only a nasal half-field of vision in the other eye.

Disorders that affect the optic nerve or retina of an eye may produce a defect in the field of vision of that eye. The characteristic change is a central scotoma, although visual field contractions or even blindness may occur. Defects in the visual fields of both eyes may occur if both optic nerves or retinas are affected, in which case visual field defects may be present in the nasal and temporal fields of both eyes. Visual fields that are restricted or contracted (tubular vision) as a result of disease of the retinas or optic nerves expand in proportion to the increased distance at which they are tested. However, the visual fields in the type of tubular vision resulting from conversion hysteria or malingering may remain unchanged when tested at different distances.

Simple confrontation tests may be performed when perimetric field study is not feasible. A test object such as a pencil with a white eraser or a small white bead pinned to the end of a stick may be used. The target is held as far to the side as possible between examiner and patient. The examiner and subject face each other at about arm's length. The subject places a hand over the left eye and looks with the right eye into the left eye of the examiner. The target is then slowly brought into the line of sight and the subject is directed to respond as soon as the target can be identified. This is repeated at intervals of 30–40 degrees around the periphery, and the reported field of the subject is compared to that of the examiner (which is assumed to be normal). The test may then be repeated for the other eye.

The ability to detect small movements in each quadrant of the normal field may also be checked by confrontation. The awareness of movement in the field of vision is the coarsest test of vision and generally is last to be affected and first to recover. Bilateral simultaneous testing of field quadrants may disclose extinction in an affected visual field that would otherwise appear to be normal.

Ophthalmodynamometry

An approximate measure of the relative pressure in the central retinal arteries may be obtained by ophthalmodynamometry. With the use of an instru-

ment of the Baillart type, pressure is exerted on the sclera of the eyeball with the spring plunger while the vessels emerging from the optic disk are observed with an ophthalmoscope. The pressure is gradually increased until the central retinal artery just begins to pulsate at a point where it or one of its branches leaves the optic disk. This reading is believed to represent the diastolic pressure in the ophthalmic artery of that eye and is usually approximately half the brachial blood pressure. (When the intraocular pressure is further increased until it equals or surpasses the systolic pressure in the central artery, pulsation ceases and the vessel collapses.) The procedure is repeated on the other eye, and the results in both eyes are recorded in mm Hg from the scale of the ophthalmodynamometer. Testing with Baillart's ophthalmodynamometer may be performed without anesthetic with the patient seated with head supported.

A difference of approximately 15% in systolic and 20% in diastolic pressures between the 2 eyes may indicate impaired carotid arterial circulation on the lower side. Decreased pressure, however, may also result from obstructive disorders of the ophthalmic artery or its terminal branches (thromboses, arteriosclerosis, masses, etc).

Electroretinography

Electroretinography may provide a measure of retinal function. At rest there is a 6-mV difference of potential between an electrode on the cornea and one on the back of the eye or the skin of the head, with the cornea positive. A characteristic sequence of potential changes, whose record is called an electroretinogram (ERG), occurs when light strikes the eye. The a, b, and c waves are responses to the turning on of a light stimulus, whereas the d wave is an added response produced when the stimulus is turned off. In monkeys, the a wave is believed to be due to activity in the outer segment of retinal receptors; the b wave originates in the inner layers of the retina; and the c wave presumably originates in pigment epithelium underlying the retina.

In humans, the ERG is obtained by briefly stimulating the eye with a high-intensity light (strobo-

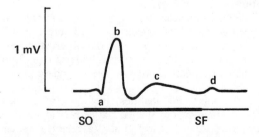

Figure 21–7. Human electroretinogram (ERG). SO = light stimulus on; SF = light stimulus off. (From Ganong WF: *Review of Medical Physiology,* 2nd ed. Lange, 1965. Redrawn from Ziv: Electroretinography. *N Engl J Med* 1961; 264:5.)

scope) and then recording the difference in potential between a contact lens electrode and an indifferent skin or scalp lead. A normal human ERG shows at least a brief small negative deflection (a wave) followed by a higher, more prolonged positive wave (b wave). More prolonged stimulation produces a prolonged c wave and a brief d wave (off effect). In disorders that diffusely affect the retinal rods and cones (retinal detachment, retinitis pigmentosa, etc), the voltage of the ERG may be greatly reduced or absent.

Visual Evoked Potentials (VEP)

The evoked electrical responses of the occipital cerebral cortex after retinal stimulation by repeated light flashes may be used to evaluate clinical disorders of the visual pathway. With use of averaging computers, the evoked response to a light stimulus can be recognized and the asynchronous background activity in the EEG can be suppressed, so that there is enhancement of the evoked cerebral response to repetitive light stimulation (50–100 flashes).

Two types of visual stimuli are used to elicit visual evoked potentials: unpatterned flashing lights and patterned stimuli (usually checkerboards with pattern reversal). Responses to unpatterned flashing lights are affected by the intensity and rate of flash, while brightness and pattern change may affect patterned stimuli responses.

The largest amplitude VEP is usually obtained with an electrode located in the midline 1–2 cm above the inion. Usually, monopolar electrode placement is used, with the occipital electrode serving as the active electrode and the earlobe or mastoid electrode as the indifferent or reference electrode. The VEP reflects stimulation mainly of the central 3 degrees of the visual field and is chiefly foveal in origin.

Optic nerve lesions can be recognized by stimulating each eye separately, since there is absent or impaired response on stimulation of an affected optic nerve. With visual pathway lesions behind the optic chiasm, a difference in response of the 2 cerebral hemispheres may occur, with a normal response in the occipital cerebral cortex of the normal cerebral hemisphere and an absent or abnormal response in the affected cerebral hemisphere.

Fluorescein Angiography

Ophthalmoscopy following the rapid intravenous injection of 5 mL of aqueous sodium fluorescein may assist in diagnosis. Repeated serial observations and photographs may be made in the filling phase (8–20 s), recirculation phase (3–5 min), and late phase (30–60 min).

Vascular abnormalities, including microaneurysms, arteriovenous shunts, and neovascularization, are detectable in the early phase. Vascular leakage can be seen later. Retinal edema or inflammation and fibrous tissue may fluoresce to a variable degree. Suspected papilledema can be associated with vascular leakage in the area of the optic disk. Retinal hemor-

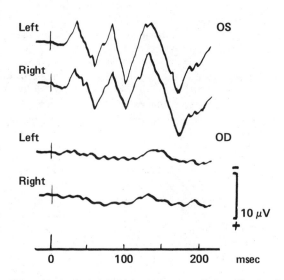

Figure 21–8. Complete right optic nerve lesion. No visual evoked occipital cortex response after stimulating right eye (OD) and good response evoked after stimulating left eye (OS). (Courtesy of M Feinsod. Reproduced, with permission, from Vaughan D, Asbury T: *General Ophthalmology*, 9th ed. Lange, 1980.)

rhages and hyperpigmented areas usually obscure underlying fluorescence.

Electronystagmography

The electronystagmogram (ENG) provides a permanent record of eye movements that may be useful for diagnostic and therapeutic purposes. Data about eye movements in various neurologic diseases may be obtained, and low-grade nystagmus may be detected.

The eye may be considered to be a dipole in which the cornea is the positive pole and the retina the negative pole. Normally, there is at least a 1-mV potential difference between the 2 poles that produces field changes when the eyeballs rotate. Electrodes placed on adjacent periorbital skin may detect these electrical changes, which can be amplified and recorded.

When the eyeballs are in midposition (forward gaze), the resting voltage obtained serves as the baseline. Horizontal eye movements conventionally produce an upward pen deflection when the eyes move to the right and a downward deflection when the eyes move to the left. Vertical eye movements are recorded by upward deflection of the pen for upward movements and downward deflection for downward movements.

Stimulation of the vestibular system by water or air caloric irrigation (see Hallpike caloric test, p 103) may be performed in conjunction with the ENG. Visual stimulators may be used with the ENG, including fixation points in the vertical and horizontal planes, a moving target for tracking, and a striped drum for optokinetic testing.

Audiometry | 22

The human ear recognizes sounds by detecting the various tones of which they are composed. Audible tones range in frequency from about 16 to 16,000 Hz.* Sound contains many harmonic frequencies that are multiples of the fundamental, or basic, frequency. In general, the loudness of a sound is correlated with the amplitude of a sound wave: the greater the amplitude, the louder the sound. Pitch correlates with the frequency, or number, of waves per unit of time: the greater the frequency, the higher the pitch. Persons who clearly perceive frequencies between 500 and 2000 Hz can hear adequately for useful communication, but they may be unable to appreciate the full quality of sounds about them.

Hearing loss becomes a significant handicap when there is difficulty in communication by speech. Beginning impairment has been defined as an average hearing level loss of 16 decibels (dB) at frequencies of 500, 1000, and 2000 Hz. A person is usually considered to be deaf when the hearing level loss for these 3 frequencies is at or above 82 dB. Early hearing loss often appears initially at 4000 Hz, both in children with conduction impairment and in adults with presbycusis.

The incidence of hearing loss rises sharply with age and is generally greatest among persons age 65 years and older. However, loss of hearing is also notable among younger people. The most common cause of deafness in active adult life is otosclerosis, which is frequently first noticed in late adolescence. Twice as many women as men have otosclerosis, although hearing impairments due to all causes are more common in males. Continuous exposure to intense noise can produce permanent damage of the inner ear. Among children, severe or total deafness may be associated with hereditary nerve deafness, birth trauma, brain defects, cerebrospinal meningitis, mental retardation, and early infections. (See pp 102–103.)

Voice Tests

The patient's perception of whispered or spoken words provides a quick rough estimate of loss of hearing. However, voice tests are apt to be inaccurate because of variations in intensity of voice even when test words are spoken by trained personnel. In unilateral loss of hearing, the better ear should be "masked," or tightly closed.

Tuning Fork Tests

Tuning forks that are free of overtones and whose vibrations fade gradually should be used. The fork should be struck against the pad of the palm or a piece of rubber.

A. Weber's Test: When hearing is normal there is no lateralization of sound to either ear when the stem of the vibrating tuning fork is held against the midline vertex portion of the skull. If the sound is referred to the poorer hearing ear, loss of hearing is due to impaired conduction in the external or internal ear. If the sound is referred to the better hearing ear, loss of hearing is attributable to poor function of the auditory nerve or the cochlea.

B. Schwabach's Test: The bone conduction hearing of the patient is compared with that of the examiner (normal ear), and time in seconds is recorded. The vibrating tuning fork is usually applied behind the ear to the mastoid area.

C. Rinne's Test: The ability to hear a tuning fork by air conduction is compared with the ability to hear by bone conduction. The vibrating tuning fork is alternately held in front of the ear and pressed against the mastoid process. In the normal ear, a fully vibrating fork of 256 or 512 Hz is heard about twice as long by air conduction as by bone conduction (positive test). Impaired function of the middle ear is indicated if hearing by bone conduction is equal to or greater than hearing by air conduction (negative test).

Watch Tick Test

Testing the patient's perception of a watch tick provides a crude estimate for hearing of frequencies of more than 2000 double vibrations per second. Results are recorded as a fraction indicating the distance at which the test watch is heard by the patient compared to the distance at which it is heard by normal ears. Ears with a high-frequency perceptive loss may be detected by this test; however, reduced hearing for watch tick may be of little clinical significance.

Electronic Audiometer Tests

These tests depend upon the use of an electronic instrument that can deliver pure tones at controlled intensities. Some instruments also contain a circuit capable of delivering speech signals from a live voice or phonograph recordings at controlled intensities. Air conduction and bone conduction receivers are provided.

*1 Hz (hertz) = 1 cycle per second (c/s).

Audiometers used for general clinical purposes usually deliver tones at octave and half-octave intervals. To produce a tone one octave higher than a preceding tone, it is necessary to double the frequency of vibrations. The range of frequencies tested usually is from 125 to 8000 Hz.

Intensities are calibrated in decibels, a physical unit based on sound pressure energy. Each decibel approximates a barely perceptible increase in loudness of the tone for a normal ear. The average loudness of the conversational voice is about 60 dB.

Pure tone threshold audiometric results may be charted, with frequencies as abscissa and intensity as ordinate. Air conduction is frequently recorded in black and bone conduction in red. Right ear results may be recorded as circles joined by a solid line and left ear results as crosses joined by a broken line. Tests for loudness recruitment may corroborate bone conduction findings or provide information on the site of the disorder in perceptive deafness.

Recruitment refers to a condition in which the perceived loudness of a tone increases much more rapidly than its intensity. A tone not heard by a patient at 35 dB may be heard normally at 38 dB and become even painful at slightly higher intensities (45 dB). Recruitment is characteristic of cochlear damage.

Loudness balancing can be tested in patients with one normal ear. Specified pure tones of one minute's duration at various suprathreshold levels are presented alternately to each ear. Interpretation depends on changes in relative loudness levels between the 2 ears at successively higher intensity levels. With lesions of the acoustic nerve or middle ear, loudness seems to increase equally in the 2 ears, whereas in cochlear lesions, loudness increases more rapidly in the affected ear.

The **short increment sensitivity test (SISI)** depends on presentation to the ear of a sustained pure tone at 20 dB above threshold that is momentarily increased by 1 dB at 5-second intervals for 20 times. In

cochlear lesions, because of recruitment, 50–100% of the increases are perceived; in lesions of the middle ear, acoustic nerve, or central pathways, few if any of the increases are perceived.

The **Békésy test** depends on comparative audiometry using an interrupted tone and a sustained tone. The tone is made louder until the patient presses a switch to indicate that the sound has been heard, after which the tone gets weaker and weaker until the patient turns off a switch to indicate that the tone is no longer heard. The process is repeated with progressively higher tones. The Békésy audiogram gives 4 distinct types of curves. In type I curve, the continuous and interrupted tone tracings are superimposed on one another. In type II curve, the 2 tracings are superimposed to about 1000 Hz, and above this the continuous tone tracing falls below the interrupted tone tracing; this type II curve is seen with cochlear damage. In the type III audiogram, the interrupted tone tracing appears normal, but the continuous tone tracing falls sharply toward zero as the frequencies increase; type III curves are very characteristic of acoustic nerve lesions. Type IV audiograms are similar to those of type II, but the continuous tone tracing falls below the interrupted tone tracing at all frequencies; type II curve is indicative of severe cochlear lesions.

The **tone decay test** resembles the continuous tone Békésy test, but a conventional audiometer is used. A continuous tone at 5 dB above threshold is presented to one ear with the opposite ear masked. When the patient no longer hears the tone (because it "decayed"), the intensity is increased 5 dB, and this is repeated for 1 min. As in the Békésy test, a diseased cochlea shows fatigue to a continuous tone and is evident by the number of times a 5-dB increment must be added. In normal or only slightly impaired cochleas, 0–15 dB must be added in one minute. In moderate or severely impaired cochleas, 15–30 dB must be added. If more than 30 dB must be added, disease of the acoustic nerve may be present.

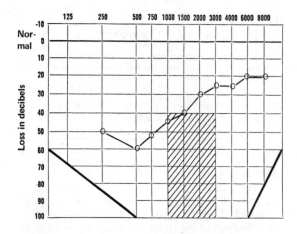

Figure 22–1. Middle ear, or conduction, deafness. Representative air conduction curve, showing greatest impairment of pure tone thresholds in lower frequencies.

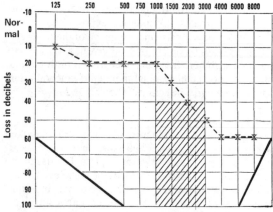

Figure 22–2. Perception, or nerve, deafness. Representative bone conduction curve of pure tone thresholds with greatest deficit in higher frequencies.

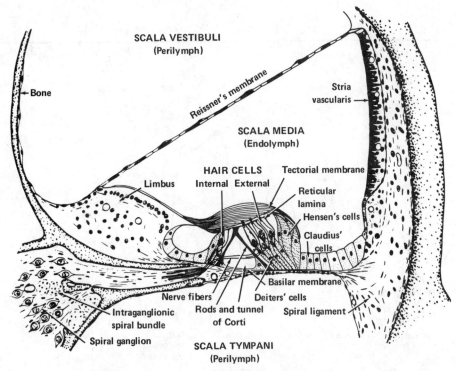

SCALA VESTIBULI
(Perilymph)

Bone

Reissner's membrane

Stria vascularis →

SCALA MEDIA
(Endolymph)

HAIR CELLS   Tectorial membrane

Limbus   Internal External

Reticular lamina

Hensen's cells

Claudius' cells

Basilar membrane

Nerve fibers   Deiters' cells

Rods and tunnel of Corti   Spiral ligament

Intraganglionic spiral bundle

Spiral ganglion

SCALA TYMPANI
(Perilymph)

Figure 22–3. Cross section of one turn of the cochlea of a guinea pig. (Reproduced, with permission, from Davis et al: Acoustic trauma in the guinea pig. *J Acoust Soc Am* 1953;**25**:1180.)

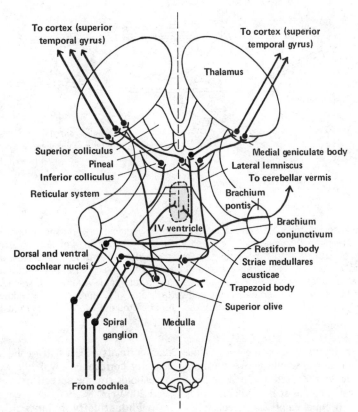

To cortex (superior temporal gyrus)

To cortex (superior temporal gyrus)

Thalamus

Superior colliculus   Medial geniculate body

Pineal   Lateral lemniscus

Inferior colliculus   To cerebellar vermis

Reticular system   Brachium pontis

IV ventricle   Brachium conjunctivum

Restiform body

Dorsal and ventral cochlear nuclei   Striae medullares acusticae

Trapezoid body

Superior olive

Spiral ganglion   Medulla

From cochlea

Figure 22–4. Simplified diagram of main auditory pathways superimposed on a dorsal view of the brain stem. Cerebellum and cerebral cortex removed. (Reproduced, with permission, from Ganong WF: *Review of Medical Physiology,* 10th ed. Lange, 1981.)

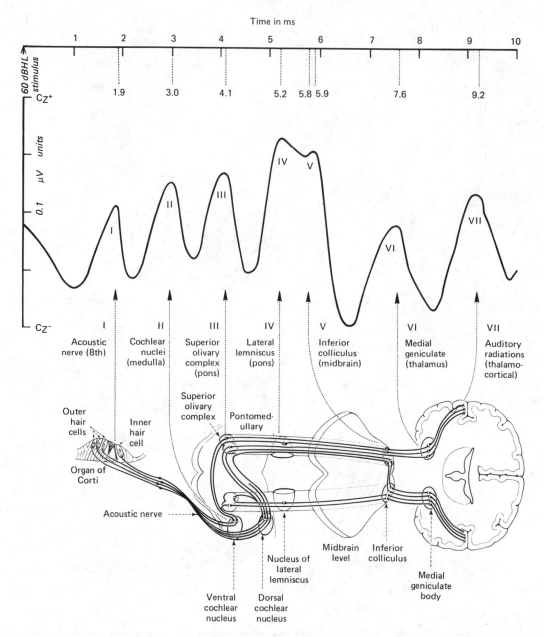

Figure 22–5. Far-field recording of brain stem auditory response latencies in humans. Proposed functional-anatomic correlations are given. Diagram shows normal latencies for vertex-positive brain stem auditory evoked potentials (waves I–IV) evoked by clicks of 60 dBHL (60 dB above normal hearing threshold) at a rate of 10/s. Lesions at different levels of the auditory pathway tend to produce response abnormalities beginning with indicated components. Intermediate latency (5.8 ms) between latencies of waves IV and V is the mean peak latency of fused wave IV/V when present. C_{Z^+}, C_{Z^-} = vertex positivity, represented by an upward pen deflection, and vertex negativity, represented by a downward pen deflection. (Reproduced, with permission, from Stockard JJ, Stockard JE, Sharbrough FW: *Mayo Clin Proc* 1977;**52**:761.)

Speech audiometry provides a measure of the ear hearing of frequencies and sounds above threshold intensities. Spondaic words used for determining speech reception thresholds consist of 2-syllable words that give approximately equal emphasis to each syllable (eg, "railroad," "baseball"). The speech reception threshold is the intensity at which an individual can correctly repeat half of the spondaic words; this usually corresponds with the average of pure tone thresholds for the speech frequencies of 500, 1000, and 2000 Hz.

Phonetically balanced words are lists of monosyllables. Selected lists of 50 words each cover the phonetic range of the English language. The test is

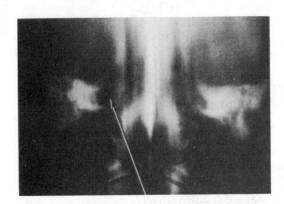

Figure 22–6. Tomogram showing enlarged acoustic meatus in patient with a neurinoma of the right acoustic nerve.

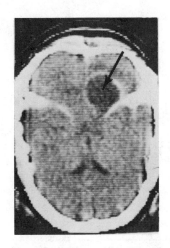

Figure 22–7. Computerized tomogram (CT scan) of neurinoma of acoustic nerve.

believed to measure the ability of the ear to discriminate speech, and the results may be graphed, with intensity as the abscissa and percentage of words repeated correctly as the ordinate. Results of this test do not always correlate well with the results of threshold tests.

Speech discrimination may be severely impaired in acoustic lesions, whereas it is hardly affected in conduction deafness. It has been suggested that speech discrimination tests may be adapted to test hearing of both ears (binaural) and compared to single ear hearing (monaural). A list of one-syllable words is given to each ear separately at an intensity adjusted to give a 50% score; then, at the same intensity, words are given to both ears. If central pathways are intact, the score should improve, whereas with central lesions involving the auditory pathways, this synergism may not be present.

Characteristic Examples
A. Middle Ear, or Conduction, Deafness:
1. Air conduction–Pure tone threshold moder-

ately or severely impaired, particularly in the lower frequencies, with much less impairment in higher frequencies.

2. Bone conduction–Approximately normal curve.

3. Speech reception threshold–Impaired to an extent similar to average of pure tone thresholds in speech frequencies.

B. Perception, or Nerve, Deafness:
1. Air conduction–Air conduction threshold for pure tones impaired with greatest deficit in the higher frequencies.

2. Bone conduction–Bone conduction threshold for pure tones impaired in fashion similar to that for air conduction.

3. Speech reception threshold–Deficit approximates the pure tone threshold deficit in the speech frequencies.

Brain Stem Auditory Evoked Response (BAER)

A brain stem auditory response consisting of 7 vertex-positive evoked potentials may be recorded from the human scalp within 10 ms of an appropriate acoustic stimulus. The first of these potentials arises in the acoustic nerve, the third in the pons, and the fifth in the midbrain. Abnormalities in the brain stem auditory response may provide evidence suggesting clinical neurologic disorders involving the brain stem (see p 236).

The short latency brain stem auditory evoked potentials may be averaged and analyzed with the aid of computer techniques. In a normal human subject with a vertex scalp (C_Z) electrode placement, a click stimulus presented to the ear may evoke typical responses with 7 wave components. These wave components are believed to come from the region of the auditory nerve (wave I), dorsal cochlear nucleus (wave II), superior olive (wave III), lateral lemniscus (wave IV), and inferior colliculus (wave V). Wave VI may

Table 22–1. Differentiation of sensorineural and conduction deafness. (AC = air conduction; BC = bone conduction.)*

	Conduction Deafness	Sensorineural Deafness
Patient's voice	Speaks softly	Speaks loudly
Effect of noisy environment	Hears best	Hears poorly
Speech discrimination	Good	Poor
Hearing on telephone	Good	Poor
Weber test lateralization	To diseased ear	To good ear
Rinne test	Negative (AC = BC)	Positive (AC > BC)

*Reproduced, with permission, from Krupp MA, Chatton MJ (editors): *Current Medical Diagnosis & Treatment 1982.* Lange, 1982.

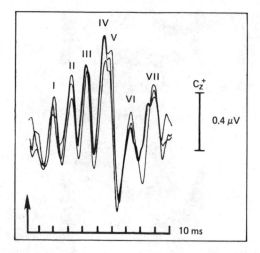

Figure 22–8. Scalp recordings of brain stem auditory response in a neurologically and audiometrically normal subject. Each of the 3 tracings is the computer average of 2048 responses evoked by 20/s 60 dBSL (SL = sensation level) left monaural clicks and recorded from vertex to left mastoid. In this figure, positivity at the vertex (relative to mastoid) produces upward pen deflections. (Reproduced, with permission, from Stockard JJ, Rossiter VS: Clinical and pathologic correlates of brain stem auditory response abnormalities. *Neurology* 1977; **27**:316.)

indicate activity of the rostral midbrain or caudal thalamus, whereas wave VII may reflect activity from the thalamus or thalamocortical projection.

A click intensity of 60 dB above the patient's hearing threshold is presented monaurally at about 11/s while the other ear is presented with white noise. The EEG recorded from the vertex to the ipsilateral ear is filtered and amplified.

Waves I, III, and V represent the volume-conducted electrical activity from the auditory nerve, pons, and midbrain, respectively, and the latencies between these potentials represent neural conduction in the connecting pathways of the brain stem auditory pathway.

Peak latencies and peak-to-peak amplitudes are measured. At least 2 separate trials and averages of 2000–4000 responses are recorded and superimposed for each ear.

The BAER may be of value clinically and is useful in demonstrating structural brain stem changes that may be associated with coma, multiple sclerosis, posterior fossa masses, and related disorders.

Psychologic tests are sometimes used to help evaluate the status of neurologic patients. Results must be considered in terms of the clinical history and findings of the particular subject tested. Psychologic tests are best used in combination or in a battery of tests, so that individual test weaknesses are minimized.

Efficiency of intellectual function may be impaired with cerebral disease, but the degree is not necessarily related to the severity of the organic disorder, especially where the lesions are small. No test specific for brain disease exists as such, although subjects with brain injuries may have intellectual impairment and increased emotional lability. Greater relative deficiency in tests involving memory, speed, or new learning than in tests involving vocabulary and information is regarded as evidence of intellectual deterioration. Patients with deterioration due to organic brain lesions, as well as schizophrenic patients, show a tendency to be rigid, stereotyped, and concrete in their concepts, with inability to perform adequately tests involving classification, categorization, or induction.

Tests of intellectual performance may sometimes give the best evidence of organic brain disorder. A variety of tests may be used to test the subject's ability to abstract, use symbols, and evaluate new experiences on the basis of past experience. Diffuse brain disorders and those with bilateral frontal lobe changes are most commonly associated with impairment of intellectual performance. The patient with organic brain disease is apt to show diminished capacities to grasp the essence of a situation and to detect slight differences or changes, difficulty in remembering 2 or more commands or following directions, limited attention span, faulty judgment, impaired memory, and, in severe cases, gross memory loss and confusion.

Obvious mental or language dysfunction may require specific tests to define the nature and severity of the disorder. Indications for such formal testing may be evident from the history or examination. For instance, simple testing of intellectual performance during neurologic examination may indicate defects in memory, calculation, judgment, or general information.

Two general types of psychometric tests are recognized. **Objective tests** are standardized from representative portions of the population and used for "quantitative" evaluation of personality traits in rela-

tion to established norms. Standard intelligence tests and personality inventories are typical examples. **Projective tests** are designed to evaluate the subject's responses to "amorphous," ambiguous, or unstructured stimuli or tasks. The responses are considered to be significantly influenced by the subject's personality. Although the responses may be compared with previously established norms, a significant variable factor is the subjective interpretation placed upon them by the examiner. The Rorschach, Thematic Apperception, and sentence completion tests are examples of this type.

OBJECTIVE TESTS

Wechsler Adult Intelligence Test

This test is used widely for measurement of intelligence of the adult population and has the reputed advantage that past formal educational background does not greatly modify test results. Intelligence quotients may be computed with due regard for anticipated decline in intelligence with advanced aging. "Global intelligence" is measured by use of 11 diversified subtests. Six of these form a verbal intelligence scale and measure abilities in verbal area, arithmetical area, and those areas dependent upon abstract reasoning (eg, ability to perceive logical relations and use of symbols). The remaining 5 subjects comprise the performance intelligence scale and depend upon the subject's ability to handle practical situations calling for performance and manipulative abilities. The 6 tests included in the verbal score are information, comprehension, arithmetic, similarities, digit span, and vocabulary. The 5 tests in the performance score are digit symbol, picture completion, block design, picture arrangement, and object assembly.

The revision known as the Wechsler Adult Intelligence Scale (WAIS) was published in 1955 and a scale for children (WISC) in 1949.

Stanford-Binet Intelligence Test

This is one of the most widely used intelligence tests and is particularly suitable for children. It consists of a selection of short problems arranged for ages 2–14 years by 6-month and one-year levels, with 3 "adult" levels of difficulty. A wide range of psychologic func-

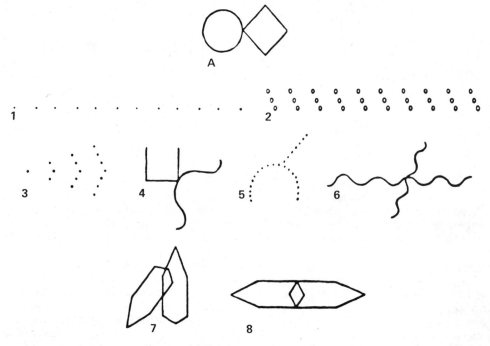

Figure 23–1. Designs to be reproduced by a patient given the Bender Gestalt test. (Reproduced, with permission, from Bender L: *A Visual-Motor Gestalt Test and Its Clinical Use.* Research Monograph No. 3. American Orthopsychiatric Association, 1938. Copyright © by American Orthopsychiatric Association.)

tions are checked, with verbal and language functions predominating. Test items vary at different age levels or appear in more difficult forms at higher levels. Performance is indicated in terms of mental age and intelligence quotient. Because of its standardization and the character of the items contained in it, the test appears to be appropriate for children of grade school years and adolescence.

Bender Gestalt Test

This is considered to be a test of visual motor function and depends upon the responses (pattern, or Gestalt) elicited by 9 standard patterns. The patterns are presented one at a time to the subject, who is requested to copy them on a sheet of paper. Interpretation of the test results depends on many factors, including the manner in which patterns are reproduced, their relationships to each other, spatial background, and temporal patterning.

Porteus Maze Test

In this performance test, the subject is asked to trace a path through a series of mazes of increasing difficulty graded by year levels. Performance in this test appears to be related to traditional intelligence quotient. The complexity of the mazes successfully solved indicates ability; the manner in which the test is done is related to aspects of personality.

Goodenough Draw-a-Man Test

This is a performance test of the ability of a subject to draw a picture of a man. The drawing is scored according to prescribed standards.

Minnesota Multiphasic Personality Index

This widely used standardized objective personality test consists of several hundred diverse statements about feelings, family matters, attitudes, events, and reactions that the subject is asked to classify as "true," "false," or "cannot say." A personality profile may be derived on the basis of 9 categories: hypochondriasis, depression, hysteria, psychopathic deviation, masculinity-femininity, paranoia, psychasthenia, schizophrenia, and hypomania. Interpretation is usually based on the profile as a whole.

Benton Visual Retention Test

This test is designed to assess visual perception, visual memory, and visual reconstructive ability. A series of simple and complex drawings are presented for 5–10 seconds. The subject must then reproduce the design after various time periods (direct copy, immediate reproduction, and reproduction after 15-second delay).

Halstead-Reitan Test

This has become one of the most popular and widely used neuropsychologic test batteries. It provides a comprehensive array of tests of cognitive and adaptive ability. Included are tests of verbal and nonverbal intelligence, concept formation, expressive and receptive language, memory, auditory perception, time perception, tactile performance, perceptual motor speed, spatial relations, finger gnosis, and double simultaneous stimulation.

PROJECTIVE TESTS

Rorschach Test

This projective test is administered by having the patient examine 10 standard cards, each of which contains an ink blot. Various aspects of the subject's responses contribute to the interpretation: content of subject's free associations regarding the ink blots; factors such as shape, color, or shading; and whether all or part of a blot is employed. Each ink blot has minimal conventionalized meanings; the responses represent functions of the patient's own personality. Feelings and motivations that are deep or unconscious may stimulate distorted responses to the test. Claims for the value of such a projection technique for evaluating organic brain damage rest upon the findings of repetition, perplexity, stereotyped responses, and confusion in such patients.

Thematic Apperception Test (TAT)

This is a projective test that depends upon the story told by the subject on viewing test material consisting of 20 picture cards appropriately selected for age and sex. Pictures differ among themselves and are intentionally unclear and ambiguous. For each picture, the subject constructs an imaginary plot or story. The themes of these plots may reveal attitude, drives, and conflicts, for the themes projected into the stories often are related to analogous themes in the subject's life. The content of the stories provides clues to the manner in which the subject perceives and thinks as well as to the subject's fears, needs, and hopes.

Figure 23–3. Card F12 of the Thematic Apperception Test. (Reproduced, by permission of the publisher, from Henry A. Murray: *Thematic Apperception Test,* Cambridge, Mass.: Harvard Univ Press, copyright 1943 by the President and Fellows of Harvard College, 1971 by Henry A. Murray.)

For use with children, a variation known as the Children's Apperception Test (CAT) has been developed.

Figure 23–2. Card V of Rorschach test. (Reproduced with permission of Hans Huber, Bern, Switzerland, publishers of Rorschach's *Psychodiagnostics.*)

Sentence Completion Test

The subject is asked to complete a number of incomplete sentences. The way the sentences are completed is thought to reveal the subject's wishes, needs, and feelings. Since different personalities show characteristic performance differences and the test itself is simple, brief, and flexible, it enjoys wide use as a corroborative test.

Make-a-Picture-Story Test (MAPS)

The test materials consist of large numbers of cutout figures and various backdrops. The patient selects figures, arranges them before a backdrop, and then tells a story about the arrangement. The patient's selection and arrangement of materials and the stories invented may reveal the subject's conscious and unconscious needs and feelings.

Word Association Test

A series of stimulus words is presented to the subject, and the reaction time, content of response, and emotion associated with each word are noted. Words selected are neutral and chosen to give diagnostic aid based on the ratio of normal to abnormal responses. Examples of words used in these tests are white, dark, woman, doctor, anger, afraid, etc.

House-Tree-Person Test (H-T-P)

The subject is requested to make a freehand drawing of a house, a tree, and a person. Information about the maturity, sensitivity, flexibility, and integration of the subject's personality may be derived from the drawings.

Section IV: Central Nervous System Disorders

Congenital Defects | 24

Several factors, singly or in combination, may contribute to the development of a congenital CNS anomaly or malformation: (1) Heredity: A tendency to develop abnormally may exist in the fertilized egg, and this tendency may be related to the existence of the same tendency in the parents or other relatives. (2) Intrinsic factors: The growth in complexity and the differentiation of some portions of the embryo are under the control of the chemical and metabolic environment of that portion of the tissue. (3) Extrinsic factors: The host or parent in which an embryo grows affects the growth of the embryo in many ways. Thus, it is assumed that for normal development to occur there should be normal uterine mucosa, adequate circulation, and proper temperature. In the developing fetus, the nervous system is particularly vulnerable to anoxia, ionizing radiations, and certain infectious diseases of the mother (German measles, mumps). (4) Critical periods: At certain phases in the early development of tissue and organs, relatively minor variations may give rise to severe abnormalities.

Genetic diseases may be inherited, characteristically along classic mendelian lines. The chromosome defect is usually considered to be at the molecular level (as a mutant gene) and thus produces no visible structural chromosomal change.

DNA, important in transmission of hereditary characteristics, is found in the chromosomes of all cells and in some viruses. Models have been constructed from x-ray diffraction studies of DNA extracted from chromosomes or viruses. DNA consists of 2 helical chains of alternate phosphate and sugar (deoxyribose) molecules linked by pairs of nitrogen bases that project from the sugar molecules on each chain. The base pairs, one a purine (usually adenine and guanine) and the other a pyrimidine (thymine and cytosine), are bound by weak hydrogen bonds. It has been suggested that adenine is always paired with thymine and that guanine is always paired with cytosine.

The particular arrangement of base pairs along the chains of the long, thin molecule of DNA constitutes a genetic code, passed on via replication of DNA. Just before mitosis of somatic cells or meiosis (reduction division) of gametic cells, DNA is thought to be present in double helical form. During mitosis or meiosis, the DNA unwinds and the 2 unwound chains then attract from their environment the proper bases to build 2 copies that duplicate exactly the original helix.

Genes and their subdivisions, gene particles, have not yet been precisely identified chemically. It is quite possible that they represent a nucleotide or several nucleotides. If this is so, then one DNA molecule may have many thousands of genes or gene particles.

Abnormalities of cell division may occur during human gametogenesis or during early division of the fertilized egg, leading to development of individuals with an abnormal chromosome constitution. Cytologic techniques have established that normally there are 46 chromosomes in humans, and improved techniques have made possible more accurate analysis and study of the normal human chromosome. Cells from normal human tissues or peripheral blood may be grown in a medium containing minute amounts of colchicine. By this treatment, mitosis is stopped at the metaphase, and many such cells accumulate in the culture. Exposure of the colchicine-treated cells to the osmotic effects of hypotonic solution for several minutes before fixation causes them to swell and thus disperses the chromosomes within. Squash or smear preparations spread the chromosomes in one optical plane, which allows accurate counting and photography. Preparations are then stained and examined under an oil-immersion lens.

Chromosomes in metaphase of mitosis appear as rod-shaped structures split longitudinally into 2 chromatids lying side by side and held together at a constricted area, the centromere, the site of spindle fiber attachment. Chromosomes vary in length and centromere position, so that individual characteristics occur. Chromosomal analysis depends upon classifying them into 7 groups based on their total length and arm ratios.

There are 22 pairs of identical nonsex chromosomes, or autosomes, and, in the male, one pair of sex chromosomes of unequal length. One of the sex chromosomes, the X, is usually the seventh largest chromosome, and the other, the Y, is frequently the largest of the smallest group. The normal female has what appears to be an identical pair of X chromosomes and no Y chromosomes.

Two main types of human chromosome abnormalities have been described: (1) an irregular number of chromosomes, and (2) altered structure of individual chromosomes. An irregular number of chromosomes may occur, eg, if one of a pair is missing or if there are more than 2 of a given pair. Altered structure of individual chromosomes includes chromosome deletion, eg, if one arm of a chromosome is broken off

Table 24—1. Sex chromosome abnormalities.*†

Phenotype	Sex Chromatin	Sex Chromosome	Chromosome Number	Clinical Picture
Female	Positive	XX	46	Normal female.
Female	Few smaller than normal Barr bodies (7%)	Xx (partial deletion)	46	Streak gonads. No secondary sex characteristics. Amenorrheic.
Female	Negative	XO	45	Turner's syndrome.
Female	Positive for 2 Barr bodies	XXX	47	Usually normal appearing female with mental retardation. Occasional menstrual disturbances and absence of secondary sex characteristics.
Female	Positive for 3 Barr bodies	XXXX	48	Normal female with mental retardation.
Female	Positive for 4 Barr bodies	XXXXX	49	Mental retardation with mongoloid facies and simian palmar crease. Skeletal defects similar to those of 49,XXXXY.
Hermaphrodite	Positive	XX	46	Variable phenotype. Both testicular and ovarian tissue in gonads.
Male	Negative	XY	46	Normal male.
Male	Positive for 1 Barr body	XXY	47	Klinefelter's syndrome.
Male	Negative	XYY	47	Undescended testes, ± mental retardation, irregularity of teeth. Tall (> 6 feet). Radioulnar synostosis.
Male	Negative	XYYY	48	Mild psychomotor retardation, inguinal hernia, undescended testes, pulmonary stenosis, simian lines, dental dysplasia.
Male	Positive for 1 Barr body	XXYY	48	Klinefelter's syndrome.
Male	Positive for 2 Barr bodies	XXXY	48	Klinefelter's with more mental retardation and testicular atrophy.
Male	Positive for 3 Barr bodies	XXXXY	49	Mental retardation, hypoplastic external genitals, and skeletal defects. Facies suggestive of Down's syndrome.

*Reproduced, with permission, from Krupp MA, Chatton MJ (editors): *Current Medical Diagnosis & Treatment 1982.* Lange, 1982.
†Normal male and normal female included for comparison.

and subsequently lost, and translocation, if 2 chromosomes exchange unequal fragments.

Autosomal trisomy syndromes occur when 3 instead of 2 chromosomes of a particular autosomal pair are present. In Down's syndrome, trisomy of chromosome number 21 occurs, so that the total number of chromosomes is 47 instead of the normal 46. Other trisomy conditions involving chromosomes of group IV (numbers 13, 14, and 15) are associated with mental defects and multiple congenital anomalies. Patients with trisomy of group V (number 17 or 18) show spasticity, ear anomalies, flexion of the fingers, deformed feet, and congenital heart disease; they usually do not survive past infancy.

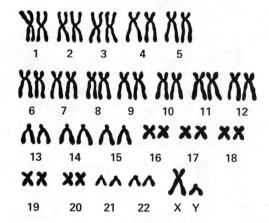

Figure 24–1. Normal male karyotypes. (Reproduced, with permission, from Krupp MA et al: *Physician's Handbook,* 20th ed. Lange, 1982.)

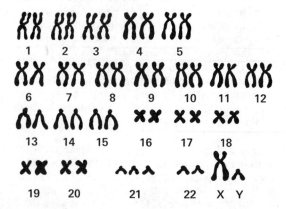

Figure 24–2. Down's syndrome, showing trisomy for chromosome number 21. (Reproduced, with permission, from Krupp MA et al: *Physician's Handbook,* 20th ed. Lange, 1982.)

Table 24—2. Partial list of autosomal disorders.*

Chromosome Defect	Signs
1q+	Peaked nose; micrognathia; long, tapering fingers; congenital heart disease; small or absent thymus
4p+	Severe psychomotor and growth retardation, microcephaly, abnormal facies, abnormal vertebrae and pelvis
4p- (Wolf's syndrome)	Severe growth and mental retardation, midline scalp defects, seizures, abnormal facies, hypospadias
4q+	Low birth weight, mental retardation, hypotonia, early closure of fontanelles
5p- (cri du chat syndrome)	Microcephaly, catlike cry, abnormal facies, low birth weight, abnormal dermatoglyphics
5q-	Long-standing aregenerative macrocytic anemia
7q+	Low birth weight, mental retardation, fuzzy hair, wide fontanelles, abnormal facies, bony abnormalities such as kyphoscoliosis, dislocated hip
8+ (trisomy 8)	Mild mental retardation, concomitant strabismus, skeletal defects of ribs and vertebrae
8p+	Small hands with short fifth fingers and dysplastic toenails
8q-	Mental retardation, limited joint mobility, rib and vertebral anomalies
9p+	Mental retardation, moderate microcephaly, brachycephaly, abnormal facies, hypoplasia of phalanges, abnormal dermatoglyphics
9p-	Mental retardation, hypertonia, abnormal facies, congenital heart disease
t(9q+:22q-) (Philadelphia chromosome)	Associated with chronic myelogenous leukemia
9+ (trisomy 9)	Microcephaly, abnormal facies, small penis, undescended testes, long flexed fingers, severe congenital heart disease
10q+	Severe psychomotor and growth retardation, abnormal facies, abnormalities of digits (webbing, wide spacing)
11p+	Mental retardation, hypotonia, abnormal facies, strabismus
11q+	Mental retardation, low birth weight, abnormal facies, congenital heart disease, renal disease
13+ (trisomy 13; trisomy D; Patau's syndrome)	Severe mental retardation; congenital heart disease; cerebral malformations, especially olfactory bulbs; abnormal facies; low birth weight
13q+d	Psychomotor retardation, microcephaly, abnormal facies, delayed and abnormal dentition, increased fetal hemoglobin
13q-	Microcephaly, psychomotor retardation, eye and ear defects, hypoplastic or absent thumbs, genitourinary anomalies
14q+	Mental retardation, failure to thrive, seizures, microcephaly, abnormal facies
15q+	Severe psychomotor retardation with normal growth, strabismus, hypotonia, seizures, abnormal facies
18+ (trisomy 18; trisomy E; Edward's syndrome)	Severe mental retardation, long narrow skull with prominent occiput, congenital heart disease, flexion deformities of fingers, abnormal facies, low birth weight
21+ (trisomy 21; Down's syndrome; mongolism)	Mental retardation, brachycephaly, prominent epicanthic folds, Brushfield spots, poor nasal bridge development, congenital heart disease, hypermobility of joints
21q- (G I deletion syndrome, antimongolism)	Mental and growth retardation, microcephaly, antimongoloid slant to palpebral fissures, hypertonia, abnormal facies, skeletal defects
22q+ (cat eye syndrome)	Coloboma (cat eye), anal atresia, severe psychomotor retardation, congenital heart disease
22+ (trisomy 22)	Mental and growth retardation, microcephaly, abnormal facies, abnormal thumbs
22q- (G II deletion syndrome)	Mental retardation with microcephaly, hypotonia, abnormal facies, syndactyly of fingers
Monosomy 22	Moderate mental retardation, antimongoloid slant of eyes, spade hands, abnormal facies

*Reproduced, with permission, from Krupp MA, Chatton MJ (editors): *Current Medical Diagnosis & Treatment 1980.* Lange, 1980.

Sex chromosome anomalies may also occur. **Klinefelter's syndrome** is characterized by an abnormal number of chromosomes (47), with an extra X chromosome, so that sex chromosome constitution is XXY. Small testes, sterility, eunuchoidism, and gynecomastia may occur.

Patients with **Turner's syndrome** have 45 chromosomes, with a single X chromosome. They are short females who fail to develop secondary sex characteristics and may have multiple congenital defects, including webbing of the neck, peripheral lymphedema, coarctation of the aorta, and hypoplasia of the nails.

Mental retardates with XXX female sex chromosomes (47 total) or with XXXY male (48 total) have also been described. In the male, these patients resemble those with Klinefelter's syndrome.

Other unusual examples reported have included sex chromosome constitutions such as XXYY, XXXX, and XXXXY.

GLOSSARY OF GENETIC TERMS

Abiotrophic disease: Genetically determined disease not evident at birth but manifest later in life.

Acquired: Not hereditary; contracted after birth or in utero.

Allelic genes: Paired, or partner, genes occupying the same locus on homologous (paired) chromosomes. Normally, they segregate from each other during reduction division or mitosis.

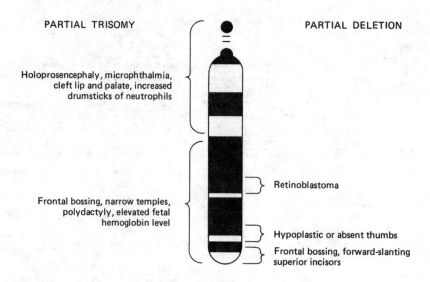

PARTIAL TRISOMY   PARTIAL DELETION

Holoprosencephaly, microphthalmia,
cleft lip and palate, increased
drumsticks of neutrophils

Retinoblastoma

Frontal bossing, narrow temples,
polydactyly, elevated fetal
hemoglobin level

Hypoplastic or absent thumbs

Frontal bossing, forward-slanting
superior incisors

Figure 24–3. Provisional phenotypic map of chromosome 13. (Redrawn and reproduced, with permission, from Lewandowski RC Jr, Yunis JJ: New chromosomal syndromes. *Am J Dis Child* 1975;**129**:515.)

Analogous: Similar in structure but not of the same origin.

Aneuploidy: Abnormal number of chromosomes. In complex aneuploidy, 2 or more chromosomes have an abnormal variation in number.

Autosomes: Chromosomes other than the sex chromosomes.

Barr body: Sex chromatin mass occurring in cells of females; considered to be X chromosome chromatin.

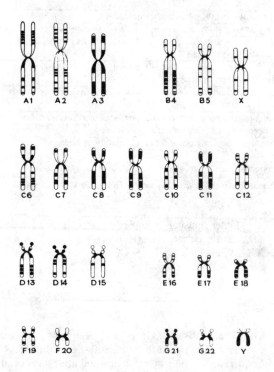

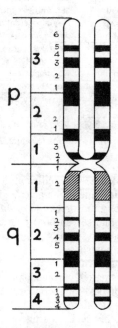

Figure 24–4. *Left:* Karyotype of normal male using Giemsa technique. Demonstrates specific banding pattern of chromosomes. (Redrawn and reproduced, with permission, from Drets ME, Shaw MW: Specific banding patterns of human chromosomes. *Proc Natl Acad Sci USA* 1971;**68**:2073.) *Right:* Fine detail of chromosome No. 1. The numbers identify the regions and banded areas designated by the Paris Conference. All chromosomes are comparably identified. (Redrawn from Paris Conference [1971]: Standardization in human cytogenetics. *Birth Defects* 1972;**8**[7]:18.)

Centromere: The cross-over point or primary constriction that divides a chromosome into 2 arm lengths.

Chimera: An individual with mosaicism.

Chromatid: The 2 halves of the chromosome.

Chromatin body: A special stainable body in the nucleus of body cells, apparently related to staining characteristics of the X chromosome.

Chromosome: A small threadlike or rodlike structure into which the nuclear chromatin divides during mitosis. It is composed of a linear arrangement of genes, each of which occupies a specific locus. Chromosome number is constant for any species. In humans, there are 22 pairs of autosomes and one pair of sex chromosomes.

Cistron: A gene specified as a hereditary unit of function.

Congenital: Existing at or before birth.

Deletion: Loss of a segment of chromosome owing to breakage of chromatid in cell division.

Diploid: Having 2 full sets of homologous chromosomes, as normally occurs in somatic cells.

Dominant: Designating a gene whose phenotypic effect largely or entirely obscures that of its allele.

Drumstick: An accessory lobe on the nucleus of neutrophilic polymorphonuclear leukocytes of females, consisting of a fine stainable thread and a round stainable head; a variant of sex chromatin.

Duplication: Repetition of a small segment of a chromosome. It may result from breakage of chromatid during cell division.

Eugenics: The science dealing with factors that can improve the hereditary qualities of future generations.

Expressivity: The degree of phenotypic expression of a trait (ie, forme fruste versus full expression).

Familial: Pertaining to hereditary or acquired traits that tend to occur in families.

Gamete (germ cell): A cell that can unite with another cell in sexual reproduction (ovum or spermatozoon).

Gene: The unit of heredity in a specific locus in the chromosomes. Alone or in combination, the gene produces a single characteristic, usually a single molecule capable of self-duplication or mutation.

Genetic carrier state: The condition in which a hereditary characteristic is not manifest in an individual but may be genetically transmitted to its offspring.

Genetic code: Sequential order of the bases (cytosine, guanine, adenine, thymine) of DNA that determines the development and metabolism of cells.

Genotype: Hereditary constitution or combination of genes of a given individual or group of genetically identical organisms.

Haploid: Having a single set of chromosomes as normally carried by a gamete.

Hereditary: Transmitted from ancestor to offspring via germ plasm.

Heterologous chromosomes: Paired chromosomes in which each member of the pair has a different configuration and genetic material (such as X and Y chromosomes).

Heterozygote (dizygotic, or fraternal) twins: Twins derived from 2 distinct fertilized ova.

Heterozygous: Having 2 dissimilar members of a hereditary factor pair with 2 genes of an allelic pair not identical.

Homologous chromosomes: Paired, or sister, chromosomes resulting from normal meiosis; each member of the pair has the same configuration and genetic material as the other.

Homozygotic (monozygotic, or identical) twins: Twins derived by division of one fertilized ovum into 2 at an early stage.

Homozygous: Having 2 members of a given hereditary factor that are similar; 2 genes of an allelic pair are identical.

Idiogram: Diagrammatic representation of chromosome complement based on measurement of chromosomes of a number of cells.

Index case: See Proband.

Inversion: Occurs after fracture of a chromatid, with the fragment reattached to the same chromosome in upside-down fashion.

Isochromosome: An abnormal chromosome in which the arms on either side of the centromere have the same genetic material in the same order.

Karyotype: Chromosomal constitution of a cell, individual, or species.

Locus: The specific site of a gene in a chromosome.

Meiosis: Cell division in maturation of sex cells, in which a normal diploid set of chromosomes is reduced to a single (haploid) set by means of 2 successive nuclear divisions and one chromosome division.

Mitosis: Cell division of a mother cell to produce 2 daughter cells of exactly the same chromosomal number and composition as the mother cell.

Monosomy: The presence of only one member of a particular pair of chromosomes.

Mosaic, mosaicism: Different constitution of adjacent tissue resulting from mutation or incorporation of tissue from a nonidentical twin; no intolerance for such tissue is evident; human blood type and sex mosaics have been identified.

Mutation: Transformation of a gene into a different gene in the same locus of the chromosome, with a new gene allelic to the normal gene from which it arose.

Nondisjunction: Failure of a sister pair of chromosomes to separate normally at cell division.

Pedigree: A table or diagram illustrating ancestral lineage; genealogy.

Penetrance: The likelihood or probability that a gene will be morphologically (phenotypically) expressed. It may depend on acquired as well as genetic factors.

Phenotype: Visible characteristics of one individual that are common to a group of apparently identical individuals.

Polyploid: Having more than 2 full sets of homologous chromosomes.

Polysomy: Occurs when one chromosome is represented 4 or more times.

Proband: Individual with a hereditary trait detected independently of the other members of the family. The first proband detected is called the index case, or propositus.

Propositus: See Proband.

Recessive: Designating a gene whose phenotypic effect is obscured by its allelic gene.

Reduction division: Separation of members of homologous pairs of chromosomes, with reduction to the haploid state.

Segregation: Separation of 2 genes of a pair in maturation, so that only one gene goes to each germ cell.

Sex chromatin: See Chromatin body.

Sex chromosome: A chromosome or pair of chromosomes that determines the sex of the individual.

Sex linkage (X linkage): The influence of sex on transmission of hereditary traits. It depends on whether X-linked genes are in the X or Y chromosomes and may be absolute or incomplete.

Sibship: Children of the same parents; sometimes used to include all blood relatives.

Somatic cells: Cells incapable of reproducing the organism.

Translocation: The attachment of extra chromosomal material to a chromosome. It may result from unequal exchange of chromosomal substance between 2 different chromosomes during cell division.

Trisomy: The presence of 3 chromosomes of one type rather than a normal pair of chromosomes.

Zygote: A cell formed by the union of 2 gametes in sexual reproduction.

·   ·   ·

Most classifications of congenital CNS lesions are based on the location and time of occurrence of a malformation. In general, there may be a primary defect involving cells, tissues, organs, embryonal layers, and organ systems, or combinations of these. Clinically important malformations are discussed in the following paragraphs.

SPINA BIFIDA GROUP

Spina bifida results from failure of the vertebral canal to close normally because of a defect in the development of vertebrae. Other abnormalities affecting the development of the spinal cord, brain stem, cerebrum, or cerebellum may be associated, as well as meningoceles, meningomyeloceles, congenital tumors, hydrocephalus, or other somatic developmental defects. Since the bony spinal column closes by the 12th week of intrauterine life, these defects are concerned with early intrauterine life. In general, 2 large

Table 24–3. Types of closure defects.*

Embryonic Origin	Type of Dysplasia	Resultant Condition
Cutaneous; somatic ecto-dermal	Cutaneous	Cutaneous defect, hypertrichosis, hypoplasia of skin, pilonidal cysts, congenital dermal sinuses
Mesodermal	Vertebral	Absence of spinous process, split spinous process, cleft in vertebral neural arch, rachischisis
	Dural	Nonfusion of dura mater
Neural; neuro-ectodermal	Neural tube	Myelodysplasia, intramedullary and extramedullary growth associated with dysraphia
	Neural crest	Ectopia of spinal ganglion

*Reproduced, with permission, from Lichtenstein: Spinal dysraphism. *Arch Neurol Psychiatry* 1940;44:792.

groups may be defined: (1) spina bifida occulta, in which there is a simple defect in the closure of the vertebra; and (2) spina bifida with meningocele or meningomyelocele, where the defect is associated with saclike protrusions of the overlying meninges and skin, which may contain portions of the spinal cord or nerve roots. Simple failure of closure of one or more vertebral arches in the lumbosacral region is a common finding on routine x-ray or autopsy examination of the spine. A slight tendency for familial incidence of this defect has been noted.

Spina Bifida Occulta

This type of defect occurs relatively frequently and is sometimes noticed as an incidental finding on x-ray examinations of the vertebral column. The bony defect, which is present usually in the lumbar or sacral spine, is due to a failure of closure of the laminas of the affected vertebrae. The defect in the spine may be palpated. Associated abnormalities such as hypertrichosis over the affected area, fat deposits, dimpling of the skin, and telangiectases of the overlying skin may occur. Symptoms may be due to the presence of intraspinal lipomas, adhesions, bony spicules, or maldevelopment of the spinal cord. Maldevelopment and deformities of the feet (valgus, varus, or cavus) and scoliosis are commonly associated.

Symptoms may not occur until late and are proportionate to functional impairment of the affected sacral spinal cord and cauda equina. Bladder and bowel dysfunction, radicular motor and sensory symptoms, and skin and vasomotor changes may occur. Muscles of one or both lower extremities may be atrophied, and alteration of tendon reflexes may occur. The finding of a spinal defect on x-ray does not necessarily imply that the patient's symptoms are due to this defect, especially since there is a likelihood of associated congenital or developmental defects. The course of patients with this disorder depends upon the extent and nature of the lesion and the associated congenital defects. Spina bifida occulta as such is compatible with a relatively normal life.

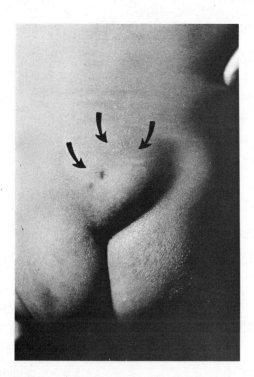

Figure 24–5. Spina bifida occulta. Fat deposit and dimpling of skin overlying spina bifida occulta of lumbosacral spine in infant.

Meningocele

Herniation of the meningeal membranes through the bony vertebral defect usually causes the appearance, low in the midline of the back, of a cystic, soft, translucent tumor.

Meningomyelocele

Nerve roots and spinal cord protrude through the bony vertebral defect and are usually adherent to the inner wall of the meningeal sac. Symptomatically, bladder and bowel incontinence, sexual impotence, and sensory and motor loss of function of the involved spinal cord and nerve roots are apt to occur. At higher levels there may be the clinical picture of complete or incomplete transection of the cord, or combined root and spinal cord symptoms similar to those of syringomyelia.

The threat of meningitis from extension of local infection is always present in meningocele and meningomyelocele. Prophylactic repair of the sac and supportive closure of the tissues over the bony defect may be performed early in life. Excision of spinal sacs that contain neural elements is usually followed by poor results. The closure of a sac, particularly a large one, may be followed by progressive hydrocephalus.

CRANIUM BIFIDUM

Midline defects of fusion of the cranial bone, most commonly occipital, usually accompanied by saclike protrusions of the overlying skin, may occur. The sac contains meninges (meningocele) or meninges and nervous tissue (encephalocele). When the defect is in the occipital region, hydrocephalus is apt to occur. The symptoms and signs depend upon the presence or absence of hydrocephalus or other associated congenital neural malformations. Treatment consists of excision of the sac and its contents, with firm closure of the dura where possible. The prognosis is poor in those cases where the sac contains large amounts of cerebral tissue in the presence of hydrocephalus or other serious neural defects.

CONGENITAL HYDROCEPHALUS

Enlargement of the head associated with the accumulation of cerebrospinal fluid within or without the ventricles of the brain may occur before birth or soon after. Congenital hydrocephalus may be communicating or noncommunicating, depending upon the presence of free flow of cerebrospinal fluid from the ventricles into the lumbar subarachnoid space. This may be determined by use of a test in which dye is injected into the lateral ventricle and its absence or presence in lumbar subarachnoid cerebrospinal fluid is determined.

Head circumference (Table 24–4) is measured by passing a tape measure over the most prominent part of the occiput and just above the supraorbital ridges. The average of normal children at birth is about 35 cm

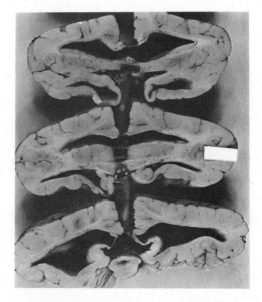

Figure 24–6. Coronal sections of brain of infant with congenital communicating hydrocephalus showing symmetric dilatation of ventricles.

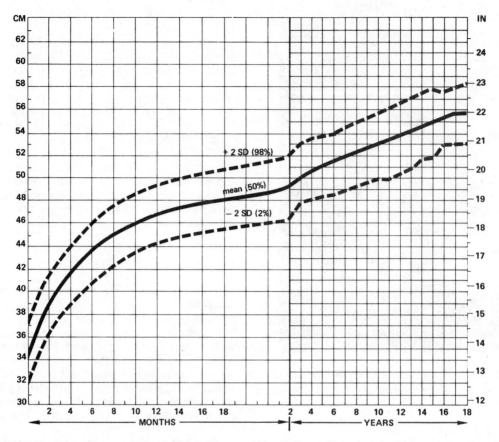

Figure 24–7. Head circumference for boys, birth to 18 years. (After Nellhaus. Reproduced, with permission, from Kempe CH, Silver HK, O'Brien D [editors]: *Current Pediatric Diagnosis & Treatment,* 6th ed. Lange, 1980.)

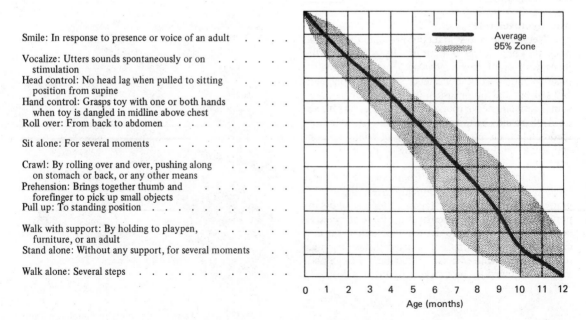

Smile: In response to presence or voice of an adult

Vocalize: Utters sounds spontaneously or on
 stimulation
Head control: No head lag when pulled to sitting
 position from supine
Hand control: Grasps toy with one or both hands
 when toy is dangled in midline above chest
Roll over: From back to abdomen

Sit alone: For several moments

Crawl: By rolling over and over, pushing along
 on stomach or back, or any other means
Prehension: Brings together thumb and
 forefinger to pick up small objects
Pull up: To standing position

Walk with support: By holding to playpen,
 furniture, or an adult
Stand alone: Without any support, for several moments

Walk alone: Several steps

Figure 24–8. Norms of development. (Adapted from Aldrich CA, Norval HA: *J Pediatr* 1946;**29**:304. Reproduced, with permission, from Kempe CH, Silver HK, O'Brien D [editors]: *Current Pediatric Diagnosis & Treatment,* 7th ed. Lange, 1982.)

Table 24—4. Head circumference of normal children. (After Stuart & Meredith.)

Age	Boys, Percentile			Girls, Percentile		
	10	50	90	10	50	90
Birth	33.5	35.3	37.0	33.4	34.7	36.0
3 months	39.2	40.9	42.1	38.5	40.0	41.7
6 months	42.7	43.9	45.4	41.4	42.8	44.5
9 months	44.5	46.0	47.1	43.2	44.6	46.3
12 months	45.5	47.3	48.4	44.3	45.8	47.7
18 months	47.0	48.7	49.9	45.5	47.1	49.0
24 months	48.0	49.7	51.0	46.4	48.1	50.1
36 months	48.9	50.4	51.9	47.5	49.3	51.1

(13.75 inches) ± 1.2 cm. In the first 4 months of life, the head increases by 5 cm (about 1.2 cm per month); during the next 8 months, it increases another 5 cm (10 cm increase at the end of 1 year). The average circumference at 2 years is 49 cm; at 3 years, 50 cm; at 4 years, 50.5 cm; at 5 years, 50.8 cm; and at 6 years, 51.2 cm.

It is assumed that defective absorption of the cerebrospinal fluid into the venous sinuses occurs in some cases. Obstruction in the midbrain as a consequence of a malformed aqueduct of Sylvius occurs in others. The functional obstruction of the foramens of Luschka and Magendie may also occur secondary to intrauterine meningitis with meningeal adhesions, congenital absence, or congenital abnormality.

Symmetric dilatation of the cerebral ventricles and atrophy of the brain are usually present. Other malformations that may be associated include porencephaly, microgyria, macrogyria, absence of the corpus callosum, spina bifida, syringomyelia, Arnold-Chiari malformation, and meningocele. Separation of the suture lines of the skull and bulging of the fontanelles may be evident. The scalp appears thin and stretched, and the lower face appears small by contrast with the upper head. Optic atrophy, mental deficiency, and spastic paralysis of extremities are frequently seen.

The heads of infants may be "transilluminated" with a flashlight held at a right angle against the head in a darkened room. In cases of hydrocephalus, porencephaly, hydranencephaly, and subdural hygroma, transillumination may be pronounced. In other cases,

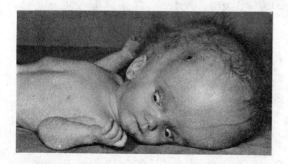

Figure 24—9. Hydrocephalus in 14-month-old infant.

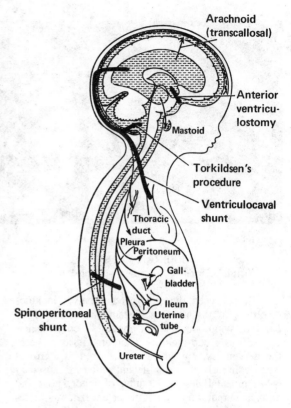

Figure 24—10. Diversionary procedures used for treatment of hydrocephalus. (Reproduced, with permission, from Logue, in: *Biochemical Aspects of Neurological Disorders,* 3rd ed. Cumings JN, Kremer M [editors]. Davis, 1968.)

where there is increased space between the brain and the undersurface of the cranium, a defect of the cranium or scalp, and subdural effusion, an unusual glowing of a side or part of the head may be noted.

In the **Dandy-Walker syndrome,** hydrocephalus occurs with atresia of the foramen of Magendie. The skull may enlarge principally in the occipital region because of the relatively large fourth ventricle, and the bitemporal diameter may remain normal.

Macewen's sign is the presence of tympany on percussion over the lateral ventricle of an infant with increased intracranial pressure and hydrocephalus.

The course of congenital hydrocephalus is usually progressively downhill, with death in the first or second year of life resulting from intercurrent infections. Occasionally, hydrocephalus may be "arrested," and the child grows into adult life with few symptoms beyond enlargement of the head. Surgery is often required, and the outcome may depend upon the success of the operation as well as the presence of other serious malformations of the nervous system. Operations for relief of hydrocephalus include excision or cauterization of the choroid plexuses and shunting procedures by which artificial connections are made between the ventricular system and cisterns or veins, or between subarachnoid spaces and body cavities.

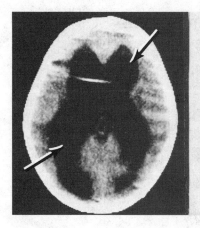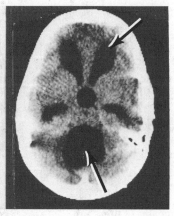

Figure 24–11. CT scan of child with hydrocephalus and ventricular shunt.

CEREBRAL PALSY
(Little's Disease, Infantile Cerebral Palsy)

Broadly used, the term "cerebral palsy" includes disorders of the nervous system characterized by paralytic symptoms in infancy or childhood. This heterogeneous group includes disorders and damage to the nervous system which are incurred in utero, at birth, or in early postnatal life and which are caused by developmental defects, trauma of labor, postnatal anoxia, intrauterine meningitis or encephalitis, cerebrovascular accidents of infancy, and kernicterus.

Various clinical types of cerebral palsy have been noted: spastic, athetoid, ataxic, rigid, and tremorous. Combinations of these groups are common, and other significant neural defects may be associated, such as speech disorders, dysphasia, apraxia, hemianopsia, and mental retardation. Brain injury may be suspected at birth because of listlessness, feeding difficulties, and poverty of movements. The rate of development of motor, speech, and intellectual faculties may be delayed. In mild cases, the defect may not be recognized for several years until it is obvious that the child is physically and intellectually inferior to others of the same age group.

The relative incidence of clinical types of cerebral palsy, classified on the basis of major motor complaints, is as follows: spastic, 65%; athetoid, 25%; rigid, tremorous, ataxic, 10%.

Infantile spastic hemiplegia is the most common form of cerebral palsy, accounting for about one-third of all cases. **Prenatal spastic hemiplegia** is uncommon (less than 5%) and is caused by brain malformations or prenatal "stroke" due to toxemia. **Natal spastic hemiplegia** is the most common type (65%). Predisposing factors include prematurity and heavy birth weight and perhaps also debility of the newborn or bleeding diathesis. Forceps trauma may injure the brain, and physiologic hazards of birth may cause injury to the fetal head, which acts as a battering ram during labor; pelvic disproportion, dystocia, or Pitocin induction may aggravate physiologic trauma. **Postnatal infantile spastic hemiplegia** is common (over 30%). It comprises over 90% of all postnatal cerebral palsies, since most postnatal brain injuries are unilateral. It is usually caused by head trauma, infection and encephalitis, and vascular damage. Motor aphasia is common only in postnatal right hemiplegia.

Mental retardation and convulsive seizures are common in all forms of infantile spastic hemiplegia. The upper extremity is usually more involved than the lower. The sensory handicap may be more disabling than the motor, because proprioception and form discrimination are lost. Failure of growth may be of cerebral origin as a result of involvement of the postcentral gyrus. Hemianopsia may follow damage to the occipital lobe.

Good results have been reported with diazepam (Valium), 2–20 mg daily, for treatment of patients with athetosis.

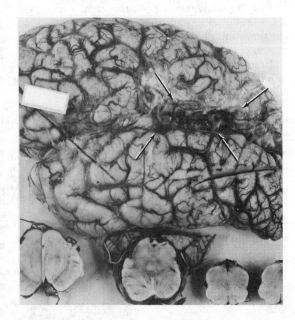

Figure 24–12. Cerebral palsy. Left frontoparietal cystic atrophy of brain of a 33-year-old woman with right hemiparesis since birth.

MENTAL RETARDATION
(See Tables 30–1 and 30–2.)

Mental retardation or mental deficiency is characterized by incomplete or slow intellectual maturation from early years. It may be caused by genetic, biologic, or other factors and usually results in social maladjustment. Poor attention span, inability to concentrate on a single activity, hyperactivity, distractibility, and anxiety may increase the problems of adjustment. Overt evidence of organic brain damage is variably present. Sometimes there are associated convulsive disorders, paralyses, ataxias, deformities, etc. Patients with organic brain damage are more likely to exhibit behavior of unpredictable nature, distractibility or inability to concentrate, hyperkinesis, impulsiveness, overreaction to environmental stimuli, and difficulties in abstract thinking.

The degree of deficiency may be assessed by psychometric tests and clinical evaluation and may vary from borderline to severe. Mental retardation is ordinarily considered to be present if the intelligence quotient (IQ) is less than 70. "Morons" are those with IQs between 70 and 50, and they correspond in intelligence to the average normal 10-year-old child. They can often learn to read and write and may possibly be self-supporting. "Imbeciles" are those with IQs between 50 and 20, and they correspond in intelligence to the average normal 7-year-old child. They are trainable and can be taught a certain degree of self-care. "Idiots" have IQs of less than 20, correspond in intelligence to the average normal 3-year-old child, and often present a severe custodial problem throughout life. Asphyxia, anoxia, and cerebral hemorrhage associated with prolonged labor or prematurity, prenatal infections, and childhood encephalitides are etiologically accountable for a large segment of this group. A family history of mental deficiency may be present in others. Associated neurologic syndromes such as tuberous sclerosis, neurofibromatosis, amaurotic familial idiocy, metabolic disorders, and mongolism are commonly present.

Among the conditions apt to be confused with mental retardation is childhood schizophrenia, or infantile autism. This condition usually develops gradually, and patients may exhibit unusual behavior for a long time before being brought to the doctor. They lose interest in siblings, parents, playmates, and school and seem to live in a world of their own, sitting inactive and apparently preoccupied for hours at a time. They are emotionally cold and show no emotional response to stimuli and environment. Motor awkwardness, mannerisms, and habit spasms are often present, and there may be a flat, mechanical quality in the voice. The clinical features of adult schizophrenia may become apparent as these children grow older.

Children with neuroses are sometimes thought to be mentally retarded. In this group, however, children

Table 24–5. Classification of mental retardation.*

	IQ	Terminology
American Psychiatric Association	70–85	Mild mental deficiency
	50–70	Moderate
	0–50	Severe
World Health Organization	50–69	Mild subnormality
	20–49	Moderate
	0–19	Severe
American Association for Mental Deficiency	70–84	Borderline
	55–69	Mild
	40–54	Moderate

*Reproduced, with permission, from Solomon P, Patch VD (editors): *Handbook of Psychiatry,* 3rd ed. Lange, 1974.

Table 24–6. Identifiable biochemical disorders often associated with mental retardation, characterized by elevated blood amino acids.*

Disease	Amino Acid Accumulated in Blood	Chief Clinical Features in Patients With Biochemical Defect
Phenylketonuria	Phenylalanine	Mental retardation Convulsions Eczema Fair hair and skin
Maple syrup urine disease	Valine Leucine Isoleucine	Mental retardation Spasticity Myoclonic seizures
Tyrosinosis	Tyrosine	Myasthenia gravis
Hyperprolinemia	Proline	Congenital genitourinary tract anomalies Renal disease Photogenic epilepsy Mental retardation
Hydroxyprolinemia	Hydroxyproline	Mental retardation Microscopic hematuria
Histidinemia	Histidine	Delayed speech development Mental retardation
Citrullinuria	Citrulline	Mental retardation Convulsions Vomiting
Hyperglycinemia	Glycine	Mental retardation Ketosis after leucine ingestion Neutropenia, thrombocytopenia Hypogammaglobulinemia
Homocystinuria	Methionine (homocystine in urine)	Mental retardation Seizures Dislocated lenses Thromboembolic phenomena
Oasthouse urine disease	Valine Leucine Isoleucine Methionine Phenylalanine Tyrosine	Mental retardation White hair Edema Unpleasant odor of urine

*Reproduced, with permission, from Efron ML et al: Simple chromatographic screening test for detection of disorders of amino acid metabolism. *N Engl J Med* 1964;**270**:1378 (as modified in: Mental retardation: A handbook for the primary physician. *JAMA* 1965;**191**:183).

Table 24–7. Identifiable biochemical disorders often associated with mental retardation, characterized by increased urinary amino acid but little or no increase in blood concentration.*

Disease	Amino Acids in Excess in Urine	Chief Clinical Features
Hartnup disease	"Neutral" amino acids Many	Mental retardation Ataxia Pellagralike rash
Joseph's syndrome	Proline Hydroxyproline Glycine	Infantile convulsions Increased cerebrospinal fluid protein
Argininosuccinic-aciduria	Argininosuccinic acid	Mental retardation Convulsions Friable hair Ataxia
Cystathioninuria	Cystathionine	Mental retardation Congenital anomalies Psychosis Pituitary disease
Hypophosphatasia	Phosphoethanol-amine	Bone disease Low alkaline phosphatase
Glycinuria, with nephrolithiasis	Glycine	Nephrolithiasis
Galactosemia	Many	Mental retardation Jaundice Cataracts
Hepatolenticular	Many, especially cystine and threonine	Cirrhosis Tremor
Cystinosis	All plasma amino acids	Vitamin D – resistant rickets Acidosis Dehydration Early death

*Reproduced, with permission, from Efron ML et al: Simple chromatographic screening test for detection of disorders of amino acid metabolism. *N Engl J Med* 1964;**270**:1378 (as modified in: Mental retardation: A handbook for the primary physician. *JAMA* 1965;**191**:183).

use neurotic symptoms as a defense against environmental stress or as an outlet for emotional conflicts. Usually, no evidence of brain damage can be found or inferred in the birth history or early life. Hyperactivity and tics are common. Stereotyped repetitions and purposeless, abrupt, involuntary tic movements are prone to occur in older children of this type.

The association of mental retardation with remediable defects in some disorders has led to a more optimistic outlook for selected patients. Thus, the adequate early surgical treatment of craniosynostosis may prevent or favorably modify associated mental retardation. The early recognition and prompt treatment of metabolic disorders such as phenylketonuria, galactosemia, and cretinism may prevent or halt the manifestations of mental retardation in these patients.

Commonly used screening tests of urine of children with mental retardation include the following:

(1) Ferric chloride: A positive (green) reaction occurs with phenylketonuria, tyrosinuria, histidinemia, and oasthouse disease.

(2) Dinitrophenylhydrazine (DNPH): A positive reaction occurs with phenylketonuria, tyrosinuria, histidinemia, oasthouse disease, maple syrup urine disease, hyperlipidemia, hyperglycemia, and Lowe's syndrome.

(3) Sodium nitroprusside: A positive reaction occurs with homocystinuria, cystinuria, and cystathioninuria.

(4) Benedict's solution: A positive reaction occurs with galactosemia, fructosemia and fructosuria, oasthouse disease, and maple syrup urine disease.

(5) Cetyltrimethylammonium bromide: A positive reaction occurs in the presence of mucopolysaccharidoses.

Laurence-Moon-Biedl Syndrome

Mental retardation, adiposogenital dystrophy, retinal pigmentary degeneration, and, sometimes, polydactylism occur in afflicted families.

Sturge-Weber Syndrome

The disease is characterized by localized calcification, cortical atrophy, an ipsilateral port wine nevus of the face or scalp, and associated convulsions. Mental retardation, hemiplegia, or hemianopsia may also occur. A characteristic pattern (cortical calcification) may be demonstrated on skull x-ray.

Lindau-Von Hippel Syndrome

Hemangioblastomas of the cerebellar hemispheres are present, often associated with angiomatosis of the retina, cysts of the kidney and pancreas, and a tendency to familial distribution.

Morquio's Syndrome

This is a familial type of osseous dystrophy characterized by mental deficiency, dwarfism, kyphosis, and impaired joint action. Onset frequently is in the first year of life. (See Gargoylism, p 381.)

MINIMAL BRAIN DYSFUNCTION IN CHILDREN

Children may have minimal brain dysfunction as a result of a variety of chronic brain syndromes. The clinical features may include (1) awkwardness, impaired free movement or coordination; (2) perceptual, intellectual, and memory deficits; (3) alterations in activity, attention, impulse control, and affect; (4) impairments of vision, hearing, and speech; and (5) subclinical seizures. Excessive clumsiness may be evident when the child is tying shoes, learning to ride a bicycle, or catching a ball. Perceptual abilities, right-left orientation, spatial relationships, and body image concept may be disturbed. An organic pattern of learning disturbance may be noted on psychologic testing. Hyperactivity and shortened span of concentration may improve greatly under treatment with dextroamphetamine (Dexedrine), amphetamine (Benzedrine), methylphenidate (Ritalin), or tranquilizers.

DOWN'S SYNDROME
(Mongolian Idiocy, Mongolism)

Mental deficiency in infants with facial and body features superficially resembling those of Mongolian origin is called mongolism. The preferred term now is Down's syndrome. Physical and mental development is retarded. Brachycephaly, flattening of the face, narrowing and slanting of palpebral fissures, epicanthus, broadening and coarsening of the tongue, shortening of stature, and congenital skeletal and visceral anomalies are frequently associated. There is often a single crease across the hand. Trisomy of chromosome number 21 occurs in most cases of Down's syndrome, which is one of the most common causes of mental retardation in children. Translocation of chromosome 21 with a member of pair number 15, 21, or 22 also occurs. Trisomy 21 cases increase in frequency with advancing maternal age. The translocation cases account for the carrier state of Down's syndrome, familial Down's syndrome, and the occurrence of Down's syndrome in younger mothers.

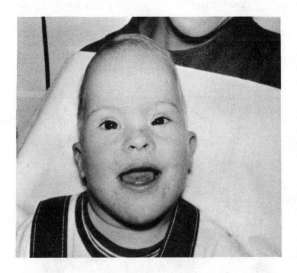

Figure 24–13. Facies of a child with Down's syndrome. (Reproduced, with permission, from Kempe CH, Silver HK, O'Brien D [editors]: *Current Pediatric Diagnosis & Treatment,* 7th ed. Lange, 1982.)

TUBEROUS SCLEROSIS
(Epiloia, Bourneville's Disease)

This congenital, sometimes familial disease begins in early childhood and is characterized by progressive mental deterioration, convulsions, and the appearance of tumors of the skin and viscera. Within the brain are numerous glial nodules, and those projecting from the walls of the lateral ventricles may sometimes be seen in air studies of the brain. The skin tumors, which resemble adenoma sebaceum, are scattered all over the body but are characteristically found about the face, nose, and lips. These skin lesions are small yellow or red-brown nodules in butterfly distribution over the nose and cheeks.

The prognosis is poor and the course progressive in the complete syndrome, with seizures increasing in frequency and the severity of the mental defect progressing. Death frequently occurs before age 30. However, abortive forms with a relatively normal life span, minimal mental defect, and seizures may also occur.

CRANIOSTENOSIS
(Craniosynostosis)

Premature closure of the skull sutures may result in malformation of the skull, with secondary effects upon the brain and eyes. Familial incidence and developmental defects of other bones (particularly of the upper extremities) may be associated. Early operation is usually advisable; the operation of choice is linear craniectomy parallel to the suture that is prematurely fused, with insertion of polyethylene film over the edges to delay closure.

Oxycephaly is characterized by a dome-shaped skull (tower skull), exophthalmos, optic atrophy, and developmental retardation. The skull is of great height, with forehead receding, face narrow and elongated, and eyeballs prominent and protruding. Headaches, papilledema from increased pressure, and secondary optic atrophy are common; mental retardation, convulsive seizures, and deafness sometimes also occur. **Scaphocephaly** results from premature closure of the sagittal suture. Deformity in the shape of the skull is characterized by lateral flattening, high vertex, increased anteroposterior diameter, and bulging forehead. Clinically, scaphocephaly resembles mild oxycephaly. **Brachycephaly** results from premature closure of the coronal suture, so that the head is flattened in the anteroposterior plane and the vault is abnormally high. The forehead is broad, nose flattened, and eyes widely separated. Brachycephaly resembles oxycephaly clinically.

KLIPPEL–FEIL SYNDROME

In this congenital condition, there is a fusion and reduction in number of the upper cervical vertebrae, producing a short neck, a low hairline, and limitation of motion of the neck. Developmental anomalies of the cervical spinal cord may also be present, such as syringomyelia, spina bifida, and other congenital defects.

NEUROFIBROMATOSIS
(Von Recklinghausen's Disease)

This congenital disorder is characterized by development of multiple tumors of the spinal or cranial nerves, tumors of the skin, and cutaneous pigmenta-

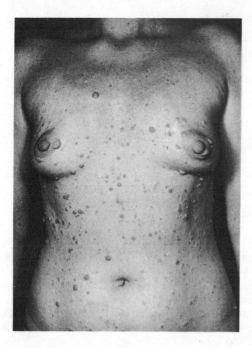

Figure 24–14. Neurofibromatosis (von Recklinghausen's disease). Multiple cutaneous and subcutaneous nodules.

tion. Changes in the skin include plexiform neurofibromas, pedunculated or sessile polyps, café au lait spots, and port wine or anemic nevi. Bone changes and local overgrowth of tissue causing hypertrophy of the tongue, face, and extremities may occur. Meningioma and gliomas of the CNS may be associated. The cutaneous manifestations together with overgrowth of skin and other tissues may produce characteristic deformities and disfigurements. The course is often relatively benign, with no shortening of life span. How-

ever, in patients with cranial nerve or spinal root lesions, disabling symptoms requiring surgery may occur.

ARNOLD–CHIARI MALFORMATION

In this anomaly, a projection of medulla and cerebellum extends through the foramen magnum and into the cervical spinal canal. It is frequently associated with spina bifida. Presumably during fetal life, fixation of the lower spinal cord or its nerve roots may exert traction on the upper cervical cord and brain stem, causing the medulla and cerebellum to herniate through the foramen magnum. Hydrocephalus is usually present. Other developmental defects may be associated, such as defects in the skull bones, spinal column, spinal cord, and meninges.

Three degrees, or types, of Arnold-Chiari malformation may occur. In type 1, there is downward displacement of the cerebellum and medulla. In type 2 there is, in addition, elongation of the fourth ventricle into the spinal cord. In type 3, there is herniation of the cerebellum through a bony defect of a cervical spina bifida.

Signs and symptoms usually are evident in the first few months of life and are related to the associated hydrocephalus and other developmental neural de-

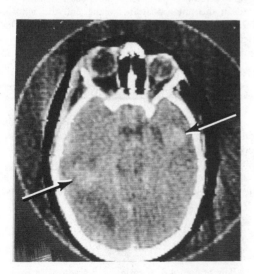

Figure 24–15. CT scan of intracerebral masses in a 5-year-old girl with neurofibromatosis and optic atrophy.

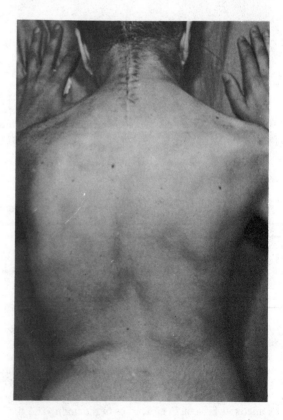

Figure 24–16. Arnold-Chiari malformation in a 31-year-old woman. Note scoliosis and atrophy of shoulders.

fects. Prognosis is poor in these cases. Hydrocephalus is attributed to obstruction of the basal cistern; compression of brain stem and stretching of cranial and cervical nerves produce other signs and symptoms. Rarely, onset of symptoms may be delayed until adult life and may simulate symptoms produced by posterior fossa tumor, syringomyelia, disseminated sclerosis, or platybasia.

Treatment of infants includes decompression of the posterior fossa and excision of the sac of the spinal region; in adults, decompression of the posterior fossa is performed.

SYRINGOMYELIA

Syringomyelia, a disease of the spinal cord and brain stem of unknown cause associated with gliosis and cavitation of spinal cord and brain stem, is characterized clinically by muscular wasting and weakness, varying types of sensory defects, signs of injury to the long tracts, and trophic disturbances. It is considered by many to be the result of imperfect closure of the neural tube, the persistence of embryonic rests giving rise to a proliferation of glial cells in the central portion of the spinal cord about the central canal.

Lower cervical cord segments are usually affected, although the disease may similarly affect the lumbar cord and brain stem. Constitutional or developmental defects are frequently associated, such as "pigeon breast," scoliosis, cervical rib, or hydrocephalus. Pathologically, there is central gliosis of the affected portion of the cord and often associated cystic cavitation with the presence of thick yellow fluid. A coincidence of syringomyelia and intramedullary tumors (gliomas, hemangiomas) has been noted.

Symptoms usually occur in the second or third decade of life and are characterized by the early loss of pain and temperature sense, with preservation of touch and deep pressure sense in the lower cervical dermatomes. The classic and most common form is that in which the cervical spinal cord is involved. Presenting symptoms may be wasting of small muscles of the hand and painless burns of the fingers or forearm.

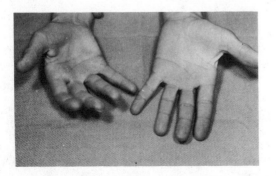

Figure 24–17. Wasting of the small muscles of the hands in a woman with syringomyelia.

Weakness and atrophy of the shoulder girdle muscles may be associated, as well as Horner's syndrome, nystagmus, and vasomotor and trophic disturbances of the upper extremities. Loss of pain and temperature sensation in the cervical and thoracic dermatomes is apt to be in a shawllike distribution (see Fig 10–9). Deep reflexes of upper extremities may be absent. As a result of long tract spinal cord damage, spasticity and ataxia of lower extremities and impaired bladder function may be present. Charcot joints are common in this disorder. **Morvan's syndrome** consists of the formation of slowly healing, painless infections of the fingers or toes in an anesthetic extremity, as in syringomyelia.

When the lumbosacral region alone is involved in syringomyelia, the clinical picture may be characterized by weakness and atrophy of the lower extremities and pelvic girdle, dissociated sensory loss in lumbosacral segments, bladder paralysis, and vasomotor and trophic disturbances of the lower extremities. When the medulla is involved (syringobulbia), atrophy and fibrillation of the tongue, loss of pain and temperature sense in the face, nystagmus, dysphonia, or respiratory stridor may occur.

After an initial rapid progression, the disease usually progresses slowly for years. New clinical signs and symptoms reflect the further involvement of CNS tissue. In spinal cases, death usually is the result of intercurrent infection; in syringobulbia, death may occur within a few months as a result of destruction of medullary nuclei.

Myelography discloses in many cases a partial or complete block in the zone of the syringomyelia, or a characteristic deformity of the contrast column may be detected. Treatment varies with the degree of clinical involvement and the evidence of block on myelographic study. Laminectomy and decompression may be performed, with needle aspiration or myelotomy through the posterior median fissure of the spinal cord in selected cases. Roentgen therapy of the affected area of the spinal cord has been advocated, but the results of such treatment are generally poor.

PLATYBASIA
(Basilar Impression)

Platybasia is a deformity of the occipital bone and upper end of the cervical spine and results from defective development. It is sometimes characterized by fusion of the atlas with the basioccipital bone and accompanied by abnormalities of the odontoid process of the axis. Signs of compression of the medulla, complete obstruction of the subarachnoid space, and hydrocephalus may occur. Symptomatically, the disease may resemble syringomyelia, multiple sclerosis, or progressive spastic paralysis. When lateral x-ray of the skull shows the dens extending above Chamberlain's line (a straight line drawn from the posterior lip of the foramen magnum to the posterior border of the hard palate), platybasia should be suspected. Surgical decompression of the foramen magnum, freeing of adhesions, and occasionally amputation of the cerebellar tonsils are sometimes indicated for treatment.

CERVICAL RIB SYNDROME
(Thoracic Outlet Syndrome)

The brachial plexus and subclavian artery may be compressed in the neck by a rudimentary cervical rib, fibrous band, first thoracic rib, or tight scalene muscle, giving rise to sensory, motor, or vascular symptoms in one or both upper extremities. The onset of symptoms has been related by some to the loss of tone in shoulder girdle muscles with age or excessive trauma to these parts incurred by lifting or straining.

Cervical ribs, rudimentary or fully developed, are relatively common although frequently asymptomatic. Although they are frequently bilateral, cervical ribs may give rise to unilateral complaints. Prominence of the lower neck above the clavicle on one or both sides may be obvious on inspection. Pressure in this region will give rise to local pain as well as pain referred to the hand and arm. Pain and paresthesia, particularly in the ulnar portion of the hand and forearm, most commonly occur. Impaired perception of pain and light touch in the hand or forearm and muscular weakness of small hand muscles may also be present. Coldness and blueness of the hand and diminished pulsation in radial and ulnar arteries may be noted. Horner's syndrome, resulting from damage to cervical sympathetics, has occurred. **Adson's test,** or maneuver, is usually positive on the affected side. In this maneuver, the patient is seated, hands resting on thighs, and is instructed to take a deep inspiration, hold the neck in full hyperextension, and then turn the head as far as possible, first to one side and then the other. Obliteration of the pulse on one side is considered a positive test. **Naffziger's syndrome** (scalenus anticus syndrome) is characterized by pain in the arm, shoulder, and neck and is associated with atrophy of the small muscles of the hand and numbness of the hand in ulnar distribution. It is caused by compression of the lowermost cord of the brachial plexus by the scalenus anticus muscle.

The clinical course is subject to considerable variations. Frequent remissions or slow progression occurs. Temporary relief may be obtained by wearing a sling support on the affected extremity. Rest in bed, traction on the neck, and the use of pillows to support the shoulders are also helpful. Surgical removal of cervical ribs, division of fibrous bands, or section of the scalenus anticus muscles may give permanent relief.

ARTERIOSCLEROSIS OF THE BRAIN

The primary pathologic change in arteriosclerosis of the brain occurs in the cerebral blood vasculature, although similar changes may be present in other systemic vessels also. The disease is predominantly one of old age and is considered by many to be a normal manifestation of the aging process in humans. Disturbances in metabolism—especially of fats—are believed to be a prominent associated change.

Pathology

Atheromatous changes in the arterial system are found relatively frequently at postmortem examination of the bodies of people who have reached middle age. Vessels of all sizes may be affected. Microscopically, one sees a combination of degenerative and proliferative changes. The muscularis is the main site of degeneration; the intima the main site of proliferation. Disseminated areas of softening of the brain, generalized atrophy, and senile plaques in the cortex are frequently found.

The most frequent and severe atherosclerotic lesions noted in an analysis of 1175 consecutive autopsies were located in 4 areas of the circle of Willis: the upper and lower basilar artery, the internal carotid artery at its trifurcation, the first third of the middle cerebral artery, and the first part of the posterior cerebral artery. Severe narrowing of vessels sufficient to cause vascular insufficiency occurred in 2% of cases as early as age 30–40 years and in as many as 6–8% in patients from age 60 to 70 years. In younger patients, vessel narrowing in the anterior part of the circle of Willis occurred in the internal carotid artery or the first part of the middle cerebral arteries. In older patients, narrowing was almost exclusively present in the posterior part of the circle of Willis in the basilar artery, the vertebral arteries, or the first part of the posterior cerebral arteries.

Clinical Findings

Headache, dizziness, tinnitus, and insomnia are common, and memory may be impaired. Personality changes are well recognized, and judgment is apt to be impaired; aphasia, delusions, hallucinations, behavior disorders, and dementia may occur in the later stages. Paralysis agitans and apoplectic syndromes are com-

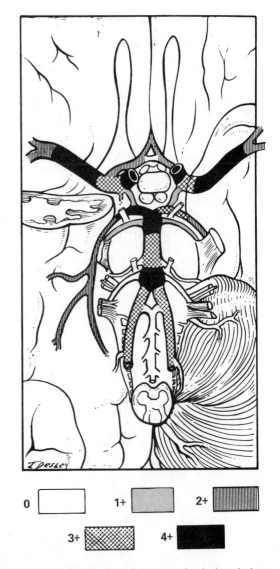

0		1+		2+	

3+		4+	

Figure 25–1. Distribution of degenerative lesions in large cerebral arteries of the circle of Willis in 1175 consecutive autopsies. Severity of lesions is illustrated by intensity of shaded areas, the darkest areas showing the most severe lesions. (Reproduced, with permission, from Baker & Iannone: *Neurology* 1961;11:23.)

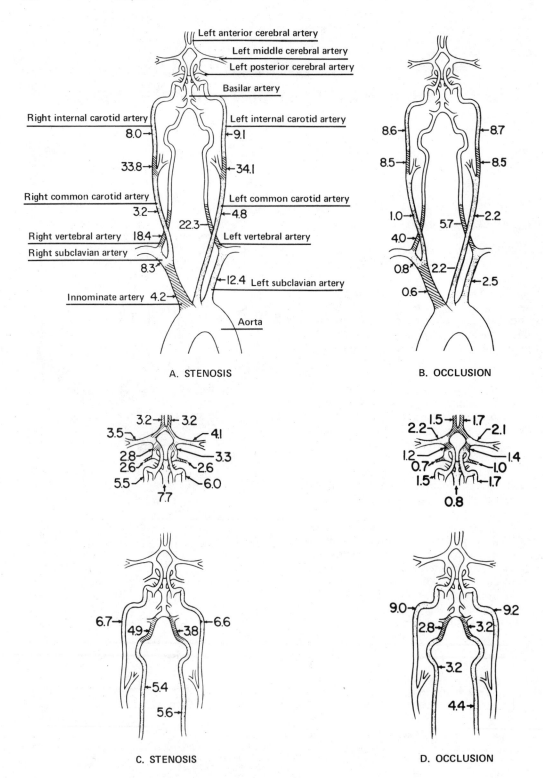

Figure 25–2. Frequency distribution of arterial lesions of 4748 patients with cerebrovascular insufficiency. Extracranial lesions in figures A and B are surgically accessible. (Modified and reproduced, with permission, from Hass et al: Joint study of extracranial arterial occlusion. *JAMA* 1968;**203**:961.)

mon complications. Evidence of arteriosclerosis of other parts such as the retina or the extremities may coexist.

Treatment & Prognosis

There is no specific therapy for the prevention or cure of this disease. Symptomatic therapy is employed as necessary.

HYPERTENSIVE ENCEPHALOPATHY

Hypertensive encephalopathy syndromes affecting the CNS are frequently encountered in essential hypertension as well as in glomerulonephritis associated with hypertension.

Pathology (Cerebrovascular Accidents)

The findings usually associated with cerebral arteriosclerosis (ie, thickening and hyalinization of the muscularis) are noted with narrowing of the lumens of the vessels and hyaline deposits beneath the endothelium. Recurrent arterial spasms associated with altered permeability of the blood-brain barrier are believed to occur prior to the onset of severe arteriosclerotic changes. Brain edema or swelling is commonly noted; many small infarcts and petechial hemorrhages may be found.

Clinical Findings

Anorexia, weakness, vomiting, headache, and dizziness are common. Transitory focal motor or sensory signs may occur, presumably as a result of temporarily altered local cerebral function. Symptoms may be accentuated by rises in blood pressure following emotional disturbances.

Convulsive seizures preceded by an aura are frequently associated with abrupt increases in blood pressure. Variable degrees of changes in the fundus are noted: narrowing of arteries, evidence of old and recent retinal hemorrhages, papilledema, exudates, and arteriovenous nicking. Cerebrospinal fluid pressure is usually elevated and protein increased, with values up to 200 mg/dL. Blood nonprotein nitrogen may be normal or only slightly elevated.

Treatment

Medical management may include the use of sedatives, salt restriction, hypotensive drugs, psychotherapy, anticonvulsant drugs, and autonomic ganglionic blocking agents. Surgical treatment, usually the removal of a portion of the lumbodorsal sympathetic chains, has been advocated in some clinics for patients with early malignant hypertension and good renal function.

CEREBROVASCULAR ACCIDENTS

The acute onset of apoplexy, or a "stroke," is usually associated with disease of the intracranial vas-

cular tree or of the blood or is due to trauma. The commonest causes of generalized or focal disturbance of brain function are cerebral vascular lesions.

The main types of spontaneous cerebrovascular accidents may be classified as (1) cerebral thrombosis, (2) cerebral hemorrhage, (3) cerebral embolism, or (4) subarachnoid hemorrhage.

Cause

Cerebrovascular accidents may occur at any age, but intracerebral hemorrhage and thrombosis are rare before age 40 years. Peak incidence for cerebral thrombosis is at age 50–70 years; for cerebral hemorrhage, 40–70 years.

Cerebral angiographic as well as postmortem studies have disclosed that in patients with cerebrovascular insufficiency there is a high incidence of occlusion or stenosis of extracranial arteries (Fig 25–2).

Pathology

A. Cerebral Thrombosis: Cerebral thrombosis is usually associated with softening of the brain (encephalomalacia); occasionally, softening of the brain occurs without demonstrable thrombosis of a cerebral vessel. By far the commonest cause is arteriosclerosis. Other causes include vasculitis, meningitis, encephalitis, thromboangiitis obliterans, periarteritis nodosa, polycythemia, dehydration, mechanical obstruction by masses, and systemic acute infections of childhood. In patients with arteriosclerosis, cerebral thrombosis is believed to follow clotting of the blood at a site where its flow is impeded by a sclerotic plaque on the vessel wall. Ischemia and infarction of brain tissue in the area supplied may follow occlusion of the cerebral artery, with congestion and edema of neighboring zones. After a few days, edema diminishes; ischemic brain may undergo necrosis (**pale infarct**). Necrotic brain tissue is liquefied and removed by macrophages; a glial and vascular scar partially replaces the destroyed brain tissue, producing shrinking of brain tissue or formation of small multilocular cysts filled with clear fluid. Occasionally, red blood cells invade the necrotic tissue area to form a **red infarct;** in these cases it has been felt that the obstructing clot (or embolus) moves distally, permitting hemorrhage through the necrotic vessel wall.

B. Cerebral Hemorrhage: Hemorrhage into the brain or meninges results from rupture of one of the cerebral vessels and in the great majority of cases is from a ruptured arteriosclerotic vessel. Other causes include rupture of congenital and mycotic aneurysms, acute infections, toxic agents, blood dyscrasias, trauma, and systemic disease. Hemorrhage deep into the substance of the brain—especially the pons and midbrain—may result from head trauma or in association with supratentorial brain tumor. Diffusely scattered hemorrhages of various sizes may result from damage to brain vessels by acute infection, toxins or drugs, acute leukemia, polycythemia, thrombocytopenic purpura, and scurvy. The mechanism of rupture of diseased vessels remains obscure. Some hemor-

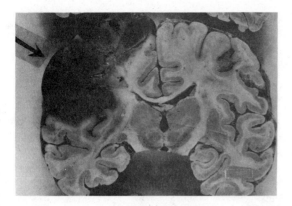

Figure 25-3. Hemorrhagic (red) infarct of right cerebral hemisphere in a 67-year-old hypertensive man.

rhages are of arterial and others of venous origin. Softening of the brain tissue about a blood vessel probably facilitates rupture of that vessel. Rupture of the vasa vasorum of medium-sized vessels may precipitate cerebral hemorrhage. Changes in caliber and tension within the vessel may contribute to rupture of a vessel.

The blood clot destroys and replaces adjacent brain tissue; neighboring brain tissue is usually softened. In large hemorrhages, the site of the ruptured vessel may not be apparent. The most common site for simple hemorrhages is the basal ganglia extending to involve the internal capsule and frequently rupturing into the lateral ventricles, where blood spreads throughout the ventricular system and into the subarachnoid space of the convexity and base of the brain. In cases where recovery ensues, blood and necrotic brain tissue are removed by macrophages. Blood is removed, and destroyed brain tissue is completely replaced by connective tissue, glia, and new blood vessels, producing a shrunken, fluid-filled area.

C. Cerebral Embolism: Cerebral embolism is the occlusion of a cerebral vessel by a small piece of blood clot, tumor, fat, air, or other substance, or a clump of bacteria. Following occlusion of the vessel,

necrosis of the area supplied by the vessel occurs. Most cerebral emboli are sterile, although emboli of patients with pulmonary infections or infective endocarditis may contain bacteria and may give rise to encephalitis, abscess, or meningitis.

The most common source of cerebral embolism is heart disease, although embolism may occur with thrombotic or suppurative processes of any part of the body or with extracranial vascular disease. Air embolism may follow lung injuries. Fat embolism may be associated with fractures of long bones. In children, cerebral emboli occur with rheumatic heart disease or infective endocarditis; in middle-aged and elderly patients, cerebral embolism frequently occurs with atrial fibrillation or coronary thrombosis. Embolus may completely or partially occlude a cerebral vessel. The area of brain tissue supplied by this vessel becomes infarcted and resolves in somewhat the same way in which resolution of a thrombotic infarct occurs. Red infarcts of the brain often occur with cerebral embolism. If the embolism is septic, encephalitis or abscess or, if infection is confined to the vessel, mycotic aneurysmal dilatation may occur. This may later rupture, giving rise to cerebral hemorrhage. Emboli to the brain are frequently multiple, and there may be infarcts to lungs, spleen, kidneys, and other viscera and peripheral vessels.

D. Subarachnoid Hemorrhage: This may be caused by head trauma, blood dyscrasias, intracranial tumor, vascular anomalies, intracerebral hemorrhages, or infectious disease. Primary subarachnoid hemorrhage refers to bleeding due to rupture of a vessel in the subarachnoid space. The vast majority of cases are due to congenital weakness of the vessel. Maldevelopment of the media, especially at the area of bifurcation, has often been noted. In older age groups, arteriosclerosis is a contributing factor. Septic emboli with mycotic aneurysms and syphilis are occasionally significant factors.

E. Recurrent Cerebral Ischemia: Recurrent cerebral ischemia with transient impairment of cerebral circulation may produce recurring attacks of approximately the same pattern depending upon which artery is chiefly affected. These ischemic episodes, formerly called "vasospasm," are considered to be a warning of impending or threatening stroke. Attacks may last a few seconds or minutes and may vary in number from a few to hundreds. These attacks appear to be closely related to atherosclerosis and thrombosis and are apt to occur when local cerebral circulation is about to fail completely. Although precipitation of attacks has been attributed to transient fall in blood pressure, this is often difficult to confirm objectively. Anticoagulants may abolish the attacks in many cases, but their specific mode of action is not known.

F. Progressive Cerebral Ischemia: Narrowing of the extracranial arteries by arteriosclerotic patches—particularly the internal carotid artery at its origin in the neck—has been incriminated in some cases of transient cerebral ischemias and infarction. Routine postmortem studies have disclosed that in

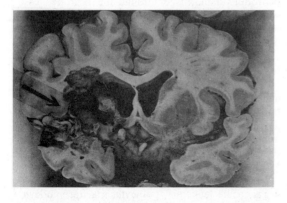

Figure 25-4. Postencephalomalacic cyst of right cerebral hemisphere.

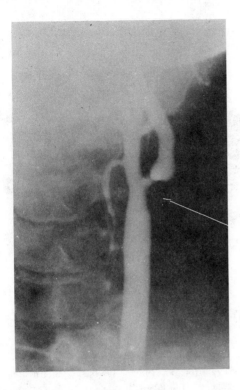

Figure 25–5. Carotid angiogram showing stenosis of the common and internal carotid arteries at the bifurcation in the neck.

patients over age 50 years, about 40% have at least one major cervical carotid or vertebral artery reduced by more than half. In patients whose history has been consistent with cerebral ischemia, high-grade cervical arterial stenosis is present in about 70% on postmortem examination. The large number of patients who have cervical arterial stenosis without ischemic symptoms emphasizes the importance of interpreting angiograms of stenosis or occlusion with due regard for the clinical features presented.

Pulseless disease (Takayasu's syndrome) is produced by progressive stenosis of the major arteries arising from the aortic arch, with consequent obliteration of peripheral radial pulses. Cerebral infarction is apt to be associated. The cause is obscure, although syphilis has been noted in some cases.

Clinical Findings

The general clinical picture is apt to be similar for "strokes" of varying causes. Premonitory symptoms are infrequent. These include headache, dizziness, drowsiness, and mental confusion. Local premonitory signs are most likely to be indicative of thrombosis. Onset is usually sudden, and maximum intensity is reached within a few hours at most. Headache commonly occurs, and stupor or coma is present during the acute phase. Focal neurologic signs (paralysis, sensory loss, and speech defects) are common. Generalized neurologic signs include headache, vomiting, convul-

sions, and coma; these are most common with cerebral hemorrhage. Nuchal rigidity is common with intracerebral or subarachnoid hemorrhage. In the period following a stroke, mental signs and symptoms (confusion, disorientation, and memory defects) are common. Early symptoms and signs vary considerably. The onset of a stroke may be violent, with the patient falling to the ground and lying inert like a person in deep sleep, with flushed face, stertorous or Cheyne-Stokes respirations, full and slow pulse, and one arm and leg usually flaccid. Lesser grades of stroke may consist of slight derangement of speech, thought, motion, sensation, or vision. Consciousness need not be altered. Symptoms may last seconds to minutes or longer and may persist indefinitely. Some degree of recovery is usual.

Survivors of the acute phase of a stroke often enter a convalescent, or chronic recovery, phase. Varied signs and symptoms may be present, usually resembling the acute manifestations and related to the location and degree of brain damage. Recovery is sometimes remarkably complete, so that altered brain function may be hardly demonstrable even with special tests (EEG, psychometrics, pneumoencephalograms, etc). Generally, however, patients have lesser grades of their initial defects (eg, hemiparesis, numbness, aphasia, hemianopsia, impaired mentation). Paralyzed limbs and parts in this later phase usually show signs of upper motor neuron disease: spastic weak muscles with little muscle atrophy, hyperactive deep reflexes, diminished or absent superficial reflexes, and pathologic reflexes such as a positive Babinski sign.

Pseudobulbar palsy is characterized by weakness of muscles supplied by the medulla oblongata (bulb), which controls talking, swallowing, and pharyngeal and tongue movements. It is caused by multiple lesions in both cerebral hemispheres, particularly thromboses in cerebral arteriosclerosis. It may occur without paralysis of the extremities and is often associated with loss of emotional control and spontaneous outbursts of laughing and crying.

Specific focal signs are associated with occlusion of particular arteries. These are outlined below:

A. Common and Internal Carotid Artery: Occlusion may be asymptomatic in young persons with a normal circle of Willis. In middle-aged or elderly patients, any of the following may occur: (1) transient attacks of hemiplegia at first, with persistent hemiparesis thereafter; (2) unilateral loss of vision (ophthalmic artery occlusion); and (3) aphasia when the dominant hemisphere is affected.

B. Anterior Cerebral Artery: This artery supplies the medial aspect of the anterior two-thirds of the cerebral hemisphere. It arises from the internal carotid artery. Its branches include the following: (1) the frontopolar artery, to the anterior portion of the medial surface of the frontal lobe; (2) the callosomarginal artery, to the posterior portion of the medial surface of the frontal lobe; (3) the pericallosal artery, to the corpus callosum and the posterior portion of the medial surface of the frontal lobe; and (4) the recurrent

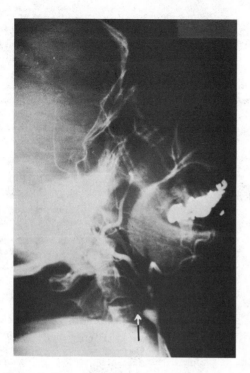

Figure 25–6. Internal carotid artery thrombosis. Occlusion of first portion of internal carotid artery just beyond bifurcation of common carotid artery, with filling of external carotid artery and branches in carotid angiogram.

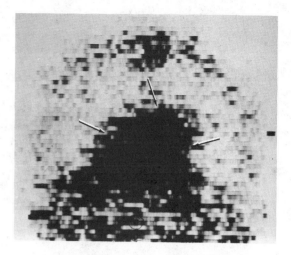

Figure 25–8. Cerebroscintigram with ^{203}Hg (posterior view) of bilateral posterior cerebral infarcts in a 56-year-old man with acute cortical blindness.

artery of Heubner, which appears at about the level of the anterior communicating artery and supplies the most anterior portion of the basal ganglia and the adjacent internal and external capsules.

Occlusion of the main trunk of the anterior cerebral artery may cause contralateral hemiplegia (affecting chiefly the lower extremity), mild sensory deficits in the contralateral lower extremity, mental confusion, and clouding of consciousness.

C. Middle Cerebral Artery: This artery supplies the greater portion of the convexity of the cerebral hemisphere. It is the largest branch of the internal carotid artery and initially lies deep within the fissure of Sylvius. Its branches include the following: (1) perforating branches to the basal ganglia, internal capsule, and thalamus (lenticular, lenticulostriate arteries); (2) the ascending frontoparietal artery, to the lateroposterior portion of the frontal lobe and the lateral portion of the parietal lobe; (3) the posterior parietal artery, to the parietal lobe; (4) the angular artery, to the posterior parietal lobe and the superior posterior temporal lobe; and (5) the posterior temporal artery, to the superior and posterior portions of the temporal lobe.

Occlusion of the main trunk of the middle cerebral artery may cause coma, contralateral flaccid hemiplegia, hemianesthesia, and hemianopsia, and profound motor and sensory aphasia if the dominant side is involved.

Occlusion of perforating branches may cause contralateral hemiplegia. Contralateral rigidity and tremor may follow.

Occlusion of the posterior parietal, angular, or posterior temporal artery may cause contralateral hemiparesis, contralateral astereognosis, contralateral homonymous hemianopsia, and sensory aphasia, agnosia, apraxia, and alexia if the dominant side is involved.

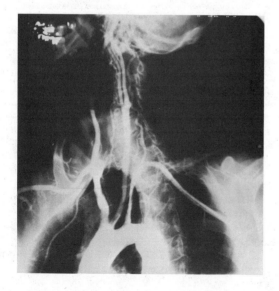

Figure 25–7. Aortic arch angiogram via left brachial catheter, demonstrating normal aortic arch and arteries in a 65-year-old man with transient cerebral ischemia attacks.

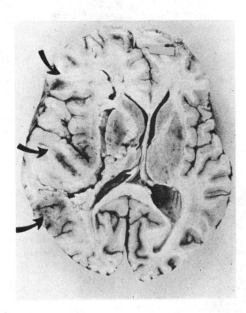

Figure 25–9. Middle cerebral artery thrombosis. Massive infarction of the cerebral hemisphere, with a shift of ventricles to the opposite side simulating the effects of intracerebral mass lesion.

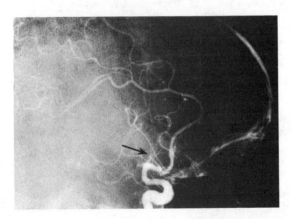

Figure 25–10. Middle cerebral artery thrombosis. Carotid angiogram showing filling of the carotid siphon and anterior cerebral artery and branches. The middle cerebral artery does not fill because of thrombosis at its origin.

D. Posterior Cerebral Artery: This artery supplies the posterior pole and the medial portion (posterior third) of the cerebral hemisphere and the inferior portion of the temporal lobe. It usually takes its origin from the basilar artery, occasionally from the internal carotid artery. Its branches include (1) the anterior temporal artery, to the inferior surface of the temporal lobe; (2) the posterior temporal artery, to the inferior surface of the temporal lobe; (3) the posterior occipital artery, to the inferior and posteromedial portion of the occipital lobe and the posterior corpus callosum; (4) the calcarine artery, to the pericalcarine cortex; and (5) collateral arteries (thalamogeniculate and thalamo-

perforating branches), to the basal ganglia and midbrain.

Occlusion of the main trunk of the posterior cerebral artery may cause contralateral hemiplegia (usually transient), contralateral hemianesthesia, contralateral homonymous hemianopsia, and sensory aphasia if the dominant side is involved. Less often, occlusion also causes ipsilateral cerebellar signs, contralateral rigidity, tremors, and choreiform movements.

Occlusion of the posterior occipital artery may cause thalamic syndrome with contralateral hemianalgesia (pain and temperature) and contralateral spontaneous dysesthesia and pain.

Occlusion of the calcarine artery may cause contralateral homonymous hemianopsia with loss of half of macular vision, and visual agnosia if the dominant side is involved.

The retrolenticular capsule syndrome consists of hemiplegia, hemihypalgesia, hemianesthesia, and hemianopsia resulting from occlusion of that branch of the posterior cerebral artery which supplies the posterior portion of the internal capsule.

E. Posterior Inferior Cerebellar Artery: This artery supplies the posterior inferior portion of the cerebellum and the lateral portion of the medulla. It arises from the vertebral artery just posterior to the basilar artery. Its branches include (1) the medial branch, to the posterior inferior portion of the cerebel-

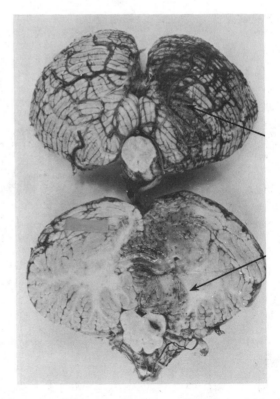

Figure 25–11. Hemorrhagic infarct in distribution of right posterior inferior cerebellar artery (Wallenberg's syndrome).

Table 25—1. Diagnosis of cerebrovascular disorders.

	Intracerebral Hemorrhage	Cerebral Thrombosis	Cerebral Embolism	Subarachnoid Hemorrhage	Vascular Malformation and Intracranial Bleeding
Onset	Generally during activity. Severe headache (if patient is able to report findings).	Prodromal episode of dizziness, aphasia, etc, often with improvement between attacks. Unrelated to activity.	Onset usually within seconds or minutes. No headache. Usually no prodrome. Unrelated to activity.	Sudden onset of severe headache unrelated to activity.	Sudden "stroke" in young patient. No headache. Unrelated to activity.
Course	Rapid hemiplegia and other phenomena over minutes to one hour.	Gradual progression over minutes to hours. Rapid improvement at times.	Rapid improvement may occur.	Variable; apt to be at worst in initial few days after onset.	Most critical period is usually in early stages.
History and related disorders	Suspect diagnosis especially if other hemorrhagic manifestations are present and in acute leukemia, aplastic anemia, thrombopenic purpura, and cirrhosis of the liver.	Evidence of arteriosclerosis, especially coronary, peripheral vessels, aorta. Associated disorders: diabetes mellitus, xanthomatosis.	Evidence of recent emboli: (1) other organs (spleen, kidneys, lungs), extremities, intestines; (2) several regions of brain in different cerebrovascular areas.	History of recurrent stiff neck, headaches, subarachnoid bleeding.	History of repeated subarachnoid hemorrhages, epilepsy.
Sensorium	Rapid progression to coma.	Relative preservation of consciousness.	Relative preservation of consciousness.	Relatively brief disturbance of consciousness.	Relatively brief disturbance of consciousness.
Neurologic examination	Focal neurologic signs or special arterial syndromes; nuchal rigidity.	Focal neurologic signs or special arterial syndromes.	Focal neurologic signs or special arterial syndromes.	Focal neurologic signs frequently absent; nuchal rigidity, positive Kernig and Brudzinski signs.	Focal neurologic signs; cranial bruit.
Special findings	Hypertensive retinopathy, cardiac hypertrophy, and other evidences of hypertensive cerebrovascular disease may be present.	Evidence of arteriosclerotic cardiovascular disease frequently present.	Cardiac arrhythmias or infarction (source of emboli usually in the heart).	Subhyaloid (preretinal) hemorrhages.	Subhyaloid (preretinal) hemorrhages and retinal angioma.
Blood pressure	Arterial hypertension.	Arterial hypertension frequent.	Normotensive.	Arterial hypertension frequent.	Normotensive.
CSF	Grossly bloody.	Clear.	Clear.	Grossly bloody.	Grossly bloody.
Skull x-ray	Shift of pineal to opposite side.	Calcification of internal carotid artery siphon visible; shift of pineal to opposite side may occur.	Pineal apt to show little if any displacement.	Partial calcification of walls of aneurysm sometimes noted.	Characteristic calcifications in skull x-rays may be present.
Cerebral angiography	Hemorrhagic area seen as avascular zone surrounded by stretched and displaced arteries and veins.	Arterial obstruction of narrowing of circle of Willis (internal carotid, etc).	Arterial obstruction of circle of Willis branches (internal carotid, etc).	Typical aneurysmal pattern in circle of Willis arteries (internal carotid, middle cerebral, anterior cerebral, etc).	Characteristic pattern showing cerebral arteriovenous malformation.
Brain scan	May show increased uptake in affected cerebral area. Most marked in 2—3 weeks, with diminution or clearing thereafter.			Apt to be normal.	Increased uptake may be seen in area of arteriovenous malformation.
Echoencephalography	May show shift of midline toward opposite side in those patients with a cerebral lesion acting as a mass.				
Computerized tomography (CT)	May show area of hematoma, infarct, etc, with distortion or shift of ventricles.				

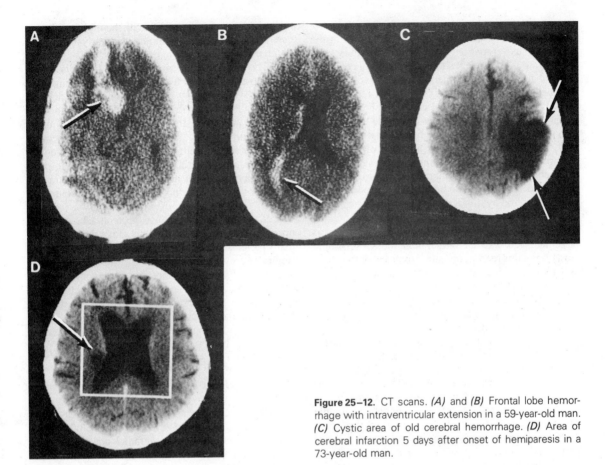

Figure 25–12. CT scans. *(A)* and *(B)* Frontal lobe hemorrhage with intraventricular extension in a 59-year-old man. *(C)* Cystic area of old cerebral hemorrhage. *(D)* Area of cerebral infarction 5 days after onset of hemiparesis in a 73-year-old man.

lum; and (2) the lateral branch, to the posterior inferior portion of the cerebellum and the lateral portion of the medulla.

Occlusion of the main trunk of the posterior inferior cerebellar artery may cause ipsilateral facial analgesia, ipsilateral Horner's syndrome, ipsilateral ataxia, and contralateral analgesia; ipsilateral weakness of the vocal cords or tongue, with contralateral hemiparesis, may also be present (Wallenberg's syndrome).

F. Superior Cerebellar Artery: This artery supplies the superior surface of the cerebellum and sends a few branches to the pons and midbrain. It arises from the anterior part of the basilar artery. Occlusion may cause ipsilateral ataxia and contralateral hemianalgesia and hemianesthesia.

G. Basilar Artery: This artery supplies the brain stem and midbrain via short paramedian and long circumferential branches. Occlusion of the main trunk of the basilar artery may cause headache, dizziness, and coma; flaccid quadriplegia, areflexia, complete anesthesia, pinpoint pupils, and hyperpyrexia.

H. Anterior Spinal Artery: Occlusion of this vessel is associated with a characteristic clinical picture and with softening of the spinal cord (myelomalacia). Symptoms include sudden paraplegia (depending on the spinal level of softening), disturbance in bowel and bladder function, and sensory disturbances (impaired perception of pain and temperature).

Differential Diagnosis

It is sometimes not possible to identify the type of vascular accident that has occurred during an individual attack. In general, however, the following criteria may be used to arrive at a probable diagnosis:

(1) Mode of onset: A relatively slow onset favors the diagnosis of thrombosis.

(2) Precipitating cause: Apoplexy occurring during or soon after exertion or emotional upset favors cerebral hemorrhage or subarachnoid hemorrhage.

(3) Preexisting diseases: A known history of hypertension favors cerebral hemorrhage. Infective endocarditis, atrial fibrillation, or previous myocardial infarction favors embolism.

(4) Associated clinical findings: Cranial nerve palsies and evidence of meningeal irritation favor subarachnoid hemorrhage.

(5) Laboratory findings: Evidence of massive bleeding into the cerebrospinal fluid usually favors subarachnoid or cerebral hemorrhage.

(6) Cerebral angiography or CT scan may disclose characteristic x-ray patterns.

Treatment & Prognosis

Immediate treatment involves bed rest with the head elevated, sedation, supportive measures, and nursing care. The patient should be placed at complete bed rest and carefully handled in order to avoid injury. Agitated patients should be given tranquilizers or sedatives as needed. Oral feedings should not be attempted in patients who are unconscious or unable to swallow. Nutrition should be maintained by means of tube feedings or parenteral measures. Catheterization may be required. Lumbar puncture removing a small quantity of cerebrospinal fluid for diagnostic purposes may be performed cautiously. Reduction of increased intracranial pressure by use of parenteral steroids (eg, dexamethasone) may be useful.

Cerebral hemorrhage is often fatal. The clot is large and acts like an intracranial mass, absorbing slowly. For this reason, operative removal of the blood clot may be indicated in patients who withstand the initial shock of hemorrhage and who show evidence of continued increased intracranial pressure on lumbar puncture or in patients who show evidence of development of papilledema.

Anticoagulant therapy has been advocated for the prevention of recurrences in cerebral thrombosis or cerebral embolism and for the treatment of carotid or basilar insufficiency. Recent studies by several groups suggest that anticoagulant therapy helps only a few individuals in any large series of patients with the clinical picture of stroke. The evidence is most promising for cerebral ischemia. The risk of hemorrhage is particularly great in hypertensive patients.

Narrowing of the extracranial arteries, especially the cervical portions of the internal carotid artery, is now being evaluated, and operative measures to correct the affected vessels are being studied.

Prognosis is usually difficult to evaluate in the early stages. The prognosis for life should be guarded; residual disability (hemiplegia, etc) is the rule. The rehabilitation of the patient with hemiplegia due to cerebrovascular accident should start early and should be intensive.

The outcome in cerebral thrombosis is determined to a great extent by the location and extent of the infarct as well as the general condition of the patient. In general, the greater the delay in improvement, the poorer the prognosis. In cerebral embolism, the underlying condition and the presence of emboli in other organs are significant factors. In intracerebral hemorrhage, the prognosis is poor, particularly in the presence of hypertension and arteriosclerosis. Intraventricular or brain stem hemorrhage is a discouraging sign.

If the patient survives the acute attack, the prognosis for life may be good. With active rehabilitation, many patients are able to walk and care for themselves. Return of useful function to the upper extremity occurs less often. Patients can be trained to achieve some degree of recovery. The prognosis for functional recovery is poor in those patients with severe residual organic mental syndrome or sensory aphasia and in those patients with profound, irreversible, or massive infarction or hemorrhage.

INTRACRANIAL ANEURYSM

Aneurysmal dilatation of blood vessels may occur as a result of arteriosclerosis, congenital abnormalities, or embolism. Intracranial aneurysms vary from the size of a pea to that of an orange, and individual aneurysms may vary in size from time to time. Larger aneurysms may erode the bones of the skull and sella turcica and compress adjacent cerebral tissue and cranial nerves. Most are located near the basilar surface of the skull, and almost half arise from the internal carotid or middle cerebral arteries. They are usually single but occasionally multiple. A coincidence of

Table 25–2. Incidence of signs and symptoms in the variously located aneurysms and vascular anomalies.*

| | Before Rupture | | | Chance of Rupture | After Rupture in Subarachnoid Space | | | | | | | | | |
| | Asymptomatic | Headache | Paresis of Cran. N. III | | Involvement of Cranial Nerves | | | | | | | Coma | Hemiparesis | Convulsions |
					II	III	IV	V	VI	VII	VIII			
Supratentorial vascular anomalies	+(†)	+	0	+	0	0	0	0	0	0	0	++	++	+
Aneurysm of internal carotid artery														
Infraclinoid	0	0	++++	+	+	++++	+++	+	+++	0	0	+	0	0
Carotid cavernous fistula	0	+	+(‡)	0										
Supraclinoid	++	++	++	+++	+	++	+	0	0	0	0	+	+	+
Aneurysm of anterior cerebral and communicating arteries	++	++	0	+++	+	0	0	0	0	0	0	+++	+	+
Aneurysm of middle cerebral artery	+	+	0	+++	0	0	0	0	0	0	0	++	++	+
Aneurysm of posterior communicating and cerebral arteries	+	+++	+	+++	0	++	+	+	+	0	0	+	+	+
Aneurysm of vertebral and basilar arteries	++	+	0	+++	0	0	0	0	0	+	+	+++	+	0

*Reproduced, with permission, from Walker: *Neurology* 1956;6:88.

†Convulsions common.

‡Syndrome of pulsating exophthalmos, bruit, and at times ocular palsies.

Rating: 0 = 0.5%　　　+ = 5.1–35%　　　++ = 35.1–65%　　　+++ = 65.1–95%　　　++++ = 95.1–100%

Table 25–3. A classification and outline of the cerebrovascular diseases.*

I. **Cerebral Infarction** (pale, red [hemorrhagic], and mixed types)
  A. Thrombosis with atherosclerosis
  B. Cerebral embolism
    1. Of cardiac origin
      a. Atrial fibrillation and other arrhythmias (with rheumatic, atherosclerotic, hypertensive, congenital heart disease)
      b. Myocardial infarction with mural thrombus
      c. Acute and subacute infective endocarditis
      d. Heart disease without arrhythmia or mural thrombus
      e. Complications of cardiac surgery
      f. Nonbacterial thrombotic ("marantic") endocardial vegetations
      g. Paradoxic embolism with congenital heart disease
    2. Of noncardiac origin
      a. Atherosclerosis of aorta and carotid arteries (mural thrombus, atheromatous material)
      b. From sites of cerebral artery thrombosis
      c. Thrombus in pulmonary veins
      d. Fat
      e. Tumor
      f. Air
      g. Complications of neck and thoracic surgery
      h. Miscellaneous: rare types
      i. Of undetermined origin
  C. Other conditions causing cerebral infarction
    1. Cerebral venous thrombosis
    2. Systemic hypotension
    3. Complications of arteriography
    4. Arteritis (see VI)
    5. Hematologic disorders (polycythemia, sickle cell disease, thrombotic thrombopenia, etc)
    6. Dissecting aortic aneurysm
    7. Trauma to carotid
    8. Anoxia
    9. Radioactive or x-ray radiation
    10. With tentorial, foramen magnum, and subfalcial herniations
    11. Miscellaneous: rare types
  D. Cerebral infarction of undetermined cause
II. **Transient Cerebral Ischemia Without Infarction**
  A. Recurrent focal cerebral ischemic attacks (previously called vasospasm, usually associated with thrombosis and atherosclerosis)
  B. Systemic hypotension ("simple faint," acute blood loss, myocardial infarction, Stokes-Adams syndrome, traumatic and surgical shock, sensitive carotid sinus, severe postural hypotension)
    1. With focal neurologic deficit
    2. With syncope
  C. Migraine
III. **Intracranial Hemorrhage** (including intracerebral, subarachnoid, ventricular, rarely subdural)
  A. Hypertensive intracerebral hemorrhage
  B. Ruptured saccular aneurysm (if unruptured see IV A)
  C. Angioma (if unruptured see IV B)
  D. Trauma
  E. Hemorrhagic disorders (leukemia, aplastic anemia, thrombopenic purpura, liver disease, complication of anticoagulant therapy, etc)

F. Of undetermined cause (normal blood pressure and no angioma)
  G. Hemorrhage into primary and secondary brain tumors
  H. Septic embolism, mycotic aneurysm
  I. With hemorrhagic infarction, arterial or venous (see under I and VII)
  J. Secondary brain stem hemorrhage (temporal lobe herniation)
  K. Hypertensive encephalopathy
  L. Idiopathic brain purpura
  M. With inflammatory disease of arteries and veins (see under VI, VII)
  N. Miscellaneous: rare types
IV. **Vascular Malformations and Developmental Abnormalities**
  A. Aneurysm—Saccular, fusiform, globular, diffuse (if ruptured see III B)
  B. Angioma (including familial telangiectasis, trigeminal encephaloangiomatosis [Sturge-Weber-Dimitri], retinalpontine hemangiomas) (if ruptured see III C)
  C. Absence, hypoplasia, or other abnormality of vessels (including variations in pattern of circle of Willis)
V. **Inflammatory Diseases of Arteries**
  A. Infections and infestations
    1. Meningovascular syphilis
    2. Septic embolism
    3. Arteritis secondary to pyogenic and tuberculous meningitis
    4. Rare types (typhus, schistosomiasis mansoni, malaria, trichinosis, etc)
  B. Diseases of undetermined origin
    1. Lupus erythematosus
    2. Rheumatic arteritis
    3. Polyarteritis nodosa (necrotizing and granulomatous forms)
    4. Cranial arteritis (temporal)
    5. Idiopathic granulomatous arteritis of aorta and its major branches
VI. **Vascular Diseases Without Changes in the Brain**
  A. Atherosclerosis
  B. Hypertensive arterio- and arteriolosclerosis
  C. Hyaline arterio- and arteriolosclerosis
  D. Calcification and ferruginization of vessels
  E. Capillary sclerosis, etc
VII. **Hypertensive Encephalopathy**
  A. Malignant hypertension (essential, chronic renal disease, pheochromocytoma, etc)
  B. Acute glomerulonephritis
  C. Eclampsia
VIII. **Dural Sinus and Cerebral Venous Thrombosis**
  A. Secondary to infection of ear, paranasal sinus, face, or other cranial structures
  B. With meningitis and subdural empyema
  C. Debilitating states (marantic)
  D. Postpartum
  E. Postoperative
  F. Hematologic disease (polycythemia, sickle cell anemia)
  G. Cardiac failure and congestive heart disease
  H. Miscellaneous: rare types
  I. Of undetermined cause
IX. **Strokes of Undetermined Origin**

*Reproduced, with permission, from *Neurology* 1958;8:405.

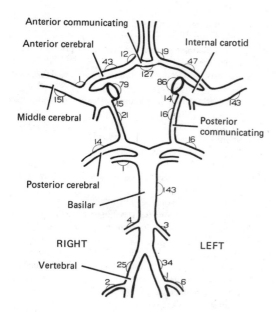

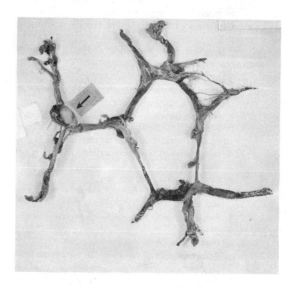

Figure 25–13. Location of intracranial aneurysms in 1023 cases. (Reproduced, with permission, from McDonald & Korb: *Arch Neurol Psychiatry* 1939;**42**:298.)

Figure 25–15. Right middle cerebral arterial aneurysm that ruptured and produced intracerebral hemorrhage.

congenital intracranial aneurysms and polycystic kidneys and coarctation of the aorta has been noted.

Pathology

Fusiform dilatation of the basilar arteries or the terminal portions of the internal carotids may occur as a consequence of diffuse arteriosclerotic changes.

Miliary, saccular aneurysms frequently occur near the bifurcation of a vessel in the circle of Willis and are associated with congenital abnormalities of the muscularis. A mycotic aneurysm, the result of an arteritis produced by bacterial emboli, is relatively infrequent. Larger aneurysms may be partially or completely clot-filled; occasionally, they may be calcified.

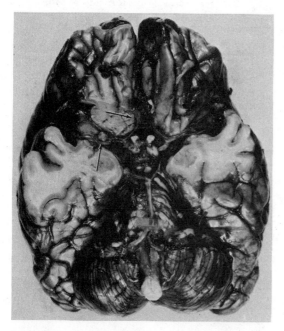

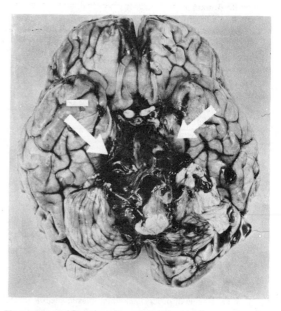

Figure 25–14. Multiple aneurysms (right middle cerebral and anterior cerebral arteries) in a woman with coarctation of aorta.

Figure 25–16. Severe subarachnoid hemorrhage secondary to intracerebral hemorrhage.

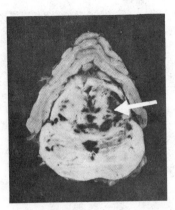

Figure 25–17. Pontine hemorrhages.

Clinical Findings

Prior to rupture, aneurysms may be asymptomatic or may cause symptoms, depending upon the location and size of the aneurysm. Headache on effort and involvement of cranial nerves II, III, and V are apt to be present. Bruit on stethoscopic auscultation over the affected site is sometimes heard.

Following rupture, the symptoms are those of acute subarachnoid hemorrhage. Recurrent unilateral headaches that clinically resemble those of migraine sometimes occur.

Diagnosis

By use of carotid or vertebral angiography with injections of meglumine diatrizoate (Renografin), sodium acetrizoate (Urokon), or other contrast media, an aneurysm may be demonstrated on x-ray.

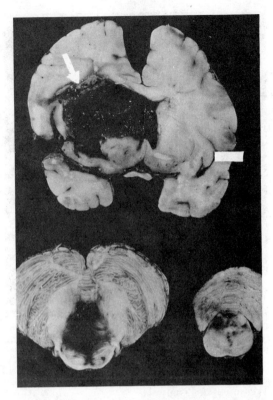

Figure 25–19. Cerebral hemorrhage with intraventricular rupture and associated pontine hemorrhage.

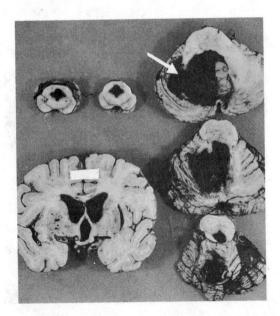

Figure 25–18. Cerebellar hemorrhage with intraventricular rupture.

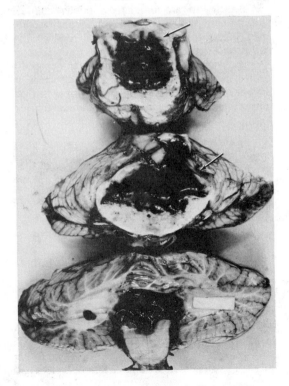

Figure 25–20. Pontine hemorrhage with rupture into fourth ventricle in a 46-year-old hypertensive woman.

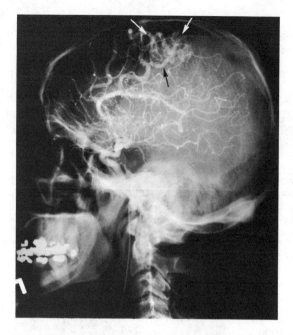

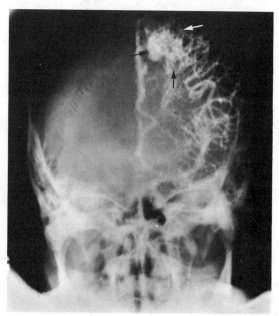

Figure 25–21. Lateral and posteroanterior views of arterial phase of carotid angiogram showing arteriovenous malformation of the left frontal lobe.

Treatment & Prognosis

Because of the high mortality rate associated with spontaneous subarachnoid bleeding and the probability of recurrence of subarachnoid hemorrhage, intracranial aneurysms are considered a serious pathologic entity. Antifibrinolytic agents such as aminocaproic acid (Amicar) may be used during active bleeding to prevent recurrence.

The choice of surgical treatment as opposed to medical treatment rests upon many circumstances, including the size and location of the aneurysm, the clinical status of the patient, the skill and experience of the surgeon, and the enthusiasm for a particular therapeutic regimen. Various surgical procedures, including "trapping" the aneurysm by applying clips on either side, clipping the neck of the sac of the aneurysm, packing muscle around the aneurysm, etc, have been successfully performed in some cases.

More recently, methods have been applied for preventing rupture of a cerebral aneurysm by spraying plastics directly on the aneurysm and the surrounding vessels, with the reported advantage that operative sacrifice of a major cerebral vessel can thus be avoided.

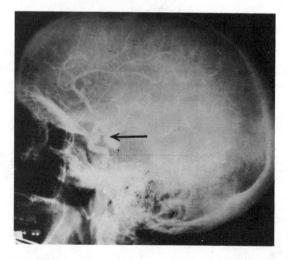

Figure 25–22. Aneurysm of the posterior communicating artery demonstrated by carotid angiogram.

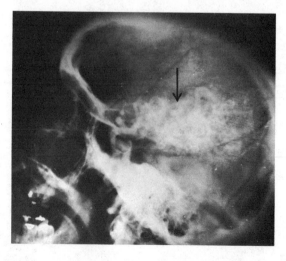

Figure 25–23. Arteriovenous aneurysm (malformation) of middle cerebral artery and vein.

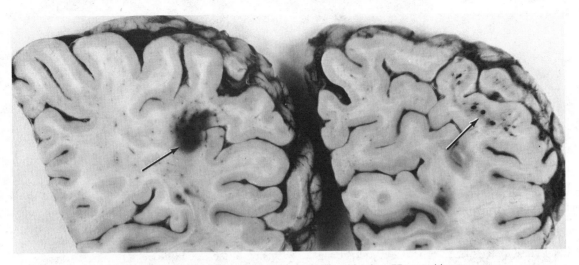

Figure 25–24. Occipital lobe arteriovenous malformation in a 77-year-old man.

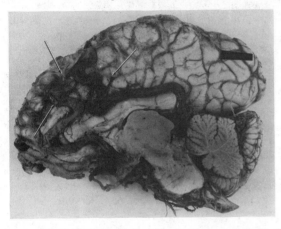

Figure 25–25. Sagittal section of brain showing arteriovenous malformation of right frontal lobe with dilated large anterior cerebral artery and draining veins.

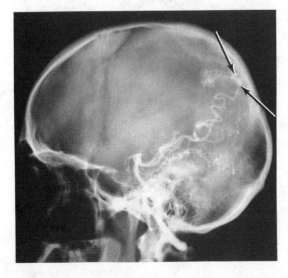

Figure 25–26. Vertebral angiogram showing left parietal arteriovenous malformation.

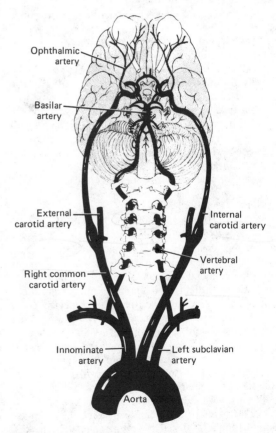

Figure 25–27. Diagram of arterial blood supply to the eyes and brain. (Reproduced, with permission, from Wylie EJ, Ehrenfeld WK: *Extracranial Occlusive Cerebrovascular Disease: Diagnosis and Management.* Saunders, 1970.)

26 | Infectious Diseases of the Central Nervous System

With Michael J. Chusid, MD

PYOGENIC LEPTOMENINGITIS

Classifications of leptomeningitis may be made on the basis of the specific causative agent. Among the commoner causes are meningococcal, pneumococcal, and *Haemophilus influenzae* infections. Less frequently, staphylococcal, streptococcal, and gonococcal organisms are isolated. *Neisseria meningitidis* (meningococcus) is the causative agent in about 40% of all cases of meningitis in adults and older children.

Pathogenesis & Pathology

Access to the subarachnoid space may be gained by an invading pyogen following a systemic or bloodstream infection. More rarely, extension from an adjacent infected area may take place.

Characteristically, the subarachnoid space contains a cloudy or milky cerebrospinal fluid. Both an exudate containing great numbers of polymorphonuclear leukocytes and tissue undergoing destruction are present in the subarachnoid space. Degenerative neuronal changes, perivascular leukocytic collections, and congestion of adjacent tissues are frequent. Evidence in the brain and spinal cord of encephalitis, brain abscess, or petechial hemorrhage is not unusual.

Clinical Findings

At onset, violent headache, severely stiff and painful neck, greatly elevated temperature, and clouding of the sensorium, with stupor and delirium, are common. As the disease progresses, nausea and vomiting, photophobia, and convulsions frequently occur. Cranial nerve palsies with diplopia, tinnitus, and choking of optic disks are well-recognized occurrences. Rigid spine, head retraction, and positive Kernig's and Brudzinski's signs are prominent features. Petechial skin hemorrhages and arthritis are commonly present; endocarditis and nephritis are rare complications.

Brudzinski's "neck" sign is positive when forcible flexion of the neck on the chest causes flexion of both legs and thighs. **Kernig's sign** is demonstrated when the recumbent patient's leg cannot be extended with the hip joint flexed at a right angle. Brudzinski's contralateral "leg" signs may be present: (1) when one

thigh is flexed at the hip, the other also becomes flexed; (2) when one leg and thigh are fully flexed and the other extended, lowering of the flexed leg causes flexion of the extended one.

Diagnosis (See Table 15–1.)

Culture of blood and of cerebrospinal fluid will usually indicate the specific pyogen causing the meningitis. The presence of coexisting or preceding infections such as otitis media or pneumonia points to potential meningitis. Exposure or contact with known meningitis cases raises the probability of occurrence.

Bacterial meningitis should be considered in all newborn infants who appear ill or do not thrive; signs of the disease are vague and nonspecific, particularly in premature infants. Anorexia, vomiting, lethargy, irritability, jaundice, respiratory distress, diarrhea, bulging fontanelles, convulsions, nuchal rigidity, fever, pyoderma, and omphalitis may occur, and pneumonitis, gastroenteritis, or other infection increases the possibility of meningitis.

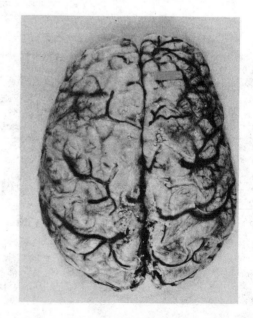

Figure 26–1. Pneumococcal meningitis. Convexity of brain covered by thick green exudate in subarachnoid space.

Michael J. Chusid is Associate Professor of Pediatrics, Medical College of Wisconsin, Milwaukee.

Treatment

Culture and sensitivity tests are of value in determining the drug of choice in treatment, but treatment should not be withheld pending the results of the tests. Occasionally, however, it is necessary to use combinations of drugs for proper treatment. Although bacteriologic studies are necessary, initial treatment cannot await final results. Since treatment must be directed toward both gram-positive and gram-negative organisms, 2 and perhaps 3 drugs should be used.

A. Meningitis of Unknown Cause:

1. Adults—Give ampicillin, 8–12 g daily intravenously.

2. Children—Give ampicillin, 200–400 mg/kg daily intravenously, and chloramphenicol, 100 mg/kg daily intravenously, while awaiting culture results.

B. Meningococcal Meningitis:

1. Penicillin—Give aqueous penicillin, 20 million units intravenously daily for at least 7 days. Ampicillin, 8–12 g daily intravenously, may be used instead.

2. Chloramphenicol—Dosage of 4 g intravenously daily for 7 days can be used in a penicillin-sensitive person.

Prophylactic rifampin orally may be useful in epidemics to reduce carrier rates and should be administered to persons in close contact with patients.

C. Pneumococcal, Streptococcal, and Staphylococcal Meningitis: Pneumococcal and streptococcal meningitis are treated with aqueous penicillin by continuous intravenous drip at a rate of 2–3 million units every 4 hours.

Staphylococcal meningitis is similarly treated if the staphylococcus is sensitive to penicillin G; otherwise, treatment is with sodium methicillin, 10–12 g daily intravenously. Treatment should be continued for 2–4 weeks.

With adequate and at times very large doses of antibiotics, the death rate is strikingly reduced. Staphylococcal meningitis carries the gravest prognosis.

The primary focus of infection should be eradicated by surgery if necessary, especially in recurrent or persistent pneumococcal meningitis.

D. *Haemophilus influenzae* Meningitis: The treatment of choice is with sodium ampicillin (adults, 10–20 g daily; children, 200–400 mg/kg daily) by intravenous drip. Chloramphenicol is very effective. Because of ampicillin resistance in many areas, ampicillin and chloramphenicol should be administered together pending the results of sensitivity tests. In untreated infants, the mortality rate is over 90%. Subdural effusion is commonly seen in infants with influenzal meningitis and is characterized by persistent vomiting, bulging fontanelles, convulsions, and persistent fever. Prompt relief follows evacuation of the effusion via subdural tap through the fontanelles.

E. Supportive Therapy: Supportive therapy, including blood transfusions and other infusions, should be employed as necessary. Subdural effusions are a common complication of purulent meningitis and should be ruled out if fever recurs after an afebrile period. Convulsions, irritability, fever, lethargy, and coma may also be associated. Subdural taps in children with open fontanelles are advantageous and should be repeated, with 15–30 mL of fluid removed at a time until the subdural space is dry; small effusions do not require removal.

Prognosis

With the advent of chemotherapy, the prognosis for survival in the pyogenic leptomeningitides is relatively good.

BRAIN ABSCESS

Localized suppurations may occur within the brain as in other portions of the body. Following acute purulent infection, pus in brain tissue may be free or encapsulated. Abscesses vary from microscopic size to an area covering most of a cerebral hemisphere.

Brain abscess is usually caused by staphylococci or anaerobes, although any of the common pyogenic bacteria may be found. The organism may gain access to the brain by direct extension from otitis media, mastoiditis, sinusitis, and infected head injuries, or, more rarely, via the bloodstream from distant sources such as pulmonary or cardiac infections.

Pathology

The abscess consists of a central necrotic and purulent area surrounded by a capsule. The central area contains debris and leukocytes. The capsule, which may take weeks to form, may have 3 layers: (1) an inner layer adjacent to the pus cavity, characterized by presence of collagenous connective tissue fibers; (2) a broader middle layer rich in connective tissue repair elements such as capillaries and fibroblasts; and (3) an external layer of connective tissue containing vessels and more phagocytes than the middle layer.

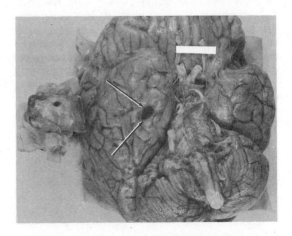

Figure 26–2. Abscess of right temporal lobe with sinus extending into adjacent temporal bone. Adherent dura and temporal bone reflected laterally.

Abscesses occurring by extension from infections of the middle ear or mastoid are usually located within the temporal lobe or cerebellum. Abscesses occurring by extension from paranasal sinuses usually occur in the frontal lobe. Abscesses following bacteremia are apt to be multiple. Metastatic abscesses are often secondary to pulmonary suppurations.

Clinical Findings

A history of evidence of preceding infection is usually present. Otitis media, mastoiditis, sinusitis, bronchiectasis, or pneumonia is frequently present. Focalizing manifestations may occur, producing visual field defects, motor and other sensory changes, aphasia, and cranial nerve palsies similar to those caused by any other intracranial mass.

Signs of increased intracranial pressure may occur, such as papilledema, headache, and slowed pulse and respirations. Mild meningeal signs may be present, such as mild rigidity of the neck and a positive Kernig's sign. Somnolence and slowing of mental processes are common. The temperature is mildly elevated and rarely exceeds 39 °C (102.2 °F) if complications such as meningitis do not occur.

Diagnosis

Brain abscesses may be confused with other clinical entities (eg, brain tumors, leptomeningitis, or encephalitis). In brain tumor, history or evidence of preceding infection is usually absent, and the cerebrospinal fluid cell count is usually normal. Leptomeningitis can usually be differentiated through a positive culture of the cerebrospinal fluid. Acute fulminating leptomeningitis is easily distinguished clinically from brain abscess; mild leptomeningitis (eg, tuberculous and syphilitic leptomeningitis) may be clinically indistinguishable. Encephalitis usually fails to exhibit the focalizing signs of brain abscess and usually provokes more profound and severe changes in the sensorium and personality.

Electroencephalography, brain scan, CT scan, and echoencephalography may help in the diagnosis and localization of brain abscess. Air ventriculography, pneumoencephalography, or cerebral angiography may be necessary to determine the site of abscess.

Brain abscesses may be located at operation with the use of needle aspiration.

Treatment

Treatment consists of operative drainage of pus. Operation may be delayed until the abscess is firmly encapsulated. If the abscess is well encapsulated and if it is practicable, excision in toto is sometimes performed. Marsupialization of the cavity, packing of the cavity, and various types of incision and drainage are commonly employed. After surgical drainage has been induced, irrigations of the abscess cavity with antibiotic solutions are helpful. Treatment of the original focus of infection (eg, a chronic mastoiditis) is sometimes necessary before a brain abscess will heal com-

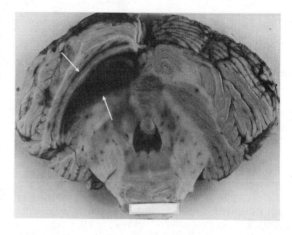

Figure 26–3. Multiple petechial hemorrhages and right cerebellar hemorrhage in a 62-year-old man with subacute bacterial endocarditis (SBE).

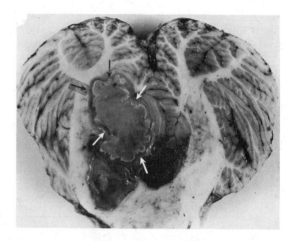

Figure 26–4. Cerebellar abscess.

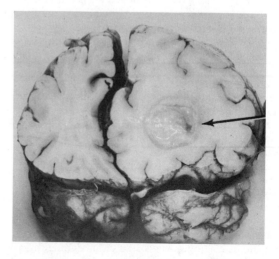

Figure 26–5. Left frontal abscess in a 63-year-old woman with osteomyelitis of the skull.

pletely. Antibiotic therapy should be based upon the results of culture and sensitivity tests.

Prognosis

Drug therapy has greatly improved the outlook for brain abscess. It has even been maintained that the formation of brain abscesses can be aborted with the use of appropriate antibiotics early in the course of infection (eg, cerebritis). Without treatment, brain abscess usually has a fatal outcome.

LESS COMMON PYOGENIC INFECTIONS

Subdural Abscess

Cerebral subdural abscess is a relatively rare form of intracranial infection that may result from extension directly from the middle ear, nasal sinuses, or meninges, or as a complication of skull fracture or septicemia. Pyogenic bacteria, particularly staphylococci, are the usual causative agents. Subdural effusions, with or without bacteria, may complicate influenzal and other types of meningitis of infancy. Symptomatology includes that of the focus of origin (nasal sinus, ear, etc) and that of intracranial extension.

If untreated, the mortality rate is high; with prompt evacuation of pus and chemotherapy, recovery is possible.

Spinal Epidural Abscess

Spinal epidural space infections, characterized by fever, headache, pain in the back, and paraparesis or complete paraplegia, may result from direct extension of local skin infections, perforating wounds, or lumbar puncture, or by metastasis through the bloodstream from remote infected areas. The usual infective organism is *Staphylococcus aureus,* although other pyogens may be causative. The midthoracic vertebral zone is the most common site, and pus is usually posterior to the spinal cord. Localized granulomatous collections may result when the organism is of low virulence.

Symptoms develop abruptly: severe pain in the back or lower extremities, followed by stiff neck, headache, malaise, and fever. Paralysis of the lower extremities may develop at any time; flaccid paraplegia may develop secondary to thrombosis of infected spinal vessels. Treatment consists of prompt surgical drainage by laminectomy and the use of appropriate antibiotics. Delay in drainage may result in permanent paralysis; in cases with transverse myelitis, little if any improvement occurs following delayed operation.

Lateral Sinus Thrombophlebitis

This is much less frequently seen since antibiotics have come into wide use. It occurs principally in infants and children and usually is secondary to otitis media and mastoiditis. Classic clinical features include fever, headache, nausea and vomiting, swelling over the mastoid area, and distention of local superficial veins. Papilledema, bulging of the fontanelles, and separation of sutures in infants, drowsiness, coma, and convulsive seizures may also occur. Chemotherapy and surgery are indicated, with removal of infected bone, exposure and drainage of the sinus, and jugular vein ligation.

In normal persons, it is necessary to compress both jugular veins to produce engorgement of the retinal veins. In unilateral sinus thrombosis, compression of the healthy side only will suffice to produce engorgement (Crowe's sign).

Cavernous Sinus Thrombophlebitis

Cavernous sinus thrombophlebitis is usually secondary to suppuration in the orbit, nasal sinuses, or upper face zone and usually spreads via the circular sinus to involve the opposite cavernous sinus. Acute onset with febrile reaction, proptosis of the eyeball, edema and chemosis of the conjunctiva and eyelids, diplopia, ptosis, and papilledema may develop. This disorder usually responds well to antibiotic treatment.

Most infections are due to *S aureus*. In other cases, *Staphylococcus albus,* streptococci, pneumococci, or *Proteus* organisms may be responsible. A semisynthetic penicillin should be given until results of sensitivity studies are reported. In children, addition of ampicillin to the treatment regimen may be required because of the possibility of *Haemophilus* infection. Adjunctive therapy with corticosteroids may be necessary if functional derangement of the pituitary is present also.

Longitudinal Sinus Thrombophlebitis

Thrombophlebitis of the superior sagittal (longitudinal) sinus may cause fever, prostration, elevated intracranial pressure, edema of forehead and anterior scalp, and engorgement of the vertex veins. There may be extension to local tributary cerebral veins, with convulsive seizures, hemiplegia, aphasia, or hemianopsia. Nonseptic thrombosis may occur, particularly in infants with dehydration and marasmus. Obstruction may be demonstrated by injection of radiopaque dye directly into the anterior superior longitudinal sinus. Antibiotics are indicated in the septic type.

Nonseptic or primary thrombosis may occur in debilitating illness. Treatment is aimed at reducing intracranial pressure and may include the use of intravenous mannitol or parenteral steroids such as dexamethasone (Decadron).

TOXOPLASMOSIS

Toxoplasmosis is caused by *Toxoplasma gondii,* a protozoan parasite found throughout the world in humans and many animals. The disease is believed to be transmitted to humans from domestic cats. The organism is found in the reticuloendothelial system, parenchymal cells, and exudates. It usually occurs in very young infants and may be fatal in its congenital form.

Findings include convulsions, hydrocephalus, chorioretinitis, psychomotor disorders, and cerebral calcifications demonstrable by x-ray. Symptomatic infection is rare in adults, and active infection is most frequent in the newborn and is often acquired in utero.

Toxoplasma organisms may be found in smears of blood, bone marrow, cerebrospinal fluid, or exudates. Serologic tests, including the Sabin-Feldman dye test, the indirect fluorescent antibody test, complement fixation tests, and neutralization tests, may be required to establish the diagnosis. Intracerebral or intraperitoneal inoculation of mice or rabbits with blood or spinal fluid may demonstrate the *Toxoplasma* organisms.

Acute infections are treated with daily administration of pyrimethamine and trisulfapyrimidines. The course of the infection is followed by means of repeated Sabin-Feldman and complement fixation tests during and after treatment.

NEUROSYPHILIS

Infection of the CNS by *Treponema pallidum* may occur early or late in the course of syphilis. In general, patients with mild early manifestations of syphilis are more apt to develop tabes and general paresis.

The clinical syndromes resulting from neurologic infection with *T pallidum* depend upon the extent of involvement of the parenchyma, blood vessels, and meninges. Although the CNS is involved by *T pallidum* within a few weeks or months of the original infection, clinical evidence of involvement may be delayed for many years.

On the basis of clinical and pathologic data, CNS syphilis may be classified as (1) **nonparenchymatous, or interstitial, neurosyphilis** (syphilitic leptomeningitis, vascular neurosyphilis), or (2) **parenchymatous neurosyphilis** (general paresis, tabes dorsalis). Combinations of the main features of 2 or more types may occur. **Argyll Robertson pupil** (common with neurosyphilis; occasionally present in epidemic encephalitis and alcoholism) consists of loss of light reflex, retention of accommodation reflex, loss of ciliospinal reflex, and imperfect dilatation of the pupil with atropine. Miosis is usually present.

Asymptomatic neurosyphilis may occur in which abnormalities of cerebrospinal fluid indicative of CNS infection are present without clinical signs or symptoms. In untreated cases, the incidence of asymptomatic neurosyphilis varies according to the duration of the infection; the highest incidence occurs in the first or second years after infection. The prognosis is good with adequate treatment.

ACUTE SYPHILITIC MENINGITIS

Acute syphilitic meningitis is often the earliest form of neurosyphilis present in a particular patient and is a frequent concomitant of early secondary syphilis. Involvement of the meninges may be diffuse or focal in type. The incubation period varies from a few months to many years, but the disease usually occurs within the first year of infection.

On pathologic examination, the pia is found to be moderately congested, and lymphocytes are collected around the blood vessels.

In severe, fully developed cases the patient may exhibit the classic findings of acute leptomeningitis, eg, headache, stupor, convulsions, fever; stiff, painful neck; cranial nerve palsies; and positive Kernig's and Brudzinski's signs.

A strongly positive blood and cerebrospinal fluid test for syphilis (serologic test for syphilis or VDRL) is usually present. The cerebrospinal fluid usually exhibits a marked lymphocytic pleocytosis.

The treatment of choice is penicillin, 15–20 million units intramuscularly in a 2- to 3-week period. The outcome of disease is usually influenced favorably by the prompt use of penicillin.

VASCULAR NEUROSYPHILIS

The blood vessels of the CNS are frequently affected by syphilis. The consequences of involvement of these vessels are generally more serious than similar involvement elsewhere in the body. Thrombosis of arteries and encephalomalacia with appearance of various focal signs are characteristic.

Proliferation of the intima, cellular infiltration of the adventitia and media, and splitting of the elastica generally make up the pathologic picture of **Heubner's endarteritis.** Some degree of associated meningitis or meningoencephalitis is usually present. Infarction of the brain occurs following occlusion or thrombosis of affected vessels.

Early in vascular neurosyphilis, few if any symptoms may be recognized. With increasing vascular involvement and subsequent parenchymal damage, headache, convulsions, stupor, and personality changes may occur. When relatively large vessels are affected in the brain, occlusion or rupture with gross cerebral hemorrhage may occur (see p 313).

Symptomatic treatment as for similar cerebrovascular lesions is indicated. Penicillin, 15–20 million units intramuscularly in a period of 2–3 weeks, is necessary.

GENERAL PARESIS

General paresis is not so common as formerly because of earlier and more frequent recognition and more effective treatment of syphilis. It usually appears many years after the primary lesion and is therefore more common in the fourth and fifth decades of life.

The frontal lobes are predominantly affected; the cerebral convolutions are atrophied and the sulci widened. The cerebral cortex is thin, and the ventricles appear enlarged. There is distortion of the normal structure of the cortex, produced by degeneration and disappearance of ganglion cells, and great increase in interstitial glial elements and blood vessels. The leptomeninges over the atrophic areas are opaque, thickened, and adherent to the underlying cortex.

Mental symptoms are believed to be primarily a reflection of frontal lobe dysfunction. Dementia, delusions, emotional changes, defective judgment, and clouding of consciousness are common. General paresis may mimic any of the classic mental and psychiatric disorders and syndromes. Tremors of fingers, lips, and tongue, slurred speech, ataxia, Argyll Robertson pupils, positive Babinski's sign, and exaggerated deep tendon reflexes are frequent findings.

The cerebrospinal fluid and serologic test for syphilis or VDRL reactions are strongly positive. The cerebrospinal fluid usually shows a moderate increase in cells (lymphocytes) and globulin.

Penicillin, 20–30 million units, is injected intramuscularly in a period of 3–4 weeks.

Without treatment, death occurs in a few years. The use of antibiotics may retard or halt the progression of the disease.

TABES DORSALIS
(Locomotor Ataxia)

This once common syndrome appears as a relatively late manifestation of syphilis. The primary lesion and the early mild signs are frequently not evident to the patient. Tabes dorsalis is relatively uncommon at present. It is much more frequent in males and whites and commonly develops 10–25 years after the initial infection.

The syndrome is more readily understood when it is remembered that it results from syphilitic infection of the posterior roots and the root entrance zone of the spinal cord, with secondary degeneration of the dorsal columns. Grossly, the spinal cord may appear smaller and atrophic, and the posterior roots are likely to be smaller than average. Microscopically, a decrease in the number of normal nerve fibers of the lumbosacral roots, cellular infiltration of the dorsal root ganglia, and degeneration of the posterior columns are evident.

Clinical Findings

Symptoms of root involvement such as shooting and girdle pains, paresthesias, and hypesthesias occur. Periodic, irregular, severely painful episodes, known as crises, sometimes occur. Ataxia and bladder disturbances are common.

Loss of sense of position and vibration, ataxia, and a positive Romberg sign are usually a result of posterior column degeneration. Hypotonia of skeletal musculature, Argyll Robertson pupils, optic atrophy,

and decreased or absent deep tendon reflexes are commonly found. Other signs include disorders involving the bladder and rectum, cranial nerve palsies, Charcot joints, and mal perforant (malum perforans pedis: painless perforating foot ulcer). Abadie's sign (presumptive evidence of tabes) is loss of the sense of pain on squeezing the Achilles tendon. Biernacki's sign (of tabes) is loss of deep pressure pain when pressure is exerted over the ulnar nerve behind the elbow. **Westphal's sign** is characteristic of tabes, but it may occur with any lesion that completely interrupts the motor or sensory neurons of the femoral nerve; it consists of absence of the knee jerk reflex. **Romberg's sign** (of posterior column disease or polyneuritis) is positive if a patient sways or falls when standing with the eyes closed and feet close together. This indicates a loss of proprioceptive sense in the legs.

Diagnosis

The blood and cerebrospinal fluid tests for syphilis (serologic test for syphilis, VDRL) are positive in about half of known cases. Increased cell count and total protein of the cerebrospinal fluid may be present. Cerebrospinal fluid is abnormal in the early stage but may be normal in the late stage.

Treatment & Prognosis

Treatment with antibiotic chemotherapy is usually effective. Penicillin, 15–20 million units intramuscularly over a 2- to 3-week period, is effective in arresting the course of the disease and in reversing the cerebrospinal fluid abnormalities. Persistence of lightning pains and crises, ataxia, bladder disturbances, and Charcot joints is usual despite antisyphilitic treatment. Phenytoin (Dilantin) or carbamazepine (Tegretol) may be useful in control of pain. Chordotomy may be necessary as a last resort for relief of excruciating pains.

If tabes dorsalis is untreated, progression occurs, with severe disability and suffering.

•   •   •

TUBERCULOUS MENINGITIS

Tuberculous meningitis differs from most other common meningitides because the course is more prolonged, the mortality rate much higher, and the cerebrospinal fluid changes less severe. It occurs most commonly in childhood. It may be referable to a focus of tuberculosis elsewhere in the body, most commonly in the peritracheal, peribronchial, or mesenteric lymph nodes, lungs, or other organs. Discharge of bacilli into cerebrospinal fluid from adjacent foci of caseation in the brain has been considered to occur in the majority of cases.

Pathology

Tubercles may be found scattered through the brain and spinal cord. Exudate is usually found over the base of the brain and is usually thick, tough, and adherent. Microscopically, the brain shows miliary tubercles whose structure is like that of tubercles found elsewhere in the body.

Clinical Findings

The presence of tuberculous lesions elsewhere in the body may sometimes be demonstrated. In children, evidence of contact with tuberculous family members should be sought.

The onset is usually gradual, with listlessness, irritability, loss of appetite, and mild fever.

During the progression of the disease, headache; vomiting; extraocular palsies; night cries; convulsions; stiff, painful neck; and positive Kernig's and Brudzinski's signs usually appear. In infants, bulging of fontanelles and peculiar shrill "meningeal" cries are apt to occur. Opisthotonos, choked disks, paralysis, and coma soon follow.

Diagnosis

The cerebrospinal fluid is frequently xanthochromic, cloudy, or opaque; is often under increased tension; and may form a pellicle and web on standing. Smear, culture, and guinea pig inoculation of the pellicle and web will demonstrate tubercle bacilli. Increased cells (lymphocytes) and total protein occur. Glucose and chlorides are usually markedly reduced in amount.

Demonstration of tuberculous infection or exposure may be better judged after chest x-rays and tuberculin skin testing.

Intracranial tuberculoma occasionally occurs and is characterized by symptomatic progression, focal

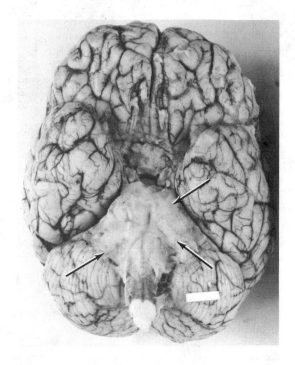

Figure 26–7. Basal view of tuberculous meningitis in a 26-year-old man.

Figure 26–6. Tuberculoma of the anterolateral region of the spinal cord. The tumor has caused analgesia and thermoanesthesia on the opposite side of the body below the level of the lesion. It was this case particularly that led Spiller to recommend chordotomy as a practical surgical procedure for the relief of pain. (Reproduced, with permission, from Cadwalader: *Diseases of the Spinal Cord.* Williams & Wilkins, 1932.)

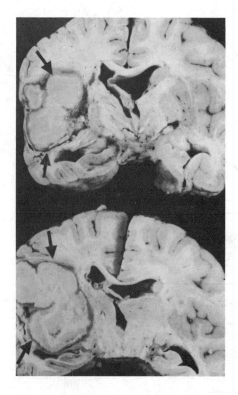

Figure 26–8. Tuberculoma of the brain in a 3½-month-old child.

signs, and evidence of increased intracranial pressure, so that it resembles an expanding intracranial neoplasm.

Tuberculous meningitis must be considered in the differential diagnosis of fever of unknown origin, especially in children under age 2 years. Confusion with viral infections of the CNS may occur, especially where symptoms of encephalitis predominate. Careful study of cerebrospinal fluid can usually rule out uncommon infections, eg, torulosis. Rarely, malignant disease may simulate tuberculous meningitis.

The prognosis is better in older than in younger children. Serial lumbar punctures are helpful in evaluation. A persistently abnormal EEG usually indicates a poor outlook, even without clinical convulsions. A normal CT scan early in the course of tuberculous meningitis is a favorable prognostic sign. Obstruction at basilar cisterns may sometimes be noted with hydrocephalus. Ultimate recovery of survivors can be determined only after prolonged clinical observation, with electroencephalographic and psychometric studies providing useful aid.

Treatment & Prognosis

Give streptomycin, 1 g intramuscularly daily for 2 weeks and then twice weekly for 60–90 days. Also give isoniazid, 10 mg/kg daily (up to a total of 300 mg daily), and rifampin, 600 mg daily for 18–24 months. Corticosteroid treatment (60 mg of prednisone daily) is given until improvement occurs and is then gradually discontinued.

Pyridoxine, 50 mg daily, is added to the therapy regimen to prevent isoniazid-induced peripheral neuropathy.

Treat symptoms as they arise; maintain good nutrition and adequate fluids.

In untreated cases, death may occur within 3 weeks of onset of symptoms. Recovery may occur with proper prolonged treatment, but severe residual defects (deafness, blindness, paralysis, hemiplegia, mental retardation, and convulsions) may occur.

FUNGAL MENINGITIS

The clinical picture of the usual case of fungal meningitis may resemble that of tuberculous meningitis. Onset of nervous system signs is gradual, and meningeal signs predominate. Occasionally, focal neurologic signs or mental syndromes are prominent. Diagnosis is established by culture of organisms — Cryptococcus, Blastomyces, Histoplasma, or Coccidioides — on Sabouraud's medium or by identification of organisms in cerebrospinal fluid or blood. The cerebrospinal fluid changes in fungal meningitis are like those of tuberculous meningitis: fluid is under increased pressure, with mild to moderate pleocytosis, increased protein, and decreased glucose and chlorides. Serologic or immunologic (counterimmunoelectrophoresis) techniques often aid in diagnosis.

Although there is no specific therapy for fungal meningitis, amphotericin B (Fungizone) has been successful, especially when therapy was begun before extensive involvement of the CNS had occurred. It may be necessary to install a permanent reservoir connected with the ventricular system to allow chronic administration of amphotericin.

EPIDEMIC ENCEPHALITIS
(Von Economo's Disease, Encephalitis Lethargica)

This disease is characterized by an acute onset of clinical manifestations of diffuse brain involvement and various sequelae. It occurred in epidemic form between 1916 and 1926 but is now quite rare. The inference has been drawn that a virus related to the virus of influenza causes this disease, since the pandemic of influenza of 1919–1920 was associated with and followed by many cases of epidemic encephalitis. However, no valid proof exists that epidemic encephalitis is caused by a virus.

Severe acute damage to nerve cells, perivascular round cell infiltration, glial proliferation, and congestion occur. Damage is especially likely to occur to nerve cells of periaqueductal gray matter and adjacent cranial nerve nuclei, the substantia nigra, the ventromedial nucleus of the thalamus, and the medial geniculate body.

Onset may be insidious or sudden and violent. Initially, headache, tinnitus, malaise, and mild fever—such as are commonly associated with upper respiratory tract infections—are apt to be present. After about 2 weeks, diplopia, sleepiness, lethargy, insomnia, and weakness of muscles may be evident. In the acute phase, progression to severe coma and death is possible.

After apparent recovery, further symptoms may appear. Forms of parkinsonism may appear later in life. Severe behavioral disturbances, especially in children, may ensue. These personality changes sometimes require institutionalization of the patient. Epilepsy, narcolepsy, and fat and water metabolic disturbances have occurred.

VIRAL ENCEPHALITIS

Many viruses may cause encephalitis. The clinical syndrome may range from malaise, headache, fever, nuchal rigidity, and nausea and vomiting to stupor, seizures, and coma. Cranial nerve palsies and focal neurologic signs may occur.

Accompanying infections in the spinal cord are common in encephalitic virus infections, and these signs and symptoms sometimes predominate and mask the features of the brain infection.

The specific type of encephalitis present in a particular patient may not be identified for weeks and perhaps never. Cerebrospinal fluid examination often

Table 26–1. Representative viral infections of the human central nervous system.

DNA-containing viruses	
Herpesvirus	Herpes simplex, varicella-zoster, cyto-megalovirus
Papovavirus	Progressive multifocal leukoencephalopathy (PML)
Poxvirus	Vaccinia
RNA-containing viruses	
Arbovirus	St. Louis, equine encephalomyelitis, California, Japanese B
Orthomyxovirus	Influenza
Paramyxovirus	Measles (SSPE), mumps
Rhabdovirus	Rabies
Arenavirus	Lymphocytic choriomeningitis
Togavirus	Rubella
Picornavirus	Poliovirus, coxsackievirus, echovirus

shows completely normal reactions, although a slight increase in cells or protein is not unusual. Isolation of a virus from the spinal fluid or blood must be attempted very early in the course of the disease if it is to have any chance of success. The titer of spinal fluid and blood as determined by serum neutralization tests may give a clue to the presence of a particular virus infection. A 4-fold rise in titer occurring with clinical progression of the disease or upon recovery is usually a positive reaction. In times of epidemic, less error is apt to be made concerning the specific cause of a case.

Arbovirus Encephalitis (See Table 26–2.)

The most common causes of viral encephalitis are the arboviruses (arthropod-borne viruses). Included in this group are St. Louis encephalitis, equine encephalomyelitis, California encephalitis, and Japanese B encephalitis.

Table 26–2. Arbovirus (arthropod-borne) encephalitis.*

	Geographic Distribution	Vector; Reservoir	Comment
California encephalitis	Throughout USA	Mosquitoes; small mammals	Mainly in children
Eastern (equine) encephalitis	Eastern part of North, Central, and South America	Mosquitoes; birds, small rodents	Often occurs in horses in the area
St. Louis encephalitis	Western and central USA, Florida	Mosquitoes; birds (including domestic fowl)	
Venezuelan encephalitis	South America	Mosquitoes	Rare in USA
Western (equine) encephalitis	Throughout western hemisphere	Mosquitoes; birds	Often occurs in horses in the area; particularly affects young children

*Reproduced, with permission, from Krupp MA, Chatton MJ (editors): *Current Medical Diagnosis & Treatment 1982.* Lange, 1982.

In **St. Louis encephalitis,** a specific virus that is transmissible to mice and able to be neutralized by the serum of convalescent patients can be isolated from the spinal fluid. Diagnosis is made by isolation of the virus from brain tissue or by development of specific neutralizing antibodies.

Two types of **equine encephalomyelitis,** eastern and western, occur in the USA and produce immunologically specific reactions. Epidemics of this equine infection occur primarily in the summer. The virus of the western type has been isolated from human blood and spinal fluid. Diagnosis can be made by neutralization tests. The virus can be isolated from the brains of fatal cases. The virus of eastern equine encephalitis has been recovered also from the blood of laboratory animals, from wild and laboratory-bred birds, and from human blood. Eastern equine encephalitis is spread by infected birds and transmitted by a mosquito that feeds on these birds and may also bite humans and other mammals. People and horses can be immunized against the disease. The mortality rate is believed to be 5–20%, and survivors may have permanent brain damage. Immune bodies in the serum can be detected in the blood of infected persons.

California encephalitis is transmitted by mosquitoes, and outbreaks occur in late summer and early fall; cases occur predominantly in children. The mortality rate is low, but sequelae such as emotional lability, learning difficulties, and recurrent seizures are noted.

Japanese encephalitis is caused by a mosquito-borne group B arbovirus in and around Japan. Clinical and laboratory findings resemble those of equine encephalomyelitis. It commonly occurs in children and has a very high mortality rate; there are severe neurologic defects in survivors.

Systemic Infections

Encephalitis may occur as a complication of systemic virus disease (poliomyelitis, rabies) or may be "postinfectious," occurring after apparent recovery from a viral infection (rubeola, rubella). Encephalitis has been known to occur following vaccination for smallpox or immunization for pertussis. Herpes simplex, infectious mononucleosis, typhus, scrub typhus, herpes zoster, rabies, trichinosis, malaria, and schistosomiasis may be associated with severe encephalitis. Administration of ACTH, corticosteroids, or both to patients with encephalitis such as measles encephalitis does not prevent CNS sequelae. Some deaths may be averted by constant, intensive therapy. Supportive measures include correction of dehydration and electrolyte imbalance by intravenous administration of appropriate fluids. In addition, intubation tracheostomy to avoid respiratory distress, treatment of bacterial complications with antibiotics, oxygen administration, anticonvulsants as necessary, and adequate nursing attention are required.

Cytomegalic Inclusion Body Disease

This disorder is a viral infection, usually latent, in

infants and children. Clinically obvious infections may occur in newborn infants following transplacental transmission and are manifested by jaundice, anemia, thrombocytopenia and hemorrhages, hepatosplenomegaly, chorioretinitis, encephalitis, and microcephaly. The disease may affect older debilitated children. Typical cytomegalic cells may be isolated from urine or adenoids in clinical and latent cases. Cytomegalovirus is readily isolated from the urine and body tissues of ill patients and can be recovered for many months after birth or after acute infection. Characteristic large inclusion bodies are present in the epithelial cells of urinary sediment. No specific treatment is effective, and the severe clinical disease is usually fatal.

Cytomegalovirus infection may also occur in immunosuppressed individuals. After massive transfusions, acute acquired cytomegalovirus disease may occur, presenting a clinical picture similar to that of infectious mononucleosis but usually without apparent CNS involvement.

Lymphocytic Choriomeningitis

This disease frequently resembles a mild attack of influenza, and the virus that causes it affects other tissues as well as the CNS and the meninges. The virus is easily obtainable from the spinal fluid and blood, and clinical diagnosis is confirmed by complement fixation and neutralization tests. The cerebrospinal fluid characteristically contains many lymphocytes but shows no change in sugar or chloride content.

Inclusion Body Encephalitis
(Subacute Sclerosing Panencephalitis, SSPE)

This subacute encephalitis of children and adolescents is characterized by progressive dementia, incoordination, ataxia, myoclonic jerks, and other focal signs. Children under age 12 years are predominantly affected, with gradual onset without fever. Although cerebrospinal fluid shows little remarkable change, the EEG usually shows widespread abnormalities with 2–4 Hz wave and spike complexes. Intranuclear and intracytoplasmic inclusion bodies are found in the neurons and occasionally in oligodendroglia of the brain. Beginning with mental deterioration, the disorder progresses to hallucinations, a stage of involuntary movements occurring at intervals of 5–10 seconds, akinetic mutism, and death. The disease usually lasts about 2 years, although survival for 8 years has been reported.

This disorder is also called **subacute sclerosing panencephalitis** (SSPE) and is considered to be a late sequela of measles. Measles antibodies in the cerebrospinal fluid and an increased serum measles antibody titer are usually present.

Coxsackievirus Infection

Symptoms and signs of meningeal involvement may occur with acute or subacute fever, headache, malaise, nausea, abdominal pain, and stiff neck. As a rule, no sensory, motor, or reflex changes occur; a coincidental infection with the virus of acute anterior poliomyelitis may occur. The course is self-limited and benign; herpangina and epidemic pleurodynia may also be caused by this type of virus. Diagnosis can be established by recovery of virus from feces or from the pharynx and by the demonstration of an increase in specific neutralizing antibodies in the sera. Enteroviruses that infect the human intestinal tract now include over 60 immunologically different agents. Twenty-nine coxsackievirus types (23 group A and 6 group B), 28 echovirus types, and 3 poliovirus types comprising this group may produce CNS involvement which is clinically indistinguishable from that produced by nonenteric viruses such as mumps and herpes simplex.

Herpes Simplex Meningoencephalitis

Severe asymmetric necrotizing inflammation, strikingly predominant in the limbic system, produces behavioral disturbances, memory loss, disorientation, olfactory and gustatory hallucinations, and focal neurologic defects including hemiparesis, hemianopsia, aphasia, and adversive and jacksonian seizures. The disease usually progresses rapidly and terminates fatally early. Characteristic intranuclear inclusions occur in affected neurons of the brain. The cerebrospinal fluid is often hemorrhagic. Brain scan, electroencephalography, and CT scan usually demonstrate a necrotic

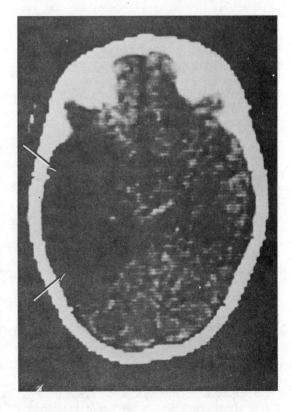

Figure 26–9. Herpes simplex encephalitis. CT scan of a 7-month-old infant showing cystlike left temporal lobe.

medial temporal lobe focus that may present as a mass lesion.

Adenine arabinoside (Ara-A) is the drug of choice in this infection, but treatment must be initiated early to reduce morbidity and mortality rates.

ACUTE ANTERIOR POLIOMYELITIS
(Heine-Medin Disease)

This acute generalized disease may occur in sporadic or epidemic forms. Most cases are now seen in immunodeficient patients who were given oral poliomyelitis vaccine or in nonimmune adults exposed to recently immunized children.

A gastrointestinal portal has been implicated as the mode of transmission. There is some question about the exact manner in which infection occurs. Experimentally, infection via the gastrointestinal and upper respiratory tracts can be effected. Multiplication of the virus in the gastrointestinal tract may continue for weeks or months after the acute infection.

The disease is most prevalent during the summer and warm periods. Invasion of the nervous system occurs as a relatively late manifestation. A stage of early viremia precedes invasion of the nervous system, which may occur from the gastrointestinal tract to the nervous system by way of the axis cylinders of the nerves.

There are 3 antigenic virus strains. Complement-fixing antigens are known for each of the 3 types of virus, and they may be prepared from tissue culture or the CNS of infected infant mice or hamsters. Inactivation of the virus by formalin, heat, or ultraviolet light liberates a soluble complement-fixing antigen. A type-specific precipitin reaction occurs when virus in sufficient concentration is used with immune animal or convalescent human serum.

Pathology

Gray matter damage is likely to occur. Changes in ganglion cells, varying in severity from mild to severe degeneration, occur especially in the anterior horn cells of the spinal cord. The lumbar and cervical enlargements of the cord are most affected. Microglia are increased early; later, remaining glial elements partake in glial scar formation.

Round cell infiltration of the spinal root ganglia may occur. Congestion and hemorrhage of the pia and arachnoid as well as the parenchyma of the cord may be present.

Clinical Findings

A. Prodromal Stage: In the prodromal, or preparalytic, phase, this disease resembles many other mild infections. One usually cannot predict which set of a group of ill patients in an epidemic will develop the severe permanent paralyses and which ones will never be severely affected. During the preparalytic phase, irritability, drowsiness, diarrhea, abdominal distress, headache, and fever of mild degree may be present.

The cerebrospinal fluid examination at this time may indicate a mild increase in the number of cells, most of which are polymorphonuclear leukocytes.

B. Paralytic Stage: The paralytic phase may come on soon after and may be accompanied by severe general symptoms, collapse, coma, and fever of 39.5–40.5 °C (103.2–105 °F). Usually 1–3 days after severe symptoms have been present, the fever drops and motor paralysis is apparent. Neck stiffness, pain, retraction, and a positive Kernig's sign are present early. In the acute phase, there may be tenderness of muscles, with painful contractions precipitated by movement or exposure to cold. Retention of urine is common but soon disappears. When muscle paralysis occurs, it may be severe and generalized, with function returning slowly in the weeks after.

C. Convalescent Stage: In general, maximum recovery occurs in the first few months after onset of paralysis, although it may require as long as 2 years.

Differential Diagnosis

The diagnosis of acute anterior poliomyelitis frequently cannot be made in the early phase of the disease. Especially in times of epidemic outbreaks, other diseases are confused with it. The major entities that are apt to be confused with poliomyelitis are meningitis, which can usually be diagnosed by adequate cerebrospinal fluid smear, culture, and cell counts; diphtheria, which can be detected by early nasopharyngeal smear and culture; and Guillain-Barré syndrome, which usually causes sensory changes, symmetric involvement, and characteristically albuminocytologic dissociation and is usually milder. Other virus infections of the nervous system may be identified by virologic and immunologic studies.

Landry's paralysis is characterized clinically by a rapid ascending paralysis usually terminating in death. It was believed to be a fulminating type of acute anterior poliomyelitis, although other causes cannot be excluded. Because of the rapid course of the disease, demonstrable pathologic changes are minimal or absent.

The **Guillain-Barré syndrome** may last for weeks or months, but recovery is the rule and is often complete, without paralytic sequelae or muscular atrophy. The components of this syndrome are as follows: (1) Motor disturbances: progressive weakness or paralysis beginning in the lower extremities and ascending to involve the trunk, upper extremities, and, occasionally, the cranial nerves. Deep reflexes are lost, but the cutaneous reflexes are preserved. (2) Sensory disturbances, including paresthesias and marked tenderness on pressure over the affected muscles; objective sensibility is only slightly disturbed. (3) Albuminocytologic dissociation: hyperalbuminosis of the spinal fluid in the absence of an increase in the number of cells is a constant diagnostic finding.

Prevention

Use of vaccine is desirable prophylactically, since the incidence of paralytic poliomyelitis is much lower in vaccinated groups. When intramuscular poliomyelitis vaccine (Salk) was used, 2 injections of 1 mL each were given at intervals of 1 month and repeated after 7 months and again after 1 year. Oral vaccine of the Sabin type is recommended as 3 doses of trivalent vaccine at intervals of 6–8 weeks, followed by one dose a year later.

Treatment & Prognosis

The patient should be kept in bed on a firm mattress with a padded footboard. Therapy in the acute phase is aimed at keeping the patient comfortable. To this end, hot packs are beneficial. When painful contractions of the muscles are no longer present, muscle reeducation should be vigorously pursued. The use of a respirator may be a necessary lifesaving measure in the acute phase when central paralysis has occurred. The patient should be watched carefully and, if signs of respiratory embarrassment develop, placed in a respirator immediately. Tracheostomy may be desirable or necessary when air passages are occluded by mucus or laryngospasm, particularly in patients in respirators. Application of removable splints may assist in prevention of stretching or injury to weak or paralyzed muscles.

The prognosis varies for different epidemics and localities. In the individual patient, the degree of functional recovery cannot be predicted in the acute phase. The early return of a mild or very slight degree of function in a muscle is a good prognostic sign for that particular muscle.

RABIES

Rabies is an acute encephalomyelitis with characteristic neuronal inclusion bodies transmitted by infected saliva of a rabid animal. Human rabies may result from the bite of an infected dog, although cats, bats, skunks, foxes, wolves, and other warm-blooded animals may also carry the virus. The incubation period in humans ranges from 10 days to 2 years. Pain appears at the site of the bite, followed by tingling; the skin becomes hypersensitive to temperature change and air currents. Periods of rage may alternate with calm intervals. Attempts to drink cause painful laryngeal spasms, so that the patient refuses to drink (hydrophobia). The patient becomes restless, with muscle spasms, laryngospasm, and extreme excitability. Convulsions occur finally, followed by death from cardiac or respiratory failure or generalized paralysis in 2–3 days.

Once symptoms have appeared, therapy is of little or no value. After a positive diagnosis of rabies in the biting animal or after the bite of an animal suspected of having the disease when the animal cannot be observed, immunization with rabies vaccine (human diploid cell culture) is recommended. In facial or severe head bites, rabies hyperimmune serum should be administered in addition to vaccine.

CHOREA
(Sydenham's Chorea)

Sydenham's chorea occurs in young individuals and is characterized by involuntary irregular movements, incoordination of voluntary movement, mild muscle weakness, and, occasionally, mental disturbances. It is generally linked with and regarded as one of the manifestations of rheumatic fever. Other clinical evidences of rheumatic fever are apt to be present.

Clinical Findings

The child becomes irritable, excitable, restless, and sleepless. Parents and friends describe the patient as being unable to keep still. The patient may grimace, become clumsy in movement, and stumble frequently. Involuntary irregular and dysrhythmic movements are the outstanding feature of this disease. Movements—especially of the extremities—are abrupt, sudden, short, quick, and jerky. Speech and trunk muscles may also be affected. Voluntary movements of affected parts are modified by the superimposed involuntary movements, which are made worse in attempted movement. Affected limbs are weaker in motor power and are hypotonic.

Diagnosis

Sydenham's chorea usually runs a limited course, with maximum disability 2–3 weeks after onset, then subsides slowly to disappear in 2–3 months. Recurrences occasionally occur. It must be differentiated from tics or habit spasms, which are characterized by stereotyped facial grimacing, blinking, smacking of the lips, and clicking noises without difficulty in articulation. There is no associated muscle weakness or evidence of rheumatic fever. Multiple tics may persist for months undiminished.

Treatment

Sedatives such as phenobarbital or tranquilizers such as phenothiazines or haloperidol (Haldol) are usually helpful. Treatment with corticotropin (ACTH) or corticosteroids may shorten the course or suppress rheumatic manifestations.

BACTERIAL NEUROTOXINS

The toxins elaborated by some pathogenic bacteria have an affinity for the nervous system.

Botulism

The poisoning that may follow ingestion of contaminated food containing the toxin of *Clostridium botulinum* is characterized by weakness of striated and smooth muscles. *C botulinum,* a gram-positive anaerobe, has spores which are heat-resistant and which may be introduced by contamination during canning and subsequently flourish, forming gas and giving a rancid taste and odor to food. Twelve to 48 hours after ingestion of contaminated food, symptoms of acute bulbar palsy may occur. Difficulty in convergence, ptosis of eyelids, paralysis of extraocular muscles, dilated pupils, difficulty in swallowing, and dysarthria are characteristic. Weakness of the muscles of the trunk and extremities may follow; the sensorium remains clear until convulsions and coma develop terminally.

Treatment should include early use of intravenous antitoxin (20,000–40,000 units 2–3 times daily). Gastrointestinal lavage, purgation, artificial respiration, and other supportive measures may also be necessary.

Diphtheria

The earliest neurologic complications of diphtheria may occur in the second or third week after the onset of infection. Paralysis of the palate and laryngopharyngeal muscles and nerves is believed to be due to local action of the toxin, producing characteristic nasal speech, regurgitation of fluid through the nose, and swallowing difficulties. Blurred vision develops as a result of accommodation paresis. About 2–3 weeks later, manifestations of generalized polyneuritis may occur, including motor weakness, peripheral sensory changes, and tenderness of muscles and nerves to pressure.

Symptomatic treatment and use of rehabilitation measures may be required.

Tetanus

Tetanus, or lockjaw, results from infection of wounds with *Clostridium tetani*, an anaerobic spore-former whose toxin may produce local or generalized muscle spasms. In the localized form, muscular spasms and contractions are limited to an involved extremity. In the generalized form, stiffness of the jaw (trismus) occurs early. Thereafter, neck stiffness, irritability and restlessness, rigidity of back muscles, and opisthotonos may occur. Rigidity of facial muscles, recurrent tonic muscle spasms, and generalized convulsions may occur spontaneously or may be elicited by external stimuli. Dysphagia, cyanosis, respiratory distress, and asphyxia may occur. Consciousness is usually preserved except during convulsions.

Prompt and adequate use of tetanus antitoxin, debridement of wounds, general anesthetics and muscle relaxants, and continuous nursing care are essential features of the treatment program.

ASEPTIC MENINGITIS

A variety of agents may be associated with aseptic meningitis, which is characterized by acute onset of fever, headache, and stiff neck. The cerebrospinal fluid shows pleocytosis, mainly mononuclear cells, with normal glucose, normal or slightly elevated proteins, and no bacteria. Recognized causes include (1) neurotropic viruses such as those of poliomyelitis, other enteroviruses, the virus of lymphocytic choriomeningitis, and arthropod-borne encephalitis virus; (2) other viruses such as the viruses of mumps, herpes simplex, herpes zoster, infectious mononucleosis, cat-scratch fever, infectious hepatitis, chickenpox, and measles; (3) spirochetes such as *Treponema pallidum* and *Leptospira;* (4) bacterial products, as in silent brain abscess or treated bacterial meningitis; (5) *Mycoplasma* or *Chlamydia;* and (6) foreign bodies such as air, contrast media, isotopes, etc, in the cerebrospinal fluid. The diagnosis depends upon isolation of the agent, rise in specific antibodies, epidemiologic features, specific details of the history, and cerebrospinal fluid findings.

EPIDEMIC NEUROMYASTHENIA
(Benign Myalgic Encephalomyelitis)

Viruses are believed to be responsible for outbreaks of epidemics of fatigue, headache, intense muscle pain, slight or transient paresis, mental disturbances, and objective evidences of diffuse CNS involvement. No causative agent has been isolated. The disease has been confused with poliomyelitis. Young and middle-aged adults are usually affected.

"SLOW" VIRUS INFECTIONS OF THE CENTRAL NERVOUS SYSTEM

Slow virus infections differ from other viral diseases in that the virus continually proliferates, slowly causing a progressive pathologic lesion, either without eliciting an antibody response or in spite of such a response. The incubation period may be up to 5 years. Scrapie, which occurs as a genetic trait in sheep, is caused by a heat-stable virus capable of producing the disease in sheep or goats when inoculated either into the CNS or peripherally. Known examples of transmissible slow virus infections of the nervous system include scrapie in sheep in England and Scotland and rida in sheep in Iceland.

Similarities have been noted in the epidemiologic, clinical, and histopathologic features of scrapie in sheep, its transmitted form in goats, and the human disease known as kuru. Kuru is a place-limited disease in an isolated Melanesian population. It is rapidly progressive, leading to death of most victims within a year.

Three neurologic diseases of humans have been shown to be caused by chronic, persistent, slow virus infections: kuru, Creutzfeldt-Jakob disease, and subacute sclerosing panencephalitis (SSPE). A viral cause has been reported or strongly suspected in other chronic nervous system disease.

Brain material from patients with Creutzfeldt-Jakob disease and kuru can produce similar diseases when injected into chimpanzees. Diseased chimpanzee brain can successfully transfer the diseases to other chimpanzees after an incubation period of months to years.

Kuru is characterized by progressive ataxia,

Table 26–3. Slow virus infections.*

Disease	Virus	Host(s)	Incubation Period	Nature of Disease
Diseases of humans				
Kuru	< 220 nm (probably < 100 nm)	Humans (chimpanzees, monkeys)	Months to years	Spongiform encephalopathy
Creutzfeldt-Jakob (C-J) disease	?	Humans (chimpanzees, monkeys)	Months to years	Spongiform encephalopathy
Subacute sclerosing pan-encephalitis (SSPE)	Measles variant	Humans	2–20 years	Chronic sclerosing panencephalitis
Progressive multifocal leuko-encephalopathy (PML)	Papovavirus	Humans	?	CNS demyelination
Diseases of animals				
Scrapie	< 50 nm, perhaps 14 nm	Sheep (goats, mice)	Months to years	Spongiform encephalopathy
Transmissible mink en-cephalopathy (TME)	35 nm	Mink (other animals)	Months	Spongiform encephalopathy
Visna	70–100 nm (oncor-naviruslike)	Sheep	Months to years	CNS demyelination
Aleutian disease of mink	25 nm	Mink	Months	Immune complex disease
Lymphocytic choriomenin-gitis (LCM)	50–150 nm	Mice (humans occasionally infected)	Months (in mice)	Immune complex disease (in congenitally or neonatally infected mice)

*Reproduced, with permission, from Jawetz E, Melnick JL, Adelberg EA: *Review of Medical Microbiology*, 15th ed. Lange, 1982.

tremors, dysarthria, and emotional lability. The incidence is higher in women and may be related to the cannibalism practices of the natives of New Guinea.

Creutzfeldt-Jakob disease, or subacute presenile dementia, is characterized by slowly progressive dementia, myoclonic fasciculations, ataxia, and somnolence. Its onset is gradual, and it is usually fatal within a few months to years. Transmission of infection in humans by surgical procedures (corneal transplant, etc) has been reported or suspected. However, in the majority of cases the mode of infection is not known. Unusual clusters of cases have been noted worldwide. About 25% of known cases have occurred in families with 2 or more victims, often not of the same generation.

PROGRESSIVE MULTIFOCAL LEUKOENCEPHALOPATHY (PML)

This unusual disease may occur late in the course of such chronic illnesses as malignant lymphoma, leukemia, sarcoidosis, carcinomatosis, or miliary tuberculosis. Rapid progressive focal or asymmetric brain disorder may be noted. Manifestations may include mental changes, impaired visual acuity, hemianopsia or blindness, aphasia, hemisensory impairment, ataxia, vertigo, nystagmus, and choreiform movements. Cerebrospinal fluid examination is usually unremarkable. Skull x-rays, pneumograms, and cerebral angiograms are normal. Electroencephalography may show diffuse slow-wave activity. Pathologically, multifocal demyelinative lesions of varying size and in varying stages of evolution are found throughout the brain, especially in the brain stem and cerebellum, although the spinal cord is usually normal. The cause is not known, but decreased resistance to infections may

be involved, since this disorder is associated with diseases in which immunologic hyporeactivity has been found. Papovavirus has been recovered from brains of some patients. The JC subtype is the virus most often isolated. A second variant, SV40 subtype, has also been isolated. Seroepidemiologic studies of antibody occurrence suggest that human infections with these papovaviruses may be common despite the rarity of clinically apparent neurologic disease.

EXPERIMENTAL ALLERGIC ENCEPHALITIS

Encephalitis may be induced in some animals by the injection of brain substances from other members of the same animal species together with adjuvants. Demyelinating disease with disseminated lesions of the brain and spinal cord may follow intramuscular injection into a monkey of its own frontal lobe brain material mixed with adjuvant. Histologically, the lesions resemble those of postinfectious encephalitis, which occurs in children after virus infections, or "postvaccinal encephalomyelitis," which occurs after repeated injections containing animal brain material.

Experimental allergic encephalitis cannot be transferred passively by serum, but it can be passively transferred with lymphoid cells. The severity of the induced lesions is not related to measurable complement-fixing antibrain antibodies, and such antibodies may even protect against lesions. Experimental allergic encephalitis is believed to be a hypersensitivity reaction to a lipoprotein of brain acting as an allergen; one such encephalitogenic protein has been isolated in pure form. Some animals developing such encephalitis show a delayed (tuberculin type) skin reaction to brain substance.

27 | Trauma to the Central Nervous System

HEAD INJURY

Emergency Evaluation

Any patient who gives a history of head injury followed by unconsciousness—and any unconscious patient who may have sustained a head injury—should receive careful neurologic evaluation. Particular effort should be made to detect focal or progressive neurologic changes. Skull x-rays should be taken as soon as possible.

The following are the most important features of the examination.

A. State of Consciousness: The depth and duration of unconsciousness usually reflect the degree of trauma. However, an initially alert and well-oriented patient may become drowsy, stuporous, and comatose as a result of progressive intracranial hemorrhage. During the first 24–48 hours it may be necessary to awaken the patient hourly to evaluate the degree of orientation, alertness, and general response to stimulation. *Caution:* Do not discharge the patient to home care unless it is certain that a responsible person will be on hand to awaken the patient from "sleep" every hour and to summon aid if complete arousal is difficult.

B. Vital Signs: Temperature, pulse, respiration, and blood pressure should be observed at intervals of one-half to 12 hours, depending upon the extent of injury.

C. Paralysis: In the stuporous or unconscious patient, paralysis can be demonstrated only by careful examination. Loss of strength and motion, although of minimal grade, may indicate intracranial hemorrhage.

D. Ocular Signs: The pupils should be observed regularly along with the vital signs. A fixed dilated pupil often means an ipsilateral epidural or subdural hemorrhage or ipsilateral brain damage. Ophthalmoscopic examination may reveal evidence of papilledema (due to intracranial pressure) or retinal hemorrhage.

E. Convulsions: Convulsions are apt to occur soon after a head injury; focal (jacksonian) convulsions suggest an irritative lesion of the contralateral cerebral hemisphere. Cerebral contusion and laceration, often in association with epidural, subdural, or intracranial hemorrhage, causes focal convulsions.

F. Nuchal Rigidity: Although nuchal rigidity may result from the subarachnoid bleeding often associated with head injuries, cervical spine injury must be ruled out by appropriate x-ray and clinical examinations.

G. Bleeding From the Ear: Otorrhagia suggests basilar fracture through the petrous pyramid of the temporal bone, but it may also occur as a result of traumatic rupture of the tympanic membrane or laceration of the mucous membranes without perforation of the drum. Subcutaneous blood over the mastoid area (Battle's sign) is suggestive of a basal skull fracture.

General Considerations

Craniocerebral injuries are frequently classified on the basis of the nature of the injury to the skull, although the prognosis for recovery depends primarily upon the nature and severity of the damage to the brain.

Closed head injuries are those in which there is no injury to the skull or in which the skull injury is limited to simple undisplaced fracture of the skull. They may be considered clinically as mild, moderate, or severe. Mild head injuries are characterized by brief loss of consciousness (seconds to minutes) without demonstrable neurologic changes (usually the same as cerebral concussion). Cerebrospinal fluid findings are usually normal. Retrograde amnesia may be present. Moderate head injuries are characterized by longer periods of unconsciousness, frequently with abnormal neurologic signs, and are often associated with cerebral edema and contusion. Severe head injuries cause prolonged unconsciousness and abnormal neurologic signs and are usually associated with cerebral contusion and laceration.

Open head injuries include scalp lacerations, compound fractures of the skull, and various degrees of cerebral destruction. If fragmentation of bone occurs, there will be extensive associated contusion and laceration of the brain. Consciousness may not be impaired at first, although depression of consciousness may occur later if progressive intracranial bleeding or edema occurs. Scalp lacerations should be sutured immediately unless they overlie a depressed fracture or penetrating wound of the skull, in which case the skin wound is treated in the operating room in conjunction with the fracture.

Fractures may be simple or compound, and linear (with no displacement of fragments), comminuted, or depressed.

Cerebral edema may follow head injury. Clinically, there is considerable variation in the severity of the findings. Focalizing signs such as convulsions, hemiplegia, and aphasia are not uncommon. Cerebrospinal fluid pressure is usually slightly increased. At operation, the brain looks very pale and swollen.

Contusion, or bruising, of the brain at or directly contralateral to the zone of impact (contrecoup injury) may be limited to superficial cortex, or associated hemorrhage into the underlying brain may also occur. Contusions frequently occur along the base of the posterior frontal lobes and the adjacent temporal lobe tips. Brain contusion is often clinically indistinguishable from concussion or laceration of the brain.

Brain laceration (a tear in the substance of the brain) usually occurs at the point of application of great force to the head or directly opposite (contrecoup effect). Lacerations involving the base of the brain usually cause death in a short time. Focal neurologic signs may persist after the acute episode has subsided. Associated subarachnoid or intracerebral hemorrhage is usually present, and the cerebrospinal fluid is bloody. Brain laceration (or contusion) may occur with no injury (or minimal injury) to the skull. The frontal and temporal lobes are common sites. Minor injuries may cause tearing of the brain and meninges and extensive hemorrhagic necrosis of the cortex and subcortical white matter. Associated hemorrhage of the basal ganglia and brain stem may also occur. Laceration of arachnoidal vessels may result in subarachnoid bleeding or the formation of subdural hematoma. Tearing of the middle meningeal artery or the dural sinuses or veins may be followed by bleeding into the extradural spaces.

Clinical Findings

A. Symptoms and Signs: Transient loss of consciousness lasting from seconds to minutes occurs classically with concussion of the brain. In coma that lasts for several hours or days, there is a likelihood of edema or contusion and laceration of the brain. The period of coma depends on the extent and site of injury; in severe cases it may last for many hours, days, or weeks.

After the patient recovers consciousness, symptoms and signs are related to the severity and nature of associated brain injury. With mild concussion, the patient may be normal within a few minutes; with laceration or contusion of the brain, mental confusion is apt to be present. Hemiplegia, aphasia, cranial nerve paralysis, and other focal neurologic signs may also be noted depending upon the nature and extent of the brain injury. The ipsilateral pupil is often dilated in dural hemorrhage.

In the recovery phase and for months thereafter, there may be complaints of headache, dizziness, and personality changes ("posttraumatic cerebral syndrome").

Loss of memory for the period immediately after recovery of consciousness (posttraumatic amnesia) and for the period immediately preceding the injury (pretraumatic, or retrograde, amnesia) may occur and is often related to the extent of brain damage.

If the patient remains unconscious, the diagnosis of a progressive intracranial hemorrhagic lesion is difficult. Vital signs (pulse rate, respirations, blood pressure) may change, although these are not reliable. In the case of deepening or unusually prolonged coma, exploratory trephination may be indicated; cerebral angiography may show pathognomonic features of subdural, epidural, or intracerebral hemorrhage. Prolonged unconsciousness is believed to indicate severe damage to the brain stem, usually due to secondary hemorrhage or compression of the brain stem.

B. Laboratory Findings: Lumbar puncture may establish the presence of subarachnoid hemorrhage and the pressure of the cerebrospinal fluid. Cerebrospinal fluid is frequently normal in all respects in brain concussion or cerebral edema. With contusion or laceration of the brain, bloody cerebrospinal fluid under increased pressure may be found.

C. X-Ray Findings: Skull x-rays should be taken as soon as the patient's physical condition permits. Cerebral angiography may help demonstrate subdural or intracerebral hematoma. A pneumogram often is useful in demonstrating ventricular distortion, shift, or dilatation following head injury. CT scans may disclose intracerebral or extracerebral hematoma, ventricular distortion, shift, or dilatation.

D. Special Examinations:

1. Electroencephalography may be of diagnostic and prognostic aid in selected cases.

2. Echoencephalograms may reveal evidence of midline shift, as with contused brain, hematomas, and cerebral edema.

3. Brain scans may show increased uptake of isotope in the area of hematoma, contusion, or edema.

4. Psychometrics are useful after the acute phase in assessing degrees and types of organic deficits.

Differential Diagnosis

The history of a blow to the head makes the cause of the unconsciousness evident; however, when a history of trauma is lacking, it is necessary to differentiate head injury from other causes of unconsciousness, such as diabetic, hepatic, or alcoholic coma, cerebrovascular accident, and epilepsy (where trauma to the head may occur during the attack).

Differentiate the neurologic findings following head injury from those caused by epidural hematoma, subdural hematoma, brain tumor, etc.

Complications & Sequelae

The complications of head injuries include vascular lesions (hemorrhage, thrombosis, aneurysm formation), infections (meningitis, abscess, osteomyelitis), rhinorrhea and otorrhea, pneumatocele, leptomeningeal cysts, cranial nerve injuries, and focal brain lesions. The sequelae include convulsive seizures, psychoses, mental disturbances, and posttraumatic cerebral syndrome.

A. Subarachnoid Hemorrhage: Bleeding into the subarachnoid space is often associated with other types of brain injury and is relatively common in

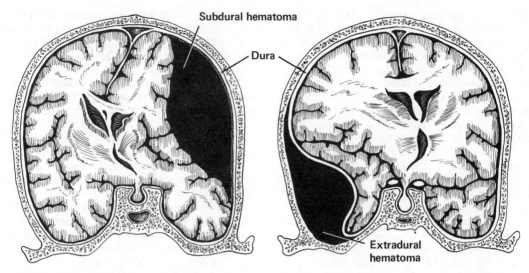

Figure 27–1. Subdural hemorrhage. (Reprinted from *Hosp Med* (Oct) 1965; 1:9, by permission of the authors and Wallace Laboratories.)

Figure 27–2. Extradural hemorrhage. (Reprinted from *Hosp Med* (Oct) 1965; 1:9, by permission of the authors and Wallace Laboratories.)

traumatized patients who have been unconscious for 1 hour or more. The clinical and diagnostic features of traumatic and spontaneous subarachnoid hemorrhage are similar. Painful stiffness of the neck and the presence of fresh blood in the cerebrospinal fluid are the usual findings.

B. Subdural Hemorrhage: Bleeding into the subdural space, which lies between the dura mater and the arachnoid, may follow relatively minor head injuries. This space is ordinarily filled with small amounts of lymphlike material and has little capacity to absorb blood. Acute subdural hemorrhage of minor degree may occur in association with other brain damage or injury and may not require surgical relief.

Chronic subdural hemorrhage or hematoma usually requires operative relief. Bleeding usually occurs originally from a subdural vein rupture. Subsequently, the hematoma increases in size and may be enveloped in a capsular mesothelial membrane. Increasing intracranial pressure and personality changes may appear weeks or months after the precipitating injury. X-rays frequently show a pineal shift to the opposite side. Specific patterns may be seen in angiograms. Evacuation of the hematoma through exploratory trephine openings may be necessary.

C. Extradural Hemorrhage: Extradural hemorrhage classically follows traumatic rupture of the middle meningeal artery or vein and may be difficult to

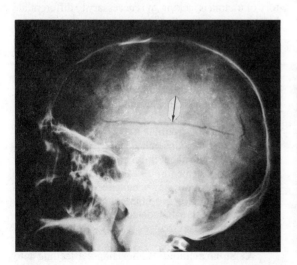

Figure 27–3. Roentgenogram showing a skull fracture.

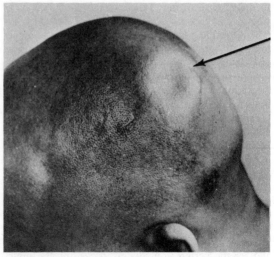

Figure 27–4. Depressed skull fracture of left parieto-occipital area.

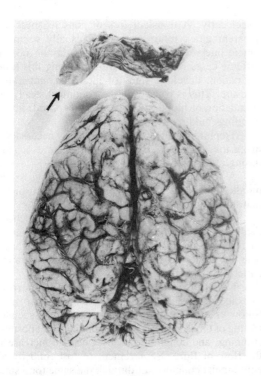

Figure 27–5. Left chronic subdural hematoma. Membranes with part of contents placed in front of brain.

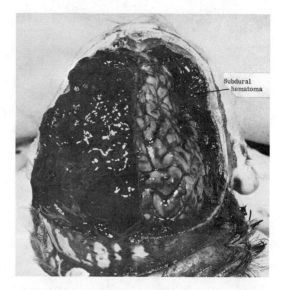

Figure 27–6. Chronic right subdural hematoma. Part of dura mater and hematoma has been reflected over left cerebral hemisphere.

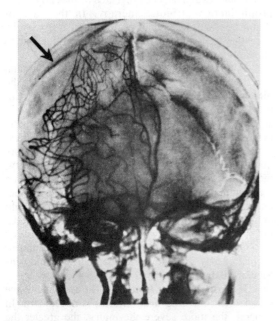

Figure 27–7. Carotid angiogram showing displacement of cerebral vessels by subdural hematoma (avascular space). (Reproduced, with permission, from Zehnder M: Die subduralen Hämetome. *Zentralbl Neurochir* 1937;**3**:339. JA Barth Verlag, Leipzig.)

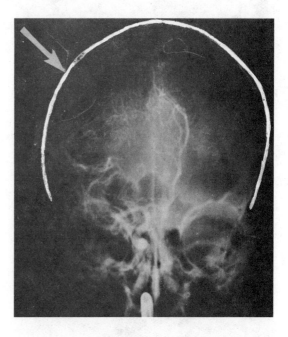

Figure 27–8. Subdural hematoma. Carotid angiogram revealing avascular space occupied by subdural hematoma.

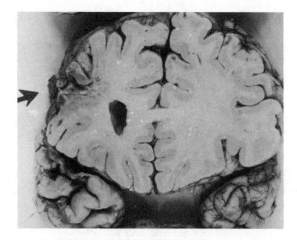

Figure 27–9. Posttraumatic epilepsy. Cerebral scar 15 years after skull fracture.

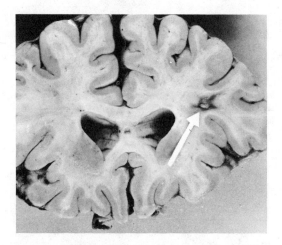

Figure 27–10. Fragments of bone from old depressed skull fracture embedded in brain.

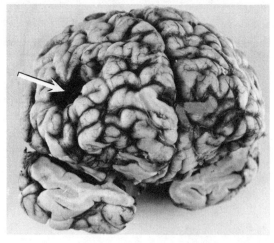

Figure 27–11. Posttraumatic cerebral atrophy. Arrow points to area of right frontal atrophy after skull fracture.

detect early. A transient loss of consciousness and apparent quick return to normal usually occur. A ''lucid interval'' lasting as long as a day or more in extreme cases customarily follows; during this time, the patient develops signs of increased intracranial pressure. This is caused by the continued steady accumulation of blood in the extradural space from the bleeding middle meningeal vessel.

Trephining of the skull is frequently necessary to make the diagnosis. Blood may then be evacuated through the trephine openings.

A fracture that is found by x-ray to cross the middle meningeal groove should raise the suspicion that this syndrome may be present.

D. Intracerebral Hemorrhage: A large subcortical hematoma may develop, but the most common findings are multiple small intracerebral hemorrhages near the contused area. The CT scan angiographic pattern is characteristic.

E. Rhinorrhea and Otorrhea: Rhinorrhea (leakage of cerebrospinal fluid from the nose) may follow fracture of the frontal bone with associated tearing of the dura mater and arachnoid. Erect posture, straining, and coughing usually cause an increase in the flow of fluid. Replacement of lost fluid by air entering the cranial vault through the same (or a similar) pathway may give rise to an aerocele. Otorrhea (leakage of cerebrospinal fluid from the ear) is usually of serious prognostic importance because it is caused by injuries to the more vital areas of the base of the brain.

Infection and meningitis are potential hazards in both instances and may be prevented by the early use of prophylactic antibiotic therapy. In the case of rhinorrhea, surgical repair of the dural tear may be necessary to stop the flow of cerebrospinal fluid and to close off a potential route of infection.

F. Cranial Nerve Paralysis: Injury to the cranial nerves may occur. Commonly affected nerves are the olfactory (anosmia), facial (paralysis), auditory (tinnitus and deafness), and optic (atrophy).

G. Posttraumatic Syndrome: The posttraumatic syndrome is more common after serious head injuries, but severe symptoms may be produced by relatively minor injuries. Headache, giddiness, easy fatigability, memory defects, and impaired ability to concentrate are common complaints. Personality changes are not uncommon. Changes of posture, exposure to sunlight or heat, exercise, and alcohol ingestion are apt to make the symptoms worse.

On pathologic examination, the brain may appear normal or may show severe cortical atrophy and ventricular dilatation.

H. Posttraumatic Epilepsy: The exact incidence of seizures following head injuries is not known. In general, the more severe the injury, the greater the possibility of seizures. Electroencephalographic studies are important in establishing the diagnosis.

I. Other Complications of Head Injuries:

1. Increased intracranial pressure may be manifested by changes in the level of consciousness, head-

ache, restlessness, unequal pupils, a slowly falling respiratory rate, a falling pulse rate, a slowly rising blood pressure, papilledema, hemiparesis, and elevated cerebrospinal fluid pressure. Rule out intracranial bleeding (subdural, epidural, or intracerebral).

2. Wound infection or osteomyelitis may be prevented by prophylactic antibiotic therapy in patients with compound or depressed fractures of the skull, rhinorrhea, otorrhea, or extensive scalp lacerations, and by meticulous aseptic technique for all dressings.

3. Pulmonary infections or atelectasis may be prevented or treated by the proper use of suction, positioning on the side, or, if necessary, intubation or tracheostomy.

4. Hyperthermia may result from injury of the hypothalamus or brain stem, local or general infection, or marked dehydration.

5. Shock usually occurs in patients with head injuries complicated by other severe injuries to the trunk and extremities and must be treated at once.

Treatment

A. Emergency Measures:

1. Treat shock if present; parenterally administered fluids and blood may be required.

2. Maintenance of an adequate airway and pulmonary ventilation is vital. The patient should be placed prone, with head turned to one side to facilitate drainage of secretions from the mouth and to keep the tongue from obstructing the pharynx. Intratracheal intubation or tracheostomy may be necessary. Give oxygen if necessary.

B. General Measures:

1. During the acute or initial phases, restlessness may be a factor. Special nursing and tranquilizers may be required. Avoid morphine because of its medullary depressant effects. Catheterization of a full bladder may relieve restlessness. Lumbar puncture and removal of a small amount of bloody cerebrospinal fluid may also relieve agitation.

2. Antibiotic treatment is always indicated if there is active bleeding or discharge from the nose or ears. Give broad-spectrum antibiotics until the danger of infection is past.

3. Continued observation is essential.

Course & Prognosis

Prognosis and course are related to the severity and site of cranial injury. With simple concussion, recovery is usually rapid. With laceration of the brain, the mortality rate may be 40–50%.

Subdural or epidural hematoma ordinarily requires prompt surgical evacuation in order to prevent death or serious neurologic complications.

In general, residual symptoms and signs in patients with head trauma are likely to be more extensive and incapacitating in those with the more severe types of brain injury. It is not uncommon, however, for patients to remain symptomatic (headache, dizziness, impaired memory, personality changes) even though neurologic diagnostic studies are negative.

Predictions regarding the clinical outcome are more accurate when made 6–12 months after the injury or when the clinical status of the patient has stabilized. Great variations occur in individual cases. A patient in whom subdural hematoma has been successfully removed may recover completely. On the other hand, many patients continue to have severe complaints after an apparently trivial head injury. A complicating factor in many cases is the role played by the "secondary gain" for the patient via lawsuits, insurance, and other types of compensation.

BIRTH INJURIES

Normal or prolonged labor may cause a variety of brain injuries. Subdural hemorrhage and tears of the dural membrane are relatively common. Following manipulation, depressed skull fracture with damage of underlying cerebral tissue may occur. Children who die within the first few months of life sometimes are found to have cortical lacerations and intracerebral bleeding.

Bloody cerebrospinal fluid is often found in normal newborn infants. This is thought to be due to mild subarachnoid hemorrhage caused by rupture of superficial brain veins.

Massive focal subarachnoid hemorrhage associated with hemorrhagic lesions in the brain parenchyma, intraventricular hemorrhages, hemorrhagic infarction, and direct traumatic bruising of the brain with

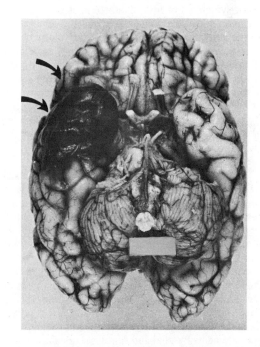

Figure 27–12. Birth injury. Hematoma of right anterior temporal lobe associated clinically with status epilepticus in a newborn infant.

local hemorrhagic diathesis have been noted in infants who died from acute birth injury. Minor extravasations of blood in the subarachnoid space and isolated petechial hemorrhages in the brain were also seen. A possible asphyxial basis for hemorrhagic lesions has been suggested under certain circumstances.

SPINAL CORD INJURIES

In general, the sequelae of spinal cord injuries are more dangerous and disabling than those of head injuries.

Concussion of the Spinal Cord

Concussion of the spinal cord is a rare disorder that is believed to be analogous to concussion of the brain. Loss of function in the spinal cord causes motor paralysis, loss of sensation, and sphincter paralysis, with subsequent return of function. The signs are believed to be due to reversible alterations of the neural tissue of the spinal cord. Edema and petechial hemorrhage with altered spinal cord circulation may occur. Assessment of ultimate disability requires an adequate posttraumatic observation period.

Contusion of the Spinal Cord

Contusion of the spinal cord may occur following fractures and dislocations of the vertebral column. Edema and mild evidence of bleeding of the pia and arachnoid may be found on pathologic examination. Severe symptoms of loss of function of the cord are present early, but the final degree of improvement can only be assessed after prolonged observation. In the acute stage, contusion of the spinal cord is associated with bloody cerebrospinal fluid. **Jolly's sign,** or position, indicates a unilateral lesion of the seventh cervical root segment. The patient holds the forearm in flexion, with the shoulder abducted. When the disorder is bilateral, the sign is called Bradburne's or Thorburn's sign.

Compression of the Spinal Cord

Fracture dislocations of the vertebral column are particularly apt to cause transverse compression, which may be complete when any severe degree of bony injury has occurred. The cerebrospinal fluid is bloody in the acute phase. It later becomes xanthochromic and may thereafter have an increased amount of protein. Partial or complete block of the subarachnoid channels may occur. Permanent severe residual defects are common, and significant improvement is rare. Loss of function below the level of the lesion may be complete. Severe and irreversible parenchymal damage with replacement of functioning neural elements by glial and fibrotic scars and formation of meningeal adhesions is the usual result.

Urinary tract infection is a common complication and may be fatal. Prevention of urologic infections and decubitus ulcers is an important aspect of the total care of the patient.

Treatment in the acute stage usually consists of correction of the dislocation with laminectomy and removal of compressing bone fragments. Orthopedic devices and braces should be used as soon as possible to encourage locomotion with the aid of crutches.

HERNIATION OF INTERVERTEBRAL DISK

In most cases, rupture or herniation of an intervertebral disk is caused by trauma. Sudden straining with the back in an "odd" position and lifting in the trunk-flexed posture are commonly recognized precipitating causes. The defect may occur immediately after an injury or following an interval of months to years.

The lumbosacral intervertebral disks (L5–S1 or L4–5) are most commonly affected, producing the clinical picture of sciatica. Herniation occasionally occurs in the cervical region (characterized by cervical radicular complaints) and rarely in the thoracic region.

Clinical Findings

A. Symptoms and Signs: These usually depend upon the location and size of the herniated or extruded disk material. Compression of a nerve root by a disk

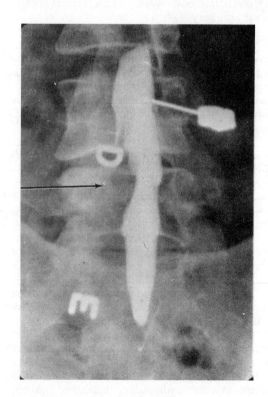

Figure 27–13. Herniated lumbar intervertebral disk demonstrated by Pantopaque myelography.

may be confined to a single nerve root; however, several roots may be compressed (eg, cauda equina by disk at L5–S1). Large lesions may even compress the spinal cord and produce symptoms commonly associated with tumors.

1. Lumbosacral disk– In the great majority of cases, (over 90%), rupture of the disk occurs at the level of the fourth or fifth lumbar interspace. This is characterized by straightening of the normal lumbar curve, scoliosis toward the side opposite the sciatic pain, limitation of motion of the lumbar spine, impaired straight leg raising on the painful side, tenderness to palpation in the sciatic notch and along the course of the sciatic nerve, mild weakness of the foot or great toe extensors, impaired perception of pain and touch over the dorsum of the foot and leg (in L5 or S1 distribution), decreased or absent ankle jerk, and radiation of pain along the course of the sciatic nerve to the calf or ankle on coughing, sneezing, or straining.

2. Cervical disk herniation (5–10% of herniated disks)–The cervical disks most commonly involved are between C5–C6 and C6–C7. Paresthesias and pain occur in the upper extremities (hands, forearms, and arms) in the affected cervical root distribution (C6 or C7). Slight weakness and atrophy of the biceps or triceps may be present, with diminution of biceps or triceps jerk. The mobility of the neck is restricted, with accentuation of radicular and neck pains by neck motion, coughing, sneezing, or straining. Long tract signs (extensor plantar response, sensory or motor impairment of lower levels, etc) occasionally occur, indicating compression of the spinal cord by the disk.

B. Laboratory Findings: Cerebrospinal fluid protein may be elevated, and complete or partial cerebrospinal fluid block is occasionally demonstrated.

C. X-Ray Findings: Spine x-rays may show loss of normal curvature, scoliosis, and narrowing of the intervertebral disk. A characteristic roentgenologic defect in the subarachnoid space is usually produced by a herniated disk and is readily demonstrable by myelography. Electromyography may be of value in localizing the site of a ruptured disk if characteristic denervation potentials can be demonstrated in muscles of a particular root distribution.

Differential Diagnosis

In tumors of the spinal cord, the course is progressive, cerebrospinal fluid proteins are elevated, partial or complete spinal subarachnoid block is present, and the myelographic pattern is distinctive.

In arthritis, neurologic findings are usually minimal or absent, and the myelogram is usually negative.

Spinal column anomalies show characteristic x-ray findings, cerebrospinal fluid findings are negative, and myelographic changes are dissimilar or absent.

Treatment
A. General Measures:
1. Lumbosacral disk–In the acute phase, bed rest, heat applied locally to the back, salicylate analgesics, and the use of a bed board under the mattress are indicated. Traction to the lower extremities is frequently beneficial. The avoidance of severe physical effort and strain is essential to minimize recurrence of symptoms after the initial episode. Low back belts, braces, or supports may be beneficial. It is important to instruct the patient in the proper methods of bending, lifting (with knees flexed), and carrying (with the object held close to the body).

2. Cervical disk–In acute exacerbations of herniated cervical disks, bed rest with cervical halter traction is indicated. In subacute or mild episodes, intermittent cervical halter traction with various devices may be employed on an outpatient basis or at home. The use of a light collar may be helpful. Local application of heat, diathermy, and similar measures may be of temporary value.

B. Surgical Measures: If the response to conservative measures is poor or recurrences are disabling, diskectomy is indicated.

Injection of the enzyme chymopapain into the diseased disk has been reported effective in relieving pain.

Prognosis

Conservative management with or without traction may bring about improvement to the point of "practical" recovery. Relief of pain usually follows removal of the damaged disk. Reversal of motor dysfunction, muscle atrophy, and skin sensory changes may occur.

LOW BACK PAIN

Low back pain may be associated with a variety of causes, and careful examination of such a patient may yield important clues regarding the site and cause of the disorders. Such a patient may be subjected to a large number of laboratory, x-ray, and diagnostic procedures with ambiguous or disappointing results. This may in turn often reflect the inadequate clinical evaluation of the patient and commonly results from failure to utilize the information that a properly conducted physical and neurologic examination may supply. The increasing overdependence of the clinician upon the laboratory is unnecessarily exaggerated when the physician fails to obtain vital information available at the bedside examination.

Inspection and palpation of the painful area are important. Since pain from nerve roots or nerves is commonly referred toward the periphery, the physician should explore the entire nerve lengths leading from the area and should note the presence of any masses or tenderness and, where possible, the size and consistency of nerves.

Rectal and vaginal examination should be included, so that local lesions and involvement of accessible lumbodorsal plexuses can be ruled out if possible.

Muscle spasm and tenderness to percussion and deep pressure may give evidence suggesting radicular irritation, particularly when associated with local deformity or restriction of spinal motion.

The range of motion of joints and the effect of movement on the pain should be determined, since pain from areas such as the hip may be referred distally, and severe distal peripheral pain may be referred to the entire limb.

The regional blood vessels and those of the extremity should be checked for adequacy of pulsation and aneurysmal dilatation.

The straight leg-raising test (**Lasègue's sign**; see Fig 5–19) should be performed. The relaxed, extended lower extremity is gently lifted from the bed or table with the patient supine. The presence and amount of pain and the extent to which the straight leg may be raised are noted. Pain and limitation of motion often accompany radiculopathy, especially that which occurs with herniated lumbar or lumbosacral disks.

In testing for the "f-ab-er-e" sign (**Patrick's sign**), the patient lies supine, and the heel of the lower extremity being tested is passively placed on the opposite knee. Then the knee on the side being tested is pressed laterally and downward by the examiner as far as it will go. The test is considered positive if motion is involuntarily restricted; pain frequently accompanies this limitation of motion. The test is positive in hip joint disease and negative in sciatica. "F-ab-er-e" is a mnemonic formula: "f" for flexion, "ab" for abduction, "er" for external rotation, and "e" for extension motions of the hip (Fig 5–18).

Kernig's sign is elicited with the patient supine. The examiner flexes the patient's hip and then extends the knee as far as possible without producing significant pain. A positive Kernig test consists of an involuntary spasm of the hamstring muscles that limits extension of the knee and often causes pain. Its clinical significance is similar to that of a positive straight leg-raising test.

Lumbar paraspinal muscle spasm frequently is noted with local radiculitis, which is due to many causes, including herniated lumbar intervertebral disk.

Passive flexion of the neck so that the chin rests on the chest may induce ascension of the spinal cord within the spinal canal. This then puts tension on the various spinal roots, causing excessive pain and indicating disease of particular nerve roots—provided motion of the spinal column was not induced and the patient was relaxed.

With the patient standing facing away from the examiner, the presence of lordosis, scoliosis, or list affecting the lumbar region is noted. The effect of flexion, hyperextension, and lateral flexion of the trunk on the pelvis is observed.

Psoas muscle spasm usually indicates disease of the psoas muscle or of the lumbar vertebrae and soft tissue adjacent to this muscle. It may be tested with the patient prone and the pelvis firmly pressed against the

table with one hand by the examiner. With the examiner's other hand grasping the ankle, the patient's leg is moved to the vertical position with the knee flexed at a right angle. The hip is passively hyperextended by lifting up on the ankle. Limitation of motion is produced by involuntary psoas muscle spasm.

Limitation of passive lumbar flexion and resulting pain often accompany disease of the lumbar or lumbosacral articulations. With the patient supine, the examiner grasps one lower extremity with both hands and moves the thigh to a position of maximal flexion. The examiner then presses firmly downward toward the table and upward toward the patient's head, passively flexing the lumbar spinal column.

CERVICAL SPONDYLOSIS

Radicular symptoms and myelopathy may result from cervical spondylosis. Symptoms develop because of direct cord and root compression and angulation by ridges on the posterior margins of the vertebral bodies, ischemia due to compression of the anterior spinal artery and veins, vascular and soft tissue changes, and trauma—although the initiating vertebral disturbance may be unknown. Spondylosis usually affects several levels, being confined to a single level in only one-fifth of cases.

The onset is variable. A high proportion of cases occur in males, who report a long duration of symptoms, and the average age at onset is in the mid 50s. Paresis, dysesthesia, and numbness of the upper ex-

Figure 27–14. Area of cervical spinal cord compression in a 57-year-old man with cervical osteoarthritis.

tremities, as well as fasciculations, atrophy, and weakness of the affected upper limbs, may occur. Hyperreflexia in the lower limbs, extensor plantar responses, and gait disturbances may also be noted in severe cases.

Loss of cervical lordotic curvature, subluxation, narrowing of intervertebral spaces, and osteophytosis may be detected in lateral cervical spine x-rays. Myelographic examination frequently demonstrates anterior indentation of the spinal cord, although complete block is infrequent.

Conservative measures include heat, massage, cervical traction, and a Minerva jacket or immobilization in a cervical collar for several months. If the response to conservative measures is poor or if there is rapid progression of neurologic signs, wide laminectomy of the affected cervical spine and section of the dentate ligaments may prove beneficial.

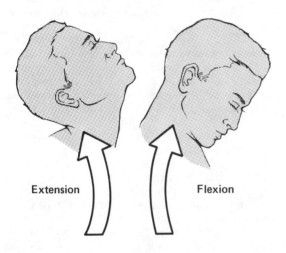

Figure 27–15. Mechanics of a whiplash injury.

Extension   Flexion

SHOULDER–HAND SYNDROME

This syndrome may result from reflex mechanisms in which shoulder pain is associated with swelling of the hand and wrist. The shoulder pain may be secondary to local trauma or may be referred from myocardial infarction, osteoarthritis of the cervical spine, cervical radiculitis, etc. In some cases, no obvious cause can be established. The vasomotor disturbance and swelling in the hand may suggest scleroderma. The shoulder difficulty may be confused with bursitis, arthritis, and gout. Treatment of underlying disease, analgesics, and physical therapy are usually necessary. Stellate ganglion block and systemic corticosteroids may be required.

ACUTE SPRAIN OF CERVICAL SPINE
(Whiplash Injury)

Whiplash refers to an injury in which the spine is suddenly and unexpectedly forced violently in one direction and then with a returning force and motion in the opposite direction. It is often associated with rear-end automobile collisions. It may be manifested by rapid onset of neck pain and headache, stiff neck with increased pain on motion, nervousness, and apprehension. The pain may be intensified by motion and improved by rest. Nausea and vomiting, radiating pains, and numbness in the upper extremities may occur. In severe cases, headaches may persist for several weeks and neck stiffness for several months. Loss of normal neck motion is often striking. Forward flexion of the neck is attempted slowly and cautiously. Muscle spasm of the neck muscles may be evident on palpation. X-rays of the cervical spine often show straightening or reversal of normal cervical spine curvature. Treatment may require analgesics, sedatives, tranquilizers, rest, heat, and massage. Cervical traction may be useful and necessary, particularly in the early phases. Neck support with a cervical collar, cast, etc, may be required.

28 | Tumors of the Central Nervous System

INTRACRANIAL TUMORS

Primary tumors generally do not resemble the carcinomas and sarcomas that are found outside the CNS and rarely metastasize outside of the CNS. The CNS is fertile soil for the growth of metastatic carcinomas and sarcomas from extraneural foci. Experimentally, certain carcinogenic agents may induce gliomas of the brain in some strains of mice.

If one includes all tumors (both primary and metastatic) of the brain, skull, and scalp in the term intracranial tumors, a convenient classification may be made: congenital, mesodermal, ectodermal, metastatic, and miscellaneous.

Pathology

A. Congenital:

1. Dermoids are frequently cystic and may contain sebaceous caseous material, hair, etc. The tumor cavity is usually lined with squamous epithelium.

2. Teratomas are developmental tumors that usually contain a greater variety of structures such as bone, muscle, fat, and nerve tissue, and they are calcified, so that they are readily seen in x-ray. They tend to lie in the midline.

3. Epidermoids, also known as cholesteatomas, or pearly tumors, occur in the bones of the skull and are made up of masses of crystalline cholesterin enclosed within a capsule of stratified squamous epithelium.

4. Chordomas are soft tumors containing much mucoid intercellular material and cords of highly vacuolated large cells. They arise from remnants of the primitive notochord.

5. Craniopharyngiomas occur mainly in children and arise from the pars tuberalis of the hypophysis. They are usually cystic, and calcifications above the sella turcica may be seen on x-ray. The tumor mass and cyst frequently become quite large and slowly compress the adjacent tissue. They contain cells arranged in stratified squamous epithelial layers or in a syncytial mass.

B. Mesodermal: Many types of **meningiomas** are recognized. Characteristically, the tumor is encapsulated and easily separated from nervous tissue. Calcified psammoma bodies and whorllike collections of cells are commonly found. Mitoses are rare. The nuclei tend to be ovoid and vesicular. **Neurinomas** are thought to arise from neurilemma sheath cells of the vestibular portion of the eighth cranial nerve, within the auditory meatus, where they grow and expand to fill the cerebellopontine angle. They are apt to be yellowish, soft, and cystic and are composed of elongated, spindle-shaped cells with ovoid nuclei that seem to run in parallel streams, with the nuclei showing a tendency to lie side by side in "palisade" formation. Mitoses are uncommon.

Tumors growing from nerves are of 2 types:

(1) True neuromas (rare) arise from actual nerve tissue, usually in connection with the sympathetic system. They are distributed beneath the skin and are often multiple.

(2) False neuromas arise from the connective tissue of the nerve trunk, usually on the spinal nerves and often in large numbers. They usually appear in the first half of life and are often hereditary. Various types include plexiform neuromas, pachydermatocele, and multiple neurofibromatosis (von Recklinghausen's disease).

A common symptom of nerve tumors is pain, usually intermittent and radiating to the periphery of the nerve. Paresthesias may occur. Treatment is by excision. In nerves that may be examined directly by inspection and palpation, abnormal masses may be seen or felt, and there may be tenderness to palpation or percussion.

Vascular tumors may occur as angiomas or hemangioblastomas. **Angiomas** are usually associated with vascular malformation elsewhere in the body and are regarded as malformations by some writers. A bruit is sometimes audible, especially if the angioma lies between relatively large arterial and venous elements. **Hemangioblastomas,** usually cystic, are apt to occur in the cerebellar hemispheres and are sometimes present in association with angiomas of the retina and other organs. The tumor usually is a relatively small nodule in the wall of the cyst cavity and is composed of many capillaries and extremely vacuolated cellular tissue arranged in small groups or cords. Reticulin stains reveal many reticulin fibers about the capillaries.

C. Ectodermal:

1. Gliomas–Glioblastoma multiforme is an infiltrative, rapidly growing cerebral tumor that occurs most frequently in middle-aged persons and is apt to invade both cerebral hemispheres via the corpus callosum. It is a multicolored tumor with grossly visible, hemorrhagic yellow and brown areas. Microscopically, the tumor is quite cellular, with many mitoses,

Table 28—1. Frequency of brain tumor types according to age and site.*

Age	Cerebral Hemisphere	Intrasellar and Parasellar	Posterior Fossa
Childhood and adolescence	Ependymomas; less commonly, astrocytomas.	Astrocytomas, mixed gliomas, ependymomas.	Astrocytomas, medulloblastomas, ependymomas.
Age 20–40	Meningiomas, astrocytomas; less commonly, metastatic tumors.	Pituitary adenomas; less commonly, meningiomas.	Acoustic neuromas, meningiomas, hemangioblastomas; less commonly, metastatic tumors.
Over age 40	Glioblastoma multiforme, meningiomas, metastatic tumors.	Pituitary adenomas; less commonly, meningiomas.	Metastatic tumors, acoustic neuromas, meningiomas.

*Reproduced, with permission, from Dunphy JE, Way LW (editors): *Current Surgical Diagnosis & Treatment,* 4th ed. Lange, 1979.

giant cells, and young glial forms (spongioblasts). Areas of necrosis are characteristic, with pseudopalisading of cells about the necrotic foci. The blood vessels within the tumor show severe proliferation of the intima and hyaline degeneration. The average survival period is about 1 year.

a. Medulloblastoma is a rapidly growing tumor of the vermis of the cerebellum and usually occurs in children. It characteristically metastasizes to the surface of the remaining CNS via the subarachnoid spaces. It is grossly red and soft and is composed of many closely packed cells, with oval nuclei and many mitoses. Pseudorosette formations in which nuclei of the cells tend to group themselves in circles or semicircles are common. The average survival period with x-ray treatment is 15 months.

b. Astrocytoma usually occurs in the cerebrum

Table 28—2. Frequency of major types of brain tumors.*

Intracranial Tumors†		Frequency of Occurrence
Gliomas		50%
Glioblastoma multiforme	50%	
Astrocytoma	20%	
Ependymoma	10%	
Medulloblastoma	10%	
Oligodendroglioma	5%	
Mixed	5%	
Meningiomas		20%
Nerve sheath tumors		10%
Metastatic tumors		10%
Congenital tumors		5%
Miscellaneous tumors		5%

*Reproduced, with permission, from Dunphy JE, Way LW (editors): *Current Surgical Diagnosis & Treatment,* 5th ed. Lange, 1981.
†Exclusive of pituitary tumors.

of adults and the cerebellum of children, although it may occur in the cerebellum of adults. It grows slowly and usually becomes cystic. It is composed of astrocytes with densely staining nuclei and scanty cytoplasm and is usually relatively acellular. Fibrillary and protoplasmic astrocytomas may be distinguished by the presence of fibrillary or protoplasmic astrocytes. The survival period averages about 6 years.

c. Oligodendrogliomas are slowly growing, solid, calcified tumors usually found in the cerebral hemispheres of adults. They are grossly firm and red, with areas of calcification, and are composed of cells with deeply staining nuclei within polyhedral spaces where the cytoplasm is hardly discernible. Mitoses are uncommon. The average survival period is about 5 years.

d. Astroblastoma is a relatively rare glioma that occurs in the cerebral hemispheres of middle-aged adults. It looks grossly and behaves clinically like glioblastoma multiforme. It contains astroblasts that arrange themselves about vessels in a radiating fashion. Giant cells and mitoses are common, and there is proliferation of the intima of smaller blood vessels. The average survival period is 3 years.

e. Spongioblastomas occur predominantly near the optic chiasm of children and in the pons, where they are apt to cause uniform enlargement and give the appearance of "hypertrophy of the pons." They are composed of spindle-shaped cells of the spongioblast series, which tend to lie in parallel rows and have large, thick processes. The average survival period of patients with spongioblastomas occurring in the brain stem is about 1 year.

f. Ependymomas occur chiefly in children. They are slowly growing and are apt to calcify and arise in or near ventricular walls. They are more common in the fourth ventricle than elsewhere and are composed of adult ependymal cells or younger ependymoblasts. Pseudorosette formation, in which the cells are arranged about a clear space or a blood vessel, is common, and blepharoplasts (small round or rod-shaped intracytoplasmic bodies) may be demonstrated. The survival period is short owing to the usual location in the fourth ventricle.

Table 28—3. Types of CNS tumors in children.*

Cell Type	Incidence	Supratentorial	Posterior Fossa
Medulloblastoma	30%	. . .	Midline cerebellum
Astrocytoma	30%	Occasional	Cerebellar hemisphere
Ependymoma	10%	Rare	Fourth ventricle
Pontine glioma	10%	. . .	Pons
Craniopharyngioma	4%	Suprasellar	. . .
Dermoid tumors and teratoma	3%	Rare	Rare
Other gliomas	8%	Uncommon	Uncommon

*Reproduced, with permission, from Dunphy JE, Way LW (editors): *Current Surgical Diagnosis & Treatment,* 5th ed. Lange, 1981.

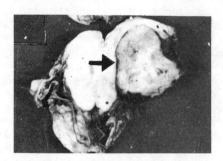

Figure 28–1. Compression of the brain stem by acoustic neurinoma.

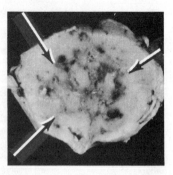

Figure 28–2. Glioblastoma multiforme of brain stem.

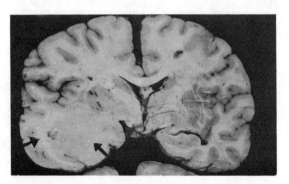

Figure 28–3. Astrocytoma of left temporal lobe.

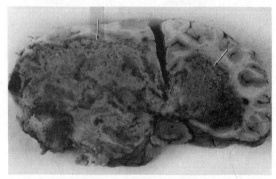

Figure 28–4. Glioblastoma multiforme in a 65-year-old woman, with extensive involvement of both cerebral hemispheres and corpus callosum.

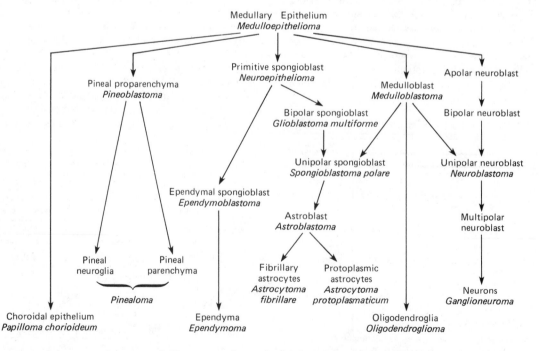

Figure 28–5. Scheme to relate types of gliomas according to the predominant cellular constitution of each group. (Reproduced, with permission, from Bailey P: *Intracranial Tumors,* 2nd ed. Thomas, 1948.)

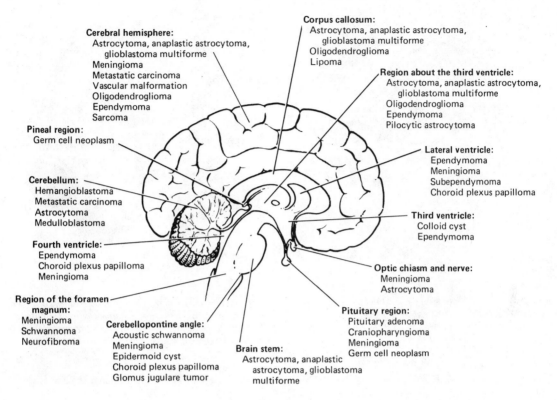

Figure 28–6. Distribution of intracranial tumors in adults. (Reproduced, with permission, from Burger PC, Vogel FS: *Surgical Pathology of the Nervous System & Its Coverings.* Wiley, 1976.)

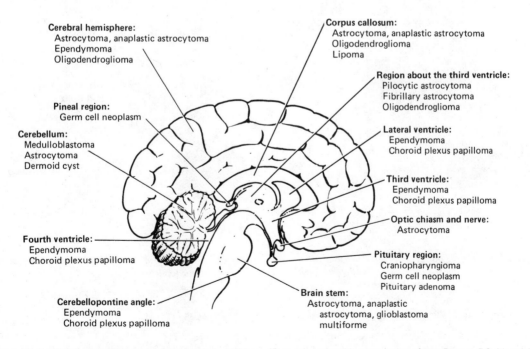

Figure 28–7. Distribution of intracranial tumors in children. (Reproduced, with permission, from Burger·PC, Vogel FS: *Surgical Pathology of the Nervous System & Its Coverings.* Wiley, 1976.)

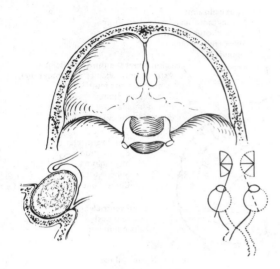

Failing vision, primary optic atrophy, and bitemporal hemianop-sia; endocrine disturbances and enlargement of sella turcica.

Figure 28–8. Pituitary adenoma.

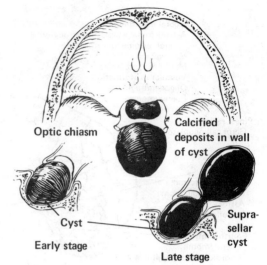

Early Stage: Failing vision, primary optic atrophy, bitemporal field defects, endocrine disturbances (hypopituitarism), suprasellar calcification (80%) in children and adolescents.
Late Stage: Headache, nausea and vomiting, papilledema.

Figure 28–9. Craniopharyngioma.

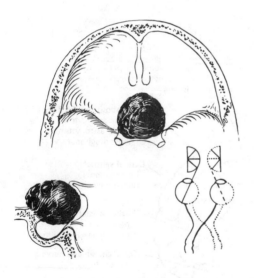

Failing vision, primary optic atrophy, and bitemporal hemianop-sia, **but** no endocrine disturbance and no enlargement of the sella turcica in middle-aged persons.

Figure 28–10. Meningioma of tuberculum sellae.

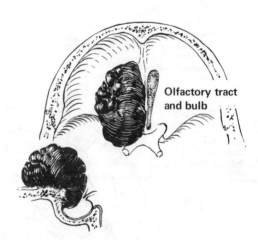

Ipsilateral anosmia and primary optic atrophy; contralateral papilledema (optic nerve).

Figure 28–11. Olfactory groove meningioma.

(Figs 28–8 through 28–15 reproduced, with permission, from Scarff: *Classic Syndromes of Brain Tumor.* Annual Clinical Conference of the Chicago Medical Society, 1953.)

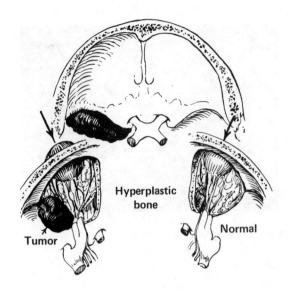

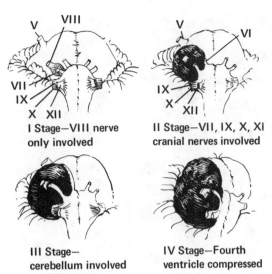

Early Stage: Unilateral exophthalmos, slowly progressing (months—years). Increased density (in x-rays): retro-orbital plate, ipsilateral side.

Figure 28—12. Retro-orbital meningioma.

First Stage: Tinnitus; later, deafness and disturbances of equilibrium.
Second Stage: Weakness of facial muscles, pain in face, dysphagia and dysarthria.
Third Stage: Ataxia and incoordination.
Fourth Stage: Ventricles compressed. Evidence of increased intracranial pressure.

Figure 28—13. Acoustic neurinoma.

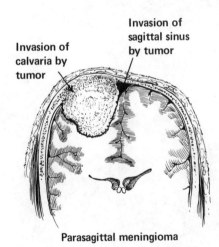

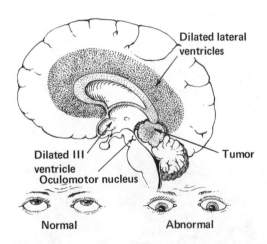

Disturbances of cerebral function, depending on localization. Focal hyperplasia and hypervascularization of the overlying bones.

Figure 28—14. Parasagittal meningioma.

Symptoms and signs of increased intracranial pressure, without lateralizing signs. Limitation of upward gaze. Abnormal pupillary reactions.

Figure 28—15. Pinealoma.

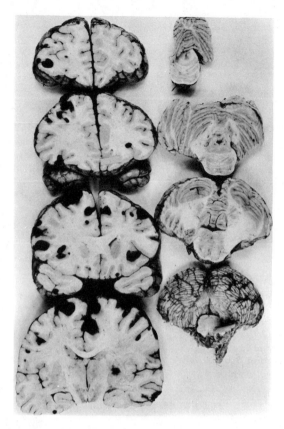

Figure 28–16. Metastatic melanoma in a 43-year-old woman.

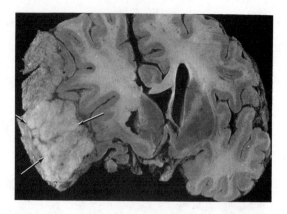

Figure 28–18. Meningioma of right cerebral hemisphere convexity in an 80-year-old man.

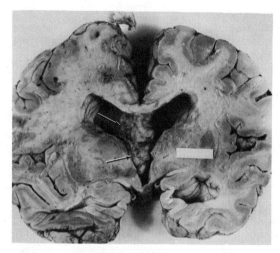

Figure 28–19. Glioblastoma multiforme of septum pellucidum in a 73-year-old woman.

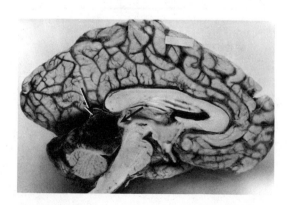

Figure 28–17. Compression of vermis of cerebellum by Hodgkin's tumor in a 65-year-old man.

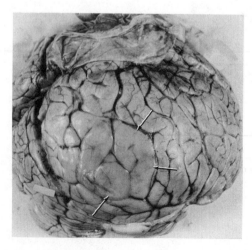

Figure 28–20. Right parieto-occipital tumor (glioblastoma multiforme) with enlargement and flattening of gyri.

Table 28—4. Classification of pituitary adenomas.*

	Secretory Product	Clinical Syndrome
Endocrine-Active[1]		
Somatotropic	Growth hormone (GH)	Acromegaly (adult), gigantism
Corticotropic	Adrenocorticotropic hormone (ACTH)	Cushing's disease, Nelson's syndrome[2]
Prolactinoma	Prolactin (PRL)	Amenorrhea-galactorrhea, impotence
Thyrotropic	Thyroid-stimulating hormone (TSH)	Hyperthyroidism
Gonadotropic	Follicle-stimulating hormone (FSH), leutinizing hormone (LH)	Too rare to characterize
Endocrine-Inactive		
Prolactinoma	Prolactin (PRL)	Hypopituitarism[3]

*Reproduced, with permission, from Dunphy JE, Way LW (editors): *Current Surgical Diagnosis & Treatment*, 5th ed. Lange, 1981.

[1] Some tumors secrete more than one hormone, most often GH-PRL and ACTH-PRL.

[2] After adrenalectomy.

[3] More than half of these tumors contain prolactin granules and the patients have hyperprolactinemia, but the prolactin does not produce the typical amenorrhea-galactorrhea syndrome, possibly because the prolactin is not biologically active.

2. Pituitary tumors—Pituitary tumors are relatively common in the anterior pituitary glands of adults. They cause erosion and expansion of the sella turcica and give the appearance on x-ray of "ballooning" of the sella turcica. Compression of the adjacent optic chiasm and hypothalamus is common.

Tumors of the pituitary may be considered to be endocrine-active or endocrine-inactive (see Table 28–4). Adenomas smaller than 1 cm are microadenomas; those larger than 1 cm are macroadenomas. Large tumors may cause a mixed endocrine picture or oversecretion with hypopituitarism. Endocrine-active tumors may produce characteristic symptoms.

D. Metastatic: These tumors usually arise from carcinomas, more rarely sarcomas, and only occasionally from melanoblastomas, hypernephromas, and retinal tumors. The most common source of metastatic tumor to the brain is bronchogenic carcinoma. Carcinomas of the breast, thyroid gland, and gastrointestinal tract also frequently give rise to brain metastases.

E. Miscellaneous: Aneurysms, tuberculomas, syphilomas, gummas, parasitic formations, etc.

Clinical Findings

A. Generalized Symptoms: The presence of a tumor may give rise to early effects mechanically, either through displacement of brain tissue or by causing a mild block in cerebrospinal fluid circulation. Headache is commonly present and is intensified or precipitated by any activity that tends to raise the intracranial cerebrospinal fluid pressure, such as stooping, straining, or exercising. Conversely, mea-

sures that reduce intracranial cerebrospinal fluid pressure may relieve headache. Nausea and vomiting are common and are not necessarily related to meals. Mental clouding, lethargy, and easy fatigability are not unusual. As the intracranial cerebrospinal fluid pressure increases, papilledema occurs.

B. Focal Signs and Symptoms: As a tumor grows, progressively greater destruction or dysfunction of tissue may occur, causing locally referable signs. In this way, involvement of the cerebrum, brain stem, cranial nerves, etc, may soon be evident through the loss or alteration of function of these parts. Tumors involving the frontal lobe tend to produce a disturbed mental state, with defective memory, impaired judgment, irritability, mood changes, and facetiousness. In left-sided (dominant hemisphere) tumor, convulsive seizures as well as loss of speech may occur. Anosmia may occur with tumors at the base of the frontal lobe.

Sensory and motor abnormalities are common in parietal lobe tumors. Motor or sensory focal seizures, contralateral hemiparesis, hyperreflexia, impaired sensory perception, astereognosis, and a positive extensor plantar response may be present. Aphasic and agnosic components may be demonstrable when the dominant side is involved.

Visual alterations and seizures preceded by an aura of lights and visual hallucinations are characteristic. Contralateral homonymous hemianopsia occurs, frequently with sparing of the macular area. Agnosia may be noted.

Psychomotor seizures and automatisms occur with temporal lobe tumors. If the dominant side is involved, sensory aphasia may be pronounced. A contralateral homonymous field defect may occur.

Cerebellar tumors are characterized by disturbances of equilibrium and coordination and the early development of increased intracranial pressure and papilledema.

Diagnosis

X-ray of the skull may show the shift of a calcified pineal gland, local erosions or hypercalcifications, and ballooning of the sella turcica. Digital markings on the inner table of the skull may be apparent following prolonged (at least 6 months) increase of cerebrospinal fluid pressure. In children, abnormal separation of the sutures is apt to occur.

Computerized tomography (CT scan) is a highly useful neurodiagnostic method that uses a computerized x-ray system for examining the brain. The x-rays are converted into electronic impulses that measure the density of small slices of the brain, and the computer reproduces from the accumulated data a graphic representation that can be seen on an oscilloscope (see Chapter 19).

Arteriography, the injection of diatrizoate (Hypaque) or diatrizoate sodium I 131 (Radio-Renografin) into the internal carotid or vertebral artery, may show displacement or obliteration of major vessels or may outline the presence of a neoplasm. In serial angiography, glioblastomas appear in the arterial

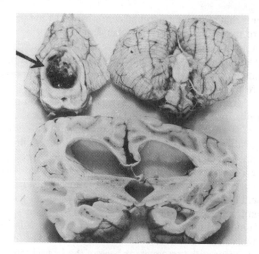

Figure 28–21. Ependymoma causing occlusion of cerebral aqueduct and obstructive hydrocephalus.

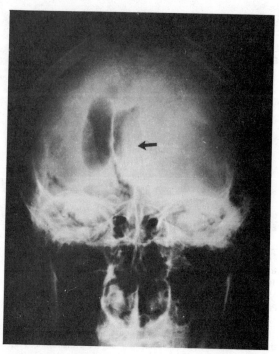

Figure 28–23. Ventriculogram of a left parietotemporal tumor, showing shift of the lateral and third ventricles to the right.

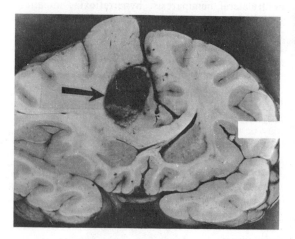

Figure 28–22. Metastatic carcinoma of right frontal parasagittal region in a 40-year-old woman.

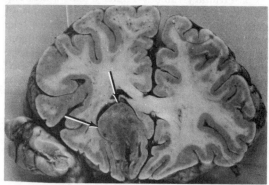

Figure 28–24. Chromophobe adenoma with suprasellar extension into right frontal lobe.

and capillary phase; astrocytomas and oligodendrogliomas are more apt to appear in the venous phase. Meningiomas appear in the arterial phases and reach greatest contrast at the end of the venous phase.

Electroencephalography often shows focal abnormalities (especially a delta focus) in association with cerebral neoplasm.

Lumbar puncture usually shows increased cerebrospinal fluid pressure (over 200 mm of water), and the total protein content is apt to be increased.

Visual field examinations may disclose classic defects caused by involvement of the optic nerve, optic tract, or rradiations (Fig 4–6).

Radioactive isotope studies, eg, with iodinated serum albumin, chlormerodrin Hg 203, etc, have been used to lateralize intracranial masses on the theory that cellular tumors, metastatic carcinomas, sarcomas, and recurrent tumors give high local concentrations and uptake that can be detected with the aid of radiation localizers.

Air ventriculography (introduction of air directly into the ventricles) may indicate obstruction, deformity, dilatation, shift, and other changes of the ventricular system produced by an intracranial neoplasm. **Air encephalography** (introduction of air via the lumbar subarachnoid spaces) is usually contraindicated when there is a strong suspicion of intracranial neoplasm.

Ultrasonic encephalography, in which ultrasonic signals are sent into the brain, may be helpful as a simple screening test to detect shift of midline structures. The ultrasonic transducer is placed against the patient's moistened temple, and waves that are reflected back are transmitted to an oscilloscope. Three

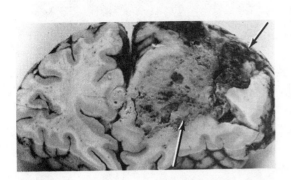

Figure 28–25. Glioblastoma multiforme of left frontal lobe.

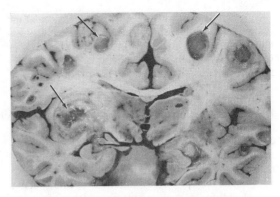

Figure 28–26. Multiple cerebral metastases from carcinoma of lung.

equidistant spikes, representing the 2 sides of the skull and the center of the brain, are usually noted. A shift of the middle spike may result from a shift of the cerebral hemisphere, as with tumor, intracerebral or subdural hematoma, etc. The B scan may localize intracranial masses.

Frozen section preparations are often used for the rapid survey of pathologic material removed at the time of operation or at postmortem examination. With the use of suitable methods, cells and nuclei, metachromatic substances, axis cylinders and myelin sheaths, glial fibers, microglia, oligodendroglia, and fat may be identified. Tissue fixed in formalin ammonium bromide shows astrocytes very well with the Cajal gold sublimate method, and microglia can be demonstrated in similarly fixed tissue by Hortega's method. Oligodendroglia can frequently be shown by the methods of Hortega or Penfield.

Paraffin sections ordinarily are employed for routine work in most laboratories and are quite suitable for making thin sections, for rapid surveys of blocks of tissue, and for handling soft or disintegrating specimens. Basic methods include (1) survey stains such as hematoxylin and eosin, cresyl violet, van Gieson,

Masson trichrome, and Mallory's phosphotungstic acid–hematoxylin; (2) glial methods (Holzer, Mallory); (3) myelin sheath stains (Weil, Heidenhain); (4) axons (Bodian); and (5) connective tissue (Perdrau, Foot, Masson, van Gieson).

Celloidin sections are useful for preparation of large blocks of tissue and for serial and interval sections. The natural structure of tissue is best preserved with this method, and various stains can be readily applied to successive sections of tissue. Contrasts in such slides facilitate study; for example, on celloidin-prepared tissue, successive sections can be stained by the Nissl method for nerve cells, the Weil method for myelin sheaths, the Holzer method for glia, and the van Gieson method for connective tissue.

Treatment & Prognosis

Cure may be achieved in some tumors, eg, meningiomas, neurinomas, dermoids, and astrocytomas, by early diagnosis and operative removal of the neoplasm. On the other hand, a deep-seated tumor such as glioblastoma multiforme, medulloblastoma, or ependymoma may be entirely unaffected and even unfavorably influenced by operation.

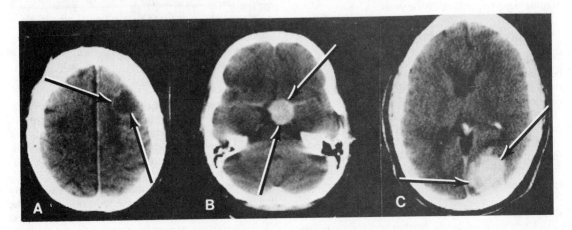

Figure 28–27. CT scans. *A:* Cerebral metastasis from carcinoma of the lung in a 78-year-old man. *B:* Suprasellar meningioma in a 60-year-old woman. *C:* Cerebral convexity meningioma in a 60-year-old man. (Courtesy of GP Ballweg.)

Prognosis varies with the type and location of the tumor. A favorable response to intensive x-ray therapy may occur with a variety of tumors, and in some cases (eg, pituitary tumors) a cure may be achieved. Reduction of increased intracranial pressure for periods of 3–10 hours may be obtained by intravenous administration of hypertonic solution of mannitol or urea. Parenteral corticosteroids, eg, dexamethasone (Decadron), 10 mg intravenously or intramuscularly every 6 hours, are sometimes highly effective in reducing cerebral edema associated with intracranial masses.

Chemotherapy of brain tumors is under active investigation in many centers. Although many chemotherapeutic agents have been used, beneficial effects have been rare. The nitrosoureas—carmustine (BCNU), lomustine (CCNU), and methyl lomustine (methyl-CCNU)—are lipid-soluble compounds that cross the blood-brain barrier easily. Their effectiveness in the treatment of animal brain tumors has led to their experimental use in patients.

In some centers, combination therapy (operative resection of tumor, radiation therapy, and chemotherapy) has been used on the theory that the more tumor removed, the more effective radiation therapy and chemotherapy will be.

PSEUDOTUMOR CEREBRI
(Benign Intracranial Hypertension)

Pseudotumor cerebri is a syndrome characterized by increased intracranial pressure, usually in the absence of neurologic manifestations other than headache or papilledema. CT scans, electroencephalography, pneumoencephalograms, and cerebrospinal fluid protein and cell count are usually normal. In some cases, this syndrome follows ear infections or may be associated with thrombi in the superior longitudinal or lateral sinus. Endocrine disorders and hormone or drug therapy may sometimes cause this syndrome. The prognosis is usually good, although complete recovery may be delayed for months or years.

TUMORS WITHIN THE SPINAL CANAL

The onset of individual tumors has sometimes been related to traumatic episodes. In general, however, there is no known relationship between the presence of primary tumors and any specific factor.

On the basis of the location within the spinal canal, neoplasms are classified as extradural (outside of the dura mater) or intradural (within the dura mater). Intradural neoplasms are either extramedullary (outside of the spinal cord) or intramedullary (within the spinal cord).

Pathology

There is a distinct relationship between the pathologic nature of a neoplasm and its location within the spinal cord.

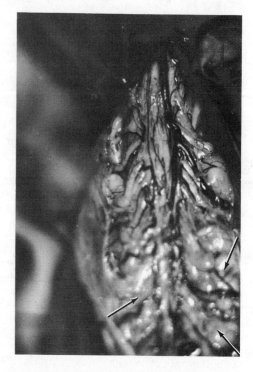

Figure 28–28. Neurinomas of lower cervical region in a 51-year-old man with neurofibromatosis.

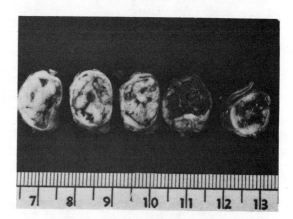

Figure 28–29. Ependymoma of spinal cord, with massive intraspinal hemorrhage.

A. Extradural: Sarcomas and carcinomas, invasive from adjacent vertebrae or metastatic from a distant source, are commonly found. Hodgkin's disease is also common. Lipomas, fibromas, neurinomas, chondromas, and angiomas also occur.

B. Intradural:

1. Extramedullary tumors—These are relatively benign in that they usually have their origin from the pia-arachnoid and the sheaths of roots of spinal nerves. **Neurinomas** are especially common in the thoracocervical area and may occur as part of a generalized neurofibromatosis. They are encapsulated and well

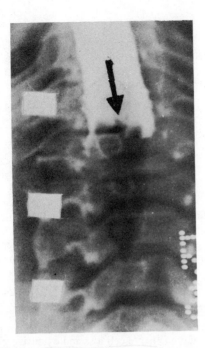

Figure 28–30. Myelogram showing defect and obstruction of iophendylate (Pantopaque) column produced by an intraspinal tumor.

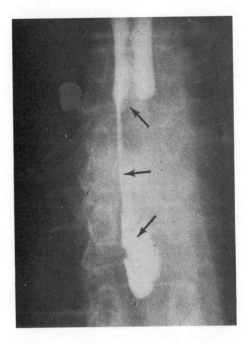

Figure 28–31. Spinal cord tumor. Myelogram showing defect and outline of spinal cord tumor (recurrent ependymoma).

circumscribed and arise from the sheath of a spinal nerve. Microscopically, they resemble intracranial neurinomas. **Meningiomas** may occur in many forms. They are usually circumscribed and encapsulated and are nearly twice as common as neurinomas. They usually arise from arachnoid membrane and are microscopically similar to those within the intracranial cavity. Rarely, a diffuse **sarcoma** occurs as part of a diffuse invasion of the intracranial and intraspinal pia and subarachnoid spaces.

2. Intramedullary tumors–Gliomas, particularly ependymomas, are the commonest intramedullary tumors. Hemangiomas and lipomas occur more rarely.

Clinical Findings

The location of the tumor largely determines its clinical manifestations. In general, as with intracranial neoplasms, slow progression and focalization of signs are the rule.

Signs and symptoms referable to the spinal nerve roots are common, eg, radicular pains and paresthesias that are made worse by exertion, coughing, or straining. Localized motor weakness, paralysis, and muscle atrophy following involvement of motor roots or anterior horns of the spinal cord also occur.

Symptoms may be related to compression of the cord, producing paraplegia, sensory loss, bowel and bladder sphincter disturbances, and similar abnormalities. The early loss of sensation occurs in intramedullary tumors, but the perianal area is apt not to become involved until late.

Diagnosis

The following diagnostic measures are of value in establishing a diagnosis of intraspinal neoplasm:

X-rays may show calcification within the tumor. Atrophy of the vertebrae with dilatation of the canal may occur, increasing the size of the interpedicular spaces. Kyphosis may occur at the level of the tumor in children.

Lumbar puncture may show a partial or complete block in the vertebral canal (Queckenstedt's sign). The total protein of the cerebrospinal fluid is usually elevated, at times to such an extent that the fluid is yellow and may clot.

Myelography may demonstrate the tumor. Iophendylate (Pantopaque) is injected above or below the suspected site of the tumor, and the outline of the tumor is then visualized under fluoroscopy or x-ray.

Electromyography has been used to localize tumors. This test is based on the assumption that normal myograms are apt to be present above the upper level of the lesion and that abnormally active myograms may be obtained at or below the upper level.

Treatment & Prognosis

Treatment consists of surgical removal followed, in some cases, by x-ray irradiation. In general, tumors of the intradural extramedullary group, eg, neurinomas and meningiomas, are readily removed by operation. Intramedullary tumors offer a less favorable prognosis, but some improvement may occur after operative removal and subsequent radiation treatment.

29 | Degenerative Diseases of the Central Nervous System

SENILE DEMENTIA

Changes within the brain as a result of the aging process may occur independently of changes in the cerebrovascular and other tissues.

Gross examination may show diffuse or focal changes. The brain may be small and the cortex relatively thin, with wide, deep sulci. The ventricles are apt to be dilated. The basal ganglia may be small and on cut section usually contain grossly visible small cystic spaces. Microscopically, the neuronal cells show atrophy, increased yellow pigment, nuclear degeneration, and degeneration of neurofibrils. Senile plaques, composed of an amorphous, granular argyrophilic substance from which fibrils radiate, are apt to be found in the lower cortical layers. Increased gliosis and decrease in nerve fibers are also apparent.

Mental changes may be profound. Memory may be poor, especially for recent events. Impairments in judgment, imagination, concentration, and attention are commonly present, as well as episodic excitement, delirium, depression, delusions, and hallucinations.

Physical stamina is diminished. Tremor, physical and mental sluggishness, and rigidity are commonly seen when the basal ganglia are significantly affected. Parkinsonian gait, posture, and facies may be apparent. Generalized epileptic seizures may occur. The Lhermitte and McAlpine syndrome refers to combined pyramidal-extrapyramidal disease due to encephalomalacia or encephalitis in the neighborhood of the internal capsule and adjacent extrapyramidal motor nuclei.

In presenile dementia, the onset of symptoms is earlier (40–60 years of age), with slow progression thereafter. Pathologically, a great number of senile plaques are found.

PRESENILE DEMENTIA
(Pick's Disease & Alzheimer's Disease)

These disorders are characterized by progressive dementia and dysphasia. In most cases, age at onset is 40–60 years. Two clinical types have been described, one characterized by mutism, immobility, and loss of spontaneity and the other by restlessness and hyperactivity. Severe atrophy of the cerebral cortex is found in both diseases; atrophy is usually restricted to the frontotemporal lobes in Pick's disease and is more diffuse in Alzheimer's disease. The course is progressive, and incapacity is complete by the time death occurs.

Alzheimer's disease is characterized by neurofibrillary degenerative changes in the neurons, loss of nerve cells, and argyrophilic plaques in the cerebral cortex and, less often, in the basal ganglia. In Pick's disease, there is nerve cell loss and extensive gliosis; the remaining neurons may show swelling and argyrophilic Pick inclusions.

The neurofibrillary tangles appear to be irregular masses of neurofilaments. Neurofilaments may take part in saltatory movements essential for axoplasmic flow and movement of specific organelles. Abnormal neurofilaments affecting axoplasmic flow might deprive the axon of essential protein and lead to neural dysfunction. Impaired intracellular function could then lead to an accumulation of toxic metabolites and cell death. Some factor affecting cytoplasmic protein may be involved in this disorder.

Recent studies have suggested that the brains of patients with Alzheimer's disease have significantly decreased concentrations of choline acetylase, the enzyme that produces acetylcholine.

PARKINSONISM
(Paralysis Agitans)

This disorder was originally described by James Parkinson, who noted "involuntary tremulous motion, with lessened motor power, in parts not in action and even when supported; with a propensity to bend the trunk forwards and to pass from a walking to a running pace, the senses and intellect being unimpaired."

Parkinsonism occurs most often in persons in their 50s and 60s. It may follow an attack of epidemic encephalitis or may be due to cerebral arteriosclerosis, carbon monoxide or manganese poisoning, trauma to the head, neurosyphilis, or cerebrovascular accidents. The precipitating cause is often unknown; in these cases, the disease is ascribed to degeneration of cells and tracts of the striate bodies and substantia nigra, with loss of cells and alteration of the remaining cells.

Disturbed metabolism of brain amines has been

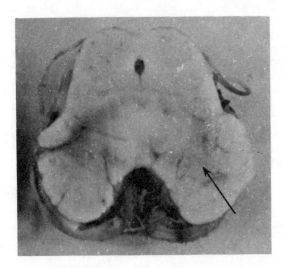

Figure 29–1. Midbrain of a 45-year-old woman with Parkinson's syndrome, showing depigmentation of substantia nigra.

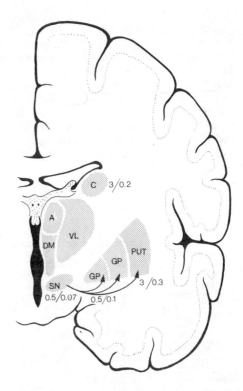

Figure 29–2. Locus of the chemical lesion in parkinsonism. The arrows represent the dopamine-containing neurons whose cell bodies are in the substantia nigra (SN) and whose axons course directly to the lenticular nucleus, made up of the putamen (PUT) and globus pallidus (GP). The connection to the caudate nucleus (C) is indirect. The figures show some representative values for the dopamine content (μg/g of tissue) in human autopsy material from control subjects (larger numbers) and those with parkinsonism. A, DM, and VL are the anterior, dorsomedial, and ventrolateral nuclei of the thalamus. (Reproduced, with permission, from Meyers FH, Jawetz E, Goldfien A: *Review of Medical Pharmacology,* 7th ed. Lange, 1980.)

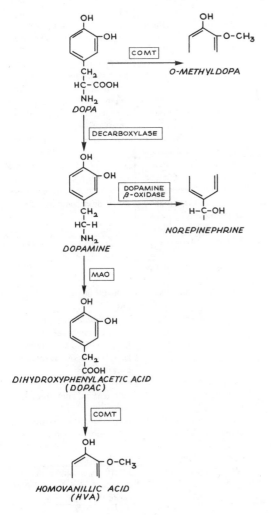

proposed as the basis for the development of parkinsonism. Abnormally low concentrations of dopamine in the basal ganglia have been reported upon postmortem examination of brains of patients with parkinsonism (Fig 29–2).

Clinical Findings

Onset is usually insidious and gradual, and progression is slow. The patient may complain of increasing rigidity and tremor, immobility of facial expression, slowness of movements, diminished swinging of the arms, and heaviness in the limbs when walking. Posture is commonly stooped, with the arms at the sides, elbows slightly flexed, and fingers adducted.

Figure 29–3 (at left). Metabolism of dopa and dopamine. (Reproduced, with permission, from Meyers FH, Jawetz E, Goldfien A: *Review of Medical Pharmacology,* 7th ed. Lange, 1980.)

Tremors of fingers, hands, and wrists usually occur. Motor power diminishes gradually throughout the body, so that movements of all kinds are carried out slowly.

Intermittent tremor (about 2–6 per second) occurs that is worse when the limb is at rest. Tremors frequently are of the pill-rolling type, involving the thumb, index finger, or wrist, and are sometimes associated with a to-and-fro tremor of the head. Emotional disturbances and fatigue are apt to aggravate the tremor.

The limb muscles on passive motion are rigid (lead pipe or cogwheel). There may be difficulty in getting out of a chair, so that several attempts to rise are made. Turning is difficult, even when standing or in bed. Movements such as adjusting a tie, buttoning a coat, and brushing hair may ultimately become difficult without assistance. Some patients have a tendency to break into a run or trot (festination gait). The patient's voice tends to become weak, low in volume, and monotonous. Oculogyric crises may occur.

Table 29—1. Antiparkinsonism drugs.

Drug	Tremor	Rigidity and Spasms	Akinesia (Weakness)	Oculogyric Crisis	Dosage	Precautions and Remarks
Trihexyphenidyl (Artane)		●	●	●	1–5 mg 3 times daily, starting at low dosage and slowly increasing. For oculogyric crisis use 10 mg 3 times daily.	May precipitate acute glaucoma in elderly persons and is contraindicated in patients with glaucoma. Blurred vision, dryness of mouth, vertigo, and tachycardia are early toxic symptoms; late symptoms are vomiting, dizziness, mental confusion, and hallucinations. The synthetic drugs are apt to cause more dizziness than the natural alkaloids and are somewhat less potent parasympatholytics.
Biperiden (Akineton)		●		●	2 mg 3–4 times daily.	
Procyclidine (Kemadrin)		●			2.5–5 mg 3 times daily after meals.	
Cycrimine (Pagitane)		●	●	●	1.25–5 mg 3–4 times daily. Dosage may be gradually increased up to the limits of tolerance.	Useful when effects of trihexyphenidyl wear off. Other remarks as for trihexyphenidyl.
Benztropine methanesulfonate (Cogentin)	●	●			0.5 mg 1–2 times daily, increasing by 0.5 mg at intervals of several days to 5 mg daily or toxicity. Often most effective as single dose at bedtime.	Side-effects similar to those of trihexyphenidyl. Best effect by combining with trihexyphenidyl or dextroamphetamine.
Diphenhydramine (Benadryl)	●				50 mg 2–4 times daily.	Reduce dosage if transient drowsiness occurs.
Orphenadrine (Disipal)	●	●			50 mg 3–5 times daily.	
Chlorphenoxamine (Phenoxene)		●			50 mg 3–4 times daily.	Valuable adjunct to other drugs.
Ethopropazine (Lysovane, Parsidol)	●	●			25–30 mg 4 times daily.	May be used in conjunction with other antispasmodic drugs. Drug is related to chlorpromazine; precautions as for this class of drugs.
Levodopa (Dopar, Larodopa, etc)	●	●	●		250 mg 3 times daily. Increase to tolerance (4–8 g daily).	Nausea and vomiting, postural hypotension, choreiform movements.
Levodopa and carbidopa (Sinemet)	●	●	●		3–6 tablets daily of Sinemet-25/250X (Carbidopa, 25 mg, and levodopa, 250 mg)	Nausea, vomiting, postural hypotension, dyskinesia.
Amantadine (Symmetrel)	●	●	●		100 mg twice daily.	Jitteriness, insomnia, depression, confusion, hallucinations, livedo reticularis.

Treatment & Prognosis

The response to medical treatment is variable, but therapy usually brings some symptomatic relief. The drugs used include derivatives of belladonna root, synthetic compounds with atropinelike action (trihexyphenidyl [Artane], cycrimine [Pagitane], etc), antihistamines, levodopa, and amantadine. The disease is slowly progressive, and the patient may live for years. As disability increases, depression, anxiety, and emotional disturbances often occur.

In carefully selected patients, surgical destruction of portions of the globus pallidus or the ventrolateral nucleus of the thalamus has proved highly beneficial.

Physical therapy should include massage, stretching of muscles, and active exercise when possible. The patient should be taught to exercise daily the muscles most severely affected, especially those of the hands, fingers, wrists, elbows, knees, and neck.

Reassurance and psychologic support are of decided value and should stress the positive aspects of the disease: (1) symptomatic relief with drugs, (2) no impairment of mental faculties, (3) slow progression over many years, and (4) active research and the hope of therapeutic breakthroughs.

Barbiturates should be avoided. Moderate use of alcohol to relax tension may be permitted. Nonbarbiturate sedatives (eg, meprobamate rather than phenothiazines) may be of value. Treatment with drugs, especially early in the disease, may produce temporary amelioration of complaints. Although significant improvement of tremor and rigidity may follow operative treatment (pallidotomy, thalamotomy) in some cases, patients selected for surgery should be free of generalized brain disease and have little akinesia and little pseudobulbar involvement (eg, loss of speech); surgery may make these patients worse.

A number of drugs have been found effective in alleviating symptoms of parkinsonism. To obtain optimal therapeutic results, drugs are often used in combination. Combinations such as trihexyphenidyl (Artane) and diphenhydramine (Benadryl), 3 times daily, may be used. Drugs should not be stopped abruptly when changing to new medications. The dosage of the new drug should be increased as the previously used drug is gradually withdrawn.

Levodopa (Dopar, Larodopa, etc) has been shown to be highly effective against the akinesia and rigidity of parkinsonism and, to a lesser extent, against tremor. Capsules (250 mg) are given 3–4 times daily and increased to tolerance over several weeks or until significant side-effects occur. Side-effects, including nausea and vomiting, postural hypotension, cardiac dysrhythmia, and choreiform movements, may respond to adjustment of dosage. Use of a peripheral decarboxylase inhibitor in combination with levodopa may permit a great reduction in levodopa dosage required for optimal therapy. Sinemet is a combination of carbidopa, a peripheral decarboxylase inhibitor, and levodopa. Patients not currently on levodopa may be started on Sinemet 10/100 (½ tablet twice daily). The dosage is gradually increased by 1 tablet every 3–4

days to an effective therapeutic level (usually 3–6 tablets of Sinemet 25/250 daily in divided doses). When patients already on levodopa switch to Sinemet, they may require only about 20% of their previous levodopa dosage.

Amantadine (Symmetrel) is an antiviral agent that has been found effective against the akinesia, rigidity, and tremor of parkinsonism. The maximum daily dosage is 200 mg (100 mg twice daily). Side-effects have been controlled by adjustment of dosage or use of concomitant medication. Side-effects include jitteriness, insomnia, abdominal uneasiness, dizziness, depression, confusion, and occasionally hallucinations. Convulsions have been reported with overdosage (800 mg daily).

CHRONIC PROGRESSIVE CHOREA
(Huntington's Chorea, Adult Chorea)

Huntington's chorea is a hereditary disease of the basal ganglia and cortex, characterized by the onset in adult life of choreiform movements and mental deterioration. Many cases in the USA have been traced to 2 brothers who emigrated to Long Island from England. The movements are abrupt and jerky, though less rapid and lightninglike than those of Sydenham's chorea. Any somatic musculature may be involved. The disease is chronically progressive and usually leads to death in about 15 years.

Treatment is symptomatic. Large doses of tranquilizers are helpful in management of the motor manifestations. Haloperidol (Haldol) and fluphenazine (Permitil, Prolixin) are especially effective.

HEPATOLENTICULAR DEGENERATION
(Wilson's Disease)

This familial disease, with signs and symptoms of injury to the basal ganglia, is accompanied by cirrhosis of the liver and, in most cases, greenish-brown pigmentation of the cornea near the scleral junction (Kayser-Fleischer ring), best seen by slit lamp examination. Changes in the cerebellum, cerebral cortex, and other parts of the nervous system may be present to a lesser degree. An increase in the excretion of copper and amino acids in the urine and a decrease in the ceruloplasmin content of blood serum suggest that damage to the liver and brain may be due to familial metabolic disturbance. A normal adult usually excretes less than 50 μg of copper in the urine in 24 hours; values above 100 μg are considered abnormal.

Onset of symptoms is usually between the ages of 11 and 25 years. Clinical features are those of liver and nervous system disorders. Evidence of liver disease, ascites, or jaundice may occur at any stage of the disease. Tremors and rigidity are the commonest early symptoms. Tremors may be of the intention type or may be alternating like the tremors observed in Parkinson's disease. Commonly, they are of the bizarre

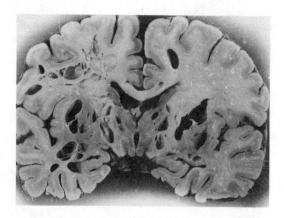

Figure 29–4. "Swiss cheese brain." Usually due to post-mortem changes produced by aerobic gas-forming bacteria.

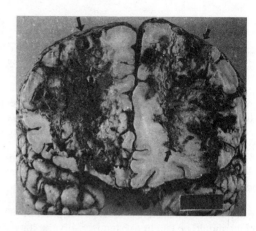

Figure 29–5. Cystic degeneration following bilateral frontal leukotomy.

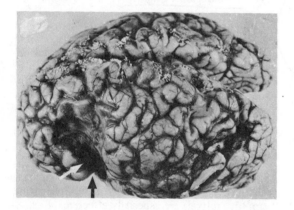

Figure 29–6. Cerebral arteriosclerosis with left cerebral cortical atrophy.

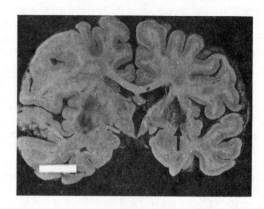

Figure 29–7. Lacunar cystic degeneration involving principally left caudate and lenticular nuclei.

"wing-beating" type, confined to and accentuated by extension of the upper extremities.

Wilson's disease is insidious in onset and progresses slowly. Partial remissions and exacerbations commonly occur, but the outcome is usually fatal within 10 years. Previously, treatment with dimercaprol (BAL) injections twice daily for 10-day periods every 2 months was recommended; however, penicillamine (250 mg 3 times daily) is an effective chelating agent suitable for oral administration that far surpasses the effect of BAL in increasing excretion of copper. Some of the specific manifestations may be ameliorated by symptomatic therapy. The full effect of dimercaprol or penicillamine therapy on the course of the disease or on longevity has not as yet been determined.

FRIEDREICH'S ATAXIA

Friedreich's ataxia is a familial and hereditary disease characterized pathologically by degenerative changes principally of the cerebellum and dorsal half of the spinal cord, and clinically by onset, in the first or second decades, of ataxia, absent deep reflexes, impaired proprioception of lower extremities, and extensor plantar responses. Scoliosis and clubbing of the feet are commonly associated, and there may be optic nerve degeneration and muscle atrophies. The disease is slowly progressive, but incapacity is complete by age 30 years. Degeneration of the posterior columns and the lateral corticospinal and spinocerebellar tracts of the spinal cord, with extensive gliosis of the posterior columns, is the rule. Sometimes there is also loss of cells of Clarke's column and atrophy of dentate nuclei and Purkinje's cells of cerebellum.

FAMILIAL SPASTIC PARAPLEGIA

This relatively rare familial or hereditary disease is characterized by the development in the first years of life of spasticity and weakness of the lower extremities. Progression is the rule, and patients are apt to become paraplegic or chair-ridden before age 15–20 years. Weakness of extremities becomes severe, and the gait becomes spastic and scissorslike. There are usually no cerebellar or sensory findings.

OLIVOCEREBELLAR & OLIVOPONTOCEREBELLAR ATROPHY

This disorder is characterized by progressive cerebellar ataxia of middle or adult life, with degeneration of the cerebellum, olives, and pons. In cases described by Holmes, degeneration of olives and cerebellum was noted; in those of Déjérine and Thomas, degeneration of olives, pontine nuclei, and cerebellum occurred. Clinically, this disease is similar to Marie's ataxia, in which optic atrophy and oculomotor palsies are apt to occur. Progressive cerebellar ataxia, impaired gait and equilibrium, scanning speech, and nystagmoid eye movements may be noted.

HEREDITARY CEREBELLAR ATAXIA WITH SPASTICITY (Sanger-Brown & Marie)

This hereditary disorder is characterized by onset of ataxia and exaggerated tendon reflexes late in life; optic atrophy and oculomotor palsies are often associated. The first symptoms may not begin until the fourth or sixth decades, with ataxia of gait and incoordination in use of the upper extremities. Mental deterioration may occur as a late manifestation.

PARENCHYMATOUS CEREBELLAR DEGENERATION

This disorder is characterized by development in middle life of cerebellar symptoms affecting predominantly the lower extremities. The course is slowly progressive and may extend over decades. The cause is not known; men are more commonly affected than women. Initially, there is difficulty with walking; the gait soon becomes wide-based, ataxic, and sometimes spastic. Nystagmus usually is not present but may occur. In the later stages, the upper extremities may also be involved.

In alcoholics, cerebellar cortical degeneration is marked in the vermis, especially in the anterior portion.

HEREDITARY ATAXIA WITH MUSCULAR ATROPHY (Lévy-Roussy Syndrome)

This disorder may be a variant of Friedreich's ataxia in which there is a great deal of muscular wasting and relatively few symptoms. Symptoms develop early in childhood and include impairment of equilibrium in walking and standing, loss of knee and ankle jerks, atrophy of muscles of the lower extremities and sometimes of hands, occasional extensor plantar responses, and kyphoscoliosis. Symptoms progress slowly, and in a large percentage of cases they seem to stop before disability becomes severe.

ATAXIA–TELANGIECTASIA

This is a familial disease characterized by onset in early childhood of progressive cerebellar ataxia, oculocutaneous telangiectasis, and severe sinopulmonary infections. Ocular dyspraxia, choreoathetosis, hyporeflexia, drooling speech, and nystagmus may also occur. Hypogammaglobulinemia has been noted. Serum IgA is reduced in most cases.

ACUTE CEREBELLAR ATAXIA OF CHILDREN

Children may show severe gait ataxia, usually of sudden onset and often shortly after a nonspecific infectious disease, with complete recovery possible within a few months. Affected patients, however, do not always recover, and severe initial manifestations are associated with slow recovery. Cerebrospinal fluid and other laboratory data obtained on initial examination have been found to be normal. Persistent neurologic defects that may occur include gait disturbance, truncal tremor, ataxia of extremity movement, abnormal eye movement, delayed and impaired speech, and signs of mental retardation.

PROGRESSIVE SUBCORTICAL ENCEPHALOPATHY (Binswanger's Disease)

This rare disorder is characterized by demyelinization of the white matter of the cerebral hemispheres associated with hypertension. The onset is usually between age 40 and 50 years, and the course is progressive over the next 1–2 years. Seizures and focal neurologic signs develop. Diagnosis is usually made at necropsy.

MARCHIAFAVA–BIGNAMI DISEASE (Primary Degeneration of Corpus Callosum)

This slowly progressive, usually fatal disease is characterized by mental symptoms with signs of focal or general brain disorder. It occurs usually in middle-aged or elderly Italian males and is associated with the finding of primary degeneration of the corpus callosum. Ingestion of crude Italian wine has been implicated as a causative factor in some cases.

CENTRAL PONTINE MYELINOLYSIS

This rare disorder usually evolves rapidly over a few weeks, resulting in coma and death. It occurs mainly in chronic alcoholics. Progressive facial and tongue weakness, emotional lability, progressive quadriparesis, bilateral extensor plantar responses, urinary incontinence, and respiratory paralysis may occur. Postmortem examination reveals a focus of demyelinization involving the basal pons.

HEREDITARY OPTIC ATROPHY
(Leber's Disease)

This disease of the optic nerve is characterized by loss of central vision, with relatively normal peripheral fields of vision. It occurs usually in males but is transmitted solely by females; onset is between age 12 and 25 years. The disease ordinarily progresses rapidly and commonly reaches its maximum extent within a few weeks. It rarely progresses to complete blindness.

STATUS MARMORATUS
(Vogt's Disease)

This disorder is characterized by the appearance in the first year of life of athetosis, dystonia, rigidity of muscles, and dysarthria. Mental deficiency is also sometimes noted. "Marble appearance" (status marmoratus) of the basal ganglia, particularly of the caudate and lenticular nuclei, is due to large bundles of abnormally situated myelin sheaths and may be related to excess formation from overgrowth of glia resulting from fetal anoxia or encephalitis.

STATUS DYSMYELINATUS

This disorder is characterized by the development, in the first year of life, of athetoid movements that are gradually replaced by rigidity and death in the second decade. There is shrinkage of the caudate nucleus, globus pallidus, and subthalamic nucleus, with failure to stain or lack of development of myelin sheaths in affected zones.

HALLERVORDEN–SPATZ DISEASE
(Pigmentary Degeneration of Globus Pallidus)

This is a rare familial disease of the basal ganglia in which there is deposition of iron-containing pigment (green, blue, or brown) in ganglion cells and interstitial tissue. It is characterized clinically by the onset at about age 10 years of gradually increasing stiffness of limbs, clubfoot deformity, dysarthria, and dementia, with progression to death usually within 20 years.

OCCULT HYDROCEPHALUS
(Normal Pressure Hydrocephalus)

Progressive dementia associated with psychomotor retardation, unsteady gait, and urinary incontinence may occur in late middle-aged patients with normal cerebrospinal fluid pressure. Mild to moderate diffuse slowing may occur on the EEG. Pneumoencephalograms or CT scans may reveal a dilated ventricular system with no sulci in the cerebral cortex. Cerebral angiography may show a stretched or elevated anterior cerebral artery. Radioisotopes such as radioiodinated serum albumin may fail to ascend the cerebrospinal fluid pathways to the cerebral convexities for 72 hours after lumbar intrathecal injection. The cause may be obstruction of subarachnoid space around the brain stem by various processes, including tumor.

Treatment by ventricular shunts may produce prompt clinical improvement.

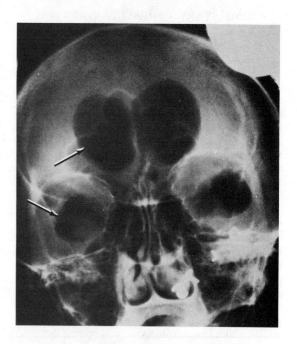

Figure 29–8. Normal pressure hydrocephalus. Pneumoencephalogram shows dilated lateral ventricles with no air over the cerebral convexity.

DYSTONIA MUSCULORUM DEFORMANS
(Torsion Spasm)

The characteristic movements of torsion spasm involve the muscles particularly of the trunk and girdle and are similar to those of athetosis but more sustained in contraction. Pathologic changes include degenerative changes in the cells of the basal ganglia, cerebral cortex, and olivary nuclei. Onset is usually gradual and the course slightly progressive. Symptoms include gait abnormalities, twisting of the pelvis, dysarthria, facial grimacing, and torticollis. Drugs that produce muscle relaxation may have palliative value. Surgical destruction of the ventrolateral nucleus of the thalamus has been reported to be beneficial in selected patients.

SPASMODIC TORTICOLLIS
(Wryneck)

Intermittent spasmodic movements of muscles of the neck are characteristic of this disorder. The head may be turned to one side, may rotate and bend in another direction, and may be forcibly flexed or extended. The most commonly affected muscle is the sternocleidomastoid of the side opposite deviation of the chin. Movements may spread to the facial and brachial muscles of both sides. The movements are adversely affected by emotional tension and may be influenced by postural changes or external stimuli. Medical treatment has proved unsatisfactory; some relief may be afforded by psychotherapy or surgery (section of spinal accessory nerve; section of anterior and posterior divisions of first 3 cervical motor roots).

DEMYELINATING DISEASES

Demyelination of the CNS often occurs with vascular lesions, infections, nutritional disorders, and other diseases. In these cases, the demyelination is secondary to destructive changes in other neural elements. There are, in addition, primary demyelinating diseases in which the reason for the presence of the lesions is obscure. Two broad groupings may be noted: (1) the multiple sclerosis type and (2) the diffuse sclerosis type.

The **multiple sclerosis type** includes classic multiple sclerosis, acute encephalomyelitis, and neuromyelitis optica. Here there is destruction of normally formed myelin. The onset of symptoms is in the late teens or early adult life, and remissions and exacerbations are common. Exogenous factors seem to be more important than inheritance in precipitating the active disease process.

The **diffuse sclerosis type** shows a diffuse type of degeneration of the white matter of the brain and is probably related to genetically determined metabolic disturbances. Two large subgroups have been noted: (1) myelinoclastic (Schilder's disease), in which there is destruction of normally formed myelin; and (2) leukodystrophies, in which there is a defect in the formation of myelin, usually associated with pigment deposition in the degenerated areas and occasionally also in nerves and other organs of the body. The onset of symptoms is commonly in infancy or early childhood, and the disease is steadily progressive, with death occurring within a few months or years after onset. Usually included in this category are spongy sclerosis (Canavan), globoid cell type (Krabbe), hyaline body type (Alexander), glycerophosphatide dystrophy (Pelizaeus-Merzbacher), and metachromatic (sulfatide) leukodystrophy.

The term **leukodystrophy** was originally proposed to designate a disorder characterized by a heritable progressive degeneration of cerebral white matter. In these disorders there is implied failure of glial cells to maintain nutrition of myelinated axons and to carry out effectively the degradation of myelin breakdown products to their final sudanophil stage of neutral fat and esterified cholesterol. Although a broad distinction has often been made between a lipidosis, with its accumulation of lipid material within the border of nerve cells, and leukodystrophy, with a major pathologic process in the axons, neurochemical research is currently modifying these views and is increasingly concerned with the presumed enzymatic defects of the various disorders.

MULTIPLE SCLEROSIS

Multiple sclerosis is usually a diffuse, chronic, slowly progressive neurologic disorder that has its onset in early adult life and is characterized by irregular, fluctuating periods of exacerbation and remission. It is now recognized with greater frequency than formerly. At one time or another, multiple sclerosis has been considered to be the result of infections, intoxications, nutritional deficiency states, lead poisoning, thrombophlebitis, and other causes. The presence of lipolytic enzyme in circulating blood and a disturbance in CNS lipid metabolism have been reported. The search for viral infections with a long latent period (slow viruses) in patients with multiple sclerosis has led to intensive but inconclusive studies of the immunologic, humoral, viral, genetic, and histocompatibility status of such patients. There is a greater incidence of the disease in the northern latitudes of North America and Europe; it is comparatively rare in the Orient. The incidence of the disease has allegedly increased in the USA.

An acute form with a sudden onset may also occur.

Pathology

Grossly, there are multiple irregular areas of degeneration that appear to have a predilection for the white matter as opposed to the gray matter of the brain and spinal cord. The lesions may vary in extent from the size of a pinpoint to more than 1 cm in diameter. Microscopically, the areas of degeneration show early demyelinization of the axon sheaths. Later, there is breakdown and disappearance of axons and subsequent glial scar formation.

Clinical Findings

The symptoms and signs frequently regress following their initial appearance. However, exacerbations usually occur, and the disease almost always becomes more severe with the passage of time. The patient usually becomes progressively more disabled and cachectic and is apt to develop some infection that

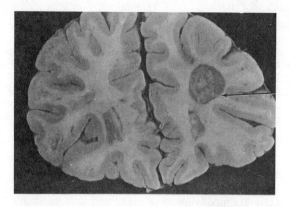

Figure 29-9. Area of demyelination of white matter of frontal lobe of a 54-year-old man with multiple sclerosis.

will prove fatal. Involvement of the medullary or hypothalamic areas by plaques usually hastens death.

Multiple sclerosis characteristically affects persons between age 20 and 40 years; onset is rare before age 12 or after age 50. Involvement of the visual system often occurs early and may be shown by impaired visual acuity or ocular motility or both. A sudden onset of severe visual impairment, usually unilateral, with pain in or behind the globe, is often an early manifestation.

Signs of multiple involvement of the spinal cord or brain may be present; nystagmus, slurred speech, intention tremor, spastic paralysis, and retrobulbar neuritis are common. The usual symptoms at onset are weakness, visual disturbances, tremor, ataxia, and paresthesias.

It is not uncommon to find the patient euphoric.

Hyperexcitability and even maniacal reactions have been observed.

Diagnosis

The diagnosis depends on a characteristic history of relapse and remission and findings referable to multiple lesions. Occasionally, multiple sclerosis is confined to a single area, in which case an inaccurate diagnosis may cause the patient to be erroneously operated upon for tumor.

The cerebrospinal fluid usually shows a first or second zone or normal colloidal gold curve, but the presence or absence of this reaction does not establish or disprove the diagnosis. Gamma globulin often is increased. Skull and spine x-rays, EEGs, cerebral angiography, pneumoencephalography, and iophendylate (Pantopaque) or air myelography may be necessary in some cases to rule out neoplasms, herniated intervertebral disks, or other disorders that may mimic multiple sclerosis.

Oligoclonal bands of IgG may be detected by electrophoresis of the cerebrospinal fluid. The concentration of myelin basic protein in cerebrospinal fluid may be increased. Visual evoked potentials to both flash and pattern reversal stimuli may demonstrate abnormalities. CT scan of the brain may sometimes demonstrate periventricular or subcortical lesions.

Treatment & Prognosis

Various treatments based upon the etiologic and pathologic theories currently in vogue have been tried, with disappointing results. Among the more common treatment methods that have been employed are fever therapy, antisyphilitic therapy, anticoagulant therapy, protein shock, and histamine desensitization. Thera-

CELLULOSE ACETATE PATTERN

NORMAL CEREBROSPINAL FLUID
(100× CONCENTRATE)

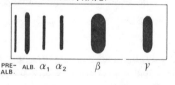

DENSITOMETER TRACING

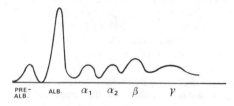

MULTIPLE SCLEROSIS
(100× CONCENTRATE)

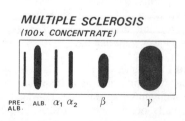

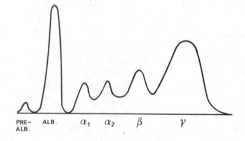

Figure 29-10. Zone electrophoresis patterns of cerebrospinal fluid from normal subject and multiple sclerosis patient. (Reproduced, with permission, from Stites DP et al [editors]: *Basic & Clinical Immunology,* 3rd ed. Lange, 1982.)

peutic claims have also been made for tolbutamide, isoniazid, vitamin B_{12}, procaine, blood transfusions, fat-free diets, steroids, vasodilators (5–10% CO_2), and histamine infusions, but their value has not been established. In some patients with disabling spasticity, diazepam, dantrolene sodium, or baclofen may be helpful.

Physical therapy and symptomatic and supportive measures may prove helpful. Particular attention must be paid to prevention of bed sores, prompt treatment of respiratory infections, and avoidance of urinary tract infections. Adequate sleep at night and rest in the afternoon have been found to make patients more comfortable. Sudden changes in temperature (external or internal) should be avoided to reduce vascular spastic phenomena. Heat makes these patients much worse, whereas cold often improves them temporarily. Rehabilitation, physical therapy, and psychotherapy are indicated to encourage patients to live with their disability and make the most of the assets they retain.

Multiple sclerosis is a chronic disease. Because of its progressive nature, the hazards of chronic invalidism usually increase the longer the patient survives. Intercurrent infections of the respiratory and urinary tracts are common. Although the prospects for cure are dim, relatively long quiescent phases are not uncommon. The course is varied and unpredictable. In almost all cases there is a remission of the initial symptoms, but with each recurrence of a symptom the chances of remission decrease. Early remissions may be remarkably complete; later in the course of the disease, remissions tend to be partial. Remissions may last several months to 2 years. A clinical course of 10–20 years is not uncommon. In a large series, the average survival after onset of symptoms was estimated at 27 years.

NEUROMYELITIS OPTICA
(Devic's Disease)

This clinical syndrome is characterized by the acute occurrence of optic neuritis and transverse myelitis. It is believed by many to be a variant or acute form of multiple sclerosis or Schilder's disease. Demyelinating lesions are found in the optic nerves, brain, and spinal cord. Devic's disease usually either terminates fatally soon after onset or improves without subsequent development of new symptoms.

ACUTE ENCEPHALOMYELITIS

This syndrome is characterized by the acute onset of neurologic signs and symptoms as a result of demyelinization of the CNS. The nervous system changes are more acute and much more severe than those usually seen with multiple sclerosis, and the disease is nonrecurrent and without exacerbations. Some of these cases probably represent postinfectious encephalomyelitis. The course is rapid and often fatal; severe residual defects are present in survivors. Cerebrospinal fluid changes may resemble those of multiple sclerosis. Lymphocytic pleocytosis (25–250 cells/μL) usually occurs.

SCHILDER'S DISEASE
(Encephalitis Periaxialis Diffusa)

Schilder's disease is rapidly progressive, characterized by widespread demyelinization of the cerebral hemispheres, with convulsions, loss of vision, mental symptoms, and motor and sensory disturbances. The demyelinization usually occurs in the white matter of one or both cerebral hemispheres. Death usually occurs within 3 years after onset. Complete dementia, quadriplegia, and decerebrate rigidity may occur in the terminal stages.

Adrenoleukodystrophy has been classed as a separate entity distinct from Schilder's disease. The disorder comprises a combination of Addison's disease, bronzing of the skin, and leukodystrophy. Although the neurologic features and cerebral lesion are like those of Schilder's disease, the adrenal atrophy and sex-linked male inheritance are distinctive.

DIFFUSE SCLEROSIS

The term diffuse sclerosis has been used to designate a number of clinical or pathologic disorders characterized by widespread diffuse loss of myelin in the white matter of the cerebral hemisphere. They usually occur in childhood and are progressive. In Schilder's disease, believed to be an acquired, or exogenous, disease, there is destruction of normally constituted myelin.

In the leukodystrophies, however, there is a defect in formation of myelin associated with a familial, chiefly infantile, usually genetically determined inborn error of metabolism. Several variants of leukodystrophy have been noted. In the Pelizaeus-Merzbacher type, the diffusely demyelinated areas are sudanophilic. In the Krabbe-Scholz type, there are large multinucleated histiocytes (globoid cells). In the Canavan spongy type, there are small cystic spaces in the white matter of the cerebral hemispheres. In the Alexander type, there are hyaline bodies, resembling Rosenthal bodies from degenerated astrocytes, around blood vessels and at subpial and ependymal surfaces. In metachromatic leukodystrophy or leukoencephalopathy, affected tissues stain metachromatically, ie, stain red with toluidine blue.

Clinically, these progressive heredofamilial disorders usually begin in the first few months of life, and death occurs within a few months or years after onset. They are often associated with nystagmus, intention tremors, ataxia, spasticity, trophic changes, dementia, and blindness.

METACHROMATIC LEUKOENCEPHALOPATHY
(Greenfield's Disease)

This form of diffuse sclerosis usually affects children or young adults; it is slowly progressive, with quadriparesis, bulbar signs, and dementia. Optic atrophy and incoordination may be superimposed. Metachromatic material is deposited within the nervous system and the kidney, where it may be found by biopsy. This abnormal material, which may be found in centrifuged urine sediment, stains a golden brown metachromatic color with toluidine blue and is soluble in certain organic solvents. Increased amounts of hexosamine are found in the white matter. Sulfatide is found in excessive amounts in brain and kidney and is responsible for the metachromatic staining of the lipid in the degenerating white matter. Pathologically, diffuse demyelination is prominent, with accumulation of metachromatic material either free in tissue or within cytoplasm of proliferated glial cells. It is also found in nerve cells, especially of the midbrain, medulla, and spinal cord, as well as in other organs such as kidney and liver. Deficiency of the enzyme arylsulfatase A has been demonstrated recently (see Table 30–1).

Metabolic & Toxic Disorders of the Nervous System

BLOOD DISEASES

POSTEROLATERAL SCLEROSIS
(Subacute Combined System Disease)

Posterolateral sclerosis is characterized by progressive degeneration of the posterior and lateral columns of the spinal cord, sometimes with degeneration of the peripheral nerves. It is usually associated with and most often described as a complication of **pernicious anemia.** Nutritional deficiency states and other forms of anemia are also commonly cited as possible causes.

The severity of the disease when associated with pernicious anemia does not necessarily parallel the blood status, which suggests that the causative factors responsible for the neural and blood changes are not identical. Degeneration of the spinal cord may develop before other clinical manifestations of pernicious anemia and may occur early in pernicious anemia rather than in the later phases.

Pathology

Although posterolateral sclerosis is usually considered to be predominantly a disease of the spinal cord, pathologic changes may also be found in the brain. The posterior and lateral columns of the spinal cord undergo the most profound pathologic changes. Degenerated demyelinized areas give the appearance of a "spongy" state under the microscope. These areas are vacuolated and areolar in appearance, and there is little evidence of glial tissue or scar formation. Degeneration of cerebral white matter and peripheral neuropathies may be present also.

Clinical Findings

The onset is characterized by tingling, numbness, and "pins and needles" sensations, first in the toes and feet and later in the fingers. Mental symptoms are not infrequent: hallucinations, disorientation, memory defects, and personality changes are apt to occur. With pronounced peripheral nerve involvement, there may also be tenderness of the calf and sole muscles, stocking distribution of impaired touch sensibility up to the level of the knees (Fig 10–10), weakness of the lower extremities (particularly in the distal segments), and depressed or absent knee and ankle jerks.

Posterior column disease may be evidenced by loss of position sense in the extremities, a positive Romberg test, an ataxic, broad-based gait, loss of the faculty of 2-point discrimination, and loss of vibratory sensation. **Lateral column disease** may be evidenced by voluntary muscle weakness, hyperactive deep muscle reflexes, spasticity of the extremities, and a positive Babinski sign.

Diagnosis

Posterolateral sclerosis should be suspected in any instance of obscure neurologic symptomatology in association with pernicious anemia or other macrocytic anemias. The diagnosis sometimes rests on a study of the factors associated with pernicious anemia or other anemias. The following studies are frequently made: (1) Gastric analysis for free hydrochloric acid, with a histamine stimulation test if necessary. (2) Bone marrow and blood smear studies. (3) Stool examination for ova and parasites. (4) Serum vitamin B_{12} levels.

The Schilling test is useful in diagnosing defective vitamin B_{12} absorption in patients with combined system disease before the onset of anemia and in differentiating pernicious anemia from megaloblastic anemias due to folic acid deficiency.

Treatment & Prognosis

Vitamin B_{12} therapy is specific, and there is usually no necessity for treatment with hydrochloric acid, liver, special diets, or folic acid. Monthly vitamin B_{12} injections may be required for life. Purified and crude liver extracts are not believed to have advantages over vitamin B_{12}. Give vitamin B_{12} (cyanocobalamin), 30 μg intramuscularly 2–3 times a week until blood values return to normal, and then 30 μg once a month; larger quantities are usually given in the presence of neurologic involvement. CNS symptoms are reversible if they are of relatively short duration but may be permanent if present longer than 6 months. Despite treatment with vitamin B_{12}, achlorhydria and an abnormal Schilling test usually persist.

The individual well-developed syndrome will usually not progress if treatment of pernicious anemia is adequate. It is very doubtful that the disease will occur at all if pernicious anemia is appropriately treated before neurologic symptoms appear. Once the disease is well established, the pathologic changes

Table 30–1. Lipid storage diseases with known enzyme defects.*

Disease	Signs and Symptoms	Major Lipid Accumulation	Enzyme Defect
Gaucher's disease	Spleen and liver enlargement, erosion of long bones and pelvis, mental retardation only in infantile form	GLUCOCEREBROSIDE — CERAMIDE–GLUCOSE	Glucocerebroside-β-glucosidase
Niemann-Pick disease	Liver and spleen enlargement, mental retardation, about 30% with red spot in retina	SPHINGOMYELIN — PHOSPHORYLCHOLINE	Sphingomyelinase
Krabbe's disease (globoid leukodystrophy)	Mental retardation, almost total absence of myelin, globoid bodies in white matter of brain	GALACTOCEREBROSIDE — GALACTOSE	Galactocerebroside-β-galactosidase
Metachromatic leukodystrophy	Mental retardation, psychologic disturbances in adult form, nerves stain yellow-brown with cresyl violet dye	SULFATIDE — GALACTOSE 3-SULFATE	Sulfatidase
Ceramide lactoside lipidosis	Slowly progressive brain damage, liver and spleen enlargement	CERAMIDE LACTOSIDE — GLUCOSE–GALACTOSE	Ceramide lactoside-β-galactosidase
Fabry's disease	Reddish-purple skin rash, kidney failure, pain in lower extremities	CERAMIDE TRIHEXOSIDE — GLUCOSE–GALACTOSE–GALACTOSE	Ceramide trihexoside-α-galactosidase
Tay-Sachs disease	Mental retardation, red spot in retina, blindness, muscular weakness	GANGLIOSIDE GM_2 — GLUCOSE–GALACTOSE–GalNAc, NeuNAc	Hexosaminidase A
Tay-Sachs variant	Same as Tay-Sachs disease but progressing more rapidly	GLOBOSIDE (AND GANGLIOSIDE GM_2) — GLUCOSE–GALACTOSE–GalNAc–GALACTOSE, NeuNAc	Hexosaminidase A and B
Generalized gangliosidosis	Mental retardation, liver enlargement, skeletal deformities, about 50% with red spot in retina	GANGLIOSIDE GM_1 — GLUCOSE–GALACTOSE–GalNAc–GALACTOSE, NeuNAc	β-Galactosidase
Fucosidosis	Cerebral degeneration, muscle spasticity, thick skin	H-ISOANTIGEN — GLUCOSE–GALACTOSE–N-ACETYL GLUCOSAMINE–GALACTOSE–FUCOSE	α-Fucosidase

*Reproduced, with permission, from Brady RO et al: *Fed Proc* 1975;**34**:1310.

may be considered irreversible, and full clinical recovery cannot be expected. Improvement of the peripheral nerve component is more likely to occur with adequate treatment. The prognosis is less favorable in patients over age 60 years.

NEUROLOGIC COMPLICATIONS OF OTHER BLOOD DISEASES

Pernicious Anemia

The neurologic complications of pernicious anemia are discussed under Posterolateral Sclerosis.

Polycythemia Vera (Osler-Vaquez Disease, Erythremia)

Thrombosis or rupture of intracranial vessels may occur. Papilledema may result from retinal circulatory changes or increased intracranial pressure. Lassitude, vertigo, tinnitus, visual disturbances, and paresthesias are commonly present. Hemiplegia, aphasia, or other focal neurologic signs usually follow cerebrovascular accident.

Sickle Cell Anemia

The neurologic features are usually those of an acute cerebrovascular lesion, ie, infarct or hemorrhage. Thrombosis of the dural sinuses, subdural or subarachnoid hemorrhage, and hemorrhage (or thrombosis) of smaller vessels may occur.

Leukemia

Petechial or gross brain hemorrhages may occur, particularly in acute types. Spotty leptomeningeal hemorrhages are common. Involvement of facial or optic nerves has been noted.

Kernicterus

Erythroblastosis fetalis, associated with Rh incompatibility of the parents, may result in severe jaundice, with staining of the brain, especially the basal ganglia, by pigment. The mortality rate is high. In some cases, survival may be associated with chorea and mental retardation. Phototherapy and exchange transfusions may prevent the accumulation of high levels of unconjugated serum bilirubin and protect the nervous system.

Thrombocytopenic Purpura

Because of the thromboses of small blood vessels, hemolytic anemia, and purpura that may occur in this disorder, a variety of neurologic manifestations are possible. The common neurologic findings are seizures, aphasia, cortical blindness, and organic mental syndrome.

Hodgkin's Disease; Lymphomas

Hodgkin's disease and other lymphomas are often associated with significant neurologic complications. Herpes zoster, spinal cord compression by epidural tumor extensions, cranial nerve palsies, peripheral neuropathies, encephalitic syndromes, epilepsy, and CNS infections with fungi or yeasts may occur.

Figure 30–2. Epidural tumor in Hodgkin's disease, with compression of thoracic spinal cord (Weil stain).

DISORDERS OF LIPID METABOLISM (LIPIDOSES)

In certain diseases, altered lipid metabolism is reflected in or associated with CNS changes.

Cerebromacular Degeneration (Tay-Sachs Disease; Amaurotic Familial Idiocy)

This is a familial disease characterized by progressive loss of vision, dementia, and paralysis, usually with a fatal outcome. The onset is within the first 6 months of life. Optic atrophy and macular degeneration (cherry-red spot in the center of a degenerated retinal area) are characteristic.

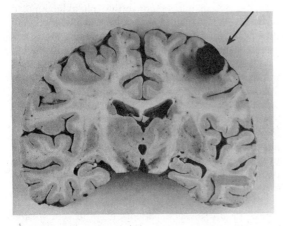

Figure 30–1. Hemorrhages of cerebral hemispheres in a 60-year-old man with myeloblastic leukemia.

Absence of hexosaminidase A (or A and B) in brain and other tissues has been noted, with accumulation of G_{M2} ganglioside in brain tissue.

Niemann-Pick Disease

This familial disease may occur in infants. It is characterized by enlargement of the spleen and liver, brownish skin discoloration, progressive blindness, and mental deterioration. The disease is considered to be due to a disturbance in phospholipid metabolism, especially sphingomyelin; it develops rapidly and leads to death within 2 years. The enzyme that hydrolyzes sphingomyelin (sphingomyelinase) is low in some patients.

Cranial Xanthomatosis (Hand-Schüller-Christian Disease)

This disease, believed to be due to a defect in cholesterol metabolism, is characterized by defects in membranous bones, exophthalmos, and diabetes insipidus. Onset is in early childhood. Multiple small cutaneous skin plaques may occur, resembling those of seborrheic dermatitis. Lymphadenopathy, hepatosplenomegaly, and anemia are often present. Reticuloendothelial system pathology consists of lipoid cell hyperplasia and histiocyte proliferation. Characteristic x-ray defects of the skull and flat bones may be noted.

The course is chronic and usually relatively benign. X-ray therapy of specific local lesions may be helpful.

Gaucher's Disease

This chronic disease is characterized by the deposition of glucocerebroside in the reticuloendothelial cells of the liver and spleen. A defect of β-glucosidase has been found in juvenile cases. It is manifested by listlessness and apathy, with head retraction. The onset is usually between age 6 and 12 months in infants. Infants are hypertonic and show bulbar symptoms. The course of the disease is variable. In children, rapid progression with early death may occur.

Supportive treatment and splenectomy for hypersplenism may be indicated.

Plasma Lipid Disturbance of Bigler

Physical and mental retardation and hepatomegaly may occur in this rare hereditary lipid disorder, with an increased plasma level of phospholipids and triglycerides.

Treatment is symptomatic.

Bassen-Kornzweig Syndrome

This rare neuromuscular disease is usually associated with ataxia, proprioceptive sensory loss, and areflexia. Weakness, corticospinal signs, peripheral nerve sensory loss, ophthalmoparesis, and kyphosis may also occur. Retinitis pigmentosa, abnormal erythrocytes (acanthocytes), and a complex lipid disorder are also present. Impaired absorption of fat and fatty acids, deficiency of β-lipoprotein in serum, and reduced total lipids, triglycerides, cholesterol, and phospholipids in serum occur.

Tangier Disease (Familial α-Lipoprotein Deficiency)

Children afflicted with recurrent peripheral neuropathy have large, orange-colored tonsils, hepatosplenomegaly, lymphadenopathy, low plasma cholesterol with normal or elevated triglycerides, and markedly decreased α-lipoprotein. There is asymmetric sensory involvement of the lower extremities and progressive distal and proximal weakness. Biopsy of bone marrow or rectal mucosa may disclose typical foam cells.

Fabry's Disease (Diffuse Angiokeratosis)

This disorder is associated with accumulation of a trihexoside (a ceramide) due to ceramide trihexoside α-galactosidase deficiency. In its early stages, the disease is characterized by multiple red vascular lesions, or angiokeratoses, on the lower half of the body. Fever, abdominal pains, extremity pains, joint involvement, and corneal dystrophy may occur. Progressive mental deterioration, seizures, and motor signs may occur, with death in the fifth or sixth decade.

DISORDERS OF AMINO ACID METABOLISM

Phenylpyruvic Oligophrenia (Phenylketonuria)

Phenylpyruvic oligophrenia is a familial disorder in which large amounts of phenylpyruvic acid are present in the urine and blood (because of faulty metabolism of phenylalanine). It is associated with mental deficiency and occurs predominantly in fair-skinned, blue-eyed blonds. Acidified urine of affected subjects turns green when tested with ferric chloride.

This disorder is inherited as a recessive trait and is due to absence of an enzyme, phenylalanine hydroxylase, that is capable of converting phenylalanine to tyrosine. Phenylalanine accumulates in the blood, and its deamination product, phenylpyruvic acid, is excreted in the urine. Mental retardation and schizoid changes usually occur if the disease is untreated, and tremors, ataxia, and hypertonicity have been occasionally noted. Serum phenylalanine levels are elevated.

A proposed screening program includes testing of blood on the day before discharge from the hospital nursery. The Guthrie inhibition assay test measures the presence of phenylalanine by the effect of a phenylalanine antagonist as inhibitor of *Bacillus subtilis*.

A diet low in phenylalanine started in the first few weeks of life in such patients may prevent mental retardation or arrest the condition in recently established cases.

Table 30—2. Syndromes associated with inborn errors of metabolism: Disorders of amino acid metabolism.*

	Amino Acids or Organic Acids Increased in Plasma	Amino Acids or Organic Acids Increased in Urine	Biochemistry	Clinical Features and Treatment
Sulfur-Containing Amino Acid				
Cystathioninuria	. . .	Cystathionine	Cystathionine cleavage enzyme deficiency; homoserine dehydratase deficiency.	Mental retardation, congenital malformations, talipes, deafness, abnormal ears and sensation. One case with high phenylalanine, one with thrombocytopenia and renal calculi. Treat with large doses of pyridoxine.
Homocystinuria	Methionine	Homocystine, homolanthionine	Cystathionine synthetase deficiency. 50% are pyridoxine-dependent. May have folate deficiency.	Mental retardation, spastic paraplegia, occasional convulsions, cataracts, lenticular dislocation, friable hair, malar flush, thromboembolic disease, bone changes. Treat with low-methionine, cystine-supplemented diet or with pyridoxine.
Cystinuria	. . .	Cystine, lysine, arginine, ornithine	Transport abnormality in renal tubules and bowel mucosa.	Somatic and occasional mental retardation; renal calculi with their complications. Treat with penicillamine, high water intake, alkalies, and sometimes low-methionine diet. Renal transplantation in severe renal failure.
Methionine malabsorption syndrome	. . .	α-Hydroxybutyric acid (also in feces)	Methionine, leucine, isoleucine, and valine: rejected by bowel wall; may be same as oasthouse syndrome.	Convulsions, episodic diarrhea, hyperventilation, mental retardation; smell as in oasthouse syndrome.
β-Mercaptolactate cysteine disulfiduria	. . .	β-Mercaptolactate cysteine disulfide	Unknown.	Severe retardation; increased tone in lower limbs; persistent sucking reflex.
Sulfite oxidase deficiency	. . .	S-Sulfo-cysteine; also sulfite and thiosulfate	Sulfite oxidase deficiency.	Spastic quadriplegia; blindness; subluxation of lenses.
Urea Synthesis Cycle				
Argininosuccinic-aciduria	. . .	Argininosuccinic acid, citrulline	Argininosuccinate lyase deficiency.	Mental retardation, ataxia, convulsions, friable hair, rough skin, coma (due to ammonia intoxication). Treat with low-protein diet.
Ornithine transcarbamylase deficiency	. . .	Generalized aminoaciduria	Ornithine carbamoyl transferase deficiency.	Episodes of vomiting, restlessness, ataxia, coma in early life (from ammonia intoxication). Treat with low-protein diet.
Citrullinuria	Citrulline, methionine	Citrulline, alanine, aspartic acid, glycine, glutamic acid, histidine, N-acetylcitrulline	Argininosuccinate synthetase deficiency.	Mental retardation; episodes of severe vomiting and coma (due to ammonia intoxication). Treat with low-protein diet.
Carbamyl phosphate synthetase deficiency	Glycine; also ammonia	Glycine	Carbamyl phosphate synthetase deficiency.	Severe vomiting, hypotonia, lethargy, and dehydration in infancy. Responds to low-protein intake.
Hyperornithinemia	Ornithine, lysine; ammonia	Homocitrulline	Unknown.	Irritability, failure to thrive, intention tremors, and myoclonic seizures.
Tryptophan Metabolism				
Congenital tryptophanuria	Tryptophan after oral load	Tryptophan	Possible tryptophan oxygenase deficiency.	Mental retardation, photosensitivity, rough hyperpigmented skin, telangiectasias of conjunctiva. Treat with nicotinic acid.

*Reproduced, with permission, from Kempe CH, Silver HK, O'Brien D (editors): *Current Pediatric Diagnosis & Treatment,* 3rd ed. Lange, 1974.

Table 30—2 (cont'd). Syndromes associated with inborn errors of metabolism:
Disorders of amino acid metabolism.

	Amino Acids or Organic Acids Increased in Plasma	Amino Acids or Organic Acids Increased in Urine	Biochemistry	Clinical Features and Treatment
Hartnup disease	. . .	Alanine, serine, glutamine, valine, leucine, isoleucine, phenylalanine, tyrosine, tryptophan, histidine; basic amino acids low	Tryptophan rejection by bowel and renal tubular epithelium.	Mental retardation in some cases, pellagra-like skin rash, ataxia, and other cerebellar signs. Treat with nicotinic acid and low-protein diet.
Indolylacryloylglycine excretion	. . .	Indolylacryloyl-glycine	Possible malabsorption defect.	Mental retardation.
Hyperserotoninemia	Serotonin	. . .	Unknown.	Flushing episodes, ataxia, seizures.
Kynureninase deficiency	. . .	Kynurenine, hydroxykynurenine; xanthurenic acid	Kynureninase deficiency. May be B_6-dependent	Infantile spasms. May respond rapidly or slowly to vitamin B_6.
Imino Acid Metabolism				
Hyperprolinemia Type A	Proline	Proline, hydroxyproline, glycine	Proline oxidase deficiency.	Familial nephritis, deafness, renal hypoplasia, epilepsy, abnormal EEG.
Type B	Proline	Not recorded	Δ'-Pyrroline-5-carboxylic acid dehydrogenase.	Convulsions, coma, mental retardation.
Hydroxyprolinemia	Hydroxyproline	Hydroxyproline, 1-methylhistidine	Hydroxyproline oxidase deficiency.	Mental retardation, moderate hematuria and pyuria.
Joseph's syndrome	. . .	Proline, hydroxyproline, iminodipeptiduria		Convulsions, raised cerebrospinal fluid protein, mental retardation.
Iminopeptiduria	. . .	Imino–C terminal peptides	Unknown.	Mental retardation, splenomegaly, exophthalmos, unusual facies.
Histidine Metabolism				
Histidinemia	Histidine	Histidine, alanine, threonine	Histidine ammonia lyase.	Slurred, inarticulate speech. Variable incidence of mental retardation. Low-histidine diet has been reported; results questionable.
Formiminoglutamic-aciduria Type A	. . .	FIGLU after histidine load	Formiminotransferase deficiency.	Somatic and intellectual retardation, round face, obesity, hypersegmentation of polymorphonuclear leukocytes.
Type B	. . .	FIGLU before and after histidine load	(?) Folic acid transport defect.	Ataxia, megaloblastic anemia, mental retardation, convulsions.
Imidazole amino-aciduria in amaurotic idiocy	. . .	Anserine, carnosine; also histidine and 1-methyl-histidine	Unknown.	Retardation, obesity, inactivity, blindness; later, increased muscle tone and decerebrate state.
Cyclohydrolase deficiency	Folic acid	No excess FIGLU	Cyclohydrolase.	Microcephaly, optic atrophy, hypsarythmia.
Carnosinemia	Carnosine	Carnosine	Carnosinase.	Grand mal seizures, myoclonic epilepsy.
Phenylalanine and Tyrosine Metabolism				
Phenylketonuria	Phenylalanine	Phenylalanine, o-hydroxyphenylacetic acid. Phenylpyruvic acid.	Phenylalanine hydroxylase deficiency.	Usually (but not always) severe mental retardation. Convulsions, eczema, fair hair and complexion. Treat with low-phenylalanine diet.
Hyperphenylalaninemia	Phenylalanine	. . .	Not precisely known; phenylalanine transaminase in some cases.	May be normal; depends on type. Treat if level of serum phenylalanine > 20 mg/dL.
Tyrosinosis (several clinical types)	Phenylalanine, tyrosine	Normal for age	Transient p-hydroxyphenylpyruvic acid oxidase deficiency.	General failure to thrive, convulsions. Temporarily responds to low-phenylalanine diet.

Table 30—2 (cont'd). Syndromes associated with inborn errors of metabolism:
Disorders of amino acid metabolism.

	Amino Acids or Organic Acids Increased in Plasma	Amino Acids or Organic Acids Increased in Urine	Biochemistry	Clinical Features and Treatment
Oasthouse syndrome	Not reported	Phenylalanine, methionine, tyrosine, (?) leucine and isoleucine, α-hydroxybutyric acid	Unknown.	Infantile spasms, with interim flaccidity and unresponsiveness, sparse hair, retardation, general unawareness.
Branched-Chain Amino Acid Metabolism				
Branched-chain ketoaciduria	Isoleucine, valine, leucine, alloisoleucine	Leucine, isoleucine, valine	Branched-chain keto acid decarboxylase. Partial and intermittent forms described.	Neonatal difficulty in feeding, anorexia, convulsions, and other CNS signs. Mild, intermittent, and thiamine-dependent forms are seen.
Hypervalinemia	Valine	Valine	Not identified.	Failure to thrive, vomiting, nystagmus.
Isovaleric acidemia	Isovaleric acid, especially after valine load	Isovaleric acid, isovalerylglycine	Isovaleric dehydrogenase.	Mental and motor retardation. Smell of sweat in skin and urine.
Hydroxylysinuria	Hydroxylysine (slight increase)	Hydroxylysine and N-acetyl hydroxylysine increased	Defect in breakdown of hydroxylysine.	Mental and physical retardation.
β-Hydroxyisovaleric acidemia	No abnormality detected	β-Hydroxyisovaleric acid, β-methylcrotonylglycine	β-Methylcrotonyl carboxylase deficiency.	Progressive hypotonia and muscular atrophy. Possibly a biotin dependency.
Methylhydroxybutyric aciduria	. . .	α-Methyl-β-hydroxybutyric acid, α-methyl-aceto-acetate	β-Hydroxy acyl dehydrogenase.	Intermittent severe metabolic acidosis, macrocephaly, retardation.
Methylmalonic aciduria	Methylmalonic acid	Glycine, lysine, methylmalonic acid	Methylmalonyl-CoA isomerase. May also be error in B_{12} metabolism.	Acute episodes of vomiting and acidosis. Failure to thrive. B_{12} therapy should be attempted (500 μg daily intramuscularly initially).
Propionyl-CoA carboxylase deficiency Type A	Propionic acid	Propionic acid	Propionyl-CoA carboxylase.	Neonatal severe acidosis.
Type B	Glycine ++; also serine, alanine, glutamic acid	Glycine	Propionyl-CoA carboxylase.	Neonatal vomiting, ketosis, neutropenia, thrombocytopenia, osteoporosis.
Dibasic Amino Acid Metabolism				
Argininuria	. . .	Arginine	Unknown.	Convulsions, hepatomegaly, dry brittle hair.
Hyperlysinemia	Lysine; also ammonia	Lysine, N-acetyl lysine, homoarginine	Lysine acylase, lysine dehydrogenase, or lysine ketoglutarate reductase.	Convulsions and coma related to protein feeding.
Saccharopinuria	Lysine	Saccharopine, lysine, histidine, homocitrulline	Saccharopine cleavage enzyme.	Short stature, retardation.
Hyperdibasic aminoaciduria	Lysine, arginine, ornithine, homocitrulline	Dibasics are normal or low	Renal and enteric transport defect.	Mental and physical retardation, failure to thrive.
Miscellaneous				
Aspartylglucosaminuria	. . .	Aspartylglucosamine	Unknown.	Coarse facies, retardation.
Hyperglycinemia	Glycine, serine, alanine, glutamic acid	Glycine, valine, leucine; taurine, serine may be low	Glycine-formyl FH_4 transferase deficiency.	Episodes of vomiting with severe dehydration, acidosis, ketosis, repeated infection, somatic and mental retardation.
Glutamicaciduria	Glutamic acid	Slight generalized increase in total amino nitrogen	Unknown.	Sparse, coarse, unpigmented hair, mental retardation, failure to thrive, other congenital malformations.

Table 30–2 (cont'd). Syndromes associated with inborn errors of metabolism: Disorders of amino acid metabolism.

	Amino Acids or Organic Acids Increased in Plasma	Amino Acids or Organic Acids Increased in Urine	Biochemistry	Clinical Features and Treatment
Raised cerebrospinal fluid glutamic acid	Proline; also, perhaps, glutamic acid, leucine	Slight generalized increase in total amino nitrogen	Unknown.	Hypertonia, hyperreflexia, failure to thrive, mental retardation.
Sarcosinemia	Sarcosine (methylglycine)	Sarcosine (methylglycine)	Sarcosine oxidase deficiency.	Hypotonia; sometimes mental and physical retardation. Limb muscle contractures also reported.
Hyperalaninemia Type A	Alanine, lactic acid, pyruvic acid	Alanine, pyruvate, lactate	Pyruvate decarboxylase.	Severe acidosis, development retardation, ataxic convulsions. Treat with thiamine, 5 mg intramuscularly daily.
Type B	...	...	Pyruvate carboxylase.	Mental retardation.
β-Aminoisobutyric aciduria	...	BAIB	Physiologic variant.	None.
β-Alaninemia	β-Alanine	β-Alanine, BAIB, taurine, GABA	Possibly β-alanine α-ketoglutarate transaminase.	Lethargy, somnolence, hypotonia, hyporeflexia, grand mal seizures.
Infantile keto-acidosis	Ketones	Lysine, glycine, phenylalanine, ketones	Muscle pyruvate kinase.	Severe ketosis with protein feeding.
Glutathionuria	Glutathione	Glutathione	Serum γ-glutamyl transpeptidase deficiency.	Moderate mental retardation.

Maple Syrup Urine Disease

This familial cerebral degenerative disease may have its onset during the first week of life and progress rapidly to a decerebrate phase and excretion of urine with a maple syrup–like odor. The clinical course is characterized by decerebrate rigidity, respiratory irregularities, and occasionally generalized seizures. Death has occurred in most cases before age 20 months. A polymer of α-hydroxybutyric acid is believed responsible for the maple syrup odor.

The amino acid pattern of the urine may be normal at birth, but increased excretion of leucine, isoleucine, and valine may occur during the later stages of the illness. A block in oxidative decarboxylation of α-keto acids has been inferred from the accumulation of these 3 keto acids together with the absence of other metabolites along the degradation pathway of leucine. Pathologically, there is a defect in myelin formation of white matter, with foci of increased severity, areas of spongy change, associated astrocytosis, and decrease in oligodendroglia.

Hartnup Disease (H Disease)

This rare genetic defect in the renal transport mechanism for tryptophan is characterized by cerebellar ataxia, mental retardation, aminoacidemia, dermatitis, and increased excretion of indole and indican compounds.

Treatment is by hydration to prevent renal calculus formation. Protein-restricted diets and niacinamide are of dubious value.

Leucine Sensitivity Disease

A genetic metabolic disorder characterized by abnormal hypoglycemia and due to leucine sensitivity has been noted. Clinical features include hypoglycemia, flushing, sweating, and convulsions.

No specific treatment is available.

Albinism

Albinism is a congenital disorder in which tyrosinase is absent from melanocytes. It is manifested clinically by absence of pigment in the skin, eyes, and hair. Photophobia, nystagmus, and defective vision may occur. The skin and hair are white; the irises and pupils are red.

Cystathioninuria

This rare disorder of amino acid metabolism—believed to be related to a deficiency of cystathionine enzyme—is associated with mental retardation. No known treatment for cystathioninuria has proved to be effective.

Citrullinuria

Mental retardation may be associated with this rare aminoaciduria of undetermined origin. Increased levels of citrulline may be demonstrated in the blood, cerebrospinal fluid, and urine. No other amino acid abnormality or renal tubular defect has been noted.

Familial Hyperprolinemia

Nerve deafness, convulsions, mental retardation,

and congenital renal hypoplasia may occur in this rare hereditary disorder. Increased levels of proline (8–10 mg/dL), characteristic aminoaciduria (proline, hydroxyproline, and glycine only), and hematuria may occur. Electroencephalographic abnormalities are also associated.

The pathogenesis is not known, and no treatment is available.

Hydroxyprolinemia

Mental retardation and abnormal urinary excretion of red and white blood cells are associated in this rare disorder with increased blood and urine levels of hydroxyproline. A low-hydroxyproline diet does not affect the plasma hydroxyproline level.

Idiopathic Hyperglycinemia & Hyperglycinuria

Mental and developmental retardation, protein intolerance, osteoporosis, neutropenia, and thrombocytopenia may occur in this rare disorder of amino acid metabolism characterized by abnormal glycinemia and glycinuria. Plasma concentration of other amino acids (leucine, glutamine) is increased without a corresponding increase in urine.

Reduction of dietary protein reduces the frequency and severity of acute episodes.

Homocystinuria

This hereditary disorder, characterized clinically by mental retardation and dislocation of lenses, occurs in children with sparse blond hair and genu valgum. The plasma homocystine and methionine levels are elevated. Urinary excretion of homocystine is increased, and the nitroprusside test of urine is positive (a magenta color develops). Absence (or lack of activity) of the enzyme cystathionine synthetase in liver is believed to cause the disease. A child born with homocystinuria may suffer from a cysteine deficiency immediately after birth, when the need for this particular amino acid is great.

Oculocerebrorenal Syndrome (Lowe's Syndrome)

This congenital hereditary disorder of unknown cause is associated with defects of the nervous system, eyes, and kidneys. Mental retardation, hypotonia, cataracts, glaucoma, metabolic acidosis, proteinuria, hyperaminoaciduria, and organic aciduria occur. Affected children look strikingly alike.

Protein-Calorie Deficiency (Kwashiorkor; Marasmus)

Deficiency of proteins and calories early in life, particularly in the first 6 months of life, may adversely affect maturation and lead to permanent mental retardation. Inadequate protein and essential amino acid intake may be at fault. Language development is usually more affected than motor development. Apathy, irritability, drowsiness, impaired learning, weakness, hypotonia, depressed tendon reflexes, and coarse tremors may occur.

DISORDERS OF CARBOHYDRATE METABOLISM

Galactosemia

This disorder may be manifested soon after birth by feeding problems, vomiting, diarrhea, abdominal distention, mental retardation, cataracts, hepatomegaly, and elevated blood and urine galactose levels. An enzyme (galactose-1-phosphate uridyl transferase) necessary for conversion of galactose to glucose is deficient in these children.

Treatment consists of excluding galactose and lactose from the diet for the first 3 years of life. If treatment is instituted before the fourth month, clinical manifestations can be prevented.

Glycogen Storage Disorders (Glycogenoses)

A number of congenital disorders associated with abnormal deposition of glycogen occur as a result of a specific enzymatic deficiency. Hepatorenal glycogenosis (von Gierke's disease) is the most common of the group. Ten clinical types are well recognized: (1) hepatorenal (von Gierke's disease), (2) generalized glycogenosis (Pompe's disease), (3) limit dextrinosis (Forbes' disease), (4) amylopectinosis (Andersen's disease), (5) muscle phosphorylase type (McArdle's syndrome; see p 423), (6) liver phosphorylase type (Hers' disease), (7) phosphoglucomutase type, (8) phosphofructokinase type, (9) phosphorylase kinase type, and (10) glycogen synthetase type. A specific and different enzymatic defect has been found in each of these glycogenoses.

Von Gierke's Disease

This rare hereditary disorder may become evident in early life by easy fatigability, hepatomegaly, and hypoglycemia and ketosis with resulting shock and convulsions. Serum glucose does not respond to the epinephrine test. Excessive glycogen deposits in the liver and kidneys are caused by deficiency of the enzyme glucose-6-phosphatase, which is required for degradation of glycogen to glucose. Treatment is aimed at nutritional improvement and correction of hypoglycemia by frequent feedings. Death usually occurs in infancy or childhood. If the patient survives, symptoms improve as the child gets older.

Gargoylism (Hurler's Disease)

This rare disorder usually becomes manifest in the early months of life. The child may resemble an achondroplastic dwarf. Mental and physical retardation, mental deficiency, hepatosplenomegaly, and optic atrophy may occur. The clinical syndrome is marked by dwarfism, infantilism, mental retardation, coarse facial features, large tongue, potbelly, kyphosis, corneal clouding, and characteristic skeletal dystrophy. Hurler's disease is due to abnormal metabolism of certain mucopolysaccharides. Dermatan sulfate and heparan sulfate are produced in excess, with abnormal deposition in the CNS and body organs and

Table 30–3. Disorders of lysosomal hydrolases.*†

Disorder	Enzyme Defect	Mucopolysaccharides In Urine	Clinical Features
Hurler's syndrome	α-Iduronidase	Heparan sulfate and dermatan sulfate	Autosomal recessive. Mental retardation, hepatospleno-megaly, umbilical hernia, coarse facies, corneal clouding, skeletal changes with gibbus.
Scheie's syndrome	α-Iduronidase (allele to Hurler mutant but probably more residual activity to natural substrate)	Dermatan sulfate and lesser amounts of heparan sulfate	Autosomal recessive. Corneal clouding, stiff joints, normal intellect. Clinical types intermediate between Hurler and Scheie are quite common.
Hunter's syndrome	Sulfoiduronate sulfatase	Heparan sulfate and dermatan sulfate	X-linked recessive. Variable mental retardation, coarse facies, hepatosplenomegaly. Corneal clouding and gibbus not present. Mild forms are seen.
Sanfilippo syndrome Type A	Sulfamidase	Heparan sulfate	Autosomal recessive. Severe mental retardation with com-paratively mild skeletal changes, visceromegaly, and facial coarseness. Types *cannot* be differentiated clinically.
Type B	α-N-Acetylglucosamini-dase	Heparan sulfate	
Type C	Acetyl-CoA:α-Gluco-saminide N-acetyltrans-ferase	Heparan sulfate	
Type D	N-Acetylglucosamine-6-sulfate sulfatase	Heparan sulfate	
Morquio's syndrome	N-Acetylhexosamine-6-sulfatase	Keratosulfate	Autosomal recessive. Severe skeletal changes, platyspon-dylisis, corneal clouding.
Maroteaux-Lamy syndrome Type A	N-Acetylgalactosamine-4-sulfatase	Dermatan sulfate	Autosomal recessive. Coarse facies, growth retardation, severe skeletal deformities with gibbus, corneal clouding, hepatosplenomegaly, normal intellect.
β-Glucuronidase deficiency[1]	β-Glucuronidase	Chondroitin sulfates A and C	Autosomal recessive. Varies from mental retardation, skeletal changes with gibbus, corneal clouding, and hepa-tosplenomegaly to mild facial coarseness, retardation, and loose joints. Hearing loss common.
Mannosidosis[2]	α-Mannosidase	Oligosaccharides in urine	Autosomal recessive. Varies from severe mental retarda-tion, coarse facies, short stature and skeletal changes, and hepatosplenomegaly to mild facial coarseness, retardation, and loose joints. Hearing loss common.
Fucosidosis[3]	α-Fucosidase	Oligosaccharides in urine	Autosomal recessive. Variable: coarse facies, skeletal changes, hepatosplenomegaly, occasional angiokeratoma corporis diffusum.
I-cell disease[4]	Multiple lysosomal hydrolases	Sialyl oligosaccha-rides in urine	Autosomal recessive, milder forms are known. Severe shortness of stature, mental retardation, early facial coarsening, clear cornea, stiffness of joints, and normal head circumference.
Sialidosis[5]	N-Acetylneuraminidase (sialidase)	Sialyl oligosaccha-rides in urine	Autosomal recessive. Mental retardation, coarse facies, skeletal dysplasia, myoclonic seizures, cherry-red macular spot.

*Reproduced, with permission, from Kempe CH, Silver HK, O'Brien D: *Current Pediatric Diagnosis and Treatment,* 7th ed. Lange, 1982.
†For further details, see McKusick VA: *Heritable Disorders of Connective Tissue,* 4th ed. Mosby, 1972. See also specific references:

[1] *J Pediatr* 1973;**82**:249.
[2] *Acta Paediatr Scand* 1973;**62**:555.
[3] *J Pediatr* 1974;**84**:727.
[4] *J Pediatr* 1971;**79**:360.
[5] *Am J Med Genet* 1977;**1**:21.

excretion of large amounts in the urine. Variations from the usual syndrome have been described as Hunter's syndrome, Sanfilippo's syndrome, Morquio's syndrome, and Scheie's syndrome.

NEUROENDOCRINE DISORDERS

PITUITARY SYNDROMES

Simmonds' Disease (Pituitary Cachexia)

Simmonds' disease may be caused by total de-struction of the anterior lobe of the pituitary by trauma, hemorrhage, tumor, etc. It produces severe asthenia and emaciation as well as reduced metabolism, temperature, and blood pressure. Psychotic symptoms may occur. The disease resembles anorexia nervosa, a psychogenic disorder of young females who voluntarily refrain from eating. In severe cases, death may ensue.

Corticotropin or corticosteroids are helpful in medical treatment.

Diabetes Insipidus

This clinical syndrome is characterized by excessive urinary excretion and fluid intake. It is associated with a deficiency of antidiuretic hormone of the posterior pituitary, sometimes with lesions of the hypothalamus.

Adiposogenital Dystrophy (Fröhlich's Syndrome)

Fröhlich's syndrome occurs in children, usually boys, and is characterized by obesity and retarded development of secondary sex characteristics. Developmental abnormalities may correct themselves at puberty. The disease is sometimes noted with tumors of the suprasellar region.

Pituitary Dwarfism

This disorder may occur in children with tumors of the suprasellar region. It is attributed to deficiency of anterior pituitary hormones. Dwarfism of various grades, retarded primary and secondary sexual development, and altered skin appearance may occur.

Cushing's Syndrome (See below.)

Acromegaly

Overgrowth of the skeleton occurs with hyperfunction of the pituitary gland and may be caused by an eosinophilic tumor of the pituitary gland. Gradual and progressive enlargement of the hands, feet, skull, and lower jaw is characteristic. The features coarsen, and there is overgrowth of facial hair. The activity of the gonads is decreased, with amenorrhea and loss of libido. A similar disorder in childhood, occurring before closure of the epiphyseal lines, results in generalized increase in size, particularly of long bones (gigantism).

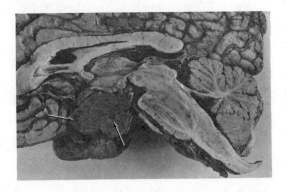

Figure 30–3. Adenoma of pituitary in a 48-year-old woman.

Inappropriate ADH Secretion (Cerebral Salt Wasting)

Excessive inappropriate secretion of antidiuretic hormone (ADH) may occur with brain injury, especially of the hypothalamic area, secondary to head trauma, infections, cerebral infarcts, etc. This syndrome is characterized by hyponatremia and hypotonicity of body fluids; urinary excretion of sodium; normal renal and adrenal function; absence of dehydration, edema, hypotension, and azotemia; and improvement of the electrolyte disorder and clinical features upon fluid restriction. Headache, confusion, somnolence, coma, convulsions, weakness, transient focal neurologic signs, and electroencephalographic signs may occur.

ADRENAL SYNDROMES

Addison's Disease

Chronic insufficiency of the adrenal cortex may result in weakness, fatigability, hyperpigmentation, hypotension, nausea, vomiting, diarrhea, irritability, and periodic hypoglycemia. The gland may be destroyed by tuberculosis, hemorrhage, or tumor. Crises may be precipitated by stress, overexertion, or infections.

Relief may follow adequate hormone therapy (adrenocortical hormones) and a high-sodium, high-calorie diet.

Primary Aldosteronism

Periodic episodes of severe muscle weakness, intermittent tetany, paresthesias, hypertension, polyuria, and polydipsia are believed to occur as a result of a tumor of the adrenal cortex that secretes aldosterone in pathologically large amounts. Laboratory findings include low serum potassium, elevated serum sodium, alkalosis, low urinary specific gravity, and an increase in the urinary excretion of sodium-retaining corticosteroids.

Cushing's Syndrome

Cushing's syndrome was attributed at one time (by Cushing) to basophilic adenomas of the pituitary gland. It is now known to occur more commonly with tumor or hyperplasia of the adrenal cortex. Symptoms include obesity, hypertrichosis, purplish abdominal striae, hypertension, polycythemia, hyperglycemia, amenorrhea, impotence, osteomalacia, acrocyanosis, somnolence, backache, easy fatigability, and, ultimately, weakness. Mental symptoms may occur. This syndrome may be reproduced by administration of corticosteroids or corticotropin. It is more common in females than in males.

Waterhouse-Friderichsen Syndrome

This syndrome consists of sudden collapse, pallor, and purpura caused by adrenal hemorrhages, usually in conjunction with a fulminating septicemic form of cerebrospinal fever (meningococcemia).

Pheochromocytoma

Hyperfunction of the adrenal medulla as a result of a tumor of the chromaffin cells of that area may give rise to constant or intermittent hypertension of moderate to severe grade. Periodic attacks of hypertension with associated palpitation, precordial distress, headache, dizziness, perspiration, and anxiety may follow intravenous injection of histamine or massaging of the abdomen in the region of the adrenals. Death may result from cerebral hemorrhage, cardiac failure, or pulmonary edema. The phentolamine (Regitine) test is used for diagnosis: 5 mg injected rapidly intravenously will produce a prompt drop in blood pressure.

In normotensive intervals, the intravenous injection of 25–50 μg of histamine base may cause a blood pressure rise of 50 mm Hg systolic and 25 mm Hg diastolic within 3 minutes. Increased 24-hour urine excretion of catecholamines occurs in most patients with pheochromocytoma. Diagnostic studies, including intravenous urography and renal angiography, may be helpful.

THYROID SYNDROMES

Cretinism

Cretinism is due to severe thyroid deficiency in early life and is characterized by retarded physical and mental development. In untreated children, dwarfism and severe mental deficiency may result.

Myxedema (Hypothyroidism)

Myxedema in adults is characterized by nonpitting edema of the subcutaneous tissues, weakness, lethargy, decreased sweating, sensitivity to cold, and enlargement of the tongue. Diagnosis may be aided by finding low T_3 and T_4 using any method of measurement, and by finding elevated serum cholesterol. The disease responds well to treatment with thyroid extract. Patients with myxedema may complain of pains or paresthesias in the hands that may be due, in some cases, to a carpal tunnel syndrome resulting from nerve compression by edematous tissue.

Graves' Disease (Hyperthyroidism)

The common neurologic alterations that may be associated with Graves' disease are tremors of the hands, exophthalmos, lid lag (von Graefe's sign), convergence weakness (Möbius' sign), infrequent blinking (Stellwag's sign), widened palpebral fissures (Dalrymple's sign), weakness of muscles, and elevated values of all tests for circulating thyroid hormone and thyroid function. **Thyrotoxic myopathy** is apt to occur in males with thyrotoxicosis. It is manifested by weakness and wasting of the pelvic girdle and shoulder girdle muscles and may superficially resemble myasthenia gravis. **Exophthalmic ophthalmoplegia** (rare) may develop in association with or independent of hyperthyroidism. It is characterized by exophthalmos and paralysis of the extraocular muscles. Edema of lids, chemosis, and papilledema may occur.

OTHER NEUROENDOCRINE DISORDERS

Parathyroid Tetany (Hypoparathyroidism)

The most common cause of parathyroid tetany is operative removal or destruction of the parathyroid glands. The disease may be associated with carpopedal spasm, convulsions, and numbness and cramps of the extremities. Cataracts may occur, and the nails may be thin and brittle. Basal ganglia calcification may be noted on skull x-ray. Decrease in the serum calcium varies with the degree of hypofunction (values as low as 4.5 mg/dL have been observed). Serum phosphorus is elevated. Relief may follow treatment with parathormone, dihydrotachysterol (Hytakerol), or a high-calcium, low-phosphorus diet.

Manifestations of hyperirritability of nerves occur when the blood calcium falls below normal. These may include the following:

A. Chvostek's Facial Sign of Tetany: Tapping over the parotid gland results in spasmodic contraction of the ipsilateral facial muscles (hyperexcitability of the facial nerve).

B. Trousseau's Sign of Tetany: A typical spasm of the hand and forearm (accoucheur's hand) occurs after compression of the brachial artery for 1–5 minutes.

C. Erb's Sign of Tetany: Hyperexcitability of the peripheral motor nerve to galvanic current; in tetany, the cathodal opening contraction current is commonly less than 5 milliamperes.

D. Hoffman's Sign of Tetany: Tetanic muscular spasms produced by electrical or mechanical stimulation of a sensory nerve. The ulnar nerve is usually selected for the test.

E. Kashida's Thermic Sign of Tetany: Development of hyperesthesias and spasms after application of hot or cold irritants.

F. Pool's Arm and Leg Signs of Tetany: (1) Tension on the brachial plexus by forcible abduction of the arm causes spasms of the muscles of the hand and arm. (2) Tension on the sciatic nerve by forcible flex-

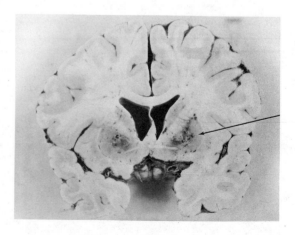

Figure 30–4. Bilateral basal ganglia calcification in a 60-year-old man with hypoparathyroidism.

ion of the thigh on the trunk with the leg extended causes spasms of the muscles of the leg and foot.

G. Schlesinger's Leg Sign of Tetany: If the hip joint is flexed and the leg extended at the knee, painful spasm of the extremity occurs in a few seconds to 3 minutes.

H. Schultze's Tongue-Dimpling Sign of Tetany: Tapping the protruded tongue with a percussion hammer causes dimpling at the point of mechanical stimulus.

Osteitis Fibrosa Cystica (Hyperparathyroidism)

Muscular weakness, thinning of the bones, and formation of renal calculi may result from excess parathyroid hormone activity, usually due to adenoma or diffuse enlargement of the parathyroid glands. Serum calcium is usually elevated, serum phosphorus decreased, and serum alkaline phosphatase increased.

Hypoinsulinism (Diabetes Mellitus)

Diabetes mellitus may be accompanied by polyneuritis, mononeuritis, diabetic coma, or cerebrovascular degenerative lesions similar to those of cerebral arteriosclerosis. In most cases, the diabetes mellitus has been known to the patient for years. However, neurologic involvement occasionally provokes a medical examination, and diabetes is discovered.

In middle-aged or elderly diabetics, dehydration may precipitate hyperosmolar nonketoacidotic coma. This may present with seizures, often focal in onset.

Hyperinsulinism

The paroxysmal occurrence of nervousness, anxiety, tremors, automatism, convulsions, and coma may be related to lowering of blood glucose level and tends to occur at times when the blood glucose may be expected to be low. Symptoms are of variable intensity and are usually relieved promptly by the administration of glucose.

DISEASES OF COLLAGEN TISSUES

Polyarteritis Nodosa

The CNS is involved in about 30% of cases of polyarteritis nodosa. Multiple peripheral neuritis is the most common neurologic finding. Damage to cerebral arteries may lead to thrombosis of small vessels, with convulsions and focal neurologic signs. In cases with exclusive or predominant localization of disease in the brain, the clinical picture may simulate encephalitis or brain tumor.

Lupus Erythematosus

Involvement of the nervous system may occur in the late stages of the disease and may be associated with thrombosis of small vessels or multiple petechial hemorrhages. Convulsions, mental symptoms, poly-

neuritis, hemiplegia, and cranial nerve palsies may occur.

Dermatomyositis

Painful erythema of the skin, tenderness, weakness, and loss of reflexes of affected muscles may occur. The muscles affected may be those of the face, extremities, jaw, or pharynx; the proximal portions of the pelvic and shoulder girdle muscles and the pharyngeal muscles are most often affected.

Treatment with corticosteroids (eg, prednisone, 60–80 mg daily) is effective in this and other collagen disorders.

MISCELLANEOUS METABOLIC DISORDERS

Temporal Arteritis

This disorder, which occurs most often in elderly women, is characterized by headache and a nodular, tender, prominent, tortuous temporal artery. Blindness sometimes occurs and is usually attributed to thrombosis of the central retinal artery. The early administration of adrenal corticosteroids may provide symptomatic relief and prevent blindness.

Serum Reactions

Most cases of nervous system complications following prophylactic administration of serum occur 1–2 days after the appearance of somatic evidence of serum sickness and about 1 week after the serum injection. Similar neurologic complications may appear, however, in the absence of any constitutional symptoms. Radiculitis, especially of the cervical roots, is the most common complaint; less often, there may be polyradiculitis and polyneuritis, myelitis, or encephalomyelitis. The vast majority of patients recover with little or no residual disability.

Amyloidosis

In amyloidosis, polyneuropathy may be associated with hepatosplenomegaly, heart failure, and macroglossia, alone or in combination. The Congo red test for amyloidosis may be positive, and amyloid may be demonstrable in a biopsied nerve. Preexisting long-standing infection or debilitating illness may precede amyloidosis. There is no effective treatment for systemic amyloidosis, and death may occur within a few years. Local amyloid "tumors" may be excised surgically; secondary amyloidosis may presumably be prevented by early treatment of infections.

Porphyria

Porphyria is a metabolic defect associated with the excretion of porphyrins in the urine. It may be associated with polyneuritis, convulsions, abdominal pains, and mental symptoms.

Acute porphyria (the most common type) is inherited as an autosomal dominant trait and is believed to be due primarily to a hepatic defect. Excretion of burgundy-red urine, pigmentation of the skin, colicky abdominal pains, convulsions, mental symptoms, and polyneuritis may develop. Acute porphyria occurs most often in females. Symptoms are apt to appear in the third decade. The mortality rate in reported cases is about 50%.

Congenital porphyria (relatively rare) is more common in males and is transmitted as an autosomal recessive trait. Manifestations become evident early in life and consist of sensitivity to light, anemia, and hepatosplenomegaly. The bone marrow appears to be the site of the metabolic error.

Liver Disorders

Confusion, delirium, stupor, or coma may occur with liver failure. Sometimes there are associated tremors and rigidity of the limbs, and extensor plantar responses. Deeper grades of "hepatic coma" usually are associated with an increased degree of slowing of frequencies in the EEG.

Reduction of cerebral oxygen consumption occurs gradually in hepatic insufficiency, and a severe depression of cerebral oxygen utilization appears necessary for the development of clinical manifestations of even moderate cerebral dysfunction. No constant relationship between the severity of hepatic disorder, the state of consciousness, and the blood ammonia level has been reported. No single pathogenic mechanism at present can account for the onset or perpetuation of hepatic coma. Among the various mechanisms alleged to affect the state of consciousness in liver dysfunction are increased blood and cerebral uptake of ammonia; slowing of the Krebs cycle, with decreased oxygen consumption; liberation of α-ketoglutarate, pyruvate, and lactate; a possible disturbance of metabolism of indolic or phenolic compounds, or both; and liberation of toxic substances into the blood as a result of liver damage, which produces neuronal disturbances in brain. Cerebrospinal fluid may have elevated α-ketoglutaramate.

Reye's Syndrome (Encephalopathy With Fatty Degeneration of Viscera)

This syndrome, to which young children seem most susceptible, does not have a clearly established cause, although viral infections and toxic and metabolic causes have been suspected. The onset leads to diagnostic confusion with other causes of coma (eg, hepatic coma). It is characterized by a recent history of upper respiratory infection or chickenpox, vomiting, lethargy, and drowsiness, progressing to coma, elevated SGOT and normal serum bilirubin levels, variable hypoglycemia, and hyperammonemia. Convulsions and decorticate and decerebrate posturing may occur. The brain shows gross cerebral edema, occasionally with evidence of herniation. The brain may show loss of neurons and fatty vacuolation about blood vessels. The liver shows diffuse steatosis with minimal inflammatory changes. The kidneys show swelling

and fatty degeneration of proximal tubules.

Therapy is usually directed to control of cerebral edema with administration of mannitol and dexamethasone and to correction of electrolyte and related imbalances.

Uremia

Acute uremia may produce confusion, agitation, apathy, depression, stupor, and coma. Nystagmus, facial paralysis, and lower cranial nerve dysfunction are common. Muscle wasting, myalgia, tremor, fasciculations, myoclonus, and transient paresis are frequent. Convulsions are also frequent, but sensory phenomena are rare. No correlations with routine blood chemistries are noted, although rapid shifts are more likely to cause symptoms. The twitchings and convulsions observed in uremia are likely to be due to a generalized metabolic lesion and not just to hypocalcemia; many symptoms may be due to hypoxia. Polyneuropathy, with greatest involvement of the most distal portions of nerves, may also occur in uremia.

Dialysis treatment of uremia may sometimes result in neurologic abnormalities such as convulsions, encephalopathy, and acute brain syndrome, which are presumably related to the very rapid correction of blood pH.

Heat Disorders

Three major clinical syndromes may occur as a result of excessively high environmental temperature.

(1) Heat cramps, characterized by painful contractions of skeletal muscles, result from loss of sodium chloride via sweat and may be prevented by dietary salt supplementation.

(2) Heat exhaustion, a more severe sodium chloride depletion with decreased plasma and interstitial fluid volume, is manifested by giddiness, pallor, sweating, vomiting, muscle cramps, and syncope. Body temperature is usually normal but may be subnormal or slightly increased. Intravenous saline generally results in rapid recovery; in less severe cases, salt deficit may be corrected orally.

(3) Heat stroke is a serious condition with a mortality rate as high as 50%. Failure of the heat regulatory mechanisms of the hypothalamus is associated with cessation of sweating, followed by thermal and anoxic damage to various organs. Body temperature usually exceeds 41 °C (105.8 °F), the skin is hot and dry, and breathing is rapid. Some disturbances of consciousness and other neurologic dysfunctions may occur. Cardiovascular, renal, hepatic, and hematologic dysfunction may also occur. Onset may be sudden or may occur after prodromes of faintness, headache, anorexia, diarrhea, ataxia, mental confusion, and polyuria. Rapid reduction of body temperature by immersion in or sponging with cold water, fanning, etc, is the primary goal of treatment. Dehydration is usually not a problem in heat stroke.

Radiation Myelopathy

Radiation myelopathy should be suspected when

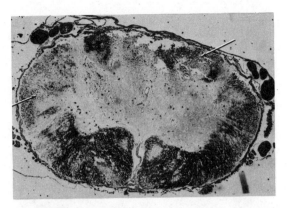

Figure 30–5. Subacute radiation myelopathy. Lower cervical spinal cord following irradiation for treatment of mediastinal Hodgkin's disease.

the spinal cord is involved and is included in an area of irradiation of adjacent tissue subjected to radiotherapy for cancer. The main neurologic lesion is usually within the segments of spinal cord exposed to irradiation. Myelography or operation may be required to exclude spinal cord compression or metastasis as the cause of the neurologic syndrome that follows irradiation. Radiation myelopathy may be designated as (1) transient radiation myelopathy, (2) radiation amyotrophy, (3) subacute radiation myelopathy, and (4) chronic progressive radiation myelopathy. (See Fig 30–5.)

Osteitis Deformans (Paget's Disease)

The neurologic complications of Paget's disease are those resulting from pressure on the CNS or the nerve roots by overgrowth of bone. Deafness, facial paralysis, visual changes, and compression of the spinal cord may occur. Secondary platybasia may take place in advanced cases.

Morgagni-Morel-Stewart Syndrome

This consists of hyperostosis of the internal table of the frontal bone in obese, hirsute women with complaints of headaches and mental disorders.

Vitamin B Complex Deficiencies

Since members of the vitamin B complex are closely associated in function and occurrence, deficiency of more than one member often occurs. It is usually advisable to provide adequate dietary or parenteral sources of all members of the B complex.

A. Thiamine (Vitamin B_1): This is the coenzyme for decarboxylation of α-keto acids (pyruvic and α-ketoglutaric acid) and is important in normal carbohydrate metabolism. Beriberi (avitaminosis B_1) results from an inadequate intake due to diet, excessive cooking of foods, etc. Early or mild manifestations include anorexia, muscle cramps and tenderness, paresthesias, and depressed reflexes. Severe or late manifestations (beriberi) include anorexia, polyneuritis, paralysis of extremities, serous effusions, subcutaneous edema,

and cardiac insufficiency. Treatment with thiamine chloride, 20–50 mg orally, intravenously, or intramuscularly daily in divided doses for 2 weeks and then 10–20 mg orally daily, is usually adequate.

B. Niacin: Pellagra may result from deficiency of components of vitamin B complex. Niacin deficiency is the principal but not the only dietary deficit in pellagra; the low tryptophan content of some foods plays a role. Mild or early manifestations include skin redness and roughness and tongue redness. Severe or late changes include marked skin roughening after exposure to light and friction, diarrhea, scarlet red atrophic tongue, stomatitis, depression, mental dullness, rigidity, and peculiar sucking reactions. Nicotinamide, 50–500 mg intravenously, intramuscularly, or orally daily, is given until symptoms subside, along with therapeutic doses of thiamine, riboflavin, and pyridoxine.

C. Pyridoxine (Vitamin B_6): Pyridoxine may be important in transamination and decarboxylation of proteins. Severe generalized convulsions occur in newborn infants and animals with dietary pyridoxine deficiencies. Neuropathies and convulsions secondary to drug effects produced by hydrazides may be prevented or alleviated with pyridoxine. In deficiency states, treatment with 10–50 mg parenterally or orally daily is usually adequate.

D. Vitamin B_{12}: Vitamin B_{12} is believed to be the extrinsic factor or effective principle lacking in pernicious anemia. Posterolateral sclerosis (see p 373) may be associated with deficiency of vitamin B_{12}.

Subacute Necrotizing Encephalomyelopathy (Leigh's Disease)

This rapidly progressive disorder occurs in infants who fail to thrive and become floppy, with impaired vision and hearing. Convulsions may occur. Subacute necrotizing encephalomyelopathy (SNEM) is associated with a lack of thiamine triphosphate in neural tissue. It is attributed to the presence of an inhibitor that prevents formation of thiamine triphosphate from thiamine pyrophosphate. The urine contains a substance that inhibits thiamine pyrophosphate–adenosine triphosphate phosphoryl transferase. In some cases, progression may be slow, with death resulting after several years.

NEUROLOGIC COMPLICATIONS OF DRUG & CHEMICAL INTOXICATIONS

Heavy Metals

A. Arsenic: The use of various arsenicals may be associated with polyneuritis, acute hemorrhagic encephalitis, or optic neuritis. Treatment with dimercaprol (BAL) may be helpful.

B. Lead: Neurologic complications of lead intoxication may take 2 forms. In adults there is usually a chronic polyneuritis, with pain, paresthesia, weakness, and stocking and glove anesthesia of extremities. Lead encephalopathy, characterized by generalized or focal convulsions with subsequent paralysis, occurs in infants. Hemiplegia, papilledema, lethargy, and coma may occur. Treatment with chelating agents (calcium disodium edathamil [EDTA, Versenate]) may be helpful. Urinary lead excretion of less than 0.15 mg/L is of doubtful diagnostic significance.

C. Manganese: Parkinsonism has been alleged to follow excessive exposure to manganese-containing dusts, which gain entrance to the body via the respiratory tract.

D. Thallium: Serious nervous system complications may occur. There may be associated optic neuritis or generalized polyneuritis. Acute severe poisoning may be associated with blindness, delirium, convulsions, and death.

E. Mercury: Organic mercurial poisoning was believed to account for the neurologic manifestations of Minamata disease. This disorder was noted among inhabitants of Minamata Bay in Japan who consumed contaminated fish and shellfish caught in the bay and developed constricted visual fields, ataxia, dysarthria, tremors, mental changes, salivation, sweating, and various extrapyramidal signs. Treatment with BAL and EDTA produced some improvement clinically.

Alcohols & Morphine

A. Ethyl Alcohol: Acute ethyl alcohol intoxication may be associated with ataxia, mental confusion, psychosis, and coma. Chronic intoxication may be associated with delirium tremens, convulsions, polyneuritis, Korsakoff's psychosis, cerebellar degeneration, mental deterioration, or Wernicke's polioencephalitis. The onset of coma is believed to indicate a blood alcohol level of 250 mg/dL. Intoxication may be characterized by drunkenness, aggressiveness, or coma, and depression of some neurons of the brain may be the cause of neurologic disorders.

Withdrawal of alcohol after heavy drinking may induce, in sequence, tremulousness and nausea, seizures and hallucinosis, and delirium tremens. Vitamin supplements and a nutritious diet will not greatly speed recovery from the preceding clinical syndromes. However, dietary deficiencies associated with alcoholism may cause Wernicke's disease, Korsakoff's psychosis, polyneuropathy, amblyopia, and pellagra. Administration of thiamine to patients with Wernicke's disease may reverse the ophthalmoplegia, ataxia, and nystagmus and relieve apathy and drowsiness. Alcoholic polyneuropathy and amblyopia may also be thus successfully treated. The psychic features of Wernicke's disease, the amnestic portion of Korsakoff's psychosis, and alcoholic dementia respond slowly and incompletely to thiamine therapy.

Korsakoff's syndrome consists of polyneuritis associated with loss of memory for recent events, confabulation, disorientation, and confusion. In **Wernicke's syndrome**, the oculomotor palsies are due to involvement of nuclei of the third or fourth cranial

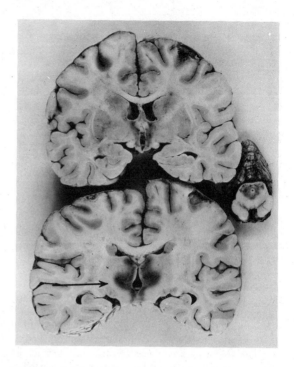

Figure 30–6. Wernicke's encephalopathy. Periventricular and periaqueductal hemorrhage, pigmentation, necrosis, and congestion in a 44-year-old alcoholic man.

nerve. Ptosis and pupillary changes are seen, as well as tremor due to involvement of the red nucleus. There may also be optic neuritis, retinal hemorrhages, ataxic gait, and muscular weakness. Progression from drowsiness, stupor, and delirium to death may occur within 2 weeks.

Quinquaud's sign, or toxic tremor, may occur in chronic alcoholism. When the patient's fingers are spread and the fingertips pressed against the examiner's hand held vertically, a series of slight shocks are felt after a few seconds, as if the phalanges of each finger were knocking together.

B. Methyl Alcohol: Acute methyl alcohol intoxication may be characterized by lethargy, headache, impaired vision, delirium, and coma. Impaired vision may persist after acute intoxication; visual acuity may be greatly reduced, and central scotomas and contracted peripheral visual fields may occur.

C. Morphine and Related Alkaloids: Acute poisoning is manifested by stupor, coma, respiratory depression, pinpoint pupils, cyanosis, and shock. Death due to respiratory failure may occur. Oxygen, artificial respiration, and a narcotic antagonist such as naloxone (Narcan) may be required. The suggested dose of naloxone hydrochloride is 0.4 mg intravenously, which may be repeated at intervals of 2–3 minutes 2 or 3 times. In addicts intoxicated by an overdose, a withdrawal reaction or an abstinence syndrome may be triggered by naloxone, so that the therapeutic level of this narcotic antagonist is best reached by increments.

Carbon Monoxide

Acute serious carbon monoxide intoxications usually terminate in coma and death. In those few who recover, hemiparesis, impaired memory, aphasia, hyperkinesia, and parkinsonism may develop.

Anticonvulsant Drugs (See Table 31–3.)

A. Hydantoins: Phenytoin (Dilantin) may produce ataxia, nystagmus, hypertrophy of the gums, and a morbilliform rash, which may be eliminated by discontinuing or reducing the drug.

B. Barbiturates: In therapeutic dosages, the barbiturate group may cause ataxia, thickness of speech, lethargy, and drowsiness. These symptoms usually disappear on reduction of dosage or withdrawal of the drug. With acute overdoses, coma, respiratory depression, cyanosis, loss of reflexes, and loss of pupillary reactions may occur. Chronic barbiturate poisoning is evidenced by mental changes, defective memory, emotional lability, nystagmus, ataxia, and tremor or weakness.

C. Bromides: Chronic bromidism may give rise to lethargy, ataxia, confusion, disorientation, delirium, and stupor. Chronic bromide poisoning is usually associated with an increased blood bromide level (above 150 mg/dL).

Chemotherapeutic Drugs

A. Streptomycin: Following high or prolonged dosage of streptomycin, vestibular and auditory nerve damage may occur, manifested by tinnitus, vertigo, and ataxia.

B. Quinine: Repeated use of quinine in large doses may be associated with visual loss (quinine amblyopia), pallor of optic disks, and papilledema.

C. Isoniazid: Excessive use of isoniazid in high dosage may cause polyneuritis, dizziness, headache, and convulsions in susceptible individuals.

D. Vincristine: This drug may cause a polyneuropathy with progressive symmetric sensory, motor, and reflex changes. Bowel and genitourinary dysfunction may also occur.

E. Procarbazine: Somnolence, confusion, agitation, and depression may be associated, and occasionally a mild polyneuropathy.

F. Cisplatin: Cisplatin may be associated with tinnitus and high-frequency hearing loss. Peripheral neuropathy may also occur.

Antihistaminic Drugs

Excessive amounts of diphenhydramine (Benadryl), tripelennamine (Pyribenzamine), and related compounds may cause drowsiness, headache, tremors, nervousness, excitement, and convulsions.

Chlorinated Insecticides

Acute poisoning with chlorophenothane (DDT), chlordane, and related compounds produces symptoms of hyperexcitability, vomiting, tremors, ataxia, and convulsions.

Stimulant Drugs

Strychnine is a component of various tonics and is commonly used in rodenticides. It may cause greatly increased reflex excitability, especially of the spinal cord. In acute intoxications, spasms of muscles (particularly extensor spasms of the extremities) of increasing severity and frequency, opisthotonos, and death from respiratory failure occur.

Picrotoxin, pentylenetetrazol (Metrazol), and nikethamide (Coramine) stimulate the spinal cord, medulla, and cerebral cortex. The principal effect of intoxication with these drugs is convulsions.

Caffeine in large doses stimulates the CNS and may cause convulsions.

Hemlock

The principal evidences of hemlock poisoning are convulsions and respiratory failure. Following ingestion of water hemlock (*Cicuta* species), abdominal pain, nausea, vomiting, diarrhea, cyanosis, convulsions, and respiratory failure may occur. Following ingestion of poison hemlock *(Conium maculatum)*, gradually increasing muscle weakness and respiratory failure may occur.

Lathyrism

A toxic agent found in the pea *Lathyrus sativus* is believed responsible for the selective pyramidal tract damage that occurs in lathyrism. This disorder, found in India and less often in Europe, is considered to be due to a variety of nitril compounds containing cyanide radicals that have been isolated from these legumes.

Snake Venoms

Snake venoms may produce pronounced neurotoxic effects. Victims generally die through paralysis of respiratory muscles. Venoms may have a pronounced curarizing effect on muscles. Weakness of limbs, oculomotor palsies, and ataxic gait appear first. Central effects, including analgesia, may also occur.

Hallucinogens

The "hallucinogens" are drugs that can produce transient schizophreniclike psychoses in humans. This group of drugs, most of which contain an indole ring in their chemical structure, includes lysergic acid diethylamide (LSD), yohimbine, harmine, ibogaine, mescaline, bufotenine, cannabis derivatives, tryptamine, and epinephrine breakdown products.

Different chemicals have been used in the past to induce "model psychoses." These include the following: (1) group composed of mescaline, DMT (N,N-dimethyltryptamine) and DET (diethyltryptamine), psilocybin, LSD, and close derivatives; (2) analogs of atropine; (3) phencyclidine (Sernyl); and (4) N-allylnormorphine.

Studies on the mode of action of hallucinogenic drugs may help ultimately in uncovering some of the biochemical features of disorders that may produce psychoses in humans.

Table 30—4. Recognition of acute intoxication in drug abuse. (Manifestations vary depending upon the individual, purity of drug, drug combinations, dosage, routes of administration, and duration of use.)

	Hallucinogens[1]	Cannabis (Marihuana)[2]	Narcotics[3]	Sedative-Hypnotics[4]	CNS Stimulants[5]
Physical signs					
Pupils	Dilated, react to light	Normal	Pinpoint, fixed	Normal	Dilated, react to light
Conjunctiva		Reddened			
Skin	Flushing, sweating, gooseflesh		Flushing, needle marks (IV)		Sweating, needle marks (IV)
Mouth		"Burnt leaves" odor	Yawning	Yawning	Dry
Respiration	Increased		Decreased, pulmonary edema (IV)	Decreased	Increased, shallow
Pulse rate	Increased	Increased	Decreased		Increased
Blood pressure	Increased	Postural hypotension	Decreased	Decreased	Increased
Deep reflexes	Hyperactive			Hypoactive	Hyperactive
Speech				Slurred	
Coordination				Incoordination, ataxia	
Psychiatric symptoms					
Mood	Range from ecstasy to panic	Euphoria	Euphoria, drowsiness	Excitement → somnolence → coma	Tense and jittery
Sensorium	Often clear		Usually dulled	Confusion	Clear (mild); confusion (severe)
Sensory perception	Distorted	Distorted			
Memory		Mild transient loss		Impaired	
Hallucinations	Any type (often kaleidoscopic)	Rare, any type			
Delusions	Variable, dose-connected	Paranoid, dose-connected			
Laboratory findings	Hyperglycemia (occasionally)		Drug detected in urine	Drug detected in blood and urine	

[1] Hallucinogens: LSD, mescaline, psilocybin, STP, DMT.
[2] Cannabis: Marihuana, hashish, THC.
[3] Narcotics: Opium, heroin, morphine, methadone, meperidine.
[4] Sedative-hypnotics: Barbiturates, chloral hydrate, meprobamate, glutethimide, chlordiazepoxide, diazepam.
[5] CNS stimulants: Amphetamines, cocaine.

Electrolytes

Depletion of electrolytes by vomiting, intestinal drainage, diet, etc, may affect the sensorium and may induce mental changes, muscular weakness, and seizures. Excessive intake of fluids may cause water intoxication and convulsions. Extremely high levels of blood sodium may cause malaise, restlessness, confusion, hallucinations, and convulsions and induce histologic changes in cerebral and renal tissues. Fluids in the form of 5% dextrose in water should be infused as needed once hypernatremia has been diagnosed.

Fatal or near-fatal acidosis may follow ingestion of large doses of ammonium chloride. The associated low serum potassium has a neuromuscular depressant tendency.

Serum magnesium and calcium may be reduced in malabsorption after resection of the small intestine or steatorrhea and may be associated with confusional states, seizures, hyperreflexia, tremors, and myoclonic jerks. Oral or intravenous magnesium salts are effective in treatment.

Neuroleptics

Neuroleptics are drugs used to treat many psychotic disorders, including those associated with organic brain syndromes, drug abuse, schizophrenia, depression, and mania. They may provide symptomatic relief from hallucinations, delusions, hyperactivity, negativism, and insomnia. Included in this group of drugs are phenothiazines, thioxanthenes, butyrophenones, dihydroindolones, and dibenzoxazepines.

Side-effects of neuroleptics may include dry mouth, blurred vision, urinary retention, ileus, glaucoma, orthostatic hypotension, impotence, inhibition of ejaculation, and cardiac arrhythmias. Extrapyramidal system side-effects may include akathisia, dystonias, parkinsonism, and tardive dyskinesia.

Tardive dyskinesia is characterized by abnormal involuntary stereotyped movements of the face, mouth, tongue, and limbs, with onset usually months or years after prolonged use of neuroleptic agents. It occurs more frequently in women after the age of 40 years and worsens under stress.

Antidepressants

Tricyclic antidepressants may produce anticholinergic effects such as blurred vision, dry mouth, constipation, urinary retention, orthostatic hypotension, and electrocardiographic changes. Monoamine oxidase inhibitors (eg, iproniazid) may produce orthostatic hypotension, hepatotoxicity, agitation, toxic psychosis, and sensitivity to exogenous amines with tyramine such as liver, cheese, sausage, etc.

Sedative-Hypnotics

This mixed group of drugs, which includes the benzodiazepines and barbiturates, has hypnotic and sedating properties, decreases anxiety, and depresses brain function. Some have anticonvulsant and muscle relaxant properties. In general, they are additive and cross-dependent. With chronic excessive use, drug dependency, tolerance, and withdrawal symptoms similar to those of alcoholism appear (see p 438).

NEUROPATHIES

Polyneuritis (Multiple Neuritis, Peripheral Neuropathy)

Polyneuritis is a syndrome characterized by widespread sensory and motor disturbances of the peripheral nerves. It may appear at any age, although it is most common in young or middle-aged adults, especially men. A noninflammatory degeneration of the peripheral nerves is usually present.

Polyneuritis may be caused by (1) chronic intoxications (eg, alcohol, carbon disulfide, benzene, phosphorus, sulfonamides); (2) infections (eg, meningitis, diphtheria, syphilis, tuberculosis, pneumonia, Guillain-Barré syndrome, mumps); (3) metabolic causes (eg, diabetes mellitus, gout, pregnancy, rheumatism, porphyria, polyarteritis nodosa, lupus erythematosus); (4) nutritional causes (eg, beriberi, other vitamin deficiencies, cachectic states); and (5) malignancies.

Four major pathologic types have been recognized: (1) axonal, or "dying back," neuropathies (eg, nutritional, toxic, some metabolic neuropathies); (2) demyelinating neuropathies (eg, postinfectious or Guillain-Barré neuropathies); (3) chronic, often hereditary neuropathies (eg, Charcot-Marie-Tooth syndrome, Déjérine-Sottas syndrome, Refsum's disease); and (4) vascular neuropathies (eg, polyarteritis nodosa, diabetes mellitus).

Symptoms usually develop slowly over a period of weeks. Notable exceptions with rapid onset may occur in infections with overlying alcoholic polyneuritis. Pains, tenderness, paresthesias, weakness and fatigability, and sensory impairment may be present. The pains may be mild or, occasionally, burning and sharp. Muscular weakness is usually greatest in the distal portions of the extremities. Impaired sensory perception, especially of vibration, is frequent; in alcoholic and arsenical polyneuritis, severe and extensive sensory defects may occur. The cutaneous sensory defect may consist of hypesthesia or anesthesia in an irregular stocking or glove distribution.

Tendon reflexes are usually depressed or absent. With paralyzed toes, the plantar response may be absent; with weak abdominal muscles, abdominal skin reflexes may be diminished or absent. Flaccid weakness and muscular atrophy of affected parts may occur, especially in the distal portions of the extremities. Footdrop with associated steppage gait may result.

Trophic changes of the skin of the extremities are manifested by a glossy red skin and impairment of the sweating mechanism. Muscles and nerves may be tender and hypersensitive to pressure and palpation.

Remove the patient from exposure to toxic agents (eg, alcohol, lead). In lead polyneuritis, calcium disodium edathamil (Versenate) may be beneficial. In arsenical polyneuritis, give dimercaprol (BAL).

Attempt to obtain optimal metabolism of nerve tissue by administration of a high-calorie diet and by liberal use of vitamins, especially of the B complex. The entire B complex can be administered with thiamine hydrochloride, 15 mg 3–4 times daily orally or parenterally, and dried yeast (brewer's yeast), 10–30 g daily.

Place the patient at bed rest and forbid use of the affected limb. If a lower extremity is affected, keep a cradle over the foot of the bed to prevent pressure of bed covers. Give analgesics as necessary to control pain. After pain has subsided, massage and passive motion may be of value. Encourage active motion at the same time. Prevent contractures by means of splints and passive stretching.

In most forms of polyneuritis, recovery may occur once the cause has been corrected. In some cases, the disorder progresses for weeks, remains stationary for a time, and goes on to slow recovery in 6–12 months. Objective sensory changes usually disappear first, and paralyses later; dysesthesias may persist during recovery.

Landry-Guillain-Barré Syndrome

In this syndrome, patients often develop polyneuritis 1–2 weeks after a mild respiratory infection or gastroenteritis. Early lower extremity weakness extends within a few days to the upper extremities and face. Facial diplegia, dysphagia, and dysarthria commonly occur. Weakness of the trunk and extremity muscles may be severe; flaccid paraplegia and respiratory muscle weakness requiring a respirator may occur.

Sensory changes are not usually present, but muscle tenderness and nerve sensitivity to pressure may occur. Symptoms may progress over a week to several weeks with variable prognosis. Death may occur as a result of respiratory failure or intermittent infection within a few weeks after onset. Gradual recovery may take days to weeks; the duration of paralysis in untreated cases is variable.

The cerebrospinal fluid usually shows "albuminocytologic dissociation,'' especially at the height of the disorder, when the total protein may be several hundred milligrams per deciliter, with few or no white cells. Alteration in the immune responses of peripheral nerve has been suggested, with hypersensitivity or autoimmune response of nerves leading to demyelination and often a mononuclear inflammatory reaction of peripheral nerves. Although good results have been reported after intensive treatment with steroids, many clinicians doubt their effectiveness.

Refsum's Syndrome

This is a hereditary (recessive) neuropathy manifested by retinitis pigmentosa, night blindness, concentric constriction of visual fields, chronic polyneuritis, progressive nerve deafness, and elevated cerebrospinal fluid protein.

Rigorous dietary fat restriction can reduce plasma levels of phytanic acid and may lead to some restoration of nerve function.

Déjérine-Sottas Syndrome (Hypertrophic Interstitial Neuritis)

This is a rare heredofamilial disease characterized by chronic progressive polyneuritis associated with collagenous degeneration of the endoneurium or sheath of Schwann, with degeneration of myelin sheaths and nerve fibers. Thickened peripheral nerves may be palpable and visible.

Peroneal Muscular Atrophy (Charcot-Marie-Tooth Disease)

This relatively rare disease is characterized by clubbing of the feet and muscular wasting that begins in the legs and later involves the muscles of the distal portion of the thigh and upper extremities. Atrophy of the leg muscles gives a characteristic ''stork leg'' appearance; atrophy usually starts in the intrinsic muscles of the feet and in the peroneal muscles. The onset of symptoms is usually before age 20 years but is sometimes delayed until age 40 or 50 years. Objective loss of sensation occasionally occurs.

Macroglobulinemia (Waldenström's Primary Macroglobulinemia)

This disorder, characterized by excess of abnormal macroglobulin in the blood, may be associated with severe polyneuropathy, generalized exhaustion, loss of weight, a bleeding diathesis (with normal clotting factors), and Raynaud's syndrome.

Neuritis

Inflammation or degeneration of the peripheral nerves may be local or widespread. **Mononeuritis** (localized neuritis) affects a small group of nerves or a single nerve trunk. Causative factors include trauma (contusion, tearing, compression, or stretching of the nerve), chronic intoxications (by alcohol or metallic poisons), and infections (local or generalized, or by extension from adjacent infected parts). The inflammatory reaction may be one of 3 types: in perineuritis

(limited to the perineurium) and interstitial neuritis (affecting the interstices), the nerves are swollen and red. Parenchymatous neuritis affects the nerve fibers themselves (myelin sheaths, axis cylinders, and neurilemmas), causing a shrunken, pale, translucent appearance. Symptoms include irritative phenomena (pain, tenderness, paresthesias), motor loss (flaccid paralysis with muscle atrophy and reaction of degeneration), sensory loss, and, at times, trophic and vasomotor changes. The prognosis depends upon the extent and character of the injury. Treatment is directed toward removal of the cause, relief of pain, and prevention of contractures.

Neuralgia

Neuralgia is a syndrome affecting various sensory nerves and characterized by sudden paroxysmal attacks of pain, usually of short duration, occurring in the distribution of the nerve fibers and not associated with pathologic changes in the nerve. An attack may be brought on by various causes, eg, local pressure, cold, movement, pressure on the nerve trunk, or stimulation of a ''trigger zone.'' Vasomotor symptoms may accompany an attack, eg, reddening of the skin, sweating, edema, tearing, and excessive salivation. The various types of neuralgia include the following: trigeminal, sphenopalatine, glossopharyngeal, superior laryngeal, cervico-occipital, brachial, intercostal, phrenic, visceral, lumbar, sciatic, and coccygeal.

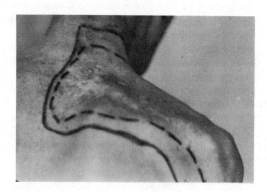

Figure 30–7. Area of sensory deficit after lower cervical rhizotomy for postherpetic neuralgia in a man with Hodgkin's disease. (Solid line = pain; dotted line = touch.)

Trigeminal (Trifacial) Neuralgia (Tic Douloureux)

Trigeminal neuralgia is characterized by a sudden attack of excruciating pain of short duration along the distribution of the fifth cranial nerve. The attack is normally precipitated by stimulation (usually mild) of a ''trigger zone'' in the area of the pain and is characterized by recurrent paroxysms of sharp, stabbing pains in the distribution of one or more branches of the nerve. The onset is usually in middle or late life, and the incidence is higher in women. The pain may be described as searing or burning, occurring in lightninglike jabs, lasting only 1–2 seconds or as long as 15 minutes. The frequency of attacks varies from many times daily to several times a month or a year. Attempts are made to immobilize the face during conversation or to swallow food without chewing in order to avoid irritating the trigger zone.

Medical treatment is sometimes unsatisfactory, but the following have often been tried before surgery is undertaken:

(1) Carbamazepine (Tegretol) is effective in the medical treatment of trigeminal neuralgia. Give 200-mg tablets 3–4 times daily until facial pain is entirely suppressed, after which medication may be slowly reduced or withdrawn. Occasional side-effects include skin rash, nausea, ataxia, dizziness, and drowsiness.

(2) Anticonvulsants, eg, phenytoin (Dilantin), 0.1 g 4 times daily, or vasodilators, eg, tolazoline (Priscoline), 50 mg 4 times daily, have been reported

to be beneficial in some cases.

(3) Massive doses of vitamin B_{12} (1 mg intramuscularly daily for 10 days) have been reported to relieve the severe pain.

(4) Injection of alcohol into the ganglion or the branches of the trigeminal nerve may produce relief from pain for several months or years. Repeated injections may be required later.

Surgery may be required if medical treatment affords no relief. Percutaneous electrocoagulation of the preganglionic rootlets under local anesthesia is effective in some resistant cases of trigeminal neuralgia.

In most cases, the paroxysms of pain are present for several weeks or months. Remissions may last from a few days to as long as several months or years. As patients become older, remissions tend to become shorter.

31 | Epilepsy

EPILEPSY

Epilepsy is characterized by sudden, transient alterations of brain function, usually with motor, sensory, autonomic, or psychic symptoms and often accompanied by alterations in consciousness. Coincidental pronounced brain wave alterations in the electroencephalogram (EEG) may be detected during these episodes.

Cause (See Tables 31–1 and 31–2.)

Epilepsy was formerly classified as "idiopathic" or jacksonian. With the development of more precise diagnostic tests and instruments, idiopathic epilepsy has been found in many cases to be caused by abnormally active brain tissue resulting from injury, infection, or unknown agents. Idiopathic epilepsy tends to run in families.

Seizures indistinguishable from those of idiopathic epilepsy may occur in such types of organic brain disease as brain tumor, cerebrovascular accident, posttraumatic cerebral scar, and intracranial infection. Metabolic disorders such as uremia, hypoglycemia, hypocalcemia, and excessive hydration may also give rise to seizures.

In children, the most common causes of symptomatic epilepsy are birth injury and anoxia, inflammatory brain lesions, cerebrovascular accidents, head injuries, and congenital brain malformations.

In susceptible individuals, physical stimuli (eg, light, sound, touch) may precipitate seizures. In some epileptics, seizures characteristically occur during sleep. Other factors may indirectly affect the susceptibility of a particular patient to seizures, eg, excessive alcohol intake, emotional tension, fatigue, or lack of food and sleep.

Seizures may occur in groups over a period of hours or days. In individual patients, the pattern of seizures is apt to be stereotyped. The patient may not be personally aware of the nature of the attacks, so that verification by a witness is desirable. Temporary postseizure paresis (Todd's paralysis) may occur, particularly with seizures arising in the motor cortex.

Pathology

Since epilepsy is a syndrome rather than a specific disease entity, it is not surprising that in most cases of idiopathic epilepsy histologic examination fails to show specific pathologic tissue alterations. Despite many biochemical and physiologic studies in patients with convulsions, the pathophysiology of convulsive seizures remains obscure. Seizures are more apt to occur in patients with organic brain lesions than in those with a normal CNS.

Pathologic Physiology

The metabolic activity of the brain varies somewhat with the state of functional activity. When there is a general increase in neuronal activity, as in convulsive states and in states of diffuse neuromuscular activity, metabolic activity is increased. However, there is no significant change in overall metabolic activity in highly localized types of cerebral function. The decrease both in oxygen consumption of brain and in activity of enzymes associated with glucose utilization in the older age groups may be due to progressive decrease in the ratio of neurons to glial cells.

Acetylcholine and cholinesterase activity has been demonstrated in every cortical layer of the normal brain and is roughly proportionate to neuron density and size. Epileptic cortical foci are reported to have elevated cholinesterase activity, and changes in the bound acetylcholine of the brain may be demonstrated before and during experimentally induced seizures in animals. These findings have been interpreted to indicate that alteration in acetylcholine metabolism occurs in conjunction with epileptic brain abnormalities.

However, other neurochemical mechanisms unrelated to acetylcholine metabolism may also be important in the production of convulsive seizures. Increased production of ammonia may immediately precede the onset of experimental seizures, and abnormalities of potassium distribution have been found in convulsed brain segments. Toxic epileptogenic agents (eg, fluoroacetate) block the citric acid cycle while producing convulsions. Inhibition of glutamine synthesis in the brain occurs after treatment with methionine sulfoxime, the toxic convulsant agent of nitrogen chloride (Agene). A deficiency of pyridoxine causes seizures in infants and animals, and certain convulsant drugs such as the carbazide series act by inducing pyridoxine deficiency. Glutamine and asparagine can reverse the defective glutamic acid metabolism of certain types of epileptogenic cortex, thus

Table 31-1. Causes of epilepsy.*

An etiologic classification of the epilepsies similar to that in use at the National Institute of Neurological Diseases and Blindness includes epilepsy due to the following causes:

Genetic and birth factors:
1. Genetic influences (idiopathic, essential, cryptogenic)
2. Congenital abnormalities (including chromosomal abnormalities)
3. Antenatal factors (infections, drugs, anoxia, etc)
4. Perinatal factors: Birth trauma, asphyxia neonatorum, perinatal infections
5. Perinatal jaundice: Prematurity

Infectious disorders:
1. Meningitis: Purulent, tuberculous, viral, parasitic, fungal
2. Epidural and subdural abscess
3. Brain abscess and granuloma: Metastatic, direct spread
4. Encephalitis: Viral
5. Other (including parasites)
6. Fever (febrile convulsions)

Toxic factors:
1. Inorganic substances (eg, carbon monoxide)
2. Metallic substances (eg, lead, mercury)
3. Organic substances: Alcohol, other
4. Drugs
5. Allergic disorders: Ingestion of foreign protein, vaccination or injection of foreign protein
6. Pregnancy
7. Other: Uremia or other toxic medical conditions

Trauma or physical agents:
1. Acute craniocerebral injuries
2. Subdural or epidural hematoma and effusion
3. Posttraumatic meningocerebral cicatrization
4. Anoxia or hyperoxia (including drowning)

Circulatory disturbances:
1. Subarachnoid hemorrhage
2. Sinus thrombosis
3. Encephalomalacia due to thrombosis, embolism, hemorrhage
4. Hypertensive encephalopathy
5. Arteriosclerosis and arterial occlusive disease, intracranial and extracranial
6. Vasospasm (eg, migraine)
7. Syncope
8. Changes in blood (anemia, hemorrhagic diathesis)

Metabolic and nutritional disturbances:
1. Electrolyte and water imbalance: Sodium, calcium, overhydration or dehydration, other
2. Carbohydrate metabolism: Hypoglycemia, diabetes mellitus, glycogen storage disease
3. Protein metabolism: Phenylketonuria, porphyria, other
4. Fat metabolism: Lipid storage diseases, other
5. Vitamin deficiency: Pyridoxine deficiency, other
6. Endocrine disorders: Menstruation, other

Neoplasms:
1. Primary intracranial tumors
2. Metastatic tumors
3. Lymphoma and leukemia
4. Blood vessel tumors and vascular malformations (eg, arteriovenous malformations, Sturge-Weber syndrome)

Heredofamilial and degenerative diseases:
1. Multiple sclerosis
2. Tuberous sclerosis
3. Cerebellar degeneration with convulsions
4. Other

Psychogenic causes

Cause unknown

*Reproduced, with permission, from Robb P: *Epilepsy.* NINDB Monograph No. 1, US Department of Health, Education, & Welfare, USPHS Publication No. 1357, 1965.

inhibiting seizures. Chronic experimental epilepsy is readily induced in monkeys by treatment of the cerebral cortex with aluminum hydroxide; other metals may also be effective. In guinea pigs with allergic encephalomyelitis, convulsive seizures have been noted to be correlated directly with marked increase of intracellular sodium and to be unrelated to water increase or potassium depletion. In one study, hamsters developed convulsive seizures after large cream meals or meals of saturated fatty acids; however, after vegetable and fish oil meals of the same size, only occasional seizures or no seizures occurred. Reduction in available oxygen in brain occurred after cream meals and varied directly with the amount of cream feedings.

Classification*

In general, an attempt should be made to determine the anatomic site of onset and the cause. On the basis of clinical findings, the seizures may be classified as follows:

*McNaughton's proposed classification of the epilepsies is given in Table 31–2.

A. Grand Mal (Tonic-Clonic Seizures): A typical aura may signal an impending attack. This aura is usually specific for the individual patient and may consist of a sensation of nausea or numbness, an odor, a visual image, or a flash of memory. Loss of consciousness usually ensues, and the patient falls to the floor. The patient may cry out and frequently incurs some bodily injury. Convulsions usually follow; the patient lies stiff and mildly rigid for as long as 1–2 minutes, and the muscles of the body are in a state of mild tonic contraction. A clonic stage follows in which rhythmic, severe, synchronous, convulsive movements of the body occur. Bowel and bladder control is frequently lost, and biting injuries to the tongue are common. More rarely, fractures of bones may occur. A variable period of sleep and stupor, lasting usually 1–4 hours, follows this phase. Responses are abnormal in a patient who is awake, and later there is little recollection of events occurring during this period. Upon full recovery from the attack, the patient frequently is aware of painful muscles.

B. Petit Mal (Absence Seizures): Seizures may occur in which the patient has a minor or abortive

Table 31–2. Classification of the epilepsies.*

Group	Attack Pattern	Electrographic Findings	Radiographic Findings	Clinical and Pathologic Findings
Focal epilepsy (cortical or subcortical)	Focal attack pattern depends on site of origin in brain. This includes focal temporal seizures with automatism. Attacks major or minor in degree.	Focal spikes, sharp waves, etc.	Cranial growth asymmetry, intracranial calcification, etc, may be present; pneumogram may show focal change, depending on type of lesion.	Clinical examination may show focal neurologic signs. Attacks secondary to a variety of lesions: agenesis and other congenital abnormalities, birth injury, focal vascular lesions and anomalies, syphilis, lead, parasites, encephalitis, degenerative diseases, diffuse vascular diseases, scar, neoplasm, abscess; or no lesion may be found.
Central or "centrencephalic" epilepsy	Attacks major or minor (true "petit mal"); little or no warning; movements symmetric. Focal attack patterns unusual. Myoclonic jerks common. Automatism may occur.	3-Hz wave and spike, bilaterally synchronous. Bitemporal 4- to 6-Hz waves.	Cranium usually normal. Pneumogram normal or may show symmetric enlargement of ventricles.	Examination usually normal. Cause usually unknown. Birth trauma and anoxia possible causative factors.
Epilepsy, unlocalized (of known cause)	Focal attack pattern unusual or varied. Attacks major or minor in degree.	Generalized multiforme (including slow spike and wave), or may be normal.	Pneumogram normal or shows diffuse changes. Usually atrophic.	Findings vary with cause: (1) diffuse cerebral lesions, as listed under focal epilepsy; (2) extracerebral causes, eg, fever hypoglycemia, cerebral anemia, anoxia.
Epilepsy, unlocalized (of unknown cause)	Focal attack pattern unusual. Attacks major or minor in degree.	Normal or indefinite.	Normal or indefinite.	Unknown or indefinite. Many patients fall first into this category. Further study may reclassify under one of the above groups.

*Modified by FL McNaughton and reproduced, with permission, from McNaughton FL: *The Classification of the Epilepsies.* Epilepsia (Third Series), Vol 1, Nov 1952.

Penfield & Erickson attempt to relate type of seizure and anatomic localization, as follows:

	Clinical Type	Localization
Somatic motor	Generalized (grand mal)	Complete motor
	Jacksonian (local motor)	Prerolandic gyrus
	Masticatory	Lower rolandic
	Simple adversive	Frontal
	Tonic postural (decerebrate, opisthotonic)	Brain stem
Somatic sensory (auras)	Somatosensory	Postrolandic gyrus
	Visual	Occipital
	Auditory	Temporal
	Vertiginous	Temporal
	Olfactory	Infratemporal
Visceral	Autonomic	Diencephalic
Psychic	Dreamy state	Temporal
	Petit mal	
	Automatism (ictal and postictal)	
	Psychotic states (secondary)	

Penfield & Erickson also relate age at onset of seizures to the presumptive cause, as follows:

Age at Onset		Presumptive Cause
Infancy	(0–2)	Birth injury, degeneration, congenital
Childhood	(2–10)	Birth injury, febrile thrombosis, trauma, cryptogenic
Adolescence	(10–20)	Trauma, obscure causes
Youth	(20–35)	Trauma, neoplasm
Middle age	(35–55)	Neoplasm, trauma, arteriosclerosis
Senescence	(55–70)	Arteriosclerosis, neoplasm

attack not associated with falling or convulsive movements of the body. Instead there is a momentary or transient loss of consciousness, so fleeting or camouflaged in ordinary activity that neither the patient nor anyone else may be entirely aware of it. The "petit mal triad," according to Lennox, includes myoclonic jerks, akinetic seizures, and brief absences, all of which usually are accompanied by the specific 3-Hz spike and wave pattern. In classic petit mal, there is sudden vacant expression, cessation of motor activity, and sometimes loss of muscle tone. Abrupt return of consciousness with resumption of mental and physical activity occurs. As many as 100 attacks a day may occur.

Myoclonic jerks of limbs or muscles may occur without evident alteration of consciousness or in association with a typical absence. Myoclonic jerks tend to occur more frequently in the morning and on going to sleep; normal individuals may have rare myoclonic jerks in drowsiness or light sleep.

Akinetic attacks are seizures of sudden, brief loss of postural tone, with the subject slumping a little before realizing it or recovering just after the body or knees touch the ground.

Myoclonus epilepsy (Unverricht's familial myoclonic epilepsy) is a familial convulsive disorder manifested by generalized seizures. It occurs usually in prepuberal girls. After several years, myoclonia (irregular, lightninglike, arrhythmic jerks of muscle groups, unaccompanied by movements of the extremities) becomes progressively more intense and widespread and is associated with gradual dementia and perhaps signs of a bulbar disorder.

C. Psychomotor Seizures (Complex Partial Seizures): This category now includes practically all types of attacks that do not conform to the classic descriptions of grand mal, focal jacksonian seizure, or petit mal. Automatisms, patterned movements, apparently purposeful movements, incoherent speech, turn-ings of the head and eyes, smacking of the lips, twisting and writhing movements of the extremities, clouding of consciousness, and amnesia commonly occur. It has been postulated that "equivalent states" exist in which the patient exhibits a behavior disturbance rather than the classic convulsion. Temporal lobe foci (spikes, sharp waves, or combinations) are frequently associated with this type of epilepsy. Accentuation of electroencephalographic abnormalities during light phases of sleep is sometimes striking.

D. Jacksonian Epilepsy (Simple Partial Seizures): Seizures due to focal irritation of a portion of the motor cortex may be confined to the appropriate peripheral area. Consciousness may be retained, and the seizure may spread over the rest of the adjacent motor cortex to involve adjacent peripheral parts. This type of seizure is most commonly associated with organic lesions such as brain tumor or scar.

E. Status Epilepticus: This serious disorder consists of a train of severe seizures with relatively short intervals or no intervals between. The patient becomes exhausted and frequently hyperthermic. Death not uncommonly occurs during attacks.

F. Epilepsia Partialis Continua (Kojevnokoff's Epilepsy): Convulsive activity of one part of the body that may continue steadily (or with brief interruptions) over long periods of time is characteristic. Localized, continuing, myoclonic seizures or focal motor seizures, usually without spread, may occur.

G. Reflex Epilepsy: Focal or generalized seizures associated with concomitant alterations in the EEG can be evoked in some patients following stimulation of a somatic trigger zone.

H. Febrile Convulsions: Fever and convulsions are commonly encountered in the very young. A febrile convulsion is apt to be the first convulsion of an epileptic child, and febrile convulsions are said to be about twice as common among children with a family history of epilepsy. Various explanations of this relationship have been offered, including the following: (1) Fever results from the liberation of heat and energy that occurs during muscular contractions caused by the seizure. (2) Fever results from hypothalamic seizure discharge. (3) Fever and convulsions both are caused by an infectious organism. (4) Excessive hydration and drugs to combat infection may cause convulsions. (5) Convulsions may result from a pathologic brain reaction induced by an infection. (6) The immature brain may respond to high fever and an infectious agent with a convulsion.

The prognosis of febrile convulsions varies. Many children subsequently develop psychomotor seizures. Nonfebrile convulsions also occur in a majority of patients with a history of febrile convulsions. Most children with a history of febrile convulsions have had only 1–2 such febrile seizures.

I. Massive Spasms (Infantile Spasms): This type of seizure is fairly common in the first 2 years of life. It is characterized by sudden strong contraction of most of the body musculature, often resulting in transient doubling up of the body and flexion-adduction of

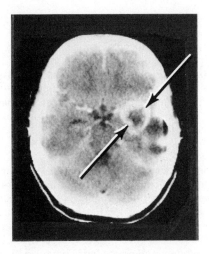

Figure 31–1. CT scan showing temporal lobe mass in a 55-year-old woman with focal motor seizures.

the limbs. Attacks may occur singly or in a series beginning with strong, prolonged contractions that become progressively weaker at progressively longer intervals. Attacks are apt to occur in children with evidence of motor and mental retardation and may disappear after age 3 years. Electroencephalography frequently shows a pattern of hypsarhythmia; a favorable response to treatment with corticotropin has been noted in some cases.

International Classification of Epileptic Seizures*

I. Partial seizures (seizures beginning locally):
   A. Partial seizures with elementary symptomatology (generally without impairment of consciousness):
      1. With motor symptoms (includes jacksonian seizures).
      2. With special sensory or somatosensory symptoms.
      3. With autonomic symptoms.
      4. Compound forms.
   B. Partial seizures with complex symptomatology (generally with impairment of consciousness) (temporal lobe or psychomotor seizures):
      1. With impairment of consciousness only.
      2. With cognitive symptomatology.
      3. With affective symptomatology.
      4. With "psychosensory" symptomatology.
      5. With "psychomotor" symptomatology (automatisms).
      6. Compound forms.
   C. Partial seizures secondarily generalized.
II. Generalized seizures (bilaterally symmetric and without local onset):
      1. Absences (petit mal).
      2. Bilateral massive epileptic myoclonus.
      3. Infantile spasms.
      4. Clonic seizures.
      5. Tonic seizures.
      6. Tonic-clonic seizures (grand mal).
      7. Atonic seizures.
      8. Akinetic seizures.
III. Unilateral seizures (or predominantly).
IV. Unclassified epileptic seizures (due to incomplete data).

Diagnosis

The diagnosis of epilepsy may be made on the basis of a history of recurrent seizures and the observation of a typical seizure. Physical and neurologic examination, skull x-rays, cerebrospinal fluid manometrics, cell and protein studies, CT scan, brain scan, cerebral angiography, and air studies may be helpful. Electroencephalography has become a most objective tool in the diagnosis of epilepsy. With the use of

*Abstracted from Gastaut H: Clinical and electroencephalographical classification of epileptic seizures. *Epilepsia* 1970; **11**:102.

provocative measures such as intravenous pentylenetetrazol (Metrazol) and barbiturates, sleep, hyperventilation, and postural changes, accurate diagnoses of epilepsy can be made with a fair degree of certainty.

Behavioral or emotional components may be so pronounced as to mask the underlying convulsive disorder. Following a grand mal episode or a series of brief seizures, patients may remain confused for minutes to hours. Disorientation, anxiety, hallucinations, paranoid delusions, excitement, and aggressive activity may be overwhelming.

Patients with petit mal, especially when attacks are frequent, may appear to be daydreaming; staring and blank spells often occur without the patient's knowledge. Impaired learning ability, short attention span, and restlessness are often associated. Petit mal status may be diagnosed as aimless wandering, erratic behavior, or incoherent speech.

Automatisms may occur, particularly with seizures of temporal lobe origin. Complex acts, movements, walking, lip-smacking, chewing movements, etc, may occur for periods of seconds to 10 minutes. An abnormal feeling of familiarity, called déjà vu—a feeling of having lived through the present situation before, including sights, sounds, thoughts, or experiences—may be present. Depersonalization, in which familiar things, faces, etc, become strange, may also appear occasionally as part of a seizure syndrome. There may be fear or depression at the beginning of a convulsion and automatic thinking of a stereotyped nature. Increased irritability, especially before grand mal episodes, and variable grades of mental dullness may be manifested. Episodic psychoses in epileptic patients may be part of the epileptic disorder.

Children with epilepsy often appear to be restless, hyperactive, aggressive, and irritable. These traits as well as learning difficulties and apparent mental retardation sometimes may be improved by adequate anticonvulsant therapy.

Complications

Fractures and soft tissue injuries may occur during seizures. Mental and emotional changes, particularly in poorly controlled epileptics, sometimes occur. Behavioral or emotional components may mask an underlying convulsive disorder. Examples are disorientation, hallucinations, excitement, incoherent speech, erratic behavior, automatisms, mental dullness, and irritability.

Treatment

The objective of therapy is complete suppression of symptoms, though in many cases this is not possible. Most epileptics must continue to receive anticonvulsant therapy throughout life. However, if seizures are entirely controlled for 3–5 years, the dosage may be slowly reduced (over a period of 1–2 years) and finally withdrawn to ascertain if seizures will recur.

The patient must be made aware of the nature of the disease and encouraged to become a member of local branches of groups interested in the welfare of epileptics, such as the Epilepsy Foundation of America. Patients may receive information regarding research and treatment from these organizations.

Epileptic patients should avoid hazardous occupations and driving. It is important to maintain a regular program of activity to keep the patient in optimal physical condition, but excessive fatigue must be avoided. Forbid all alcohol. Treat emotional factors as indicated. Impress upon the patient the absolute necessity of faithful adherence to the drug regimen. An epilepsy identification card should be carried at all times.

Major anticonvulsant drugs include hydantoin derivatives (phenytoin, mephenytoin, and ethotoin), oxazolidinediones (trimethadione and paramethadione), carbamazepine, barbiturates (phenobarbital, mephobarbital, metharbital, and primidone), and succinimides (phensuximide, methsuximide, and ethosuximide).

Monitoring blood levels of antiepileptic drugs has increased the safety and efficacy of drug therapy in epilepsy. For most patients, the effective blood levels of the major anticonvulsants (in μg/mL) are phenytoin, 10; phenobarbital, 15; primidone, 5; ethosuximide, 40; and carbamazepine, 4.

Except in status epilepticus, no specific treatment is usually given during an attack other than to protect the patient from injury. Anticonvulsant measures (Table 31–3) in the 4 principal types of epilepsy are as follows:

A. Grand Mal: *Caution:* Never withdraw anticonvulsant drugs suddenly.

1. Phenytoin sodium (Dilantin)–This is the drug of choice. Give 0.1 g after the evening meal for 3–7 days, increasing dosage by 0.1 g daily every week until seizures are brought under control. If attacks are severe and frequent, it may be necessary to begin on the first visit with 0.3 g daily. The average dose is 0.4–0.6 g daily. After convulsive seizures are controlled, the dosage may be reduced if desired, but the dosage should immediately be raised again if symptoms return. A therapeutic serum level of phenytoin is 10–20 μg/mL.

2. Phenobarbital–If the patient is on maximum dosage of phenytoin and there is inadequate response, give phenobarbital in addition to phenytoin, increasing the dosage as with phenytoin, while maintaining full dosage of phenytoin. Some clinicians prefer to begin with phenobarbital and maintain without phenytoin if possible. In many cases, the 2 drugs used in combination are more effective than either drug used alone.

3. Mephenytoin (Mesantoin)–If excessive gum hypertrophy results from the use of phenytoin, mephenytoin may be tried in its place. The dosage is the same. This drug may be effective where grand mal and petit mal coexist. Do not change suddenly to mephenytoin but gradually substitute for phenytoin. Combinations of both may prove more useful than the individual drugs.

4. Other drugs–Bromides, primidone (Myso-

line), mephobarbital (Mebaral), or ethotoin (Peganone) may be tried (Table 31–3).

B. Petit Mal: Ethosuximide (Zarontin) is very effective in petit mal and is the drug of choice in many centers. Valproic acid (Depakene) is effective in refractory or atypical cases of petit mal. Other succinimides (methsuximide [Celontin] and phensuximide [Milontin]) and the diones (trimethadione [Tridione] and paramethadione [Paradione]) are highly effective. Unfortunately, trimethadione is not an entirely safe drug, since it causes bone marrow depression in some patients. *Caution:* Whenever this drug is used, perform a complete blood count once or twice a week for the first month, then every 2 weeks for 2–3 months, and monthly thereafter. Begin with 0.3 g daily and increase the daily dose by 0.3 g every 7 days until attacks are controlled. Do not give more than 2 g daily.

If grand mal seizures occur also, trimethadione may aggravate this tendency; it may therefore be necessary to administer medication for grand mal seizures simultaneously and in some cases to stop the trimethadione. Paramethadione (Paradione) is said to be less toxic than trimethadione. It is almost equally effective in petit mal attacks and may be effective where other drugs fail. Observe precautions as for trimethadione.

Phenobarbital, acetazolamide (Diamox), or mephobarbital (Mebaral) may prove useful (Table 31–3).

C. Status Epilepticus: In many centers, the drug of choice is diazepam (Valium) given intravenously. Diazepam (5–10 mg) injected slowly intravenously (taking at least 1 minute for each 5 mg) is highly effective and may be repeated in 2–4 hours if necessary. Hypotension and respiratory depression may occur occasionally as side-effects. Resuscitative facilities should be readily available when intravenous diazepam or other parenteral anticonvulsant drugs are used for status epilepticus. Amobarbital sodium (Amytal Sodium), 0.4–1 g intravenously, may be given. Phenobarbital sodium, 0.4–0.8 g injected slowly intravenously, may be used. Paraldehyde, 1–2 mL diluted in a triple volume of saline and given slowly intravenously, is an effective alternative. If the convulsion continues, repeat the intravenous dose *very slowly and cautiously* or give 8–12 mL intramuscularly. Phenytoin sodium (Dilantin Sodium) may be injected intravenously at a rate not to exceed 50 mg/min; a total dosage of 1000 mg may be required. General anesthesia may be used if all measures fail. Phenytoin sodium (Dilantin Sodium), 250–500 mg intramuscularly daily, or phenobarbital sodium, 30–60 mg intramuscularly 4 times daily—*or both*—may be required until the patient is able to take medication orally.

D. Psychomotor Epilepsy: Patients must be watched and guarded to prevent injury to themselves or others. Phenytoin (Dilantin), with or without phenobarbital, as for grand mal epilepsy, is the drug of choice. Carbamazepine (Tegretol) may be effective in

Table 31—3. Drugs used in epilepsy.

Drug	Average Daily Dose	Indications	Toxicity and Precautions
Phenytoin sodium (Dilantin)	0.3—0.6 g in divided doses	Safest drug for grand mal, some cases of psychomotor epilepsy. May accentuate petit mal.	Gum hypertrophy (dental hygiene); nervousness, rash, ataxia, drowsiness, nystagmus (reduce dosage).
Mephenytoin (Mesantoin)	0.3—0.5 g in divided doses	Grand mal, some cases of psychomotor epilepsy. Effective when grand mal and petit mal coexist.	Nervousness, ataxia, nystagmus (reduce dosage); pancytopenia (frequent blood counts); exfoliative dermatitis (stop drug if severe skin eruption develops).
Ethotoin (Peganone)	2—3 g in divided doses	Grand mal.	Dizziness, fatigue, skin rash (decrease dose or discontinue).
Trimethadione (Tridione)	0.3—2 g in divided doses	Petit mal.	Bone marrow depression, pancytopenia, exfoliative dermatitis (as above); photophobia (usually disappears; dark glasses); nephrosis (frequent urinalysis; discontinue if renal lesion develops).
Paramethadione (Paradione)	0.3—2 g in divided doses	Petit mal.	Toxic reactions said to be less than with trimethadione. Other remarks as for trimethadione.
Phenacemide (Phenurone)	0.5—5 g in divided doses	Psychomotor epilepsy.	Hepatitis (liver function tests at onset; follow urinary urobilinogen at regular intervals); benign proteinuria (stop drug; may continue if patient is having marked relief); dermatitis (stop drug); headache and personality changes (stop drug if severe).
Carbamazepine (Tegretol)	0.3—1.2 g in divided doses	Psychomotor epilepsy, grand mal epilepsy.	Diplopia, transient blurred vision, drowsiness, ataxia; bone marrow depression (frequent blood counts).
Phenobarbital	0.1—0.4 g in divided doses	One of the safest drugs for all epilepsies, especially as adjunct. May aggravate psychomotor seizures.	Toxic reactions rare. Drowsiness (decrease dosage); dermatitis (stop drug and resume later; if dermatitis recurs, stop drug entirely).
Mephobarbital (Mebaral)	0.2—0.9 g in divided doses	As for phenobarbital.	As for phenobarbital. Usually offers no advantage over phenobarbital and must be given in twice the dosage.
Metharbital (Gemonil)	0.1—0.8 g in divided doses	Grand mal. Especially effective in seizures associated with organic brain damage and in infantile myoclonic epilepsy.	Drowsiness (decrease dosage).
Primidone (Mysoline)	0.5—2 g in divided doses	Grand mal. Useful in conjunction with other drugs.	Drowsiness (decrease dosage); ataxia (decrease dosage or stop drug).
Bromides (potassium or sodium)	3—6 g in divided doses	All epilepsies, especially as adjuncts. Rarely used now. Effective at times when all else fails.	Psychoses, mental dullness, acneiform rash (stop drug; may resume at lower dose).
Phensuximide (Milontin)	0.5—2.5 g in divided doses	Petit mal.	Nausea, ataxia, dizziness (reduce dosage or discontinue); hematuria (discontinue).
Methsuximide (Celontin)	1.2 g in divided doses	Petit mal, psychomotor epilepsy.	Ataxia, drowsiness (decrease dosage or discontinue).
Ethosuximide (Zarontin)	750—1500 mg in divided doses	Petit mal.	Drowsiness, nausea, vomiting (decrease dosage or discontinue).
Acetazolamide (Diamox)	1—3 g in divided doses	Grand mal, petit mal.	Drowsiness, paresthesias (reduce dosage).
Valproic acid (Depakene)	1—2 g in divided doses	Petit mal, petit mal variant, myoclonic and akinetic seizures.	Nausea and vomiting, drowsiness (decrease dosage or discontinue).
Clonazepam (Clonopin)	1.5—20 mg in divided doses	Petit mal, petit mal variant, myoclonic and akinetic seizures.	Drowsiness, ataxia, agitation (decrease dosage or discontinue).
Chlordiazepoxide (Librium)	15—60 mg in divided doses	Mixed epilepsies. Useful in patients with behavior disorders; also in status epilepticus (by intravenous infusion).	Drowsiness, ataxia (decrease dosage or discontinue).
Diazepam (Valium)	8—30 mg in divided doses		
Meprobamate (Equanil, Miltown)	1.2—2 g in divided doses	Absence attacks, myoclonic seizures.	Drowsiness (decrease dosage or discontinue).
Dextroamphetamine sulfate (Dexedrine)	20—50 mg in divided doses	Absence and akinetic attacks. Counteracts sleepiness. Useful in narcolepsy.	Anorexia, irritability, insomnia (decrease dosage or discontinue).
Methamphetamine (Desoxyn)	2.5—10 mg in divided doses		

Table 31—4. Pharmacologic properties of 6 antiepileptic drugs.*

Drug	Dosage (mg/d)	Expected Blood Level Average (µg/mL)	Expected Blood Level Range (µg/mL)	Time to Reach Steady-State Blood Levels (d)	Serum Half-Life (h)	Effective Blood Level (µg/mL)	Toxic Blood Level (µg/mL)	Protein-Bound (%)
Phenytoin	300	10	5–20	5–10	24 ± 12	>10	>20	90
Phenobarbital	120	20	10–30	14–21	96 ± 12	>15	>40	40–50
Primidone	750	8	5–15	4–7	12 ± 6	>5	>12	0–50
Phenobarbital	†	24	5–32	14–21	–	–	–	–
Carbamazepine	1200	6	3–12	2–4	12 ± 3	>4	>8	70
Valproic acid	1500	50	40–70	2–4	12 ± 6	>50	>100	90
Ethosuximide	1000	60	40–100	5–8	30 ± 6	>40	>100	0

*Reproduced, with permission, from Penry JK, Newmark ME: The use of antiepileptic drugs. *Ann Intern Med* 1979;**90:**207.
†Derived from primidone.

doses up to 1.2 g daily. Give 200-mg tablets, usually 4–6 daily. Phenacemide (Phenurone) is also effective. Give initially 0.5 g 3 times daily and increase (until symptoms are controlled) up to 5 g daily in 3–5 equal doses. Mephenytoin (Mesantoin), mephobarbital (Mebaral), primidone (Mysoline), acetazolamide (Diamox), and methsuximide (Celontin), alone or in combination with other drugs, are frequently useful.

E. Massive Spasms: Treatment is difficult, and the spasms are usually quite resistant to therapy. Metharbital (Gemonil), mephobarbital (Mebaral), methsuximide (Celontin), and meprobamate (Equanil, Miltown) may be helpful; corticotropin (ACTH) or the corticosteroids are also reported to be effective.

Prognosis

In epilepsy due to identifiable lesions, the outcome varies with the underlying disease. In idiopathic epilepsy, skillful use of anticonvulsant drugs causes significant improvement in the great majority of cases.

NARCOLEPSY

Narcolepsy is a chronic clinical syndrome characterized by intermittent episodes of uncontrollable sleep. Sudden transient loss of muscle tone in the extremities or trunk (cataplexy) and pathologic muscle weakness during emotional reactions may also occur. Inability to move in the interval between sleep and arousal (sleep paralysis) and hallucinations at the onset of sleep (hypnagogic hallucinations) may also occur. Attacks of sleep may occur several times daily and last from minutes to hours. Sleep attacks may occur under appropriate or inappropriate circumstances, with or without forewarning. The nocturnal sleep of narcoleptics is usually unremarkable. Narcolepsy may be associated with moderate to severe obesity. Cataplectic attacks, with loss of muscle tone and weakness, may occur under acute emotional stimulation, particularly with surprise. The Kleine-Levin syndrome (of hypersomnia and bulimia, believed to be related to narcolepsy) usually occurs in young males and is characterized by episodes of excessive hunger (bulimia) and somnolence. Clouding of the sensorium and amnesia for portions of the attacks may occur.

Treatment

Treatment with stimulant drugs in sufficient dosage at proper intervals often gives satisfactory results.

A. Amphetamine Sulfate (Benzedrine): The average dose is 10–20 mg 3 times daily, but more may be required for some patients. The optimal dosage may be determined by starting with 10 mg each morning and increasing the dosage as necessary to control symptoms.

Table 31—5. Drugs commonly used in the treatment of seizures.*

Seizure Type	Drug	Usual Total Daily Dosage (g)	Minimum Number of Doses per Day	Therapeutic Blood Level (µg/mL)
Generalized tonic-clonic and partial seizures	Phenytoin (Dilantin)	0.1–0.4	1	10–20
	Phenobarbital (Luminal)	0.1–0.4	1	15–40
	Primidone (Mysoline)	0.5–2	3	5–12
	Carbamazepine (Tegretol)	0.3–1.2	3	4–8
	Valproic acid (Depakene)	1–2	3	50–100
Absence seizures	Ethosuximide (Zarontin)	0.75–1.5	2	40–100
	Valproic acid (Depakene)	1–2	3	50–100
	Clonazepam (Clonopin)	1.5–20 mg	2	20–80 ng/mL

*Reproduced, with permission, from Krupp MA, Chatton MJ (editors): *Current Medical Diagnosis & Treatment 1982.* Lange, 1982.

B. Dextroamphetamine Sulfate (Dexedrine):
Give 5 mg each morning initially and increase as
necessary. Long-acting capsules (Dexedrine Span-
sules) are available in 5-, 10-, and 15-mg doses.

C. Ephedrine Sulfate: Ephedrine is not as satisfactory as amphetamine but is helpful in many cases.
The average dose is 25–50 mg 2–4 times daily.

D. Methylphenidate Hydrochloride (Ritalin):
Used in doses of 5–10 mg 3–4 times daily (or more if
necessary).

E. Imipramine (Tofranil): May be effective in
reducing attacks of cataplexy. Used in doses of 25 mg
3–4 times daily.

Prognosis

Narcolepsy usually persists throughout life. Although the attacks of somnolence and sleep may be
relieved by medical treatment, the cataplexy and attacks of muscular weakness that accompany emotional
reactions (laughing, crying) are usually not affected by
drug therapy.

BREATH–HOLDING ATTACKS

These attacks, which occur in infants and children, are usually precipitated by emotional distress,
eg, fright, pain, frustration, or anxiety. The child begins to cry, temporarily stops breathing, becomes limp
or stiff, and loses consciousness. The episode is usually brief and is associated with cyanosis; recovery
from the episode is usually rapid and complete. In
some cases, however, the rigid phase may be followed
by a series of jerks or tonic-clonic generalized seizures, after which the infant may appear sleepy or fall
asleep. These attacks are benign and generally cease
by the time the child is 3 years old; they are not
considered to be epileptic in origin, although there may
be improvement under treatment with anticonvulsant
drugs such as phenytoin or phenobarbital.

Syncope (fainting) is a symptom complex in which there is a sudden, brief loss of consciousness and decreased muscle tone. Sensations of lightheadedness, dizziness, weakness, giddiness, and decreased motor power may precede the full episode. Some episodes of syncope may be aborted or prevented by lying down.

Syncopal attacks usually involve one or more of the following pathophysiologic mechanisms: (1) impaired cerebral circulation, (2) impaired cerebral metabolism, and (3) psychosomatic alterations.

Differential Diagnosis of Syncope

Some clinical conditions are characterized by episodic disturbances that superficially resemble and must be differentiated from syncopal attacks.

A. Epilepsy: Those varieties not associated with pronounced motor convulsive manifestations, such as petit mal and some psychomotor types, are frequently considered as fainting by patients and their families. Careful history taking and electroencephalographic studies will usually assist in differentiation (see Chapter 31).

B. Narcolepsy: This disorder is characterized by a propensity to sleep, even when the patient is well rested. It is sometimes associated with **cataplexy,** a symptom in which there is sudden loss of muscular tone without loss of consciousness, usually precipitated by acute emotional stimuli (eg, fright, laughter).

C. Labyrinthitis: Disturbances of the vestibular mechanism may be associated with episodic dizziness and exacerbated by certain postures and motions. Attacks are often associated with nausea and vomiting, tinnitus, deafness, or nystagmus. Loss of consciousness does not usually occur.

VASODEPRESSOR SYNCOPE
(Vasovagal Syncope, Simple Fainting)

The commonest variety of syncope is vasodepressor syncope. It may be precipitated by fear, anxiety, or pain (eg, preceding or during surgical procedures), or psychic shock (eg, the sight of blood). It is more apt to occur with the patient in the standing position.

Among the possible basic reactions contributing to syncopal episodes are the following: physiologic effects of the fear reaction; tissue damage; reaction to pain, especially from deep structures; reflex reactions to injury of certain areas (eg, testicles, blood vessels, alimentary tract); impaired cerebral circulation (arteriosclerosis), reduced blood volume, and peripheral vasodilatation.

In the early phase there may be motor weakness, epigastric distress, perspiration, restlessness, yawning, and sighing respirations. The subject may appear anxious and may have a pale face and cold, moist extremities. After several minutes, lightheadedness, blurring of vision, and sudden loss of consciousness with decreased muscle tone may appear. If the patient remains erect, a brief but mild convulsion may follow. The syncope is associated with a rapid drop in arterial blood pressure and a slowing of the heart rate. Loss of consciousness may occur at about 75 mm Hg systolic blood pressure. The recumbent position usually aids in retarding further progression or in preventing recurrence of symptoms. In severe syncopal episodes, signs and symptoms similar to those of primary shock may occur, ie, extreme pallor, weak pulse, shallow respirations, and flaccid muscles.

Electroencephalographic changes occur after the onset of unconsciousness. These consist of the abrupt appearance of diffuse, high-amplitude, very slow wave activity.

Treatment of the individual episode consists of ensuring that the patient remains recumbent until full recovery is achieved. After resuming the erect position, the patient should move about actively. In individuals with frequent recurrences of syncopal attacks, psychologic evaluation and treatment may be indicated.

CAROTID SINUS SYNCOPE

Three types of carotid sinus syncope have been described. This classification is based on the pathophysiologic mechanisms involved: (1) Cardiodepressor (vagal), in which pressure on the carotid sinus causes slowing of the heart rate and consequent severe fall in blood pressure. (2) Vasodilator (vasomotor), in which critical fall in blood pressure occurs without significant decrease in heart rate after pressure on the

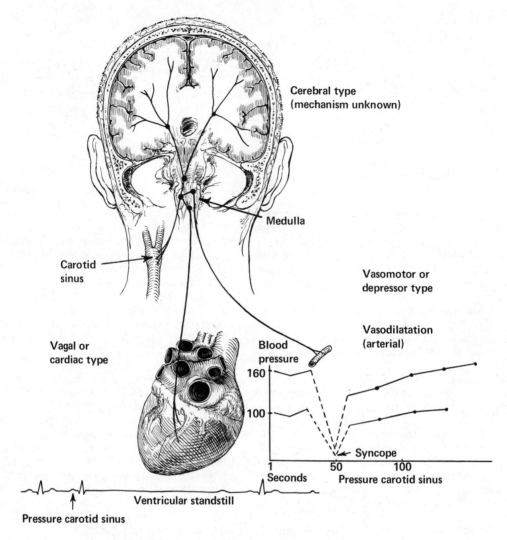

Figure 32–1. The mechanisms of syncope in carotid sinus hypersensitivity.

carotid sinus. (3) Central (cerebral), in which the loss of consciousness following pressure on the carotid sinus is not associated with fall in blood pressure.

Dizziness or loss of consciousness associated with wearing of tight collars or abrupt turning of the neck suggests the possibility of a hypersensitive carotid sinus. Focal seizures occasionally follow the syncopal episode.

Simultaneous blood pressure, electrocardiographic, and electroencephalographic studies are of value in the analysis of individual cases. In elderly or debilitated individuals, there is a great risk of accidentally precipitating a cerebrovascular accident by stimulation of a hypersensitive carotid sinus, so that this is best not done on such patients.

The central type of carotid sinus syncope may be confused with cerebral ischemia due to cerebral artery occlusion in patients with cerebrovascular disease and with hysterical syncope. Occlusion of the common carotid artery below the carotid sinus will not affect patients with the cerebral type of carotid sinus syncope, whereas patients with inadequate collateral circulation (thrombosis of the opposite internal carotid artery, etc) may show syncope, etc. In hysterical syncope, massage of some portion of the neck other than the carotid sinus may induce syncope in the recumbent patient.

Treatment

Conservative medical management requires the education of the patient in regard to the influence of turning, tight collars, etc, and the use of drugs such as atropine and ephedrine. In selected intractable cases, surgical denervation of the carotid sinus may be performed with satisfactory results.

Correct all abnormalities whenever possible. Eliminate emotional problems and forbid use of tight collars. In severe cases, denervation of the sinuses may be necessary. Local anesthesia of the carotid sinuses abolishes all types of carotid sinus syncope.

A. Vagal Type: Atropine sulfate, 0.4–0.6 mg 3–4 times daily (or more, if needed), will usually abolish attacks. Ephedrine sulfate or hydrochloride, 25 mg, with phenobarbital, 15 mg 3–4 times daily, or amphetamine sulfate, 5–10 mg, may be used.

B. Vasomotor Type: Ephedrine and phenobarbital as above will usually prevent attacks.

C. Cerebral Type: Drugs are of no value.

ORTHOSTATIC HYPOTENSION
(Postural Hypotension)

This type of syncope is characterized by repeated fainting episodes associated with a sudden drop in arterial blood pressure whenever the patient assumes the erect position. Recognized contributing factors leading to the occurrence of orthostatic hypotension are prolonged convalescence and recumbency, faulty reflex postural adaptation, sympathectomy, peripheral venous stasis, chronic anxiety, and use of antihypertensive drugs. When vasodepressor syncope was induced in healthy young normal subjects by head-up tilt and administration of sodium nitrite, loss of consciousness and severe electroencephalographic changes did not appear until the blood pressure fell to approximately 25 mm Hg. This degree of hypotension was associated with marked increase in cerebral arteriovenous oxygen difference, indicating considerable reduction in cerebral circulation. Slowing of heart rate or cardiac arrhythmia usually preceded loss of consciousness, and relative bradycardia persisted for 2–4 minutes after return of consciousness and restoration of blood pressure.

Idiopathic orthostatic hypotension (Shy-Drager's syndrome) may be associated with dysarthria, rigidity, tremor, ataxia, monotonous speech, diplegia, vertigo, and incontinence; degenerative changes in the autonomic ganglia, basal ganglia, and cortex may be found.

Treatment is directed toward the underlying cause when possible. Withdraw or reduce the dosage of hypotensive drugs. Caution the patient against rising too rapidly from the sitting or lying position. If abdominal ptosis is present, an abdominal belt may help. Elastic stockings may be of value. Vasoconstrictor drugs may be tried but usually do not help.

Ephedrine sulfate, up to 75 mg daily, may be useful. Fludrocortisone acetate has also been reported to be effective in daily doses of 0.1 mg or more.

CARDIAC FUNCTIONAL CHANGE

Syncopal attacks may occur as a consequence of sudden cardiac functional change. In the **Stokes-Adams syndrome,** syncope occurs with evidence of a slow pulse and electrocardiographic changes indicative of a high grade of atrioventricular block (Fig 32–2). Attacks of syncope in this syndrome may vary greatly in frequency and may occur in both sleeping and waking states. In intervals between episodes, the patient may be quite comfortable. If the period of unconsciousness is prolonged, convulsions are apt to occur. Patients may expire during an attack of this syndrome. The use of a Holter monitor may show cardiac arrhythmia as a cause of syncope.

Reflex heart block may contribute to some types of syncopal episodes. It may be a consequence of hypersensitivity of the carotid sinus, in which the syncope follows physical stimulation of the carotid sinus; viscerovagal reflexes, such as may occur following distention or irritation of a viscus, producing syncope; oculovagal reflexes, such as occur after pressure on the eyeball; or postural changes.

Syncope may also be associated with other varieties of cardiac disorders, as follows: (1) Coronary and myocardial insufficiency. Syncopal episodes may occur with angina pectoris attacks; sometimes convulsions and sudden death may occur thereafter. (2) Paroxysmal tachycardia. Sudden impaired cardiac output may lead to syncope. (3) Aortic stenosis. Precipitation of syncope by exertion occurs in this condition. (4) Congenital heart disease. Syncope associated with sudden intense exertional efforts is well recognized in this group.

IMPAIRED BRAIN METABOLISM

Impaired cerebral metabolism may be the most significant factor in the production of some types of syncope. Examples of such varieties of syncope are those associated with the following: (1) anoxemia, as in patients with congenital heart disease; (2) severe chronic debilitating anemias; (3) hypoglycemia, as in "labile diabetics" after overexertion or failure to eat after taking insulin; (4) acidosis, as in some patients with uncontrolled diabetes mellitus; (5) drug intoxication, as with barbiturates; (6) acute alcoholism; and (7) hyperventilation with associated respiratory alkalosis and tetany.

IMPAIRED BRAIN CIRCULATION

Impairment of the cerebral circulation may also lead to syncopal attacks. Syncope associated with transient focal neurologic findings is relatively common among elderly patients with arteriosclerotic cerebrovascular disease. Dizziness followed by syncope can occur following abrupt head movements in patients with head injuries. Transient episodes of lightheadedness or unconsciousness are commonly encountered in hypertensive encephalopathy, where they may be secondary to local impaired blood flow associated with narrowing of vessels. Lightheadedness and, more rarely, syncope may be present as manifestations of migraine, a disorder that in its initial phase is associated with diminished cerebrocranial arterial blood flow. One of the varieties of syncope in people with hypersensitivity of the carotid sinus is associated with

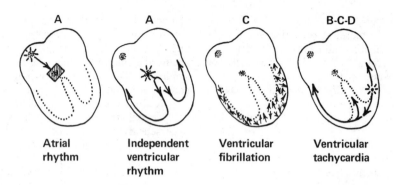

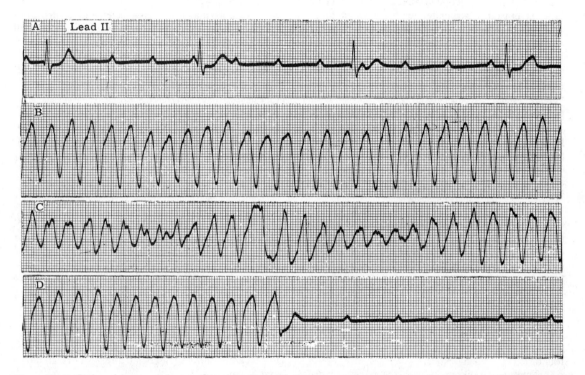

Figure 32–2. Stokes-Adams syndrome. Complete heart block with ventricular tachycardia, ventricular fibrillation, and ventricular asystole. **A:** Complete heart block. The atrial rate is 92, the ventricular rate 25. **B:** Ventricular tachycardia. The ventricular rate is 200. The QRS complexes are wide, undulating waves. **C:** Ventricular fibrillation interspersed with ventricular tachycardia. The QRS complexes are more bizarre during the period of ventricular fibrillation and vary in size and configuration from beat to beat. **D:** Ventricular tachycardia terminating in ventricular asystole. Atrial activity is now seen. The patient died shortly thereafter. This tracing illustrates the arrhythmias associated with the Stokes-Adams syndrome. (Reproduced, with permission, from Goldman MJ: *Principles of Clinical Electrocardiography,* 11th ed. Lange, 1982.)

profound abrupt fall in blood pressure and consequent impaired cerebral circulation (see above). In patients with intracerebral neoplasms or vascular malformations, displacement, engorgement or occlusion of intracranial blood vessels may be related to the syncopal episodes sometimes encountered.

Sudden syncope during the terminal phase of micturition may occur in young males shortly after they assume the upright posture following a period of recumbency and sleep; sudden decrease of reflex vasoconstriction on emptying a full bladder during motionless standing may be important. Syncope after

coughing ("cough syncope") may be related to sudden increase in venous pressure, rise in cerebrospinal fluid pressure, or concussionlike effect produced by the coughing; loss of consciousness may precede a fall in peripheral arterial blood pressure.

Treat the specific cause whenever possible. Consciousness may be restored in hyperventilation by rebreathing into a paper bag, breath-holding, or administration of 5–10% CO_2 with oxygen by mask. Recurrent attacks of hyperventilation syndrome suggest that psychiatric consultation should be considered.

SYNCOPE IN HYSTERIA

Syncope may occur as a hysterical feature. Psychologic evaluation may indicate that in such individuals the syncopal episode symbolizes an expression of a repressed drive. The syncopal episode in hysteria is usually not associated with evidences of anxiety. Women are especially apt to have this type of episode, particularly during adolescence. Other features of hysterical personality may be prominent. In hysterical fainting, the EEG usually shows no significant changes during the period of unconsciousness.

VERTIGO
(Dizziness)

The terms "vertigo" and "dizziness" are generally used to denote the subjective sensation of rotatory movement, either of the individual or of the environment, and imply an inability to orient the body in relation to surrounding objects. Vertigo is found mainly in disease processes involving the labyrinths, the vestibular portion of the eighth cranial nerve, and their nuclei or connections. True vertigo is usually manifested by nystagmus, falling to one side, and abnormal reaction to tests of vestibular function. Among the more common causes are Meniere's syndrome; acute labyrinthitis; organic brain damage involving the vestibular nerve, its end organs or connections, or the cerebellum; and drug and chemical toxicity.

Dizziness is a common complaint, and a broad systemic survey may be required to determine its specific cause. In a model dizziness clinic in which all patients with "dizziness" were accepted, Drachman and co-workers collected data in a highly organized protocol on relevant medical, neurologic, otologic, cardiac, and other problems in 125 patients. Vestibular disorders were found in 38%, hyperventilation syndrome in 23%, multiple sensory disorders in 13%, psychiatric disorders in 9%, brain stem cerebrovascular accidents in 5%, other neurologic disorders in 4%, and cardiovascular disorders in 4%.

A practical diagnostic approach to the patient with dizziness is illustrated in Fig 32–3. Treatment is based upon accurate diagnosis of the underlying disorder.

MENIERE'S SYNDROME
(Paroxysmal Labyrinthine Vertigo)

Meniere's syndrome is characterized by recurrent episodes of severe vertigo associated with deafness and tinnitus. It is encountered most often in men in the age group from 40 to 60 years. The cause is not known, but "endolymphatic hydrops" with marked dilatation of the cochlear duct is suspected. Meniere's syndrome may follow head trauma or middle ear infection, but many cases develop without apparent damage to the nervous system or ear.

Intermittent severe vertigo, which may appear to throw the subject to the ground, is the principal symptom. Brief loss of consciousness occasionally occurs in an attack. "Spinning" of surrounding objects is often noted. Nausea, vomiting, and profuse perspiration are

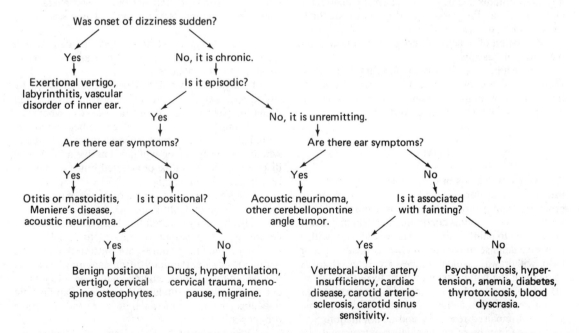

Figure 32–3. Practical diagnostic approach to patient with dizziness. (Modified and reproduced, with permission, from Clairmont AA, Turner JS Jr, Jackson RT: Dizziness: A logical approach to diagnosis and treatment. *Postgrad Med* [Aug] 1974;**56**:139.)

often associated. The attacks may last from a few minutes to several hours. The frequency of attacks varies considerably even in the same patient. Headache, nerve type hearing loss, and tinnitus occur during and persist between attacks. Hearing loss is apt to be progressive and is unilateral in 90% of cases. Nystagmus may occur during attacks of vertigo. An altered labyrinthine response is often demonstrated by means of the caloric, or Bárány, test. There is increased sensitivity to loud sounds. Audiometric tests show recruitment, decreased speech discrimination, and a nerve type hearing loss (see Chapter 22).

Treatment

Reassurance is important, since many of these patients have a marked psychic overlay. A salt-free diet and ammonium chloride, 1–2 g 4 times daily, may be helpful. Diuretics such as acetazolamide (Diamox) and chlorothiazide (Diuril) may also be used. Nicotinic acid, 50–100 mg intravenously 2–3 times daily, or 100 mg orally 5–6 times daily, has been found useful. The antihistamines, especially diphenhydramine hydrochloride (Benadryl) and dimenhydrinate (Dramamine), in doses of 50–100 mg 3–4 times daily, appear to be of benefit to some patients. Parenteral diphenhydramine or dimenhydrinate—or atropine sulfate, 0.6 mg—may stop the acute attack.

Destructive surgery on the labyrinth or vestibular nerve may be necessary in a few severe cases.

Prognosis

Meniere's syndrome is a chronic recurrent disease that persists for several years. Remission or improvement of vertigo after treatment is often noted; however, tinnitus and deafness usually are unaffected and permanent. Progression is slow and sometimes stops before complete deafness occurs.

Cessation of attacks of vertigo may follow complete loss of hearing.

Procedures that destroy or interrupt an affected vestibular portion of acoustic nerve (such as destruction of the labyrinth or section of the acoustic nerve) may prevent further attacks of vertigo.

COMA

Whereas the loss of consciousness in syncope is usually brief in duration and sudden in onset, more prolonged and profound loss of consciousness is described as coma. In this condition, a patient may show no reaction to painful stimuli or may react only with a primitive defense movement such as corneal reflex or limb withdrawal. Milder grades are referred to as semicoma; the patient may attempt to push away an offending stimulus. Still lesser grades are referred to as stupor or confusion and are characterized by variable grades of impaired reactivity and disorientation.

Coma may be of intracranial or extracranial origin. Examples are given below:

A. Intracranial: Head injuries, cerebrovascular accidents, CNS infections, tumors, convulsive disorders, degenerative diseases, increased intracranial pressure, psychiatric disorders.

B. Extracranial: Vascular (shock or hypotension, as with severe hemorrhage, myocardial infarction, arterial hypertension); metabolic (diabetic acidosis, hypoglycemia, uremia, hepatic coma, addisonian crisis, electrolyte imbalance); intoxications (alcohol, barbiturates, narcotics, bromides, analgesics, ataractics, carbon monoxide, heavy metals); miscellaneous (hyperthermia, hypothermia, electric shock, anaphylaxis, severe systemic infections).

Clinical Findings

A. History: Interrogate the patient during lucid intervals. Valuable information may also be obtained from the patient's friends, relatives, and attendants. Inquire specifically about the patient's occupation; previous physical, mental, or emotional illness; trauma, the use of alcohol and drugs, epilepsy, and hypertension.

B. Physical Examination: Place particular emphasis on vital signs, evidence of injury or intoxication, and neurologic abnormalities. Do not assume that sensory disturbances are due to alcoholic intoxication merely because an alcoholic breath is detected. Inspect the head and body carefully for evidence of injury. Discoloration of the skin behind the ear often is associated with skull fracture (Battle's sign).

Examination should include evaluation of motor responses to pain, respiration pattern, pupil size and reactions, and vestibulo-ocular reflexes.

Observe respiration, which may be deep and labored (suggesting diabetic acidosis) or of the Cheyne-Stokes type. Puffing out of one cheek with each expiration indicates paralysis of that side of the face.

Spontaneous movements may indicate which areas are normal parts or may represent the onset of focal motor convulsions.

Paralysis of extremities may be determined by lifting each extremity and allowing it to fall. In light coma the paralyzed limb will fall heavily, whereas a normal limb will gradually sink to the bed. Vigorous stimulation of the feet may cause a normal leg to react, whereas a paralyzed leg will not. Passive motion may disclose diminished tone of affected limbs in acute or recent flaccid hemiplegia.

Decerebrate rigidity or the presence of tonic neck reflexes suggests dysfunction at a brain stem level.

Check the eyes carefully. Hemianopsia may be demonstrable in stupor by failure to flinch when threatening hand gestures are initiated from the hemianopsic side. Pupillary differences may be of vital diagnostic importance; enlarged pupils are often present with ipsilateral subdural hematoma. Papilledema indicates elevated intracranial pressure and is a grave prognostic sign.

Oculomotor paralysis of one eye is often associated with a ruptured aneurysm of the anterior portion of the circle of Willis. The oculocephalic reflex

Table 32–1. Glasgow Coma Scale. A practical method of assessing changes in level of consciousness based upon eye-opening, verbal, and motor responses. The response may be expressed by the sum of the scores assigned to each response. The lowest score is 3 and the highest score is 15.*

	Examiner's Test	Patient's Response	Assigned Score
Eye-opening	Spontaneous	Opens eyes on own.	4
	Speech	Opens eyes when asked to do so in a loud voice.	3
	Pain	Opens eyes when pinched.	2
	Pain	Does not open eyes.	1
Best motor response	Commands	Follows simple commands.	6
	Pain	Pulls examiner's hand away when pinched.	5
	Pain	Pulls a part of body away when pinched.	4
	Pain	Flexes body inappropriately to pain (decorticate posturing).	3
	Pain	Body becomes rigid in an extended position when pinched (decerebrate posturing).	2
	Pain	Has no motor response to pinch.	1
Verbal response (talking)	Speech	Carries on a conversation correctly and tells examiner where and who he or she is and the month and year.	5
	Speech	Seems confused or disoriented.	4
	Speech	Talks so examiner can understand words but makes no sense.	3
	Speech	Makes sounds examiner cannot understand.	2
	Speech	Makes no noise.	1

*Slightly modified and reproduced, with permission, from Rimel RN, Jane JA, Edlich RF: Injury scale for comprehensive management of CNS trauma. *JACEP* 1979;**8**:64.

(doll's head maneuver) and cold caloric (ice water) oculovestibular reflex may be altered or absent in brain stem lesions or dysfunction.

Pronounced nuchal rigidity usually signifies meningeal irritation (meningitis, subarachnoid bleeding) or herniation of the cerebellar tonsils due to intracranial tumor or vascular accident.

C. Laboratory Findings: Catheterize the patient if necessary and examine the urine especially for protein, blood, glucose, and acetone. Determine hemoglobin, white blood cell count, differential count, and hematocrit. Draw blood for assessment of blood gases, electrolytes, pH, nonprotein nitrogen, glucose, and blood ammonia when indicated (for diagnosis of uremia, diabetic coma, or hepatic coma). Lumbar puncture should be considered when meningitis, encephalitis, or subarachnoid hemorrhage is suspected. Cerebrospinal fluid examination and culture may be helpful. Special studies may be indicated, eg, blood cultures and analysis of body fluids for evidence of toxins. Skull x-rays, electroencephalography, brain scan, CT scan of head, cerebral angiography, and pneumography are valuable aids when brain tumor or subdural hematoma is suspected. Order chest x-ray and other x-rays as indicated.

Irreversible coma due to cerebral death may be suspected (in the absence of hypothermia or drug intoxication) on the basis of the absence of response to noxious stimuli, absence of spontaneous movements or respirations, areflexia, and a flat, isoelectric EEG for 24 hours.

Treatment

A. Emergency Measures: The immediate objective is to maintain life until a specific diagnosis has been made and appropriate treatment can be started.

1. Maintain adequate ventilation–First determine the cause of any respiratory difficulty (eg, obstruction, pulmonary disease, depression of respiratory center, vascular collapse).

Keep airways open. Place the patient in the prone or lateral recumbent position and turn the patient's head to the side, keeping it well extended. *Never* put the patient in the supine position or keep the patient's head in a flexed position. If necessary, pull the tongue forward with fingers or forceps and maintain in an extended position (eg, by pharyngeal airways). Aspirate mucus, blood, and saliva from the mouth and nose with a lubricated soft rubber catheter. If no suction apparatus is available, use a 25- to 50-mL syringe. Endotracheal catheterization or tracheostomy may be necessary. (***Caution:*** If the endotracheal tube remains in place for more than 2 hours, there is danger of laryngeal edema and further obstruction upon its removal.) The services of a trained anesthetist or otolaryngologist are desirable.

Artificial respiration may be administered if respirations have ceased or are failing. Passive hyperventilation to achieve a P_{CO_2} of 25–30 mm Hg may be used to treat increased intracranial pressure. Closed cardiac massage may be necessary.

Oxygen may be administered by mask, catheter, or tent as indicated.

2. Shock–Institute immediate treatment if patient is in shock or if shock is threatened. A minimum blood pressure of 80–90 mm Hg is usually considered adequate to maintain cerebral perfusion.

3. Glucose–Give 50 mL of 50% dextrose solution after blood samples have been drawn for laboratory tests. In alcoholic subjects, give 100 mg of thiamine chloride intravenously before the glucose to avert potentiation of Wernicke's encephalopathy by the glucose.

B. General Measures: The patient must be observed constantly. Change body positions every 30–60 minutes to prevent hypostatic pneumonia and skin ulcerations. Catheterize the patient if coma persists for longer than 8–12 hours and the patient fails to void. If necessary, insert an indwelling catheter (with appropriate aseptic technique).

Provide proper fluid and nutrition with intravenous glucose, amino acids, and saline solutions for the first few days until the patient is able to take fluids by mouth. If the patient is comatose for more than 2–3 days, tube feedings should be employed.

Whenever possible, avoid sedative or other depressant medications until a specific diagnosis has been made. Sedation with paraldehyde or barbiturates may be necessary for mild restlessness in coma that is not due to barbiturate or other drug toxicity.

Intravenous mannitol. Increased intracranial pressure (eg, in brain tumor, head injury, brain swelling) may be reduced for 3–10 hours by intravenous administration of a hypertonic solution of mannitol. Usually, 500 mL of a 20% solution of mannitol is given over 15–20 minutes.

The use of parenteral corticosteroids such as dexamethasone (Decadron), 30–40 mg daily in divided doses, may be effective in reducing cerebral edema.

C. Specific Measures: Treat specific causes, such as fevers, infections, and poisonings. In the absence of hypothermia or sedation, irreversible brain damage or brain death may be suspected when there is areflexia, loss of spontaneous respirations, fixed dilated pupils, motor and sensory paralysis, and an isoelectric (flat) electroencephalogram for 24 hours.

Headache is a common symptom that may be due to a wide variety of causes, including emotional disorders, head injuries, migraine, fever, intracranial vascular disorders, dental disease, intracranial masses, or diseases of the eyes, ears, or nose.

Clinical Disorders Associated With Headache

Certain types of headache are frequently observed to be associated with specific clinical entities. Throbbing, pulsating headache is more likely to be encountered in vascular diseases such as migraine, arterial hypertension, and intracranial vascular malformations. Pressure headache, a sensation of tightness with a constricting, bandlike feeling about the head, is often due to emotional disorders. A steady, dull headache is often encountered in patients with intracranial masses or head injuries.

The most severe headaches are believed to be those associated with migraine, meningitis, high degrees of fever, and ruptured intracranial aneurysms. A relatively prolonged, minor grade of headache may occur with such serious disorders as intracranial hematoma, brain tumor, or abscess.

Since headache may occur as a symptom of many clinical disorders, it may not always be possible to determine the cause in a given case despite elaborate diagnostic procedures. The choice of a particular study frequently reflects the tentative diagnosis and, indirectly, the physician's clinical orientation. Thus, the internist may feel that no patient with headache has been adequately studied without allergy tests; the psychiatrist may consider an elaborate psychometric assay essential; and the neurosurgeon may not feel satisfied until pneumoencephalographic, angiographic, and cervical myelographic studies as well as CT scans have been exhausted. In some clinics, routine skull x-rays and EEGs are made as initial "screening" tests in all patients with headaches, and further specific test procedures are then adapted to the particular diagnostic needs as necessary. Among the clinical types are the following:

A. Traumatic Headache: Following head injury, with or without obvious evidence of injury to the skull and adjacent soft tissues; following injury to the upper cervical spine or its associated soft parts (ligaments, muscles, fascia, and intervertebral disks).

B. Inflammatory Headache: Associated with paranasal sinusitis, mastoiditis, meningitis; febrile systemic illnesses, especially those with acute onset of high fever or fluctuations in temperature; myositis or arthritis involving tissues of the head or neck; or angiitis, as in temporal arteritis.

C. Tumor Headache: Associated with primary or metastatic tumors of the head and neck or intracranial hematoma (eg, subdural, intracerebral).

D. Vascular Headache: Migraine, histaminic cephalalgia, intracranial aneurysms and vascular malformations, essential hypertension, and syncope (recovery phase).

E. Metabolic Headache: Hypothyroidism, ovarian dysfunction, anemias and blood dyscrasias, and drug intoxications (eg, alcohol, carbon monoxide).

F. Emotional Headache: Anxiety or pain, conversion neuroses.

G. Miscellaneous: Neuralgias (occipital, trigeminal), ocular disorders (refractive errors, glaucoma), or following lumbar puncture.

Pathogenesis

According to H.G. Wolff, the following 6 basic mechanisms are commonly involved in the production of headaches from an intracranial source: (1) Traction on veins that pass to the venous sinuses from the brain surface and displacement of the major venous sinuses. (2) Traction on the middle meningeal arteries. (3) Traction on the large arteries at the base of the brain and their main branches. (4) Distention and dilatation of intracranial arteries. (5) Inflammation in or about any of the pain-sensitive structures of the head. (6) Direct pressure on the cranial and cervical nerves containing many afferent pain fibers from the head.

A. Areas of Pain: Whereas the skull, the brain parenchyma, the choroid plexuses, and most of the dura mater and pia-arachnoid are not sensitive to pain, the tissues covering the cranium, especially the arteries, are sensitive to pain.

B. Modification by Physical Measures: Under some conditions, the characteristics of headaches may be modified by physical measures. Abrupt increase in intracranial pressure, as is produced by coughing, sneezing, or straining, will usually exaggerate most headaches associated with intracranial masses or bleeding. Headache following lumbar puncture is usually made more severe by elevating the head and improved by lowering the position of the head relative to the rest of the body. Manual compression of the common carotid artery in the neck or the major cranial branches of the external carotid artery may relieve the headache of migraine. Headaches following head injuries are frequently made worse by abrupt alteration in position of the head. Pressure headaches associated with emotional disorders may be greatly relieved by local gentle massage of the affected region. Nocturnal headaches of the migraine type sometimes are exaggerated by the recumbent position and relieved when the patient stands erect.

Classification of Headache*

A. Vascular Headaches of Migraine Type: Recurrent attacks of headache, widely varied in intensity, frequency, and duration. The attacks are commonly unilateral in onset; are usually associated with anorexia and, sometimes, with nausea and vomiting; are preceded by, or associated with, conspicuous sensory, motor, and mood disturbances in some cases; and are often familial.

Evidence supports the view that cranial arterial distention and dilatation are importantly implicated in the painful phase but cause no permanent changes in the involved vessel. Listed below are particular varieties of headache, each sharing some, but not necessarily all, of the above-mentioned features:

1. "Classic" migraine–Vascular headache with sharply defined, transient visual and other sensory or motor prodromes or both.

2. "Common" migraine–Vascular headache without striking prodromes and less often unilateral than classic and cluster migraine. Synonyms are "atypical migraine" or "sick" headache. Calling attention to certain relationships of this type to environmental, occupational, menstrual, or other variables are such terms as "summer," "Monday," "weekend," "relaxation," "premenstrual," and "menstrual" headache.

3. "Cluster" headache–Vascular headache, predominantly unilateral on the same side, usually associated with flushing, sweating, rhinorrhea, and increased lacrimation; brief in duration and usually occurring in closely packed groups separated by long remissions. Identical or closely allied are erythroprosopalgia (Bing); ciliary or migrainous neuralgia (Harris); erythromelalgia of the head or histaminic cephalalgia (Horton); and petrosal neuralgia (Gardner and others).

4. "Hemiplegic" migraine and "ophthalmoplegic" migraine–Vascular headache characterized by sensory and motor phenomena that persist during and after the headache.

5. "Lower-half" headache–Headache of possibly vascular mechanism, centered primarily in the lower face. In this group there may be some instances of "atypical facial" neuralgia, sphenopalatine ganglion neuralgia (Sluder), and vidian neuralgia (Vail).

B. Muscle-Contraction Headache: Ache or

sensations of tightness, pressure, or constriction, widely varied in intensity, frequency, and duration, sometimes long-lasting, and commonly suboccipital. It is associated with sustained contraction of skeletal muscles in the absence of permanent structural change, usually as part of the individual's reaction during life stress. The ambiguous and unsatisfactory terms "tension," "psychogenic," and "nervous" headache refer largely to this group.

C. Combined Headache, Vascular and Muscle-Contraction: Combinations of vascular headache of the migraine type and muscle-contraction headache prominently coexisting in an attack.

D. Headache of Nasal Vasomotor Reaction: Headaches and nasal discomfort (nasal obstruction, rhinorrhea, tightness, or burning), recurrent and resulting from congestion and edema of nasal and paranasal mucous membranes, and not proved to be due to allergens, infectious agents, or local gross anatomic defects. The headache is predominantly anterior in location and mild or moderate in intensity. The illness is usually part of the individual's reaction during stress. This is often called "vasomotor rhinitis."

E. Headache of Delusional, Conversion, or Hypochondriacal States: Headaches of illnesses in which the prevailing clinical disorder is a delusional or a conversion reaction and in which a peripheral pain mechanism is nonexistent. Closely allied are the hypochondriacal reactions in which the peripheral disturbances relevant to headache are minimal. These also have been called "psychogenic" headaches.

Note: The foregoing represent the major clinical disorders dominated by headache—those that are particularly common, and in which headache is frequently recurrent and disabling.

F. Nonmigrainous Vascular Headaches Associated With Generally Nonrecurrent Dilatation of Cranial Arteries:

1. Systemic infections, usually with fever.

2. Miscellaneous disorders, including hypoxic states, carbon monoxide poisoning, effects of nitrites, nitrates, and other agents with vasodilator properties; caffeine-withdrawal reactions; circulatory insufficiency in the brain (in certain cases); postconcussion reactions; postconvulsive states; "hangover" reactions; foreign-protein reactions; hypoglycemia; hypercapnia; acute pressor reactions (abrupt elevation of blood pressure, as with paraplegia or pheochromocytoma); and certain cases of essential arterial hypertension (eg, those with early morning headache).

G. Traction Headache: Headaches resulting from traction on intracranial structures, mainly vascular, by masses:

1. Primary or metastatic tumors of meninges, vessels, or brain.

2. Hematomas (epidural, subdural, or parenchymal).

3. Abscesses (epidural, subdural, or parenchymal).

4. Post-lumbar puncture headache ("leakage" headache).

---

*Reproduced, with permission, from Friedman AP et al: *JAMA* 1962;**179**:717.

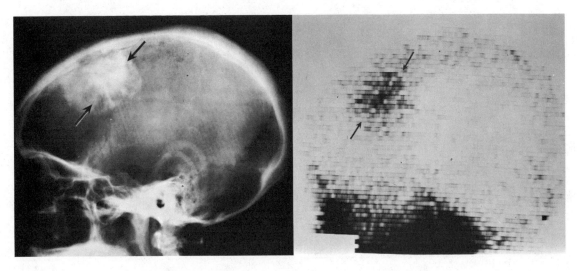

Figure 33–1. Left parasagittal meningioma visualized by external carotid angiogram and lateral cerebroscintigram in a 34-year-old woman with headaches and recent seizures.

5. Pseudotumor cerebri and various causes of brain swelling.

H. Headache Due to Overt Cranial Inflammation: Headaches due to readily recognized inflammation of cranial structures, resulting from usually nonrecurrent inflammation, sterile or infectious.

1. Intracranial disorders–Infectious, chemical, or allergic meningitis; subarachnoid hemorrhage; postpneumoencephalographic reaction; arteritis; and phlebitis.

2. Extracranial disorders–Arteritis and cellulitis.

I–M. Headaches Due to Disease of Ocular, Aural, Nasal and Sinusal, Dental, or Other Cranial or Neck Structures:

I. Headache due to spread of effects of noxious stimulation of ocular structures (as contraction of muscles, trauma, new growth, or inflammation).

J. Headache due to spread of effects of noxious stimulation of aural structures (as by trauma, new growth, or inflammation).

K. Headache due to spread of effects of noxious stimulation of nasal and sinusal structures (as by trauma, new growth, inflammation, or allergens).

L. Headache due to spread of effects of noxious stimulation of dental structures (as by trauma, new growth, or inflammation).

M. Headache due to spread of pain from noxious stimulation of other structures of the cranium and neck (periosteum, joints, ligaments, muscles, or cervical roots).

N. Cranial Neuritides: Caused by trauma, new growth, or inflammation.

O. Cranial Neuralgias: Trigeminal (tic douloureux) and glossopharyngeal. The pains are lancinating (''jabbing''), usually in rapid succession for several minutes or longer; are limited to a portion or all of the domain of the affected nerve; and are often triggered by end organ stimulation. Trigeminal neuralgia must be distinguished, in particular, from cluster headache (A3), with which it is often confused.

Note: So-called chronic posttraumatic headache may arise from one of several mechanisms. Such headache may represent sustained muscle contraction (B), recurrent vascular dilatation (A2), or, rarely, local scalp or nuchal injury (M). In some patients, the pain is part of a disorder characterized by delusional, conversion, or hypochondriacal reactions (E).

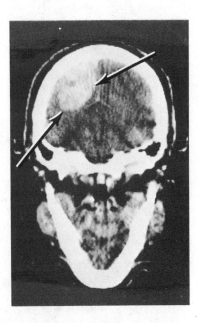

Figure 33–2. CT scan showing meningioma in a 60-year-old man with severe vertex headaches.

Table 33—1. Some differential diagnostic features of various types of headaches.*

Characteristics	Migraine Typical	· Atypical	· Hybrid	Histaminic Cephalalgia	Hypertensive Headache	Tension Headache	Muscle Tension Headache
Age at onset	Childhood, adolescence, early adult	Adolescence, early adult		Early or middle adult	Any	Any	Any
Periodicity	+ Often with menses or ovulation	+	+	+ Often seasonal	–	–	–
Location	Quadrantic, hemicranial, or whole head	Quadrantic, hemicranial		Quadrantic, hemicranial	Occipital, frontal, rarely vertex	Frontal, generalized	Occipital, nuchal, shoulders
Severity, I–IV	II–IV	I–IV	I–IV	IV	I–IV	I–III	I–II
GI disturbance	+ –	+ –	+ –	–	–	–	–
Cortical disturbance	+ –	+ –	+ –	–	– (unless encephalopathy)	–	–
FH migraine	+ –	+ –	+ –	–	Often	–	–
Nasal stuffiness and rhinorrhea	+ – Uni- or bilateral	+ –	+– Unilateral	+ Unilateral	–	–	–
Conjunctivitis and lacrimation	+ – Uni- or bilateral	+ –	+– Unilateral	+ Unilateral	–	–	–
Character of pain	Throbbing, bursting, viselike	Stabbing, waxes and wanes		Knifelike, shooting; throbbing	Throbbing or steady, dull	Constant, may throb	Stiff, sore, with superficial tenderness
Duration of pain	Hours to days	2–12 hours		Minutes to 2 hours	2–3 hours usually	4–16 hours	2–3 hours
Night pain	Rarely wakens unless associated with hypertension	Often wakens from sleep		Always wakens from sleep	Wakens 4–6 AM	–	–
Other features	Often an unconscious but marked hostility toward an individual or situation. Ambitious, perfectionist, inflexible, meticulous, restrained, "time-bound."			Ulcer not infrequent. Ulcer and cephalalgia exacerbate and remit simultaneously.	Hypertension or vascular hyperreactor	Follows stress	Often associated with arthritis of cervical spine
Precipitants	Fatigue—physical, mental, emotional. Vasodilators.			Vasodilators, histamine	Widened pulse pressure	Fatigue, stress	Muscle tension
Relief of acute attack	Gynergen, dihydroergotamine, Cafergot			Dihydroergotamine	Upright posture, thiocyanates	Rest	Change of posture, heat, massage

*Reproduced, with permission, from Macy: *J Am Med Wom Assoc* 1950;**5**:352.

Clinical Findings

Headaches are of variable duration; in the same patient, different periods of distress may occur. Pressure headaches, commonly present in tension states of emotional origin, may persist for days or weeks. Brief, paroxysmal, prostrating headache of less than 30 minutes' duration may occur in migraine.

Periodic recurrence of headache is a recognized phenomenon. In women with migraine, intracranial vascular malformations, or intracranial aneurysms, headaches are prone to occur at the time of the menstrual period. Seasonal variations in the incidence of headaches are sometimes related to the coincidental increase of emotional tension in migraine patients. Headaches associated with paranasal sinus or nasal disorders are more frequent when upper respiratory infections are most common.

Associated local tenderness at the site of a headache sometimes occurs with head injury, migraine, osteitis, or myositis.

The location of a headache may provide a clue to its origin. Headaches of the pressure type due to emotional disorders may start in the occiput and upper neck and then radiate frontally. Unilateral, recurrent headache suggests migraine, intracranial vascular malformation, or aneurysm of that side. Headache associated

Table 33–1 (cont'd). Some differential diagnostic features of various types of headaches.

Myofibrositic Headache	Rheumatic Headache	Temporal Arteritis	Arteriosclerotic Headache	"Allergic" Headache	Headache With Brain Tumor	Psychogenic Headache
Usually adult	Adult	55 years or older	Late adult	Any	Any	Adult
–	–	–	–	May be seasonal	–	–
Occipital, nuchal, shoulders	Occipital, nuchal, shoulders	Distribution of temporal artery	Temporal artery or deep	Vertex, band	Any	"All over"
I–III	II–IV	IV	I–III	I–III	I–IV	0–I
–	–	–	–	–	–	–
–	–	–	–	–	+–	–
–	–	–	–	–	–	–
–	–	–	–	+– Bilateral	–	–
–	–	–	–	+– Bilateral	–	–
Superficial, with superficial tenderness	Exquisite superficial tenderness	Knifelike, shooting, stabbing, throbbing, with marked superficial tenderness	Dull, steady, or may be ticlike	Tight band, weight, or bursting	Any	Constant invariable ache
Days to weeks	Months	2–6 months	Minutes to weeks	2–3 hours usually	Any	"All the time"
May prevent sleep, does not waken	Prevents sleep	Prevents sleep	Does not waken unless associated with hypertension	–	+–	–
Normal sedimentation rate. No fever, no nodules.	Elevated sedimentation rate, Globulin ±, Low grade fever ±, Lymphocytosis ±, Muscle nodules	Malaise, weakness, fever, night sweats, weight loss, leukocytosis, anemia, elevated sedimentation rate, loss of vision	Other evidence of arteriosclerosis	Other stigmas of allergy	Other findings of brain tumor	Other features of psychiatric illness
Dampness, cold	Dampness, cold	–	–	Allergen	Sudden change in CSF or blood pressure, body position	–
Heat, massage, vasodilators, salicylates	Heat, massage, vasodilators, salicylates	Opiates, steroids	Salicylates, vasodilators, histamine subcutaneously	Nasal vasoconstrictors, antihistamines	Salicylates, opiates	Psychotherapy

with dental, paranasal, or eye disease is apt to be frontal in location at the onset.

Increasingly severe headache suggests the possibility of an enlarging intracranial mass (brain tumor, aneurysm, subdural hematoma).

General Nonspecific Treatment Measures

These include physical and mental rest, sedatives, and analgesics. Sedatives should be used only as a temporary measure and should not be used as a substitute for a complete work-up and specific therapy. Narcotics are generally contraindicated except in terminal disease. Because of their antipyretic activity, analgesics constitute specific therapy in febrile headaches. They should not be administered for prolonged periods indiscriminately; their routine use often obscures important pathology.

MIGRAINE

Migraine is characterized by paroxysmal attacks of headache that are usually localized to one side of the head. The headache may be preceded by psychologic or visual disturbances and sometimes is followed by drowsiness. It is said to affect about 8% of the population. It is more frequent among women than men and occurs more commonly among persons with a background of inflexibility and shyness in childhood and with perfectionistic, rigid, resentful, and ambitious character traits in adult life. There is commonly a history of similar headaches in blood relations.

The headache of migraine is believed to result from vascular changes. An initial episode of cerebral, meningeal, and extracranial arterial vasoconstriction is believed to occur (accounting for the visual and other prodromal phenomena), followed by dilatation and distention of cranial vessels, especially of the external carotid artery. Increased amplitude of pulsation is said to determine the throbbing nature of the headache. Rigid, pipelike vessels result from persistent dilatation, and the headache becomes a steady ache. A phase of muscle contraction, with pain, is believed to follow. According to Wolff and associates, during severe and long-lasting headaches of the migraine type, neurokinin, an extremely powerful vasodilator polypeptide, may be found in body fluids. They reported that an enzyme capable of forming neurokinin and called neurokinin-forming enzyme (NFE) is contained in body fluids. Intradermally injected tissue fluids containing mixtures of neurokinin and NFE induce pain, lower the pain threshold, increase capillary permeability, and heighten vulnerability to injury.

Migraine often begins in childhood; about one-half of migraine patients report their initial attack before age 15 years. Characteristically, the headache occurs in episodes associated with gastrointestinal or visual symptoms (nausea and vomiting, scintillating scotomas, photophobia, hemianopsia, blurred vision). Methysergide maleate (Sansert) may be effective in reducing the number and severity of migraine attacks, although it lacks the capacity to terminate an existing headache. The recurrent increased reactivity of cranial blood vessels is reduced, thus preventing the crises of vasoconstriction and vasodilatation that characterize the migraine attack.

Ophthalmoplegic migraine. The association of migraine and ophthalmoplegia may in some cases be due to aneurysm or tumor, but in others no apparent cause can be shown by cerebral angiograms, surgical exploration, or postmortem study. The paralyses usually occur after many years of simple migraine, and in the attack, paralysis occurs several hours or days after the headache phase.

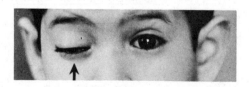

Figure 33–3. Ophthalmoplegic migraine. Severe recurrent right oculomotor paralysis in a child with associated migraine headaches. Carotid angiogram normal. Neostigmine (Prostigmin) and edrophonium (Tensilon) tests negative for myasthenia gravis.

Onset of paralysis is sudden and subsidence gradual. The oculomotor, trochlear, or abducens nerves may be involved singly or in combination. Occasionally, vasoconstrictor drugs relieve the ophthalmoplegia. Edema of cranial vessels at the end stage of migraine, with direct pressure of the edematous arteries on adjacent cranial nerves or interference with vasa vasorum to cranial nerves peripherally, has been considered the likely cause.

Prevention

Methysergide maleate (Sansert) may be effective in preventing vascular headaches. The average daily dose is 2–4 tablets (2 mg each), preferably one tablet with each meal. This drug is contraindicated in pregnancy, peripheral vascular disease, and severe arteriosclerosis. Retroperitoneal fibrosis has been reported in some cases following methysergide therapy. Drug administration should not be continued for longer than 6 months, and a drug-free interval of 3–4 weeks should follow each course of treatment.

The use of sedatives, tranquilizers, antidepressants, diuretics, propranolol, or psychotherapy may help to reduce the frequency and severity of attacks.

Treatment

In most cases, treatment with ergotamine or similar drugs is effective. Psychotherapy is useful in reducing the frequency of attacks.

A. Treatment of Acute Attack:

1. Ergotamine tartrate (Gynergen) is the treatment of choice; 0.25–0.5 mg intramuscularly will relieve headache within an hour in most cases. Administer the drug as early in the attack as possible. Do not repeat more often than once weekly. Oral or sublingual administration is less effective; if the patient vomits, it is impossible to know how much of the drug has been absorbed. The dosage is 4–5 mg sublingually or orally; continue with 2 mg every hour until headache has disappeared or until a total of 6 mg has been administered.

Toxicity: Do not administer ergotamine to patients in septic or infectious states, to those who have peripheral vascular or arteriosclerotic heart disease, or to pregnant women. A few patients complain of numbness and tingling of extremities and some muscle pains and tension.

2. Dihydroergotamine (DHE 45), in doses of 1 mg intramuscularly or intravenously, may be substituted for ergotamine tartrate. Repeat in 1 hour if necessary.

3. Ergotamine with caffeine (Cafergot) or atropine is sometimes more effective by the oral route alone and requires a smaller total dose. It is available as suppositories for rectal use if vomiting prevents oral administration.

4. Pressure on the external carotid artery or one of its branches early in the attack may abolish pain. Oxygen, 100% by nasal mask, may relieve the acute attack.

B. General Measures: Until the drug begins to

relieve headache, have the patient at rest in a chair. After headache has been relieved, the patient should rest in bed for at least 2 hours in a quiet, darkened room without food or drink. This will promote relaxation and is necessary to prevent another attack from occurring immediately.

C. Aborting an Attack: The patient who feels an attack of migraine coming on should seek relaxation and rest in bed in a quiet, darkened room. The following drugs may help: pentobarbital, 0.1 g orally; ergotamine tartrate (Gynergen), 3–4 mg sublingually; or even aspirin, with or without codeine. An ergotamine inhaler may be effective.

CLUSTER HEADACHES
(Histaminic [Horton's] Cephalalgia)

"Histaminic cephalalgia" is characterized by a sudden onset of severe unilateral pain. The pain is of short duration and subsides abruptly. Associated signs include redness of the eye, lacrimation, rhinorrhea or stuffiness of the nostril, swelling of the temporal vessels on the affected side, and dilatation of the vessels of the pain area. The headache involves the orbital area, frequently radiating to the temple, nose, upper jaw, and neck. Typical attacks can be induced by injections of small quantities of histamine diphosphate. Attacks occur most frequently during sleep. Pain does not appear to follow distribution of a particular cranial nerve, and no trigger areas are noted. Attacks tend to develop in clusters ("cluster headache"), while remissions and exacerbations occur spontaneously. More males than females (6:1) are affected. This type of headache is considered to be identical to or closely allied with erythroprosopalgia of Bing, ciliary neuralgia of Harris, and petrosal neuralgia of Gardner.

Diagnosis may be aided by a positive **histamine test:** 0.35 mL of concentrated solution of histamine diphosphate (2.75 mg/mL) injected subcutaneously usually brings on a typical headache in 20–40 minutes in susceptible persons.

Methysergide maleate (Sansert), 2 mg 2–3 times daily with meals, is highly effective in treatment. This drug is contraindicated in pregnancy, vascular disease, and arteriosclerosis. Histamine desensitization by means of frequent subcutaneous injections of increasing doses of histamine diphosphate over a period of several weeks has also been advocated as an effective type of treatment. Management of the acute phase is similar to that for migraine. Ergotamine derivatives, bed rest, inhalations of oxygen, and cold compresses may be necessary. Long-range management usually requires adequate psychologic evaluation and treatment.

TENSION HEADACHES

Tension headaches are by far the most commonly encountered of all types of headache. However, since emotionally disturbed patients may have headaches due to other causes, a complete and adequate history and examination is always necessary.

Tension headaches seem to have no precise localization and usually do not conform to the distribution of cranial or peripheral nerves of roots. Patients characterize the headache as being dull, drawing, pressing, burning, or vague in character. Medications, including potent analgesics, may not give complete relief. Exacerbation of complaints and association with anxiety, worry, or other emotional upsets are not always obvious to the patient.

Mild sedatives and analgesics are usually required, as well as psychiatric evaluation and treatment. Recognition and alleviation of fundamental emotional causes may require extensive and painstaking efforts on the part of the physician.

HEADACHES DUE
TO MENINGEAL INVOLVEMENT

These headaches are the most severe, but they usually respond to analgesics. Manifestations and specific treatment depend upon the type and site of underlying disease.

Analgesics should be given as needed if pain is not too severe. Narcotics may be necessary. Lumbar puncture, performed very cautiously, may sometimes be used to relieve headache associated with increased intracranial pressure (eg, subarachnoid hemorrhage, hypertension, nephritis; not in posterior fossa tumors).

Lumbar puncture headaches are believed to be due to leakage of the cerebrospinal fluid from the puncture site. If headache is mild upon arising, analgesics such as acetylsalicylic acid, 0.3 g every 2–3 hours, may suffice. Codeine may be necessary. If lumbar puncture headache is very severe, it can be alleviated by lying down. Intrathecal injection of small quantities of sterile normal saline may afford relief in severe cases.

34 | Neuromuscular Disorders

Clinical Features of Neuromuscular Disorders

Characteristic clinical features may be associated with neuromuscular disorders, so that a careful history and examination often provide highly informative clues and are essential for intelligent and accurate diagnosis and treatment.

Patients with neuromuscular disease may describe specific functional motor impairment resulting from difficulty in contracting or sustaining contraction of particular muscle groups. Patients may have trouble lifting their head from the pillow or rolling over in bed, and in arising from a low chair they may have to push themselves up with their hands. They may be unable to cross their knees without using their hands to flex the thigh. Walking may be difficult because their ankles tend to turn or their feet to "flop." Ascending or descending stairs, squatting and standing up, or lifting a leg into a car may be difficult. Upper extremity weakness may result in inability to lift heavy objects, turn doorknobs, or hold the arms overhead.

Extraocular muscle weakness may produce diplopia and drooping of eyelids. Lip muscle weakness may interfere with clear enunciation, whistling, sucking with a straw, or expanding a balloon. A changed facial expression or a "frozen," fixed expression may be noted. Jaw muscle weakness may lead to tiring of the jaws or inability to bite hard. Regurgitation, nasal speech, dysphagia, and dysarthria may be caused by weakness of the muscles of the pharynx, palate, and tongue. Food may be trapped between the teeth and the cheeks in the presence of facial and tongue weakness. It should be noted that impaired motor performance resulting from spasticity, rigidity, stiffness, pain, and functional or psychiatric disorders may be readily confused—by the patient as well as by the unwary examiner—with true or primary muscle weakness.

Inspection, palpation, and percussion of peripheral nerves and muscles and tests of muscle strength and muscle stretch reflexes may yield valuable diagnostic information. Several peripheral nerves are susceptible to direct palpation and percussion. Palpation of nerves in the axillas, the radial nerve above the lateral humerus, the ulnar nerve at the elbow, or the peroneal nerve just below the head of the fibula may disclose tenderness, abnormal thickening, or masses.

Muscle size and bulk vary greatly depending upon age, sex, body habitus, occupation, nutritional status, physical training, etc. Atrophy of a muscle usually means that the muscle was once longer and is now shorter. Inspection and palpation of the muscle, comparison with neighboring muscles and with homologous muscles of the opposite side, and observation of general muscular development should be carried out. Altered contour and shape of a muscle often confirm a diagnosis of suspected atrophy. Repeated examination at intervals may be necessary to determine the true status of a muscle or group of muscles. Muscle atrophy caused by muscle or lower motor neuron disease is usually associated with significant muscle weakness, but muscles atrophied from disuse, systemic disease, or senility may still show vigorous contraction. Hypertrophy of muscle may be obvious in the increased size of that muscle, although in the presence of atrophied neighboring muscles a normal muscle may appear hypertrophied by contrast.

The term "fibrillation" is reserved for spontaneous independent contractions of individual muscle fibers. These are so minute that they cannot be observed through the intact skin. Denervated muscle may show electromyographic evidence of fibrillations 1–3 weeks after the muscle has lost its nerve supply, and these fibrillations usually persist for a year or so. Fasciculation twitches may be seen, palpated, and even heard with the aid of a stethoscope. Fasciculations are usually seen better in oblique lighting in a well-lighted room. Light percussion of affected muscle activates fasciculations, and administration of neostigmine to susceptible persons greatly increases their twitches. Spontaneous fasciculations may vary because of the length and number of muscle fibers involved. They can result from any disease producing degeneration or irritation of the lower motor neuron and may be seen in poliomyelitis, spinal cord disease, motor root and peripheral nerve disease, and amyotrophic lateral sclerosis. Spontaneous fasciculations are occasionally noted in persons without recognizable neurologic or muscular disease and are referred to as benign fasciculations. Fasciculations present for several months unassociated with other clinical or electrical signs of denervation usually turn out to be benign.

Contraction fasciculations disappear upon relaxation of muscle and are thus differentiated from spontaneous fasciculations, which persist in resting, relaxed muscle. Contraction fasciculations may occur during weak muscular contractions and usually are seen in tense persons who cannot relax and also in poliomyelitis and amyotrophic lateral sclerosis.

Twitches of normal muscle may result from shivering as a result of cold. Patients should be kept warm when being observed for spontaneous fasciculation. Tremors may resemble fasciculations, and the tongue is best observed for fasciculation while it lies at rest in the mouth to avoid confusion with the increased tremors associated with tongue protrusion.

Myokymia is a benign form of muscle twitching that usually occurs without apparent cause but sometimes is associated with infection or metabolic disorders. Spontaneous, brief, tetanic contractions of motor units or groups of muscle fibers occur, sometimes producing a continual undulation of muscle surface. The movements of myokymia are slower and more prolonged than the brief twitchings of fasciculation, with which they may be confused.

Sharp percussion of normal muscle usually causes it to contract. The muscle fibers that have been directly percussed contract, causing a brief longitudinal depression in the muscle. This muscular excitability may persist even in the absence of the stretch reflex, so that direct percussion of the muscles should be avoided in the study of stretch reflexes. Persistence of a strong muscular contraction after stimulation has ceased is typical of myotonia and is usually referred to as the myotonic reaction. It may also occur when myotonic muscle contraction is produced voluntarily, mechanically, or electrically. When myotonia is suspected, it may be demonstrated after the patient has strongly grasped the examiner's hand for about 5 seconds, after which contraction persists when the patient tries to release the examiner's hand quickly on command. Percussion myotonia may be demonstrated by sharp percussion (with the tip of a reflex hammer) of the thenar eminence, tongue, deltoid, etc; the portion of the muscle struck contracts, producing a visible crease or depression in the percussed muscle that persists for several seconds. Normal muscles, in contrast, produce a much briefer and less pronounced contraction. Myoedema, which occurs occasionally in normal persons and more often in debilitated states and myxedema, is characterized by the formation of a small elevation, or hillock, at the site of the percussed muscle and is unaccompanied by electrical activity of underlying muscle.

Palpation of muscle may disclose muscular tenderness that may be distinguished from tenderness of superficial skin and subcutaneous tissue by the response to gentle touching, pressing, and squeezing of the overlying skin. Local phlebitis, with associated findings such as linear tenderness, local warmth, and a firm tender vessel, must also be differentiated. The consistency of muscle tends to vary greatly among different individuals. The atonic muscle resulting from acute denervation is flabby upon palpation. Increased consistency, ranging from rubberiness to woodenness, may occur with muscular dystrophy, polymyositis, and muscular contractures. Some muscles may be found upon palpation to be diffusely affected, whereas in others, increased consistency may be localized and patchy. Spastic, rigid, and tender muscles are generally of increased consistency.

Contractures of muscles may be detected by passive motion of joints, because there is usually a limited range of motion of the joint owing to tightening of the affected muscle tendon. True contracture, usually considered to be due to changes in the fibrous and elastic supporting tissue of muscle, must be distinguished from muscle spasm or structural joint changes. Contractures of muscles occur most often in the back extensors; shoulder adductors and internal rotators; hip flexors, extensors, and adductors; and forearm flexors and pronators as well as in other flexors of the extremities.

Evaluation of the strength of individual muscles is an important but difficult part of the muscle examination (see Chapter 9). The degree to which the patient cooperates must be gauged in assessing psychogenic factors and elements. Apparent improvement or progression of a motor disorder depends upon adequate and accurate motor testing. In some disorders such as muscular dystrophy, the localization and pattern of weakness—and in other disorders such as myasthenia gravis, the character of the muscle weakness—provide important clues about the nature of the neuromuscular disorder.

Muscle stretch reflexes may be useful in distinguishing primary muscle disease from that secondary to peripheral nerve disorders. In primary muscle disease, the stretch reflex usually remains intact until profound muscular wasting and weakness occur, whereas in peripheral nerve or anterior horn cell disorders, diminished stretch reflex often occurs very early. The amplitude of response, the rapidity with which it occurs, and its duration should be noted. In myxedema, the reflex duration time is lengthened. Clinical evaluation of a stretch reflex depends upon comparison with reflexes from other muscles and the opposite side.

Classification

The neuromuscular disorders include a number of chronic diseases that are characterized by progressive weakness and atrophy of certain groups of muscles. It is customary to differentiate atrophies from dystrophies: **muscular atrophies** result from a neural lesion involving either the cell body or axon of the lower motor neuron. **Muscular dystrophies** result from primary disease of the muscle itself. Muscular weakness and atrophy and loss of tendon reflexes may occur, however, in many dissimilar diseases.

Table 34–1. Differential diagnosis of atrophies and dystrophies.

Atrophies	Dystrophies
Generally occur late in life.	Occur in childhood.
Affect distal muscle groups, eg, the small muscles of the hand.	Affect the proximal muscle groups, eg, the hip and shoulder girdle.
Show fasciculations.	No fasciculations.
May show spastic phenomena.	No spastic phenomena.
No familial incidence.	Generally familial.

PROGRESSIVE MUSCULAR
(OR NUCLEAR) ATROPHIES
(Motor Neuron Disease)

The progressive muscular atrophies are due to nuclear involvement of the lower motor neuron by progressive lesions. Since the causative agent is usually unknown, the classification has been based upon the level of involvement rather than upon the cause. Diet, deficiency states, inflammatory conditions, vascular disorders, and toxic processes have been implicated in some cases. The term "motor system disease" has also been used to refer to this group of diseases.

Syndromes similar to those occurring naturally have been associated with specific causes. A group of cases has recently been found secondary to chronic mercury poisoning, and in some of these the lesions appeared limited to the lower motor neuron, thus resembling the clinical features of progressive muscular atrophy. A familial syndrome with clinical and pathologic features of amyotrophic lateral sclerosis, Parkinson's disease, and Alzheimer's disease in natives in Guam has been extensively studied.

A pyrimidine analog, 5-fluoroorotic acid, which was found to interfere with production of nucleic acid in nerve fibers, produced neurologic disorders following its intrathecal injection into cats. One or 2 days after injection, spontaneous contractions of muscle fibers, myoclonic jerks, and augmented muscle tone and reflexes occurred; in severe cases, flaccid paralysis with loss of reflexes and severe muscle atrophy occurred. Impaired biosynthesis of nucleic acid in nerve cells, with formation of defective coenzymes and abnormal RNA molecules, is believed related to the neurologic disorder. Spongy disorders of spinal cord white matter and more severe neurologic changes occurred after the second week.

Aran-Duchenne atrophy (myelopathic muscular atrophy) is the adult form of progressive spinal muscular atrophy. It is a rare disorder of middle age that starts in the small hand muscles with atrophy and fibrillations and slowly extends to involve the arms, shoulders, and trunk muscles. A degenerative lesion is found in the cervical gray matter of the cord. It may occur as the first stage of amyotrophic lateral sclerosis (see below).

Werdnig-Hoffmann paralysis is a hereditary form of progressive spinal muscular atrophy that occurs in infants and starts in the pelvic girdle and thighs and spreads to the extremities. Associated adiposity may produce a pseudohypertrophy.

True bulbar palsy is caused by a nuclear involvement of the last 4 or 5 cranial nerves and is characterized by twitchings and atrophy of the tongue, palate, and larynx; drooling; dysarthria; dysphagia; and finally respiratory paralysis. True bulbar palsy is usually a manifestation of amyotrophic lateral sclerosis.

Amyotrophic lateral sclerosis is a combined upper and lower motor neuron lesion that may involve the spinal or bulbar levels or both. It is a chronic progressive disease of unknown cause associated with fasciculation and atrophy of the somatic musculature. It is predominantly a disease of middle life, with onset usually between age 40 and 60 years. Amyotrophic lateral sclerosis occurs in all races and in all parts of the world. A high incidence has been noted among natives of Guam and the Mariana and Caroline Islands. The possibility of a dominant inheritance was suggested by the marked familial aggregation of cases. Degeneration of the motor cells of the spinal cord and brain stem and, to a lesser extent, of the motor cortex may occur, with secondary degeneration of the lateral and ventral portions of the spinal cord. There may be spastic weakness of the trunk and extremities, with associated hyperactive deep reflexes and extensor plantar responses. If the fibers of the bulbar nuclei become involved, pseudobulbar or bulbar paralysis may appear. The initial symptom is often weakness and wasting of the extremities (usually the upper extremities). The course is progressively downhill without remission. The average duration of life from the appearance of the first symptom is about 3 years.

Hereditary Proximal Neurogenic Atrophy
(Wohlfart-Kugelberg-Welander Disease)

As a result of electromyography, nerve conduction tests, and muscle biopsies, some cases formerly classified as limb girdle muscular dystrophy have been shown to be neurogenic in origin. The onset of symptoms in this disease is usually in childhood, but it may be delayed. Most patients are males. Weakness and muscular wasting start in the proximal muscles of the extremities, although the distal muscles may also be affected. Fasciculations of muscles may be observed. Associated skeletal abnormalities occur. The disease is very slowly progressive and compatible with a relatively normal life span.

PROGRESSIVE MUSCULAR DYSTROPHY

This disease of unknown cause shows a strong hereditary trend and may occur in several members of a family. It is characterized by a chronic progressive disturbance of the skeletal musculature. There are several variants, depending upon the site of initial muscular involvement and the distribution of apparent hypertrophy and atrophy. A defect in creatine metabolism, possibly due to muscle wasting, is usually present. Striated muscle is chiefly affected. On cut section the muscle fibers may appear swollen, indistinct, and homogeneous, with disturbed striations; some fibers may be hypertrophic and others atrophic. The late stages are characterized by fibrosis and fatty infiltration of muscles.

Elevation of various serum enzymes may be noted in patients with muscular dystrophy. Two serum transaminases, aldolase, and 2 types of dehydrogenase occur in their highest levels early in childhood muscular dystrophy and taper toward normal several years later. Serum creatine phosphokinase has also been

Figure 34–1. Patients with muscular dystrophy rise from a prone position by laboriously "climbing up upon themselves" (Gowers' maneuver).

reported to be greatly increased in patients with progressive muscular dystrophy. The possibility that some forms of muscular dystrophy may be "molecular diseases" similar in pathogenesis to the abnormal hemoglobin diseases has been inferred from abnormal spectrophotometric absorption spectra of the myoglobin in 2 forms of muscular dystrophy.

A general metabolic dysfunction may produce a neuromuscular disorder resembling one of the typical clinical types. Proximal myopathy may occur in late middle life in association with cancer.

Pseudohypertrophic Type (Duchenne)

This type occurs in early youth and is characterized by bulky calf and forearm muscles (that are quite soft as a result of infiltration by fat and fibrous tissue) and progressive atrophy and weakness of the thigh, hip, and back muscles and shoulder girdle. It usually occurs in males and rarely in females, with onset in the first 3 years of life. It is considered to be X-linked and recessive, with a high mutation rate (rarely, autosomal recessive). Symmetric early involvement of the pelvic girdle muscles and, later, of the shoulder girdle muscles occurs. In about 80% of cases there is pseudohypertrophy, particularly of the calf muscles but sometimes of the quadriceps and deltoids. Steady and rapid progression usually leads to inability to walk within 10 years. The gait becomes

waddling, and there is difficulty in going up or down stairs. These patients characteristically rise from the recumbent position by "climbing up upon themselves" (Fig 34–1). When an attempt is made to lift a patient with this disorder by grasping the torso under the arms, the loose shoulder girdle permits the head to slip through the examiner's hands. Lordosis frequently develops from the weakness of the trunk muscles. Late in the disease, the patient becomes too weak to move or stand unaided. Progressive deformity results, with muscular contractures, skeletal distortion, and atrophy. In the past, death from inanition, respiratory infection, or cardiac failure usually occurred in the second decade of life, but with current antibiotic, supportive, and intensive care, patients often reach the middle years of life.

Facioscapulohumeral Type (Landouzy-Déjérine)

Atrophy begins early in life and affects the muscles of the face, shoulder girdle, and upper arms; the muscles of the forearms are not involved. It occurs in either sex, with onset at any age from childhood until late adult life. It is transmitted usually as an autosomal dominant, occasionally with sex limitation. Abortive cases are common. Initially, the face and shoulder girdle muscles are involved and later the pelvic girdle muscles. Muscular pseudohypertrophy, contractions, and skeletal deformity are the rule. The characteristic

**Familial
Myelopathic**

INFANTILE

Infantile muscular
atrophy (Werdnig-
Hoffman)

ADULT

Hypertrophic
interstitial
neuritis
(Déjérine-Sottas)

JUVENILE

Peroneal muscular
atrophy (Charcot-
Marie-Tooth)

JUVENILE

Familial
ataxia
(Friedreich)

**Familial
Myopathic**

ADULT

Myasthenia
gravis
(Wilks, Erb)

JUVENILE

Familial peri-
odic paralysis
(Cavaré)

JUVENILE

Progressive mus-
cular dystrophy
(Erb-Landouzy)

JUVENILE

Myotonia
(Thomsen)

ADULT

Myotonic
dystrophy
(Deleage)

**Sporadic
Myelopathic**

The mannikin representative of each
disease shows the distribution of
atrophy, which is quite varied and
yet characteristic of each disease.
Muscles most affected are shown
solid black; those not regularly
affected are cross-hatched.

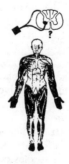

INFANTILE

Amyotonia congen-
ita (Oppenheim)
(myopathic?)

ADULT

Progressive mus-
cular atrophy
(Aran-Duchenne)

OLD

Amyotrophic lat-
eral sclerosis
(Charcot)

Figure 34–2. Classification of muscular atrophies. (Modified and reproduced, with permission, from Aring & Cobb: The
muscular atrophies and allied disorders. *Medicine* 1935;**14**:77.)

facial involvement, with drooping of the eyelids, is known as "myopathic facies" and the thickened over-hanging lip as "tapir lip." The weakened shoulder girdle causes "winging" of the scapula. The absence of forearm involvement gives a "Popeye the sailor" appearance. The disease progresses insidiously, with prolonged periods of apparent arrest, and most patients survive and remain active to a normal age.

Limb Girdle Type (Erb)

This form of muscular dystrophy involves the shoulder and pelvic girdles. The face is not affected. It occurs in either sex, with onset usually in the second or third decade but occasionally late in the first decade or in middle life. It is usually transmitted as an autosomal recessive characteristic. Primary involvement of either shoulder girdle or pelvic girdle muscle is noted, with spread to the other after a variable period. Muscular pseudohypertrophy occurs uncommonly. Abortive or static cases are uncommon. Variable severity and rate of progression may occur, but severe disability usually is present 20 years after onset. Muscular contractions and skeletal deformity come on late in the course of the disease. Most patients become severely disabled in middle life, and the life span is shortened.

Distal Myopathy

First described by Gowers, this form of benign muscular dystrophy occurs rarely in both sexes. Starting between age 40 and 60 years, the disease begins in the small muscles of the hands and in the feet and legs. It appears to be inherited as an autosomal dominant.

Ocular Myopathy

Muscular dystrophy may affect external ocular muscles, producing ptosis, diplopia, and possibly complete external ophthalmoplegia. Although formerly most such patients were considered to have progressive nuclear ophthalmoplegia, tissue examination of involved muscles in recent cases has indicated that some of these were examples of muscular dystrophy of the extraocular muscles. In some cases of muscular dystrophy of the external ocular muscles, there has been associated upper facial muscle weakness, dysphagia, and atrophy and weakness of neck, trunk, and limb muscles.

McARDLE'S SYNDROME

A myopathy characterized by weakness, stiffness, pain, and prolonged contracture of the skeletal muscles with moderate exercise results from the hereditary absence of muscle phosphorylase, leading to an inability to convert glycogen to glucose in muscle. A transient myoglobinuria is noted. The myopathy may not be noted in resting muscles. Treatment includes limitation of physical exercise and adequate diet. Glucagon given intramuscularly 3 times daily has been reported to be helpful.

FAMILIAL PERIODIC PARALYSIS

Hypokalemic periodic paralysis is a rare disorder in which the victim is seized by periodic attacks of flaccid paralysis lasting from a few minutes to several hours. Between attacks the patient is apparently normal. A severe attack may cause death from respiratory paralysis. A "cadaveric" electric reaction accompanies the attack. Decrease in serum potassium and serum phosphate is associated. Treatment includes oral administration of potassium salts. Attacks in susceptible individuals may be produced by injection of hypertonic glucose, insulin, desoxycorticosterone, or epinephrine or by water diuresis or excess sodium intake.

During attacks, the muscle potassium and sodium are not significantly elevated, and the muscle becomes electrically unexcitable. Membrane potentials recorded by microelectrodes within the muscle cell do not disclose hyperpolarization. During attacks, increased fluid may be noted in large vacuoles within the endoplasmic reticulum of muscle cells. Accumulation of abnormal glycogen breakdown products in these vacuoles may cause the influx of electrolytes and water into muscle cells to preserve ion balance.

Treatment is with potassium chloride, 5–10 g orally when the diagnosis has been made and then 5 g 2–4 times daily during acute episodes as needed to prevent weakness or paralysis. In respiratory paralysis, give a prepared solution containing 1 g of potassium chloride in 50–60 mL of distilled water very slowly intravenously. *Caution:* This is a dangerous procedure.

Patients with this disease should avoid high-carbohydrate foods. Routine administration of potassium chloride enteric-coated tablets, 8–12 g 3 times daily, prevents attacks. Acetazolamide (Diamox), 250–750 mg orally daily, may be effective in preventing recurrence of attacks.

With adequate treatment, the prognosis is excellent. Death may result from respiratory paralysis, but this is rare.

Adynamia episodica hereditaria, or **hyperkalemic periodic paralysis,** described by Gamstorp, is a disorder in which an increase in serum potassium accompanies paralytic attacks. Muscle weakness may be provoked in these patients by administration of potassium chloride or by rest after physical exertion. Onset is usually in the first decade. Attacks occur during rest after physical exertion. Mild paresthesias of the limbs usually precede attacks, and if exercise is begun at this stage, paralysis may be aborted.

CONGENITAL MYOPATHIES

Central core disease is a congenital myopathy with onset probably before the first month of life. Proximal muscle weakness, most severe in the lower extremities, results in delayed walking. The disability tends to remain stationary after the patient learns to walk. Hypotonia occurs, but deep tendon reflexes are normal, and muscle wasting is not extensive. The principal histologic change is in the anatomic arrangement and histochemical characteristics of aberrant fibrillary bundles found in the center of muscle fibers; frequent large fibers and central nuclei are also noted. The primary biochemical abnormality causing central core disease has not yet been identified. This disorder is one of many disorders of infancy associated with hypotonia, so that it must be considered in the differential diagnosis of such children ("floppy infant").

Nemaline myopathy was so named because of the threadlike forms observed in the muscle fibers. It is congenital and, until adolescence, does not appear to be progressive. The diagnosis is made by muscle biopsy. Within affected muscle fibers are noted numerous rod-shaped structures containing a contractile protein of the myosin family but lacking myosin adenosine triphosphatase activity and myosin antigenicity.

Megaconial myopathy is characterized by hypotonia and progressive proximal weakness in the young child. It is associated with giant mitochondria in affected muscle cells.

Pleoconial myopathy of childhood, with a striking increase in mitochondria of muscle cells, is associated with proximal muscle weakness and wasting. Episodic flaccid paralysis and salt craving may also occur.

Myotubular myopathy of adolescents is characterized by progressive weakness and wasting of the limbs, perhaps more marked distally, with ptosis, facial diplegia, and loss of reflexes. Muscles show the persistence of central nucleation in affected tissues and give the appearance of myotubes, or fetal muscular elements.

Fingerprint body myopathy of infancy is characterized by generalized weakness and hypotonia. Mild tremors of the extremities, decreased tendon reflexes, and mental retardation are associated. Muscle biopsy discloses abnormal inclusions with concentric lamellas resembling fingerprints in pattern.

Multicore myopathy of infants is characterized by diffuse muscle atrophy with proximal weakness, hypotonia, and hyporeflexia. Biopsy of muscle discloses decreased mitochondria with or without sarcomere disintegration.

Congenital muscular dystrophy is associated with severe hypotonia at birth. In the benign form, gradual improvement may occur; in the severe form, there is rapid progression. Muscle contractures may occur, and sucking and swallowing difficulties are present at birth. Muscle biopsy shows hypertrophy and degeneration of muscle fibers.

POLYMYOSITIS

Muscular atrophy and weakness may be secondary to widespread local inflammatory changes. In chil-

dren, this disorder may be confused with progressive muscular dystrophy, although its course is apt to be more rapid. Muscles are sometimes tender and indurated. Muscle biopsy discloses variations in muscle fiber size, with necrosis, active phagocytosis, and cellular infiltration. Corticotropin or corticosteroid drugs may be helpful. Regeneration of muscles may occur, and spontaneous recovery is frequent.

Polymyositis and dermatomyositis occur most commonly in middle age, affecting women more than men, and are characterized by proximal limb and girdle muscular weakness and, to a lesser extent, distal and neck muscular weakness. Associated features may include dysphagia, muscular stiffness, pain, induration, and atrophy.

MYOGLOBINURIA

Myoglobin may be found in the urine in idiopathic spontaneous hemoglobinuria, crush injuries of muscle, following extreme muscular exertion, or following ingestion of certain toxic agents. Myoglobinuria is suspected when a dark urine gives a positive reaction for occult blood in the absence of red blood cells in a person without evidence of hemolytic disease. The idiopathic type may be familial and associated with paroxysmal muscle pains and weakness and may prove fatal. The term "paroxysmal paralytic myoglobinuria" has been suggested for the group in which the disease is precipitated by exertion, starts in young adult life, has a high familial incidence with many repeated attacks, and is frequently complicated by weakness and atrophy. Absolute identification is made by spectrophotometric studies of the abnormal urine.

MYASTHENIA GRAVIS

This disorder, characterized by marked weakness and fatigability of muscles, is believed to affect the motor apparatus at the myoneural junction. Although almost any muscle in the body may be affected, the disease shows a special affinity for muscles innervated by the bulbar nuclei (face, lips, eyes, tongue, throat, and neck). The cause is essentially unknown, although some investigators consider myasthenia gravis to be a metabolic disorder. Dysfunction at the myoneural junction has been inferred from chemical and biologic studies.

Pathologic examination has failed to demonstrate consistent specific changes in the CNS, peripheral nerves, or muscles. Abnormalities of the thymus gland, including enlargement and tumor formation, have been described in some patients. It has been suggested that myasthenia gravis is an autoimmune disease, since multiple autoantibodies (including anti-skeletal muscle antibody) have been found in the sera of patients with this disorder. Myasthenia gravis may be caused by an autoimmune reaction to postsynaptic receptor protein with a destructive reaction involving the postsynaptic membranes.

Clinical Findings

There is usually pronounced fatigability of muscles, with consequent weakness and paralysis. The muscles innervated by the bulbar nuclei are especially susceptible. Weakness of the extraocular muscles results in diplopia and strabismus. Ptosis of the eyelids may become most apparent late in the day. Speech and swallowing difficulties may be recognized after prolonged exercise of these functions. Difficulty in the use of the tongue and a high-pitched, nasal voice may be present. A snarling, nasal ("myasthenic") smile may be evident.

Women are more often affected than men, and the disease appears most commonly between age 20 and 30 years.

Other somatic musculature may also be affected, resulting in generalized weakness. Fatigability of the deep tendon reflexes, with increasing diminution in response on repeated tendon tapping, is sometimes demonstrable. After a short rest, a single stimulus may then produce a strong muscle contraction. The Jolly reaction refers to the unusual fatigability of muscle upon repeated electrical stimulation, with pronounced capacity to recover after a short rest.

Diagnosis

A. Neostigmine (Prostigmin) Test: Prompt relief of symptoms (appearing within 10–15 minutes and lasting up to 4 hours) follows the subcutaneous injection of neostigmine methylsulfate, 1.5 mg, in most cases of myasthenia gravis. Atropine sulfate, 0.6 mg, is administered simultaneously to counteract side reactions. Observations are made 30 minutes later. If dysphagia is present, the response to neostigmine may be readily observed fluoroscopically as the patient swallows a thin barium paste.

B. Edrophonium (Tensilon) Test: Edrophonium is a quaternary ammonium salt that exerts a direct stimulant effect on the neuromuscular junction. Intravenous injection of 10 mg of edrophonium may relieve weakness within 20–30 seconds. Intramuscular injection of 25–50 mg may produce improvement lasting for several hours. Intravenous injection of 2–3 mg may be used as a test dose to distinguish myasthenic crisis (which improves) from overtreatment intoxication (no change) in myasthenic patients under treatment.

C. Other Studies and Tests:

1. In myasthenia gravis, EMG recording shows temporary decremental diminution in amplitude of contraction when peripheral nerve is stimulated electrically at frequencies of 3/s to 10/s.

2. Because of the coincidence of thymoma or thyroid disease, patients with myasthenia gravis should be studied for these disorders.

3. In most patients with myasthenia gravis, acetylcholine receptor antibodies can be detected in the blood. However, the antibody titer is unrelated to the clinical status of the patient.

Treatment

A. Emergency Treatment: Sudden inability to swallow or respiratory crises may occur at any time. The patient should always carry 2 ampules of 0.5 mg of neostigmine methylsulfate (Prostigmin), to be given immediately subcutaneously or intramuscularly if severe symptoms develop. The patient should be placed under medical care at once; if additional neostigmine is needed, 1 mg may be given parenterally 2–3 times in 1 hour until an adequate response is obtained.

Progressively and potentially fatal weakness of the muscles of respiration may occur in spite of the administration of increasingly large amounts of neostigmine. A tracheostomy set, oxygen equipment, suction apparatus, and respirator should be available. After endotracheal intubation or tracheostomy is performed, place the patient in a respirator and give oxygen as needed. Withhold neostigmine. Maintain fluid and electrolyte balance during the period of artificial respiration. After a few days, it is usually possible to decrease gradually the time spent in the respirator. In patients who survive the crisis, remissions may occur, in some instances lasting for several years.

Cholinergic crisis due to overtreatment with anticholinesterase drugs may resemble myasthenic crisis due to exacerbation of myasthenia gravis. The edrophonium chloride (Tensilon) test may help distinguish the two. Monitoring of motor strength and pulmonary function in an intensive care unit is desirable during such crises.

B. General Measures: Inform the patient about the disease, using simple lay terms. Maintain good nutrition and health.

C. Specific Measures:

1. Pyridostigmine bromide (Mestinon), an analog of neostigmine, is at times more effective in treatment of bulbar muscle weakness. Give 0.6–1.5 g daily at intervals spaced to provide maximal relief. Long-acting tablets (Mestinon Timespan), 180 mg each, are especially useful at bedtime.

2. Give Neostigmine bromide, 15 mg orally 4 times a day, and increase (up to 180 mg daily) as required to give relief.

3. Ambenonium chloride (Mytelase) is twice as long-acting as neostigmine and has fewer side-effects. Start with 5 mg 3 times daily and increase as necessary. The average dose is 5–25 mg 4 times daily.

4. Edrophonium chloride (Tensilon) may relieve myasthenic weakness: 10 mg intravenously gives relief in 20–30 seconds; 25–50 mg intramuscularly gives improvement lasting for hours; 2–3 mg intravenously may be used as a test dose for patients under treatment to distinguish between myasthenic crisis (improvement) and overtreatment (no change).

5. Ephedrine sulfate, 12 mg with each dose of neostigmine, often enhances neostigmine action.

6. Side-effects of treatment with anticholinesterase drugs (eg, abdominal cramps, nausea and vomiting) may be ameliorated or prevented by adding atropine or atropinelike drugs to the therapeutic regimen as necessary.

D. Surgical Measures: Beneficial effects have been reported from removal of the thymus gland. In some centers, thymectomy is considered for all patients under age 60 years who are seriously disabled by myasthenia gravis and are otherwise in good general health. Thymectomy is best performed in centers experienced with this type of surgery and with the pre- and postoperative management of thymectomy patients. A preoperative course of corticosteroids may be necessary in candidates for thymectomy, and corticosteroids are often required postoperatively, especially in thymoma cases.

For thymoma, the recommended treatment is thymectomy following a 3000-R course of x-ray therapy to the thymus over a period of 3–6 weeks.

E. Corticotropin and Corticosteroids: Encouraging results have been reported with short-term courses of massive corticotropin (ACTH), long-term periodic corticotropin injections, and long-term oral prednisone (100 mg on alternate days). Long-term alternate-day treatment with high single doses of prednisone has been reported to produce excellent clinical responses, especially in older and male patients. Complications of such treatment include cataracts, hypertension, diabetes mellitus, fluid retention, and osteoporosis.

The early phase of corticosteroid treatment may be associated with increased weakness. Prednisone may be started in a dosage of 10–20 mg daily and gradually increased to 80–100 mg daily over a period of weeks to months.

Management of Newborn Infants of Myasthenic Mothers

Immediately after delivery, children of patients with myasthenia gravis may have severe signs of the disease. Immediate treatment with neostigmine is necessary to preserve life. After a few days the symptoms may disappear, and the child thereafter usually does not suffer from myasthenia.

Prognosis

Spontaneous remissions occur frequently, but relapse is the rule. Pregnancy usually produces amelioration, although exacerbations may also occur at this time.

Myasthenic crisis, with sudden death from apparent respiratory failure, may occur. Survival of crisis may be followed by a remission. Overtreatment with neostigmine may produce muscle weakness simulating myasthenic crisis.

In myasthenic crisis, the mortality rate may be reduced by withdrawing anticholinesterase medications for about 72 hours after onset of respiratory difficulty or arrest and instituting early tracheostomy with positive pressure respiration using a cuffed tracheostomy tube.

AMYOTONIA CONGENITA
(Oppenheim's Disease; Benign Congenital Hypotonia)

Amyotonia congenita is a rare congenital disorder of children characterized by marked atony of the muscles. It is not progressive. Oppenheim thought it represented a delay in muscular development. Others claim it to be due to agenesis of the lower motor neurons and classify it as a fetal form of spinal muscular atrophy of the Werdnig-Hoffmann type. Numerical deficiency of the anterior horn cells has been reported on pathologic examination.

Oppenheim felt that in the infants in his study, the generalized hypotonia, muscle weakness, and areflexia affecting infants from birth had as its most characteristic feature a tendency to recover with the passage of time. This, he felt, distinguished this disorder from the spinal muscular atrophy of Werdnig and Hoffmann. Muscle biopsy and electrodiagnostic studies may be of value in diagnosis.

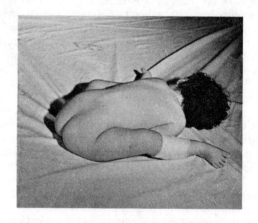

Figure 34–3. Child with hypotonia, hyporeflexia, and muscle weakness.

MYOTONIA CONGENITA
(Thomsen's Disease)

Myotonia congenita is a rare heredofamilial disorder characterized by localized or generalized myotonia. Hypertrophy and hypertonicity of the muscles may occur, rendering them rigid and unyielding. The disease has occurred in 5 successive generations in the family of Dr. Thomsen, who first described it. Although it usually is not serious, the increased muscle stiffness makes it difficult for its victims to enjoy physical activity. Some have periodic attacks of generalized muscular spasm. Typically, the disorder is present from birth, and there is stiffness and difficulty in relaxation of the entire voluntary musculature. Stiffness is usually accentuated by cold and relieved by exercise, and generalized muscular hypertrophy is common. It is inherited usually as an autosomal dominant characteristic. Quinine has been used successfully

Figure 34–4. Myotonia congenita. Hypertrophied myotonic shoulder muscles of young brother and sister.

in relieving hypertonicity. Acetazolamide may help occasionally.

MYOTONIA ATROPHICA
(Dystrophia Myotonica; Steinert's Disease; Myotonic Dystrophy)

Myotonia atrophica is a rare heredodegenerative disease of adult life that appears to be a mixture of Thomsen's disease and muscular dystrophy. There is hypertonicity of some muscles, usually of the tongue and the fist-making muscles of the hand, together with atrophy and weakness of the face, jaw muscles, peronei, and other muscles. In both myotonia congenita and myotonia atrophica, the patient characteristically grasps an object and then is unable to release it immediately. Myotonia, muscle atrophy (especially of face and neck), cataracts, early baldness, testicular atrophy, and evidence of dysfunction of other endocrine glands usually occur. Serum gamma globulin concentration is frequently reduced in myotonic dystrophy (IgG or 7Sγ fraction of immunoglobulins) as a result of increased catabolism of this protein.

Paramyotonia congenita is a relatively rare disorder characterized by myotonia which increases in the presence of cold, intermittent flaccid paresis which is not necessarily dependent upon cold or myotonia, and a hereditary pattern dependent upon a single autosomal dominant gene. It has been suggested that paramyotonia congenita is identical with or closely related to hyperkalemic periodic paralysis.

"STIFF MAN" SYNDROME
(Progressive Fluctuating Muscular Rigidity & Spasm)

This is a disorder of unknown cause and pathogenesis characterized by stiffness, tightness, or rigidity of the muscles and painful spasms of the muscles of the limbs and back. Boardlike rigidity of the back and abdominal muscles, stiff gait, and a tendency to fall like a "wooden man" may be noted intermittently.

Diazepam (Valium) has been reported to produce dramatic improvement in patients in doses of 10–15 mg 4 times daily.

GENERALIZED MYOSITIS OSSIFICANS

This progressive familial disease begins in early childhood and is often accompanied by congenital anomalies of the digits. Interstitial tissue shows the earliest changes; swellings in muscles are noted that gradually are transformed into bony-hard lumps. Respiratory muscles may be affected, and progressive respiratory embarrassment is prone to occur in some patients.

CONGENITAL NEUROMUSCULAR DISORDERS

Some congenital disorders of muscle or of the lower motor neurons are essentially nonprogressive. The following classification has been found useful.

Congenital Absence of Muscle
This relatively common defect appears to affect certain muscles more than others. The pectoralis major, trapezius, serratus anterior, and quadratus femoris muscles are reported to be most commonly absent. The defect may be asymptomatic or may be associated with other developmental defects.

Congenital Neuromuscular Disease With Localized or Restricted Weakness
A. Congenital Facial Diplegia, External Ophthalmoplegia, and Related Abnormalities: Congenital weakness of the facial muscles, the lateral rectus muscles (Möbius' syndrome), and other muscles supplied by the cranial nerves may coexist with other congenital defects. Although the site of primary pathology is generally considered to be at the levels of the cranial nerve nuclei, not many confirmatory pathologic studies have been reported.

B. Congenital Ptosis: Isolated weakness of the levator palpebrae muscle may be unilateral or bilateral. Affected individuals go about frequently with neck extended and brow furrowed in attempts to compensate for ptosis. Congenital Horner's syndrome may also occur, with slight ptosis, defective iris pigmentation, and miosis.

C. Congenital Neuropathies and Radiculopathies: Unilateral facial weakness related somehow to pregnancy or the birth process is common, and the prognosis for recovery from this and similar cranial nerve palsies in the first year of life is excellent. Traction palsies (Erb and Klumpke; see p 118) are usually attributed to brachial plexus injuries but may result

Table 34—2. Classification of neuromuscular disorders by age of patient at onset.*

Presenting at birth	**Adults**
Infantile spinal muscular atrophy (Werdnig-Hoffman disease)	Muscular dystrophy (various types)
Benign infantile hypotonia	Motor system diseases:
Congenital muscular dystrophy	Amyotrophic lateral sclerosis
Central core disease	Progressive muscular atrophy
Nemaline myopathy	Progressive bulbar palsy
Congenital hypoplasia of muscle	Myotonic dystrophy (Steinert's disease)
Other metabolic myopathies	Thyrotoxic myopathy
Early childhood (usually progressive)	Potassium periodic paralysis (various types)
Progressive muscular dystrophy (usually Duchenne type)	Sarcoid myopathy
Glycogen storage diseases	Peroneal muscular atrophy (Charcot-Marie-Tooth disease)
Some cases of infantile spinal muscular atrophy	Proximal familial neuromuscular disease
Juvenile myasthenia gravis	**Onset at any age**
Other early life myopathies and neuromyopathies	Trichinosis
Late childhood and adolescence (often progressive)	Dermatomyositis and polymyositis (with or without associated
Muscular dystrophy, various types	malignancy in adults)
Myotonia congenita (Thomsen's disease)	Polyarteritis with motor (and sensory) neuropathy
Potassium periodic paralysis (various types)	Myasthenia gravis
Other rare conditions	Drug-induced myopathies (steroid and chloroquine)

*Reproduced, with permission, from Pearson CM, Price HM: Muscle biopsy: Why? how? and when? *Hosp Med* (Feb) 1966;**2**:34.

from injury at the spinal root level instead. The congenital and birth palsies must be distinguished from those acquired in the first few days after birth from injections, trauma, infection, etc.

Congenital Neuromuscular Disorders Associated With Contracture & Deformity About Joints

At birth, infants with neuromuscular disease may have contractures and fixed deformities about one or more joints. Associated local weakness, atrophy, or

absence of muscle or other congenital disorders such as myelomeningocele, spina bifida, etc, may also occur.

A. Congenital Clubfoot: This is considered to be one of the most common congenital musculoskeletal deformities, and the term clubfoot is applied to any fixed, abnormal posture of one or both feet. Plantar flexion and inversion of the foot is the most common position, and more than one member of a family, usually a male, may be affected. In a few instances, abnormalities of the spinal cord and peripheral nervous

Table 34—3. Classification of neuromuscular diseases by chief site of involvement.*

Chiefly involving proximal muscle groups
Muscular dystrophies
Polymyositis and dermatomyositis
Thyrotoxic myopathy
Sarcoid myopathy
Proximal familial neuromuscular disease
Chiefly involving distal muscle groups
Motor system diseases
Myotonic dystrophy
Distal muscular dystrophy
Peroneal muscular atrophy
Other peripheral motor neuropathies
Proximal or distal distribution, or both
"Floppy infant" syndrome
Poliomyelitis
Myasthenia gravis
Potassium periodic paralyses
Myotonia congenita
Dystrophic ophthalmoplegia
Steroid and chloroquine myopathy
Other rare syndromes

*Reproduced, with permission, from Pearson CM, Price HM: Muscle biopsy: Why? how? and when? *Hosp Med* (Feb) 1966; **2**:34.

Table 34—4. Comparison of major histologic findings during active phase of common neuromuscular disorders.*

	Muscular Dystrophy	Polymyositis	Neurogenic Atrophy
Random muscle fiber atrophy	++	++	−
Group (or motor unit) atrophy	−	−	++
Muscle fiber hypertrophy	++	±	±
Muscle fiber regeneration	±†	++	−
Central nucleation	++‡	+	−
Focal necrosis and phagocytosis of muscle fiber	±†	++	−
Inflammatory cell infiltrate	±†	++	
Endomysial connective tissue proliferation	++	+ to ++	− (+ late)
Fat cell proliferation	+ to ++	+	− (+ late)
Vasculitis	−	+ to ++	−

*Reproduced, with permission, from Pearson CM, Price HM: Muscle biopsy: Why? how? and when? *Hosp Med* (Feb) 1966; **2**:34.

†May be found early in the course of the Duchenne type of muscular dystrophy.

‡Most common in myotonic dystrophy.

system have been described, but in most cases no pathologic changes in the nervous system can be established.

B. Congenital High Shoulder (Sprengel's Deformity): The scapula is broader and shorter than usual. It is usually rotated and elevated, so that the lower angle lies closer to the spine than normally. Extensive fibrosis in the upper portion of the trapezius muscle and absence or replacement by fat and connective tissue of the lower portion of the trapezius have been noted.

C. Congenital Torticollis: Typically, there is contracture of the sternocleidomastoid muscle, with the occiput inclined toward that side and the chin deviated up and toward the opposite side. The head may be bent laterally, the face broadened, the frontal prominences minimized, and the occiput exaggerated on the affected side. The involved sternocleidomastoid muscle is often firmer than normal to the touch. Extensive fibrosis occurs within the residual fibers of the affected sternocleidomastoid muscle. The cause is not known, but presumably it antedates birth. Spontaneous recovery may occur or may be aided by physical therapy, a cast, or a collar. Surgical measures directed at the muscle or its nerve supply, when necessary, may be therapeutically effective.

D. Deformity About Several Joints (Arthrogryposis Multiplex Congenita): This syndrome refers to a condition in which multiple joints are deformed or bent in association with contracture of muscle. An imbalance of muscle strength about the joints resulting from neural or myopathic disease usually occurs without primary disorders of the joints. In disorders of neuropathic origin, the lower limbs are usually abducted, flexed, or extended at the hips, extended at the knees, and plantar flexed at the ankles. In those of myopathic origin, the hips are adducted and the knees and ankles flexed. Associated anomalies such as absence of the lower limbs, hemivertebrae, fusion and deformity of the ribs, scoliosis, meningomyelocele, and genitourinary disorders may occur.

Congenital Neuromuscular Disorders With Nonprogressive Generalized Weakness & Hypotonia

Many disorders may present as nonprogressive congenital conditions with generalized hypotonia, eg, amyotonia congenita, Down's syndrome, cretinism, arachnodactyly, and Turner's syndrome. Some CNS diseases may present with mental retardation and generalized hypotonia, although weakness may not be the most prominent feature. Congenital myasthenia

Table 34–5. Suggested classification of the floppy infant.[*]

Paralytic conditions (weakness with incidental hypotonia)
Proximal spinal muscular atrophies—neurogenic atrophies
  (1) Infantile spinal muscular atrophy (Werdnig-Hoffmann)
  (2) Benign variants (including Kugelberg-Welander)
Congenital myopathies
  (1) Structural—Central core disease, nemaline myopathy, myotubular myopathy, mitochondrial abnormalities, miscellaneous
  (2) Metabolic—Glycogenoses
Other neuromuscular disorders
  (1) Muscular dystrophy—Early onset Duchenne dystrophy
  (2) Congenital muscular dystrophy
  (3) Dystrophia myotonica
  (4) Myasthenia gravis
  (5) Periodic paralysis
  (6) Polymyositis
  (7) Peripheral neuropathies

Nonparalytic conditions (hypotonia without significant weakness)
Disorders of the central nervous system
  (1) Nonspecific mental deficiency
  (2) Hypotonic cerebral palsy, athetosis, ataxia
  (3) Metabolic disorders: abnormalities of amino acids, abnormalities of mucopolysaccharides, lipidoses
  (4) Mongolism
  (5) Birth trauma, intracranial hemorrhage, anoxia
Hypotonia-obesity syndrome (Prader-Willi)
Connective tissue disorders
  (1) Congenital laxity of the ligaments
  (2) Marfan's syndrome
  (3) Ehlers-Danlos syndrome
  (4) Osteogenesis imperfecta
  (5) Arachnodactyly
Metabolic, nutritional, endocrine
  (1) Hypercalcemia, renal tubular acidosis, rickets, celiac disease, hypothyroidism
Acute illness
  (1) Infection
  (2) Dehydration
Miscellaneous: Congenital heart disease
Benign congenital hypotonia; essential hypotonia

[*]Reproduced, with permission, from Dubowitz V: *The Floppy Infant.* Spastics International Medical Publications. The Lavenham Press Ltd, Lavenham, Suffolk, 1969.

gravis, polyneuritis of infancy, progressive muscular dystrophy, and polymyositis may sometimes be mistaken for amyotonia congenita. The syndrome of the ''floppy infant''—the flaccid, limp, slack, hypotonic child—usually presents a diagnostic challenge because of the many clinical entities with which it may be associated.

35 | Selected Psychiatric Disorders

Neurologic disorders are frequently associated with psychiatric symptoms, either as a result of primary involvement of the cerebral cortex or because of psychic reactions to unpleasant or progressive chronic disability. Conversely, psychiatric disorders may mimic neurologic disorders (eg, conversion reaction and psychophysiologic disturbances), and the differentiation may at times be exceedingly difficult. Any type of psychiatric disturbance may occur in neurologic disease.

Neurologic diseases of insidious onset (eg, multiple sclerosis, brain tumor, paresis) are often considered to be of psychogenic origin during their early phases. It is important to diagnose neurologic disorders when they are present and perhaps masked by other symptoms. One should not be misled even when there is overwhelming evidence of psychiatric disturbance. This is especially true for those neurologic disorders that may be amenable to therapy (eg, infections, toxins, injury).

ACUTE BRAIN SYNDROME
(Acute Organic Brain Syndrome)

The acute brain syndromes are a group of disorders of perception and interpretation, usually associated with delirium. They are often reversible and may result from temporary impairment of brain function secondary to a variety of causes, including systemic or CNS infection, exogenous or endogenous intoxication, trauma, cerebrovascular disease, convulsive disorders, intracranial tumors, and metabolic disorders such as anoxia and dehydration.

The onset may be abrupt or gradual. Acute brain syndromes are most common in old age and childhood and are more apt to occur among people with dependent, unsophisticated personalities in deprived social circumstances. The clinical course may be benign, ending in complete remission, or the disorder may progress to irreversible brain damage or death.

The clinical features (often reversible) may include the following: (1) disorientation, particularly with respect to time; (2) memory impairment, especially for recent events; (3) impaired intellectual function, especially in comprehension, learning, calculation, and knowledge, with poor concrete ideation,

perseveration, and confabulation; (4) impairment of judgment and planning ability; and (5) labile or shallow emotional responses. Great alterations in mental function may occur within brief periods. Delirium, usually associated with impaired perceptions, visual hallucinations and illusions, and increased psychomotor activity, may occur; or there may be stupor, with apathy and mental retardation.

An organic cause must be sought even in patients with a past history of social maladjustment and psychic stress and numerous emotional upsets. Clinical features related to headache, vomiting, impaired vision, convulsions, paralyses, incoordination, and paresthesias should be carefully investigated. Psychologic testing may disclose patterns suggestive of organic intellectual and memory impairment. Physical and neurologic examination and appropriate laboratory studies (blood, cerebrospinal fluid, x-rays, EEG, etc) should be carried out.

Whenever possible, treatment should be specifically directed against an established cause. Supportive measures are usually of great importance. The patient is best kept in a cool, quiet room with subdued lighting. Supervision is essential to protect the patient and others from injury. Sedatives and tranquilizers may be required for excessive agitation or aggression. Additional nursing and supportive measures required may include maintenance of hydration and electrolyte balance, reduction of fever, vitamin supplements, attention to bladder and bowel function, and skin care.

CHRONIC BRAIN SYNDROME
(Chronic Organic Brain Syndrome)

Chronic brain syndromes consist of usually permanent, often diffuse impairment of cerebral function that may be almost imperceptible clinically. Although the manifestations may ultimately become milder, some degree of impaired judgment, memory, orientation, comprehension, and affect usually persists. This is apt to be the case even if the underlying pathologic process subsides or responds to specific treatment.

Chronic brain syndrome may be due to many of the same underlying disorders that cause acute brain syndromes, and the differentiation may sometimes be based upon the demonstration of permanent impair-

Table 35—1. Classification (DSM-III, modified) of the American Psychiatric Association.*

DISORDERS USUALLY FIRST EVIDENT IN INFANCY, CHILDHOOD, OR ADOLESCENCE

Mental retardation
Mild
Moderate
Severe
Profound
Unspecified

Attention deficit disorder
With hyperactivity
Without hyperactivity
Residual type

Conduct disorder
Undersocialized, aggressive
Undersocialized, nonaggressive
Socialized, aggressive
Socialized, nonaggressive
Atypical

Anxiety disorders of childhood or adolescence
Separation anxiety disorder
Avoidant disorder
Overanxious disorder

Other disorders of infancy, childhood, or adolescence
Reactive attachment disorder of infancy
Schizoid disorder of childhood and adolescence
Elective mutism
Oppositional disorder
Identity disorder

Eating disorders
Anorexia nervosa
Bulimia
Pica
Rumination disorder of infancy
Atypical eating disorder

Stereotyped movement disorders
Transient tic disorder
Chronic motor tic disorder
Tourette's disorder
Atypical tic disorder
Atypical stereotyped movement disorder

Other disorders with physical manifestations
Stuttering
Functional enuresis
Functional encopresis
Sleepwalking disorder
Sleep terror disorder

Pervasive developmental disorders
Infantile autism
Childhood onset pervasive developmental disorder
Atypical

Specific developmental disorders
Reading
Arithmetic
Language
Articulation
Mixed specific
Atypical specific

ORGANIC MENTAL DISORDERS

Dementias arising in the senium and presenium
Primary degenerative dementia, senile onset
Primary degenerative dementia, presenile onset
Multi-infarct dementia

ORGANIC MENTAL DISORDERS (Cont'd)

Substance-induced
Alcohol
Intoxication
Idiosyncratic intoxication
Withdrawal
Withdrawal delirium
Hallucinosis
Amnestic disorder
Dementia associated with alcoholism
Barbiturate or similarly acting sedative or hypnotic
Intoxication
Withdrawal
Withdrawal delirium
Amnestic disorder
Opioid
Intoxication
Withdrawal
Cocaine
Intoxication
Amphetamine or similarly acting sympathomimetic
Intoxication
Delirium
Delusional disorder
Withdrawal
Phencyclidine (PCP) or similarly acting arylcyclo-
hexylamine
Intoxication
Delirium
Mixed organic mental disorder
Hallucinogen
Hallucinosis
Delusional disorder
Affective disorder
Cannabis
Intoxication
Delusional disorder
Tobacco
Withdrawal
Caffeine
Intoxication
Other or unspecified substance
Intoxication
Withdrawal
Delirium
Dementia
Amnestic disorder
Delusional disorder
Hallucinosis
Affective disorder
Personality disorder
Atypical or mixed organic mental disorder

ORGANIC BRAIN SYNDROMES
Delirium
Dementia
Amnestic syndrome
Organic delusional syndrome
Organic hallucinosis
Organic affective syndrome
Organic personality syndrome
Atypical or mixed organic brain syndrome

*Modified slightly as to form and reproduced, with permission, from *American Psychiatric Association; Diagnostic and Statistical Manual of Mental Disorders,* 3rd ed. Washington, DC, APA, 1980.

Table 35–1 (cont'd). Classification (DSM-III, modified) of the American Psychiatric Association.

SUBSTANCE USE DISORDERS
Alcohol abuse
Alcohol dependence (alcoholism)
Barbiturate or similarly acting sedative or hypnotic abuse
Barbiturate or similarly acting sedative or hypnotic dependence
Opioid abuse
Opioid dependence
Cocaine abuse
Amphetamine or similarly acting sympathomimetic abuse
Amphetamine or similarly acting sympathomimetic dependence
Phencyclidine (PCP) or similarly acting arylcyclohexylamine abuse
Hallucinogen abuse
Cannabis abuse
Cannabis dependence
Tobacco dependence
Other, mixed or unspecified substance abuse
Other, specified substance dependence
Unspecified substance dependence
Dependence on combination of opioid and other nonalcoholic substance
Dependence on combination of substances, excluding opioids and alcohol

SCHIZOPHRENIC DISORDERS
Schizophrenia
    Disorganized
    Catatonic
    Paranoid
    Undifferentiated
    Residual

PARANOID DISORDERS
Paranoia
Shared paranoid disorder
Acute paranoid disorder
Atypical paranoid disorder

PSYCHOTIC DISORDERS NOT ELSEWHERE CLASSIFIED
Schizophreniform disorder
Brief reactive psychosis
Schizoaffective disorder
Atypical psychosis

AFFECTIVE DISORDERS
Major affective disorders
    Bipolar
        Mixed
        Manic
        Depressed
    Major depression
        Single episode
        Recurrent
Other specific affective disorders
    Cyclothymic disorder
    Dysthymic disorder (or depressive neurosis)
Atypical affective disorders
    Atypical bipolar disorder
    Atypical depression

ANXIETY DISORDERS
Phobic disorders (or phobic neuroses)
    Agoraphobia with panic attacks
    Agoraphobia without panic attacks
    Social phobia
    Simple phobia
Anxiety states (or anxiety neuroses)
    Panic disorder
    Generalized anxiety disorder
    Obsessive compulsive disorder (or obsessive compulsive neurosis)
Posttraumatic stress disorder
    Acute
    Chronic or delayed
Atypical anxiety disorder
SOMATOFORM DISORDERS
Somatization disorder
Conversion disorder (or hysterical neurosis, conversion type)
Psychogenic pain disorder
Hypochondriasis (or hypochondriacal neurosis)
Atypical somatoform disorder
DISSOCIATIVE DISORDERS (OR HYSTERICAL NEUROSES, DISSOCIATIVE TYPE)
Psychogenic amnesia
Psychogenic fugue
Multiple personality
Depersonalization disorder (or depersonalization neurosis)
Atypical dissociative disorder
PSYCHOSEXUAL DISORDERS
Gender identity disorders
    Transsexualism
    Gender identity disorder of childhood
    Atypical gender identity disorder
Paraphilias
    Fetishism
    Transvestism
    Zoophilia
    Pedophilia
    Exhibitionism
    Voyeurism
    Sexual masochism
    Sexual sadism
    Atypical paraphilia
Psychosexual dysfunctions
    Inhibited sexual desire
    Inhibited sexual excitement
    Inhibited female orgasm
    Inhibited male orgasm
    Premature ejaculation
    Functional dyspareunia
    Functional vaginismus
    Atypical psychosexual dysfunction
Other psychosexual disorders
    Ego-dystonic homosexuality
    Psychosexual disorder not elsewhere classified

FACTITIOUS DISORDERS
Factitious disorder with psychologic symptoms
Chronic factitious disorder with physical symptoms
Atypical factitious disorder with physical symptoms

Table 35–1 (cont'd). Classification (DSM-III, modified) of the American Psychiatric Association.

DISORDERS OF IMPULSE CONTROL NOT CLASSIFIED ELSEWHERE	**PERSONALITY DISORDERS (Cont'd)**
Pathologic gambling	Antisocial
Kleptomania	Borderline
Pyromania	Avoidant
Intermittent explosive disorder	Dependent
Isolated explosive disorder	Compulsive
Atypical impulse control disorder	Passive-aggressive
	Atypical, mixed, or other
ADJUSTMENT DISORDERS	
With depressed mood	**CONDITIONS NOT ATTRIBUTABLE TO A MENTAL DISORDER THAT ARE A FOCUS OF ATTENTION OR TREATMENT**
With anxious mood	
With mixed emotional features	Malingering
With disturbance of conduct	Borderline intellectual functioning
With mixed disturbance of emotions and conduct	Adult antisocial behavior
With work (or academic) inhibition	Childhood or adolescent antisocial behavior
With withdrawal	Academic problem
With atypical features	Occupational problem
	Uncomplicated bereavement
PERSONALITY DISORDERS	Noncompliance with medical treatment
Paranoid	Phase-of-life problem or other life circumstance problem
Schizoid	Marital problem
Schizotypal	Parent-child problem
Histrionic	Other specified family circumstances
Narcissistic	Other interpersonal problem

ment of brain function in the chronic group. The most common causes of chronic brain syndrome are chronic alcoholism, cerebrovascular disease, senility, presenility, multiple sclerosis, head trauma, convulsive disorders, brain tumors, and neurosyphilis.

The usual clinical picture is one of slow deterioration in memory, confusion, irritability, stereotyped behavior, and delusional somatic complaints. Disorientation for time, place, and person is often present. Confabulation—to fill the gaps of memory deficit—is encountered in Korsakoff's psychosis. The patient often becomes untidy, mentally dull, rigid, and self-centered. Evidence of associated or underlying organic brain disease such as that associated with cerebrovascular disease or brain tumors may be apparent on examination. Laboratory studies and special tests may provide significant clues to the underlying brain changes and the cause.

In addition to treatment of the underlying disease (when feasible), symptomatic and supportive treatment, supervision, nursing care, sedation, and the use of tranquilizers are frequently necessary. Since the underlying disease may be untreatable, custodial care in a suitable environment is often required.

THE PSYCHOSES

Psychoses may occur without known or recognizable physical cause or structural brain changes. A characteristic feature is personality disintegration of variable degree, with failure to properly evaluate external reality. The ability to work and to relate adequately to other people is impaired. The psychoses are characterized by withdrawal and bizarre or asocial behavior. Outbursts of antisocial, dangerous, or self-destructive behavior are likely to occur. Borderline and ambulatory psychotic states may also occur, and in these cases the individual may make a marginal type of adjustment without the necessity of hospitalization.

A great many patients in mental institutions have psychotic disorders. The onset is commonly during adolescence, although it may be at any time from infancy to old age. Psychotic breaks frequently occur in persons whose behavior and thinking have always been different from those of others. The psychoses may last from a few hours to years or even most of a lifetime.

AFFECTIVE PSYCHOSES
(Major Affective Disorders)

Affective reactions are those psychotic disorders in which mood change is the principal symptom.

Manic-Depressive Psychosis

The manic-depressive state is characterized by abnormal mood swings with increased or decreased psychomotor activity. Over a period of many years, the same patient may have isolated attacks of mania and depression (''bipolar''), although in some patients one type of reaction tends to recur (''unipolar''). This disorder is most common in young adults and occurs

Table 35—2. Diseases causing dementia.*

Diffuse parenchymatous diseases of the CNS	**Normal pressure hydrocephalus**
So-called presenile dementias	**Deficiency diseases**
Alzheimer's disease	Wernicke-Korsakoff syndrome
Pick's disease	Pellagra
Kraepelin's disease	Marchiafava-Bignami disease
Parkinsonism-dementia complex of Guam	Vitamin B_{12} and folate deficiency
Huntington's chorea	**Toxins and drugs**
Senile dementia	Metals
Other degenerative diseases	Organic compounds
Hallervorden-Spatz disease	Carbon monoxide
Spinocerebellar degenerations	Drugs
Progressive myoclonus epilepsy	**Brain tumors**
Progressive supranuclear palsy	**Trauma**
Parkinson's disease	Open and closed head injuries
Metabolic disorders	Punch-drunk syndrome
Myxedema	Subdural hematoma
Disorders of the parathyroid glands	Heat stroke
Wilson's disease	**Infections**
Liver disease	Brain abscess
Hypoglycemia	Bacterial meningitis
Remote effects of carcinoma	Fungal meningitis
Cushing's syndrome	Encephalitis
Hypopituitarism	Subacute sclerosing panencephalitis
Uremia	Progressive multifocal leukoencephalopathy
Dialysis dementia	Creutzfeldt-Jakob disease
Metachromatic leukodystrophy	Kuru
Vascular disorders	Behçet's syndrome
Arteriosclerosis	Syphilis
Inflammatory disease of blood vessels	**Other diseases**
Disseminated lupus erythematosus	Multiple sclerosis
Thromboangiitis obliterans	Muscular dystrophy
Aortic arch syndrome	Whipple's disease
Binswanger's disease	Concentration camp syndrome
Arteriovenous malformations	Kufs' disease
Hypoxia and anoxia	Familial calcification of basal ganglia

*Reproduced, with permission, from Wells CE: *Dementia,* 2nd ed. Davis, 1977.

more frequently in women than in men. A familial tendency has been noted, and relatively minor events may trigger an acute episode.

The patient in the manic phase demonstrates flight of ideas, increased psychomotor activity, and emotional excitement. Other features include bizarre dress, hallucinations, hypersexuality, grandiose delusions, and even delirium.

The depressed phase is characterized by difficulty in thinking, psychomotor retardation, and depression. In severe cases, hallucinations and self-accusatory delusions may occur; suicidal tendencies are often prominent at this time. Stupor or clouding of consciousness may also occur.

Mixed types also occur, in which the cardinal symptoms of both phases are present, such as in agitated depression or maniacal stupor. This is most apt to occur when a patient in the depressed or manic phase is undergoing a shift to the opposite mood.

During acute episodes, hospitalization is usually required. Electroshock therapy may be effective in shortening the depressive phase as well as the acute manic phase. Antidepressant drugs may also prove effective. Drugs currently used include tricyclic compounds and lithium. Lithium carbonate may prevent recurrent manic attacks. In the manic phase, continuous tub baths (sedative hydrotherapy), sedative-hypnotics, and phenothiazine tranquilizers may be useful. Psychiatric care after the acute episode is usually desirable. Recovery from a single episode usually occurs, although recurrences are frequent.

The acute phase may last from a few days to many years. Onset in early life usually implies a lifelong history of recurrence of hyper- and hypoactive moods and behavior.

Psychotic Depression

These patients are severely depressed and have difficulty in relating to reality. Delusions and hallucinations may be present. There usually is no history of recurrent depressive episodes or mood swings, but a history of an external precipitating factor directly related to the onset of the depression can often be elicited. The prognosis is usually good, and treatment, consisting of psychotherapy, drugs, or electroshock therapy, is usually effective.

Table 35–3. Commonly used antidepressants.*

	Usual Daily Oral Dose (mg)	Usual Daily Maximum Oral Dose (mg)
Tricyclic and Tetracyclic Compounds		
Tertiary amines		
Imipramine (Presamine, Tofranil)	150–200	300
Trimipramine (Surmontil)	75–150	200
Amitriptyline (Elavil, Endep)	150–200	300
Doxepin (Adapin, Sinequan)	150–200	300
Secondary amines		
Desipramine (Norpramin, Pertofrane)	150–200	300
Nortriptyline (Aventyl, Pamelor)	100–150	200
Protriptyline (Triptil, Vivactil)	15–40	60
Maprotiline (Ludiomil)	150–200	300
Piperazine		
Amoxapine (Asendin)	150–200	300
Monoamine Oxidase Inhibitors		
Tranylcypromine (Parnate)	20	30
Phenelzine (Nardil)	45–60	90
Isocarboxazid (Marplan)	10–20	30

*Reproduced, with permission, from Krupp MA, Chatton MJ (editors): *Current Medical Diagnosis & Treatment 1982.* Lange, 1982.

Involutional Psychosis

Psychotic disturbances characterized by depression may occur during the involutional period of life, particularly in women in association with the menopause. Insomnia, increasing agitation, somatic delusions, and feelings of unreality may gradually appear. Marked depression, with agitation, may become so profound that precautions against suicide must be instituted. These disorders usually respond favorably to electroshock and drug therapy, especially if these are instituted early. Supportive psychotherapy and psychiatric supervision are advisable.

SCHIZOPHRENIA

The schizophrenias are characterized by progressive withdrawal from the environment, as manifested by specific alterations of the ability to think, feel, and relate to the external world. The schizophrenias are the largest group of severe behavioral disorders. Although schizophrenia occurs most often in adolescents and young adults, it may occur at any age from childhood to middle age. The schizophrenic reaction may be of brief duration, or it may be protracted over many years or be present throughout the entire lifetime of the patient.

Patients with schizophrenia have deficits in awareness of social or interpersonal realities. Defects in associative function, changes in affect, and ambivalence are noted. Auditory hallucinations with persecu-

tory meaning frequently occur. Delusions are usually persecutory in type, although delusions of grandeur and imaginary diseases also are noted. Memory disturbances, including amnesias, are common. Speech and writing may show blocking, poverty of ideas, incoherence, and delusional content. The speech may be characterized by affected mannerisms, substitutions, and accidental associations. Catatonic symptoms, including catalepsy, stupor, hyperkinesia, and stereotyped speech, movement, expression, and mannerisms, may also occur.

The physical examination usually does not produce any remarkable findings, although schizophrenics tend to have an asthenic habitus, autonomic instability, weight loss, poor motor coordination, and an awkward gait.

Treatment usually includes psychotherapy, the use of psychopharmacologic agents, and electroshock therapy in selected patients. The prognosis is variable,

Table 35–4. Commonly used antipsychotics.*

	Chlorpromazine Ratio	Usual Daily Oral Dose	Usual Daily Maximum Dose†
Phenothiazines			
Chlorpromazine (Thorazine and other trade names)	1:1	100–200 mg	1 g
Thioridazine (Mellaril)	1:1	100–200 mg	600 mg
Mesoridazine (Serentil)	1:2	50–100 mg	400 mg
Piperacetazine (Quide)	1:8	20 mg	160 mg
Butaperazine (Repoise)‡	1:8	20–50 mg	150 mg
Perphenazine (Trilafon)‡	1:10	8–16 mg	64 mg
Trifluoperazine (Stelazine)‡	1:20	5–15 mg	60 mg
Fluphenazine (Prolixin, Permitil)‡	1:50	2–10 mg	60 mg
Thioxanthenes			
Chlorprothixene (Taractan)	1:1	100–200 mg	600 mg
Thiothixene (Navane)‡	1:20	5–10 mg	80 mg
Butyrophenone			
Haloperidol (Haldol)	1:50	2–5 mg	50 mg
Dihydroindolone			
Molindone (Moban, Lidone)	1:15	50–100 mg	225 mg
Dibenzoxazepine			
Loxapine (Loxitane, Daxolin)	1:10	50–75 mg	200 mg

*Reproduced, with permission, from Krupp MA, Chatton MJ (editors): *Current Medical Diagnosis & Treatment 1982.* Lange, 1982.
†Can be higher in some cases.
‡Indicates piperazine structure.

although an acute onset, catatonic symptoms, and a marked degree of affective disturbance are usually asociated with a better prognosis; whereas onset at a young age, slow progress, and the absence of overt anxiety indicate a poor prognosis.

A variety of clinical types have been distinguished on the basis of the predominance of some of the symptoms.

Paranoid Schizophrenia

Patients become suspicious and interpret even indifferent events and objects as threats to themselves. They feel that others are conspiring against them, and they hear voices that talk about and to them. This may lead to violent action, as in fleeing from or turning against a supposed tormentor. As the disorder becomes more chronic, ideas of omnipotence and delusions of grandeur may appear.

Catatonic Schizophrenia

The principal signs are stupor, mutism, negativism, and peculiarities of gait. Periods of catatonic excitement may occur, with impulsive activity, self-disregard, sleeplessness, and repetitious overactivity. In the akinetic phase, the patient may show waxy flexibility, refusal to swallow, and automatic responses to commands. The onset is often acute, and the patient's mood may alternate between mania and melancholia.

Hebephrenic Schizophrenia

This is an acute psychosis followed by deterioration but without paranoid or catatonic features. The onset is usually between age 12 and 25 years. Pronounced feelings of mental and physical incapacity, pathologic sensations, emotional dulling, grotesque silliness, and sexual preoccupation are the principal features. Hebephrenic schizophrenia includes acute noncatatonic forms characterized by melancholia, mania, amentia, and twilight states.

Simple Schizophrenia

Patients become intellectually and affectively impoverished, with diminishing ability to make competent judgments and to work and care for themselves. They appear stupid and finally show a picture of severe dementia. Simple schizophrenia is slowly progressive over a period of many years. Institutional care is usually required.

THE NEUROSES

The neuroses are personality disturbances in which there is no gross impairment of perception or ability to interpret reality and no severely antisocial behavior. They are frequently precipitated by environmental factors. The cause appears to lie in early life conditioning, although the patient's current life situation triggers the actual neurotic symptoms. The major types of neurotic reactions are classified according to the predominant reaction.

ANXIETY NEUROSIS

Anxiety is characterized by feelings of apprehension or tension when faced with real or symbolic danger. In some patients, continuous or recurrent symptoms result from "free-floating" anxiety; this syndrome is seen in young adults and is known as anxiety neurosis. Complaints include palpitations, tremors, headache, dizziness, chest pains, choking, faintness, and dyspnea. Attacks are precipitated by emotional or physical stress. Crowded areas (eg, public gatherings) often form the setting of attacks. Increased irritability and inability to tolerate mild annoyances may make hospitalization necessary. The patient may have a sensation of impending disaster. Attacks may last from a few minutes to hours and may assume panic proportions.

Physical examination may reveal excessive perspiration of hands, tremors, mild tachycardia, or flushed face and neck.

Anxiety may be of brief duration or may last many years, with exacerbations and remissions. Treatment includes a complete medical work-up to reassure the patient, the use of sedatives and tranquilizers, and psychotherapy.

PHOBIC NEUROSIS

In some cases, anxiety is precipitated only by a particular object or situation that symbolically represents a neurotic conflict. Neurotic reactions in children are frequently of this kind. Elaborate efforts to avoid the phobia-inducing object cause the patient's life to become increasingly isolated.

Treatment consists of psychotherapy directed toward achieving insight, so that the patient can overcome the phobia and the personal meaning it represents.

HYSTERICAL NEUROSIS
(Conversion Hysteria)

Insupportable anxiety may be converted into impairment of motor or sensory function. The resulting handicap is often dramatic and bizarre, but despite apparent paralysis, blindness, paresthesias, etc, the patient seems remarkably undisturbed. Patients with immature, unsophisticated backgrounds are most susceptible. Amnesia and dissociation of ideas may occur and represent avoidance mechanisms. In peacetime, this syndrome is more apt to occur in women.

Conversion symptoms may at times be difficult to distinguish from organic symptoms, but in general the patient's apparent illness will have atypical features.

For example, anesthetic areas are frequently of the "stocking and glove" type rather than corresponding to anatomic nerve distribution; paralyses vary in degree and distribution from time to time; visual fields in hysterical blindness may be the same at varying distances from the eyes, and the patient appears able to avoid obstacles. Hysterical attacks of variable types occur and may be difficult to distinguish from epileptic seizures. However, patients with hysterical seizures usually do not become unconscious, do not hurt themselves, and do not lose bladder or bowel control.

Treatment by suggestion, persuasion, hypnotism, and sedation may be effective. In resistant or severely disabled patients, psychotherapy is usually required. Removing the patient from a threatening situation often has a beneficial effect on symptoms.

OBSESSIVE–COMPULSIVE NEUROSIS

In this type of neurosis, obsessive thoughts or compulsive acts dominate the patient's behavior. Obsessive thoughts tend to persevere and usually cannot be put out of consciousness; compulsions are repetitious acts, usually of a ritualistic, stereotyped character. The typical patient is clean and neat, polite, perfectionistic, indecisive, and unimaginative, but with superior intellectual capacity. Anxiety and depression occur if the ritual is interrupted. Rituals include repetitive hand washing, object touching, and prolonged dressing. Obsessive thoughts may relate to death, sex, or other subjects disturbing to the patient.

Psychiatric treatment is often difficult and may be of little help in severe cases.

PERSONALITY DISORDERS

A person's character structure is reflected in the habitual attitudes and reaction patterns displayed in relationships with other people. Personality, or character, disorders consist of inappropriate exaggeration of one or more aspects of behavior. Lifelong patterns of action and behavior, rather than specifically identifiable mental or emotional symptoms, characterize the personality disorders. They are usually distinguished by deeply ingrained, maladaptive patterns of behavior that differ perceptibly from psychotic and neurotic changes and are often recognizable at adolescence or even earlier.

Paranoid Personality

This behavioral pattern is characterized by hypersensitivity, rigidity, suspicion, jealousy, envy, excessive self-importance, and the tendency to blame others and ascribe evil motives to them.

Cyclothymic Personality

In this behavior pattern, there are recurring periods of depression and elation not readily attributable to external circumstances.

Schizoid Personality

This pattern is manifested by shyness, seclusiveness, oversensitivity, avoidance of competition or close relationships, and—often—eccentricity. Autistic thinking, inability to express hostility, and aggressive feelings occur. Peculiar or "offbeat" ideas and behavior may be present.

Explosive Personality

In this pattern there are gross outbursts of rage or of verbal or physical aggressiveness strikingly different from the patient's usual behavior. Such patients are usually considered excitable, aggressive, and hyperresponsive to external pressure.

Obsessive-Compulsive Personality

This behavioral pattern is characterized by excessive concern with conformity and strict adherence to high standards of conscience. These persons may be rigid, overinhibited, overconscientious, overdutiful, and unable to relax easily.

Hysterical Personality

In this pattern there is excitability, emotional instability, overreactivity, and self-dramatization. The self-dramatization is usually attention-seeking in nature and often seductive. Such persons tend to be immature, self-centered, vain, and usually dependent on others.

Asthenic Personality

Easy fatigability, low energy level, lack of enthusiasm, marked incapacity for enjoyment, and hypersensitivity to stress mark this behavior pattern.

Antisocial Personality

Such persons are basically unsocialized, and their behavior pattern brings them into conflict with society. They seem incapable of significant loyalty to individuals, groups, or social values. They are generally selfish, callous, impulsive, irresponsible, and unable to feel guilt, and they do not learn from experience or punishment. They tend to blame others or offer plausible rationalizations for their behavior.

Passive-Aggressive Personality

This behavior pattern is characterized by both passivity and aggressiveness. The aggressiveness may be expressed by obstructionism, pouting, procrastination, intentional inefficiency, or stubbornness. Persons in this group tend to be helpless and indecisive or to react to frustration by irritability, temper tantrums, and destructive behavior.

Inadequate Personality

Persons of this type show unadaptability, ineptness, and social incompatibility. Although they have no obvious physical or mental deficit, they respond inadequately to intellectual, emotional, social, and physical demands.

SEXUAL DEVIATIONS
(Paraphilias)

Sexual deviation refers to the condition of those persons whose sexual interests are directed primarily or exclusively toward nonhuman partners or objects, toward sexual acts not usually associated with coitus, or toward coitus performed under bizarre circumstances. Although many deviates find these practices distasteful, they are unable to substitute normal sexual behavior for them.

Homosexuality has been removed from the list of paraphilias by the American Psychiatric Association (DSM-III; see pp 431–433).

Sexual deviates exhibit sexual behavior contrary to accepted cultural codes and customs. Similar symptoms may occur with mental disorders such as schizophrenia, the psychoneuroses, or senile psychosis; these disorders must therefore be ruled out. Some of the more common deviations are the following: (Combinations of these may occur.)

A. Fetishism: Substitution of some object (eg, shoe, garment) for the genitals.

B. Transvestism: Sexual pleasure obtained from wearing the clothing of the opposite sex. This is usually associated with homosexuality and with the desire to be accepted as a member of the opposite sex.

C. Voyeurism: Sexual pleasure obtained from observation of exposed genitals or the sexual activity of others.

D. Zoophilia (Bestiality): Sexual relations with animals.

E. Pedophilia: Use of a child for sexual purposes.

F. Exhibitionism: Sexual deviation in which there is a compulsive need to expose one's body, especially the genitals.

G. Sadism: Sexual pleasure derived from acts of cruelty to others. (Sexual activity may occur concurrently.)

H. Masochism: Sexual pleasure derived from the experience of pain.

ALCOHOLISM

Alcoholism refers to the condition of patients whose alcohol intake damages their physical health or their personal or social functioning, as well as to those to whom alcohol is essential for normal functioning. There are 3 principal types.

A. Episodic Excessive Drinking: In this condition, alcoholism is present and the person becomes intoxicated at least 4 times yearly. Intoxication refers to the state in which coordination or speech is definitely impaired or behavior is clearly altered.

B. Habitual Excessive Drinking: In this state, the alcoholic becomes intoxicated more than 12 times yearly and is overtly under the influence of alcohol more than once a week, even though frank intoxication is absent.

C. Alcoholic Addiction: In this type, the patient is dependent on alcohol and suffers withdrawal syndrome when deprived of it.

Alcoholism is common among people with personality or character disorders and may also occur in many types of psychosis and neurosis. During periods of intoxication, the patient may have increased feelings of importance. Following an acute alcoholic bout, however, such a person often feels considerable self-blame and self-contempt.

Severe changes may occur in the peripheral and central nervous systems in patients with alcoholism, including Korsakoff's syndrome, Wernicke's syndrome, polyneuropathy, cerebellar degeneration, etc (see pp 388–393).

DRUG DEPENDENCE

The term drug dependence is used for patients who are addicted to or dependent on drugs other than alcohol, tobacco, and ordinary caffeine-containing beverages. The patient may be dependent on opium; opium alkaloids and their derivatives; synthetic analgesics; barbiturates; other hypnotics, sedatives, or tranquilizers; cocaine; hashish or marihuana; other psychostimulants or amphetamines; hallucinogens; or other substances. Withdrawal symptoms are usually present when the drug is abruptly stopped.

Drug addicts often have neurotic or psychopathic backgrounds with excessive emotional dependence upon others. They are apt to use any means, legal or illegal, to obtain the funds necessary to secure their drugs.

Acute intoxication in drug abuse is a constant threat and a serious neurologic problem; its early recognition and treatment may be essential for survival and recovery. The abstinence or withdrawal syndrome from drug abuse may include early restlessness, yawning, lacrimation, sweating, piloerection, pupillary dilatation in the first 12–14 hours, and, later, abdominal cramps, muscle cramps and aches, diarrhea, hypertension, agitation, insomnia, anorexia, profuse sweating, and weight loss. Seizures and coma may occur 24–48 hours after withdrawal (see pp 388–391).

GLOSSARY OF
PSYCHOLOGIC TERMS

Abreaction: Emotional discharge resulting from conscious recall of repressed intolerable experience.

Acting out: Expression of unconscious emotional feelings or conflicts through actions.

Acute stress, or situational, reaction: Acute emotional reaction related to extreme emotional stress.

Adjustment: Adaptation of individual to the environment.

Affect: Emotional feeling tone. Emotion and affect are synonyms.

Affective disorder: Severe disorder of mood; manic depressive psychosis.

Aggression: Physical, verbal, or symbolic forceful attacking action.

Agitation: Chronic restlessness; often an expression of emotional tension.

Ambivalence: Concurrent opposing emotions toward the same object.

Amnesia: Pathologic loss of memory; may be organic or emotional (or both) in origin.

Anal eroticism: Pleasurable experience of anal function. Common in childhood; in later life, may appear in disguised and sublimated forms.

Anxiety: Feeling of apprehension that may be marked and continuous.

Autism (autistic or dereistic thinking): Thinking that gratifies unfulfilled desires unrealistically; not in accord with reality, logic, or experience.

Blocking: Impaired recall or interruption of thought or speech, usually due to emotional factors.

Circumstantiality: Speaking and thinking that is indirect, overly detailed, parenthetical, or irrelevant.

Compensation: Attempt to make up for real or fancied deficiencies.

Complex: Group of related ideas with strong common emotional tone.

Compulsion: Irresistible drive to do something often contrary to best judgment or desire.

Confabulation: Imaginary filling-in of memory gaps, usually unconsciously.

Conflict: A conscious or unconscious clash between opposing emotional forces.

Confusion: Lack of orientation with respect to persons, place, and time.

Conversion: Transformation of emotions into physical manifestations.

Countertransference: Therapist's conscious or unconscious emotional reaction to the patient.

Cyclothymia: Alternating periods of depression and elation, decreased and increased psychomotor activity, apathy and excitement.

Déjà vu: Subjective feeling that an experience has occurred previously.

Delirium: Mental disorder characterized by disorientation and confusion.

Delusion: False belief that cannot be corrected by reason.

Dementia praecox: Obsolete term for schizophrenia.

Denial: Denying existence of important elements that would otherwise cause anxiety and conflicts.

Dependency needs: Infantile needs for love, protection, and nutrition; may continue beyond infancy in overt or hidden forms.

Depersonalization: Feelings of unreality regarding self or environment.

Depression: Profound, unrealistic morbid sadness.

Disorientation: Impaired awareness of self in relation to space, time, and person.

Displacement: An unconscious mental mechanism in which emotion is transferred from its original object to a more acceptable substitute object.

Dissociation: An unconscious defense mechanism; a splitting off of emotion from idea, object, or situation.

Drive: A basic urge; motivation.

Echolalia: Automatic repetition of phrases and words; frequent in schizophrenic patients.

Echopraxia: Automatic imitation of another's movements.

Ego: Part of the personality that possesses consciousness, deals with reality and the outside world; the conscious self.

Eidetic image: Vivid mental image that may be a dream, memory, or fantasy.

Emotion: Subjective feeling such as fear, grief, anger, joy, or love.

Empathy: Awareness of meaning and significance of emotions and behavior of other persons.

Euphoria: Feeling of physical and emotional well-being.

Fantasy: An imaginary sequence of events or mental images.

Flight of ideas: Skipping from one idea to another. Ideas are apt to be fragmentary and related only by chance association.

Free association: Unselective verbalization of whatever comes to mind.

Fugue: Amnesia and physical flight from a particular environment.

Hallucination: False sensory perception of external object in the absence of the object.

Hypochondriasis: Persistent marked and continual concern with physical or emotional health, accompanied by somatic complaints without apparent organic cause.

Hysteria: Disorder arising from emotional conflicts, usually with dramatic physical clinical features, characterized by immaturity, dependency, and use of defense mechanisms of conversion and dissociation.

Id: Part of the personality that contains instinctive and unconscious drives.

Ideas of reference: Continual impression that speech and behavior of other persons have reference to oneself.

Identification: Attempt to pattern oneself after another.

Illusion: Misinterpretation of a real, external experience.

Inhibition: Unconscious interference with, or restriction of, instinctual drives.

Insight: Self-understanding; one's understanding of the origin and nature of one's behavior and attitudes.

Intelligence: Potential capacity to understand, recall, and integrate previous experience and to learn to meet new situations.

Introjection: Unconscious symbolic taking within the self of loved or hated external objects; the converse of projection.

Isolation: Excessively being alone by choice.

Lability: Rapidly changing emotions.

Libido: Psychic drive or energy, usually associated with the sexual instinct.

Loose associations: Lack of continuity in thinking, with random unconnected thoughts and speech.

Mania: Mental illness with increased excitability, acceleration of thought, speech, and motor activity, and a grandiose, elated mood.

Mannerisms: Stereotyped body movements frequently repeated.

Megalomania: Grandiose thoughts of self-importance, power, or wealth.

Melancholia: Pathologic dejection, often with psychosis.

Mutism: Failure to talk.

Narcissism: Self-love and interest. Normal in early childhood.

Negativism: Resistance and opposition to advice or suggestions; normal in late infancy.

Neologism: New word or combination of words coined by the patient; common in schizophrenia.

Neurosis: Emotional disorder due to unresolved unconscious conflicts with minimal loss of contact with reality. Types include anxiety reaction, phobic reaction, conversion reaction, and obsessive-compulsive reaction.

Nihilism: Delusion of nonexistence of self or part of self.

Obsession: Persistent intrusive unwanted impulse or idea that cannot be eliminated by reasoning.

Organic psychosis: Mental syndrome found with organic brain disease and usually associated with disorientation, impaired memory and judgment, intellectual deficiency, and behavioral changes.

Paranoia: A rare, slowly developing chronic psychotic disorder characterized by persecutory or grandiose delusions, with the rest of the personality essentially normal.

Perseveration: Recurrence or repetition of speech or activity.

Phobia: Persistent unrealistic fear of external objects or situations such as heights, open spaces, dirt, etc.

Psychopath: Person whose behavior is highly amoral or antisocial, with little anxiety or guilt.

Psychosis: Severe emotional illness characterized by abnormal patterns of feeling, thinking, and acting and loss of contact with—or serious distortion of—reality.

Rationalization: Making motives, feelings, behavior more acceptable by ascribing acceptable or worthwhile motives to such as might otherwise be intolerable or unacceptable.

Reaction formation: Development of behavior and attitudes based on the opposite of unacceptable impulses.

Regression: Return to more infantile modes of gratification.

Repression: Purposeful but unconscious forgetting.

Resistance: Psychic defenses against bringing repressed thoughts or impulses into awareness, thus avoiding anxiety.

Restitution: Attempt to assuage unconscious guilt feelings by making reparation.

Schizoid: Refers usually to traits of shyness, introspection, and introversion.

Schizophrenia: Severe psychosis, usually with retreat from reality, delusions, hallucinations, and regressive behavior. Types: (1) **Paranoid,** characterized by delusions of persecution and megalomania. (2) **Catatonic,** characterized by marked immobility. (3) **Hebephrenic,** characterized by shallow, inappropriate emotions and unpredictable, childish behavior. (4) **Simple,** characterized by withdrawal, apathy, inability to relate effectively to others.

Secondary gain: External gain derived from illness (disability payments, attention, etc).

Sensorium: State of mental clarity and consciousness at a given time.

Sublimation: Diversion of unacceptable, instinctual drives into acceptable channels.

Substitution: Replacement of an unattainable goal, emotion, or object by one more acceptable or attainable.

Superego: Censoring force of the personality, conscience; contains morals and ethics of the individual; in our culture, derived largely from parents.

Suppression: Conscious efforts to overcome unacceptable thoughts or desires.

Surrogate: A substitute person.

Symbolization: An abstract representation of a particular object, idea, or constellation of ideas.

Undoing: Symbolically acting out in reverse, usually repetitiously, an unacceptable prior action.

Verbigeration: Stereotyped, apparently meaningless, irrelevant verbal responses to questions.

Appendix

THE NEUROLOGIC EXAMINATION

HISTORY

A complete history of the nature, onset, extent, and duration of the presenting complaint and associated complaints must be taken. Previous diseases, personal and family history, occupational data, and social history should be recorded. It may be desirable or necessary to interview relatives and friends. It is occasionally advisable to record portions of the history verbatim.

Detailed information is particularly important in regard to the following:

(1) Headache: Duration, time of onset, location, frequency, severity, progression, precipitating circumstances, associated symptoms, and response to analgesics.

(2) Seizures and episodic loss of consciousness: Character of the individual episode, age at onset, frequency, duration, mental status during and after episodes, associated signs and symptoms, aura, type and effectiveness of previous treatment.

(3) Pain: Onset, progression, frequency, characteristics, effect of physical measures, associated complaints, type and effectiveness of previous treatment.

(4) Visual disturbances: Previous similar or related changes, progression or remissions, scotomas, acuity changes, diplopia, field changes, associated phenomena.

PHYSICAL EXAMINATION

A general physical examination should always be made. In particular, the circulatory, respiratory, genitourinary, gastrointestinal, and skeletal systems should be studied. A record of the temperature, pulse rate, respiratory rate, and blood pressure is routinely made. Note especially deformity or limitation of the head, neck, vertebral column, and joints. The scalp and skull are inspected and carefully palpated for localized thickening of the skull, clusters of abnormal scalp vessels, depressions of the skull, abnormal contours and asymmetry of the skull, and craniotomy and other operative scars. Percussion may disclose local scalp or skull tenderness over diseased areas and, in hydrocephalic children, a tympanitic "cracked pot" sound. Auscultation of the skull and neck for bruits is carried out; if bruits are present, the effect of separate carotid artery compression is also noted.

NEUROLOGIC EXAMINATION

Mental Examination

Mental changes are frequently encountered in clinical neurology, and an understanding of them is helpful for diagnosis and treatment. Mental deterioration, confusion, excitement, mania, lethargy, apathy, anxiety, depression, neurotic behavior, psychotic reactions, personality disturbances, and character disorders may be associated with neurologic disease. The type of mental disturbance is not specific for any given neurologic disorder, although impaired intellectual functioning is very common in cerebral disease. The insidious onset of certain neurologic disorders (eg, brain tumor, multiple sclerosis, paralysis agitans), with remissions and exacerbations, frequently results in the faulty diagnosis of psychogenic illness. Early neurologic disease may occur without significant physical, laboratory, x-ray, or other special diagnostic findings. Drugs used in treatment may further complicate the clinical picture.

A. General Behavior: Speech, appearance, cooperation, posture, general attitude, characteristic mannerisms, motor behavior. The patient's appearance (including condition of clothes and hair, facial expressions, attitude, peculiarities, and rapport with environment) and conduct (including activity, postures, gestures, and changeability) are evaluated both during the interview and on the basis of information and observations obtained from family, friends, and others. Speech and stream of thought are examined, with special attention to spontaneity, relevance, and coherence. Distractibility, flights of ideas, blocking, punning, rhyming, neologizing, and stereotypy are noted, and verbatim examples recorded.

B. Mood: Anxiety, depression, apathy, fear, suspicion, irritability, elation, aggression, etc. Note the patient's general emotional state based on appearance and conduct. Obtain patient's own statement of his or her mood and make an objective estimate of mood. Check for suicidal ruminations.

C. Sensorium: Orientation, retention, alertness, stupor, coma. When possible, check orientation for time, place, person, situation, and self.

D. Level of Intelligence: Vocabulary, judgment, cultural outlook, general information, etc. Intellectual performance tests, including calculation, judgment, retention, similarities and differences, etc, should be evaluated.

Evidence of an organic brain disorder may be disclosed by tests of intellectual performance. The subject's ability to abstract, use symbols, and evaluate new experiences on the basis of past experience may be judged with the aid of the following tests:

1. Memory–Details and dates of recent and remote events should be elicited, including items such as birth date, marriage date, names and ages of children and relatives, specific details of past few days, orientation with regard to time, place, and person, educational history with dates and names.

2. General information–Should be adapted to patient's background. Usually include names of President and Vice-President, governor of state, capitals of European countries and American states; current events in politics, sports world, etc; identification of world figures and leaders.

3. Similarities and differences– Compare wood and coal; iron and silver; book, teacher, and newspaper; president and king; dwarf and child; lie and mistake.

4. Calculation–Subtract 7s from 100, etc. ($100 - 7 = 93$; $93 - 7 = 86$; $86 - 7 = 79$, etc); add, multiply, or divide single numbers and make them more difficult depending upon patient's background, eg, 3×5, 4×3, 16×3. Count from 1 to 20 and backward from 20 to 1. Calculate interest at 6% for 18 months.

5. Retention–Repeat digits in natural or reverse order. (Normally, an adult can retain 7 forward and 5 backward.) After instruction, ask the subject to repeat a list of 3 cities and 3 two-digit numbers after a pause of 3 minutes.

6. Judgment–Ask patient for symbolic or specific meaning of simple proverbs, eg, "A stitch in time saves nine." "The rolling stone gathers no moss." "People who live in glass houses should not throw stones." The content of a simple story or paragraph from a newspaper or magazine may be read and the patient's retention, comprehension, and formulation observed.

7. Memory and comprehension–The examiner tells a story, which is then retold in the patient's own words. The patient is also asked to explain the meaning of the story. Two commonly employed stories are the "Cowboy" and "Gilded Boy" stories, which are given below.

Cowboy story. A cowboy went to San Francisco with his dog, which he left at a friend's while he went to buy a new suit of clothes. Dressed in his brand new suit of clothes, he came back to the dog, whistled to it, called it by name, and patted it. But the dog would have nothing to do with him in his new coat and hat, and it gave a mournful howl. Coaxing was of no avail, so the cowboy went away and put on his old suit, and the dog immediately showed its wild joy in seeing its master as it thought he ought to be.

Gilded boy story. At the coronation of one of the popes, about 300 years ago, a little boy was chosen to play the part of an angel. In order that his appearance might be as magnificent as possible, he was covered from head to foot with a coating of gold foil. The little boy fell ill, and although everything possible was done for his recovery except the removal of the fatal golden covering, he died within a few hours.

E. Content of Thought: Obsessions, phobias, delusions, compulsions, recurrent dreams or nightmares, depersonalization, hallucinations. Special preoccupations and disorders of content are checked, with attention to special topics of concern to the patient and the form they take.

F. Language: Comprehension of spoken language; ability to read and write. Recognition and ability to name familiar objects; capacity for verbal and nonverbal means of expression; ability to recognize errors; spontaneous or automatic speech.

G. Insight: Patient's own evaluation and explanation of the illness.

Coordination, Gait, & Equilibrium

A. Simple Walking Test: Posture, gait, coordinated automatic movements (swinging of arms), and ability to walk a straight line and to make rapid turning movements are observed as the patient walks. A detailed and full description of the gait should be recorded. Certain abnormal gaits are highly characteristic of some clinical disorders (see p 172).

B. Romberg Test: The patient stands with heels and toes together and eyes closed. Increased swaying commonly occurs in patients with dysfunction of cerebellar or vestibular mechanisms. Patients with disease of the posterior columns of the spinal cord may fall when their eyes are closed, although they are able to maintain their position well with the eyes open.

C. Finger-to-Nose and Finger-to-Finger Tests: In the finger-to-nose test, the patient places the tip of a finger on his or her nose. In the finger-to-finger test, the patient attempts to approximate the tips of the index fingers after the arms have been extended at the side. Dysmetria, with overshooting of the mark, is often observed in cerebellar disorders (see p 172).

D. Toe-Finger Test: The supine patient touches the examiner's finger with his or her great toe and holds it there until the examiner moves the finger to a new position 15–45 cm (6–18 inches) away, the patient then following the examiner's finger with the toe.

E. Heel-to-Shin Test: The patient places one heel on the opposite knee and then moves the heel along the shin.

F. Rapidly Alternating Movements of Fingers: In this test, the patient rapidly flexes and extends the fingers or taps the table rapidly with extended fingers. Good rhythm cannot usually be maintained in cerebellar disease.

G. Supination and Pronation of the Forearm: Supination and pronation are tested in continuous rapid alternation. The inability to perform these movements speedily and smoothly is a feature of adiadokokinesia (see p 172).

H. Rebound Phenomenon: The inability to stop a strong active movement to avoid striking an obstacle is known as the "rebound phenomenon." Its presence in the upper extremity may be demonstrated by the sudden release by the examiner of the patient's strongly flexed upper extremity, whereupon the hand of the flexed extremity may strike the patient's shoulder, neck, or face.

Sensation (See Chapter 10.)

Sensory examination is a difficult and wearing procedure for both the patient and the physician. The patient should be well rested and must be reassured and in a cooperative frame of mind before a sensory examination is attempted. Abnormalities, especially of minor degree, should be checked by frequent reexamination and charted. The following modalities are tested:

A. Pain: The ability to perceive pinprick or deep pressure.

B. Temperature: The ability to detect and distinguish between warm and cold. (Use a test tube of warm water and one of cold water.)

C. Touch: Ability to perceive light stroking of the skin with cotton.

D. Vibration: The ability to feel the "buzz" of a tuning fork (C = 128 Hz) applied to the bony prominences. After the tuning fork has been set into maximum vibration, the duration of the perception of the vibration is timed with the base of the fork applied to the malleoli, patellas, iliac crests, vertebral spinous processes, and ulnar prominences.

E. Sense of Position: This is tested by having the patient determine the position of the digits of the toes and fingers when these are grasped by the examiner. The digit is grasped on the sides and the patient, with eyes closed, attempts to determine whether the digit is moved upward or downward. The larger joints of the extremities are tested if impairment is demonstrated in the digits.

F. Passive Motion: Ability to perceive passive movements of the extremities, especially the distal portions.

G. Stereognosis: The capacity to recognize the forms, sizes, and weights of objects is tested. A familiar object such as a coin, key, or knife is placed in the patient's hand, and the patient is asked to identify the object without looking at it.

H. Two-Point Discrimination: The shortest distance between the 2 separated points of a compass or calipers at which the patient perceives 2 stimuli is compared for homologous areas of the body. (Normal: finger tips, 0.3–0.6 cm; palms of hands and soles of feet, 1.5–2 cm; dorsum of hands, 3 cm; shin, 4 cm.)

I. Topognosis: After first making sure that the patient's eyes are closed, the examiner touches the patient's body. The patient then points to the spot touched, thereby enabling the examiner to assess the patient's ability to localize tactile sensation. Similar areas of both sides of the body are compared.

J. Double Stimulation: Two stimulations are presented together to both sides of the body in homologous areas (simultaneous homologous) or to nonhomologous areas (simultaneous nonhomologous). Two stimulations are similarly carried out on one side of the body.

Reflexes (See Chapter 12.)

The following reflexes are routinely tested, and the response elicited is graded from 0–4+.

A. Deep Reflexes:

1. Biceps reflex–The examiner places a thumb on the patient's biceps tendon (the patient's elbow being flexed at a right angle) and then strikes the thumb. Normally, a slight contraction of the biceps muscle occurs.

2. Triceps reflex–With the patient's elbow supported in the examiner's hand, the triceps is sharply percussed just above the olecranon. Contraction of the triceps, with extension of the forearm, usually results.

3. Knee reflex–The patellar tendon, after being located by palpation, is tapped lightly with a percussion hammer with increasing force until contraction of the quadriceps muscle can be elicited. The patient may be seated on the edge of a table or bed, with the legs hanging loosely. In bed patients, the subject's knees are flexed over the supporting arm of the examiner, with the heels resting lightly on the bed.

4. Ankle reflex–This is best elicited by having the patient kneel on a chair, with ankles and feet projecting over the edge of the chair; the Achilles tendon is then struck with a percussion hammer. The reflex is frequently obtained with difficulty in bed patients, where the optimum position is one in which the thigh is externally rotated and the knee flexed at about a 45-degree angle.

B. Superficial Reflexes:

1. Abdominal reflex–With the patient lying supine with relaxed abdominal muscles, the skin of each quadrant of the abdomen is briskly stroked with a pin from the periphery toward the umbilicus. Normally, the local abdominal muscles contract, causing the umbilicus to move toward the quadrant stimulated.

2. Cremasteric reflex–In men, stroking the skin of the inner side of the proximal third of the thigh causes retraction of the ipsilateral testicle.

3. Plantar response–With the thigh in slight external rotation, the outer surface of the sole of the foot is stroked lightly with a large pin or wooden applicator from the heel toward the base of the little toe and thence inward across the ball of the foot. Normal plantar response usually consists of plantar flexion of all toes, with slight inversion and flexion of the distal portion of the foot. In abnormal responses, there may be extension of the great toe, with fanning and flexion of the other toes (Babinski).

C. Clonus: In patients with exaggerated reflexes, clonus (repeated reflex muscular movements) may be elicited. In the wrist, clonus is sometimes elicited by forcible flexion of the wrist. Patellar clonus may be elicited by a sudden downward movement of the patella, with consequent clonic contraction of the quadriceps muscle. Ankle clonus is tested by quickly dorsiflexing the foot, producing clonic contractions of the calf muscles.

Motor System (See Chapter 9.)

The power of muscle groups of the extremities, neck, and trunk is tested. Where an indication of diminished strength is apparent, testing of smaller muscle groups and of individual muscles is performed. Care must be exercised so that apparent weakness is not confused with real weakness of muscles. Retesting or concealment from the patient of the object of a given test movement may sometimes indicate more power than on the patient's initial test. Atrophy or hypertrophy of muscles is judged by inspection and palpation and by measurement of the circumferences of the limbs in the case of the musculature of the extremities. The differences between the 2 sides may be related to the handedness or occupation of the subject. Abnormal movements are noted, and the influence upon them of postural and emotional change, intention, and voluntary movements is recorded.

Muscle tone (tonus) is judged by palpation of the muscles of the extremities and passive movements of the joints by the examiner. Increased or decreased resistance to passive movement is carefully described. Tone alterations, including clasp-knife spasticity, plastic or cogwheel rigidity, spasms, contractures, and hypotonia, are noted. Involuntary movements, including tremors, athetosis, chorea, tics, and myoclonus, are described. Earliest upper motor neuron weakness is usually found in the dorsiflexors of the wrist and ankle. Fatigue usually increases all types of motor weakness and in myasthenia gravis may induce actual paralysis. Barré's sign is failure to maintain the legs in vertical position with the patient lying face down and the legs flexed vertically at the knees. Mingazzini's sign is failure of the patient lying in the supine position to maintain the thighs vertically with the knees flexed at right angles and the legs parallel to the table.

Pendulousness, the motion of a passively displaced extremity when it is permitted to swing freely, is increased in hypotonia, markedly reduced in rigidity of extrapyramidal origin, and irregular in pattern—though normal or slightly diminished in duration—in spasticity.

The Cranial Nerves (See Chapter 4.)

A. Olfactory Nerve (I): (See p 88.) Use familiar odors such as peppermint, coffee, menthol, or vanilla, and avoid use of irritant substances such as ammonia and vinegar. A test substance is rapidly passed toward the subject from a distance of about 1 meter, and the

patient must then identify the substance with eyes shut and one nostril held closed. Obstruction of the nasal passages, as by a cold or septal deformity, should be excluded by having the patient sniff with each nostril alternately occluded. Complete or unilateral anosmia may be of significance in the absence of intranasal disorders.

B. Optic Nerve (II): (See p 90.)

1. Visual acuity test–A Snellen chart may be used. Measure visual acuity as 20/size read and determine whether improvement is obtained with correction. Jaeger or related test charts can be used at the bedside, where the patient (wearing glasses if they are ordinarily required) reads a series of sentences or figures in various sizes of type at a reading distance of about 30 cm (12 inches). Cruder tests may be employed in individuals with severe defects, in whom the ability to count fingers and detect hand movements and changes from dark to light is noted. (See Chapter 21.)

2. Ophthalmoscopic examination–Each optic fundus must be examined as part of the neurologic examination. If necessary, the pupils may be dilated with eucatropine (Euphthalmine) or homatropine (after the pupillary reflexes have been noted). Details of the ophthalmoscopic examination should include the color, size, and shape of the optic disk; the presence of a physiologic cup; the distinctness of the optic disk edges; the size, shape, and configuration of the vessels; and the presence of hemorrhage, exudate, or pigment. (See Chapter 21.)

3. Visual field test–The visual fields may be roughly tested by confrontation, with the patient seated about 1 meter from the examiner. With the left eye covered, the patient looks at the examiner's left eye. The examiner raises both hands from a position where they can barely be seen in the 2 lower quadrants, and the patient signifies when the moving hands of the examiner rising in the lower quadrants first become visible. The upper quadrants are similarly tested, with the examiner's hands moving downward. The left eye of the patient is then tested against the right eye of the examiner.

More accurate visual field determination requires the use of a perimeter or tangent screen (see p 281). Visual field examinations are indicated in the evaluation of patients with known visual disturbances, abnormalities of the fundus, suspected supratentorial tumors, and disorders of the hypophyseal area.

C. Oculomotor (III), Trochlear (IV), and Abducens (VI) Nerves: (See p 93.) Strabismus, nystagmus, ptosis, exophthalmos, and pupillary abnormalities may be detected on initial examination. Ocular movements are tested by having the patient follow the movement of an object or light to the extremes of the lateral and vertical planes. A subject with defective vision is requested to look at his or her own hand, which is then appropriately moved. In patients with diplopia, the use of red celluloid or glass placed over one eye will facilitate the examination. The area of the visual field where diplopia is noted and where the divergence between the 2 images is greatest is carefully noted.

The size and shape of each pupil are noted. The reactions of both pupils to a bright light flashed into one eye in a darkened room while the patient gazes into the distance are noted. The direct light reaction refers to the response of the pupil of the illuminated eye; the consensual light reaction refers to the reaction of the opposite pupil, which is carefully shielded from the stimulating light.

In testing the accommodation-convergence response, the examiner asks the subject to focus alternately on 2 objects, one distant and the other 15 cm (6 inches) from the subject's face.

D. Trigeminal Nerve (V): (See p 98.) The ability to perceive pinprick or the touch of a bit of cotton is tested over the face and anterior half of the scalp. The oronasal cavity sensation is tested by reaction to a pinprick. The corneal reflex is tested by approaching the cornea from the side and touching it with a strand of cotton as the patient looks upward. Care must be taken not to touch the eyelashes or conjunctiva. The motor function of the trigeminal nerve is tested by palpating the contraction of the masseter and temporalis muscles induced by a biting movement of the jaws. The patient's ability to move the mandible from side to side is noted, and the capacity to open the jaw against resistance in the midline is tested. With the opening of the mouth, deviation of the mandible to one side becomes more obvious.

E. Facial Nerve (VII): (See p 99.) The facial expression and mobility and facial symmetry are noted. Smiling, whistling, baring the teeth, and puckering the lips are maneuvers performed by the patient that can be used to assess the voluntary movements of the lower facial musculature. Maneuvers such as closing the eyes or wrinkling the forehead are ways of testing the upper facial musculature.

Taste sensation of the anterior two-thirds of the tongue is tested by application of small quantities of test solutions to the protruded tongue with cotton applicators. The test solutions used are sweet (sugar), bitter (quinine), salt (saline), and sour (vinegar). As each taste is perceived, the subject responds by pointing to a labeled card. Between tests, the tongue is irrigated with water.

F. Cochlear Nerve (VIII): (See p 103.) The subject's ability to hear the examiner's voice in ordinary conversation is noted. The ability to hear the sound produced by rubbing the thumb and forefinger together is then tested for each ear at distances up to a few centimeters. The farthest distance from either ear at which the ticking of a loud watch or the spoken voice is heard may be measured.

With the aid of a tuning fork vibrating at 256 Hz, air and bone conduction are tested for each ear as follows: the vibrating tuning fork is placed on the mastoid process and then in front of the ear (Rinne's test). Normally, the vibrating tuning fork is heard for several seconds longer when placed in front of the ear after it no longer can be heard on the mastoid. In injury

to the auditory nerve (''nerve deafness''), there may be complete or partial inability to hear the vibrating tuning fork. When partial hearing remains, air conduction exceeds bone conduction. In disease of the middle ear with impaired hearing (''conduction deafness''), the bone conduction of the tuning fork is better than the air conduction.

Where loss of hearing is unilateral, the sound of a vibrating tuning fork (256 Hz) placed on the bridge of the nose or over the mid vertex of the scalp may be lateralized to one ear; in normal subjects, the sound is heard equally well in both ears (Weber's test). In deafness due to middle ear disease, the sound is heard in the affected ear.

G. Vestibular Nerve (VIII): (See p 103.) The caloric test is frequently employed to evaluate vestibular function: The ear drum is first examined to make certain no perforations exist. Irrigation of the ear canal with ice water is performed on the suspected pathologic side first (the reaction on this side may be minimal). The patient is seated with head tilted slightly forward in order to test the vertical canals (or lies supine with the head tilted back at an angle of 60 degrees in order to test the horizontal canals), and a slow, steady irrigation of the external auditory canal is carried out, with the reservoir about one foot above the level of the patient's head. Irrigation is continued until the patient complains of nausea or dizziness or until nystagmus is detected. This normally takes 20–30 seconds. If no reaction occurs after 3 minutes, the test is discontinued. Time of onset of initial symptoms, time of onset and direction of nystagmus and past-pointing, and results of the Romberg test are noted after irrigation is completed. (See also Hallpike test, p 103.)

Modifications of the galvanic test may be adapted for the purpose of judging vestibular function: The patient stands balanced astride a board about one foot square whose undersurface is divided in the middle by a projection 3 inches wide. An electrode is applied to the mastoid process and the other (indifferent) electrode is placed on the subject's back. Current from the battery is increased gradually (through a rheostat), and note is made of the amount of current in milliamperes necessary to cause loss of balance on the part of the patient. A response to galvanic stimulation may be present in the absence of a response to caloric stimulation, in which case the pathologic disorder is believed to be chiefly in the labyrinth.

H. Glossopharyngeal Nerve (IX): (See p 104.) Taste over the posterior third of the tongue is tested (in a manner similar to that described under the facial nerve for the anterior two-thirds of the tongue). Sensation (usually touch) is tested on the soft palate and pharynx. The pharyngeal, or gag, reflex response is tested bilaterally.

I. Vagus Nerve (X): (See p 106.) The swallowing function is tested by noting the patient's ability to drink water and eat solid food. The pharyngeal wall contraction is observed as part of the gag reflex. Movement of the median raphe of the palate and uvula when the patient says "ah" is recorded. In unilateral paralysis of the vagus, the raphe and uvula move toward the good side, and the posterior pharyngeal wall of the paralyzed side moves like a curtain toward the good side. The character, volume, and sound of the patient's voice are recorded. With the aid of a dental mirror, the position of the vocal cords may be visualized by indirect laryngoscopy. The resting heart rate and the bradycardia produced by pressure on the eyeball (oculocardiac reflex) or pressure on the carotid sinus may be influenced by lesions involving the vagus nerve.

J. Accessory Nerve (XI): (See p 107.) The subject is instructed to rotate his or her head against resistance applied to the side of the chin to test the function of the opposite sternocleidomastoid muscle. For testing both sternocleidomastoids together, the subject flexes the head forward against resistance placed under the chin. Shrugging a shoulder against resistance is a way of testing the trapezius muscle function.

K. Hypoglossal Nerve (XII): (See p 109.) The tongue is examined for atrophy and for fasciculations or tremors when it is protruded and when it is lying at rest in the mouth. Deviation of the tongue on protrusion is tested. Deviation to the same side occurs with lesions of the hypoglossal nerve.

When the examination has been completed, a summary of the findings should be recorded and a tentative diagnosis made. Plans for further study and treatment may then be made.

NEONATAL NEUROLOGIC EXAMINATION

The neonatal neurologic examination is usually performed 36–60 hours after birth. Repeat examinations at weekly intervals may be desirable. The examination should be planned so that little stimulation of the infant occurs initially.

General Status

Observe motor pattern and supine and prone body posture; evaluate reflexes throughout the examination.

In normal infants, the limbs are flexed, the head may be turned to the side, and kicking movements of the lower limbs may occur. Extension of the limbs may occur with intracranial hemorrhage, opisthotonos with kernicterus, and asymmetry of the upper limbs with brachial plexus palsy. Paucity of movements may occur with anoxia; reduced movement or paralysis may occur with brachial plexus palsy and meningomyelocele.

Infants normally become more reactive during the examination and cry. In anoxia or intracerebral hemorrhage, the infant reacts very little.

Cranial Nerves

A. Optic Nerve (II): Test blink response to light.

Ophthalmoscopic examination should be made at the end of the examination.

B. Oculomotor, Trochlear, and Abducens Nerves (III, IV, VI): Size, shape, and equality of the pupils and pupillary responses to light are checked. Lateral rotation of the head causes rotation of the eyes in the opposite direction ("doll's eye reflex").

C. Trigeminal and Facial (V, VII) Nerves: A finger or nipple placed between the lips is sucked (sucking reflex). In the rooting reflex, the infant's mouth will open and turn toward the stimulus if a fingertip touches the baby's cheek.

D. Auditory Nerve (VIII): Blink response or startle response occurs in reaction to loud noise. The baby is carried and held up by the examiner, who then makes several turns to the right and then to the left. A normal baby will look ahead in the direction of rotation and when rotation stops, look back in the opposite direction (labyrinthine reflex).

E. Glossopharyngeal and Vagus (IX, X) Nerves: The ability to swallow is noted.

Motor Systems

Spontaneous and induced motor activity are noted. If the infant is inactive and quiet, the Moro reflex may be used to induce movement. The infant may be placed in the prone position to induce movement.

A. Incurvation Reflex (Galant's Reflex): With the infant prone, tactile stimulation of the normal thoracolumbar paravertebral zone with a finger produces contraction of the ipsilateral long muscles of the back, so that the head and legs curve around the stimulated area and the trunk moves away from the stimulus.

B. Muscle Tone: Muscle tone is assessed by palpation of muscles during activity and relaxation. Resistance to passive extension of the elbows and knees is noted.

C. Limb Motion: The infant's ability to move a limb from a given position is checked.

D. Joint Motion: The infant's hip and knee joints are flexed to check the pull of gravity when the infant is held head down in vertical suspension.

Reflexes

A. Grasp Reflex: Stimulation of ulnar palmar surfaces causes forceful grasp of hands.

B. Traction Response: Contraction of shoulder and neck muscles occurs when a normal infant is pulled from the supine to a sitting position.

C. Stepping Response: The normal infant may make stepping movements when held upright with the feet just touching the table.

D. Placing and Supporting Reactions: Drawing the dorsum of the foot across the lower edge of a moderately sharp surface (edge of examining table) normally produces flexion at the knee and hip, followed by extension at the hip (placing reaction). If the plantar surface comes in contact with a flat surface, extension of the knee and hip may occur (positive supporting reaction).

E. Moro Reflex: The Moro reflex is present in normal infants. A sudden stimulus (loud noise, etc) causes abduction and extension of all extremities, with extension and fanning of digits except for flexion of the index finger and thumb. This is followed by flexion and adduction of the extremities.

F. Others: The knee jerk, plantar responses, ab-dominal reflexes, and ankle clonus are tested with the infant quiet and relaxed.

Sensation

Withdrawal of the stimulated limb and sometimes also the unstimulated limb may be caused by pinprick of the sole of the foot.

Table 1. Development screening (Dr. Sally Provence), first year.[*]
(Adapted from Gesell et al.)

Age (Month)	Posture and Locomotion		Handling of Toys (Rattle and Bell)	Social and Language	
Birth 1	Supine: Asymmetric posturing	Prone: Lifts head briefly	Focuses on rattle in line of vision	Reduces activity when talked to	
2		Prone: Lifts head halfway	Follows rattle with eyes briefly Actively (not reflexly) holds rattle when placed in hand	Smiles socially when stimulated	
3	Supine: Symmetric posturing predominates	Prone: Lifts head high; chest up			
4			Puts toys to mouth	Laughs aloud: "belly laugh"	
5	No head lag when pulled to sit			Squeals	
6	Rolls, supine to prone		Reaches out, grasps toy with 1 hand	"Talks" to toys (spontaneously)	
7	Sits briefly when placed	Pivots in prone	Transfers toy from hand to hand — Bangs table with toy Handles toy in each hand	Consonants (da, da etc.) Imitates sounds: "razzing," etc	
8	Sits alone (steady)		Grasps small toy with thumb and index finger		
9	Creeps (hands and knees)	Pulls to standing	Bangs 2 toys together	Dada-Mama (specific) Extends toy to person without releasing it	Waves "bye" or pat-a-cakes
10			Explores bell; pokes clapper		
11	Walks with 2 hands held	Cruises at rail			
12	Walks with 1 hand held		Finds toy behind screen	Two "words" besides Mama, Dada	Understands "Give it to me" (request and gesture)

[*]Reproduced, with permission, from Silver HK, Kempe CH, Bruyn HB: *Handbook of Pediatrics,* 7th ed. Lange, 1967.

Table 2. Average development from one to four years.*
(Adapted from Provence.)

	Motor Development	Crayon and Paper	Self-Help and Plays with Toys	Language
12 months	Walks alone.		Enjoys "putting in and taking out."	
		Imitates scribbling.		Three to 6 words, mostly names.
15 months	Creeps upstairs. Releases ball with slight toss toward examiner.		Shows or offers toy. Builds tower of 2 blocks.	Jargon.
				Names a few pictures.
18 months	Walks upstairs with 1 hand held. Climbs into adult chair. Walks fast, runs stiffly. Seats self in small chair. Hurls ball (overhand). Squats in play. Kicks ball on floor (imitatively).	Scribbles spontaneously. Strokes imitatively (imitates examiner's motion).	Hugs a doll or teddy bear. Feeds self with some spilling. Builds tower of 3—4 blocks. Turns pages of book (2—3 at once).	Understands simple verbal directions.
21 months	Walks upstairs, holding rail. Walks downstairs with 1 hand held.		Builds tower of 5—6 blocks. Handles cup well.	Combines 2—3 words spontaneously.
2 years	Walks up and down stairs alone. Jumps from low object.	Imitates vertical and circular strokes when demonstrated.	Pulls on simple garment. Explores drawers, cupboards, etc. Plays alongside other children. Builds tower of 6—7 blocks. Turns page of book singly.	Begins to use pronouns. Uses 3-word sentences. Refers to self by name. Verbalizes immediate experiences.
2½ years	Walks on tiptoe (after demonstration).	Holds crayon with fingers. Imitates vertical and horizontal strokes.	Can help put things away. Builds tower of 8 blocks.	Refers to self by pronoun. Gives full name.
3 years	Alternates feet going upstairs. Pedals tricycle.	Imitates a cross (demonstrated). Copies a circle from picture.	Puts on shoes. Knows a few rhymes. Can feed self with little spilling. Understands taking turns. Unbuttons clothes.	Tells sex. Uses plurals. Names 6—8 objects in picture book. Understands 2 prepositions. Repeats 3 numbers.
3½ years	Balances on 1 foot briefly.		Washes hands and face.	Understands 3 prepositions.
4 years	Skips with 1 foot. Throws ball well overhand.	Copies a cross from picture. Draws a "man" with 2 parts.	Plays with other children (real social interchange). Washes hands and face, brushes teeth. Laces shoes. Has dramatic play.	Understands 4 prepositions (on, under, behind, beside).

*Reproduced, with permission, from Silver HK, Kempe CH, Bruyn HB: *Handbook of Pediatrics,* 7th ed. Lange, 1967.

Name: _____

WHEELCHAIR ACTIVITIES
Propel: forward, backward, turn _____
Open, through, and close door _____
Up, down ramp _____
Bed to wheelchair _____
  Wheelchair to bed _____
Wheelchair to straight chair _____
  Straight chair to wheelchair _____
Wheelchair to easy chair, couch _____
  Easy chair, couch to wheelchair _____
Wheelchair to toilet (high toilet seat, regular seat) _____
  Toilet to wheel chair _____
  Adjust clothing _____
Wheelchair to tub _____
  Tub to wheelchair _____
Wheelchair to shower (chair in stall shower, or tub) _____
  Shower to wheelchair _____

TRAVEL:
Wheelchair to car - (with curb, without curb) _____
  Car to wheelchair - (with curb, without curb) _____
Place wheelchair in car - on street _____
Drives own car? _____

SELFCARE ACTIVITIES
HYGIENE (TOILET ACTIVITIES)
Comb, brush hair _____
Brush teeth _____
Shave (electric razor, safety razor), put on make up _____
Turn faucet _____
Wash, dry hands and face _____
Wash, dry body and extremities _____
Take bath (wheelchair, walking) _____
Take shower (wheelchair, walking) _____
Use urinal, bedpan _____

EATING ACTIVITIES
Eat   with spoon _____
Eat   with fork _____
Cut meat _____
Handle: straw, cup, glass _____

DRESSING ACTIVITIES
Undershirt -- bra _____
Shorts -- panties _____
Slip-over garment _____
Shirt -- blouse _____
Slacks -- dress _____
Tying neck tie -- bow _____
Socks -- stockings _____
Shoes (laces, buckles, slip-on) _____
Coat, jacket _____
Braces, prosthesis, corset _____

Institute of Rehabilitation Medicine
New York University Medical Center
PHYSICAL THERAPY
ACTIVITIES OF DAILY LIVING
INITIAL EVALUATION

NAME: _____
ROOM: _____
CHART #: _____

Date of Initial Test _____

            Mr.
            Miss
Name: Mrs. _____

Address: _____
                                              Age: _____ M.D. _____
                              Vocation: _____
Onset Date: _____ Lesion: _____ flaccid spastic   Admission Date: _____
Disability: _____
History: _____

Method of Recording Test and Progress

Symbol For Grade

$\sqrt{}$ - Patient can perform activity independently
A - Patient needs assistance
S - Patient needs supervision
L - Patient has to be lifted
X - Activity is not indicated

If there is more than one method or item listed with an activity, circle which indicated

BED ACTIVITIES
Moving in bed: Lying, sitting _____
Roll to right: to left _____
Turn on abdomen _____
Manage: pillows, blankets _____
Sit up _____
Reach objects on night table _____
Operate signal light _____

Figure 1. Activities of daily living. (Courtesy of Institute of Rehabilitation Medicine, New York University Medical Center.)

Name: _____

HOME SITUATION

Note suggestions for adaptation next to each line or check when so indicated. In special instances, diagram of lay-out will be advisable.

Location: Urban _____ Suburban _____ Rural _____

Floor _____ Rooms _____ Elevator _____ (self-service _____) None _____

APARTMENT: Walk-up _____

Floors _____ Rooms _____ Elevator _____ (self-service _____) None _____

PRIVATE HOUSE:

ENTRANCE: Door _____ #steps _____ Railing: right _____ left _____ none _____ ramp _____

Note floor if in private home: bedroom _____ living room _____ kitchen _____

bathroom _____

BATHROOM:

Door: width _____ Tub _____ Shower over tub _____ Stall shower _____

Information uncertain: (explain) _____

APPLIANCES

Wheelchair:

8" casters _____

Wheels: vertical tips _____

Pneumatic tires _____

Cushion: seat _____ back _____

Back: snap-raised _____

Semi-reclining _____

Footrests: removable _____

adjustable _____

stationary _____

Armrests: removable _____

desk _____

stationary _____

Brakes: lever-toggle _____

Assistive Devices	L	R	Description	Crutches		Apparatus
Prosthesis				Axillary		
Short leg				Lofstrand		
Long leg				Quad Cane		
Pelvic Band				Standard Cane		
Knight Spinal				Walker		

Name: _____

MISCELLANEOUS HAND ACTIVITIES

Write name and address _____

Manage: watch _____

match or cigarette lighter _____

cigarette _____

book, newspaper _____

handkerchief _____

lights; chain, switch, knob _____

telephone: receiver, dial, coins _____

handle: purse, coins, paper money _____

WALKING ACTIVITIES

Open, go through, and close door _____

Walking outside _____

Walking carrying _____

STANDING UP AND SITTING DOWN

Up from wheelchair _____

Down on wheelchair _____

Up from bed _____

Down on bed _____

Up from straight chair _____

Down on straight chair _____

Up from straight chair at table _____

Down on straight chair at table _____

Up from easy chair _____

Down on easy chair _____

Up from center of couch _____

Down on center of couch _____

Up from toilet _____

Down on toilet _____

Adjust clothing _____

Into car, on curb, up curb _____

Out of car _____

Down on floor _____

Up from floor _____

Drives own car _____

CLIMBING AND TRAVELING ACTIVITIES

Up flight of stairs (railing, no railing) _____

Down flight of stairs (railing, no railing) _____

Into and out of car, taxi _____

Walk one block and back _____

Down curb, cross street, on curb _____

Into bus _____

Sit down, get up from bus seat _____

Out of bus _____

Figure 2. Activities of daily living. (Courtesy of Institute of Rehabilitation Medicine, New York University Medical Center.)

NORMAL LABORATORY VALUES

HEMATOLOGY

Bleeding time: 1–7 minutes (Ivy).

Cellular measurements of red cells: Average diameter = 7.3 μm (5.5–8.8 μm).
Mean corpuscular volume (MCV): Men, 80–94 fL; women, 81–99 fL (by Coulter counter).
Mean corpuscular hemoglobin (MCH): 27–32 pg.
Mean corpuscular hemoglobin concentration (MCHC): 32–36 g/dL red blood cells (0.32–0.36%).
Color, saturation, and volume indices: 1 (0.9–1.1).

Clot retraction: Begins in 1–3 hours; complete in 24 hours.

Coagulation time (Lee-White): At 37° C, 6–12 minutes; at room temperature, 10–18 minutes.

Fragility of red cells: Begins at 0.45–0.38% NaCl; complete at 0.36–0.3% NaCl.

Hematocrit (PCV): Men, 40–52%; women, 37–47%.

Hemoglobin: [B] Men, 14–18 g/dL (2.09–2.79 mmol/L); women, 12–16 g/dL (1.86–2.48 mmol/L). (Serum hemoglobin: 2–3 mg/dL.)

Platelets: 150–400 thousand/μL (0.15–0.4 × 10^{12}/L).

Prothrombin: [P] 75–125%.

Red blood count (RBC): Men, 4.5–6.2 million/μL (4.5–6.2 × 10^{12}/L); women, 4–5.5 million/μL (4–5.5 × 10^{12}/L).

Reticulocytes: 0.2–2% of red cells.

Sedimentation rate: Less than 20 mm/h (Westergren); 0–10 mm/h (Wintrobe).

White blood count (WBC) and differential: 5–10 thousand/μL (5–10 × 10^9/L).

Myelocytes	0 %
Juvenile neutrophils	0 %
Band neutrophils	0–5 %
Segmented neutrophils	40–60%
Lymphocytes	20–40%
Eosinophils	1–3 %
Basophils	0–1 %
Monocytes	4–8 %

BLOOD (B), PLASMA (P), OR SERUM (S) CHEMICAL CONSTITUENTS

Below are listed the specimen used, the source—blood [B], plasma [P], or serum [S]—the fasting state, and the normal values. Values vary with the procedure employed.

Acetone and acetoacetate: [S] 0.3–2 mg/dL (3–20 mg/L).

Aldolase: [S] 3–8 units/mL (Sibley-Lehninger). Men, < 33 units; women, < 19 units (Warburg and Christian).

α-Amino acid nitrogen: [S, fasting] 3–5.5 mg/dL (2.2–3.9 mmol/L).

Ammonia*: [B] 80–110 μg/dL (47–65 μmol/L) (diffusion method).

Amylase: [S] 80–180 units/dL (Somogyi). 148–330 IU/L.

α$_1$-Antitrypsin: [S] 210–500 mg/dL.

Ascorbic acid: [P] 0.4–1.5 mg/dL (22.7–85.3 μmol/L).

Base, serum: [S] 145–160 mEq/L (145–160 mmol/L).

Bicarbonate: [S] 24–28 mEq/L (24–28 mmol/L).

Bilirubin: [S] Total, 0.2–1.2 mg/dL (3.4–20.4 μmol/L). Direct, 0.1–0.4 mg/dL (1.7–6.8 μmol/L).

Calcium: [S] 8.5–10.5 mg/dL; 4.2–5.2 mEq/L (2.1–2.6 mmol/L) (varies with protein concentration).

Calcium, ionized: [S] 4.25–5.25 mg/dL; 2.1–2.6 mEq/L (1.05–1.3 mmol/L).

β-Carotene: [S, fasting] 50–300 μg/dL (0.9–5.58 μmol/L).

Ceruloplasmin: [S] 25–43 mg/dL (250–430 mg/L).

Chloride: [S] 96–106 mEq/L (96–106 mmol/L).

Cholesterol: [S] 150–280 mg/dL (3.9–7.28 mmol/L). (See Lipid Fractions.)

Cholesteryl esters: [S] 65–75% of total cholesterol.

CO$_2$ content: [S or P] 24–29 mEq/L (24–29 mmol/L).

---

*Do not use anticoagulant containing ammonium oxalate.

Complement: [S] C3 (β_1C), 100–190 mg/dL; C4 (β_{1E}), 20–60 mg/dL.

Copper: [S or P] 100–200 μg/dL (16–31 μmol/L).

Cortisol: [P] 8:00 AM: 5–20 μg/dL; 8:00 PM: < 10 μg/dL (138–552 nmol/L).

Creatine kinase: [S] 10–50 IU/L at 30° C. Varies with method.

Creatinine: [S] 0.7–1.5 mg/dL (62–132 μmol/L).

Epinephrine: [P] < 0.1 μg/L.

Ferritin: [S] Women, 20–120 ng/mL; men, 30–300 ng/mL.

Folic acid: [S] 4–25 ng/mL; (9.1–57 nmol/L) [RBC] > 140 ng/mL (> 318 nmol/L).

Glucose: [S, fasting] 65–110 mg/dL (3.6–6.1 mmol/L).

Iron: [S] 50–175 μg/dL (9–31.3 μmol/L).

Iron-binding capacity, total: [S] 250–410 μg/dL (44.7–73.4 μmol/L). Percent saturation: 20–55%.

Lactate: [B, special handling] Venous: 4–16 mg/dL (0.44–1.8 mmol/L).

Lactate dehydrogenase (SLDH): [S] 55–140 IU/L at 30° C; SMA, 100–225 IU/L at 37° C; SMAC, 60–200 IU/L at 37° C.

Lipase: [S] 0.2–1.5 units/mL (mL of 0.1 N NaOH).

Lipid fractions: [P, S] Desirable levels: HDL cholesterol, > 40 mg/dL; LDL cholesterol, < 180 mg/dL; VLDL cholesterol, < 40 mg/dL. (To convert to mmol/L, multiply by 0.026.)

Lipids, total: [S] 450–1000 mg/dL (4.5–10 g/L).

Magnesium: [P] 1.8–3 mg/dL (0.75–1.25 mmol/L).

Nonprotein nitrogen (NPN)*: [S] 15–35 mg/dL (10.7–25 mmol/L).

Norepinephrine: [P] < 0.5 μg/L.

Osmolality: [S] 275–295 mosm/kg of water.

Oxygen:
Capacity: [B] 16–24 vol% (varies with hemoglobin concentration).
Arterial content: [B] 15–23 vol% (varies with hemoglobin concentration).
Arterial % saturation: 94–100% of capacity.
Arterial P_{O_2} (Pa_{O_2}): 80–100 mm Hg (10.67–13.33 kPa) (sea level). (Varies with age.)

Pa_{CO_2}: [B, arterial] 35–45 mm Hg (4.67–6 kPa).

pH (reaction): [B, arterial] 7.35–7.45 (H^+ 44.7–45.5 nmol/L).

Phosphatase, acid: [S] 1–5 units (King-Armstrong), 0.1–0.63 units (Bessey-Lowry).

Phosphatase, alkaline: [S] 5–13 units (King-Armstrong); adults, 0.8–2.3 (Bessey-Lowry); SMA, 30–85 IU/L at 37° C; SMAC, 30–115 IU/L at 37° C.

Phospholipid: [S] 145–200 mg/dL (1.45–2 g/L).

Phosphorus, inorganic: [S, fasting] 3–4.5 mg/dL (1–1.5 mmol/L).

Potassium: [S or P] 3.5–5 mEq/L (3.5–5 mmol/L).

Protein:
Total: [S] 6–8 g/dL (60–80 g/L).
Albumin: [S] 3.5–5.5 g/dL (35–55 g/L).
Globulin: [S] 2–3.6 g/dL (20–36 g/L).
Fibrinogen: [P] 0.2–0.6 g/dL (2–6 g/L).

Prothrombin clotting time: [P] By control.

Pyruvate: [B] 0.6–1 mg/dL (70–114 μmol/L).

Serotonin: [B] 0.05–0.2 μg/mL.

Sodium: [S] 136–145 mEq/L (136–145 mmol/L).

Specific gravity:
[B] 1.056 (varies with hemoglobin and protein concentration).
[S] 1.0254–1.0288 (varies with protein concentration).

Sulfate: [P or S] as sulfur. 0.5–1.5 mg/dL (156–468 μmol/L).

Transaminases: [S]
Glutamic-oxaloacetic (SGOT), 6–25 IU/L at 30° C; SMA, 10–40 IU/L at 37° C; SMAC, 0–41 IU/L at 37° C.
Glutamic-pyruvic (SGPT), 3–26 IU/L at 30° C; SMAC, 0–45 IU/L at 37° C.

Transferrin: [S] 200–400 mg/dL (23–45 μmol/L).

Triglycerides: [S] < 165 mg/dL (5.4 mEq/L or 1.9 mmol/L). (See Lipid Fractions.)

Urea nitrogen*: [S] 8–25 mg/dL (2.9–8.9 mmol/L).

Uric Acid: [S] Men, 3–9 mg/dL (0.18–0.53 mmol/L); women, 2.5–7.5 mg/dL (0.15–0.45 mmol/L).

*Do not use anticoagulant containing ammonium oxalate.

Vitamin A: [S] 15–60 μg/dL (0.53–2.1 μmol/L).

Vitamin B₁₂: [S] > 200 pg/mL (> 148 pmol/L).

Vitamin D: [S] Cholecalciferol (D₃): 25-hydroxycholecalciferol, 10–80 ng/mL; 1,25-dihydroxycholecalciferol, 21–45 pg/mL.

Volume, blood (Evans blue dye method): Adults, 2990–6980 mL. Women, 46.3–85.5 mL/kg; men, 66.2–97.7 mL/kg.

Zinc: [S] 50–150 μg/dL (7.65–22.95 μmol/L).

HORMONES, SERUM OR PLASMA

Pituitary:
Growth (HGH): [S] Adults, 1–10 ng/mL (by RIA).
Thyroid-stimulating (TSH): [S] < 10 μU/mL.
Follicle-stimulating hormone (FSH): [S] Prepuberal, 2–12 mIU/mL; men, 1–15 mIU/mL; women, 1–30 mIU/mL; castrate or postmenopausal, 30–200 mIU/mL (by RIA).
Luteinizing hormone (LH): [S] Prepuberal, 2–12 mIU/mL; men, 1–15 mIU/mL; women, < 30 mIU/mL; castrate or postmenopausal, > 30 mIU/mL.
Corticotropin (ACTH): [P] 8:00–10:00 AM: up to 100 pg/mL.
Prolactin: [S] 0–20 ng/mL.
Somatomedin C: [P] 0.4–2 U/mL.

Adrenal:
Aldosterone: [P] Supine, normal salt intake, 2–9 ng/dL; increased when upright.
Cortisol: [S] 8:00 AM, 7–18 μg/dL; 5:00 PM, 2–9 μg/dL.
Dopamine: [P] < 135 pg/mL.
Epinephrine: [P] < 80 pg/mL.
Norepinephrine: [P] < 400 pg/mL.
Also see Miscellaneous Normal Values.

Thyroid:
Thyroxine, free (FT₄): [S] 0.8–2.4 ng/dL.
Thyroxine, total (TT₄): [S] 4–11 μg/dL (by CPB); 5–14 μg/dL (by RIA).
Thyroxine-binding globulin: [S] 2–4.8 mg/dL.
Triiodothyronine: [S] 80–220 ng/dL.
Reverse triiodothyronine: [S] Adult 30–80 ng/dL.
Triiodothyronine uptake (RT₃U): [S] 25–36%; as TBG assessment (RT₃U ratio), 0.85–1.15.
Calcitonin: [S] < 400 pg/mL.

Parathyroid: Parathyroid hormone levels vary with method and antibody. Correlate with serum calcium.

Islets:
Insulin: [S] 4–25 μU/mL (0.17–1.04 μg/L).

Stomach:
Gastrin: [S, special handling] Up to 100 pg/mL. Elevated, > 200 pg/mL.
Pepsinogen I: [S] 25–100 ng/mL.

Kidney:
Renin activity: [P, special handling] Supine, normal sodium intake, 1–3 ng/mL/h; standing or while on low-sodium diet or diuretics, 3–6 ng/mL/h.

Gonad:
Testosterone: [S] Prepuberal, < 100 ng/dL; men, 300–1000 ng/dL; women, 20–80 ng/dL; luteal phase, up to 120 ng/dL.
Estradiol (E₂), RIA: [S, special handling] Men, 12–34 pg/mL; women, menstrual cycle 1–10 days, 24–68 pg/mL; 11–20 days, 50–186 pg/mL; 21–30 days, 73–149 pg/mL.
Progesterone, RIA: [S] Follicular phase, 20–150 ng/dL; luteal phase, 300–2400 ng/dL; pregnancy, > 2400 ng/dL; men, < 100 ng/dL.

Placenta:
Estriol (E₃), RIA: [S] Men and nonpregnant women, < 0.2 μg/dL.
Chorionic gonadotropin: [S] Normal men and nonpregnant women, none detected.

NORMAL CEREBROSPINAL FLUID VALUES

Appearance: Clear and colorless.

Cells: Adults, 0–5 mononuclears/μL. Infants, 0–20 mononuclears/μL.

Chlorides (as NaCl): 120–130 mEq/L (120–130 mmol/L).

Glucose: 50–85 mg/dL (2.8–4.7 mmol/L). (Draw serum glucose at same time.)

IgG: 2–6 mg/dL (0.02–0.06 g/L).

Pressure (reclining): Newborn, 30–80 mm of water. Children, 50–100 mm of water. Adults, 70–200 mm of water (avg = 125).

Proteins, total: 20–45 mg/dL (200–450 mg/L) in lumbar cerebrospinal fluid.

Specific gravity: 1.003–1.008.

RENAL FUNCTION TESTS

p-**Aminohippurate (PAH) clearance (RPF):** Men, 560–830 mL/min; women, 490–700 mL/min.

Creatinine clearance, endogenous (GFR): Approximates inulin clearance (see below).

Filtration fraction (FF): Men, 17–21%; women, 17–23%. (FF = GFR/RPF.)

Inulin clearance (GFR): Men, 110–150 mL/min; women, 105–132 mL/min (corrected to 1.73 m² surface area).

Maximal glucose reabsorptive capacity (Tm$_G$): Men, 300–450 mg/min; women, 250–350 mg/min.

Maximal PAH excretory capacity (Tm$_{PAH}$): 80–90 mg/min.

Osmolality: On normal diet and fluid intake: range 500–850 mosm/kg of water. Achievable range, normal kidney: dilution 40–80 mosm; concentration (dehydration) up to 1400 mosm/kg of water (at least 3–4 times plasma osmolality).

Specific gravity of urine: 1.003–1.030.

MISCELLANEOUS NORMAL VALUES
(Urine [U], Serum [S])

Addis urine sediment count: Maximum values per 24 hours are as follows:

Red cells, 1 million
White and epithelial cells, 2 million
Casts, 100 thousand
Protein, 30 mg

Aldosterone: [U] 2–26 μg/24 h (5.5–72 nmol); varies with sodium and potassium intake.

Catecholamines: [U] Total < 100 μg/24 h. < 10 μg epinephrine (< 55 nmol); < 100 μg norepinephrine/24 h (< 591 nmol); varies with method.

Congo red test: [S] More than 60% retention in serum after 1 hour.

Cortisol, free: [U] 20–100 μg/24 h (0.55–2.76 μmol).

Fecal fat: Less than 30% dry weight.

11,17-Hydroxycorticoids: [U] Men, 4–12 mg/24 h; women, 4–8 mg/24 h. Varies with method used.

Insulin tolerance: (0.1 unit insulin/kg IV.) [S] Glucose level decreases to half of fasting level in 20–30 minutes; returns to fasting level in 90–120 minutes.

17-Ketosteroids: [U] Under 8 years, 0–2 mg/24 h; adolescents, 2–20 mg/24 h. Men, 10–20 mg/24 h; women, 5–15 mg/24 h. Varies with method used.

Lead: [U] < 0.12 mg/24 h (< 0.57 μmol).

Metanephrine: [U] < 1.3 mg/24 h (< 6.6 μmol) or < 2.2 μg/mg creatinine. Varies with method.

Porphyrins: [U]
Delta-aminolevulinic acid: Adult, 1.5–7.5 mg/24 h (11.4–57.2 μmol).
Coproporphyrin: < 230 μg/24 h (< 345 nmol).
Uroporphyrin: < 50 μg/24 h (< 60 nmol).
Porphobilinogen: < 2 mg/24 h (< 8.8 μmol).

Urobilinogen: [U] 0–2.5 mg/24 h (< 4.23 μmol).

Urobilinogen, fecal: 40–280 mg/24 h (68–474 μmol).

Vanillylmandelic acid (VMA): [U] Up to 7 mg/24 h (< 35 μmol).

SELECTED REFERENCE TEXTBOOKS

CLINICAL NEUROLOGY

Adams RD, Victor M: *Principles of Neurology*, 2nd ed. McGraw-Hill, 1981.

Aita JA: *Neurologic Manifestations of General Diseases*. Thomas, 1964.

Alpers BJ, Mancall EL: *Clinical Neurology*, 6th ed. Davis, 1971.

Baker AB: *Clinical Neurology*, 3rd ed. Hoeber, 1971.

Bannister R: *Brain's Clinical Neurology*, 5th ed. Oxford Univ Press, 1978.

Benson FD: *Aphasia, Alexia and Agraphia*. Churchill Livingstone, 1979.

Bickerstaff ER: *Neurological Examination in Clinical Pictures*, 4th ed. Blackwell-Mosby, 1980.

Bray PF: *Neurology in Pediatrics*. Year Book, 1969.

Brock S, Krieger HP: *The Basis of Clinical Neurology*, 4th ed. Williams & Wilkins, 1963.

Dalessio DJ: *Wolff's Headaches and Other Pains*, 4th ed. Oxford Univ Press, 1980.

DeJong RN: *Neurologic Examination*, 4th ed. Hoeber, 1979.

DeMyer W: *Technique of the Neurologic Examination*, 3rd ed. McGraw-Hill, 1980.

Dimond SJ: *Neuropsychology*. Butterworth, 1980.

Dyck PJ, Thomas PK, Lambert EH: *Peripheral Neuropathy*. Saunders, 1975.

Elliott FA: *Clinical Neurology*, 2nd ed. Saunders, 1971.

Farmer TA: *Pediatric Neurology*, 2nd ed. Hoeber, 1976.

Feiring EH (editor): *Brock's Injuries of the Brain and Spinal Cord and Their Coverings*, 5th ed. Springer, 1974.

Fenichel G: *Neonatal Neurology*. Churchill Livingstone, 1980.

Ford RD: *Diseases of the Nervous System in Infancy, Childhood and Adolescence*, 6th ed. Thomas, 1973.

Gardner E: *Fundamentals of Neurology*, 6th ed. Saunders, 1975.

Gilroy J, Meyer JS: *Medical Neurology*, 3rd ed. Macmillan, 1979.

Goldstein K: *Language and Language Disturbances*. Grune & Stratton, 1948.

Haymaker W: *Bing's Local Diagnosis in Neurologic Diseases*, 15th ed. Mosby, 1969.

Heilman KM, Valenstein E: *Clinical Neuropsychology*. Oxford Univ Press, 1979.

Holmes LB et al: *Mental Retardation*. Macmillan, 1972.

Jennett B: *Introduction to Neurosurgery*, 3rd ed. Heineman, 1977.

Matson DD: *Neurosurgery in Infancy and Childhood*, 2nd ed. Thomas, 1969.

Matthews WB, Miller H: *Diseases of the Nervous System*, 2nd ed. Lippincott, 1975.

Mayo Clinic: *Clinical Examinations in Neurology*, 4th ed. Saunders, 1976.

Menkes JH: *Textbook of Child Neurology*, 2nd ed. Lea & Febiger, 1980.

Merritt HH: *A Textbook of Neurology*, 6th ed. Lea & Febiger, 1979.

Monrad-Krohn GH, Refsum S: *Clinical Examination of the Nervous System*, 12th ed. Hoeber, 1964.

Morariu MA: *Major Neurological Syndromes*. Thomas, 1979.

Penfield W, Jasper H: *Epilepsy and Functional Anatomy of the Human Brain*. Little, Brown, 1954.

Plum F, Posner JB: *The Diagnosis of Stupor and Coma*, 3rd ed. Davis, 1980.

Reitan RM, Davison LA: *Clinical Neuropsychology*. Halstead, 1974.

Rose CF: *Paediatric Neurology*. Blackwell, 1980.

Rosenberg RN: *Neurology*. Grune & Stratton, 1980.

Scheinberg P: *Modern Practical Neurology*, 2nd ed. Raven Press, 1981.

Smith B: *Principles of Clinical Neurology*. Year Book, 1965.

Spillane JD: *An Atlas of Clinical Neurology*, 2nd ed. Oxford Univ Press, 1976.

Strub RL, Black FW: *The Mental Status Examination in Neurology*. Davis, 1977.

Swaiman KF, Wright FS: *The Practice of Pediatric Neurology*. Mosby, 1975.

Van Allen MW, Rodnitzky RL: *Pictorial Manual of Neurological Tests*, 2nd ed. Year Book, 1980.

Vick NA: *Grinker's Neurology*, 7th ed. Thomas, 1976.

Vinken PJ, Bruyn GW: *Handbook of Clinical Neurology*. Elsevier, 1975.

Walshe FMR: *Diseases of the Nervous System*, 11th ed. Williams & Wilkins, 1970.

Walton JN (editor): *Brain's Diseases of the Nervous System*, 8th ed. Oxford Univ Press, 1977.

Walton JN: *Essentials of Neurology*, 4th ed. Lippincott, 1976.

Wartenberg R: *Diagnostic Tests in Neurology*. Year Book, 1953.

Wechsler IS: *Clinical Neurology*, 9th ed. Saunders, 1963.

Weisenberg TH, McBride KE: *Aphasia*. Oxford Univ Press, 1935.

Williams SD: *Modern Trends in Neurology*. Series 6. Butterworth, 1975.

Youmans JR: *Neurological Surgery*, 2nd ed. Saunders, 1981.

NEUROANATOMY

Afifi AK, Bergman RA: *Basic Neuroscience*. Urban & Schwarzenburg, 1980.

Arey LB: *Developmental Anatomy*, 7th ed. Saunders, 1965.

Bailey P, von Bonin G: *The Isocortex of Man*. Univ of Illinois Press, 1951.

Barr M: *The Human Nervous System*, 3rd ed. Harper & Row, 1979.

Bossy J: *Atlas of Neuroanatomy and Special Sense Organs*. Saunders, 1970.

Bourne H: *The Structure and Function of Nervous Tissue*. 6 vols. Academic Press, 1968, 1969, 1972.

Brodal A: *Neurological Anatomy in Relation to Clinical Medicine*, 3rd ed. Oxford Univ Press, 1980.

Carpenter MB: *Human Neuroanatomy*, 7th ed. Williams & Wilkins, 1976.

Crosby E, Humphrey T, Lauer E: *Correlative Anatomy of the Nervous System*. Macmillan, 1962.

Curtis BA, Jacobson S, Marcus EM: *An Introduction to the Neurosciences*. Saunders, 1972.

Elliott HC: *Textbook of Neuroanatomy*, 2nd ed. Lippincott, 1969.

Everett NB: *Functional Neuroanatomy*, 6th ed. Lea & Febiger, 1971.

Hausman L: *Clinical Neuroanatomy, Neurophysiology, and Neurology*. Thomas, 1958.

Haymaker W, Woodhall B: *Peripheral Nerve Injuries*, 2nd ed. Saunders, 1953.

House EL, Pansky B: *A Functional Approach to Neuroanatomy*, 2nd ed. McGraw-Hill, 1967.

Jensen D: *The Human Nervous System*. Appleton-Century-Crofts, 1980.

Krieg WJS: *Brain Mechanisms in Diachrome*. Brain Books, 1957.

Krieg WJS: *Functional Neuroanatomy,* 3rd ed. McGraw-Hill, 1966.

Kuntz A: *The Autonomic Nervous System,* 4th ed. Lea & Febiger, 1953.

Larsell O, Jansen J: *The Comparative Anatomy and Histology of the Cerebellum.* Univ of Minnesota Press, 1972.

Mettler FA: *Neuroanatomy,* 2nd ed. Mosby, 1948.

Netter FH: *The Ciba Collection of Medical Illustrations.* Vol I: *Nervous System.* Ciba, 1953.

Noback CA, Demarest R: *The Human Nervous System: Basic Principles of Neurology,* 3rd ed. McGraw-Hill, 1980.

Pansky B, Allen DJ: *Review of Neuroscience.* Macmillan, 1980.

Papez JW: *Comparative Neurology.* Hafner, 1961.

Peele TL: *The Neuroanatomic Basis for Clinical Neurology,* 3rd ed. McGraw-Hill, 1977.

Ranson SW, Clark SL: *The Anatomy of the Nervous System,* 10th ed. Saunders, 1959.

Rasmussen AT: *The Principal Nervous Pathways,* 4th ed. Macmillan, 1952.

Sarnat HB, Netsky MG: *Evolution of the Nervous System,* 2nd ed. Oxford Univ Press, 1981.

White JC, Smithwick RH, Simeone FA: *The Autonomic Nervous System,* 3rd ed. Macmillan, 1952.

NEURORADIOLOGY

Binder GA, Haughton VM, Ho KC: *Computed Tomography of Brain.* Little, Brown, 1979.

Davidoff LM, Dyke C: *The Normal Encephalogram,* 3rd ed. Lea & Febiger, 1951.

Davidoff LM, Epstein BS: *The Abnormal Pneumoencephalogram,* 2nd ed. Lea & Febiger, 1955.

Davidoff LM, Jacobson HG, Zimmermann HM: *Neuroradiology Workshop.* Vols I and II. Grune & Stratton, 1961, 1963.

Decker K, Shehadi WH: *Clinical Neuroradiology.* McGraw-Hill, 1966.

Di Chiro G: *An Atlas of Detailed Normal Pneumoencephalographic Anatomy,* 2nd ed. Thomas, 1971.

Du Boulay GH: *Principles of X-Ray Diagnosis of the Skull,* 2nd ed. Butterworth, 1980.

Ecker A: *The Normal Cerebral Angiogram.* Thomas, 1951.

Epstein BS: *Pneumoencephalography and Cerebral Angiography.* Year Book, 1966.

Epstein BS, Davidoff LM: *An Atlas of Skull Roentgenograms.* Lea & Febiger, 1953.

Gonzalez E, Grossman CB, Palacios E: *Computed Brain and Orbital Tomography.* Wiley, 1976.

Krayenbühl H, Yasargil MG: *Cerebral Angiography,* 2nd ed. Lippincott, 1968.

Leeds NE, Taveras JM: *Dynamic Factors in Diagnosis of Supratentorial Brain Tumors by Cerebral Angiography.* Saunders, 1969.

Newton TH, Potts DG: *Radiology of the Skull and Brain,* 2nd ed. Mosby, 1980.

Pendergrass EP, Schaeffer JP, Hodes PJ: *The Head and Neck in Roentgen Diagnosis,* 2nd ed. Thomas, 1956.

Quisling RG: *Correlative Neuroradiology.* Wiley, 1980.

Raimondi AJ: *Pediatric Neuroradiology.* Saunders, 1972.

Robertson EG: *Pneumoencephalography,* 2nd ed. Thomas, 1967.

Salamon G, Huang HP: *Computed Tomography of the Brain.* Springer, 1980.

Schöbinger RA, Ruzicka FF Jr: *Vascular Roentgenography.* Macmillan, 1964.

Shapiro R: *Myelography,* 3rd ed. Year Book, 1975.

Taveras JM, Wood EH: *Diagnostic Neuroradiology,* 2nd ed. Williams & Wilkins, 1976.

Wilson MC: *The Anatomical Foundation of Neuroradiology of the Brain,* 2nd ed. Little, Brown, 1972.

NEUROPATHOLOGY

Adams RD, Denny-Brown D, Pearson CM: *Diseases of Muscle,* 2nd ed. Hoeber, 1962.

Adams RD, Sidman RL: *Introduction to Neuropathology.* McGraw-Hill, 1968.

Bailey P: *Intracranial Tumors,* 2nd ed. Thomas, 1948.

Bailey P, Cushing H: *A Classification of Tumors of the Glioma Group.* Lippincott, 1926.

Bethlem J: *Myopathies,* 2nd ed. Elsevier, 1980.

Biggart JH: *Pathology of the Nervous System,* 3rd ed. Williams & Wilkins, 1961.

Blackwood W, Corsellis JAN: *Greenfield's Neuropathology,* 3rd ed. Year Book, 1976.

Blackwood W, Dodds TC, Sommerville JC: *Atlas of Neuropathology,* 2nd ed. Williams & Wilkins, 1965.

Courville CB: *Pathology of the Central Nervous System,* 3rd ed. Pacific Press Publishing Association, 1950.

Crome L, Stern J: *The Pathology of Mental Retardation.* Little, Brown, 1967.

Dekaban A: *Neurology of Infancy,* 2nd ed. Williams & Wilkins, 1970.

Dubowitz V: *Muscle Disorders in Childhood.* Saunders, 1978.

Dubowitz V, Brooke M: *Muscle Biopsy.* Saunders, 1974.

Fishman R: *Cerebrospinal Fluid in Disease of the Nervous System.* Saunders, 1980.

Fudenberg HH et al (editors): *Basic and Clinical Immunology,* 4th ed. Lange, 1982.

Haymaker W, Adams RD: *Histology and Histopathology of the Nervous System.* Thomas, 1982.

Innes JRM, Saunders LZ: *Comparative Neuropathology.* Academic Press, 1962.

Jawetz E, Melnick JL, Adelberg EA: *Review of Medical Microbiology,* 15th ed. Lange, 1982.

Junqueira LC, Carneiro J: *Basic Histology,* 3rd ed. Lange, 1980.

Malamud N, Hirano A: *Atlas of Neuropathology,* 2nd ed. Univ of California Press, 1974.

McComas A: *Neuromuscular Function and Disorder.* Butterworth, 1977.

Merritt HH, Fremont-Smith F: *The Cerebrospinal Fluid.* Saunders, 1937.

Minckler J: *Pathology of the Nervous System.* McGraw-Hill, 1972.

Russell DS, Rubinstein LJ: *Pathology of Tumors of the Nervous System,* 4th ed. Williams & Wilkins, 1977.

Schochet SS, McCormick WF: *Essentials of Neuropathology.* Appleton-Century-Crofts, 1979.

Slager UT: *Basic Neuropathology.* Williams & Wilkins, 1970.

Smith JF: *Pediatric Neuropathology.* McGraw-Hill, 1974.

Tedeschi CG: *Neuropathology: Method & Diagnosis.* Little, Brown, 1970.

Walton JN: *Disorders of Voluntary Muscle,* 4th ed. Little, Brown, 1981.

Zacks SI: *Atlas of Neuropathology.* Harper, 1971.

Zimmermann H, Netsky M, Davidoff LM: *Atlas of Tumors of the Nervous System.* Lea & Febiger, 1956.

Zülch KJ: *Atlas of Gross Neurosurgical Pathology.* Springer, 1974.

Zülch KJ: *Brain Tumors,* 2nd ed. Springer, 1965.

NEUROPHYSIOLOGY

The American Physiological Society: *Handbook of Physiology.* Section I: *The Nervous System* (formerly *Neurophysiology*). Brookhart AM, Mountcastle VB (editors). Vol 1. *Cellular Biology of Neurons.* (2 parts.) Kandel ER (editor). Williams & Wilkins, 1977.

The American Physiological Society: *Handbook of Physiology.* Section I: *Neurophysiology.* Magoun HW (editor). 3 vols. Williams & Wilkins, 1959, 1960.

Aminoff MJ: *Electrodiagnosis in Clinical Neurology.* Churchill Livingstone, 1980.

Aminoff MJ: *Electromyography in Clinical Practice.* Addison-Wesley, 1978.

Bard P: *Medical Physiology,* 11th ed. Mosby, 1961.

Brazier MAB: *The Electrical Activity of the Nervous System,* 4th ed. Macmillan, 1977.

Campbell HJ: *Correlative Physiology of the Nervous System.* Academic Press, 1965.

Chatfield P: *Fundamentals of Clinical Neurophysiology.* Thomas, 1956.

Cohen HL, Brumlik JE: *Manual of Electroneuromyography,* 2nd ed. Harper & Row, 1976.

Dimond SJ, Beaumont JG: *Hemisphere Function in the Human Brain.* Halstead, 1974.

Eccles JC: *The Physiology of Nerve Cells.* Johns Hopkins Univ Press, 1957.

Eccles JC: *The Physiology of Synapses.* Academic Press, 1964.

Eccles JC: *The Understanding of the Brain,* 2nd ed. McGraw-Hill, 1977.

Eliasson SG et al: *Neurological Pathophysiology,* 2nd ed. Oxford Univ Press, 1978.

Eyzaguirre C: *Physiology of the Nervous System,* 2nd ed. Year Book, 1975.

Fulton JF: *Physiology of the Nervous System,* 3rd ed. Oxford Univ Press, 1949.

Fulton JF: *Textbook of Physiology,* 17th ed. Oxford Univ Press, 1955.

Ganong WF: *Review of Medical Physiology,* 10th ed. Lange, 1981.

Goodgold J, Eberstein A: *Electrodiagnosis of Neuromuscular Diseases,* 2nd ed. Williams & Wilkins, 1978.

Grant R: *Muscular Afferents and Motor Control.* Interscience, 1966.

Guyton AC: *Structure and Function of the Nervous System,* 3rd ed. Saunders, 1981.

Jasper HH, Ward AA, Pope A: *Basic Mechanisms of the Epilepsies.* Little, Brown, 1969.

Katz B: *Nerve, Muscle and Synapse.* McGraw-Hill, 1966.

Lenman JAR, Ritchie AE: *Clinical Electromyography,* 2nd ed. Lippincott, 1977.

Luria AR: *Higher Cortical Functions in Man.* Basic Books, 1966.

Martini L, Ganong WF: *Frontiers in Neuroendocrinology.* Raven Press, 1980.

Ochs S: *Elements of Neurophysiology.* Wiley, 1965.

Ruch T et al: *Neurophysiology,* 3rd ed. Saunders, 1972.

Schaltenbrand G, Woolsey CN: *Cerebral Localization and Organization.* Univ of Wisconsin Press, 1964.

Sherrington C: *The Integrative Action of the Nervous System.* Yale Univ Press, 1947.

Smorto MP, Basmajian JV: *Electrodiagnosis: A Handbook for Neurologists.* Harper & Row, 1977.

Tower DB (editor): *The Nervous System.* Raven Press, 1975.

Walsh FB: *Physiology of the Nervous System,* 2nd ed. Little, Brown, 1964.

NEURO–OPHTHALMOLOGY

Adler FH: *Physiology of the Eye,* 5th ed. Mosby, 1970.

Ashworth B: *Clinical Neuro-ophthalmology.* Lippincott, 1973.

Bender M: *The Oculomotor System.* Hoeber, 1964.

Cogan DG: *Neurology of the Ocular Muscles,* 3rd ed. Thomas, 1968.

Cogan DG: *Neurology of the Visual System.* Thomas, 1968.

Duke-Elder S, Wybar KC: *System of Ophthalmology.* Vol 2: *The Anatomy of the Visual System.* Mosby, 1961.

Glaser JS: *Neuro-ophthalmology.* Harper & Row, 1978.

Harrington DO: *The Visual Fields,* 5th ed. Mosby, 1981.

Kestenbaum A: *Clinical Methods of Neuro-ophthalmologic Examination,* 2nd ed. Grune & Stratton, 1961.

Smith LA: *Neuro-ophthalmology Update.* Masson, 1977.

Spiegel EA, Sommer I: *Neurology of the Eye, Ear, Nose and Throat.* Grune & Stratton, 1944.

Vaughan D, Asbury T: *General Ophthalmology,* 9th ed. Lange, 1980.

Walsh FB, Hoyt WF: *Clinical Neuro-ophthalmology,* 3rd ed. Williams & Wilkins, 1969.

Walsh TJ: *Neuro-ophthalmology.* Lea & Febiger, 1978.

Wolintz AH: *Essentials of Clinical Neuro-ophthalmology.* Little, Brown, 1976.

ELECTROENCEPHALOGRAPHY

Bennett DB et al: *An Atlas of Electroencephalography in Coma and Cerebral Death.* Raven Press, 1975.

Blume WT: *Atlas of Pediatric Electroencephalography.* Raven Press, 1981.

Fois A: *Clinical Electroencephalography in Epilepsy and Related Conditions in Children.* Thomas, 1963.

Fois A: *The Electroencephalogram of the Normal Child.* Thomas, 1961.

Gastaut H et al: *The Physiopathogenesis of the Epilepsies.* Thomas, 1969.

Gibbs FA, Gibbs EL: *Atlas of Electroencephalography.* Vol 1, 1950; Vol 2, 1952; Vol 3, 1964; Vol 4, 1979. Addison-Wesley.

Gibbs FA, Gibbs EL: *Medical Electroencephalography.* Addison-Wesley, 1967.

Glaser G: *EEG and Behavior.* Basic Books, 1963.

Goldensohn E, Koehle R: *EEG Interpretation.* Futura, 1975.

Hill D, Parr G: *Electroencephalography,* 2nd ed. Macmillan, 1963.

Hughes RR: *An Introduction to Clinical Electro-encephalography.* Williams & Wilkins, 1961.

Kellaway P, Petersen I: *Automation of Clinical Electroencephalography.* Raven Press, 1975.

Kellaway P, Petersen I: *Clinical Electroencephalography of Children.* Little, Brown, 1968.

Kellaway P, Petersen I: *Neurologic and Electroencephalographic Correlative Studies in Infancy.* Grune & Stratton, 1964.

Kiloh LG et al: *Clinical Electroencephalography,* 3rd ed. Butterworth, 1972.

Klass DW, Daly DD (editors): *Current Practice of Clinical Electroencephalography.* Raven Press, 1979.

Kooi KA: *Fundamentals of Electroencephalography,* 2nd ed. Harper, 1978.

Kugler J: *Electroencephalography in Hospital and General Consulting Practice.* Elsevier, 1964.

Laidlaw J, Stanton JB: *The EEG in Clinical Practice.* Livingstone, 1966.

Niedermeyer E, Lopes de Silva: *Electroencephalography*. Urban & Schwarzenburg, 1981.

Schwab RS: *Electroencephalography in Clinical Practice*. Saunders, 1951.

Spehlmann R: *EEG Primer*. Elsevier, 1981.

Strauss H, Ostow M, Greenstein L: *Diagnostic Electroencephalography*. Grune & Stratton, 1952.

Werner SS, Stockard JE, Bickford RE: *Atlas of Neonatal Electroencephalography*. Raven Press, 1977.

NEUROCHEMISTRY

Adams CWM: *Neurohistochemistry*. Elsevier, 1965.

Barbeau A, Growdon JH, Wurtman RJ: *Choline and Lecithin in Brain Disorders*. Raven Press, 1979.

Barker JL, Smith TG Jr: *The Role of Peptides In Neuronal Function*. Dekker, 1980.

Burn JH: *The Autonomic Nervous System for Students of Physiology and of Pharmacology*, 5th ed. Davis, 1975.

Cohen M: *Biochemistry of Neural Disease*. Harper, 1975.

Cummings JN, Kremer M: *Biochemical Aspects of Neurological Disorders*. 3rd series. Davis, 1968.

Davison AN: *Biochemistry and Neurological Disease*. Lippincott, 1976.

Davison AN, Dobbing J: *Applied Neurochemistry*. Davis, 1969.

Delgado JMR, DeFeudis FV (editors): *Behavioral Neurochemistry*. Halstead, 1977.

Elliott KAC, Page IH, Quastel JH: *Neurochemistry*, 2nd ed. Thomas, 1962.

Folch-Pi J: *Chemical Pathology of the Nervous System*. Pergamon Press, 1961.

Harlow HF, Woolsey CN: *Biological and Biochemical Bases of Behavior*. Univ of Wisconsin Press, 1958.

Hemmings G: *The Biochemistry of Schizophrenia and Addiction*. University Park Press, 1981.

Himwich HE: *Brain Metabolism and Cerebral Disorders*, 2nd ed. Halstead, 1976.

Himwich W (editor): *Biochemistry of the Developing Brain*. 2 vols. Dekker, 1974.

Kety S, Elkes J: *Regional Neurochemistry*. Pergamon Press, 1961.

Kumar S: *Biochemistry of Brain*. Pergamon Press, 1979.

Lajtha A: *Handbook of Neurochemistry*. Plenum Press, 1972.

Martin DW Jr, Mayes PA, Rodwell VW; *Harper's Review of Biochemistry*, 18th ed. Lange, 1981.

Martin L, Ganong WF: *Neuroendocrinology*. Academic Press, 1966.

McIlwain H: *Practical Neurochemistry*, 2nd ed. Little, Brown, 1976.

Quastel JH, Quastel DMJ: *The Chemistry of Brain Metabolism in Health and Disease*. Thomas, 1961.

Richter D: *Neurochemical Aspects of Neurological Disorders*. Davis, 1965.

Roberts P: *Biochemistry of Dementia*. Wiley, 1980.

Scharrer E, Scharrer B: *Neuroendocrinology*. Columbia Univ Press, 1963.

Siegel GJ et al: *Basic Neurochemistry*, 3rd ed. Little, Brown, 1981.

Tower D: *Neurochemistry of Epilepsy*. Thomas, 1960.

Triggle DJ: *Chemical Aspects of the Autonomic Nervous System*. Academic Press, 1965.

Waelsch H: *Biochemistry of the Developing Nervous System*. Academic Press, 1955.

NEUROPHARMACOLOGY

Calne DB: *Therapeutics in Neurology*, 2nd ed. Blackwell, 1980.

Cooper JR, Bloom FE, Roth RH: *The Biochemical Basis of Neuropharmacology*, 3rd ed. Oxford Univ Press, 1978.

Dreisbach RH: *Handbook of Poisoning: Diagnosis & Treatment*, 10th ed. Lange, 1980.

Glaser GH, Penry JK, Woodbury DM: *Antiepileptic Drugs: Mechanisms of Action*. Raven Press, 1980.

Goodman LS, Gilman A: *The Pharmacological Basis of Therapeutics*, 6th ed. Macmillan, 1980.

Grollman A, Grollman EF: *Pharmacology and Therapeutics*, 7th ed. Lea & Febiger, 1970.

Iversen LL: *Handbook of Psychopharmacology*. Plenum Press, 1975.

Iversen SD, Iversen LJ: *Behavioral Pharmacology*, 2nd ed. Oxford Univ Press, 1981.

Klawans HL (editor): *Clinical Neuropharmacology*. Raven Press, 1981.

Kutt H, McDowell F: *Clinical Neuropharmacology*. Churchill Livingstone, 1979.

Mercier J: *Anticonvulsant Drugs*. Pergamon Press, 1973.

Meyers FH, Jawetz E, Goldfien A: *Review of Medical Pharmacology*, 7th ed. Lange, 1980.

Prasad KN, Vernadakis A: *Mechanisms of Neurotoxic Substances*. Raven Press, 1981.

Roizin L, Shiraki H, Grčević N (editors): *Neurotoxicology*. Raven Press, 1977.

Schildkraut JJ: *Neuropsychopharmacology and the Affective Disorders*. Little, Brown, 1970.

Snyder SH: *Perspectives in Neuropharmacology*. Oxford Univ Press, 1970.

Turner PH: *Clinical Aspects of Autonomic Pharmacology*. Lippincott, 1969.

Wilder BJ, Bruni J: *Seizure Disorders: A Pharmacological Approach to Treatment*. Raven Press, 1981.

Woodbury DM et al: *Pharmacology of Antiepileptic Drugs*. Raven Press, 1971.

Index*

*The following are indexed under the nouns: arter(ies), atroph(ies), column(s), dystroph(ies), foramen(s), gangli(a), lobe(s), muscle(s), nerve(s), nucle(i), plexus(es), potential(s), reflex(es), sinus(es), sulc(i), tract(s), vein(s), ventricle(s).